THE
CAMBRIDGE
ECONOMIC HISTORY

GENERAL EDITORS: M. M. POSTAN, Professor Emeritus of Economic History in the University of Cambridge; D. C. COLEMAN, Professor of Economic History in the University of Cambridge; and PETER MATHIAS, Chichele Professor of Economic History in the University of Oxford

VOLUME VII, PART 2

THE
CAMBRIDGE
ECONOMIC HISTORY
OF EUROPE

VOLUME VII

THE INDUSTRIAL ECONOMIES
CAPITAL, LABOUR, AND
ENTERPRISE

PART 2
THE UNITED STATES,
JAPAN, AND RUSSIA

EDITED BY

PETER MATHIAS

*Chichele Professor of Economic History
in the University of Oxford,
and Fellow of All Souls College*

AND

M. M. POSTAN

*Professor Emeritus of Economic History
in the University of Cambridge,
and Fellow of Peterhouse*

CAMBRIDGE UNIVERSITY PRESS

CAMBRIDGE · LONDON · NEW YORK · MELBOURNE

1978

Published by the Syndics of the Cambridge University Press
The Pitt Building, Trumpington Street, Cambridge CB2 IRP
Bentley House, 200 Euston Road, London NWI 2DB
32 East 57th Street, New York, NY 10022, USA
296 Beaconsfield Parade, Middle Park, Melbourne 3206, Australia

© Cambridge University Press 1978

First published 1978

Printed in Great Britain
by the Anchor Press Tiptree, Essex

Library of Congress Cataloguing in Publication Data (Revised)
Main entry under title:

The Cambridge economic history of Europe from the decline
of the Roman empire.

Includes bibliographies and indexes.

Vol. 2 planned by Sir John Clapham and Eileen Power,
edited by M. Postan and E. E. Rich.

CONTENTS: v. 1. The agrarian life of the middle ages.
v. 2. Trade and industry in the middle ages.
v. 3. Economic organization and policies in the middle ages.
1. Europe – Economic conditions. 2. Europe – History.
I. Clapham, Sir John Harold, 1873–1946, ed.
II. Power, Eileen Edna, 1889–1940, joint ed.

HC240.C3   330.9′4   41–3509

ISBN 0 521 21590 0 part 1
ISBN 0 521 21591 9 part 2
ISBN 0 521 21124 7 the set of two parts

CONTENTS

THE UNITED STATES

CHAPTER I

Capital Formation in the United States during the Nineteenth Century

By LANCE E. DAVIS, Professor of Economics, California Institute of
Technology, and
ROBERT E. GALLMAN, Professor of Economics, University of
North Carolina at Chapel Hill

CHAPTER II

The United States: Evolution of Enterprise

By ALFRED D. CHANDLER, JR, George Straus Professor of Business History,
Harvard University

JAPAN

CHAPTER III

Capital Formation in Japan

By Kazushi Ohkawa, Professor Emeritus of Economics, Hitotsubashi University, and
Henry Rosovsky, Professor of Economics, Harvard University

CHAPTER IV

Factory Labour and the Industrial Revolution in Japan

By Koji Taira, Professor of Economics, University of Illinois

CHAPTER V

Entrepreneurship, Ownership, and Management in Japan

By Kozo Yamamura, Professor of Economics, University of Washington

RUSSIA

CHAPTER VI

Capital Formation during the Period of Early Industrialization in Russia, 1890–1913

By ARCADIUS KAHAN, Professor of Economics, University of Chicago

CHAPTER VII

Labour and Industrialization in Russia

By OLGA CRISP, Reader in Economic History, School of Slavonic and East European Studies, University of London

NOTES

BIBLIOGRAPHIES

TABLES

THE UNITED STATES

JAPAN

RUSSIA

ILLUSTRATIONS

THE UNITED STATES

JAPAN

Capital Formation in the United States during the Nineteenth Century[1]

I. *Introduction*

One of the grand themes of the literature on economic development relates to the behaviour of the investment rate in the early stages of modern economic growth. Economists from Adam Smith onward have given capital formation an important role in economic growth, and a considerable literature has grown up around the notion that modernization involves a rise in the share of income invested. The American record displays a very prolonged and pronounced long-term movement in this share, a movement that has not as yet received a very full analytical treatment.

The fraction of American real net national product devoted to investment rose from an average value of perhaps 6 or 7 per cent in the first four decades of the nineteenth century, to between 10 and 12 per cent in the decades just before the Civil War, to 18–20 per cent in the decades between the Civil War and the First World War (see Table 1). This development is one of the most striking aspects of American nineteenth-century economic growth, and we have chosen it as the organizing theme of this chapter. We have brought together the evidence on the volume and composition of saving, investment, income, and the capital stock and have attempted to answer two questions: (1) What role did the dramatic increase in the investment share play in American economic development? (2) How can the increase in the share be accounted for?

The chapter is organized in the following way. Section II briefly examines the analytical apparatus employed in the rest of the chapter. Section III provides quantitative measures of the effects of capital formation and the increase in the investment share on the growth rate as well as a discussion of the meaning of those measures. Section IV attempts to sort out the factors responsible for the increase in the investment share. It appears, for example, that the supply of savings in the US increased very rapidly, even relative to the abundant investment opportunities of the nineteenth century. Section V considers the forces that might have produced this rate of savings. One of these forces – the development of capital markets and other systems of intermediation – is explored in greater detail in sections VI and VII. The first of these sections is devoted chiefly to a survey of relevant analytical possibilities;

Table 1. *Net National Capital Formation in the USA, 1805–1900,*
as a percentage of NNP (at 1860 prices)

1805–40	6·2–7·0
1834–43	9·5
1839–48	10·2
1844–53	11·4
1849–58	12·1
1869–78	17·8
1874–83	17·6
1879–88	17·1
1884–93	19·2
1889–98	19·7
1894–1903	18·4

SOURCES. *1805–40.* The average annual increase in the real capital stock (at 1860 prices) between 1805 and 1840, divided by the average real net national product (1860 prices) for 1799, 1809, 1819, 1829, and 1839. The average annual increase in the real capital stock was computed by subtracting the real capital stock in 1805 from the real capital stock in 1840 and dividing by 35. The real capital stock in 1840 (including net claims on foreigners) was taken from the sources cited in Lance E. Davis, Richard A. Easterlin, William N. Parker, *et al., American Economic Growth: An Economist's History of the United States* (New York, 1972), 34. The real capital stock in 1805 was estimated in two ways: (*a*) by extrapolation from 1850 (1850 figure from sources cited in *ibid.*) on constant-price estimates in Raymond W. Goldsmith, 'The Growth of Reproducible Wealth of the United States of America from 1805 to 1950', in Simon Kuznets (ed.), *Income and Wealth of the United States: Trends and Structure,* Income and Wealth, ser. II (Cambridge, 1952); (*b*) by summing up agricultural inventories (crops and animals) and all other components of the capital stock, the latter estimated in the manner described immediately above, the former derived as the average of figures for 1800 and 1810, taken from worksheets underlying Robert E. Gallman, 'Changes in Total Agricultural Factor Productivity in the Nineteenth Century', *Agricultural History,* XLVI, 1 (January 1972), 204. Real net national product in 1799, 1809, 1819, and 1829 was estimated by extrapolation from 1839 on estimates of real gross domestic product in Paul A. David, 'The Growth of Real Product in the United States before 1840: New Evidence and Controlled Conjectures', *Journal of Economic History,* XXVII, 2 (June 1967). Use of the David estimates probably results in a modest understatement of average national product before 1839 and, therefore, a modest overstatement of the net investment rate. (See the citations in note 6 below.) See, also, the effort to estimate net investment in *fixed reproducible* capital as a fraction of product before 1840 in Lance E. Davis and Robert E. Gallman, 'The Share of Savings and Investment in Gross National Product during the 19th Century, United States of America', in F. C. Lane (ed.), *International Conference of Economic History,* Bloomington, Indiana, 1968 (Paris, 1973).

1834–43 to 1894–1903. Computed from data on worksheets underlying chap. 2 of Davis *et al., American Economic Growth.*

Note. The estimates in this table differ somewhat from the series contained in Simon Kuznets, *Capital in the American Economy: Its Formation and Financing* (Princeton, 1961). The chief reason lies in the fact that the Kuznets figures are deflated on the base 1929, while the data underlying the series in this table are deflated on the base 1860, although there are also substantive differences of lesser importance. See Robert E. Gallman, 'Gross National Product in the United States, 1834–1909', in Dorothy S. Brady (ed.), *Output, Employment and Productivity in the United States after 1800,* Studies in Income and Wealth, 30 (New York, 1966).

the second, to the empirical record. Section VIII is a summary of conclusions.

Wherever possible we have dealt with the full period 1800–1900,
but limitations of data have frequently obliged us to confine our attention to the years 1840–1900.

II. *Analytical Models*

The phenomenon of a long-term rise in the real net investment share
has been the subject of considerable scholarly attention. Two important
schools of thought have emerged, differing chiefly in their appraisals
of the main consequences of a change in the investment share. On the
one hand, the school associated with the names of W. W. Rostow and
W. A. Lewis base their work fairly clearly on the ideas of Roy Harrod
and Evsey Domar.[2] Harrod and Domar, interested in exploring the
requirements for stable growth, assume that the marginal capital–
output ratio is constant, an assumption they regard as empirically
warranted. Rostow and Lewis, interested not in questions of stability
during growth, but in the factors responsible for the transition to
modern growth, adopt the notion of a stable capital–output ratio and
make the long-term rate of growth a variable, responsive to changes
in investment. An extreme statement of their position (which neither
would accept without qualification) would be that the rate of growth
varies directly and proportionately with the investment share. Thus a
doubling of the investment share would double the rate of growth of
output.

A quite different result is derived from a model associated with the
name of Robert Solow.[3] In the Solow model, a rise in the investment
share will produce a temporary increase in the rate of growth of output.
However, assuming that the rates of growth (and employment) of the
other factors do not change, the increase in the rate of change of the
capital stock (implicit in the rise of the investment share) will lead to
a decline in the marginal product of capital and a rise in the marginal
and average capital–output ratios, while the rate of change of output
will return to its original value. In other words, in the long run the
capital–output ratio will respond to a change in the investment share,
but the rate of growth of output will not.

Rostow and Lewis established for their models parameters that they
believe to be typical of the experience of industrialization. Their
judgements in these matters are similar, but in order to avoid continual
minor qualifications that contribute little to an understanding of the
issues, we concentrate in what follows on the work of one of the two.

Since Rostow's interests are the more clearly historical, we choose to deal with him.

According to Rostow, the net investment share is typically at a level of about 5 per cent in the 'preconditions' or late pre-modern stage; it rises to a level of about 10 per cent in the two or three decades of the 'take-off' or early modernization stage and stabilizes at the new level. Since (according to Rostow) the marginal capital–output ratio tends to be at a level of 3·0 or 3·5 to 1 during this period, the rate of growth of output increases from roughly 1·5 per cent to about 3·0 per cent per annum, and per capita output definitely begins to rise.[4]

These are very clear quantitative predictions, and in some measure they are borne out by US experience. The investment share probably averaged within one or two percentage points of the predicted 5 per cent level in America in the first four decades of the nineteenth century (Table 1), and at that time modern growth – in the sense of industrialization – had barely begun. Also, the share did rise from the 1840s onward, and the timing of the increase appears to be coincident with rapid modernization. But in other respects the account sketched by Rostow does not correspond very well with the events of US history.

First, Rostow anticipates that the investment share will rise over a relatively short period, say two decades. He conceives of the movement as a relatively sudden one, a shift from a path of negligible growth to a path of quite rapid growth. But the American record shows that more than five decades intervened between the low investment rates of the beginning of the century and the peak rates toward the end of it.

Second, the increase in the US investment share is very much more pronounced than the 'take-off' theorists have led us to expect. The share roughly triples, reaching the extraordinary level of nearly 20 per cent by the end of the century.

Third, and most important, assuming a stable capital–output ratio of 3·0 or 3·5 to 1 and the investment shares already described, American real national product would have been increasing at a rate of between 1·8 and 2·3 per cent per annum in the early decades of the century, and between 5·6 and 6·6 per cent per annum in the late decades of the century.[5] Since the population of the US was growing at a rate of almost 3 per cent per year before 1840, the computed rate of growth of real national income for the early part of the century implies a persistent decline in per capita product of between 0·7 and 1·2 per cent per year, a result almost certainly inconsistent with historical fact. Furthermore, the rate of growth of real national product toward the end of the nineteenth century appears to have been less than 4 per cent, rather than the 5·6–6·6 per cent computed with the aid of the Rostow model (see Table 2).

Indeed, the pattern of US nineteenth-century growth is very nearly the converse of the pattern predicted by Rostow. The highest rates of growth were achieved in the ante-bellum years. The rates fell across the decades dominated by the Civil War and rose thereafter, but they never again reached the pre-war average level. We do not know how fast growth proceeded before 1840, but David has advanced an estimate of 4·5 per cent per annum, and while this figure has been subject to some criticism, few would now be prepared to place the rate at much less than 4·0 per cent.[6] This means that the increase in the investment share across the first fifty or so years of the century may have been accompanied by a rise in the growth rate – of, say, 0·5–1·0 per cent – but that during the remainder of the century the investment share and the growth rate tended to move in opposite directions (Tables 1 and 2).

Table 2. *Rates of Growth of Real Net National Product and Real Net National Product per Capita, 1799–1899 (per cent)*

	NNP	NNP per capita
1799–1838	4·0–4·5	1·0–1·5
1839–54	4·9	1·7
1854–74	3·3	0·7
1874–99	3·7	1·6

SOURCES.

National product: see Table 1.
Population: US Bureau of the Census, *Historical Statistics of the United States: Colonial Times to 1957* (Washington, 1960), Series A-2.

The growth rate and investment share data lead inexorably to two important conclusions. First, since the rate of growth tended to decline and the investment share to rise during the last five or six decades of the nineteenth century, the capital–output ratio, far from being stable, must have been rising. Second, the level of the capital–output ratio in the early decades of the century must have been much lower than the values discussed so far – 3·0 or 3·5 to 1. Indeed, assuming that an investment share of about 6·5 per cent was typical of the decades before 1840 and that the growth rate ran around 4·0 per cent, the economy must have been moving in the direction of an average ratio of about 1·6 to 1 (i.e. 0·065/0·040 = 1·625).

These rather striking conclusions are supported by the available direct measures of the capital–output ratio, which show a value of 1·6 for 1840, rising steadily to 3·7 by the end of the century (see Table 3). The initial value is exceptionally low, and the advance very prominent indeed. The investment experience of the period appears to call for a different interpretative model from the one provided by Lewis and Rostow.

The predictive performance of the Solow model is a good deal better. As indicated previously, the chief long-term effect of a rise in the net investment share, according to this model, is an increase in the capital–output ratio, precisely the result described by American experience. The historical record does not exhibit unequivocally the short-term acceleration of the rate of growth of output that is associated, in the Solow model, with an increase of the investment share. For

Table 3. *Ratio of National Capital Stock to Net National Product, 1840–1900 (1860 prices)*

1840	1·6
1850	1·8
1880	2·4
1890	3·3
1900	3·7

SOURCE. See the sources cited in Table 1.

example, the investment share rose sharply between the decades centred on 1853 and 1873 (Table 1), while over this interval the rate of growth of output actually fell (Table 2). But model and history are easily reconciled in this instance. The model treats the labour supply as an exogenous variable, and the prediction of acceleration arises from a simplifying assumption – that the rate of change of the labour supply remains constant. With the labour supply growing at a constant rate, an increase in the investment share necessarily produces a short-term rise in the rate of growth of total factor inputs, and thus an acceleration in the rate of change of output (in the absence of diseconomies of scale). A change in the simplifying assumption will alter this result. In the historical case, the period 1853–73 was one during which the rate of growth of all factor supplies – land, labour, and capital – declined. Thus the empirical finding of retardation in the rate of change of output is not inconsistent with the Solow model. (Nor, it should be added, is it inconsistent with the idea that the increase in the investment share had a positive effect on the rate of growth of output, holding it at a level higher than it otherwise would have achieved.)

The lineage of the Rostow model can be traced back to the Keynesian system, in which the level of investment determines employment and output, whereas Solow's work derives from neoclassical ideas. The neoclassical system, with its competitive factor and product markets and variable factor prices and proportions, comes closer to approximating nineteenth-century American conditions than does the Keynesian system, and this is no doubt the reason why the Solow model performs better than the Rostow model in this context.

Working with essentially neoclassical ideas it is possible to set out an analytical system that permits one to explore both the effects of capital formation on growth and the sources of the increase in the American net investment share. In a thoroughly competitive system, the income obtained by each factor, in equilibrium, is equal to the value of the marginal product of the factor multiplied by the number of units of the factor in use. Since factor incomes exhaust the total national product, the elasticity of output with respect to any given factor can be taken as the fraction of total income earned by the factor, which provides a means of estimating the effects of capital formation on economic growth. We adopt this approach in section III.[7]

The analytical apparatus that we propose to use to explore the factors responsible for the rise of the investment share is also consistent with the spirit of the neoclassical model. We assume that the economy consists of a number of competitive and complementary economic units, each characterized by its own production function and each operated by a profit-maximizing entrepreneur. These units are linked together because (1) they draw from the same pool of resources, (2) they sell at least a part of their output in the same market, and (3) they use the output of other units as inputs to their production process. Each firm chooses to invest in those activities whose discounted stream of future income exceeds their cost. Savings are done largely by individuals who are utility-maximizers and select bundles of present and future (savings) consumption that maximize utility, given the constraint of income. The rate of interest represents the price of savings and investment, and as such it provides the firms with the appropriate rate at which to discount future earnings and provides the savers with the measure of the value of future consumption to compare with the current consumption forgone. In sections IV–VII we elaborate this model and apply it to the historical case.

III. Contribution of Capital Formation to Economic Growth

The contribution of capital formation to economic growth depends upon the rate of growth of the capital stock and the elasticity of output with respect to capital. If appropriate conditions are met, the elasticity of output with respect to capital can be measured by the share of national income earned by capital, as we have indicated above. The elasticity estimate in principle refers to incremental changes, while we propose to use it to deal with very large changes. This consideration, together with the rather rough nature of the underlying evidence, urges a cautious approach to the results of the calculations we will carry out, a point to which we will return.[8]

The rate of growth of the capital stock would be a simple figure to compute in an economy in which the distribution of the stock among types of capital and the characteristics of the various types of capital were unchanging. Neither condition was met in the nineteenth-century American economy. The structure of the stock and the costs and output capacities of the different types of capital shifted over time.

There are two broad approaches to the measurement of the rate of change of such a stock; each approach (let us call them A and B) rests on a different method of estimating the size of the stock itself. First, one might measure the capacity of the stock to produce output. The effects of any embodied technical changes would thus be attributed to the capital stock, rather than being identified separately as consequences of technical change. Let us identify this measure as Measure A. The second approach measures the resources embodied in the stock – that is, the inputs used to produce the stock. There are in turn two variants of this latter approach. In the first, actual inputs – expressed in constant prices – are taken to constitute the value of the stock. In the second, the value of the stock is calculated in terms of the inputs required, given the techniques of production in use in a base year. Let us call the measures associated with these methods Measures B1 and B2. There are obvious conceptual and practical difficulties involved in the assembling of series corresponding to each of these measures (for example, the effort to deal with inputs of capital into capital production in connection with Measure B1 leads one into an infinite regress), but these difficulties can be set aside for the moment.[9]

Each of the three measures has a specific, relevant meaning, and it would be desirable to have series corresponding to each. Comparing rates of change of these series, one could identify the quantitative significance of changes in productivity in the capital-goods sector and changes in the productivity of capital. Various facets of the effects of capital formation on growth could also be appraised. But unfortunately we have only one, not three, constant-price capital stock series for the US in the nineteenth century; what is more troubling is that we cannot be absolutely sure of the conceptual content of the series.

Three important components of the series – inventories, transportation, and public utilities – are chiefly based on measures of the B2 type. The remaining components were derived by deflating current price estimates by price indices. In order to know the meaning of the resulting figures, one must know something about the materials from which they were constructed.[10]

The price indices are available in considerable detail and are intended to express changes in the value of capital goods of constant quality. That is, they are intended to capture the effects of (for example) changes in techniques of production in the capital-goods industries, but not the effects of changes in the quality of capital. But these intentions may have been imperfectly realized, and the indices may reflect quality changes in some measure.[11]

The current-price capital stock series are probably expressed in some combination of book and market values. However, two considerations suggest that market values are dominant. First, the stock data appear to be roughly consistent with the flows of net investment, and the latter are expressed in market prices.[12] Second, the stock was growing so fast during the nineteenth century that at each date a large fraction of the stock consisted of capital that was of very recent vintage. On relatively conservative assumptions, one can infer that 75 to 85 per cent of the depreciable capital stock must have been ten years old or less; over 90 per cent of the value of the stock of machines and equipment must have been ten years old or less; and over half must have been five years old or less.[13] Since the stock was so young, the opportunity for the emergence of large deviations between book value and market value was very limited.

If the current-price stock data refer to market valuations, and if the price indices fail to reflect quality changes, then the process of deflation would tend to produce a series approximating Measure A. That is, the price indices would eliminate any price changes due to general influences (e.g. monetary changes) and also any changes due to productivity gains in the capital-goods sector, but they would not eliminate the effects on prices of changes in quality. To the extent that the price indices do reflect quality changes, the deflated series correspond with Measure B2. Since we know that large components of the total stock series – for example, inventories (see above) – reflect the B2-type measure, and since the effects of quality changes were probably imperfectly eliminated from the price indices, it seems probable that the total capital series, in constant prices, corresponds most nearly – although imperfectly – with Measure B2: that is, it reflects the real value of the inputs into capital – technique held constant – rather than the capacity of capital to produce output. This means that our quantitative estimates of the effects of capital formation on economic growth will be largely net of the effects of embodied technical changes.

We can now turn to a consideration of the contribution of capital formation to American growth. The first thing to notice is that the capital stock grew with exceptional rapidity. Between 1800 and 1900 it probably increased roughly eighty-five-fold. Since population was about fourteen and one-half times as large at the end of the period as at the beginning, the implication is that the per capita supply of capital was about six times as large in 1900 as it was a century earlier.

The data for the period before 1840 cannot be regarded as very accurate. But the same general pattern emerges from the post-1840 data. The capital stock increased by 23·4 times between 1840 and 1900, as compared with advances of 4·4 times for population, 5·1 times for the labour force, and 5·7 times for land in production. All of the chief components of the stock increased dramatically, inventories by a factor of almost ten, buildings and other improvements to land by a factor of about twenty-five, and machines and equipment by an extraordinary factor of almost seventy. As indicated previously, the average age of capital – especially machinery and equipment – was very low; thus, if American entrepreneurs were sensitive to technical changes, the stock was always relatively modern. It seems reasonable to attribute at least a part of the high level of American per capita income in the nineteenth century to the size and productivity of the capital stock.

The elasticity of output with respect to capital – income earned by capital expressed as a share of total national income – was apparently quite small, roughly 0·19. But the low elasticity combined with the high rate of growth of capital had a substantial impact on the rate of growth of output, accounting for slightly more than one percentage point of the aggregate growth rate between 1840 and 1900. Since real net national product increased at a rate of just under 4 per cent per annum, the growth of the capital stock was responsible for over one-quarter of total growth. What is more striking is the fact that almost four-tenths of the increase in real income per capita can be accounted for by the expansion of capital stock. Just over half the gain can be attributed to the increase in the volume of land improvements (buildings etc.), just under one-quarter to the growth of the stock of inventories, and just under one-quarter to the rate of change of equipment and machinery.

For the twentieth century, Denison finds that capital formation had a somewhat smaller effect, accounting for 0·73 percentage points of the growth rate of real national income in the US between 1909 and 1929, and only 0·43 percentage points between 1929 and 1957, roughly one-quarter of aggregate growth in the earlier period and 15 per cent in the later.[14]

The preceding remarks refer to the contribution of capital formation to American growth. The question raised in section II related to a somewhat different issue, however. There we asked how the increase in the investment share affected growth. To answer this question, one must engage in a more elaborate counter-factual exercise than those previously conducted in this section.

The model used to generate our estimate of the contribution of capital formation to American growth is as follows:

$$\dot{O} = k\dot{K} + l\dot{L} + n\dot{N} + \dot{T},$$

where $\dot{O}$, $\dot{K}$, $\dot{L}$, and $\dot{N}$ equal the average annual percentage rates of change of output, the capital stock, land, and labour respectively; k, l, and n equal the elasticity of output with respect to capital, land, and labour respectively; and T equals total factor productivity change. We have estimates of the historically experienced values of all of these variables, and the values for $\dot{O}$, k, and $\dot{K}$ were used to reach our conclusion concerning the fraction of total output growth accounted for by the growth of the capital stock. We can approach the question of the impact of the rise in the investment share within the same framework.

The question of how the rise in the investment share affected growth implies another question, that of how the rate of growth would have differed had the investment share not risen. Given the assumed relationship, one can see that had the investment share not risen the capital stock would have grown more slowly, and thus the rate of growth of output would have been lower. Of course, if the rate of growth of the capital stock had been smaller, the rates of change of the labour supply, the land supply, and total factor productivity might also have been different. But we are interested in the direct relations between the investment share and the rate of growth (in a supply-side model) and can afford to ignore these aspects of the problem, at least for the moment.

Had the rate of growth of capital been lower than the historically observed value, the distribution of income among factors of production – the output elasticities – might also have been different. But the historical evidence suggests that the distribution of income has varied only modestly over time, despite marked differences among rates of change of factor supplies. Consequently, we can probably assume that elasticities would not have been very different from those observed historically even if the capital stock had grown more slowly.

It appears, therefore, that the counter-factual question can be answered if we can solve the equation for $\dot{O}$ and $\dot{K}$, on the assumption that the investment share remained constant at the pre-1840 level and that all other variables were at the levels historically experienced between 1840 and 1900.

We have one equation and two unknowns. However, one of the unknowns, $\dot{K}$, can be approximated by $\dot{O} + \dot{C}$, where $\dot{C}$ is the rate of change of the capital–output ratio. (Since $\dot{C}$ in this instance must be low, the approximation should be close.) We know the value of the capital–output ratio at the beginning of the period (1840), and therefore in order to calculate $\dot{C}$ we only need to know the value the capital–output ratio would have taken in 1900, had the investment share remained fixed at the pre-1840 level. This assumed 1900 value can be approximated by $i/\dot{O}$, where i is the share of investment in national product before 1840, a value we know. One can then find $\dot{C}$ from the following expression:

$$C_{1900} = i/\dot{O} = C_{1840}\,(1 + \dot{C})^{40},$$

where C_{1900} and C_{1840} refer to the capital–output ratio in those two years. Rearranging terms we get:

$$\dot{C} = \sqrt[40]{\frac{i/\dot{O}}{C_{1840}}} - 1$$

and substituting into the previous equations:

$$\dot{K} = \dot{O} + \left(\sqrt[40]{\frac{i/\dot{O}}{C_{1840}}} - 1 \right)$$

$$\dot{O} = k\left[\dot{O} + \left(\sqrt[40]{\frac{i/\dot{O}}{C_{1840}}} - 1 \right) \right] + l\dot{L} + b\dot{N} + \dot{T},$$

which leaves us with only one unknown. While the effort required to solve this equation would be disproportionate to the value of the result, we can simplify the problem and get an approximation to the desired result by letting $\dot{C}$ (which would be small in any case) assume a value of zero. That is, if the capital–output ratio is held constant, $\dot{K}$ and $\dot{O}$ are equal, and we can substitute the latter for the former in the equation:

$$\dot{O} = k\dot{K} + l\dot{L} + n\dot{N} + \dot{T}$$
$$\dot{O} = k\dot{O} + l\dot{L} + n\dot{N} + \dot{T}$$
$$\dot{O} - k\dot{O} = l\dot{L} + n\dot{N} + \dot{T}$$
$$\dot{O} = (l\dot{L} + n\dot{N} + \dot{T})/(1 - k)$$

Solving for $\dot{O}$ we obtain:

$$\dot{O} = 3 \cdot 7 \text{ per cent}$$

Since the historically experienced value of $\dot{O}$ was 4·0 per cent the calculations imply that the rise in the capital–output ratio accounted for 0·3 percentage points, or less than one-tenth, of the rate of growth of output. It will be observed, however, that if the capital–output ratio had remained at the 1840 level and if the rate of growth of output had fallen to 3·7 per cent, the logic of the model implies that the share of investment in national product would have fallen to 5·9 per cent (1·6 × 0·037, the capital–output ratio multiplied by the rate of growth of output), a level lower than that experienced before 1840. It follows that if the investment share had remained fixed at the pre-1840 level, the rate of growth of output would have been somewhat greater than 3·7 per cent, and the disparity between the observed and counter-factual rates of growth would have been slightly smaller than 0·3 per cent.

The significance of the rise in the investment share can be seen not only in the context of the aggregate growth rate but also in the context of the contribution of capital formation to growth. We have seen that the increase of the capital stock accounted for over 1 percentage point of the growth rate of output. We now see that something less than three-tenths of this effect can be attributed to the rise of the investment share, by no means an insignificant value.

So much the simple models and the numerical analysis can tell us. But it should be clear that the effort to obtain precise quantitative results does a certain violence to historical reality. As we will see, one aspect of American history reflected in the increase of the investment share and the rise of the capital–output ratio was a series of structural changes, associated with industrialization, urbanization, and the westward movement. To ask what would have happened if the investment share had held a fixed value and if the capital–output ratio had risen only modestly is to ask what would have happened had these structural changes been sharply moderated. This latter question brings to the fore the relationships among capital formation, the supply of land in production, urban development, immigration, and the labour supply. Had these structural changes been curtailed, the volume of land in production would probably have increased less, the flow of immigrants would have been more limited, and the labour supply would thus have grown more slowly. With total factor supplies increasing at smaller rates, total factor productivity change would probably have been less pronounced. One is tempted to say that the rise in the investment share was far more important than the measurement described in the previous paragraph suggests, since it was associated with structural changes that had massive effects on the American economy. But this says too much, since it asserts a clear causal line running from changes in the investment share to structural shifts, and we have no basis for making so strong a statement. What is clear is that capital formation was associated in many subtle ways with the broad range of shifts experienced by the American economy in the nineteenth century. The 'contribution' of capital formation, at this level, cannot be readily distinguished from the 'contributions' of other factors – indeed, the term 'contribution' in this context is perhaps inappropriate. Our simple model describes the way in which incremental changes are made and does not confront the nature of large changes. The numerical results must be seen in this light. They show what would have happened if capital formation had behaved differently, and if there had been no significant direct effects on other factor supplies or the like; therefore, they abstract from the nature of large changes. That the model deals with only a restricted aspect of change does not make it unusual, however. The full, accurate, and precise analysis of large economic changes remains an elusive desideratum.

IV. *Increase in the Capital–Output Ratio*

A. ANALYTICAL POSSIBILITIES

The share of real net national product invested and the capital–output ratio both rose over at least the last six decades of the nineteenth century; as it happens, the forces underlying both these developments can be explored most easily if we focus initially on the second of them.

In an economy of the type described in section II, the measured capital–output ratio might rise for any (or all) of three reasons. First, the composition of final demands might change in such a way as to raise the profitability of capital-intensive industries. Entrepreneurs would then bid factors of production into these industries at a higher rate than formerly; the relative importance of these industries would then grow; and this increased importance would raise the average capital–output ratio for the entire economy.

Secondly, technical change might be capital-using and labour- and/or land-saving. Entrepreneurs, responding to the new opportunities, would alter factor proportions, and it is probable that the capital–output ratio would rise.

Finally, relative factor prices might shift in favour of capital. Such a change might be due to an increase in the savings rate that produces a decline in the rate of interest, or to a reduction in the price of capital arising out of improved methods of capital production. With the cost of capital declining relative to other factor costs, entrepreneurs would be induced to change factor proportions, and this substitution would probably increase the capital–output ratio.

There might of course be interrelationships among these three sources of change. For example, the opportunities presented by a shift in final demand or capital-using technical change could be more fully exploited in the presence of ample supplies of savings than if savings were scarce. A change in the structure of the economy might alter income flows and thus affect savings. For example, an increase in capital-intensity due to changes in the structure of demand or to biased technical change might raise the share of income flowing to property, and if property income made an important contribution to savings, the savings rate might rise. Finally, changes in the structure of the economy might encourage the development of financial intermediaries, with consequences for the cost of capital.[15]

If one considers how the historical relevance of these three explanations might be tested, the following possibilities emerge. If a change in the composition of the economy lay behind the increase in the capital–output ratio, one might be able to identify the fact by direct observation of changes in the structure of output and the level of the capital–output ratio in the various producing entities. In principle the observations should be conducted at the level of the plant, but in practice some degree of aggregation must be accepted.

A shift in the economy toward capital-intensive activities would have to be accommodated by either an increase in the investment share or a decline in the rate of growth of output or some combination of the two. (As we have seen, in the American case both phenomena occurred; that is, the investment share rose and the rate of growth declined.) Unless fortuitous, exogenous factors accomplished these ends, the shift would have to be accompanied by a rise in the rate of interest, since the changes generate an increase in the demand for capital relative to the demand for consumer goods.

Finally, a shift toward capital-intensive activities would involve a shift in demand favouring capital over other inputs. One would therefore expect the relative cost of capital to rise, other things being equal. If that were the case, one would expect entrepreneurs to substitute other inputs for capital, and capital–output ratios – at the industry level – would tend to decline. The rise in the average capital–output ratio for the economy as a whole would be due exclusively to structural changes – that is, to changes in the relative importance of the various industries.

In summary, if the increase in the national capital–output ratio were due exclusively to changes in the structure of demand, one would expect to find (a) a shift in the composition of the economy favouring capital-intensive activities, (b) a rise in the rate of interest, (c) a rise in the relative cost of capital, and (d) decreases in the capital–output ratio at the industry level.

If the rise in the average national capital–output ratio were occasioned by technical changes that were capital-using, one would expect to find the capital–output ratio rising within certain industries. But there is no good reason for supposing that capital-using technical change would emerge across the whole spectrum of economic activity at the same time. It would be more likely to appear here and there, so that capital-deepening would not necessarily be widely diffused across the economy. In fact, one should find evidence of capital-shallowing in some industries. The effects of capital-using technical change on the relative cost of capital ought to be the same as the effects of the structural changes previously described: that is, given the increased demand for capital, the cost of capital ought to rise relative to other factor costs. Entrepreneurs in industries unaffected by the capital-using technical changes would therefore be induced to substitute against capital, with the effect of reducing the capital–output ratio within their industries. One would therefore expect to find capital-deepening in some industries and capital-shallowing in others, if the rise in the national capital–output ratio were due entirely to capital-using technical change.

Finally, if capital-deepening were due to a decline in the cost of capital relative to other factor costs, one should be able to observe the phenomenon directly, although the assembly and appraisal of evidence would not be simple. The cost of capital has three components: the price of capital goods, the rate of interest and the depreciation rate. The depreciation rate cannot be regarded as an independent factor, since the principal long-term changes in the rate – the only changes we are able to measure – simply reflect shifts in the composition of the capital stock. If the decline in the relative cost of capital were due to a reduction in the rate of interest (relative to other factor costs), one would expect to find capital-deepening quite widely diffused across the economy. If, on the other hand, it were due to a decline in the prices of capital goods (relative to other factor costs), the effects are not so easily set out. Presumably not all capital prices would be falling (relatively), and those falling would not necessarily be falling at the same rate. Consequently, some industries might not experience capital-deepening. Presumably the pattern of price change would be reflected in the pattern of change of the capital stock. That is, the composition of the capital stock would tend to shift. The capital goods experiencing relative price declines would assume a larger relative importance in the capital stock.

In summary, of the three basic sources of a rise in the capital–output ratio, two – structural change and a decline in the relative cost of capital – are in principle directly observable. Widely diffused capital-deepening constitutes indirect evidence consistent with a decline in the relative cost of capital. Other things being equal, there is no reason why either structural change or capital-using technical change should be associated with *general* capital-deepening, but there is reason for these developments to be associated with a rise in the relative cost of capital. The rise might, however, be moderated if the effects of these developments on income flows or financial intermediaries increased the savings rate.

With this background, we turn to the empirical record with the object of determining which of the three reasons for capital-deepening are relevant to the nineteenth-century American experience.

B. THE EMPIRICAL RECORD

There is evidence that the composition of the American economy changed drastically in the nineteenth century, and there is reason to suppose that the changes were to an important degree a consequence of alterations in demand, the latter due in no small measure to the interaction between an enduring demand structure – describable roughly by Engel curves – and a rising per capita income. It is more difficult to come to a final conclusion as to the effects of these compositional shifts on the average capital–output ratio. The problem is one of adequate data. The answer requires detailed capital–output estimates, expressed in constant prices; but constant-price output data are available only for broad industrial sectors, and there are few adequate constant-price capital figures even at this level of aggregation. Current-price estimates of depreciable capital (i.e. capital exclusive of inventories) can be assembled for each industrial sector (Table 4) and for regional constituents of agriculture (Table 6 below). Evidence bearing on the components of the manufacturing sector also exists (Table 5 below), but the capital concept involved is considerably broader than the one described (it includes land and intangibles). For the very important non-commodity sector, few reliable data are available. From this mixed evidence a hazy picture emerges.

Constant-price data are very nearly limited to broad industrial sectors. These data suggest that compositional changes probably made for capital-*shallowing*. Of the three main divisions of the economy – agriculture, industry, and services – the output of industry grew the fastest, while the capital–output ratio of this sector was probably the lowest of the three (Table 4). The average annual rates of change of real value added (real net output) by the three sectors over the period 1840–1900 were roughly as follows: agriculture, 2·6 per cent; industry, 5·2 per cent; services, 4·2 per cent.[16] The shift in the distribution of output among the three sectors – holding the capital–output ratio of each fixed at the 1840 level – would have tended to lower the average national capital–output ratio. The point is worth underlining, since so much has been written about the capital requirements of the industrial sector and the tendency for industrialization to raise the capital–output ratio. The data suggest that this was not so in the American case.

Yet this result is not quite acceptable. It may reflect an unsatisfactory classification system rather than a substantive finding. The fact is that farm housing is treated as part of the capital stock of the agricultural sector, while the housing occupied by industrial workers is not counted as part of industrial capital. If the two sectors were treated comparably in this matter, the structural shift might very well be observed to have had consequences different from those recorded above. But the data necessary to make the required adjustments are not available.

If we accept the data as they stand, and if the current-price series on depreciable capital can be made to do service for the required (but

Table 4. *Ratios of Depreciable Capital to Net Income Originating, by Industrial Sectors, 1840–1900 (current prices)*

	Agriculture	Mining and manufacturing	Services[a]
1840	1·2	0·9	1·2
1850	1·6	0·9	1·6
1860	1·7	0·9	2·1
1870	1·5	1·0	2·3
1880	1·6	1·2	2·4
1890	1·9	1·3	2·8
1900	2·1	1·5	2·8

[a] Includes construction and a few other commodity-producing industries of minor significance.

SOURCE. Davis and Gallman, 'Share of Savings and Investment', Table 10.

Note. The data underlying this table differ in important respects from the data underlying Table 3. They are expressed in current rather than constant prices. The capital stock data exclude inventories, whereas the data underlying Table 3 include them. The estimates of income originating were necessarily produced by a procedure differing from, and inferior to, the procedures used to obtain the net national product estimates underlying Table 3. Without much doubt the income-originating series describe rates of change that are biased in an upward direction. Thus the capital–output ratios contained in this table tend to *understate* the temporal increases in the sectoral capital–output ratios.

unavailable) constant-price series on total capital, it is clear that the upward pressure on the national ratio was occasioned by capital-deepening within each of the sectors (Table 4). For agriculture, the development came late and was of modest dimensions, while in industry it was confined to the decades after 1860, although it was prominent during that period. Within the services sector, the change was of long duration, persistent and pronounced. Since urban housing and transportation are included in the services sector, we may be observing here the effect of industrialization on the demand for non-farm housing (mentioned above) and transportation: that is, the upward movement of the services ratio may be a reflection of the growth of the industrial sector, a point to which we will return.

The sectoral evidence involves a substantial degree of aggregation. One would like to know what was going on within these sectors. Specifically, one would like to know whether or not the changes in the sectoral ratios reflected shifts in the composition of these sectors.

The best evidence we have on this subject relates to manufacturing and suggests that capital-deepening was widespread within the sector. While the structure of output shifted somewhat over time, the changes had only modest impacts on the sectoral capital–output ratio. Creamer's findings for the period from 1880 onward, which relate to both current-price and constant-price data, make this very clear.[17] The current-price data in Table 5, while much weaker, nonetheless suggest that these developments were of even longer duration. The data show that the upward pressure on the ratio occurred within most of the industries composing manufacturing. In every one of these industries but two or three, the capital-output ratio was higher in 1880 than it was thirty years earlier, and most of the change appears to have come in the ten years between 1870 and 1880, which is consistent with the findings for the sector as a whole (Table 4). Interestingly enough, the capital–output ratios of the so-called heavy industries do not appear to have been generally higher than those of the light industries, nor do they appear to have risen more sharply over time. Once again, the evidence tends to run against the conventional view, in this instance the notion that heavy industry was capital-intensive and that the development of this industry demanded masses of investment.

The data necessary to classify agricultural operations by type of production are not available, but regional data are probably fairly good proxies for the required classifications, since the regions specialized in different types of agricultural production. The regional evidence suggests that the capital–output ratio did vary among farms specializing in different kinds of output, but there is no indication that changes in the structure of output across the last part of the nineteenth century

Table 5. *Manufacturing Sector Capital–Output Ratios and Value Added, by Industry Group, 1850–80 (current prices)*

A. Ratios of Capital to Value Added

		1850	1860	1870	1880
1	Ordnance	1·2	1·3	1·0	2·0
2	Food and kindred products	1·8	1·6	1·6	2·0
3	Tobacco products	0·8	0·9	0·7	0·7
4	Textile mill products and apparel	1·5	1·4	1·4	1·5
5	Lumber products	1·2	1·2	1·2	1·7
6	Furniture	0·6	0·8	1·0	1·0
7	Pulp, paper, and allied products	1·5	1·3	1·6	1·6
8	Printing	0·8	1·0	0·9	1·0
9	Chemicals and products of petroleum and coal	1·4	1·4	1·5	1·9
10	Rubber products	1·0	1·4	1·1	1·0
11	Leather and leather products	0·7	0·8	0·8	1·0
12	Stone, clay, and glass	1·0	0·9	1·2	1·3
13	Primary metals and fabricated metals	1·5	1·4	1·3	1·7
14	Machinery and professional instruments	1·1	1·0	1·2	1·5
15	Transportation equipment	0·6	0·8	0·9	1·1

B. Distribution of Value Added among SIC Minor Commodity Groups[a] (per cent)

		1850	1860	1870	1880
1	Ordnance	0·4	0·3	0·3	0·3
2	Food and kindred products	11·4	12·4	13·1	13·3
3	Tobacco products	1·6	1·9	2·5	2·9
4	Textile mill products and apparel	23·1	21·8	18·2	22·9
5	Lumber products	10·7	10·3	11·6	8·7
6	Furniture	3·2	2·5	3·2	2·7
7	Pulp, paper, and allied products	1·5	1·7	1·7	2·2
8	Printing	2·3	2·9	3·5	4·1
9	Chemicals and products of petroleum and coal	4·1	3·9	3·7	4·1
10	Rubber products	0·4	0·3	0·5	0·5
11	Leather and leather products	13·9	11·4	10·5	8·4
12	Stone, clay, and glass	3·0	4·2	4·7	4·0
13	Primary metals and fabricated metals	12·3	11·0	12·3	11·6
14	Machinery and professional instruments	6·1	7·7	9·1	9·9
15	Transportation equipment	6·1	7·6	5·0	4·3
	Totals	100·1	99·9	99·9	99·9

[a] Certain Minor Commodity Groups have been combined (e.g. 'Textile Mill Products' and 'Apparel'). The 'Miscellaneous' SIC Group has been excluded.

SOURCES. Census returns, classified according to US Department of Commerce, *Standard Industrial Classification Manual* (Washington, 1945). For a discussion of the data and the system of classification, see Gallman, 'Gross National Product', 42–52, and Robert E. Gallman, 'Commodity Output, 1839–1899', in William N. Parker (ed.), *Trends in the American Economy*, Studies in Income and Wealth, 24 (Princeton, 1960), 13–15 and 56–60. Non-manufacturing industries returned by the census have been excluded, but otherwise the census data have not been corrected. 'Value added' is defined is value of output minus value of materials consumed in production.

tended to raise the sectoral capital–output ratio (Table 6). The suggestion, once again, is that capital-deepening was widely diffused.

The services sector is more difficult to disaggregate and is, in any case, a sector that poses severe conceptual and measurement problems, so that the available evidence is unusually treacherous. Nonetheless, there is some evidence that the relative expansion of the transport and

Table 6. *Relative Agricultural Capital–Output Ratios and Distribution of Agricultural Income among Regions, 1880–1900*

	Relative capital–output ratios (national average = 100)			Distribution of income (per cent)		
	1840	1880	1900	1840	1880	1900
Northeast	115	183	190	40·7	22·4	14·7
New England	149	227	210	10·9	4·4	3·1
Middle Atlantic	103	172	185	29·8	18·0	11·6
South	62	51	62	43·7	28·9	30·5
South Atlantic	61	53	67	21·7	10·8	9·9
East South Central	59	56	68	17·6	11·1	9·5
West South Central	77	37	55	4·4	7·0	11·1
West	166	91	91	15·7	48·8	54·8
East North Central	175	100	111	13·4	29·1	23·3
West North Central	104	84	92	2·3	15·3	24·1
Mountain and Pacific	—	55	69	—	4·4	7·4
Totals				100·1	100·1	100·0

SOURCES. Regional distribution of agricultural output: Richard A. Easterlin, 'Interregional Differences in Per Capita Income, Population and Total Income, 1840–1950', in Parker (ed.), *Trends in the American Economy*, Tables A-1, A-2, and A-3.

Regional distribution of agricultural capital: Capital estimates from Robert E. Gallman and Edward S. Howle, 'Fixed Reproducible Capital in the United States, 1840–1900' (unpublished paper presented to Seminar on the Application of Economic Theory and Quantitative Techniques to Problems of Economic History, Purdue University, February 1965; mimeographed). The estimates are distributed among states on the basis of census data. Capital includes only buildings and equipment.

urban-housing components – both capital-intensive – played a role in the increase of the sectoral ratio.[18] That is, the service sector is the only one of the three in which compositional changes appear to be responsible for the increase in the capital–output ratio. As noted above, this development is no doubt associated with the growth of the industrial sector.

In summary, examination of the detailed data on capital–output ratios suggests that structural changes – specifically the growing relative importance of urban housing and railroads – had something to do with the rise in the average national capital–output ratio. But the full explanation of the increase in the average ratio does not lie here. The ratios in the component parts of the economy were also rising, which suggests either that the economy was experiencing capital-using technical change and/or that the relative price of capital was declining. The fact that the phenomenon was a general one argues for the latter explanation.

There are two other lines of evidence that tend to support this conclusion. We argued previously that if structural shifts or capital-using technical changes had been the only factors behind the increase in the capital–output ratio the rate of interest would have risen. The evidence shows that the nominal rate actually declined over the long run (Table 9 below). But the nominal rate is not precisely the rate required in this context. For example, in the years between 1870 and the mid-1880s the price level declined persistently. Lenders could anticipate receiving not only the nominal rate of interest but also an appreciation in the real value of their debt instruments. Presumably they understood this and therefore the nominal interest rate reflected only part of the real return they expected when they agreed to lend. The interest rate required in the present context is the real rate – i.e. the nominal rate adjusted upward to reflect anticipated price declines, or downward to reflect anticipated price increases – since it is the real rate that gives the clearest reflection of changes in the demand for capital relative to the supply of savings.

Unfortunately, there is no way to observe historical anticipations of price change directly. In econometric work they are most often estimated as the weighted average of past changes, the more recent changes receiving heavier weights than the more remote. The theory underlying such calculations is that anticipations are formed by experience and that the more recent the experience, the more important it is. However, experience involves more than a knowledge of the magnitude of past changes. It also creates an appreciation of patterns of change. Thus, for example, after an extended period of price decline, at least some investors would begin to expect future price increases, on the ground that in the past price changes had followed a roughly cyclical pattern. A simple way to deal with this development econometrically is to permit actual future price changes to influence the value of the estimate of anticipated change. Thus, for example, one might estimate the anticipated price change in 1840 as some average of actual price changes in 1840 and in the years preceding and succeeding that date.[19] Other systems of estimation are easily devised, but the nature of the data available does not warrant more sophisticated treatment.

It should be clear that estimates derived by weighting actual price changes will depend on the number of observations used and the weights assigned to them. No very compelling case can be made for the selection of one system as against another, but once selected a

Table 7. *Index Numbers of Estimated Real Interest Rates, 1840–1900 (base: 1840 = 100)*

	Index A		Index B	
	(1)	(2)	(1)	(2)
1840	100	100	100	100
1850	79	65	77	61
1860	95	(52)	97	(49)
1870	119	108	104	93
1880	103	82	88	66
1890	76	70	63	57
1900	31	32	10	13

SOURCES AND NOTES. Computed by adjusting nominal interest rates for anticipated price changes. Nominal rates were adjusted upward in years in which price declines were anticipated, and vice versa. The data on nominal interest rates were taken from sources described in the notes to Table 9 (Index A resting on data from the first source, Index B on data from the second source). The price data used were from Bureau of the Census, *Historical Statistics*, Series E-1 and E-13. Anticipated price changes (expressed in percentile form) were estimated as weighted averages of actual price changes. The averages underlying Indexes A(1) and B(1) refer to past price changes (eight years, with weights running from 1 to 8). The averages underlying Indexes A(2) and B(2) were constructed by combining the data underlying Indexes A(1) and B(1) with data on future price changes (four years, weighted 6, 4, 2, and 2). See text.

The indexes are highly speculative. Estimates of price anticipations are highly volatile, as are the underlying price series. The bracketed index numbers for 1860 are especially speculative, since they incorporate the effects of price changes during the Civil War. While some investors no doubt anticipated war in 1860, and some may have expected price increases due to war, the formula used in the calculation of the index number probably accords too heavy a weight to this sentiment.

system should be followed consistently to minimize the effects of the investigator's preconceptions on the measures he produces. It should also be clear that no very great significance can be attached to the value obtained for any given year. At best we can hope to obtain a rough idea of the general trend of the real interest rate.

Table 7 contains four sets of index numbers describing the changes in the real rate of interest between 1840 and 1900. They are based on two different nominal-interest-rate series and two methods of computing anticipated price changes – one depending entirely on past changes, and the other giving some weight to future changes. (See the notes to the table.) Broadly speaking, all four describe the same general movements, and the consistency of the results from the four series increases one's confidence in them. The long-term drift of the real rate of interest was downward, with an interruption between 1850 and 1870 (perhaps

Table 8. *Index Numbers of Cost of Capital Relative to Cost of Labour, 1840–1900 (base: 1840 = 100)*

	A		B	
	(1)	(2)	(1)	(2)
1840	100	100	100	100
1850	98	92	100	93
1860	79	(70)	82	(72)
1870	74	87	61	76
1880	81	58	76	46
1890	54	47	47	39
1900	48	45	40	37

SOURCES AND NOTES. Column A depends upon the interest rates in Table 9, column 4; Column B upon the interest rates in Table 9, column 5.

The estimates of labour cost represent weighted averages of the wage-rate indexes in Table 9, the weights representing shares of agriculture and all other sectors in real national income, derived from Davis *et al.*, *American Economic Growth*, 55, and the wage rates underlying Table 9 below.

The cost of capital was computed from the formula $q(i + d - \dot{q})$, where q is the price index of capital goods, i the nominal rate of interest, d the depreciation rate, and $\dot{q}$ the expected rate of change of the price index of capital. Calculations were made from the data in or underlying Table 9. The expected rate of change of the price index of capital was calculated as (1) the average rate of change of the price index across the preceding decade (Indexes A(1) and B(1)) and (2) the weighted average rate of change of the price index across the preceding decade (weight: 2) and the succeeding decade (weight: 1) (Indexes A(2) and B(2)). See the notes to Table 7.

The rationale behind the use of this cost-of-capital formula is as follows. We want a measure of the annual rental per new machine, or other piece of capital – a measure conceptually similar to the wage rate. The annual rental must be sufficient to cover the opportunity costs of the funds tied up in the new piece of capital and to return the price of the new piece of capital during its lifetime. The rental rate must therefore cover the interest rate and the depreciation rate, plus any capital losses (or minus any capital gains) that are anticipated in the coming year.

The formula can also be written in the following way: $q(r + \dot{p} + d - \dot{q})$ where r is the real rate of interest, $\dot{p}$ is the anticipated rate of change of the general price level and $r + \dot{p}$ is, of course, the nominal rate of interest. In this formulation it becomes clear that the adjustment for anticipated price change is an adjustment of the real rate of interest for the anticipated change in the price of capital *relative to* the anticipated change in the general price level.

The bracketed figures for 1860 incorporate effects of the Civil War (see note to Table 7 above).

confined to 1860–70). The suggestion is, then, that the supply schedule of savings increased somewhat faster across the full period than did the demand schedule for investment, a finding that supports our previous statement that changes in the structure of demand do not fully account for the observed rise of the capital–output ratio.

The findings that capital-deepening was widely diffused and that the long-term path of the real rate of interest was downward suggest that the increase in the capital–output ratio may have been occasioned by a reduction in the relative cost of capital. The fragmentary direct evidence of the relative cost of capital is consistent with this idea. Table 8 presents four sets of index numbers of the cost of capital relative to the cost of labour. The differences among the four variants are of the same nature as are the differences among the four series in Table 7. (See the notes to the two tables.) All four series in Table 8 show very pro-nounced downward long-term trends in the relative cost of capital for the full period. The testimony concerning the period 1860–80 is mixed. Two of the series indicate a modest rise in the relative cost of capital during 1860–70, followed by a pronounced decline; the other two record a decline followed by a rise. In the latter two cases the value of the index number is roughly the same in 1880 as in 1860; in the former two, it is markedly lower. These diverse results are produced by the price-anticipation estimates, it should be said; leaving anticipa-tions out of account, one obtains a persistent decline in the relative cost of capital over the entire period 1840–1900.

It seems clear, then, that the drift of the relative cost of capital was such as to encourage entrepreneurs to substitute capital for labour, and thus to tend to raise the capital–output ratio. This factor did not operate with equal force across each decade of the period, and there may have been a limited movement in the opposite direction in at least one decade; but these represent only modest qualifications to the main conclusion.

It is of some interest to see how the various components of the rela-tive cost of capital behaved. The rate of depreciation rose persistently, roughly in step with the wage rates of labour (Table 9), the increase reflecting a shift in the composition of the capital stock. The importance of depreciable capital – such as equipment, machinery, and structures – grew relative to non-depreciable capital – inventories – and within the class of depreciable capital, short-lived components – equipment, machinery – increased in importance as compared with long-lived components (Tables 11 and 12 below). Thus the ratio of capital con-sumption to the value of the capital stock necessarily grew. Changes in the depreciation rate therefore did not operate to lower the relative cost of capital.

Table 9. *Index Numbers of Components of the Cost of Labour
and the Cost of Capital, 1840–1900 (base: 1840 = 100)*

	1	2	3	4	5	6	7
					Interest rates		
	Farm wage rate	Non-farm wage rate	Price of capital goods	Average rate on property[a]	Rail-road bonds	Short-term[b]	Rate of depreci-ation
1840	100	100	100	100	(100)[c]	—	100
1850	104	106	95	100	100	100	110
1860	131	122	104	95	98	106	(120)[c]
1870	133	184	124	110	90	81	(135)
1880	112	151	100	85	64	76	150
1890	133	164	95	70	52	60	150
1900	140	166	88	65	44	54	(150)

[a] Estimates of ratio of property income (all types) to value of land and capital.
[b] Decade averages: 1840–9, 1850–9, etc.
[c] Bracketed figures represent extrapolations or interpolations.

SOURCES. Wage rates: Stanley Lebergott, 'Wage Trends, 1800–1900', in Parker (ed.), *Trends in the American Economy*, 462.

Price of capital goods: implicit price index of the capital stock, derived from worksheets underlying chap. 2 of Davis *et al.*, *American Economic Growth*.

Interest rates:

Average rate on property: Davis *et al.*, *op. cit.*, 38.

Railroad bond rates: Paul J. Uselding, 'Factor Substitution and Labor Productivity Growth in American Manufacturing, 1839–1899', *Journal of Economic History* XXXII, 3 (September 1972), 672.

Short-term rates: Erastus A. Bigelow, *Tariff Questions Considered in Regard to the Policy of England and the Interests of the United States* (Boston, 1862), and Frederick R. Macauley, *Some Theoretical Problems suggested by the Movement of Interest Rates, Bond Yields, and Stock Prices in the United States since 1856* (New York, 1938). Data were averaged first by year and then by decade.

Rate of depreciation: ratio of capital consumption to value of capital stock (current prices), the former computed on the assumption that the annual rate of capital consumption for improvements was 2·5 per cent, and for equipment 10·0 per cent; the latter, taken from worksheets underlying chap. 2 of Davis *et al.*, *op. cit.*

The decline in the relative cost of capital was clearly due to the fact that both the price index of capital goods and the interest rate fell as compared with the indexes of wage rates, the drop in the interest rate being particularly marked. The price index of capital goods has, of course, a two-sided effect on the cost of capital. For example, when it is falling, it reduces the base against which cost calculations are made, but it also produces a positive value for the price-anticipation term in the cost-of-capital formula. Thus the downward pressure on the cost of capital originating in the reduced price level is moderated by the effects

Table 10. *Price Indexes of GNP and Components of Investment, 1839–99 (base: 1860 = 100)*

	1	2	3	4	5	6	7	8	9
		All	All fixed	Total	Railroads				Manufacturer's
		capital	capital	construc-					produced
	GNP[a]	(stocks)[b]	(flows)	tion	(Fishlow)[c]	(Ulmer)	Houses	Factories	durables
1839	94	96	100	98	(100)[c]	(104)[c]	—	—	109
1844	90	—	96	92	99	103	109	76	109
1849	96	91	99	95	94	100	95	107	113
1854	105	—	99	98	108	109	87	107	106
1859	102	100	100	98	100	100	98	—	105
1869	138	119	110	114		172	134	94	100
1874	128	—	109	116		167	—	—	94
1879	104	96	94	112		129	122	107	68
1884	108	—	93	120		146	—	—	51
1889	98	91	77	110		143	132	89	42
1894	91	—	72	96		131	—	—	35
1899	93	85	85	108		144	—	—	39

[a] GNP estimates are unadjusted for inventory changes.
[b] Capital stock price indexes refer to 1840, 1850, etc.
[c] Indexes in brackets are for 1840.

SOURCES. Cols. 1, 3, 4, and 9: Gallman, 'Gross National Product, 1834–1909', 26 and 34, or underlying worksheets.
Col. 2 is col. 3 of Table 9 above, shifted to the base 1860 without reweighting.
Col. 5: Albert Fishlow, *American Railroads and the Transformation of the Ante-bellum Economy* (Cambridge, Mass., 1965), 389.
Col. 6: Melville J. Ulmer, *Capital in Transportation, Communications, and Public Utilities: Its Formation and Financing* (Princeton, 1960), 275–6, indexes shifted to the base 1860 without reweighting.
Cols. 7 and 8: Brady (ed.), *Output, Employment and Productivity*, 110 and 111.

of price reductions on anticipations. With this in mind it becomes fairly clear that the movements of the interest rate were of greater importance in reducing the cost of capital than were the movements of the price index of capital.

The components of the price index of capital behaved in quite disparate ways (Table 10). Most of the downward pressure on the index after 1860 arose out of the prices of factories and manufactured producers' durables, chiefly the latter. Furthermore, the durables price index captures a very general movement, a movement that affected the prices of industrial and farm machinery, office and railroad equipment, shipping, and even (although to a lesser degree) hand tools.[20] These phenomena are reflected in the shifting composition of investment flows and stocks. Investment in durables increased relative to

Table 11. *Distribution of Net Investment among Types of Investment, 1839–48 to 1884–93 (at 1860 prices) (per cent)*

	Manu-factured producers' durables	Construction	Inventory changes	Changes in claims against foreigners	Total
1839–48	5·1	61·2	28·1	+5·6	100·0
1844–53	9·4	69·2	24·5	−3·1	100·0
1849–58	8·5	74·3	21·8	−4·6	100·0
1867–78	13·9	72·3	20·1	−6·5	99·8
1874–83	21·5	58·2	20·4	−0·1	100·0
1879–88	24·6	56·6	21·1	−2·3	100·0
1884–93	23·5	54·8	15·0	+6·8	100·1

SOURCE. Calculated from data on worksheets underlying chap. 2 of Davis *et al.*, *American Economic Growth*.

investment in improvements, and the movement appears to have been very general, affecting virtually all the main industrial sectors (Tables 11 and 12). The price indexes of factories and durables fell relative to the GNP price index, suggesting that the supply schedules for these goods must have been shifting outward with unusual speed, presumably due to exceptionally fruitful technical innovation, improved materials supplies, or the like (e.g. improved supplies of machine tools).[21]

The price indexes of railroads and houses, on the other hand, rose well above the levels of the other fixed capital-goods price indexes and also above the GNP price index, in the period 1860–70, and remained relatively high to the end of the century. The railroad price index is almost certainly biased in an upward direction.[22] Still, the general pattern observed may be realistic. Furthermore, the behaviour of these two

Table 12. *Distribution of Stocks of Depreciable Capital between Equipment and Improvements, by Industrial Sectors, 1840–1900 (at 1860 prices) (per cent)*

	Agriculture		Manufacturing and mining		Transportation and public utilities		All other		Total	
	Eq.	Imp.	Eq.	Imp.	Eq.	Imp.	Eq.	Imp.	Eq.	Imp.
1840	15·2	84·8	45·3	54·7	15·1	84·9	13·8	86·2	18·3	81·7
1850	15·6	84·4	44·2	55·8	19·5	80·5	10·9	89·1	17·4	82·6
1860	16·1	83·9	48·7	51·3	21·6	78·4	12·8	87·2	18·6	81·4
1870	14·7	85·3	48·8	51·2	24·0	76·0	16·2	83·8	22·2	77·8
1880	23·9	76·1	62·0	38·0	22·4	77·6	22·1	77·9	29·2	70·8
1890	27·3	72·7	64·4	35·6	23·7	76·3	27·3	72·7	34·4	65·6
1900	34·0	66·0	67·2	32·8	27·9	72·1	29·1	70·9	39·1	60·9

SOURCE. Gallman and Howle, 'Fixed Reproducible Capital'.

price indexes is consistent with our prior conclusion that the growth of the railroads and urban housing arose out of a structural shift in the economy and that the increases in the capital–output ratio due to this shift reflected primarily demand, rather than supply, phenomena.

In summary, the quantitative evidence indicates that the observed increase in the national capital–output ratio reflected both a shift in the structure of demand favouring capital-intensive activities and a decline in the relative cost of capital. None of the evidence gives very strong reason for believing that capital-using technical change played a leading role.

It goes without saying that the data are not adequate to permit us to distribute the responsibility for the observed increase in the capital–output ratio among the sources of the increase that we have identified. However, the preceding discussion has indicated that the interest rate had a particularly important role to play in the behaviour of the cost of capital. Both the nominal and the real rates of interest declined during the period, at a time when the demand for capital was increasing rapidly. The suggestion is that the supply of savings was increasing even faster. The remaining sections of this chapter are devoted to a discussion of the forces bearing on the increase in the volume of savings. The following sub-section, which deals with the quantitative evidence on the savings rate, serves as an introduction to this material.

C. THE SAVINGS RATE

The general tendency for the rate of interest to fall suggests that the supply schedule of savings was shifting outward faster than the demand schedule of investment. But while we have some fairly comprehensive and strong data on the conventional *demands* for savings, the evidence on saving itself is less adequate. We know that real net investment and real capital consumption – the two claims on saving – each increased faster than national product, so that the share of real gross investment in national product also increased (Tables 1, 13, and 14). We know also that the price index of investment goods tended to fall relative to the price index of GNP. These two developments were compensatory, at least in direction, and would be consistent with a rising, constant, or declining share of savings (current prices) in national product.

But what, in fact, happened to the savings share? The available data – which are gathered in the first column of Table 14 – suggest that it rose, and that the post-war values of the savings share were probably about half again as large as the pre-war values. Beyond these statements it would be unwise to go. In view of the limited number of observations in the ante-bellum years (and the wide variations in the values of

Table 13. *Share of Gross Domestic Investment Accounted for by Capital Consumption, 1834–43 to 1889–98 (at 1860 prices) (per cent)*

1834–43	23·7
1839–48	29·1
1844–53	26·0
1849–58	29·5
1869–78	30·3
1874–83	30·5
1879–88	37·0
1884–93	38·2
1889–98	41·7

SOURCE. Calculated from data on worksheets underlying chap. 2 of Davis *et al.*, *American Economic Growth.*

Table 14. *Share of Gross Investment in GNP, 1839 to 1889–98, at current prices and at 1860 prices (per cent)*

	Current prices	1860 prices
1839	(15)[a]	(15)[a]
1844	12	12
1849	14	13
1854	18	18
1859	(15)[b]	(15)[b]
Mean 1839–59	15	15
1869–78	18	24
1874–83	19	24
1879–88	21	25
1884–93	23	28
1889–98	23	30

[a] Bracketed items for 1839 incorporate estimates of inventory change based on experience for 1839–49.
[b] Bracketed items for 1859 incorporate estimates of inventory change based on experience for 1849–59.

SOURCE. Calculated from data on worksheets underlying chap. 2 of Davis *et al.*, *American Economic Growth.*

these observations) one cannot speak with much confidence of pre-war trends. The increase in the savings rate between the pre-war years and the first post-war decade for which we have data seems rather small – 3 percentage points – compared with the rise across the rest of the century – 5 percentage points. But one should not make too much of this. The timing of the rise is much affected by the estimates of the value of inventory changes – the weakest component of the investment series, and one particularly ill designed to trace out short-term movements of inventory changes accurately. Furthermore, the current-price variant of this component of investment is measured in the table as the change in the value of stocks. Thus, during periods of rising prices the increment in the value of stocks, due exclusively to the price rise, is treated as a component of saving, while during a period of falling prices, the loss in value of inventories (a capital loss) is treated as dis-savings. This aspect of the measure has little significance for the estimates in Table 14, except for the estimate relating to the decade 1869–78, a decade during which prices were falling markedly. If we ignore the estimated dis-savings arising out of price declines of inventoried goods in that decade, the savings rate changes from 18 per cent to almost 21 per cent, and the picture emerging from Table 14 is altered markedly with respect to the timing of the increase in the savings rate. While the concept underlying the estimates in Table 14 may well be the appropriate one in this context, the results are so sensitive to the particular concept of saving that is being used that one is unwilling to make strong assertions concerning the exact timing of the rise in the savings rate – especially in view of the known measurement weaknesses of the estimates involved.[23] What can be said is that the savings rate appears to have gone up, and by a substantial amount.

We have been dealing with conventional concepts of saving and investment, the national product, and the national capital stock. What would happen if we were to introduce unconventional components? Would the savings rate be shown to rise faster or more slowly than the conventional record shows? Would the timing of the changes be altered in any significant way?

The answers to these questions seem clear enough, in a general way. The most important unconventional component of savings and investment omitted from the previous account is surely the clearing and breaking of farm land and the construction of fences, sheds, barns, and cabins from farm materials. While we cannot know with any exactitude how important these items were, we do know that they constituted a significant but declining fraction of total investment activity.[24] The best estimates currently available suggest that the savings rate would have to be adjusted upward by about 2 percentage points in the two decades before the Civil War and in the decade 1869–78 and by negligible amounts thereafter, if we were to take into account savings carried out in this form.[25] No doubt the relative importance of this type of saving and investment was considerably greater in the decades before 1840. In some measure, then, the rise in the savings rate, conventionally measured, reflects the diversion of savings from unconventional – and usually unmeasured – forms into conventional forms, a point to which we will return.

Most of the remaining unconventional types of savings have grown relatively more important, rather than less, over time. One could argue that consumer durables should be treated as a form of investment, and Juster and Lipsey find that if this convention were adopted the decline in the American gross investment rate since the early twentieth century would be converted into a modest rise.[26] The change produced in the nineteenth-century record would be equally striking. In current price magnitudes, consumer durables accounted for less than 3 per cent of GNP in 1839, but the share rose to 4·8 per cent by 1859 and to 5·7 per cent in 1869–78. In constant prices, the rise was even more

Table 15. *Share of GNP Accounted for by Consumer Durables,*
1839 to 1899–1909, at current prices and at 1860 prices (per cent)

	Current prices	1860 prices
1839	2·8	2·0[a]
1844	3·7	2·7[a]
1849	4·7	3·9[a]
1854	4·9	4·6[a]
1859	4·8	—
1869–78	5·7	6·2
1874–83	5·3	6·4
1879–88	5·6	7·4
1884–93	6·8	8·1
1889–98	5·9	8·0
1894–1903	5·6	7·5
1899–1909	5·9	7·2

[a] The four ante-bellum figures refer to decade averages: 1834–43, 1839–48, 1844–53, and 1849–58 respectively.

SOURCES. Gallman, 'Gross National Product', 26 and 27. The GNP estimates were adjusted for inventory changes, using data in worksheets underlying chap. 2 of Davis *et al.*, *American Economic Growth.*

marked (see Table 15). If durables were counted as part of savings and investment, the fraction of American product saved and invested would show a larger increase – particularly over the period from 1839 (1834–43) to 1869–78 – than the conventional measures exhibit.[27]

The same kind of development, although somewhat less pronounced, would occur if one were to count as savings and investment American expenditure of resources on formal education – investment in human capital. Fishlow has shown that these expenditures – including forgone earnings of students – comprised small but growing shares of American GNP over the last half of the nineteenth century. How a measure of the wider concept of investment in human capital – including, for instance, on-the-job training – would behave cannot be known with certainty, but the chances are good that it would also rise relative to GNP.[28]

Finally, it is necessary to consider the effects of the slave system, and the abolition of that system, on the savings rate. To the slave-owning planters, slaves were a form of investment, a repository for savings. Could the dramatic rise in the real investment share and the less dramatic, but still pronounced, increase in the savings share between 1860 and the post-war years reflect no more than the Emancipation and the efforts of Southerners to rebuild their asset positions by intensive conventional savings efforts? While one cannot absolutely rule out such an interpretation, it does not seem to have substantial merits. Certainly one would suppose that the loss of assets by planters might shift their savings functions. However, concomitant with these developments was a pronounced decline in Southern income. In 1870, real per capita Southern income was only about six-tenths as high as it had been in 1860 and it was not until 1880 that the pre-war level was again attained. By then the share of the South in US national income had fallen to 15 per cent.[29] It seems likely that the effects of any shift in the Southern savings function would have been swamped by the changes in per capita income and, more particularly, by the declining relative importance of the South.[30]

In summary, it appears that in part the measured rise in the conventional savings rate reflects a shift from unconventional to conventional forms of saving. But that is only part of the story. The savings rate – including unconventional components of saving – almost certainly did rise. In the following sections we consider the factors that were responsible for the increase in the savings rate.

V.   Savings

Models of economic growth often associate savings with property income or some component thereof, a convention dating back at least as far as the work of David Ricardo. It may be appropriate, then, to begin our examination of the forces bearing on the US savings rate by considering the changing distribution of income between labour and property.

Estimates of the functional distribution of income in the US during the nineteenth century have been made in two separate ways. They have been derived directly from data on factor supplies and rates of remuneration and they have also been obtained by fitting aggregate production functions to estimates of inputs and national product.

The most recent direct estimates suggest that property income accounted for about 32 per cent of national income, the value changing from one date to the next but exhibiting no long-term tendency to rise or fall.[31] However, for present purposes – the analysis of savings behaviour – we need information on gross magnitudes rather than net magnitudes: that is, we require data describing the share of gross property income in gross national product.

The data contained in Table 13 above indicate that capital consumption constituted a growing fraction of gross domestic investment (expressed in constant prices), and we may also suppose that it was a growing fraction of gross national investment (expressed in current prices). Since capital consumption represents a component of gross property income, it follows that the fraction of gross national product accounted for by property income was also growing. However, the increase may not have been very pronounced. For example, if we assume that the share of property income in national income was, on average, 32 per cent in each of the periods 1839–59, 1869–88, and 1888–98 (see above), that the share of gross national product saved and invested (current prices) was about 15 per cent, 20 per cent, and 23 per cent respectively for these periods (see Table 14), and that the share of capital consumption in gross national investment (current prices) in the three periods was about 28 per cent, 34 per cent, and 40 per cent respectively (see Table 13), then it follows that the share of gross property income in gross national product (current prices) was about 35 per cent, 37 per cent, and something over 38 per cent. In fact, the procedure probably overstates the rise in the property income share.[32] But in any case, the measured increase, by itself, is insufficient to account for the observed rise in the gross savings rate (Table 14).

The production function estimates describe a somewhat more pronounced increase in the property income share, although one may doubt that the results are altogether relevant to our present interests. According to the most recent set of estimates, property income composed 38 per cent of gross domestic product in 1834/6–1853/7, 45 per cent in 1869/73–1888/92, and 46 per cent in 1888/92–1903/7; while income flowing to capital, alone, was 27 per cent, 35 per cent, and 37 per cent of gross domestic product in the same three periods.[33] But the production function estimates were of course obtained from constant-price series, which is probably the chief reason why they deviate from the direct estimates, which were obtained from current-price figures.[34] Since we require current-price estimates for present purposes, the direct estimates are the more suitable. But even if we were to accept the production function results, we would still be obliged to conclude that changes in the share of property income in gross national product cannot fully explain the rise of the savings rate, since the advance of the latter is more prominent than the increase of the former (see Table 14).

We conclude that property income accounted for an increasingly large fraction of gross national product and that the rise of the savings rate may in some measure be due to this development. But the behaviour of the savings rate cannot be explained entirely in these terms. There must have been other factors at work, and it is likely that these factors were somewhat more important than were changes in property income. In the following sections we explore these possibilities. We adopt Goldsmith's taxonomy and divide savers into corporations, governments, and individuals, treating each group separately.

A. CORPORATE SAVINGS

Since the beginning of the twentieth century, corporations have accounted for about one-fifth of total savings. Moreover, while the sector's savings–income ratio has displayed no long-term trend, it has been substantially greater than the ratio for the unincorporated business sector. In the period from 1840 to 1900 the corporate sector almost certainly grew relative both to the unincorporated business sector and to the rest of the economy. Those decades saw an expansion in the absolute and relative importance of non-agricultural activities, a great increase in the average size of business enterprise, as firms adjusted to new technologies and to larger geographical markets, and a succession of legal innovations that made it easier and less costly to acquire corporate status. From a cursory glance, it would be easy to conclude that the growth of the corporate sector could go a long way toward explaining the observed increase in the aggregate savings–income ratio. On closer examination, however, the evidence, although tenuous, suggests that we cannot depend upon the growth of the corporate sector to explain as much of the observed shift as we could if the nineteenth-century corporations had behaved like their twentieth-century descendants.

For the past fifty years, corporations have tended to save about one-half of their net income. To some degree, however, that behaviour rests on the relationship between owners and managers on the one hand and present tax laws on the other. Given the divorce between management and control, there is a great incentive for corporate managers to retain earnings, since such earnings provide the basis for their salaries and power. At the same time, given the treatment of capital gains under the income-tax laws and the monopolistic character of the securities exchanges, there is an almost equally strong incentive for stockholders to take their profits in the form of share appreciation rather than as dividends. Taken together, these three factors appear to go a long way toward explaining the high savings propensities displayed by modern corporations.

In the nineteenth century, these forces were much weaker. First, there was almost certainly a greater overlap between owners and managers. In the case of the New England textile industry, for example, most officers were major stockholders, and the rest of the shareholders tended to be closely linked to the management group through both family and business ties.[35] What evidence we have suggests that ownership and control were at least as closely linked in other manufacturing industries, and there appears to have been substantial overlap in the early transport industry as well.[36] Thus, there was less reason for management to retain earnings to enhance their own salaries or power. Secondly, there was no income tax, and the absence of such a tax (or more precisely the absence of preferential treatment for capital gains) must have made dividends relatively more attractive than retentions to stockholders. On the other hand, the unorganized state of the formal capital markets during most of the nineteenth century probably worked to increase corporate savings. The formal securities markets were less well organized, and the market for industrials was particularly thin. The chronicler of the Boston Stock Market (the most important industrial market) warned his readers not to trust his own price quotations because manufacturing shares were so seldom traded, and even as late as the 1890s there was no great volume of manufacturing shares traded on any of the nation's security exchanges.[37] Even the British, far more sophisticated investors than their New World cousins, were doubtful about the American Securities market. In 1893, with the words 'The Committee prefer in general to hold securities which are regularly quoted and dealt in, which very few of the best industrial bonds appear to be', the finance committee of the Sun Fire and Life Insurance Companies insisted that their American subsidiary sell their newly acquired Procter and Gamble bonds.[38] To the extent that markets were thin, reinvestment must have been proportionately more costly, and there should have been some stockholder pressure towards greater retention.[39] Despite this partial offset it appears that the pressures leading toward corporate savings were less intensive in the nineteenth century than in the twentieth, and what direct evidence there is tends to bear out this conclusion.

Although data on the behaviour of nineteenth-century corporations are notoriously poor, those that we have suggest that the corporate sector grew relative to the rest of the economy, but that those new corporations were not heavy savers. For the seven states covered by

Table 16. *New Business Incorporations in Seven US States, 1830–1909, by Decade*

	Connecticut	Maine	Maryland	Massachusetts	New Jersey	Ohio	Pennsylvania
1830–9	44[a]	178	178	n.d.	178	430	409
1840–9	142	226	123	n.d.	159	376	366
1850–9	548	364	n.d.	168[b]	561	619[c]	1,045
1860–9	583	384	n.d.	758	924	1,762	n.d.
1870–9	n.d.	636	1,027	773	1,101	3,048	n.d.
1880–9	884	2,586	1,062	1,549	3,859	5,945	4,181[d]
1890–9	1,483	4,820	2,024	2,335	11,355	8,059	5,995
1900–9	3,083	9,571	3,600	8,771	19,805	19,640	13,474
Ratio of 1900–9 to 1840–9	21·7	42·3	29·3	—	124·6	52·2	36·8

[a] 1837–9 only.
[b] 1852–9 only.
[c] 1850, 1851, 1856–9 only.
[d] 14 July 1879 to 31 December 1889.

SOURCE. G. Heberton Evans, *Business Incorporations in the United States, 1800–1943* (New York, 1948).

Evans's study (see Table 16), the number of new corporations increased about thirtyfold between the 1840s and the first decade of the
present century.[40] As to corporate behaviour, the most detailed work
is almost certainly Paul McGouldrick's study of the New England
textile industry.[41] For the period from 1836 to 1885, the firms in his
sample saved only about 0·2 per cent of their income, and their savings
were negative as often as they were positive (see Table 17). McGouldrick argues that the savings behaviour of the firms in his textile sample
was probably typical of most absentee-owned manufacturing corporations in the period, and his conclusions appear to be borne out by a

Table 17. *Savings Ratios of New England Cotton Textile Firms
(Baker Sample), 1836–85 (per cent)*

	Undistributed profits divided by total profits	(Gross) Undistributed profits + depreciation divided by sales	(Net) Undistributed profits divided by sales
1836–40	20·5	6·6	2·6
1841–5	17·9	7·9	3·2
1846–50	—13·7	4·2	—2·0
1851–5	3·1	5·3	0·3
1856–60	8·7	5·3	0·8
1861–5[a]	—14·6	2·4	—1·7
1866–70	—18·7	1·4	—1·4
1871–5	13·2	4·1	1·1
1876–80	18·9	4·8	1·2
1881–5	—3·0	3·6	—0·2
Aug. 1836 to 1885	2·7	4·2	0·2

[a] 1861, 1864, and 1865 only.

SOURCE. Paul F. McGouldrick, *New England Textiles in the Nineteenth Century:
Profits and Investments*, Harvard Economic Studies, 131 (Cambridge, Mass., 1968).

study of the business histories of the period. Since the 0·2 per cent rate
is no higher than that observed in the non-corporate business sector,
it appears that the shift to the corporate form of organization in the
manufacturing sector can account for none of the observed rise in the
savings–income ratio.

Outside of manufacturing, the increase in corporate activity –
particularly in transportation – probably does help explain the upward
drift in the ratio. Railroads appear to have retained a substantial proportion of their profits; and, while their behaviour does not seem to
have changed over the period, the increase in their relative share of
total economic activity should have produced some increase in the

share of savings in national income. An examination of the savings behaviour of eleven eastern railroads suggests that these lines were saving (gross) about one-half of their income in the ante-bellum decades (see Table 18) and that that figure, although subject to substantial year-to-year fluctuations, never fell below 30 per cent over any half-

Table 18. *Gross Savings Ratios of Railroads in Eleven New England and Middle Atlantic States (per cent)*

1830–4	69
1835–9	31
1840–4	43
1845–9	69
1850–4	48
1855–9	64

SOURCE. Henry V. Poor, *History of the Railroads and Canals of the United States*, 1 (New York, 1860).

decade between 1830 and the Civil War. It appears that for the transportation sector at least, structural change – change triggered by technical developments in transportation and by the pressure of demand – did contribute to the observed changes in the national propensity to save.

B. GOVERNMENT SAVINGS

For the modern period, Goldsmith has shown that government makes a small but significant contribution to the nation's stream of savings. For the period 1897–1949, all three levels of government (federal, state, and local) account for about 10 per cent of total savings; however, that contribution would bulk much larger were it not for the propensity of the federal government to dis-save during periods of war and depression. If the years of the First World War and the period from 1930 to 1949 are excluded, state governments saved about one-sixth of their income, the federal government about one-eighth, and local governments about one-twelfth. But direct contributions to the savings stream are not the only way that governments affect the savings and investment process; they can also operate indirectly by changing laws in a manner which, while involving no governmental tax or expenditure decisions, affects the behaviour of private savers and investors.

(1) *Direct Investment*

Among the direct contributions made by government to the savings stream, we should distinguish two types: physical capital in the

traditional sense, and expenditures made on human capital (primarily
education and health). If we include both types, it appears that during
the nineteenth century local governments saved substantially more than
did state governments or the federal government.

In terms of expenditures on physical capital, the federal government's
contributions to the nation's capital stock were relatively small. As a
fraction of receipts capital expenditure amounted to only about 5 per
cent over the period from 1831 to 1900, although as a fraction of
expenditures the number was slightly higher (see Table 19). No

Table 19. *Federal Government Finances: Receipts and Expenditures
on Physical Capital Items, 1831–1900*

	1 Receipts (million dollars)	2 Expenditure on physical capital (million dollars)	2:1 (per cent)
1831–5	151·4	9·6	6·3
1836–40	153·1	11·7	7·6
1841–5	104·4	4·3	4·1
1846–50	154·8	5·5	3·3
1851–5	302·9	13·4	4·4
1856–60	298·2	21·8	7·3
1870	396·0	8·4	2·1
1875	284·0	17·9	6·3
1880	333·5	13·3	4·0
1885	323·7	15·3	4·7
1890	403·1	19·0	4·7
1895	324·7	26·3	8·1
1900	567·2	28·7	5·1

SOURCES. 1831–60: Davis R. Dewey, *Financial History of the United States* (New
York, 1915).
1870–1900: John B. Legler, 'Regional Distribution of Federal Receipts and Expenditures in the Nineteenth Century: A Quantitative Study' (unpublished Ph.D. dissertation, Purdue University, 1967).

matter which measure is used, the contribution was certainly small, and
it was so small partly because of the substantial constitutional questions
raised by federal expenditures in this area – a point raised explicitly by
Andrew Jackson at the time of his veto of the Maysville Road Project.[42]
That the concern was real can be clearly seen in a breakdown of the
actual projects undertaken by the federal government. Between 1815
and 1860, the most important category of capital expenditures (about
one-third of the total) consisted of expenditures made on lighthouses
(clearly an area of federal authority). An additional 30 per cent was
spent on federal buildings (again an area in which federal authority was
not challenged). The remaining four-tenths was divided (about evenly)

Table 20. *Grants to States for Educational Purposes (acres)*[a]

	Common schools[b]	Granted directly for universities,[c] seminaries, normal schools, etc.	Agricultural and mechanic arts colleges[f]	Grants given indirectly for education[d e]	Total
Alabama	911,627	142,160	240,000[f]		1,293,787
Arizona	8,093,156	692,080	150,000[g]		8,935,236
Arkansas	933,778	46,080	150,000[g]	46,080	1,175,938
California	5,534,293	46,080	150,000[g]	500,000	6,230,373
Colorado	3,685,618	46,080	90,000		3,821,698
Connecticut			180,000[g]		180,000
Delaware			90,000[g]		90,000
Florida	975,307	92,160	90,000[g]		1,157,467
Georgia			270,000[g]		270,000
Idaho	2,963,698	446,080	90,000		3,499,778
Illinois	996,320	46,080	480,000[g]		1,522,400
Indiana	668,578	46,080	390,000	23,040	1,127,698
Iowa	988,196	46,080	240,000	500,000	1,774,276
Kansas	2,907,520	46,080	90,000		3,043,600
Kentucky			330,000[g]		330,000
Louisiana	807,271	46,080	210,000[g]		1,063,351
Maine			210,000[g]		210,000
Maryland			210,000[g]		210,000
Massachusetts			360,000[g]		360,000
Michigan	1,021,867	46,080	240,000		1,307,947
Minnesota	2,874,951	92,160	120,000		3,087,111
Mississippi	824,213	69,120	210,000	23,040	1,126,373
Missouri	1,221,813	46,080	330,000		1,597,893
Montana	5,198,258	298,560	140,000		5,636,818
Nebraska	2,730,951	46,080	90,000	46,080	2,913,111
Nevada	2,061,967	46,080	90,000[g]	500,000	2,698,047

State					
New Hampshire			150,000[g]		150,000
New Jersey		112,703	210,000[g]		210,000
New Mexico	8,711,324		250,000		9,074,027
New York			990,000[g]		990,000
North Carolina	2,495,396	416,080	270,000[g]		270,000
North Dakota	724,266		130,000	24,216	3,041,476
Ohio	1,375,000	69,120	630,000[g]		1,447,602
Oklahoma		800,000	250,000		2,425,000
Oregon	3,399,360	46,080	90,000	500,000	4,035,440
Pennsylvania			780,000[g]		780,000
Rhode Island			120,000[g]		120,000
South Carolina			180,000[g]		180,000
South Dakota	2,733,084	416,080	160,000		3,309,164
Tennessee			300,000		300,000
Texas			180,000[g]		180,000
Utah	5,844,196	456,080	200,000		6,500,276
Vermont			150,000[g]		150,000
Virginia			300,000		300,000
Washington	2,376,391	446,080	90,000		2,912,471
West Virginia			150,000		150,000
Wisconsin	982,329	92,160	240,000	546,080	1,860,569
Wyoming	3,470,009	336,080	90,000		3,896,089

[a] Not including swamp lands, some of which were used to promote education.

[b] The area granted for common schools consists of certain specified sections of each township. See US Land Office Report for 1922, pp. 34-9.

[c] 'Universities, seminaries, normal schools and *others*' includes: schools of mines, scientific schools, military institutes, reform schools, educational-charitable, and educational-penal institutions are found in only a few states. See *ibid*.

[d] The five states coming under this head all used the half-million-acre grant for the benefit of the common schools.

[e] The saline grants all went into the common schools, with one exception: Indiana used the lands for graded schools.

[f] For mining and mechanic arts.

[g] These states received agricultural college scrip which was used for locating lands in other states.

SOURCE. Benjamin H. Hibbard, *A History of the Public Land Policies* (Madison, Wisconsin, 1965), 344-5.

between rivers and harbours on the one hand and canals on the other – both areas in which the federal government now assumes a major role. Even the small amount spent on highways bulks large in comparison with what was to follow over the last four decades of the century. In that later period, less than 1 per cent of investment expenditures went into roads and canals, while rivers and harbours absorbed 60 per cent, public buildings 25 per cent, and lighthouses the remaining 15 per cent.

In the area of human capital, the record of the federal government is mixed. The nineteenth century passed with only minute expenditures in the area of public health. While the present century has seen an almost exponential increase in that budget item, even the Public Health Service was not established until 1912. Expenditures on the nation's health exceeded one thousand million dollars in 1960, but had totalled less than three million (out of a budget of over five hundred million) at the turn of the century.

Although it is difficult to value precisely, the contribution of the federal government to education was almost certainly greater. At university level, West Point was the first institution to offer engineering training; and land grants made under the Morrill Act (1862) provided substantial impetus for expansion of training in agriculture and the mechanical arts.[43] At the primary and secondary level, the effort was both earlier and quantitatively more significant. The Ordinance of 1787 committed the government to education, and the ensuing enabling legislation provided that one section of land in each township (one-thirty-sixth of the total) be reserved for the support of the common schools.[44] Some similar requirement was included almost every time a law was passed bringing a new state into the Union. Altogether, all forty-eight continental states received some federal land for the support of education, and while Delaware received only ninety thousand acres, Arizona benefited from almost nine million (see Table 20).

The federal government also added to the intangible capital stock through its expenditures on the agricultural extension service and the agricultural experiment stations. Although the dollar totals were small, when combined with the resources contributed by the states they did help to underwrite the growth of agricultural productivity. In 1888, the federal government spent about three-quarters of a million dollars for the maintenance of the agricultural experiment stations, and that level of expenditure was maintained throughout the rest of the century. It is impossible to calculate the return on this investment or even to enumerate all the advances underwritten, but it is interesting to note that a rust-resistant wheat was developed and the initial work on hybridization in corn undertaken under the aegis of these programmes.[45]

Table 21. *Aggregate State Government Social Overhead Expenditures, in Current Prices (million dollars) and as a Percentage of Total Expenditures, 1820–1902*

Decade[a]	All social overhead		Transportation		Education		Agriculture		Miscellaneous	
	$m	%	$m	%	$m	%	$m	%	$m	%
1820–9	2·59	47·8	2·32	42·8	0·213	3·9	0·009	0·2	0·048	0·9
1825–34	4·80	60·3	4·62	58·1	0·148	1·9	0·001	0·0	0·029	0·4
1830–9	9·77	64·0	9·11	59·7	0·633	4·1	0·001	0·0	0·023	0·2
1835–44	9·17	59·1	8·16	52·6	0·889	5·7	0·005	0·0	0·121	0·8
1840–9	5·78	46·7	4·78	38·6	0·891	7·2	0·013	0·1	0·104	0·8
1845–54	4·59	30·6	2·45	16·3	1·83	12·2	0·198	1·3	0·113	0·8
1850–9	6·41	31·0	2·97	14·3	2·87	13·9	0·430	2·1	0·144	0·7
1855–64	7·20	16·7	2·67	6·2	3·83	8·9	0·555	1·3	0·146	0·3
1860–8[b]	9·15	16·2	2·74	4·8	4·63	8·2	1·54	2·7	0·237	0·4
1865–73[b]	15·8	26·1	3·76	6·2	10·6	17·6	1·05	1·7	0·303	0·5
1869–78	21·7	32·3	3·16	4·7	17·6	26·3	0·611	0·9	0·273	0·4
1874–83	24·2	33·5	2·43	3·4	21·0	29·1	0·622	0·9	0·143	0·2
1879–88	26·6	34·2	2·51	3·2	23·1	29·8	0·825	1·1	0·121	0·2
1884–93	36·1	37·5	2·83	2·9	31·5	32·7	1·53	1·6	0·211	0·2
1889–98	45·9	37·5	3·07	2·5	40·0	32·6	2·59	2·1	0·241	0·2
1894–1902	54·7	37·3	3·40	2·3	47·5	32·3	3·46	2·4	0·368	0·3

[a] Annual averages for overlapping decades (state fiscal years) except as noted.
[b] Nine state fiscal years.

SOURCE. Charles F. Holt, 'The Role of State Government in the Nineteenth Century American Economy, 1820–1902: A Quantitative Study' (unpublished Ph.D. dissertation, Purdue University, 1970), 50.

For the states, additions to the capital stock represented a substantially larger portion of total expenditures. In 1820, expenditures on transportation, education, and agricultural investment (research, extension, and land conservation) amounted to almost one-half of total state spending. This fraction rose to almost two-thirds during the 1830s, then fell to between 30 and 40 per cent in the 1840s and – except for the Civil War decade – remained at that level throughout the rest of the century (see Table 21).

While the total shows little variation after 1840, the composition of the total changed. Expenditures on agriculture were never large, but they increased steadily and accounted for about 10 per cent of the total at the turn of the century. Transportation dominated capital expenditures through the 1840s (when it constituted between 80 and 90 per cent

Table 22. *New York City: Budget Expenditures by Decennial Periods, 1830–90*

	1 Per capita expenditure (dollars)	2 Total expenditure	3 Physical capital	4 Human capital	5 3 + 4	6 (3 + 4)/2 (per cent)
			(thousand dollars)			
1830	3·43	642	171	27	198	31
1840	5·13	1,455	369	99	468	32
1850	6·53	2,818	784	382	1,166	41
1860	12·14	7,564	1,792	1,440	3,232	43
1869	28·14	18,164	3,752	3,345	7,097	39
1880	24·66	17,539	2,713	3,678	6,391	36
1890	23·09	30,466	4,270	4,540	8,810	29

SOURCE. Edward D. Durand, *The Finances of New York City* (New York, 1898), 376.

of the total), amounted to about one-half through the Civil War, but declined steadily from there on. By the end of the century, transportation was absorbing less of the states' resources than the agricultural sector. Expenditures on education, on the other hand, increased dramatically. Amounting to only a little more than 5 per cent of capital expenditures in 1820, they grew to account for about one-half of the total by mid-century. The proportion changed but little over the ensuing two decades, but began to increase again in the 1870s. By the end of the century, expenditures on education amounted to about 90 per cent of capital expenditures and almost one-third of total state spending.

We know least about city expenditures, but from scattered budgets it appears that in the early years capital expenditures constituted a smaller proportion of total expenditures than they did for the states;

but on a per capita basis the absolute levels were much higher in both
the early and the later periods. In the case of New York, for example,
expenditures on transportation, public utilities, health, and education
amounted to about 30 per cent of total city spending in 1830 and ranged
between 30 and 40 per cent over the remainder of the century (see
Table 22). Like the state figures, city education expenditures rose over
time, but for the cities the rise dates from an earlier period.[46] Spending
on education, which amounted to only about one-eighth of capital
expenditures in 1830, had risen to account for over half by the time
of the Civil War. This increase occurred despite concurrent massive
increases in expenditures on lighting, water, streets, and sewers and
was part of a fourfold increase in per capita city expenditures.

New York appears to have been fairly typical of large cities in the
period. An examination of the budgets of Baltimore, Milwaukee, St
Louis, and Philadelphia indicates that capital expenditures accounted
for between one-third and 40 per cent of all spending over the last half
of the century, and that education absorbed about one-half of that
total.

(2) Indirect Activities

In the nineteenth century (as now) all levels of government were
involved in a number of activities that had a significant effect on the
private savings and investment process. Cities and states, for example,
often guaranteed private debt. Thus, while not directly participating
in the process of capital formation, they reduced risk and lowered
interest charges by interposing themselves between savers and investors.
The result was probably an increase in the total savings and investment
flow, and their interposition certainly turned the direction of that flow
away from short-term investments into longer-term social–overhead
capital.[47] The issues of the Pennsylvania Railroad, for example, were
guaranteed by both the city of Philadelphia and the state of Pennsylvania. Similarly, Maryland and the city of Baltimore both used their
credit to support the construction of the Baltimore and Ohio Railroad.
As a proportion of total activity, government guarantees were probably
more important early in the century than they were later, but there
are cases of government underwriting private investment throughout
the century.[48]

Similarly, state and federal land grants to railroads and canals appear
on the budget of no governmental unit, but they certainly were a
major influence on the pace of accumulation and on the profile of the
nation's capital stock. By increasing the revenues attached to investment
in transportation, they may have accelerated the pace of capital

accumulation, and they certainly guided the savings stream into investment in transport.[49]

Finally, new laws often affected the savings and investment processes, although at times the effect may have been unintentional. General incorporation acts made it possible to offer a far wider range of paper securities to potential investors and must have moved savings from sectors dominated by unincorporated businesses to manufacturing and transportation.[50] The selective effects of the tariff must have altered profitability and redirected the stream of American investment away from the largely unprotected agricultural sector towards the manufacturing sector, where profits were partly protected by the increasing import taxes. Government regulation of financial intermediaries, designed to increase economic stability and protect depositors and shareholders, also made it more difficult to accumulate and mobilize capital and should therefore have reduced the rate of accumulation and biased the stream of savings away from 'risky' activities and towards 'safe' ones.[51]

It appears that the increase in the investment activities carried on by cities probably contributed to the rise in the savings–income ratio, but the total impact was probably not large. Changes in the direct economic activities of other levels of government do not appear to have contributed significantly to the increase in the ratio, although they may have had an impact on the profile of the capital stock that those savings produced.

C. PERSONAL SAVINGS

With the exception of some relatively small increments produced by the shift in the composition of output towards industries marked by savings rates which were higher than average (particularly transportation) and by the growth of cities, it appears that any autonomous increase in the savings–income ratio must have been rooted in the personal savings sector.

Since the personal savings sector was always much larger, much more diverse, and subject to a much wider range of motivation than either the corporate or governmental sectors, merely narrowing the source of the increase in the savings–income ratio to that sector does not improve our understanding of the increase very much. The personal sector includes not only rich and poor but also persons and unincorporated businesses (both farm and non-farm). Logically, the increase in the savings ratio could have come from (1) a change in consumer preference between current and future income, (2) an increase in per capita income, if savings are income-elastic, (3) an increase in the net return to savers, if savings are interest-responsive, and/or (4) a shift in the composition of the group that makes up the personal savings sector.

Important though a change in consumer tastes might have been to an explanation of the rise in the savings–income ratio, we have no way of directly observing this phenomenon. In terms of indirect observation, an examination of the exogenous changes that might have affected consumers' willingness to save leads to some very mixed results. Goldsmith has examined the motivations for saving among present-day consumers and has concluded that the most important are the desires to acquire durable tangible assets, to provide for future expenditures (particularly retirement, estate provision, future expenses, and emergencies), and to accumulate enough capital to enter business. It is likely that the same motives dominated the consumption–savings decision a hundred and fifty years ago, but how they affected the savings–income ratio is much less clear. In terms of future expenditures, it appears that there were forces at work that would tend to increase the savings rate. The need for formal education was increasing, and therefore the savings rate might have increased as parents were forced to take cognizance of the increase in expenses (particularly the fall in family income that was the opportunity cost of income forgone when students remained in school) related to the rise in the average period of school attendance.[52] Probably more important were the pressures induced by the need to provide some retirement income. As life expectancies increased, the proportion of people in the older age groups rose dramatically. Persons over sixty accounted for only 4 per cent of the population in 1830, but this figure had risen to 7 per cent by 1910. At the same time the movement from agricultural to non-agricultural activities and from employer to employee status must have made it more difficult for a worker to move from full labour-force participation to retirement at a rate that he desired. Similarly, the same shift, while probably increasing per capita income, almost certainly also increased the variance of income. This greater uncertainty should also have led to a higher savings rate. Tending to offset these forces, however, was the effect of the reduction of self-employment opportunities. As the probability of entering one's own business declined, there must have been a tendency to reduce savings made in anticipation of entering business. It is difficult to assess the total impact of these exogenous forces on consumer preferences, but on net it appears that the retirement, unemployment, insurance, and educational motives probably outweighed the decline in the need for business accumulation and, taken together, probably explain a part of the upward movement in the savings ratio.

The importance of the second and third alternative explanations of the increase in the ratio (rising per capita income and increases in the net return to savers) depends upon the income- and interest-elasticity of savings. If income rose (as it did) and if savings were income-elastic, then the ratio of savings to income should have risen. Recent work, however, tends to indicate that, over time, savings are not income-elastic, although in the cross section, higher incomes are associated with higher rates of saving. There is no obvious reason to believe that the situation a century and a half ago differed markedly from the present. Along similar lines, the increase could have been the product of higher interest rates, if savings increase when interest rates rise. While the data (see Table 9 above) indicate that gross rates were falling, improvements in intermediation could have raised net rates. Moreover, the same improvements should have reduced the variance of the returns and – if the typical saver was risk-averse – should have increased the attractiveness of any given certainty equivalent. While studies of the recent past suggest that savings do not respond to changes in interest rates, the recent period – unlike the nineteenth century – was not one of substantial structural change. Moreover, most studies have indicated that the majority of savers are risk-averse, and reductions in uncertainty should therefore make savings more attractive. Taken together, structural change, the increase in net returns, and the reduction in variance may have contributed substantially to the rise in the savings ratio. We feel the question is important enough to examine in detail, and it is taken up in the next section.

Finally, there may have been shifts in the composition of the private sector, and that is the subject to which we now turn. In the recent past, farmers have tended to save more than non-farmers, but this has not always been the case. In the period 1897–1913 (the earliest period of Goldsmith's study), farmers were very heavy borrowers, and their savings rate was only about a quarter (3 per cent as opposed to 12) of that of their urban peers. If this earlier behaviour pattern had been characteristic of nineteenth-century farmers, then we might be able to explain the rise in the savings ratio in terms of the movement from farm to non-farm enterprise. Unfortunately, everything we know about farm behaviour in the nineteenth century suggests that farmers – just as they do today – saved more of their income, not less, than did non-farmers. In this case the movement out of agriculture should have worked to reduce, not increase, the savings ratio. How can this apparent paradox be explained?

Consider the following scenario. In the early part of the century, the farm sector was characterized by a high savings–income ratio if all types of savings are included. At the same time, however, the capital market was very poorly developed, particularly in the rural areas. As a result farmers borrowed very little. Savings chiefly took the form of the substitution of labour time for leisure – labour invested in 'unconventional' capital items like land clearance and building improvements, since these activities were closely linked to the farmer's income and social position and since there were few alternative forms in which he could hold his savings. These unconventional savings are not included in the usual capital-formation figures; and, as we have seen, when they are included the observed increase in the savings ratio is damped. Moreover, the existence of nearly free land on the frontier meant that little of farm expenditure was directed at land acquisition. Over time, however, two things occur. Changes in the savings and investment opportunities alter the stream of savings from unconventional to conventional forms, and at the same time the size of the farm sector declines relative to the non-farm sector. The two trends tend to offset each other in the conventional series. Later, as capital markets improve, the farm sector becomes a heavy net borrower, and a substantial portion of loan finance probably goes into land purchases, which do not appear in savings at all. Although the data are weak, they do attest to a massive increase in agricultural borrowing in the decades after the Civil War. Severson's study of Champaign County, Illinois, shows a tripling of mortgage credit between 1865 and the late 1870s; and Ladin's work on Tippecanoe County, Indiana, indicates that even in that already well-developed area, mortgage credit increased by about 25 per cent over the same period.[53] At a more general level, the census of mortgages covering the decade of the 1880s shows continuing increases across most of the West.[54] We can also note the rising complaints about the rising real burden of farm debt during the Granger and Populist periods, and they certainly suggest heavy borrowing.[55] In addition, we can observe the innovation, growth, and expansion of the mortgage banks that began in the 1870s, spread throughout the East gathering mortgage capital for Western farms in the 1880s, and finally succumbed to the drought of the late eighties and the agricultural depression of the early nineties.[56] Finally, we can see that farm mortgages still amounted to $2·0 thousand million in 1896, and that that figure had risen to $3·2 thousand million by 1910.[57]

A similar paradox arises out of an examination of the effects on the savings rate of the shift from employer to employee status. Goldsmith attributes a portion of the recent fall in the ratio to this trend, and the evidence suggests that the movement can be traced back into the last century. Unincorporated businesses, however, have until recently been characterized by low levels of savings, most likely the product of the high rate of failure and the inclusion in dis-savings of the losses of initial investments incurred by the unsuccessful entrepreneurs. Since any reading of nineteenth-century economic history suggests no less high a rate of failure among unincorporated businesses at that time, it may well be that the movement towards general incorporation made a contribution to the upward drift in the aggregate function.

While the impact of changes in the industrial structure and ownership status may be open to question, there can be little doubt that the changes in the age structure of the population must have had a substantial effect on the savings–income ratio. Recent studies have shown that savings rates among the young are very low, while the highest rates are observed among the age groups between forty and sixty-five. Over the eight decades from 1830 to 1910, the proportion of the male population under twenty declined from 56 to 41 per cent while the proportion of those between forty and sixty rose from 11 to 19 per

Table 23. *Age Structure of the Male Population, 1830–1910*
(per cent)

	Under 20 (as % of total)	40–60 (as % of total)
1830[a]	56	11
1840[a]	54	11
1850	52	14
1860	51	14
1870	50	15
1880	48	16
1890	45	16
1900	44	18
1910	41	19

[a] White only.

SOURCE. Bureau of the Census, *Historical Statistics*, 10.

cent (see Table 23). As long as most savings took the form of direct labour contribution, the real effect of the adverse age structure on savings rate in the early period was probably partly ameliorated. A farmer who drew on his leisure time to clear the 'south forty' would probably be helped by his children, so we might expect a smaller difference between the savings habits of the young and the old. However, the ratio as conventionally defined must have reflected the change in the age structure. As savings took more conventional forms, it is likely that both real and accounted savings behaviour began to resemble that which characterizes the twentieth century. Under these conditions the change in the age composition of the population must have made a substantial contribution to the observed upward shift in the savings–income ratio.

We have already seen that over time there appears to be no certain correlation between income and savings; however, every study indicates a strong positive cross-section correlation between savings and income. To the extent that the correlation persists, we expect an increase in the savings–income ratio if income becomes unequally distributed.

In the case of the United States, indirect evidence relating to changes in the distribution of economic activity among industrial sectors and between urban and rural districts indicates that there may have been increases in the skewness of both the income and wealth distributions between, roughly, the middle and the end of the nineteenth century. Direct information on the wealth holdings of the very rich in 1840, 1850, 1860, and 1890, while of a very doubtful character, nonetheless tends to support these inferences. The only direct evidence of income distribution that we have for the period derives from the administration of the income taxes of the late 1860s and early 1870s, the ill-fated tax of 1894 (declared unconstitutional before all returns were in), and the modern income tax, beginning in 1912. The most recent analyst of these data, Lee Soltow, concludes that they show that the distribution of income *among the rich* did not grow more unequal over time, although he is unprepared to place much weight on the 1894 evidence and thus leaves open the possibility that the period was characterized by a stage of growing inequality followed by a stage of diminishing inequality, a pattern consistent with the Kuznets model. Soltow's evidence can be generalized into a statement about the distribution of income between rich and poor only by extrapolation of the tail of the curve captured by the tax data – which is of course a treacherous procedure.

The direct information on income and wealth distribution is not necessarily inconsistent (for reasons indicated above, as well as for the reason that income and wealth are different concepts), but neither does it serve to form a clear picture. While the evidence favourable to the notion that inequalities widened during the latter part of the century seems somewhat weightier to us than does the evidence to the contrary, all the evidence is so tenuous that it is the better part of wisdom to render the Scottish verdict of 'not proven'.[58]

It appears, then, that there were forces at work to underwrite an increase in the aggregate savings ratio in the period after the Civil War, but these forces were less strong in the earlier period. Instead, it appears that in the years before the Civil War there was a gradual substitution of conventional for unconventional savings, and these 'new' savings are more easily picked up by the historical record. This conclusion is consistent with the interest series, which show little or no

decline from 1840 to 1860 and a steady decline thereafter. Furthermore'
while there may well have been a substitution of savings for consumption, a great part of the increase can probably be attributed to structural
changes in the economy – to the increase in the relative importance of
property income, in general, to the growth of the high-savings transportation sector, to the growth of cities, to changes in the age structure
of the population (magnified perhaps by the shift from farm to non-
farm savings and from unconventional to conventional savings) and
possibly to the redistribution of income in the direction of greater
inequality.

VI.   *The Savings–Investment Process: Some Analytical Considerations and Historical Realities*

We assume that investors are profit-maximizers and that they will
invest if the cost *to them* of the investment is less than the present value
of the net revenues that *they* expect to earn from the investment.
Because dollars tomorrow are worth less than dollars today, future
revenues and costs will weigh less heavily in the decision-making
process than will the costs incurred or the revenues earned today; and
it is the rate of interest at which the investor can borrow and lend that
is used to discount those future revenues. Changes in the rate of interest
can, therefore, make a particular investment appear more or less
attractive even if nothing else changes. Moreover, given an array of
investment alternatives (from most to least profitable), the investor
will push his investment margin until the present value of the last item
on that array exactly equals its cost. Improvements in financial intermediation will reduce the rate of interest that the potential investor
must pay and will – other things being equal – cause the investor to
push farther along the array. Moreover, at high rates of interest
investors will tend to choose items characterized by fairly quick
payoffs; but declines in the rate of interest will make long-term
investments appear more attractive. It is the revenues farthest removed
that are the most heavily discounted, and it is the present value of assets
with a preponderance of such revenues that changes the most when the
rate of interest varies. Capital-market improvements which reduce the
rate of interest will, therefore, have their greatest effect on the demand
for long-term investment.

In periods of high interest rates, investments tend to be biased towards assets with short payoff periods, and the poorer the state of

development of the capital markets the higher interest rates tend to be. But at the same time, if an economy is to develop, substantial investment in social overhead and other slow-payoff capital frequently must precede industrialization. In the case of American development, the movement into the Northwest Territory had to be underwritten by heavy investment in land-clearing, structures, and fences, and any shift of the focus of economic activity off the East Coast had to be based on a massive extension of the transportation network. How were these investments effected?

In the case of agriculture, somewhat paradoxically, it was the poor state of market development that made it possible to overcome the apparent dilemma. Not only were the capital markets extremely primitive, but the labour market was little better. Thus, for the farmer who was fully employed in agriculture only during the peak seasons, there was no market in which he could sell his residual services in the off-peak periods. While he would never have chosen a long-term investment if he had been forced to make that investment in cash, a Western farmer would frequently choose to invest his labour in such activities during the parts of the year when his farm did not require his full attention. It was not that he was irrational; it was only that the opportunity cost of his labour was valued only as leisure, and the long-term investments in farm improvements were the only investment alternatives open to him. Because of the high interest rate, the discounted stream of future income from those investments was still very low, but the costs of making the investment were even lower, since they involved little but labour services, and there was no alternative use that could command a positive price.

Fortunately for American development, many of the capital improvements that were required in agriculture in the period from 1820 to the 1850s were those that were amenable to direct investment of labour. They required little that could not be provided by the farmer himself, and within broad limits they could be made gradually as spare time permitted. Forests covered the eastern third of the country, and land-clearing, although necessary, required little but a strong back and yielded as a by-product the timber that was almost the only non-labour input required in the construction of fences, houses, barns, and other farm structures (see Table 24).[59]

Similarly, to the extent that canal construction projects (or even the railroad construction sites) were located within commuting distance from the farm, it was possible for the farmer to invest by exchanging labour services for ownership or debt instruments. While the returns from these scraps of symbolic capital were likely to be long delayed and their present value was low, they remained profitable investments

Table 24. *Farm Labour Force: Percentages in Farm–Building Construction and in Land-Clearing, 1850–9 and 1900–9*

	Labour force (thousands)		In land-clearing (%)		In building construction (%)		Clearing plus construction (%)	
	1850–9	1900–9	1850–9	1900–9	1850–9	1900–9	1850–9	1900–9
Northeast	900	1,108	7·3	2·3	4·3	3·1	11·6	5·4
South	1,767	3,406	9·9	2·3	3·4	1·7	13·3	4·0
Midwest	830	1,890	17·7	1·7	5·7	3·9	23·4	5·6
West	336	2,691	16·8	3·4	5·5	3·4	22·3	6·8
United States	3,833	9,095	11·6	2·3	[4·3][a]	3·0	[15·9][a]	5·3

[a] 4·1 in the source.
[b] 15·1 in the source.

SOURCE. Primack, 'Farm Construction as a Use of Farm Labor', 122.

as long as the only alternative use for the farmer's labour was leisure.[60] The United States clearly benefited from the 'work ethic', since such values greatly reduced the valuation placed on leisure and made investments in agriculture and the local infrastructure appear profitable.

While farmers did contribute their labour services to canal-building and to railroad construction, the sparseness of population coupled with the limited distance that such an investor could travel and still operate his farm made it impossible to finance the entire transport network (or even a major portion of it) in this manner. However, investment in these projects frequently appeared profitable to landowners along the right of way even when they were not profitable to other investors. If the railroad or canal company could have practised perfect price discrimination, it would have been possible for them to receive all the rents attributable to locations near the system. However, no one has ever found a practical way of enforcing a rate structure that could accomplish that end. As a result, a part of the increase in income attributable to the development of transportation accrues as locational rent to property-owners along the right of way. The owners realize these extra rewards in the form of increases in the value of their land, and a rational landowner would have a different view of the present value of a railroad that went near his property than would a potential investor who lived far away. To the landowner, returns from the investment would consist both of the interest or dividend stream that would accrue to any investor and also the decapitalized stream of locational rent.[61] In these cases, long-term investment in transportation might appear profitable to those living near the project, even if it were profitable to no one else. Studies of railroads in the eastern North Central region show that a substantial portion of their shareholders were drawn from this group.[62] In fact, there were many cases in which such reasoning led to the construction of railroads ahead of demand and as a result left stockholders disappointed with the returns. Since those stockholders were also voters, and since they lived close together, promoters often found themselves facing not only dissident stock-holders but angry legislators as well.

In nineteenth-century America, government policies also altered the parameters of the investment decision and produced a substantial change in the profile of the capital stock even if those policies did not increase the rate of capital accumulation (though they may have done that as well). In the 1820s and 1830s, states (and sometimes local govern-mental units) often borrowed on their own accounts and then lent the funds to private companies – often in transport, but occasionally in banking and manufacturing as well. This substitution of government debt for private debt made capital expansion by these firms more attractive at any time when the rate at which the government unit could borrow was below the rate at which the private firms could acquire funds directly. Even today, the rates on government issues are usually less than those on private issues, and this difference was even more pronounced in the very primitive capital markets of the early nineteenth century.[63] Later, both the states and the federal government made land grants in support of transportation development. To the potential investor, expected revenues were no longer limited to the earnings of the project but were supplemented by the earnings from the sale of land, and the supplement should have moved some of the projects into the economically viable category.[64] Costs were also reduced since the road or canal did not have to pay for its right of way; however, in almost every case the affected roads were being built through empty Western lands, and the cost aspect of the subsidy was probably small. Fogel's work on the Union Pacific indicates that the public did not view the nation's first transcontinental railroad as the most desirable of all investments, even when the potential revenues from the sale of land were included, and it does not appear unreasonable to conclude that without the grants the construction of the trans-continental roads would have been delayed.[65]

We have seen that the railroads (and the canals) were unable to capture all the locational rents, and the possibility of 'free riding' may have dissuaded some who owned land along the right of way from investing, even if recomputed present value was greater than cost.[66] If the road were built, the locational rent could accrue to those who did not invest as well as to those who did, and each owner may have waited for someone else to make the commitment. When this occurred, local government units frequently paid a subsidy to the railroad and then recaptured the rents through taxes on the land whose value had increased. The government used its power of coercion to discipline the potential free-riders. Such subsidies were particularly prevalent in the Midwestern states, where the great choice of feasible routes offered plentiful opportunities for competitive bidding between communities – each trying to benefit at the expense of the others. When such bidding occurred, the railroads were able to extract almost all of the locational rent, but the investments were made.[67] Once again, government action made the long-term investments more attractive than they would otherwise have been and changed the shape of the nation's capital stock.

VII *Financial Intermediation*

The growth of financial intermediaries and the development of the capital markets is a subject for a separate essay; however, it is impossible to understand the savings and investment process without touching on it. To the extent that savings and investment are interest-responsive, improvements in intermediation will induce savers to save more and capital-users to invest more, and they may therefore produce an upward shift in the savings–income ratio. Moreover, if all sectors are not initially endowed with equivalent sets of financial institutions, or if developments are not uniform in all sectors, changes in the capital markets and in the structure of intermediation affect not only the size of the savings–investment stream but also the spatial, industrial, and functional distribution of that stream.

Improvements in intermediation can affect the savings–investment process in any of three ways. They can reduce transaction costs and therefore increase net returns to savers and/or reduce the gross payments that a capital-using firm must make to realize any particular net amount. They can reduce the uncertainty discounts attached to any particular investment and therefore increase the net (after discount) returns to the saver who chooses that investment. They can increase the liquidity of any asset and, to the extent that the saver is risk-averse, make that asset appear 'safer' and therefore a better buy at any given rate of return.

Transactions costs can be divided into two categories, search costs and negotiation costs. The former include the costs incurred by the capital-user as he seeks a savings accumulation and the costs borne by the saver as he searches for an outlet for his accumulation. The latter include both the costs of bargaining between saver and investor and the purely administrative costs involved in effecting the transaction. Since intermediation can reduce both search and negotiation costs, improvements in intermediation will usually yield a greater rate of utilization of external savings by potential deficit spending units and, to the degree that savings are interest-responsive, will yield a higher rate of savings.

Where institutional structures are few and primitive and financial markets not well developed, search costs are high; and there were few financial institutions in the United States at the beginning of the nineteenth century. Moreover, since information once obtained can be used by many people at little additional cost, there are usually substantial economies of scale inherent in any institutionalization of the search procedure. In the 1870s, it paid no Western farmer to travel eastward and search out mortgage finance among Eastern savers, and it paid few Eastern savers to journey westward in search of opportunities to invest their funds in the farms of the Great Plains. It did, however, pay a firm to maintain offices in the West to collect information on potential capital-users and to make loans to those who appeared to be good risks, and to maintain offices in the Eastern cities to act as depositories for savers. For any single transaction the cost would have been prohibitive; for a thousand it was cheap. Thus were the land mortgage companies born. The costs of bringing hundreds of savers together with hundreds of farmers who wanted to use those savings was only marginally more expensive than bringing one saver in contact with one farmer. The cost of search per loan declined dramatically, the net return earned by savers rose, and a steadily swelling stream of finance moved from the Eastern cities to the Western farms.[68]

Similarly, a firm faced with negotiating a thousand individual loans of $100 might well find the administrative costs prohibitive. If they could negotiate a single loan of $100,000 with a savings bank, which in turn could accept the thousand deposits at no more cost than an entry in a passbook, the total administrative cost per dollar lent would fall to a tiny fraction of its former level, and the entire transaction could become economically viable.[69] While the early New England textile firms used to borrow occasionally from individuals, there is no record of their ever having turned to the working classes for their financial needs. As soon as the Provident Institute for Savings in the Town of Boston opened its doors in 1819, it began to acquire the savings of the city's workers, and the textile firms became its steady customers. Over the period from 1814 to 1860, that one institution appears to have accounted for almost 40 per cent of the industry's long-term loan finance.[70] The nineteenth century saw a rapid increase in the number of savings banks, and these spread throughout the Northeast. There were no savings banks in 1800; in 1820 there were only ten, with deposits of $1 million; in 1860 there were almost 280, with assets of $150 million; and by 1910 the figures had reached 637 banks and $3.3 thousand million.[71] Moreover, after the Civil War, the deposit function was also gradually spread among commercial banks as well, and by 1910 they held an equal amount in savings deposits.[72] Nor were those deposits confined to the Northeast; they came from all over the country.

Not only were transactions costs reduced by financial innovation in the nineteenth century; innovations designed to make savings 'safer' were made as well. To the farmer whose savings took the form of reduced leisure and whose investment took the form of labour devoted to land-clearing, the question of safety was largely irrelevant. As the economy became more specialized, however, savers and the users of those savings seldom coincided. If savings were to earn any positive return (since hoards could be stolen, one might argue that they had a negative return) they had to be surrendered to someone. In the absence of intermediation, such surrenders tended, to the extent that they were indivisible, to be subject to substantial variance in return; and regardless of indivisibility they were almost always illiquid. Savers are risk-averse, and they heavily discount assets with a high variance in yield; moreover, they frequently discount illiquid assets in the same fashion. Once again, to the extent that savings were interest-responsive such discounts must have reduced the savings rates, and under any circumstances must have biased the savings stream away from such forms of savings.

To reduce variance, insurance was introduced. Intermediaries could pool the accumulations of many individual savers and invest that pool in a wide variety of assets. They would thus insure the owners against fluctuations in the value of any particular asset. Commercial banks, savings banks, trust companies, and life assurance companies all performed this function in the nineteenth century. Aside from a few commercial banks, none of these institutions existed in the United States at the beginning of the century, but many were started and grew rapidly over the course of that century, particularly in the decades following the Civil War.

Liquidity was provided by the development of formal markets that, by the end of the century, provided a place where the stocks and bonds issued by governments, public utilities, and transportation companies could easily be turned into cash and a not-quite-so-ready market for the issues of the growing manufacturing sector.

Finally, the uncertainty discounts placed by the saver on little-known investments were reduced by innovations that lowered the price of information and by intermediaries who interposed themselves (as a known quantity) between the saver and the demander of those savings (frequently an unknown quantity). The formal securities markets provide a good example of institutions capable of providing inexpensive information; and banks, insurance companies, and a myriad of other institutions acted to substitute the known investment alternative for the unknown.

The history of the development of intermediation can be broken down into three parts: (1) changes outside the financial sector itself – that is, changes in the attitudes of savers that make them willing to substitute symbolic capital for real capital in their investment portfolios, and increases in the supply of such capital; (2) the development of intermediate institutions capable of issuing secondary symbolic capital and interposing themselves between savers and investors; and (3) the growth of formal markets in which symbolic capital (both direct and from intermediate institutions) can be easily bought and sold. The nineteenth century saw all three developments in the United States.

The supply of symbolic capital was increased as legal innovations changed the structure of business. At the beginning of the nineteenth century almost all firms were organized as partnerships or sole proprietorships. Although no laws precluded their issuing symbolic capital, their limited life and unlimited liability drastically limited the marketability of such issues. From the point of view of the sale of symbolic capital, corporations possessing unlimited life and limited liability were a much more attractive institutional form; but corporate charters could be granted only by special act of the legislature. At first such charters were only grudgingly granted, but gradually the process became easier. Finally, states began to adopt general incorporation acts that made incorporation easy and removed it from the political process. The number of corporations grew rapidly in response to this decrease in the price of organization, and the supply of symbolic capital was greatly increased. General incorporation became important in the 1840s and 1850s (by 1860 at least thirteen states had some form of general incorporation) and had spread through most of the rest of the country by 1880. At the latter date, among non-Western states only Mississippi, Kentucky, South Carolina, Delaware, Florida, and Vermont were without general incorporation laws.[73]

Savers' attitudes also changed. Traditionally willing only to invest in assets that he could 'touch', the saver through his experience with government debt instruments (particularly US Civil War issues) and to a lesser extent with transport issues (often of companies located near his home and frequently guaranteed by the state or local government) gradually became willing to hold scraps of paper representing real assets located far away in both space and experience. At mid-century, a few highly sophisticated persons (mostly rich and living in the East and Northeast) constituted almost the entire domestic market for symbolic capital. By 1890 financiers had begun to look at the Midwest as a potential market for corporate bonds, and by the end of the First World War a significant fraction of middle America had become a source of potential stock speculators.[74]

While legal and psychological changes made it easier for Americans to channel their savings into symbolic capital, improvements in the securities market reduced the transactions costs associated with them and increased the liquidity of such investments. New York had a stock and bond exchange in the last decade of the eighteenth century, and by the third decade of the nineteenth century important markets also existed in Boston and Philadelphia, with minor markets in such scattered cities as Detroit and St Louis. The next two decades saw the demise of the Second Bank of the United States, the rapid development of New York as a commercial and financial centre, and the invention of the telegraph. Together, these diverse developments underwrote the centralization of the nation's securities markets in New York and permitted savers to accrue the economies of scale as well as the greater liquidity inherent in a single centralized exchange.[75]

At the same time, specialized institutions designed to smooth the flow of funds through markets and intermediaries were innovated. In the securities market private bankers became underwriters and merchandisers of new issues.[76] The giant firms of the early twentieth century had their beginnings in the ante-bellum activities of firms like Prime, Ward and King; they matured during and after the Civil War, as Jay Cooke and his imitators discovered first that government and then that railroad bonds could be merchandised; and they reached maturity at the end of the century as the investment banking firms underwrote large manufacturing as well as government, railroad, public utility, and shipping issues.[77] There were the German-Jewish firms (Kuhn–Loeb, for example) and the old Boston houses that had come to banking through textile merchandising (Kidder Peabody and Lee Higginson are two examples); but most important and innovative were the firms that grew up around J. Pierpont Morgan. Morgan dominated railroad finance after 1873 and moved into industrial finance at the turn of the century. While United States Steel may have been the most spectacular of his financial projects, there was hardly a railroad or large manufacturing firm that at some point in its history did not draw on the services of his firm.[78]

In a similar fashion, the development of the commercial-paper houses made it possible for a country locked into a unit banking structure effectively to mobilize short-term bank finance across regional boundaries. In both the short- and long-term markets there tended to be excess demand for capital in the South and West and an excess supply in the East. The commercial-paper house purchased short-term commercial paper from banks in the regions of excess demand, which it sold to banks in the areas of excess supply. In so doing, they had by 1910 created a national market for short-term capital. The first paper houses were organized in the 1840s in the eastern United States, but growth was slow. Three decades passed before they moved into the Midwest; but before another thirty years had gone by, they had spread over most of the rest of the country. Dominated by a few large New York firms (Goldman Sachs was one) they operated efficiently in every region except the South.[79]

The nineteenth century also saw the emergence of a variety of financial intermediaries capable of capturing the economies of scale involved in search and negotiation, of providing insurance against the risk of wide fluctuations in the price of a single asset, and able to reduce uncertainty by interposing their symbolic capital between the saver and the unknown firm that demanded those savings. Chronologically the first of these intermediaries were mutual savings banks. Begun for philanthropic purposes in the second decade of the century, they were widely introduced in New England and the Middle Atlantic States; and throughout the century they remained the most important non-bank intermediary. The savings banks were followed by the savings and loan associations (a product of the cooperative movement of the 1840s) and by the life assurance companies, today the most important of the non-bank intermediaries.

We have already seen that the deposit function of the commercial banks became important in the decades after 1870. We know much less about the growth of trust companies, although the Massachusetts Hospital Life Insurance Company (a trust company), begun in 1823, was almost certainly the nation's largest financial enterprise in the ante-bellum decades.[80] Life assurance companies became significant in the early 1840s, when an adequate mortality table was developed and the mutual principle was first applied in that industry. Their most rapid growth, however, occurred after the Civil War with the introduction of tontine insurance, industrial policies, and new mass marketing techniques.[81]

No discussion of intermediation can, however, be concluded without mentioning the commercial banks, which stood at the centre of the entire savings and investment process. They were lenders of first resort for most business firms; they acted as an intermediary, accepting savings deposits and then investing these funds in both loans and issues of symbolic capital; they provided the finance that was necessary if the securities market was to function; it was their paper in which the commercial-paper houses dealt; and their ability to create money made it possible for them to influence the savings rate directly. As in much of the financial sector, the years after 1840 and particularly those after 1870 were marked by a rapid growth of commercial banking. In the early nineteenth century, it required an act of a state legislature to obtain a commercial bank charter.[82] Free banking, however, was adopted by New York and Michigan in 1838, and by 1870 almost every state had introduced that institution in some form.[83] In addition, after 1863 the National Banking Act provided an alternative route to charter, and while the tax placed on state banknotes initially all but destroyed non-national banks, the innovation of checking accounts made it possible for them to compete from the early 1870s onward (see Table 25).[84] Although the data are notoriously bad, there were probably fewer than a thousand banks with assets of under $750 milllion in 1840, and even as late as 1860 the numbers appear to have been about 1,500 banks and $1 thousand million. Thereafter growth was more rapid. Assets had tripled by 1875, tripled again by 1898, and yet again by 1914.

Table 25. *Commercial Banks in the USA, 1870–1910*

	State Banks		National Banks	
	Number	Assets ($ million)	Number	Assets ($ million)
1870	174[a]	149[a]	1,612	1,566
1880	650	882	2,076	2,035
1890	2,250	1,743	3,484	3,062
1900	4,659	2,625	3,732	4,944
1910	13,257	24,482	7,145	9,897

[a] Estimate.

SOURCE. Bureau of the Census, *Historical Statistics*, 626–32.

Recently John James has argued that the growth of commercial banking played an important role in the development of capital mobility as well as in capital accumulation. He finds that there was close association between the increase in the number of banks and the decline in interregional interest rate differentials.[85]

Taken together, the development of the financial markets, the growth of intermediation, and the changes in saver attitudes toward (and the supply of) symbolic capital probably account for a substantial portion of the observed rise in the savings–income ratio. In addition, they had an equally substantial impact on the form of savings and on the profile (both industrial and geographical) of the investment stream, a stream that ultimately determines the shape of the capital stock.

VIII. *Conclusions*

The nineteenth century saw a transformation of the United States. In 1800, its borders had encompassed a land area of less than nine hundred thousand square miles, population was only slightly in excess of five million, and three-quarters of the labour force were engaged in agriculture. By 1910, the population had increased to more than ninety million and lived in an area that had expanded to over three million square miles. Economic transformation was equally spectacular. Agriculture occupied only three workers in ten, and manufacturing – an activity that had employed almost no one at the beginning of the century – was absorbing about one worker in four. The country had become the world's largest producer of both agricultural and manufactured products and had probably assumed that position in the service sector as well. In the course of the century, the Civil War had almost torn the nation apart politically; the westward movement had turned two-thirds of the land area from largely unoccupied and unannexed wilderness into an economically important producer; and the growth of the domestic transportation network had united the entire nation into a single market. An important thread in any attempt to weave an explanation of this transformation is the strand that relates savings to investment – the process of capital accumulation, mobilization, and investment. This essay is an attempt to delineate the processes of savings and investment and to relate them to the national transformation.

The data (crude as they are) indicate incontrovertibly that there was a marked upward movement in the ratio of investment to income over the course of the last six decades of the nineteenth century. This increase appears to have made a substantial contribution to the relatively high level of per capita income and to its rate of growth – both important features of American economic history. The contribution of the high rate of investment was channelled both through the rate of increase in the capital stock and through the age structure of the stock (a structure that implied a heavy bias toward young, and thus more productive, capital). The bulk of this chapter has been devoted to an attempt to explain and analyse the increase in the investment ratio.

It is possible that the increase in the ratio is merely a statistical artefact following from the way that investment is defined. Standard definitions have been used in most of this essay, and such definitions exclude important components of investment, conceived in a broader way, such as the accumulation of consumer durables, investment in human capital, and some parts of farm capital formation. However, the evidence suggests that proper allowance for unconventional components of investment would not alter our conclusion that the net investment ratio did, in fact, rise, although it would moderate and perhaps alter the timing of the observed increase. Since both sales of consumer durables and investment in human capital appear to have grown more rapidly than the traditional components of the capital stock, their inclusion in measured investment would make the upward movement in the ratio even more pronounced. The inclusion of land-clearing, however, would dampen the trend in the early decades.

Logic suggests that the observed increase could have been rooted in either the investing sector or the saving sector, or both. On the investment side, it could have come from (1) a shift in the composition of final demand towards capital-intensive industries, (2) technical change biased towards capital, or (3) a change in relative factor prices that made capital cheaper compared with land and labour. On the savings side, the change could have been triggered by (1) a shift in the savings–consumption preferences of consumers, government, or business, (2) a shift within the savings sector that increased the proportion of high savings units, and/or (3) institutional changes that reduced the delivered cost of savings or increased the apparent returns to savers without increasing costs to savings-users.

Given these theoretical considerations, it is possible to examine the evidence and begin to isolate some of the factors that underlay economic growth and development in the United States. If the increase had been solely a function of changes in final demand, we would be able to observe the process in data bearing on the structure of output and sectoral capital–output ratios. Moreover, if such changes were important, we would expect capital-shallowing at the industry level, as firms responded to induced changes in relative prices. The evidence, however, suggests that the increase in the capital–output ratio was a generally pervasive movement characterizing not only the most broadly defined sectors (agriculture, manufacturing, and services) but the component industries of these sectors as well.

The sectoral comparison, however, suggests that changes in final demand contributed in part to the observed increase. While capital-deepening occurred in all three broad sectors, it was much more pronounced in the service sector. Moreover, within that sector most of the increase can be attributed to the increasing importance of the transportation and urban housing industries. From the point of view of understanding the process of development, it is useful to note that both industries were the recipients of an increase in demand derived from the general process of industrialization. The increase in transportation can be traced to changes induced by increased specialization, and that for urban housing to the population agglomerations that accompanied the widespread introduction of the factory system and the growth of the manufacturing sector.

A casual reading of history might lead one to conclude that the explanation of the increase in the investment–income ratio could be found in the course of technical change. Certainly technology had changed. Reapers and pickers had replaced labour in the harvesting of grain; large steel mills had replaced forges and bloomeries; and railroads had made long-distance transport an economic reality. While technical change certainly occurred, it is unclear how much of that change was merely a response to changes in relative prices and how much was 'pure' change. The breadth of the capital-deepening movement, however, makes one suspect that a substantial portion was of the former variety.

Other evidence, too, makes the 'relative' price argument particularly appealing. The century was marked by a series of technical advances that dramatically reduced the costs of materials that were major inputs to capital-goods production. The development of a specialized machine-tool industry reduced the costs of machines, and it is not surprising that the evidence indicates a rising proportion of producers' durables in the investment stream. Slightly later, the development of the Bessemer and open-hearth processes greatly reduced the price of steel and made it possible to substitute steel for wood in the structural members of factories and commercial buildings. It is little wonder that the relative price of that component of the capital stock fell substantially over the last decades of the century. The evidence also indicates that beginning some time between 1860 and 1880 the savings–income ratio began to rise. Such an increase should have triggered a decline in the interest component of the cost of investment goods and contributed further to the decline in the relative price of capital.

While changes on the demand side contribute something to our explanation of the rise in the share of investment in national income, there are strong implications that supply-side developments were at least equally important. We have no way of directly observing consumer tastes, but indirect evidence suggests that they may have shifted away from consumption and towards savings. As the economy became more commercialized, it is likely that the temporal variance of the income stream increased, and the probability of being forced to retire before one chose must have increased. Both would tend to induce consumers to save an increased portion of their income. In addition, the growing importance of cities must also have tended to increase the aggregate ratio. Cities were always relatively high savers, but in the course of the nineteenth century, their propensity to save appears to have increased as they added education, sewers, and street lighting to their traditional capital-formation activities. Finally, some changes in the composition of the personal savings sector appear to have contributed to the upward shift. The evidence on the effect of the change in occupational and ownership composition of the sector is ambiguous, but the changing age structure of the population must have tended to cause the savings ratio to rise, while shifts in the income distribution may have operated in the same direction.

It is interesting to note how many of the factors that appear to have directly underwritten changes in the savings ratio are related to the process of industrialization. It is true of the factors that appear to have changed consumer taste; the relative growth of cities is related to the same process, and structural factors appear also to have worked in the direction of increasing the inequality of the income distribution.

Similarly, the institutional changes in the financial markets that appear to have contributed to the drift are also largely associated with industrialization. Increasing demand for finance channelled to new and different regions and industries greatly increased the rewards attached to successful attempts to accumulate and mobilize capital. As a result a myriad of financial institutions were invented and introduced. Mortgage banks and commercial-paper houses moved funds across geographic boundaries; savings banks and insurance companies accumulated savings and made those accumulations available to business; the commercial banks both mobilized and – through their ability to engender forced savings – accumulated capital; and formal securities markets made investments appear more liquid and greatly widened the geographical and occupational areas over which these debt and equity instruments could be traded.

In part these intermediaries reduced search and negotiation costs, and these reductions increased net returns to savers and/or reduced net costs to potential investors. Either should cause an increase in the savings and investment rates. In a different dimension, they provided insurance against inter-investment variation in return as they substituted a claim on a part of a portfolio of assets for a single investment. Finally, they sometimes increased liquidity – not only are stocks and bonds often more marketable than the assets they represent, but it is usually easier to withdraw funds from a savings account than it is to sell a direct asset. Both insurance and greater liquidity made savings appear safer, and to the extent that savers are risk-averse, they certainly increased net (of risk) returns and they probably increased the rate of savings as well. Thus, the developments in the financial sector – developments that in large measure were a part of the movement toward commercialization and industrialization – appear to account for a substantial proportion of the rise in the investment–income ratio.

CHAPTER II

The United States: Evolution of Enterprise[1]

I. *Introduction: Modern Business Enterprise*

Large business enterprises have come to dominate American production, distribution, transportation, finance, and services. Such enterprises have been products of, and prime movers in, the rapid industrialization of the United States. Indeed, this new institutional form now plays a major role in all the urban and industrial economies of the non-Communist world. Giant business organizations have become hallmarks of the twentieth century.

Modern business enterprise makes use of more workers, managers, owners, machines, materials, and money than any other economic institution in history. Because of its size, it is impersonal in tone and bureaucratic in organization. Its managers, workers, and owners cannot possibly come to know one another. Its control requires the creation of a carefully defined hierarchy of offices, each with its own functions and responsibilities. The lines of authority, responsibility, and communication among offices are also carefully defined. Detailed accounts and other statistical and financial data flow through these channels. Control through statistics has become a basic managerial art. The managers of these enterprises make their careers in a single industry and often in a single firm. They are rarely, if ever, owners of their enterprises, for nearly all the enterprises are 'publicly owned' corporations in a legal sense, and their stock is held by thousands or even tens of thousands of shareholders. In only 15·5 per cent of the 200 largest corporations in 1963 did an individual, family, or group hold as much as 10 per cent of the stock. These multitudes of shareowners cannot possibly manage their complex and often multi-industrial companies. While today's corporations are 'publicly' owned, the owners are primarily private individuals, not the government. The federal government has taken a significant part in the management of the American economy since the depression of the 1930s: it has done this indirectly, however, through its monetary and fiscal policies and by becoming a major consumer and contractor. The government-owned and -operated enterprise remains a rarity in the American economy.

The evolution of the structure and function of large-scale enterprise has been central to the operation, organization, and performance of a modern industrial economy. It is within the enterprise – public or private – that the factors of production are combined and inputs become outputs. The introductory chapter to this volume pointed to the classic factors of production: land (raw materials or non-reproducible capital), capital (assets created by man or reproducible capital), and labour (the population willing and able to contribute to production). Since Jean-Baptiste Say, economists have also considered the role of the entrepreneur who transformed the factors of production from inputs into outputs and who took the financial risk involved in carrying out the transformation. Recently the concept of the entrepreneur has of necessity been enlarged to include the business unit or enterprise that came to carry out these entrepreneurial functions. In addition, emphasis has been placed on the role played by the entrepreneur or the enterprise in allocating the factors of production for future as well as current outputs of goods and services. The decisions made by the entrepreneur or within the enterprise thus affect not only the current output of an economy but also the direction of its future growth.

It is, then, within the enterprise that much of what economists call the 'residual' (defined in the introductory chapter as the proportion of output that cannot be explained by the growth of input) is created. Two elements of the enterprise affect this proportion. One is the organizational design through which the factors of production are combined for current output and in which the planning for future output takes place. The other is the training, experience, skills, and intelligence of the people responsible for transforming the factors of production into goods and services.

During the second half of the nineteenth century, when the large corporation began to replace the individual entrepreneur or partnership as the significant decision-making unit in the American economy, organizational design became more than the placing of machinery and equipment within the factory, office, or mine and the outlining of procedures for the workers to follow. It became the design by which the day-to-day activities of many sub-departments or units within a single firm were co-ordinated, controlled, supervised, and evaluated and through which long-term investments in plant and personnel were determined. Improvements in organizational design could bring fuller use of the units within the firm and sounder planning for resource allocation and could therefore enhance the current and future productivity of the enterprise.

The quality of management was even more important to the productivity of an enterprise than its organizational design. That design was, after all, only there to assist the men in charge of carrying out day-to-day operations and responsible for long-term investment decisions. As the enterprise grew, the supervising and planning tasks increased. Those responsible for them became full-time managers, and indeed management itself became a lifetime career and one that became increasingly professional. Training took longer, often including a formal and specialized education. Soon different types of managers had their own professional societies and their own specialized journals.

The primary reason for the growing importance of organizational design and professional management to the productivity of the enterprise – and with it the productivity of an economy – was that, as it grew large, the firm often became multi-unit. It expanded by adding new units – factories, sales and purchasing offices, mines, transportation divisions, and laboratories. The function of the enterprise then became not only to combine the factors of production within single operating units but to co-ordinate the flow of goods, information, and instructions between the units so that the transformation of inputs into outputs within each might be carried on more efficiently. And as an enterprise became multi-unit, the long-term allocation of resources began to require decisions about units carrying on different types of functional activities, in different geographical regions, and producing different types of goods and services.

In the United States the modern multi-unit enterprise appeared only after 1840, when the new technologies of production and transportation permitted an unprecedented increase in the speed, volume, and regularity of the processes of production and distribution. Before the coming of the new technology, nearly all enterprises were small, and nearly all were managed by their owners. One or two partners or a handful of stockholders raised the funds, acquired the equipment, hired the labour, and made both day-to-day operating decisions and long-term investment ones. The operations of such small personal partnerships required little in the way of formal organizational design. They rarely needed the services of even a single salaried manager, and when they did the managers worked closely with the owners. In their operation and performance these small personal enterprises were similar to those that had carried on economic activity in the West for more than half a millennium.

Though the size and internal operations of the business enterprise in America remained little changed from the nation's beginning until the 1840s, its activities during that period became increasingly specialized. In those years business enterprise evolved in a manner suggested by Adam Smith's definition of the relationships between specialization and the extent of the market. As the American market expanded, the firm became increasingly specialized, carrying on a single function – production, distribution, transportation, finance, or other services – and handling a single product or service. The evolution of enterprise before 1840 can be described as one of institutional specialization.

After the 1840s, however, the process became primarily one of institutional integration – that is, the combination and integration of the activities of several units. Before 1850, even the largest business enterprises in the United States rarely operated as many as two or three factories, or mines, or transportation lines, or buying or selling offices. By 1900, however, many American firms had become multi-unit; they had also become multi-functional. A single enterprise had come to manage not only several manufacturing units but also a number of selling, purchasing, mining, and transportation units as well. In the twentieth century, such multi-functional enterprises began to diversify their product lines by moving into new industries, and to enlarge their market by moving into other countries. Modern enterprise became multi-industrial and multi-national. Expansion through the addition of new units, new functions, new products, and new regional markets not only changed the activities and structure of the American firms, but also changed the structure of many industries and of the national economy as a whole.

The evolution of enterprise in the United States thus falls into three broad chronological periods. The first, occurring from the formation of the national economy in the late eighteenth century to the 1840s, was one in which the expansion of the market encouraged specialization in business. This specialization in turn helped to establish the nation's basic business institutions. During the second period, from 1840 to the First World War, new technologies revolutionized the processes of transportation, production, and distribution and encouraged the rise of the modern integrated multi-unit business enterprise. In the third period, from the 1920s to the present, multi-unit enterprises appeared in nearly all sectors of the economy. In manufacturing and distribution they continued to grow through diversification into new product lines and new overseas markets. It was during this period that the large impersonal managerial enterprise came to dominate most sectors of the American economy.

II. *The Specialization of Traditional Enterprise: 1790s to 1840s*

The colonial business world was a personal one, where the volume of goods handled was small, the pace was slow, and the role of the family critically important. The most pervasive enterprise was the family farm. Even in 1790 only 202,000 out of 3,930,000 Americans lived in towns or villages of more than 2,500; and of the 2,881,000 workers, 2,069,000 laboured on farms. Only in the South, where the crops were suited to cultivation by slave labour, did the production of staples become more than a family affair. The small amount of manufacturing done outside the home and farm was done by artisans in shops. Occasionally the artisan employed a few apprentices and journeymen, who were usually treated as part of the family. Lumbering continued to be a by-product of land-clearing, although in Maine and North Carolina timber was regularly harvested for masts, spars, barrels, and staves. There was little mining in the colonies. The only sizeable economic unit in either mining or manufacturing was the 'iron plantation', where the ore was mined, wood converted into charcoal, and iron refined into pigs. These plantations – with their rural setting, the seasonal nature of their work, the use of indentured servants and occasionally slaves – had much in common with the rice and tobacco plantations of the Southern colonies.

The activities of all these producing units were tied together by the merchant. He marketed their products and supplied them with raw materials, tools, and furnishings. This all-purpose businessman dominated the economy. Typically a resident of a coastal port, he exported, imported, retailed, and wholesaled all types of products. He took title to the goods he purchased for his regular customers, and he acted as an agent for merchants of other ports, taking their goods on consignment and selling for a fixed commission. He handled the economy's finance and transportation as well as distribution. He made long-term loans to planters, farmers, and artisans to enable them to clear land and improve their facilities; he provided short-term loans to finance the crops and the manufactured goods as they were in transit. In co-operation with other merchants, he arranged for the building of ships to carry these goods and, often with other partners, was a shareholder in these ships. As a partner or on his own account he instructed, but only in the broadest terms, the ship's captain, the supercargo, or his own agent or correspondent in a distant port, telling them what and how much to buy and sell. In all these activities he personally knew nearly all the individuals involved. Even his agents in London, the West Indies, or other North American colonies were usually relatives or trusted friends.

With the coming of political independence this personal, family business world began to change. The break with Britain disrupted old trading patterns and led to the opening of new areas to American merchants, including the Baltic, the Levant, China, and the East Indies. The continuing growth of population and the rapid expansion west into Kentucky, Tennessee, and Ohio, north into Maine, and southwest from Georgia enlarged domestic markets. After the outbreak of the wars of the French Revolution, the carrying trade with Europe and the West Indies again boomed. The swift growth of the new cotton trade, however, was probably the most important single factor in stimulating

and expanding economic activities in the United States and in bringing
the specialization of enterprise and the depersonalization of business
activity.

A. EXPANSION OF THE MARKET AND THE
SPECIALIZATION OF ENTERPRISE

Specialization of enterprise would certainly have come in the United
States during its first fifty years even without the rise of the cotton
trade. Specialization was already appearing in the distribution of goods
in New York, Philadelphia, and other large towns, where an increasing
number of retail stores and shops concentrating on a few lines of goods
had already been established. It was coming, too, in manufacturing in
New England and in parts of the middle states with the beginning of
a domestic or putting-out system and the first use of simple machines.
Yet the new high-volume cotton trade was primarily responsible for
the reorientation and expansion of American commerce.

Cotton, which was not grown commercially in the United States
until 1786, was in effect a brand new crop. By 1793, when Eli Whitney
patented the cotton gin, annual exports were already 550,000 lb. By
1800 they reached 20 million lb; by 1807, 66 million; by 1810 (the
year when Jefferson's embargo was lifted), 93 million; and by 1815
(after the close of the War of 1812), 83 million. In 1815 the value of
cotton exports stood at $17·5 million. By 1825 it had risen to $37
million, and by 1840 $64 million. The volume and value of these
exports contrast vividly with the modest expansion of the older crops
– tobacco, rice, and sugar. Exports of tobacco, for example, were
valued at $8 million in 1815 and only $10 million in 1840.

Cotton brought commercial agriculture to broad regions of the
South which, because of climate and soil, were unable to grow the older
staples. Moreover, cotton moved westward in the South a generation
before wheat moved west in the North. Cotton plantations provided
an important *initial* market to the farmers in the new Western settlements, in an era when lack of transportation facilities made it costly to
ship their corn, hogs, whiskey, horses, and mules to the East or to
Europe.

Besides stimulating the spread of agricultural units which specialized
in one major crop, cotton brought specialization to commerce. The
unprecedented volume of the cotton trade helped to make New York
the nation's leading city and initiated the swift decline of the all-
purpose general merchant. From the start the cotton trade was handled
by specialized merchants – wholesalers who did not take title to the
goods (except when they wanted to speculate), who concentrated on

a single line of products, and who were paid for their services by fixed commissions. Because they had no control of fluctuating prices set by the international forces of supply and demand, they preferred not to take the risk of having title to the goods. New men, rather than existing merchants, took up this new trade and devised the new type of enterprise. In New York City, they were at first agents of British textile firms who came to sell cloth and yarn and to make arrangements for obtaining raw cotton. In the cotton ports and particularly in the new interior towns – Columbia, Augusta, Macon, Montgomery, Jackson, and Natchez – Southerners and a surprisingly large number of New Englanders became factors for planters who had recently cleared the land in the rich black belt of Alabama and Georgia and the bottom lands along the Mississippi River.

The cotton factors marketed the planter's crops, purchased supplies and equipment for him, and provided him with credit when he needed it. In the larger towns the volume of trade was great enough to permit the rise of another active set of specialists – brokers who were not attached to any specific clients but brought together buyers and sellers of cotton for a commission. By the 1820s, an intricate network of brokers, commissioned merchants (who also acted as freight-for-warders, insurers, and financiers), and shippers moved the cotton crop from the interior to the Southern ports and then to New York and to Europe.

For the small cotton farmers in the South and the Western farmers who were beginning to grow grain in volume, storekeepers were the first businessmen on the chain from the interior to the seaboard. They carried out the same functions of marketing, purchasing, and financing for the farmers that the factors did for the large planters. The difference was that the country storekeepers took title to the crops they purchased and to the goods they brought from the East to sell to the farmers.

The flow of manufactured goods, tea, coffee, wines, and other products coming from the East and Europe to the South and West followed much the same network. Merchants handling these products preferred to buy and sell on commission rather than taking title to the goods. Nearly all importers and other suppliers to the domestic markets concentrated increasingly on a single specialized line of products, such as dry goods, wet goods (liquor), hardware, drugs, groceries, jewellery, or musical instruments. As the older cities grew and new ones appeared, the number of specialized retailers handling these same lines of goods also increased.

Because of the complexities of international trade, importers often took title to the merchandise. Also, dry-goods merchants purchased textiles at auctions which began in 1815 when the British decided to dump their surplus goods on the American market. These merchants and, to a lesser extent, buyers of hardware and other manufacturers continued to use the auctions up to the 1830s. Those specialized wholesalers who took title to the goods they handled became known as jobbers. Until the coming of the railroad and the telegraph, however, the jobbers remained relatively few in number and were concentrated in New York and Philadelphia. Both jobbers and commission agents sold to retailers in their own towns and sometimes to commission merchants in the South and West. Their best customers, however, were the cotton factors and country storekeepers who came regularly twice a year to New York to buy for their clients or to stock their stores.

The increased volume of trade led to specialization not only in the distribution of goods but also in their transportation. The most important development in transportation during the decades after 1790 was the rapid rise of common carriers (i.e. transportation enterprises that accepted any goods delivered to their pier or office), which after 1815 began increasingly to operate on a fixed schedule. Prior to 1790, the only common carriers were a small number of stagecoach and wagon lines. Their numbers grew as many turnpikes and other roads were built in the first part of the nineteenth century. After the War of 1812 came the packet lines connecting New York and Liverpool and then other major American and European ports. The first of these was started in 1818 by some of the same agents of British firms who initiated the cotton trade between New York and the South. At about the same time, steamboat lines began to appear on the Mississippi River and then on the bays, sounds, and rivers of the East. By the 1820s, the new specialized transportation companies were being increasingly used by the commission agents and jobbers to ship goods in and out of the interior of the United States. Only in trades over the more distant seas – to Asia, Africa, and Latin America – did all-purpose merchants, who owned their own vessels in which they shipped their own goods, continue to operate in the traditional way.

Specialization came even more quickly in finance than in transportation. Before the Revolution, there were no chartered banks in the colonies and no incorporated fire or marine insurance companies. A small number of banks were founded before 1800, and a good many more before the outbreak of the War of 1812. These early banks permitted the merchants to pool their capital, provided them with a safe place to deposit their funds, gave them a more certain source of long-term capital and short-term credit, and finally made possible the issuing of notes to provide a much-needed circulating medium. Just as important, the new financial institutions permitted the merchants to turn banking activities over to specialists. The boards of directors of these banks set general policies as to loans, discounts, and deposits. At first the members of the firm decided on each loan. Soon, however, the full-time salaried cashiers and presidents were making the loans by themselves, as well as carrying on all the routine work involved in these financial transactions.

As commerce moved into its new patterns after the close of the Napoleonic wars, the number of banks increased rapidly. In 1816 the nation could claim a total of 246, with thirty-eight being chartered in that year alone. Growth levelled off in the 1820s, and the number of banks stayed at a little above 300 during the rest of that decade. Except for the Second Bank of the United States, chartered in 1816, these banks remained essentially local in their activities, although many in the South and West had correspondents in New York or Philadelphia. Under the efficient administration of Nicholas Biddle, the Second Bank – with branches in all parts of the country – concentrated on financing the movement of crops, especially cotton. But with its demise in 1836, the major experiment in branch banking came to an end. As a result, the country did without an effective central banking system until the formation of the Federal Reserve System in 1913.

The rise of specialized insurance companies was similar to the coming of banks. By pooling resources in specialized insurance firms, merchants and then the commissioned agents and specialized shipping firms could get cheaper rates. The salaried employees of the new firms – the appraisers and inspectors – could concentrate on the more technical and routine aspects of the business. The first marine insurance company was incorporated in 1792; by 1800 there were twelve, and by 1807 there were forty. Fire insurance was somewhat slower in developing. Until the great fire of New York in 1835, such insurance was written on a small local scale, often by marine insurance companies. In the field of life assurance, one or two companies had existed even before the Revolution; but expansion was slow. Only a handful operated until the mid-1840s, when the first mutual life assurance company was formed. Only after the country began rapidly to industrialize and urbanize did life assurance become a significant business.

Expanding markets after 1790 affected manufacturing as well as agriculture, trade, and finance. Artisans who produced on order for local customers began to expand output by manufacturing for distant, unknown buyers. Increased output was achieved in three ways: the enlargement of an artisan's work force by the addition of journeymen and apprentices, the introduction and expansion of a domestic or putting-out system, or the application of machinery.

The first method – expansion of the work force – was used in the more skilled and luxury trades. It was also important in the building and construction industries. The putting-out system – which had appeared in a few cases even before 1790 – began to be used in the making of simple furniture and of such clothing as shoes, straw hats, gloves, lace, and stockings; in the weaving of sailcloth, sheets, and finer linens, all of which were made from flax; and in the production of cotton and wool cloth. In these trades an artisan or merchant obtained the raw materials, got them to the households to be processed, and arranged for the delivery of the finished goods to a commission agent or jobber in the closest city or town.

In the United States, more than in Britain or in continental Europe, the application of machinery rather than the putting-out system or the addition of apprentices was the method used to increase production for rapidly growing distant markets. Much of this machinery came from Britain, but many of the new machines were improved or even invented by ingenious Yankee tinkerers. Machinery came early in the processing of agricultural crops. As early as 1785, Oliver Evans constructed a mechanized flour mill on the Brandywine Creek in Delaware. Such mills expanded in number and size as the centre of milling moved west from the small streams near Philadelphia, Wilmington, Baltimore, and Richmond to Rochester and Buffalo in western New York. Machinery too became important in lumbering. This industry, using numerous small water-powered saws, grew rapidly after 1815, developing its own specialized wholesalers and retailers. Machinery also came to be widely used in the manufacturing of products made from wood, including clocks, furniture, mill work (panelling, mantels, doors, etc.), handles for axes, hoes, and other implements, gun stocks, hat blocks, and shoe lasts. In the 1830s, improved furnaces and the development of crude metal-processing machines encouraged the production of simple metal products, such as shovels, hoes, ploughs, saws, axes and other edged tools, gun barrels, nuts, bolts, and nails. However, it was not until iron, copper, and brass began to be produced in quantity through new techniques in the late 1830s and 1840s that metal products were manufactured by machinery in any volume.

It cannot be too strongly stressed that until coal and steam power came to be used on a large scale during the 1840s, American mills and shops remained small, family-run businesses, many being operated only seasonally. Even in the 1830s, an enterprise capitalized at over $100,000 and employing over a hundred men was extremely rare, and those capitalized at $50,000 and employing as many as fifty workers were considered very large. Those processing agricultural crops worked only in the autumn and into the winter. Lumbering, like meat-packing (still not a mechanized operation), was winter work. So, too, was the production of clocks, furniture, mill work, and other wood products made by machine. The production of shoes, hats, and other goods by the putting-out system was also concentrated in the winter or in slack periods in the cycle of growing crops. Before the 1840s, the small mills relied on part-time workers from nearby farms, whose pay was often in kind rather than in cash. The working of the simple machines, made largely out of wood and powered by water, required little in the way of direct continuous supervision.

The major exception to this description of American manufacturing before the 1840s was the textile industry. The small spinning mills, the first of which was Samuel Slater's venture at Pawtucket, Rhode Island, in 1789, spread slowly until 1807. Then Jefferson's embargo of that year, by cutting off British imports, led to a sharp increase in their numbers. These mills were similar to those in other manufacturing, although somewhat larger in capitalization and work force. They relied on families recruited from nearby farms, whose primary work was in the mill but who continued to be paid in goods as much as in cash. Some of the yarn these mills produced was put out to be woven in households. Most of it was sold to more distant markets through the network of commission merchants and jobbers that was then being created to handle the distribution of imported manufactured goods.

The basic change began when Francis Cabot Lowell arranged for the building of the first water-powered weaving looms in the United States and then combined them with spinning machines in a single integrated textile factory completed in 1815 at Waltham, Massachusetts, just west of Boston. By placing many spinning and weaving machines in the same building, powered by the same source, Lowell was able to produce plain coarse white cloth at a greatly reduced cost per yard. Except for the government armouries at Springfield, Massachusetts, and at Harpers Ferry, Maryland – two very special cases – this integrated cotton mill was the first true factory in the United States. The work within the enterprise was systematically subdivided. The large permanent force of 300 workers carried on specialized routine work for wages paid regularly and in cash.

This new form of manufacturing required more than technological innovation. To obtain the necessary work force, Lowell tapped an unused supply of labour – girls from the New England farms who had finished their schooling but were not yet married. To be assured of producing an uninterrupted flow of cloth, Lowell and his associates built their own machine shops and bleaching works. To get the funds required not only for building the factory but also for buying unprecedented amounts of cotton and paying the large labour force, they incorporated their company, capitalized it first at $600,000 and then at $1 million, and sold its stock to a number of Boston families. They marketed their output through the existing commission network but placed all sales in the hands of a single agent, who because of the high volume of business readily accepted a commission of only 1 per cent.

For a time, the power loom gave a new lease of life to the smaller mills, particularly in Rhode Island. These manufacturers purchased looms which were manufactured in Massachusetts and Rhode Island and which sold for less than $100 apiece. But the small mills, which rarely employed more than fifty people and used as much as $50,000 capital, had difficulty in competing with the large integrated factory. The high profits of Lowell's company, which ranged from 8 per cent to 13 per cent semi-annually even during the depressed years of 1819–21, encouraged the rapid spread of the factory. In 1822 men associated with the Waltham innovator began to build a planned industrial town named after Lowell on the banks of the Merrimack River in northern Massachusetts. By the end of the decade this town contained more than ten of the largest integrated factories. Other New Englanders quickly followed the example of the Boston associates by building similar factories along the Merrimack and the Connecticut and on the smaller rivers in Maine, Connecticut, and Vermont. Soon others appeared in New York, New Jersey, and Pennsylvania. By the 1840s these factories were driving the smaller mills out of business. In the late 1820s and 1830s, the same form of factory system began to be applied to the spinning and weaving of woollens and then to finished products like carpets, hosiery, and rope.

Yet before the 1840s the factory, with its large permanent labour force and its requirements of sizeable fixed and working capital, remained concentrated in the textile industry. A Treasury Department report on manufacturing establishments in the ten most industrialized states in the Northeast, made in 1832, listed 105 manufacturing establishments capitalized at over $100,000. Of these, eighty-eight were textile companies and twelve were ironworks, most of these the ancient type of 'iron plantation'. (The remaining five companies made nails and hoops, firearms, glass, salt, and hydraulic equipment.) Of the thirty-two firms listed in the report as employing more than 250 workers, thirty were textile factories (the other two included an iron company and a nail-and-hoop works).

The factory became important in American industries other than textiles only after low-cost coal and iron became available in the United States. In many industries, too, the appearance of the factory had to wait until steam power had improved transportation enough to enlarge the market by reducing transportation costs. Just as important, steam-powered transportation permitted a regular and steady flow of raw materials into the establishment and of finished goods out, which was so essential for continuous operation of costly plant and equipment, winter and summer. For except along the coast, ice prevented volume transportation of freight during the winter months in the region of the country where manufacturing was concentrated. Factories appeared in textiles earlier than in other American industries because machinery could be made of wood and driven by leather belting rather than iron gears, because production could be concentrated on a simple cheap product, and because a steady flow of raw cotton could be moved in and finished cloth moved out by using existing water routes and distribution channels.

Until the 1840s, then, the dominant forms of business enterprise in the United States remained small and not very different from those that had handled production, distribution, finance, and transportation in Europe since the Renaissance. Nevertheless, the growing volume of economic activity began after 1790 to alter drastically the institutional structure of the United States economy. It had encouraged a specialization of enterprise that led to the initial development of new types of business firms in the United States. In doing so, it brought to an end the personal business world of the all-purpose colonial merchant. The cotton factor, the commission merchant, the jobber, the broker, the managers of common carriers (including packet, steamboat, and canal lines), the bank cashiers, the insurance appraisers and inspectors, the mill-owners, and the factory treasurers and managers dealt regularly with men they did not know personally. The growing impersonalization and specialization meant that the flow of goods had to pass through an increasingly long and complex chain of business units from the producers of the raw and semi-finished materials to the manufacturer and then to the final consumer.

The flow was, of course, still relatively slow and indirect. Subject on the vagaries of wind, water, ice, and flood, it moved hesitantly and unsteadily through the many specialized units on the route from the producer to the consumer. No single institution or group of men attempted to guide or control this flow. Such co-ordination appeared to be carried out by impersonal and invisible market forces of supply and demand. So, too, did the long-term investment of resources for future production, distribution, and transportation. Because market forces had such a free rein, and because the business units in the economy were small and required little capital investment, the American economy in the 1830s came to be operated in a way that was quite similar to that described by the classical economists.

B. PRECURSORS OF MODERN MANAGEMENT

Because the units remained small, there was before the 1840s little specialization within the enterprise. Nearly all businesses were run by their owners. None yet required the carefully developed internal organization, the detailed statistical data, and the cost-accounting methods that have become hallmarks of modern enterprise. The merchant – still the central businessman in the economy – had no need for such techniques. In fact, specialization in handling a single product and function – and the practice of receiving payment by commission rather than from the actual buying and selling of goods – made the internal management of an agent's business less complex than was that of his predecessor, the all-purpose colonial merchant. The commission agent had fewer goods to oversee. He had less concern about seeing to it that materials kept moving through his warehouses. He, like the earlier colonial merchant, found entirely adequate the methods of book-keeping and accounting developed five hundred years before in Italy. Double-entry accounts indicated profits and losses for different ships, different commodities, and different transactions with other merchants. These accounts were used only to show a firm's current profit and loss. They were never intended as a means of appraising costs or of evaluating accurately the financial success or failure of past operations. As Stuart Bruchey has written about the early-nineteenth-century merchants, 'Experience was of far lesser importance than fresh news.'

For the new specialized financial institutions – banks and insurance companies – past experience quickly became as important as current news, but at first this resulted in only minor innovations in technique. The cashier, the bank president, and the appraiser, who were the first salaried employees in American corporations, had little difficulty in modifying existing business procedures to account for deposits, loans, and note issues, or funds paid in as insurance premiums and paid out as claims. Earlier experience in the mercantile world also helped them as they began to take over strategic as well as routine decisions from their part-time boards of directors.

Nor did the owners of farms, shops, mills, packet steamboats, wagon lines, or other common carriers, feel the need for new business methods. Accounting and internal organization remained largely private personal arrangements. There were only two exceptions to this general rule: on the Southern plantations and in the Northeastern textile factories, internal subdivisions of labour required arrangements to assure regular supervision and co-ordination of the work of the sub-units.

The plantations had their full-time managers – the overseers – who supervised the daily work of (say) fifty to a hundred slaves. But the overseer's task required very little in the way of systematic management. The co-ordination of the activities of the slaves was done by following simple routines within traditional seasonal patterns. Rarely did the overseer and planter trouble themselves about keeping careful accounts. Those that existed for the plantation were usually maintained by the planter's factor and kept in the regular mercantile way. These accounts told the planter or his factor very little about real cost, profits, or efficiency of operation. The plantation, an ancient agrarian institution, had no impact at all on the development of modern business enterprise.

The textile factory, on the other hand, was a genuine precursor of modern industrial enterprise. Yet it was only a precursor, not a pioneer in the new methods. One reason was that the men who managed the enterprise were merchants by experience and were wedded to traditional mercantile methods. Another was that technology and financing raised few entirely new problems. Maintaining and operating the textile mills did not require the skill and precision that were soon to be needed in the railroads and metal-working industries. Wooden machines and leather-belting transmission systems were easily made and repaired in the building. Each phase of the process could be carried out on one factory floor. In most factories, the raw cotton, which had been stored outside the premises, was cleaned, placed on wooden cylinders, and carded on the first floor; spun into yarn on the second; dressed on the third; woven into cloth on the fourth; and trimmed, measured, and folded for shipping on the fifth. The overseers or foremen on each floor could easily maintain a constant watch on all the operatives in their departments. The mill agent (factory manager) could personally keep in touch with the flow of materials from one department to the other.

Accounting, too, was simple. Although Lowell and his successors appreciated from the start the importance of having available large sums of working capital, nearly all of this went for just two items – raw cotton and wages. The remaining expenses were lumped into a single account, which sometimes included a certain percentage of total cost for wear and tear. Normally, however, such depreciation was handled merely by putting aside funds out of the profits of an exceptionally good year. The operating and accounting needs did not create difficult problems for the managers of textile factories.

In fact, there was so little need for a central management of these enterprises that the functions of the business were carried on quite apart from one another. The treasurer (the full-time representative of the board of directors and normally a merchant living in Boston) handled money and materials. He not only concerned himself with obtaining working and fixed capital, borrowing and paying dividends, but also purchased the raw cotton. The mill agent ran the factory. He lived in the factory town and involved himself solely with the management of personnel and machines and with the movement of materials within the factory. The finished cloth was marketed by a selling firm, which was normally a completely separate enterprise. Increasingly, the marketing firm took on more functions than just getting the goods into the distribution network at a 1 per cent commission. It assumed the financial responsibility for marketing, handled insurance and some banking services for the manufacturer, remained an important source of capital, and made decisions as to the quality, style, and quantity of the goods that the factory should produce. Throughout most of the nineteenth century, however, the critical functions of production, marketing, and finance remained under the control of different men, who often did not see each other for weeks at a time. The separation of functions, as well as the continuing mercantile practices of finance and administration, meant that the textile factory contributed little to the techniques of modern management.

Thus, while the growing domestic markets within the United States during the half-century after 1790 brought the rise of specialized economic units operating within an impersonal market economy, neither the size of the market nor the complexity of technology required the building of modern large-scale enterprises. Although the relations between enterprises had become relatively impersonal, those within the enterprise remained highly personal in the traditional style. Only in textiles had the modern impersonal factory appeared before 1840; and even the largest textile companies had few of the attributes of the modern business enterprise.

III. *The Rise of Modern Enterprise: 1840s to the First World War*

Modern enterprise had its beginnings and its first growth in the decades between the 1840s and the First World War. Its rise was affected by both expanding markets and increasingly complex technologies. The American market grew even more rapidly after 1840 than it had before. During the decade of the 1840s, heavy waves of immigration from Europe began to reach the US, and the flow would continue for the rest of the century. This swiftly growing population – from 17·1 million in 1840 to 63·1 million in 1890 – meant that most of the available agricultural land would be taken up in this period. At the same time, the urban population began to increase at a much faster rate than that of the countryside. Even with the high rate of population growth, productivity reached new heights, so that per capita income – and therefore buying power – rose rapidly after 1840. According to Richard A. Easterlin, per capita income went from $65 in 1840 to $95 in 1880 and $113 in 1900.

In the period after 1840 expanding markets were, however, no longer the dominant influence on the evolution of enterprise in the United States. That influence became technology. While growing markets encouraged the specialization of units combining the factors of production, the new technology led to the integration of many specialized units within the enterprise as a whole.

The new technologies, by revolutionizing the processes of transportation, distribution, and production, greatly increased the speed and volume of the output of goods and services. The new speed and volume required, in turn, an increase in the numbers of managers to plan and supervise the new processes. This increase in the velocity of activity also demanded the development of new organizational procedures and designs to permit the more efficient use of the much larger amounts of materials, men, and machines used in the processes of production and distribution.

Central to these fundamental changes was the adoption of a new prime mover – steam – and the use of a basic source of energy – coal. The application of steam to transportation came with a rush. Americans were pioneers in the use of steamboats on rivers, lakes, and sounds. Then in 1830, only a year after George Stephenson had conclusively demonstrated the practicality of the steam locomotive for land transportation at the Rain Hill trials in England, Americans began to build their own locomotives and railroads. By 1840 they had constructed 3,000 miles of track. At first, however, the new railroads only supplemented existing water transportation. Only in the late 1840s and the 1850s did this new fast, regular, all-weather form of transportation begin to generate a revolution in the distribution of American goods.

The adoption of new production techniques came more slowly. Americans had known of the utility of steam power since James Watt's invention was commercialized in the 1770s. They knew that coke had long been used in British blast furnaces, and they were also aware of the rapid spread in Britain of the rolling and puddling techniques for processing pig iron, developed by Henry Court in the 1780s. During the early years of the nineteenth century they had also learned of British innovations in the employment of high heat for volume production of sugar, alcohol, and beer. In this same period, Americans (Eli Whitney being the best-known pioneer in the field) began to work out techniques for using interchangeable parts in the fabrication and assembly of metal implements and machinery. Despite all these impressive technological advances, Americans before the 1840s had made very little use of steam power or of the new coal-using production methods in the furnace, metalworking, and refining industries.

A primary reason for the delay in adopting these new technologies lay in the lack of coal in the East – the most industrialized part of the United States. Before the canals into the anthracite fields of eastern Pennsylvania were completed in the early 1830s, the only available coal came from small mines on the James River in Virginia or low-grade deposits in Nova Scotia or was brought in ballast from Britain. At first the output of the anthracite mines was used largely to heat homes in the seaport cities. Then in the late 1830s and the 1840s anthracite was increasingly employed in manufacturing and transportation. In the thirties America's modern iron industry had its beginning in eastern Pennsylvania, as bar and sheet iron was produced from pig iron by coal using puddling and rolling methods. In the next decade anthracite coal was used to produce the pig itself. In the late 1830s and 1840s the availability of fuel for steam power and for firing furnaces made possible for the first time high-volume production of cutlery and metal tools and implements. Then in the late 1840s and 1850s the new sources of iron and fuel led to an increasing use of interchangeable parts in the production of machinery made of metal. It was also in the fifties that the use of super-heated steam and other modern techniques were developed in sugar and other distilling and refining industries.

The availability of coal thus lowered the cost and increased the output of the individual units of production. Steam quickly replaced water power. As the decade of the forties closed, a steam-driven factory was still a rarity. Within two decades, half the horsepower used in American manufacturing was generated by steam. By 1900, all but one-eighth of the horsepower generated was steam-produced. The consumption of coal in the United States increased enormously – from 8·3 million tons in 1850 to 79·3 million in 1880, and to 258·7 million in 1900.

As coal, a new source of energy, was making possible a great expansion in the production of goods, a revolution in transportation and communication lowered the cost and increased the speed of their distribution. In the decade of the 1850s the railroad crossed the Appalachians and spread swiftly into the Mississippi Valley. By 1860, 30,000 miles of track had been laid down, creating the basic railroad network east of the Mississippi River. By 1869 the Pacific had been reached; and by 1875, with over 74,000 miles of track in operation, the nation's basic overland transportation system had been constructed. The massive building that began again after the depression of the 1870s largely filled in the existing network. Only in parts of the West did new lines continue to open up areas to railroad transportation.

As the railroad marched across the continent, so too did the telegraph. Invented in 1844, it began to be used commercially in 1847. Railroad managers quickly found the telegraph an invaluable aid to assuring safe and efficient operation of trains; and telegraph promoters realized that the railroads provided very convenient rights of way. Because the telegraph was easier and cheaper to build than the railroad, it reached the Pacific first, in 1861. By that date 50,000 miles of wire were in operation. Two decades later, according to the Census of 1880, 31,703,000 messages were sent in a year over 291,000 miles of wire. The telephone, commercialized in the 1880s, at first only supplemented the telegraph. Until the development of the 'long lines' in the 1890s, the telephone was used almost wholly for local conversations. Thus, where the railroad improved communication by speeding the movement of mail, the telegraph and then the telephone permitted almost instantaneous communication with nearly every part of the nation.

These several converging forces – the coming of cheap coal, steam and iron; the lowering of the cost and increasing the speed of transportation and communication as the new railroad and telephone networks spread; the assurance that the railroads could move materials quickly, regularly, and on schedule in all seasons; and the growing demand, reflecting the expansion of population and per capita income – all encouraged the rapid spread of the factory. The factory, or the works, with its permanent work force, its costly machines and other equipment, and its reliance on coal for power and heat, quickly replaced the home, farm, or small shop or mill as the basic manufacturing or processing unit in the United States. The Census of 1880 reported that of the three million workers employed in mechanical industries at least four-fifths worked in factories. In the non-mechanical, heat-using industries – furnace, foundry, distilling, and refining – the proportion of the workers so employed was certainly even higher.

The operations of the new factories and works required, for the first time in manufacturing, that close attention be paid to internal organization and to the recruitment and training of managers. The new speed and flow of goods through the enterprise, as well as the increasing subdivision of work and the increasing technological complexity of the production processes, demanded careful planning and scheduling to ensure that the machines and equipment, and their operators, were steadily employed. Nevertheless, the operation of the most complex of the new factories was less difficult than that of even a small railroad.

By the 1850s the application of steam and iron to transportation had created some of the largest business enterprises the world had yet seen. During the next fifty years, the railroads required the co-ordination and control of more money, men, and equipment than any other business. No other demanded such careful minute-to-minute operation, and no other called for such large expenditures of capital. The only other type of enterprise whose technology called for as much centralized control was that of operating the new telegraph network. Thus the new commercial uses of steam and iron (and electricity in the case of the telegraph) which helped to revolutionize transportation and communication in the United States also led to the building of the first modern business enterprises in that country – that is, the first to co-ordinate, supervise, appraise, and plan for a number of specialized operating units.

To manage such enterprises in transportation and later in manufacturing demanded the services of a new sub-species of economic man – the full-time salaried professional manager. Such men had rarely been merchants or artisans. They were a new breed of businessmen, trained as civil or mechanical engineers. Such training took place at first on the job, later in colleges and universities. Indeed, the nation's first engineering schools were a response to the needs of these new enterprises for professional engineers. These men were also one of the first groups of Americans to develop their own professional associations. Their training, their experience, and their whole life-style differed as radically from those of the merchants who had run the pre-industrial economy as the new business techniques that they came to use differed from those of the older mercantile world.

A. THE RAILROADS – THE NATION'S FIRST BIG BUSINESS

Because all the problems of financing and administering large-scale enterprise had to be met by the railroads, railroad executives were forced to become pioneers of modern management. From the start the construction and operation of American railroads involved impressive amounts of money and numbers of employees. By the mid-1850s, at least fifteen railroad companies had a fixed capital investment of over $5 million. The capitalization of the four large interregional lines connecting the East with the Mississippi Valley, which were completed between 1851 and 1854, ranged from $17 million to $35 million. The largest manufacturing enterprises – the older integrated textile mills and the new integrated rail mills – were rarely capitalized at over $1 million. Even the working capital used by the East–West trunk lines ran between $2 million and $3 million annually, whereas that of textile mills was normally between $300,000 and $500,000. Finally, the railroads had up to 4,000 employees who carried out a wide variety of jobs, while the textile mills rarely hired more than 1,500 workers who carried out similar tasks.

The massive financial requirements of a railroad had two important results: one was external to the enterprise, the other internal. The large sums of money that were needed to build railroads in the 1850s caused the rise of the specialized investment-banking house in the United States and the centralization and institutionalization of the nation's money markets on Wall Street. Of the more than $1 thousand million invested in American railroads by 1859, over $700 million had been provided after 1850. During this period, modern methods of buying, selling, and transferring securities were worked out. So, too, were the standard modes of speculation, such as the use of puts and calls, selling short, and buying on margin.

The present-day instruments of finance, including those used in financing industrial corporations during and after the 1890s, were also developed at this time. Because the railroads had to rely on distant investors rather than local businessmen for capital, bonds began to be used more extensively than stocks in raising funds. The promoters of the railroads and those who lived along their lines preferred to maintain a semblance of control by taking stocks; but Eastern and European investors considered bonds a safer investment. First-mortgage, second-mortgage, and third-mortgage bonds, income and debenture bonds, and even convertible bonds appeared, as did a variety of preferred stocks. Because of the different types of issues and their large amounts, the treasurer of a sizeable line spent all his time raising and helping to allocate fixed and working capital. He did not have time to act as a purchasing agent too, as did the treasurer of a textile mill. In fact, he needed a senior officer under him to supervise the internal transactions of the enterprise.

This officer – the comptroller – was created because railroads, unlike textile or iron mills, had many employees who handled money. In the textile mill, the only employee (besides the treasurer) who was involved in financial transactions was the mill agent, who supervised the weekly paying of the hands. On a railroad, however, conductors, station agents, and freight and passenger agents received monies daily, every penny of which had to be accounted for. The comptroller's office also assisted in pricing and costing. Whereas a textile mill turned out one or two products and purchased only one raw material (the price of which was set by international markets), a railroad handled and had to set charges on a vast number of commodities. Pricing was only partly determined by the rates set by a few competitors. Costs, too, were far more difficult to determine than in a textile mill. Many more items were involved. Fixed costs were much larger. Variable costs, which fluctuated with different routes and equipment, were much harder to compute. Depreciation and obsolescence involved far greater sums of money. For these reasons, modern cost-accounting began – in the United States – on the railroads and not in the early textile mill or iron planatation.

The operation of a large railroad raised even more difficulties than did the management of its financial activities. A mill . agent could personally view the activities of every worker under his charge within half an hour, but the general superintendent of a large railroad needed a week even to check on all the personnel, equipment, yards, switching stations, and buildings (depots, terminals, offices, round-houses, and repair shops) for which he was responsible. Moreover, no other common-carrier companies – those operating stagecoaches, wagons, canal boats, or river or coastal steamers – built or maintained their own rights of way; only rarely did the turnpikes or canals act as the operators of transportation enterprises using their rights of way. The railroads, however, had to operate their own trains, usually on a single track over a distance of many miles. Their operation required exceedingly close supervision to prevent collisions and – an even more complex problem – to assure a steady use of locomotives, cars, and other equipment in the carrying of through and way freight in both directions along the line.

The first railroads to confront these operating challenges in their most exacting form were the longest lines joining major sections of the country. As long as the lines remained short, their administration remained relatively simple. Thus on the forty-four-mile Boston and Worcester line, trains left three times a day from each terminal. After safely meeting at the midpoint, Framingham, each moved on to its destination without fear of collision. A single superintendent could personally supervise and co-ordinate the work of the managers in charge of each of four different functional activities: movement of trains and of traffic, maintenance of way, maintenance of locomotives and rolling stock, and accounting and finance. But on the longer roads completed in the 1850s to connect distant commercial centres, such as New York City and the Lake Erie ports, Philadelphia and Pittsburgh, or Baltimore and Wheeling, management became more complex.

These larger roads were built in sections of seventy-five to one hundred miles, and when a new division went into operation it was given the same functional structure as the original unit. By the mid-1850s several roads had built from three to five divisions and were integrating their operations. To co-ordinate, control, and evaluate the work of several similar operating units, the companies set up central offices consisting of a general superintendent and of the executives responsible for the four functional activities for the line as a whole. At this point, the new top managers had to define the relationship of the functional officers at headquarters with those in each of the operating divisions. They had to indicate where the lines of authority lay between the central office and the regionally defined but functionally organized operating divisions.

In the 1850s Daniel C. McCallum, general superintendent of the New York and Erie, and J. Edgar Thomson, general superintendent and then president of the Pennsylvania, solved this basic management problem by making a distinction between line and staff responsibilities. Each had the president of his road delegate his authority to the general superintendent and through him to the manager on each of the divisions in charge of transportation, who now took the title of division superintendent. The managers of the line of authority were given power to order the movements of trains and traffic (that is freight and passengers), as well as any emergency maintenance of equipment and roadbed. The executives in the other functional departments (maintenance of way, maintenance of equipment, and finance) became designated as staff officers (see Fig. 3). They set standards and evaluated, promoted, hired, and fired managers in their departments; but they could not give orders concerning the movements of men and track. The line executives ordered when and where the maintenance crews carried out their work and when the repair shops had to complete their duties. In the terminology of the day, the line managers handled men; the functional or staff managers handled things.

By spelling out line and staff relationships, the managers of the early railroads devised an organizational design, a *structure*, that carefully defined the lines of authority, responsibility, and communication. The relationships were outlined in organizational charts, the very first of such devices to appear in American business. The top executives quickly developed elaborate daily, weekly, and monthly reports to flow up these communications channels and the various standardized orders and circular letters to move down them. Almost at once, they began to use for managerial purposes the detailed flow of operating information so essential for the co-ordination and control of the daily movement of hundreds of locomotives and thousands of cars over hundreds of miles of track. They also began as early as the 1850s to use costs and other statistical information to evaluate the performance of the managers within each of the regional operating divisions.

During the 1860s the attention of the managers of large railroads turned from organizational design to cost-accounting. The high fixed capital investment created the challenge. The large initial investment demanded a careful separation of construction from operating accounts, a realistic provision for depreciation, and a complex evaluation of costs in relation to trains run and traffic carried. From the 1840s on, railroad men emphasized the dangers of including current operating expenses in the construction and capital accounts. By 1859, the executives on the Pennsylvania were calculating annual depreciation on rails, ties, and 'running machines'. To meet the resulting costs, the Pennsylvania set up a 'contingency and renewal fund'. The amounts deducted for depreciation were placed in safe investments. The more usual way to account for depreciation, however, was to charge renewal to current operating accounts and to consider them as restoring 'value' that had been lost by wear and tear. Such 'renewal' accounting became standard for railroads by the 1870s.

Far more complex than the task of perfecting the capital accounts was the computation of operating expenses. Not only did a great many more types of accounts have to be kept than in a textile factory or iron mill, but many more of these costs remained constant whether the plant and equipment was used or not. Albert Fink, civil engineer, bridge-builder, and then president of the Louisville & Nashville Railroad, devised in the late sixties a formula for obtaining cost per ton-mile involving seventy different accounts. Twenty-nine of these items he considered as constant costs, nine as more constant than variable, and thirty-two as more variable than constant. Fink and the other railroad men used their analyses of costs, much as McCallum had done earlier, to evaluate the performance of the several divisions and departments, and also as a basis for setting rates.

Many factors affected rate-making even after the basic costs had been computed. Competition from water routes and from other railroad lines had some impact. Rates varied as to the type of traffic. The small, light, valuable products could carry high rates; but heavy freight such as coal, cattle, and wheat could only be moved with low rates. Empty cars on a return trip further affected the rate structure, as did the sizes of shipments. Large lots cost less per unit to move than small ones. Moreover, nearly all 'through rates' had to be decided co-operatively by the roads along the route, as did the share of the total rate which each would receive. By the 1860s, rates had to be set for hundreds of different types of goods, usually placed in one of several major freight classifications, and the railroad had to deal with a great number of shippers as well as agents of competing and connecting roads. Rate-making became a highly skilled job. Freight and passenger agents were soon placed in a separate functional organization, the Traffic Department (see Fig. 3).

In the late 1860s and the 1870s, the work of the Traffic Department increased enormously. The expansion of railroad mileage meant a higher volume of shipments, and the railroads also began to take over the business functions formerly carried out by other specialized enterprises. In the 1840s express and fast freight companies were formed to assure safe and prompt movement of goods across the many newer railroad routes and the older steamboat, sailing, and canal lines. By the 1860s, these express companies had their own railroad cars with distinctive markings, their own delivery wagons, and their networks of offices. During the Civil War, however, most of the major railroads began to take over these transportation companies and soon incorporated their activities into their own enlarged Traffic Departments. The railroads themselves, not the former specialized transportation companies, guaranteed delivery of most products from one commercial centre to another.

This came to be done through the systematic interchange of freight cars among the many roads. By the late 1870s, every large railroad company had a separate office whose sole task was to keep tabs on its cars being used on other lines and on the cars of other lines that were using its track. Such organizational arrangements, perfected by the 1880s, permitted the free and rapid interchange of cars and traffic throughout the country.

By the 1880s the new national transportation system was essentially complete. The building of bridges and the construction of tracks within terminal cities physically linked the major railroads in the years immediately following the Civil War. In the 1870s and 1880s railroad managers, working through industry and professional associations, began to standardize equipment and procedures. The standardization movement included the adoption of standard time in 1883 and the final conversion to standard gauge in 1886. But probably most important of all to the efficient operation of the new national transportation system were those arrangements between firms that permitted cars to move from one commercial centre to another in any part of the country across several railroad systems without a single transshipment.

Albert Fishlow has pointed out that the productivity of American railroad services grew at a faster rate in the second half of the nineteenth century than did that of any other sector in the economy. He credited these increases partly to improved technology (in particular heavier locomotives, larger rolling stock, and heavy steel rails), partly to the standardization carried out by industry-wide associations, and partly to the normal economies of scale and specialization resulting from the growth of the firm and of the system as a whole. But, he stresses, these developments accounted for only half the productivity increase from 1870 to 1910. He suggests that the growing experience of the work force was one factor in making up this residual. Another factor, which Fishlow does not mention, was the increased training and experience of the managers who co-ordinated the flow of trains and traffic and the development of organizational designs and procedures to assure the continuing and steady use of equipment within and between railroad enterprises. One result of this increased productivity was a much lower cost of transportation. As Fishlow points out, by 1910 'real freight rates fell more than 80 per cent from their 1849 level and real passenger charges 50 per cent'.

Although inter-firm co-operation greatly increased the speed and lowered the cost of transportation between one commercial centre and another, it failed to assure the railroads that they would always have enough traffic to meet the costs of operating and maintaining their massive capital equipment. After the nation's main lines were completed, the pressure to keep their capital employed created an irresistible temptation to attract business from competing roads by cutting rates on traffic. This was particularly true in periods of economic depression, when the volume of business fell off. For many roads, financial solvency depended on the continuing flow of through traffic. To protect themselves from competition for such traffic, the railroads during the depression of the 1870s organized informal and then formal cartels to allocate traffic and revenue among competing firms – the largest and most influential being the Southern Railway and Steamship Association and the Eastern Trunkline Association. But these and other regional associations formed to operate traffic and money pools were unable to prevent rate-cutting and rate wars.

The failure of the cartels in the early 1880s forced the major roads into a strategy of creating extended systems that would assure their own entry into the major commercial centres in their region. They aimed at obtaining what one railroad president termed 'self-sustaining' systems where 'each line must own its own feeders'. The decision to expand by purchasing, leasing, or building new units greatly increased the number of operating divisions on a single road. It also required raising huge amounts of capital. As a result financiers, particularly investment bankers, came to sit on railroad boards and have a say in the overall strategy of expansion. For many railroads such expansion proved financially disastrous. The resulting financial and administrative reorganizations were carried out in the 1890s by leading investment bankers such as J. P. Morgan & Company, and this increased still further the influence of the financiers in the top management of American railroads.

When the reorganizations of the nineties were completed, about twenty-five large railroad systems operated two-thirds of the nation's mileage and carried the major share of its goods and passengers. Nearly all these systems ran between the interior and the coasts, and those few interior systems that did not have their own outlets to the seaboard were closely allied with others that did. After 1900 the regional boundaries of the large railroad systems remained much the same until the middle of the twentieth century, when the railroads began to become technologically obsolete.

To manage their greatly enlarged transportation empires, the new systems fashioned still larger management units. This resulted in the creation of two new levels of middle and top management. A number of territories managed by general superintendents were combined into an organization headed by a general manager with his staff (see Fig. 3). The largest systems had two to five such regional organizations, which were in turn supervised by a vice president in charge of operations and his staff. On the Pennsylvania, the Burlington, and the Santa Fe, the general managers had the same degree of autonomy and profit responsibility that the division managers of large industrials such as General Motors and du Pont came to have later in the twentieth century; while the general executives in the corporate headquarters concentrated on evaluating the performance of the operating divisions and allocating resources for future operations.

The experience of the great private enterprises that operated the new forms of communication – the telegraph and the telephone – had many parallels with that of the railroads. Many telegraph companies sprang up, and because nearly all messages were long-distance and not local, co-operation among these enterprises in the handling of such messages was essential. As a result, consolidation came quickly. By the late 1850s, a decade after the telegraph became commercially practicable, six regional systems were operating nearly all the mileage constructed. By 1866 these had been consolidated into one large company, Western Union. At its start, Western Union was already managing a network of over 2,500 offices, and it continued to add from 500 to 1,000 a year. The new consolidated enterprise administered this network through a number of regionally defined offices, whose managers were responsible for supervising groups of operating units, for maintenance and repairs, and for the development of procedures to assure a smooth and steady flow of messages between towns and cities in all parts of the United States.

The telephone, in its early years, differed from the telegraph in that it was used primarily for local rather than long-distance messages. In the 1880s, local companies using Alexander Graham Bell's patents and equipment operated the first telephone enterprises. In the nineties, as local companies became interconnected and patents expired, the Bell interests maintained control over these many units by means of the American Telephone & Telegraph Company, which operated the nation's 'long lines' or through traffic. The operations of AT&T were soon managed through a regionally defined administrative structure similar to that used at Western Union.

From their beginning, then, the new forms of transportation and communication were operated through multi-unit enterprises. These enterprises, therefore, pioneered in the ways of modern big business. By making possible an unprecedented level of speed, regularity, and volume of transportation and communication, they in turn expanded the market for American producers of goods and services. The lowering of the cost of distribution and the increase in volume made possible by the railroad and the telegraph encouraged first the rise of the new techniques of modern mass marketing and mass production and then the coming of the large industrial enterprise that integrated mass production with mass distribution.

B. THE RISE OF MASS MARKETING

Between the 1850s and the 1880s a revolution occurred in American marketing, based largely on the new forms of transportation and communication. Within a single generation, the modern types of mass-marketing enterprises replaced the merchants who had for so long handled the distribution of goods.

By the 1840s these merchants not only had become specialized in handling a single line of commodities or products but also followed the farmer west into the Mississippi Valley. As the nation expanded geographically, so too did the chain of middlemen responsible for the distribution of its agricultural commodities and finished goods. Cotton and wheat moved from the farms to the processors, and dry goods and hardware from manufacturers to farmers, through the hands of at least three or four merchants, each residing at a major point of trans-shipment.

As soon as the railroads and telegraph provided fast, reliable all-weather transportation and communication, the chain of middlemen began to disappear. Commission merchants were replaced almost overnight by marketing enterprises that purchased on their own account directly from the farmer or the manufacturer and sold directly to the processor or local retailer, or in some cases to the ultimate consumer.

In the marketing of agricultural crops, the commission merchants quickly lost out to commodity dealers who purchased corn, wheat, and cotton at the railhead, stored and shipped the commodities, and sold them directly to processors. To finance these transactions, the dealers relied extensively on the grain, cotton, and other exchanges formed in the 1850s and the 1860s on the basis of telegraphic communication.

In the distribution of manufactured or processed goods, the full-line, full-service wholesalers (who specialized in the same product lines as their predecessors, such as dry goods, hardware, drugs, and groceries) began to buy directly from the manufacturer and sell directly to the local retailer. These new wholesalers pioneered in the developing of modern marketing techniques such as branding, advertising, and the use of an extensive sales force. Before the railroads, country storekeepers in the South and West had come twice a year to the Eastern cities to purchase their goods. After 1850 the new wholesalers sent salesmen out and delivered their goods directly to those retailers.

The modern mass retailers – the department store, the mail-order house, and the chains – which were increasingly to replace the whole-saler, also had their beginnings in this same period. First came the department store, which catered to the growing urban markets; then came the mail-order houses – Montgomery Ward and Sears Roebuck – which concentrated on the rural markets. Although the A&P and Woolworth's had become large by the 1880s, few other retail chains were formed before 1900.

All the new mass marketers had extensive purchasing and selling organizations. Mass distributors of finished goods had buying offices in the major commercial and manufacturing centres in the northeastern United States and in Europe. For each major line these enterprises had a buying staff, which set the prices paid, volume, and specifications of their purchases and arranged for the shipment of the goods to the offices or departments responsible for marketing that line. These marketing or operations offices handled the advertising, the actual selling, and the delivery of goods to the customer. For all managers, the criterion of successful performance was volume, or in their terms 'stock turn'. Increased stock turn meant increased profits without raising margins or prices. These new enterprises thus created integrated networks of buying and selling units carefully designed to co-ordinate a high-volume flow of goods across the new transportation systems from processors directly to the retailers or final consumers.

These basic changes in the processes of distribution were purely organizational ones. The new mass marketers required little in the way of new technology or extensive capital investment of their own. They reorganized the processes of distribution in order to exploit more effectively the new means of transportation and communication. Al-though data on increased productivity similar to those of Fishlow on the railroads do not exist, it is clear that the volume of trade that could be handled by a single enterprise had increased enormously, and that the unprecedented stock turn permitted high profits along with low prices. Before 1840 only the largest mercantile houses had annual sales of over half a million dollars. In 1865, shortly after Marshall Field had started his wholesale dry-goods and clothing establishment in Chicago, its sales reached $9·5 million. Five years later, after it had added some new lines and had begun to expand into retailing, sales rose to $17·2 million. By 1889, with little expansion in personnel or capital equipment, they were over $31·0 million. The volume of sales attained by A. T. Stewart, John Wanamaker and other mass marketers in New York and Philadelphia was even larger. The new retail tycoons, including Field, Stewart, Wanamaker, the Strauses of Macy's, and the Rosenwalds of Sears, quickly ranked among the wealthiest men in the nation. At the same time their prices were so low that small shopkeepers began to ask the states and then the federal government for legislation to protect them from such competition.

The greatly increased speed and volume of the business of the new mass marketers not only reduced the unit cost in the actual distribution of goods but also lowered the cost of financing this distribution. Prior to 1850, trade in cotton, grain, and other commodities was carried on largely by 90-day or 120-day bills carrying 5 to 7 per cent annual interest. Retailers taking title to goods usually needed credit for six months to a year. On the other hand, the high stock turn developed by the new mass marketers permitted them to generate a large cash flow which could be used to pay for new inventory on a cash, or at most a 30-day, basis. Commodity dealers, by using a system of hedging on the exchanges, were able to finance the movement of crops at a very small cost. The amount of savings resulting from lower financing expenses and greater speed and volume made possible by the organizational revolution in mass marketing has not been computed; but it does seem safe to assume that the organizational design and quality of management of these new types of enterprises lowered the cost of marketing and increased the productivity of the processes of distributing goods in the United States.

C. THE COMING OF MASS PRODUCTION

Whereas mass marketing required only organizational innovation, mass production required also new technology and extensive investment in capital equipment. Mass production, it should be pointed out, was more than just factory production. Mass-production techniques are those that permit a factory or a works to produce continuously or in large batches. Such methods made possible a fast 'throughput' of materials within the plant. High throughput was as basic to mass production as high stock turn was to mass marketing. The greater the throughput for a given plant and set of equipment, the lower the unit costs and the greater the possibility of increased profits.

High throughput could be obtained and then increased in a number of ways. Machinery and equipment could be improved and operated at higher speeds. The amount of energy used could be increased. The organizational design and administrative procedures could be adapted and improved to ensure a continuing steady and regular flow of materials from one part of the process of production within the plant to the next, and to permit more efficient use of the equipment and the workers who handled it. Finally, both workers and managers could become more skilled at their tasks. Except for this last, all these ways of increasing throughput (and the volume output per unit of inputs) increased the ratio of capital, materials, energy, and managers to the size of the work force. Mass-production processes thus became capital-intensive, materials-intensive, and manager-intensive.

The possibility of increasing throughput varied with the technology of the production processes. The potential for expanding the speed and volume of production was low in industries where mechanization had merely resulted in the replacement of manual labour by relatively simple machines. This was the case in the making of cloth, wood, apparel, shoes, saddlery, furniture, and flooring, and in the printing of books, journals, and magazines. Once the basic machinery was perfected, better-trained workers and managers could raise the productivity of the plant, but the primary way to increase output was to add more machines and more workers. Industries using such processes of production remained labour-intensive (i.e. with a high ratio of workers to capital) until well into the twentieth century. Theirs continued to be factory production similar to that of the early textile mills of the Merrimack Valley. The one change in organization was that all the activities of such manufacturing enterprises came to be centralized under the control of a single person or office (see Fig. 1).

In the refining and distilling industries, by contrast, modern high-speed, high-volume continuous or large-batch mass-production techniques came very quickly. By 1869 – a decade after the drilling of the first commercial oil well – petroleum refineries had been designed which required almost no manual labour at all. The tasks of the work force were largely in packaging the final product. More intensive use of energy through the development of superheated steam distillation and 'cracking' at high temperatures further increased the speed and volume of output. For example, by 1870 cracking permitted as much as a 20 per cent expansion in the yields of kerosene from ordinary distillations. Similar innovations occurred in the refining of sugar, cottonseed oil, and linseed oil, in the brewing of beer, and in the distilling of whiskey, industrial alcohol, sulphuric acid and other chemicals. Production units in these industries quickly became very capital-intensive, energy-intensive, materials-intensive, and manager-intensive. In such industries, expansion in the size of the plant made possible much greater economies of scale than in the labour-intensive mechanical ones. For example, when the Standard Oil Trust reorganized its refinery capacity in 1883 and concentrated almost two-fifths of American refinery production in three huge refineries, the unit cost dropped from 1·5 cents a barrel to 0·5 cents a barrel. A comparable concentration of two-fifths of the nation's output of textiles or shoes in three plants would, of course, have been impossible.

In other industries, particularly those processing agricultural products, a comparable rate of throughput was achieved with the invention of continuous-process machinery and the designing of continuous-process plants. In the late 1870s and the early 1880s such innovations appeared in the making of cigarettes, the milling of flour, oats, and other grains, the canning of soups and milk, and the production of soap and photographic film. These industries quickly became capital-, materials-, and manager-intensive. However, once the machinery and the plant design had been perfected, the potential for still further increases in productivity remained limited. This was also true of the refining and distilling industries.

It was then in the furnace and foundry industries, particularly the metal-making and metalworking ones, that the greatest continuing potential existed for increasing the velocity of volume of throughput by improvements in equipment, a more intensive use of energy, better organizational design, and improved managerial skills. In the metal-making industries, it was the integration of several operations within a single works that provided the greatest opportunity for increased productivity from such methods; in the metalworking ones, it was the subdivision of the processes into more specialized units that created such an opportunity. And it was in these industries that modern American factory or works management was perfected.

In the metal-making industries, the most dramatic example of rapidly increasing productivity came in works that integrated blast furnaces, rolling mills, and finishing mills to make rails, wire, sheets, and structures. The adoption of the Bessemer and open-hearth processes enormously increased the volume of output through the adoption of massive machinery and an intensive use of energy. Moreover, as emphasized by Alexander J. Holley, the engineer who built nearly all the new Bessemer works in the United States, the larger output of American over British mills came not only from improved converters and other equipment but from the careful layout of plants which included as many as seventy buildings and thirty miles of internal railway. Holley also noted, 'Better organization and more readiness, diligence and technical knowledge on the part of the management have been required to run the works up to their capacity, as their capacity has become increased by better arrangements and better appliances.'[2] As Peter Temin has pointed out concerning the last decades of the century:

The speed at which steel was made was continually rising, and new innovations were constantly being introduced to speed it further. Steam and later electric power replaced the lifting and carrying action of human muscle, mills were modified to handle steel quickly and with a minimum of strain, and people disappeared from the mills. By the turn of the century, there were not a dozen men on the floor of a mill rolling 3,000 tons a day, or as much as a Pittsburgh rolling mill of 1850 rolled in a year.[3]

As the steel and other metal-making works became capital- and energy-intensive, they also increased the ratio of managers to workers, for the increased speed and volume of materials through the plant intensified the need for supervision and control.

The organizational design and the operating procedures of the new iron and steel enterprises owed much to the railroads. The connection between the railroads and the iron and steel industry had always been close. The first Bessemer rail mills were financed by railroads. The steel industry's foremost entrepreneur, Andrew Carnegie, received his business training as division superintendent of the Pennsylvania's Pittsburgh Division. J. Edgar Thomson and Thomas Scott, leading executives of that road, joined Carnegie in financing the construction of the largest and the most efficient of the early Bessemer works, the J. Edgar Thomson Works, begun in 1873 near Pittsburgh.

Carnegie brought W. P. Shinn, an experienced professional manager, from the Pennsylvania Railroad to become the general manager of the new works. Shinn introduced and modified railroad accounting and cost techniques, including a voucher system employed in the locomotive shops. His daily cost sheets and other data were used to determine costs and prices and to evaluate departmental performance. No order was accepted until its costs had been carefully estimated. Summarized weekly and monthly reports went to the company's board of managers, made up largely of department heads, and to Carnegie himself. According to one of the company's executives, 'the minutest detail of cost of materials appeared from day to day and week to week in the accounts and soon every man in the place was made to realize it. The men felt and often remarked that the eyes of the company were always on them through the books.'4 Furthermore, as Temin points out, Carnegie used his accounts to evaluate the technological innovations introduced to expand output and to lower costs. And where Carnegie pioneered others quickly followed, not only in the making of iron and steel but in the production of copper, zinc, glass, and paper.

It was in the metalworking industries, however, that improvements in machinery, organizational design, and managerial performance made the most difference to productivity. Because metal was more difficult to shape than cloth, wood, or leather, and because (owing to its hardness) it could be worked to much finer tolerances and much more precise specifications than could other materials, new and improved machinery permitted a greater increase in the speed and output of metal goods than did the use of machines in shaping wood, cloth, and leather. Between the 1850s and 1880s major innovations occurred in milling, grinding, and stamping machines, in lathes, and in other equipment for cutting and working metal. Indeed, the history of the American machine-tool industry in its most innovative years is largely the story of providing equipment for the metalworking industries. These innovations involved not only machine design but also the development of metal alloys which improved the cutting edges of tools and therefore sped up their operation.

Organizational design and managerial skills were particularly critical for increasing output and productivity in the metalworking industries because their processes of production permitted a greater subdivision of labour than was possible in other industries. Such subdivision, by increasing the number of sub-departments within a works, made more difficult the managerial tasks of maintaining a steady throughput. These managerial tasks became the most difficult in those enterprises which mass-produced machinery and other products through the fabrication and assembling of interchangeable parts. These included firms making firearms, locks, clocks, watches, sewing machines, typewriters, cash registers, harvesters, threshers and other complex agricultural machinery, electrical machinery, and pumps and other heavy equipment. These enterprises also used a wider variety of greater number of raw and semi-finished materials than did any other type of manufacturing industry.

During the 1850s and 1860s the men in charge of these metalworking enterprises concentrated on improving their machinery and plant design. Only after the depression of the 1870s created pressures to cut costs did they begin to pay close attention to improving organizational design. The innovators in the new systematic or 'scientific' methods of shop and factory management were nearly all mechanical engineers connected with the metalworking industries. In fact, the history of the 'scientific management' movement in the United States can best be followed in the *Proceedings* of the meetings of the American Society of Mechanical Engineers, founded in 1880. By the middle of the eighties organizational design had become one of the Association's top concerns. At its annual meeting in 1886, Henry R. Towne (its president and also the head of the Yale & Towne Lock Company), in a presidential address entitled 'The Engineer as an Economist', urged its members to concentrate on shop management and shop accounting:

Under the head of Shop Management fall the questions of organization, responsibility, reports, systems of contract and piece work, and all that relate to the executive management of works, mills and factories. Under the head of Shop Accounting fall the questions of time and wage systems, determination of costs, whether piece or day work, methods of booking, distribution of the various expense accounts, the ascertainment of profits, and all that enters into the system of accounts which relates to the manufacturing departments of a business, and to the determination and record of its results.[5]

One technique to improve both shop management and accounting which the society discussed in its early meetings was the 'shop-order' system of tickets and cards. This method was first fully developed in sewing-machine enterprises, which appear to have borrowed it from railroad locomotive shops. It required the plant superintendent to give each order a number and a special set of cards and tickets. The foreman of each shop or sub-department then recorded the amounts of materials and labour used on each order and on each item in that order as it passed through his bailiwick. One copy of the ticket stayed in that shop, and a master copy accompanied the order through the remaining departments of the works. The latter provided gross costs for each order from all departments. A compilation of the copies of the former could permit a review of the materials and labour expended by one shop or department over a specific period of time. Such information provided accurate data on prime costs (labour and materials) by product and by process. It also made possible controls over the flow of goods through the factory and over inventories of raw and semi-finished materials. Finally, such data permitted managers to evaluate the performance of the sub-units and of the factory as a whole.

In order to get workers and foremen to accept such new control procedures, Towne in the late 1880s proposed a plan by which the employees as well as owners received the benefits of the resulting increases in productivity. By this scheme any reduction in costs through more efficient planning of time, more effective use of materials and machines, and the introduction of better equipment would be shared equally between the company and the workers, with the hands getting 30 to 40 per cent of the savings involved and the foreman getting 10 to 20 per cent. Modified by another engineer, Frederick Halsey, this plan was adopted in a number of American metalworking plants.

Then Frederick W. Taylor of the Midvale Steel Company, which produced a variety of machined castings and parts, entered the scene. He had earlier instituted at Midvale a shop-order method of control and other systematic ways to raise output. In 1895 he delivered an influential paper before the Society of Mechanical Engineers, in which he explicitly addressed himself to improving the gain-sharing plans of Towne and Halsey. In the first place, he pointed out, such plans erred in basing costs and the resulting savings to be shared on past experience. Instead, they should be based on a standard time and output to be determined 'scientifically', through careful job analyses and time-and-motion studies of the work involved. Secondly, Taylor wanted to add the stick to the carrot. Whereas Towne rewarded workers if they exceeded normal output and cut costs, Taylor would also punish by reducing a worker's pay if he failed to meet the standards set.

To carry out his plan, Taylor expected to eliminate the shop foreman altogether. He proposed to form a planning department which would administer the factory as a whole and would do so through a number of highly specialized bosses or 'functional foremen'. The planning department would handle job analyses and time-and-motion studies; it would also set standards of output. After reviewing orders received at the plant, it would – on the basis of its analysis and its information – schedule the flow of current orders and set the daily work plan for each operating unit in the factory. In addition, it was to refine the shop-order systems of control and to keep constant check on 'costs of all items manufactured with complete expense analysis and complete monthly comparative cost and expense exhibits'. Finally, it was to have charge of hiring and firing. Such careful, impersonal, overall control would permit each worker to concentrate on doing a single highly specialized and routine task.

Taylor's goal of extreme internal specialization was rarely achieved in American industry. As his critics were quick to point out, these proposals failed to pinpoint the authority and responsibility for the flow of materials through each sub-unit or even through the factory as a whole. In the plants reorganized by practitioners of 'scientific management', the sub-departments continued to be managed by foremen. These foremen remained generalists rather than specialists, stayed on the line of authority from the president through the general manager or superintendent, and remained responsible for the control of through-put in their units. The planning office became the plant manager's staff (see Fig. 2). The new staff offices included those for personnel, accounting, inspection, power and works engineering, product design, methods, production efficiency, and orders. The last was usually responsible for scheduling the flow of materials through the plant, while the department of production efficiency concerned itself with design, with the movement of men (based on time-and-motion studies), and with setting wage rates.

After 1900 the most dramatic increases in productivity within the metalworking industries came from improvements in metals used in machine tools and in the increased use of energy applied to the move-ment of materials through the processes of production. Taylor himself played an important part in intensifying the velocity of production in 1899, when he and an associate developed high-speed steel, an alloy that permitted the cutting of metals at much greater speeds. Such increases in speed, in turn, made possible an even more radical re-organization of shop practices.

A decade later, Henry Ford and a few close associates were at work in developing what became the best-known innovation for applying power to the movement of materials. The huge demand for the Model T Ford, first produced in 1908, caused these men to concentrate inten-sively on improving plant design and specialized machinery in order to boost the pace of production. By 1913 they had perfected the moving assembly line. The new production process cut the labour time needed to produce an automobile, from twelve hours and eight minutes in early 1913 to one hour and thirty-three minutes in the spring of 1914. By that time the Highland Park plant in Detroit was turning out vehicles at the rate of more than a thousand per day. The moving assembly line, the culmination of half a century of improvements in machinery, factory design, and the application of energy, quickly became and remained the symbol of modern mass production.

The resulting new velocity, volume, and efficiency of production made it possible for Henry Ford to build the cheapest car in the world, pay the highest wages in the world, and become one of the wealthiest men in the world. Indeed, the men whose enterprises were the first to use the new methods of mass production quickly amassed some of the nation's largest fortunes. This was not only true of Ford, Rockefeller, and Carnegie, but also of Duke, Eastman, Swift, Armour, McCormick, Westinghouse, the du Ponts, and others. Yet in all cases these pioneering enterprises were involved in more than mass production. All the firms that made their owners so wealthy were among the first in their industries to combine mass production with mass distribution.

D. THE COMING OF THE MODERN INDUSTRIAL ENTERPRISE

The distinctive feature of the large modern industrial enterprise is that it integrates mass production with mass distribution. Such large integrated enterprises first appeared in the United States suddenly and dramatically in the 1880s. Until that time nearly all American business firms carried out only a single economic function. They manufactured, or marketed, or mined, or transported. But by 1900 a relatively small number of large multi-functional, integrated firms had come to dominate many major American industries.

In two decades after 1880 manufacturers followed two different routes to large size. One group, finding the existing mass marketers unable to handle effectively the distribution and selling of their high-volume output, grew large by building national and usually international marketing organizations. Then they integrated backward by creating extended purchasing networks. The other group – those that found the existing marketing channels satisfactory – grew big through merger. Those who took the second route began by putting together informal combinations and then more formal cartels. Then they consolidated their small (usually family) partnerships into a single legal enterprise in the form of a trust or a holding company. In the next step the plants of the constituent companies came to be centralized under the control of a single manufacturing department. Finally the consolidated enterprise began to build large marketing and purchasing organizations and to move to control supplies of raw and semi-finished materials. Either route to large size led to the formation of enterprises that created administrative networks to co-ordinate the flow of materials from the suppliers of raw materials through the processes of production to the retailers and often the ultimate consumers.

The first enterprises to integrate mass production with mass distribution – those that found the existing marketing channels inadequate – were of three types.

One group comprised producers of semi-perishable, low-priced packaged goods who had devised and put into production in the late 1870s and early 1880s high-volume mechanical continuous-process machinery and plants. These included the makers of cigarettes (Duke's American Tobacco), matches (Diamond Match), breakfast cereal (Quaker Oats), canned goods (Campbell, Heinz, and Borden), soap (Procter & Gamble), and photographic equipment (Eastman Kodak).

The new continuous-process machinery permitted an enormous increase in volume. For example, when the Bonsack cigarette machine was perfected in the late 1880s, forty machines could meet the current world demand. The manufacturers in all these new continuous-process industries then built extensive, often worldwide sales networks to match their production capabilities. To assure a steady flow of materials into their plants, they added large purchasing networks. Though they often continued to employ wholesalers to handle the actual distribution, they became responsible for scheduling the flow of goods from the factories to these wholesalers and to large retailers. In selling they concentrated on advertising more than on the use of salesmen.

The second group of manufacturers to become large by building a network of national and often international branch sales offices were the makers of brand-new types of machines which were mass-produced by the fabricating and assembly of interchangeable parts and which required specialized marketing services. Such services included sales demonstration, installation, after-sales service and repair, and consumer credit. Such enterprises were makers of sewing machines (Singer), complex agricultural machinery (McCormick Harvester, John Deere, and J. I. Case), and the newly invented office machinery (Remington Typewriter and National Cash Register). In the 1880s firms producing heavier machinery (Otis Elevator, Western Electric, Westinghouse, Edison General Electric, Babcock & Wilcox, and Worthington Pump), built similar global marketing organizations. In their marketing, these firms relied more on the use of salesmen than on advertising.

In the same decade of the 1880s, a third type of manufacturing firm began to build comparable integrated enterprises. These firms, however, were forced to do so because of their reliance on new technology for mass distribution rather than on that of mass production. When the processors of fresh meat (Swift, Armour, Morris, and Cudahy) began to use refrigerated railroad cars to market their products, they could no longer rely on the existing wholesalers. They had to put together a national network of branch offices with refrigerated warehouses and sales facilities. They then created large buying organizations. The makers of beer who moved into the national market in the 1880s (Pabst, Schlitz, and Anheuser Busch) followed much the same pattern. Because of the perishable nature of their products, these producers devised even more sophisticated and intricate techniques than did the makers of cigarettes and soap to assure a continuing flow from the purchase of the raw materials through the processes of production to the retailer or ultimate consumer.

All three types of enterprises that grew large by building extensive sales and purchasing organizations had much in common. All used new mass-production techniques. All concentrated their production in a small number of large plants. They were clustered within a small number of industries (the 'two-digit' industrial groups 20, 21, 35, and 36 – food, tobacco, machinery, and electrical machinery – in the Standard Industrial Classification of the US Department of Commerce). All of these firms dominated their own smaller ('four-digit') industries. These latter industries were, almost from their very beginnings, oligopolistic or monopolistic. They never were competitive in the traditional sense.

A sizeable number of these first oligopolists also became the nation's first multi-nationals. After extending their marketing organizations abroad, they often built manufacturing facilities in foreign countries largely because of local tariffs and other restrictions. They then began to supply these plants from local sources. In a short time their overseas activities were operated through autonomous, integrated subsidiary enterprises.

Finally, because these enterprises successfully combined the advantages of high throughput and high stock turn, they were self-financed. The cash flow generated from the high-volume output and sales provided ample funds for both working and fixed capital, so these pioneering firms rarely went to capital markets for funds. When supplementary funds were needed, they obtained them through short-term loans from local commercial banks. As a result, the ownership of these firms remained in the hands of the founder, a few close associates, and their families.

Those enterprises that took the second route to large size, the manufacturers who found the existing channels satisfactory, moved toward merger primarily because of temporary over-capacity. In the 1870s, the prices of manufactured goods dropped rapidly. In a wide variety of industries the response to the price drop was the formation of cartels operating through trade associations. In the 1880s a small number of refining and distilling enterprises using mass-production techniques moved beyond the cartel and merged its members into a single multi-unit enterprise. These were the first and, in fact, almost the only industrial trusts. These consolidations then centralized the manufacturing facilities into a few large plants in order to obtain the economies of scale permitted by their technological processes of production. The very first of these, Standard Oil, after consolidating its refining, began to integrate vertically by buying or building marketing units and then by obtaining and producing some of its own raw materials. The cottonseed oil, linseed oil, and lead trusts quickly followed Standard's example. The two other trusts – sugar and whiskey – were content to exploit the competitive advantage of low-cost, high-volume production. After the passage of the New Jersey holding-company law in 1889, a number of consolidations occurred before 1893 in a wider variety of industries.

Then after the depressed middle years of the 1890s came the most significant merger movement in American history. Mergers occurred in all types of industries. One reason was that the depression again gave convincing proof of the difficulty of maintaining cartels. Another was that after the passage of the Sherman Anti-trust Act in 1890, federal court rulings appeared to declare the cartel illegal and the holding company legal. Still another cause was the realization by promoters and financiers of the sizeable profits available through promotion of such mergers. But certainly one of the most important reasons for the merger movement at the turn of the century was the desire of manufacturers to imitate the success of those enterprises that in the 1880s had consolidated production and had then integrated mass production with mass distribution.

In any case, manufacturers soon learned that mergers were rarely successful unless the constituent companies actually did consolidate production into a single manufacturing department and actually did build national marketing and purchasing networks. Those mergers that continued to use the holding company as a means to maintain earlier cartels (such as National Cordage, National Salt, and American Malting) were generally financial failures. Even those that did consolidate and vertically integrate continued to be successful and to dominate their industries only if they were able to combine the advantages of mass production with those of mass distribution. This occurred when their production was capital-intensive, energy-intensive, and manager-intensive, using large-batch or continuous-process techniques, and in some cases when its products required special marketing services such as demonstration, installation, service and repair, and consumer credit.

These conditions for success existed for the mergers in industries producing semi-perishable packaged goods such as sugar, biscuits, candy, whiskey, and other distilled products. They also existed for the mergers in industries producing standardized but relatively complex machinery, such as shoe and printing machinery (all these were in the same SIC groups – 20 and 35 – that grew large by internal growth). They also occurred in the oil, rubber, and explosives industries and in some chemical industries (SIC groups 28, 29, and 31) and in some of the glass and paper industries (SIC groups 26 and 32) which used continuous or large-batch techniques of production. These new consolidated and integrated enterprises quickly dominated their industries and began to join the ranks of the nation's early multinationals.

Large-scale enterprises resulting from merger and integration also proved successful in the capital-intensive steel, iron, and nonferrous-metals industries (SIC group 33). Here, high-volume production required careful scheduling and co-ordination of the flow of raw materials into the plants and of finished goods out to the consumer. The resulting organization differed somewhat from that of enterprises making more standardized mass-produced items in that their marketing organizations remained much smaller, while their purchasing departments and especially their raw-materials-producing departments were much larger. While these industries became oligopolistic, the dominant firms in them did not become multi-national as did the oligopolists created by mergers in the metal mass-production and continuous-process industries.

On the other hand, in those industries where the integration of mass production with mass distribution did not bring advantages, mergers were less successful. The new integrated mergers failed to play a dominant role in those industries where the process of manufacturing was labour-intensive, where the application of additional energy did not necessarily speed up the process, where selling required little in the way of special marketing services, and where scheduling of production and distribution was less critical. One or more of these characteristics occurred in the following industries: textiles, leather, lumber, clothing, hats, shoes, saddlery, furniture, carriage-making, and other wood-processing industries; cigars and many foods; simple metal fabricated products and machinery which did not require special installation, service, or credit; specialized machine tools and instruments; and printing and publishing. In these industries, the adding, combining, and integrating of many units failed to provide any special competitive advantage in terms of lower cost or greater customer satisfaction. In these businesses, single-unit enterprises – selling through mass marketers or manufacturers' agents – continued to compete successfully against large integrated corporations. Such industries remained highly competitive until well into the twentieth century. Although the Sherman Anti-trust Act had been passed in 1890, it clearly had little impact on the outcome of the nation's first great merger movement. Technology and marketing, not legal constraints, were the critical factors in determining the size of firms and the structure of industries.

E. ORGANIZATION-BUILDING

The enterprises that grew large through merger took on eventually the same organizational design as did firms that initially became large by building their own marketing and purchasing networks. The internal structure of integrated enterprise became in nearly all cases a centralized one with functional departments (see Fig. 4). Yet the two different paths to growth did affect the nature and size of the resulting management. The reason was that the two paths brought different financial and administrative problems.

The merged enterprise, for example, was unable to rely on current cash flow to finance its activity. For in centralizing its activities, the merged firm often reorganized large sectors of major American industries. Old plants were closed down, others modernized, and new ones located to take advantage of changing markets and supply. Such reorganization demanded large sums of money. Moreover, the merger itself often required outside funds, particularly if some of the firms joining a consolidation insisted on cash as well as securities in exchange for their stock. So the mergers of the 1890s led industrial enterprises for the very first time to rely on Wall Street and other capital markets for funds. By the First World War industrial securities had become almost as acceptable in investment portfolios as those of railroads and governments.

One result of such financing was that investment bankers began to sit on the boards of the new industrial corporations. Of more importance, the stock ownership – already dispersed through the process of merger – became even more widely scattered. At the same time salaried managers had to be hired to run the new departments, and salaried executives moved into the new central corporate offices. The firms resulting from merger, therefore, had a larger number of middle and top managers than did those that grew from internal expansion. In these merged enterprises ownership became separated from management from almost the very beginning. Such firms can be properly termed 'managerial enterprises' to distinguish them from those that grew internally and whose stock continued to be held by the entrepreneur or a small group of associates who had founded the enterprise or by their families. Those large firms where the owners continued to have a say in top management decisions, particularly decisions on long-term investment, might then be called 'entrepreneurial enterprises'.

For the salaried executives heading the new managerial enterprises, the first and most pressing task was the creation of an organizational design through which their consolidated properties were to be managed. The aim of such a design was to maintain and if possible increase the velocity and volume of output of the different constituent operating parts. The hope was to make the productivity of the whole higher than the parts could have achieved separately. When Charles R. Flint, the organizer of the United States Rubber Company and other consolidations, was asked in 1899 to describe 'the benefits of consolidated management', he replied:

The answer is only difficult because the list is so long. The following are the principal ones: raw material, bought in large quantities is secured at a lower price; the specialization of manufacture on a large scale, in separate plants, permits the fullest utilization of special machinery and processes, thus decreasing costs; the standard of quality is raised and fixed; the number of styles reduced, and the best standards are adopted; those plants which are best equipped and most advantageously situated are run continuously in preference to those less favored. In case of local strikes or fires, the work goes on elsewhere, thus preventing serious loss; there is no multiplication of the means of distribution – a better force of salesmen takes the place of a larger number; the same is true of branch stores; terms and conditions of sales become more uniform, and credits through comparisons are more safely granted; the aggregate of stocks carried is greatly reduced, thus saving interest, insurance, storage and shop-wear; greater skill in management accrues to the benefit of the whole, instead of the part; and large advantages are realized from comparative accounting and comparative administration . . . The grand result is, a much lower market price . . .[6]

None of the economic advantages of consolidation, however, came automatically. Their realization demanded the same amount of attention to internal organization and statistical data as had the operations

BASIC ORGANIZATIONAL FORMS IN MODERN BUSINESS ENTERPRISE

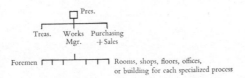

Fig. 1. Simple subdivided single-unit enterprise. Used by factories employing a simple technology from the 1840s onwards.

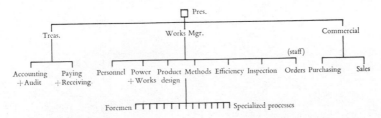

Fig. 2. Simple subdivided single-unit enterprise. Used by manufacturing enterprises employing a complex technology after the 1890s.

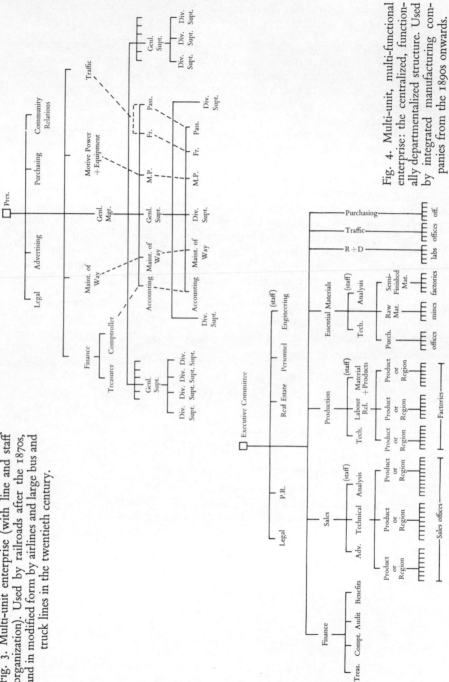

Fig. 3. Multi-unit enterprise (with line and staff organization). Used by railroads after the 1870s, and in modified form by airlines and large bus and truck lines in the twentieth century.

Fig. 4. Multi-unit, multi-functional enterprise: the centralized, functionally departmentalized structure. Used by integrated manufacturing companies from the 1890s onwards.

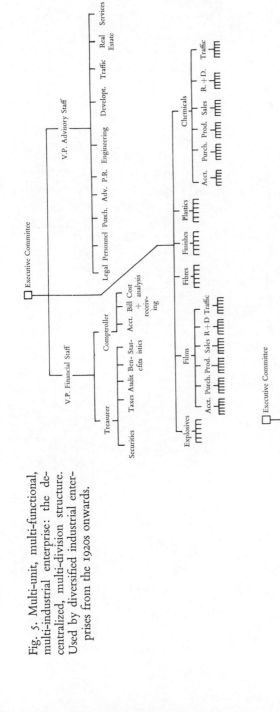

Fig. 5. Multi-unit, multi-functional, multi-industrial enterprise: the decentralized, multi-division structure. Used by diversified industrial enterprises from the 1920s onwards.

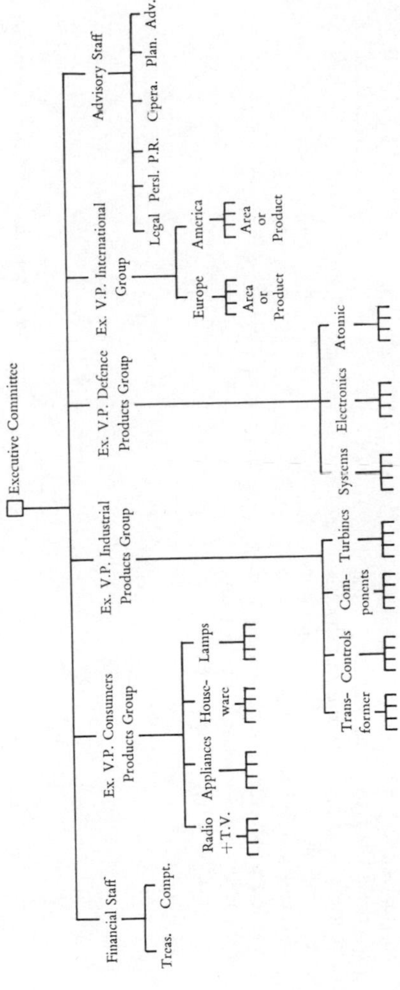

Fig. 6. Multi-unit, multi-functional, multi-industrial, multi-national enterprise.

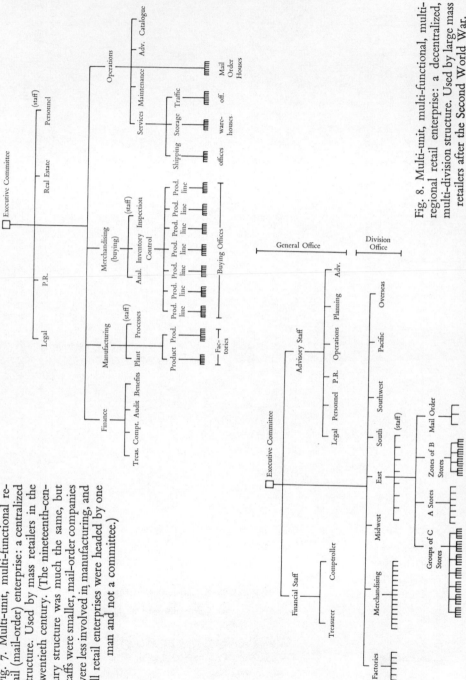

Fig. 7. Multi-unit, multi-functional retail (mail-order) enterprise: a centralized structure. Used by mass retailers in the twentieth century. (The nineteenth-century structure was much the same, but staffs were smaller, mail-order companies were less involved in manufacturing, and all retail enterprises were headed by one man and not a committee.)

Fig. 8. Multi-unit, multi-functional, multi-regional retail enterprise: a decentralized, multi-division structure. Used by large mass retailers after the Second World War.

of the first large railroads fifty years before. Moreover, the challenges differed from those that had arisen for the railroads and for the founders of industrial entrepreneurial enterprises. The senior executives in the new consolidated enterprises had to transform an agglomeration of widely scattered, hitherto competing manufacturing units and sales firms into a single manageable whole. In some companies, such as du Pont or International Harvester, these changes came quickly. In others, such as US Steel and even Standard Oil, the transformation took many years. Quickly or slowly the organization-builders, by restructuring their own new enterprises, reshaped not only the structure of many industries but also that of the larger economy.

Their task included the building both of the functional departments and of a central office to co-ordinate, appraise, and plan the work of the departments and of the enterprise as a whole (see Fig. 4). In building new plants and modernizing old ones, the new production department – where manufacturing processes permitted – adopted the new methods of scientific factory management and so helped to spread such ideas as Taylor's through many American industries. Purchasing, no longer done through small jobbers, was carried out by a central purchasing department that bought in large volume from many areas of the nation and the world. In many companies two departments were created – one to handle the massive flows of raw materials, the other to buy in smaller amounts of other supplies (though still in bulk) for the company's offices and factories. A traffic department took charge of scheduling the movement of raw and semi-finished materials to the plants and of the finished goods from the plants to distributing points and frequently to the customers themselves. Often, too, these materials and products were carried in company-owned ships, railroad cars, and later trucks. The sales department took over wholesaling and occasionally retailing from jobbers and manufacturers' agents. Salaried salesmen worked out of branch offices which in turn reported to regional executives in the central headquarters. The central sales office worked closely with the production, traffic, and purchasing departments to schedule orders and deliveries. It adjusted general price policy to meet short-term fluctuations in demand and the actions of competitors. The financial department developed cost-accounting procedures which the central office used to establish general pricing policies and evaluate the performance of the many operating units. In formulating such accounting and statistical data, financial executives blended the costing methods developed by the practitioners of scientific factory management with those of the railroads. Finally, some consolidated companies in the more technologically advanced industries formed research and development departments to concentrate on the improvement of products and processes.

In creating these functional departments, the executives of the new managerial enterprises often elaborated on the experience of the earlier entrepreneurial enterprises. On the other hand, in setting up the central offices, they pioneered in developing methods and procedures of modern general management. In the entrepreneurial enterprise, top management remained small and personal. In the consolidated mergers, top management became collective, and the process of making group decisions became increasingly systematized and rationalized. The top management group, usually meeting as an executive committee of the board of directors, included the president and chairman of the board and the heads of the functional departments. At du Pont, Bethlehem Steel, and some of the other consolidated firms, the vice president heading each of the functional departments was specifically charged with overall supervision and planning, while the department's 'director' (who did not sit on the top committee) was responsible for day-to-day administration.

The executive committee evaluated, co-ordinated, and planned the work of the departments and of the corporation as a whole. Appraisal became relatively routine, based on comparative statistics developed by the financial department. Co-ordination became systematized by means of interdepartmental co-operation in the scheduling of flows through the enterprise's many units. Long-term planning and the allocation of resources – including skilled personnel as well as money and materials – soon became the executive committee's most difficult task, and the one that took up most of its time. In making such allocations, the committee began to ask for long-range forecasts of changes in demand and technology, both inside and outside the industry.

In both its evaluation and planning, the executive committee's basic criterion was the rate of return on investment. The formula for determining the rate became more sophisticated. At du Pont and then at other large enterprises, it came to include turnover on total capital as well as the ratio of earnings to sales. 'Turnover' was defined as the ratio of sales to total current investment in existing plant and working capital, and as turnover grew larger, so did the rate of return. This concept permitted the results of changing throughput and stock turn to be incorporated into the company's basic statistical and accounting data.

By the First World War, the new centralized, functionally departmentalized structure of the modern industrial enterprise was not only being perfected in manufacturing industries but was also being adopted by the large retailing enterprises (see Fig. 7). In the early years of the twentieth century, department stores, retail chains, and mail-order houses greatly expanded their lines, their volume, and often the number of their outlets. Some had integrated backwards by acquiring control of manufacturing facilities. In all cases, they continued to schedule the flow, to design the product, and to set the price and quality for all the lines of goods that passed over their counters and through their delivery offices.

Then the sharp post-war recession of 1920–1, which was the first prolonged drop in demand for industrial products since the merger movement at the turn of the century, suddenly revealed a basic weakness in the new administrative controls, particularly in those enterprises whose processes of production and distribution required large inventories of raw and semi-finished materials. Some companies – those which marketed perishable products and which had from their beginning co-ordinated the flow of goods by daily telegraphic communication between their purchasing, processing, and selling units – had relatively little difficulty in contracting output. But such communication could not protect the electrical, automobile, and other companies mass-producing machinery, or some metal, chemical, and rubber firms using large-batch and continuous-process production, or even the mass retailers. Here raw and semi-finished materials had to be ordered and transportation arranged weeks and sometimes even months before the completion of the final product. As a result, the post-war recession led to a rapid overstocking of inventory and created for many companies a sharp though temporary financial crisis.

This post-war inventory crisis caused General Motors, General Electric, du Pont, Sears Roebuck, and others to tie nearly all routine activities to carefully forecasted demand. Scheduling of purchasing, production, employment, deliveries of finished goods, and even setting prices (for prices depended on unit cost which in turn depended on volume of throughput) came to be based on annual forecasts of demand adjusted periodically to reports of actual sales. These forecasts in turn rested on the size of national income, the state of the business cycle, normal seasonal variations, and the anticipated share of the market. As output, flows, and pricing were being calibrated to short-term forecasts, investment decisions for future production were being tied more systematically to long-term ones. With the development of such forecasts the internal structure of the large American business enterprise was virtually completed. After the 1920s, changes within the multi-functional enterprise producing a single line of products were essentially only modifications of existing forms or procedures.

Thus, by the 1920s the institutional arrangements for the production of goods and services in the modern American economy had become clearly defined. Large, integrated enterprises controlled the flow, quantity, and price in the industries where tight operational control of high-speed, high-volume production and distribution was needed to reduce costs and to increase productivity. And these industries had become the most important to the health and growth of a modern industrial and urban economy. Robert Averitt in *The Dual Economy* has defined forty-one key industries in the American economy by using seven criteria: those that lead in disseminating technological advances, in capital-goods production, and in inter-industrial dependence (that is, in having high backward and forward linkages); those having the greatest price/cost effect and the greatest wage-setting effect on other industries; those in leading growth sectors; and the full-employment bottleneck industries. By 1919, the hundred largest industrial enterprises in the United States were operating in thirty-four out of thirty-eight industries. (Three electronics industries had not yet been created.) They were absent only from two machine-tool and two instrument-making industries. Moreover, all but a handful of these industries had already become concentrated. On the other hand, very few of the top hundred operated in the older industries that processed natural fibres, wood, leather, or some vegetable products or that did simple shaping of metals. In these unconcentrated industries, small manufacturers continued to buy and sell through jobbers or manufacturers' agents. Yet even in these unconcentrated industries, the large enterprises operating at the centre of the economy played an increasingly important role in controlling the flow of goods and in setting prices, not only because of their domination in the major industries but also because they purchased from and sold to the smaller single-function, single-unit enterprises.

IV.   *Modern Business Enterprise since the First World War*

After the First World War the large integrated enterprise continued to grow in size and influence. In production and distribution its activities became more and more diverse. At the same time this form became increasingly used in other sectors of the economy. Such growth had relatively little effect on the basic processes and procedure by which the large multi-functional enterprise carried out its function of transforming inputs into outputs. It did, however, have an impact on the way in which top management handled its tasks, particularly that of investing in the factors of production for future output of goods and services.

As the large enterprise expanded in size, it added new staff departments to the central office. The need for hiring on a large scale in the

1920s and that of dealing with labour unions in the 1930s led to the creation of labour relations departments. The desire for the good will of stockholders and the larger community brought departments for public and stockholder relations. Of even more importance was the growth of departments of research and development in the companies with technologically complex processes and products.

A. EVOLUTION OF ENTERPRISE IN PRODUCTION AND DISTRIBUTION

As might be expected, the major developments in the evolution of enterprise after the First World War resulted from the continuing interaction between changing technology and changing markets. When the national income and aggregate demand began to level off in the late 1920s and then declined drastically in the 1930s, those enterprises with heavy investments in research and development embarked on a new strategy of growth. They used their laboratories to apply scientific concepts systematically to the development of new products for new markets. The strategy of product diversification, in turn, led to the adoption of a new type of 'decentralized' structure, consisting of autonomous and integrated operating divisions and a general office that appraised and planned the work of the divisions and the corporation as a whole.

The large, integrated enterprises in the most technologically advanced American industries had the best opportunity to take up the new strategy. They became multi-industrial as well as multi-functional. They had the necessary technological and managerial skills for this; besides, their oligopolistic position helped them keep making profits even in the great depression. Furthermore, precisely because these firms had accumulated vast resources in trained manpower and in facilities, their executives were under greater pressure than those of smaller firms to find new markets as old ones ceased to grow.

It was natural, therefore, that enterprises which had the greatest resources invested in research and development were the first to diversify and the ones to grow most rapidly by a continuing strategy of diversification. In 1929, over two-thirds of the personnel in organized industrial research were concentrated in five industries: the electrical industry with 31·6 per cent, the chemical industry with 18·1, machinery with 6·6, metals with 6·6, and rubber with 5·9. As Michael Gort has pointed out in a detailed study of product diversification, chemical companies were the major diversifiers during the 1930s – that is, they added more new product lines than did enterprises in any other industrial group. They were followed in order by those in electrical machinery, transportation machinery, primary metals, and rubber. Moreover, the industries into which these diversifying enterprises moved were (in order) chemicals, machinery, fabricated metals, electric machinery, food, and stone–glass–clay. This pattern of inter-weaving diversification continued well beyond the Second World War.

The histories of individual firms emphasize Gort's more general points. In the 1920s, chemical firms like du Pont, Union Carbide, Allied Chemical, Hercules, and Monsanto, all moved into new industries, each from its own specific technological base (for example, the du Pont's base was nitro-cellulose chemistry, and Union Carbide's carbon chemistry). In the same decade, the great electrical manu-facturers – General Electric and Westinghouse, which had up to that time concentrated on manufacturing light and power equipment – diversified into the production of a wide variety of household appli-ances, as well as radio and X-ray equipment. During the depression decade of the 30s, General Motors (and to a lesser extent other auto-mobile companies) began to make and sell diesel locomotives, ap-pliances, tractors, and aeroplanes. Makers of primary metals, particularly copper and aluminium companies, turned to producing kitchenware and household fittings. Some rubber companies started to develop the potentialities of rubber chemistry. Others used their distribution net-works to sell a wide variety of products often made by others. In the 1930s, too, food companies began to use their marketing facilities to handle new lines of goods which they soon came to process them-selves.

Most of these same firms came to adopt the new decentralized struc-ture to meet the needs of the new strategy. This structure was first perfected by professional managers at du Pont to permit planning, co-ordinating, and appraising the performance activities of a multi-industry enterprise. Its adoption made easier the move from one industry to another (see Fig. 5). Each autonomous division handled all the functions involved in the production and distribution of a single major line of products. The internal organization of these divisions was similar to that of the large, integrated multi-functional enterprises. A division's boundaries were defined by the markets it served. The divisions concentrated on assuring close co-ordination among purchas-ing, manufacturing, and marketing. They continued to integrate mass production with mass distribution. The general office consisted of a few top executives and large advisory and financial staffs, usually functionally defined. It appraised regularly and continually the per-formance of the divisions; using in its evaluation as a criteria of per-formance the changing share of the market as well as the rate of return on investment. The general office concentrated even more on long-term planning, particularly on deciding how the enterprise's resources were to be allocated among the divisions and in what functions, products, and regions the enterprise should contract or expand its operations. General officers were relieved of day-to-day duties so that they had the time to evaluate and plan for the corporation as a whole – and so that long-term strategic decisions would be less influenced by short-term operating ones.

By the outbreak of the Second World War, the diversified, decentralized industrial corporation, although still few in numbers, was already becoming the most dynamic form of modern industrial enterprise. In manufacturing, the older integrated, centralized, functionally departmentalized firm remained dominant in industries where less attention was given to research and development and where, as in the case of gasoline, tyres, and to some extent automobiles, heavy investment was tied up in a single product line. In retailing, the older centralized form of enterprise expanded as the number and types of chains in groceries, drugs, and other consumer items grew during the 1920s and 1930s. As a result, the older types of specialized jobbers and retailers began to decline. New single-function specialized firms appeared, however, in new specialities such as accounting, labour relations, public relations, and management consulting.

B. RECENT EVOLUTION OF ENTERPRISE IN FINANCE, TRANSPORTATION, AND COMMUNICATION

Changing markets and changing technology also brought as important mutations in the structure and functions of business enterprise in the ancillary areas of finance, communication, transportation, and other services, as they did in production and distribution.

In finance, an increasing volume of activity encouraged the spread of modern bureaucratic organization. As early as the 1890s, insurance companies, particularly those specializing in life assurance, built large centralized organizations covering the nation; they usually subdivided on regional lines and were structured like railroads and other multi-unit, single-function enterprises. Banks, because of the local nature of their business, remained for a time relatively small. By the First World War, however, they had begun to expand their activities by adding branches in the state within which each was chartered. In 1900 only eighty-seven American banks had branches. By 1915 the number had risen to 397, and by 1930 to 741. By the 1930s also many had branches in foreign countries.

For companies managing the older communications networks and those beginning to enter the new mass entertainment and communications fields, organizational change came from technological innovation more than from market expansion. By the 1920s, developments in electricity, electronics, and photography created two brand-new industries – motion pictures and radios. Large modern enterprises appeared quickly in the first, for in motion pictures production was costly and technologically complex; distribution was carried out on an international scale and required carefully co-ordinated scheduling and extensive advertising. Once the technology was standardized, radio followed the pattern of the electric-utility industry. Large multi-functional firms produced the equipment (including mass-produced receiving sets), and small local firms handled the broadcasting. However, enough economies occurred in providing the same services in different cities to encourage the formation of broadcasting chains or networks. For the same reason, newspaper chains began to appear in some number after the First World War. Finally, in the management of the long-established communication networks, the younger American Telegraph & Telephone replaced the older Western Union as the dominant firm as the long-distance telephone made the telegraph increasingly obsolete.

In transportation the internal combustion engine began after the First World War to break the railroads' hold on the nation's passenger traffic and later on freight transport as well. By 1940, the new patterns were clear. In air transportation, where operational precision was as essential for safe and efficient operations as it was on the railroad, a few large, carefully structured companies were beginning to dominate the air routes. Truck and bus lines, however, required far less operational precision, less complex equipment, and less capital; small firms were able to compete effectively with large ones even on long hauls. Also during the 1920s and 1930s (for both technological and financial reasons) local electric-power utilities were combined into multi-unit regional firms and were organized in much the same way as the nineteenth-century railroads.

In many sectors, but above all in the central sectors of production and distribution, the Second World War put a capstone on the institutional developments of the previous generation and set the stage for the impressive growth of the modern industrial enterprise and of the economy itself in the post-war years.

In the first place, wartime demands for new, technologically complex products such as synthetic rubber, high-octane gasoline, radar and electronic anti-submarine devices, and a wide variety of weapons brought a pooling of scientific and technological knowledge and led to a major expansion in the systematic application of science in American industry. As a result, petroleum, rubber, metals, and a number of food companies developed new capacities for producing a variety of chemicals and synthetic materials. Electrical and radio companies, small as well as large, old as well as new, acquired the facilities for production of a wide range of electronic products.

In the second place, the requirements of mobilizing the economy led to the pooling and expansion of managerial procedures and controls whose use was still largely concentrated in the leading techno-logically advanced, integrated enterprises. During the war, small single-function and single-unit firms (usually as subcontractors for the larger concerns), learned about the modern methods of forecasting, account-ing, and inventory control. In addition, the war brought full employ-ment for the first time since 1929. The continuance of a vast national mass market was further assured when early in 1946 Congress passed the Employment Act, which committed the federal government to maintaining maximum employment and the largest possible aggregate demand. This commitment to supporting the mass market – together with the spread of industrial technology and the increased knowledge of administrative techniques – all promised a post-war economic expan-sion which the large integrated and diversified industrial enterprise was in the most strategic position to exploit.

C. TRENDS AFTER THE SECOND WORLD WAR

The post-war evolution of American business enterprise can be noted only briefly: events are still too close to permit a thorough historical evaluation. Yet some of the trends growing directly out of earlier experiences can be ascertained. In the first place, changes in markets and technology encouraged the continued growth of the large enter-prise and its spread into nearly all areas of the modern industrial–urban economy. Indeed, these years mark the triumph of modern bureau-cratic enterprise. Aided by the new federal commitment, aggregate demand grew steadily at a healthy rate for twenty years after the war, with the gross national product (in constant prices) rising from \$309·9 million in 1948 to \$722·5 million in 1969. This growth provided a mass market far greater than any previously known in history; regional markets became as big as the national market had been in the late nineteenth century. In technology, the electronics revolution (including automation); the high-speed computer; the development of new plastics; artificial fibres, and metal alloys; and the continuing systematic application of science to industry all profoundly affected nearly every sector of the American economy.

In finance and retailing, as well as in many consumer services, the

great post-war market was probably more important than technological change in stimulating the spread of modern enterprise. New
electronic machinery did allow greatly increased speed and volume of
work performed in individual banking and insurance firms. Of even
more significance in banking was the continuing spread of branch
banking and the consolidation of many small units within major
urban, suburban, and state areas into large bureaucratic enterprises. In
food retailing, chain stores had a continuing boom, with new grocery
stores and supermarkets enjoying immense popularity. Chains in the
hotel, restaurant, and other service industries grew in number and
expanded in size. The older mass retailers – department stores, merchandise chains, and mail-order houses – became large enough to decentralize
and divisionalize along regional lines (see Fig. 8). As a result of this
massive growth of chains, the number of single-unit jobbers, retailers,
and even hotels and restaurants declined more rapidly since the war
than before it.

In manufacturing, on the other hand, technology had the greatest
impact. Automation, the computer, and the new materials (such as
plastics) intensified the velocity and expanded the volume throughput
in existing mass-production industries and permitted the use of high-
volume techniques in many of the older industries where they had not
yet been adopted. Thus, the new technology encouraged the spread of
the integrated multi-functional enterprise and therefore, oligopoly in
the textile, paper, glass, and some metal-fabricating industries. Technology also changed the mass communications and entertainment industry
by permitting television to replace both motion pictures and radio as
the most popular mass medium. Because of the huge capital requirements and the complex scheduling needed, a few television broadcasting
chains of great size (most of them outgrowths of radio chains) quickly
dominated the industry. In transportation, the pre-war trends initiated
by earlier technological innovations were accelerated. Airline companies grew in size and complexity but not in number. In the movement
of goods by truck, more large firms appeared, but large and small
companies continued to compete side by side.

Still more significant than the spread of multi-unit and multi-
functional enterprises has been the post-war growth of the diversified
multi-industry firms. Here technology has been all-important. Increasing concentration on research and development turned more and more
integrated enterprises to a strategy of expansion through diversification.
It has also encouraged firms which had already diversified to move into
still other product lines. By the 1960s, nearly all of the leading companies in the fields of chemicals, electrical machinery, rubber, glass,
paper, and transportation vehicles, as well as many food companies,

operated in more than ten industries (industries defined as 'four-digit' by the Standard Industrial Classification). Most of the large metal, oil, and machinery firms came to operate in from three to ten such industries. In order to obtain the maximum return from their new investments, nearly all of these enterprises had by the 1960s adopted the multi-divisional structure with its autonomous operating divisions and its evaluating and planning general office.

One reason for the widespread acceptance of the multi-divisional structure in technologically advanced industries was that it institutionalized the application of science and technology to the development of new products and processes. The research department in such organizations tested the commercial viability of new products generated either by the central research staff or by the operating divisions. The executives in the general office, freed from day-to-day operational decisions, determined whether or not new products used enough of the company's present facilities or would develop enough useful new ones to warrant its production and sale. If they agreed that it did, and the potential market was similar to the firm's current ones, then production and sales were handled through an existing division. If the market was quite different, a new division was formed. The institutionalizing of research and development permitted a new business concept to appear – that of the product cycle. Strategies became designed to obtain the maximum return from a new product as it moved through the cycle from its initial commercialization to full maturity.

The multi-divisional structure also made it easier for the large integrated enterprise to meet the demands of the federal government for military and advanced scientific hardware, and to reach the rapidly growing overseas markets. During the years of the Cold War, the government required a wide variety of weapons, ranging from aircraft carriers, missiles, and submarines to conventional guns and tanks, as well as nuclear reactors for the Atomic Energy Commission and the spaceships with all their accoutrements for the National Aeronautics and Space Administration. To handle these markets, the companies merely added a separate division or groups of divisions for atomic energy weapons or for government business in general (see Fig. 6).

More significant in the recent evolution of modern enterprise than post-war government demand was overseas expansion. A number of the American corporations that grew large through vertical integration had become multi-national before the First World War (that is, they had invested directly in plant, equipment, and personnel in foreign countries). A few more began overseas operations in the 1920s. The depression and then the war slowed – indeed almost stopped – expansion abroad. Then in the 1950s and early 1960s, particularly after the opening of the European Common Market, there was a massive drive for foreign markets. Direct American investment in Europe alone rose from $1·7 thousand million in 1950 to $24·5 thousand million in 1970. This 'American challenge' was spearheaded by the 200 firms that accounted for more than half of the direct investment made by United States companies abroad. These 200 were nearly all in the capital-intensive, technologically advanced industries and were those that had already adopted the multi-divisional form of organization.

Overseas investment, in turn, had an impact on the structure of the diversified enterprise. When a company first began to move abroad, it usually created an international division to supervise and co-ordinate overseas activities and to recommend investment decisions abroad to the corporation's senior executives. However, as the operations and investment decisions grew larger and more complex, the international division tended to disappear. Where the product divisions were strong, they took over the international business of the lines they were already handling domestically. For those companies which still concentrated on one dominant line of business, such as oil, copper, some food, and drink (e.g. Coca-Cola), the operating divisions became geographical, each covering a major area of the globe. A very few multi-nationals developed a matrix form of structure with overseas managers reporting to regional divisions on some matters and product divisions on others. In all cases, the multi-divisional form was extended from a national to a worldwide basis, with investment decisions continuing to be made at the general office and day-to-day co-ordination of throughput being handled by the divisions.

During the 1960s a major variation of the diversified, multi-divisional enterprises appeared on the American business scene. This was the conglomerate. The conglomerate differed from the older multi-industrial, multi-national enterprise in its strategy (and therefore in the nature of its capital investments) and in its organizational structure. The large diversified enterprise had grown primarily by direct investment of plant and personnel in industries related to its original line of products. It moved into markets where its managerial, technological, and marketing skills and resource gave it a competitive advantage. The conglomerate, on the other hand, expanded entirely by the acquisition of existing enterprises, and not by direct investment into its own plant and personnel, and it often did so in totally unrelated fields. With the exception of a few large oil companies looking for diversified investments, the acquiring firms were not usually in the capital-intensive, high-technology, mass-production, mass-distribution industries. They were, rather, in industries such as textile and ocean shipping, where small enterprises remained competitive, or they were in those industries producing specialized products to individual orders, such as the machine-tool and defence and space industries. The creators of the first conglomerates embarked on strategies of unrelated acquisition when they realized that their own industries had little potential for continued growth, and when they became aware of the value of a diversified product line and a strategy based on the product cycle. The acquiring firm tended to purchase relatively small enterprises in industries that were not yet dominated by large oligopolies. Because these small enterprises had not become wholly managerial, the acquiring firms were in some cases able to provide them with new administrative and operational techniques.

The structure of the new conglomerates reflected their strategies of growth. Their general offices were small and the acquired operating units were permitted even more autonomy than the divisions of the large diversified firm. The difference in the general office of a conglomerate was not in the size of the financial or legal staff or in the number of general executives. Indeed, many conglomerates came to have even more general executives than did the older, diversified majors. The difference came in the size and functions of the advisory staff. The conglomerate had no staff offices for purchasing, traffic, research and development, sales, advertising, or production. The only staff office was one for corporate planning (i.e. for the formulation of the strategy to be used in investment decisions). As a result, the conglomerates can concentrate on making investments in new industries and new markets and can withdraw from existing ones more single-mindedly than can the older large diversified companies; on the other hand, the conglomerates have been far less effective in monitoring and evaluating their divisions and in taking action to improve divisional operating performance. Moreover, because conglomerates do not possess centralized research and development facilities or staff expertise concerning complex technology, they have been unable to introduce new processes and products regularly and systematically into the economy. The managers of conglomerates have become almost pure specialists in making investments. They differ, however, from the managers of banks and mutual funds in that they make direct investments for whose management they are fully responsible, rather than indirect portfolio investments which rarely carry responsibility for operating performance.

As the history of the conglomerate suggests, recent changes in the large enterprises had more of an effect on the formulation of investment strategy than on short-term day-to-day operations. The techniques for managing the functional departments within an integrated business organization (either a division or a firm) have continued to be improved but not basically changed. On the other hand, the newer diversified enterprises and even the older vertically integrated ones have enlarged and systematized the operation of their top general office. By the 1950s nearly all large enterprises, no matter what route they had taken to large size, had become managerial. Management had become separated from ownership. Salaried career managers, rather than entrepreneurs or a handful of associates or their families, made long-term investment as well as short-term operating decisions in nearly all American companies. Top management had become collective. Assisted by large financial and advisory staffs, the top group concentrated increasingly on long-term investment strategy.

The continued growth of the large enterprise, particularly as it moved into new industries and new areas, has intensified three underlying trends in the process of making long-term investment decisions. One was the rationalizing of the process through the development of systematic procedures such as capital budgeting and forecasting based on increasingly sophisticated information obtained from within and outside the firm. Another has been the specialization of the investment decision process by placing it in the hands of senior executives who were relieved of day-to-day operating activities. The third trend has been the constantly broadening scope of investment decisions by private business enterprises. Firms which by 1900 were already making such decisions for major industries were by the middle of the twentieth century making massive direct investments in not one but many industries, and in not one but many countries.

In the years after the First World War, the large bureaucratic enterprise became even more powerful. It acquired control of an increasing share of the nation's economic activities, as well as a growing part of the industrial production of Europe and the rest of the world. In 1947 the 200 largest companies here in the United States (many of which were not yet fully diversified or divisionalized) accounted for 30 per cent of the value added and 47·2 per cent of total manufacturing assets. By 1963, after most of these enterprises had adopted the new strategy and the new structure, they were responsible for 41 per cent of the value added and 56·3 per cent of assets. By 1968 that last figure had risen to 60·9 per cent. These giant enterprises generated by far the largest share of funds and provided most of the personnel involved in industrial research and development that has been so instrumental in economic growth. These same firms were the prime contractors used by the government during the Second World War and then in the two decades of the Cold War. They are the companies which played a key role in its atomic energy and space programmes; and they are the same enterprises that present the 'American challenge' to Europe and to other overseas areas.

V.   Conclusion

The evolution of the private business enterprise in the United States from the small personal partnership to the giant, impersonal, multi-industry, global corporation has been the organizational response to changing and expanding markets and changing and ever more complex technologies. As the new technologies of a continuing industrial revolution permitted a massive increase in the supply of inputs, rapidly expanding markets continued to maintain the demand for outputs. To handle the huge increase in the volume of inputs being transformed into outputs, the enterprises carrying out this transformation had to pay close attention to their internal organization and had to obtain the services of many full-time managers. Otherwise, inputs could not be transformed to outputs at the speed and volume made possible by the new technology and expanding markets. The resulting changes in the size and structure of the enterprise affected not only the operation and productivity of the individual units of production but also the structure and performance of the American economy as a whole.

In the evolution of American enterprise, markets and technology have always played a larger role than tariffs, taxes, subsidies, anti-trust laws, and government legislation or regulation. Only since the 1930s has the federal government come to play a significant role in the management of the American economy; and it has done so primarily by assuming responsibility for maintaining aggregate market demand through fiscal and monetary policy, by becoming a large customer, and by encouraging the systematic improvement of technology by providing funds for research and development.

During the fifty years after the ratification of the Constitution in 1789, the expansion of the market had a greater impact on the evolution of enterprise than did technological innovation. In the early years of the nineteenth century the growing demand for agricultural products, particularly from the industrializing areas of Europe, encouraged specialization of the activities of individual enterprises. This process of institutional specialization resulted in external economies that have been recognized by economists since the writings of Adam Smith. In fact, such specialization led to the formation of all of the basic types of business institutions involved in the production, distribution, transportation, and financing of goods and services in the American economy. Until the 1840s, the co-ordination of the activities of these increasingly specialized units was carried out primarily by forces of supply and demand, the 'invisible hand' of the market.

In the decades after 1840 technology played a larger role in the evolution of enterprise than did expanding markets: indeed, technology itself began to expand the market. New technologies revolutionized the processes of transportation, distribution, production, and finance. In so doing they fundamentally altered the structures and functions of business enterprises. Institutional integration rather than institutional specialization became central to the evolution of the enterprise. Centralized control over the intermediate units in the overall processes of production and distribution helped to make possible a continuous and steady use of the new and costly capital equipment within each unit. Maintenance of flow was critical for these capital-intensive facilities, because costs per unit fell as volume rose and rose sharply as volume fell. As the business enterprise began to grow through the addition and integration of new units, the co-ordination of the flow of goods from one specialized unit to another came to be carried out in many sectors by large, geographically extended bureaucratic organizations. The visible hand of management came to replace the invisible hand of market forces.

The transformation came first in transportation and communications. Within a generation after the railroad and the telegraph became extensively used, a relatively few very large, hierarchically structured enterprises, manned by scores and even hundreds of managers, co-ordinated the flow of trains, traffic, and messages across the nation's new transportation and communications systems. As the speed and volume of transportation and communication increased, a new type of enterprise – the mass marketer – replaced the merchants who for centuries had been responsible for the distribution of goods. The new mass marketers made possible still greater increases in the velocity and volume of the distribution of goods. They did so by creating administrative networks that co-ordinated the flow of goods from the factories and processing plants directly to the retailers and increasingly to the ultimate consumer and, on a smaller scale, from the suppliers of the raw materials to the manufacturer or processor.

The increase in the speed and regularity of transportation and distribution and the lowering of their costs encouraged the swift adoption of the factory in the United States and led to the development of new processes of mass production. These new methods appeared in those industries where an intensified use of energy, further division of labour, improved machinery, and better plant design all permitted impressive increases in the volume and velocity of output. In those industries where the technology of production permitted high-volume output and where the standardization of the product permitted high-volume marketing, the processes of mass production and mass distribution were integrated within a single firm. Such enterprises created administrative networks that came to co-ordinate the flow of goods from the supplier of raw materials through the processes of production to the retailer or ultimate consumer.

After the First World War, the changes in the activities and structure of the enterprise had more of an impact on the allocation of inputs for future production than in the processing of current ones; that is, they had more impact on investment decisions than on operating ones. In order to ensure the continuing employment of their large investments in men, materials, and machines, as well as their highly developed technical and managerial skills, large enterprises began – as the demand for existing products levelled off – to diversify into new lines and move into new geographical areas. In these diversified and global enterprises the operating divisions continued to have the task of co-ordinating the processes of production and distribution with current market demand, while the senior executives of the general office concentrated on long-term allocation and investment decisions. In this way, decisions as to both future and current production became determined in many sectors of the economy by the heads of large administrative networks. Such decisions were made on the basis of estimates of future changes in markets and technology, and not – as had been the case earlier – by relying on the invisible hand of market forces expressed in the price of investment capital, that is in changing interest rates.

The evolution of enterprise in the United States, then, was part of an organizational revolution that was an essential component of the industrial revolution. Organizational change made possible the exploitation of a new technology in such a way that a rapidly growing population was able to increase its per capita income. The creation of a new economic institution – the large, multi-unit business enterprise – and of a new economic class – the full-time salaried managers – made possible the increasing velocity and volume of output essential to maintaining the productivity and growth of a rapidly expanding economy. Without the development of the new organizational design, and without the recruitment and training of a new set of men to co-ordinate the transformation of inputs into outputs, neither the 'external economies' of an enlarged market nor the 'internal economies' of a large enterprise would have been fully realized. The creation of the new managerial enterprise and of the new managerial class were vital to fulfil the promise of the new technology. Organizational innovation, like technological change, has been central to the process of modernization.

CHAPTER III

Capital Formation in Japan[1]

I. *Introduction*

This chapter analyses the relationship between the input of capital and economic growth in Japan during the past century. Our presentation follows the broad framework set forth by Solow and Temin in the introductory chapter and is complementary to the next two chapters (by Taira and Yamamura), which deal with the inputs of labour and entrepreneurship.

The assigned task of exploring the role of investment in Japan necessarily imposes a certain sectoral as well as temporal emphasis. Only relatively little attention will have to be devoted to agriculture, since this sector never became an important recipient of either public or private capital. In Japan, at least, an understanding of the advances created by a rising level of investment deals largely with the growth of modern non-agricultural industry. This also means that (unlike Taira and Yamamura) we must concentrate especially on the history of the twentieth century, when factories, machines, and new social overhead implements reached sizeable dimensions for the first time. Of course, no attempt will be made to slight the crucial transitional years of the Meiji era or even the preceding years of Tokugawa rule, but one should always keep at the forefront the sharp distinction between the hesitant beginnings of economic modernization in the late nineteenth century and its full flowering during the past sixty-odd years.

One further limiting item should be mentioned at the outset. We are concerned with the 'input' of capital – i.e. with the investment rather than the saving side of the equation. How the necessary funds were raised – by individuals, banks, the state, or foreigners – will be treated only as a side issue, but to a considerable extent this matter has been studied by other authors.

Finally, a word or two about the organization of the argument. The chapter is divided into three principal sections. We begin by discussing the pre-modern background of the Japanese economy, focusing on certain broad trends during the Tokugawa era, which lasted from the early 1600s until 1868. This will give the reader a suitable base line from which to judge subsequent events. This is followed by an analysis of capital formation during the Meiji era, which concentrates on approximately the last third of the nineteenth century. In this section the scope expands well beyond capital inputs because of the mixed nature of the economy at that time. The third section deals with the twentieth century and is in two parts. First we examine the evidence concerning investment in greater detail, and secondly we attempt to provide an interpretation of the role of capital in twentieth-century growth.

II. *The Pre-Modern Background*

No country in the history of the world has risen to international prominence as quickly as Japan. One hundred years ago, this insignificant kingdom located in a remote corner of East Asia was of little interest to those concerned with global political or economic affairs. At that time the European powers occupied centre stage, and the United States was just emerging as a major contestant for world power. In Asia – if Russia is considered a European country – only India and China were relatively well known, but neither of these vast countries had an effective voice in international affairs. India was a colony, and China mattered only in the sense that her population and resources appeared attractive to countries with commercial and/or colonial ambitions. This was the situation a century ago, and in most ways this description retained its validity until the beginning of the twentieth century.

Today the scene is radically different. Europe's role has been considerably diminished, and colonialism is largely a thing of the past. Russia and the United States have assumed the position of superpowers; China remains a question mark; most African and Asian countries are independent. But Japan has changed most of all: at present she is one of the major industrial powers of the world. The size of her GNP exceeds that of any other country except the Soviet Union and the United States. Japan leads the world in shipbuilding and is second in steel production. Japanese goods of high and sophisticated value-added content – cars, cameras, computers, etc. – are consumed in large quantities throughout the world. In fact, today the Japanese are considered serious competitors in nearly all levels and types of economic activity, and it took Japan much less than a hundred years to achieve this astonishing transformation.

It must be self-evident that Japan's transformation or modernization was not confined to economics alone. One can no longer call the Japanese remote or of little concern to the rest of the world. In nearly all facets of current life – ranging from mutual-security arrangements to architecture and religion – the Japanese occupy positions of world importance. Perhaps this is especially true because Japan is an Asian and non-white country. Until now, Japan is the only country of non-European origin to have achieved modernization, and those who would like to derive 'lessons' from this event are legion.

The economic transformation of Japan has been the most celebrated aspect of her modern history. As we shall demonstrate, especially for the past sixty years or so this transformation can be conceived in terms of a series of growth phases – or developmental 'waves' – consisting of a spurt and followed by a period of less rapid growth. The greatest growth spurt began after the destruction of the Second World War and the ensuing years of reconstruction and rehabilitation. Frequently this spurt has been called Japan's 'economic miracle', which started in 1952–4 and appears to have ended around 1973. However, there were earlier spurts and earlier waves of growth. During the 1930s the Japanese economy developed at a most impressive pace, which was abruptly interrupted by the events leading up to the Second World War. Similarly, the years between the end of the Russo-Japanese War (1905) and the end of the First World War (1918) witnessed very rapid development, followed by much slower growth during the 1920s. These three spurts, as well as the years in between, all illustrate a similar developmental pattern: growth based on the ever more speedy absorption of modern Western technology. In this process, changes in the rate of *private* investment are especially crucial.

There was, however, one critical phase in Japan's modern economic growth which does not fit into the twentieth-century pattern based on the absorption of Western technology. This is the development of the economy during the years of the Meiji era – roughly from the 1860s until the outbreak of the Russo-Japanese War.[2] Although we will not be primarily concerned with this period of 'initial' modern economic growth, some background is needed to place the later events in proper historical perspective. To appreciate fully how Japan has developed since the early 1900s it is necessary to describe the economic conditions pertaining at that time. One also has to understand what economic forces created these conditions. In short, we must provide a brief review of Meiji economic history and perhaps even of some of its antecedents.

Where should one begin? The temptation in a review of this type is to go back further and further; it is all too easy to become a victim of what Marc Bloch once referred to as the historian's 'obsession with origins'. By considering the significance of 'AD 1868' or 'Meiji 1', the dimensions of the problem can be made clearer. On one side – pre-1868 – lies the 'traditional' or 'feudal' rule of the Tokugawa, when from the economic point of view it was rather difficult to distinguish

Japan from other backward countries in Asia. On the other side of 1868 lies the modern era ushered in by the Restoration of the Meiji emperor, who formally headed a new government dedicated to – among other things – economic growth. These statements are not necessarily incorrect, but they are highly oversimplified. Neither Tokugawa Japan (1603–1868) nor Meiji Japan can be compartmentalized so easily.

Japan was ruled by the Tokugawa family for over two hundred years. These were rich, eventful years from the cultural, economic, and social point of view, and it is impossible to give an adequate overview of this period in a few lines. Yet, in considering Japanese economic growth in this century, is there anything that needs to be said about the Tokugawa shogunate? The answer is Yes, because although Japan remained in a state of relative economic backwardness under Tokugawa rule, her condition – even prior to the Restoration – must not be confused with those countries where economic and other types of backwardness were closely combined.[3] And this situation was a most important asset for future economic development.

That Japan was operating with a relatively backward economy during the seventeenth and eighteenth centuries and most of the nineteenth is not at all difficult to ascertain, even though quantitative evidence is sparse and of poor quality. To begin with, we know that the overwhelming majority of the population at this time were peasants of a rather familiar Asian type. Their output constituted the major share of total product. These peasants cultivated small, often irrigated plots (average size perhaps slightly less than one hectare), and many of them must have been living on the border of subsistence at least during the first half of this period. Production techniques varied from region to region, with the Southwest generally ahead of the Northeast. Broadly speaking, however, it is clear that their agricultural technology was traditional and that yields were well below their potential level even in terms of existing practices. Very little capital equipment was employed by the peasants; the use of organic fertilizers was highly restricted (chemical fertilizers were unknown); and scientific practices such as seed selection and optimum sowing dates were largely unknown. Double-cropping was also employed at well below optimal levels. These observations can be put in general terms. Agricultural technology falls into three clear types: biological, chemical, and mechanical. The Tokugawa years saw some biological and chemical innovations. Significant mechanical improvements, such as the use of machinery, did not occur until after the Second World War.

To cite solid figures for all these assertions is nearly impossible, but reasonable guesses are not out of the question. Towards the end of

Tokugawa rule – i.e. in the middle of the nineteenth century – roughly
80 per cent of the people were officially classified as peasants. Not all
those designated as peasants in the official class structure actually
engaged in farming. Some worked in crafts or trade and lived (sometimes illegally) in cities. But most of the peasants must have engaged
mainly in cultivation of the soil, and certainly the Tokugawa regime
was anxious to see this situation maintained, since taxation of the
peasantry was its main source of income. Perhaps, then, the figure of
80 per cent exaggerates the rural nature of Tokugawa Japan. However,
even scaling it down to 75 or 70 per cent does not change the picture
of a society in which the average inhabitant was an Asian peasant. And
the presumption is that in a society of this type the level of income per
capita – an *average* concept – is low. Of course, 'low' implies a comparative standard, and to cite actual numbers (usually expressed in US
dollars) would only confuse the issue. Following the reasoning of
Simon Kuznets, we can simply say that – other things being equal – the
greater the share of the entire gainfully employed population employed
in agriculture, the lower the level of income per capita.

When one turns to the non-agricultural sectors of the Tokugawa
economy it becomes obvious that other things were, in fact, equal.
Non-agricultural production consisted of crafts and services. Craft
output frequently combined beauty and usefulness; services were often
very sophisticated. Nevertheless, these sectors were untouched by the
liberating forces of the industrial revolution which made men more
productive. Machinery was not in use except in the most unusual
circumstances; units of production were small; steam power had not
been introduced. In essence, agriculture and non-agriculture resembled
one another: both used labour-intensive methods that depended for
gains in productivity on the skills of the individual worker. Fixed
capital was only a minor element in the production function.

There is no more revealing evidence concerning Tokugawa Japan
than her demographic balance and her international contacts. To begin
with the latter, we must recall the famous 'closing of the country'
(*sakoku*) decree issued in 1637 by the third shogun of the Tokugawa
line. The reasons for this drastic step are not entirely clear to this day.
Some scholars believe that Shogun Iemitsu feared internal strife fo-
mented by *rōnin* (masterless samurai) and closed the country to prevent
these malcontents from securing outside help. Others espouse the more
likely explanation that an external threat was the main cause. According
to this view, Iemitsu understood the danger of Western expansionism –
specifically, of the sword following the cross – in the Philippines and
China. He feared that Japan's turn was coming. Whatever the shogun's
motives, the 'closing of the country' has to be taken quite literally:

no Japanese was permitted to leave Japan, and if someone did so and returned he was to be put to death. Foreigners were not allowed to visit or to reside in Japan. Only two minor exceptions were made: the Dutch and the Chinese retained extremely limited trading rights at Nagasaki. In order to take advantage of these rights, however, Dutch and Chinese traders lived as virtual prisoners in the far South of the country. The *sakoku* decrees remained in effect for well over two hundred years. They were fully lifted only in the 1860s, when the Tokugawa had reached the last tottering years of what had been an illustrious reign. By then, isolation had become a deeply ingrained tradition, and objection to its abandonment was strong even in the second half of the nineteenth century. Now, however, outside pressure from the major Western powers could no longer be resisted. Commodore Perry and his ships made their point in an unmistakable manner.

What were the consequences of this long self-imposed isolation? These are difficult to trace out unambiguously; yet there is little reason to believe that *sakoku* had only negative effects. To be isolated from empire-building Europeans may have been advantageous; to be left alone may have created sources of inner national strength. All of this is possible; but from the economic point of view, a closed country also meant a necessary condition of relative backwardness – not so obviously in the seventeenth century, when the policy was begun, but very obviously by the time the nineteenth century opened. In the intervening years the Western world – more precisely, Great Britain – had given birth to the industrial revolution. From then on the absence of international contacts meant the availability of only second-best technology and organization; and this remains true today.

Japan's demographic balance before the Meiji Restoration is equally revealing. The first real population census took place only in 1920, but experts agree on the broad magnitudes of earlier figures. In the 1860s, total population was around thirty million. At the start of the Tokugawa era, population is estimated to have been approximately twenty to twenty-five million. These figures convert into the low rates of natural increase typical of less-developed areas before the introduction of modern medical and social advances. Students of Japanese demography have pointed to another phenomenon of equally great interest: between the late seventeenth or early eighteenth centuries and the 1840s – for roughly one hundred and fifty years – the population remained stable; growth began again in the 1840s. The reasons for stability are again not entirely clear, but it has frequently been asserted that infanticide (*mabiki*) was an important means of achieving a zero growth rate. In general, we think that population at this time was a representative variable for the entire economy: change took place, but its pace was slow.

What has been said up to now is only half the story. Some pages earlier we cautioned against confusing Tokugawa Japan with many backward countries today or with some of Japan's near and far neighbours in the nineteenth century. Although unable at that time to avail herself of modern technology and most scientific advances, Japan nevertheless was a vigorous, advanced, and effective traditional society. In many ways it was more advanced than many countries in Africa or Latin America today. This deserves special stress, because there is no denying that we tend inevitably to associate low per capita income with poor organization, corruption, lethargy, and under-nourishment. And this gives a false picture of Japan before the Restoration.

A few illustrative details should be helpful. The pre-Restoration governmental structure was effective at both central and local levels. Central government – the capital and the major cities – was under direct Tokugawa control. Local authority was in the hands of Tokugawa vassals. The entire country was divided into about two hundred 'baronies' or 'fiefs', each headed by a lord or *daimyō*. A *daimyō* was responsible for the affairs of his fief, but he was also closely watched by the central authorities, and with sufficient cause his office could be taken away. In return for exercising local authority, *daimyō* received the rights to an income stream originating in their fiefs; its most important form was the privilege of levying a yearly harvest tax, with which they supported themselves and their retainers. Tokugawa administration has frequently been described as 'centralized feudalism', and this is quite accurate. As shogun, the head of the House of Tokugawa was the leading lord of the land: he was the largest individual fiefholder, and his revenues and the number of his retainers exceeded those of all other lords. At the same time, all other lords were – directly or indirectly – vassals of the Tokugawa; this was the 'centralized' part of the feudalism.

The road system of pre-modern Japan was in keeping with the centralized nature of government. Major arteries criss-crossed the country, and both goods and people moved relatively rapidly by nineteenth-century standards. A special word must be added about the institution of *sankin kōtai* (alternate residence), since it has often been linked to the quality of the roads. According to this Tokugawa regulation, the lords had to alternate their place of residence between the national capital (Edo, since renamed Tokyo) and their local capitals. The wives and children of lords had to remain present in Edo all of the time. Normally, the lord and selected retainers spent one year in the capital and one year in the provinces. The idea behind this regulation was simple: hostage families encouraged the lord's good behaviour, and his frequent absences in Edo prevented the creation of a local power base to rival that of the shogun. The resulting movements of people, sometimes in the colourful *daimyō* processions so well depicted by Hiroshige, no doubt contributed to the development of everything connected with travel – roads, inns, restaurants, etc.

Government and roads are part of a broader picture of competence and efficiency. The Japanese knew what they were doing, even though their efforts were circumscribed by very labour-intensive technology. Much of this can be seen by focusing briefly on some of the items used in everyday life under the Tokugawa. Housing was usually well designed and well engineered and satisfied the people's needs. The same can be said of clothing. Indigenous dress was beautiful and functional and was specifically designed to fit harmoniously into the traditional way of doing things. Japanese cuisine performed equally well. It was nutritious, attractive, and somewhat bland; these were exactly the characteristics most desired. Of course the point is not at all that the average Japanese in (say) 1850 was adequately fed, housed, and dressed: probably this was not true. But the point is that the means of satisfying these wants were available within the traditional society; indeed, when a wider choice became available, traditional means often continued to be preferred.

For a more complete picture of Tokugawa life, other points should also be stressed: the vigour of urban culture inside the large cities (Edo, Kyoto, and Osaka were among the largest cities in the world at that time); the high average standards of education, ensuring that approximately 40 to 50 per cent of all males had benefited from some formal schooling; the official class structure of *bushi* (samurai), farmers, and merchants, which was conservative in intent but which did supply the country with a group of leaders largely of samurai and 'gentry' farmer background. None of these points can be treated in detail, but they all add up to an important premise: in Tokugawa Japan the gap between economic and 'other' backwardness was unusually large, and this made the prospect of modern economic growth all the more promising.

III. *The Meiji Restoration and its Aftermath*

The term 'Restoration' refers to January 1868, when the last Tokugawa shogun 'voluntarily' surrendered power and returned the task of governing to the Imperial family, and specifically to the young

Emperor Meiji. Without a doubt this was an epochal event in Japanese history, and it can stand comparison with many other great dates in national histories. The Restoration was so crucial that many volumes have been devoted to its interpretation, and there are available any number of social, political, and cultural interpretations. In the general study of 'modernization' – today such a popular subject – the Meiji Restoration is one of the most important and favoured examples. Our own focus, however, must be quite narrow. We shall confine ourselves to outlining the main economic trends from the 1860s to the turn of the century as necessary background information.

Why did a Restoration occur, and why did it occur in 1868? These are questions which undoubtedly will never be answered with precision. Students of the period have suggested many reasons for this change of government: a renewed foreign threat which made continued isolation impossible and called instead for modernization; the presence of a group of discontented lower-ranking samurai from outlying domains who saw their own opportunities for advancement blocked and who wanted power and glory for themselves; a secular economic deterioration as a result of rising expenditures by the Tokugawa (and other domains) without the means further to increase revenues. All of these – and others – contain much truth, and it is not really necessary for us to delve into this subject more deeply. The main point is that Japanese modernization – economic, political, and social – began, at least symbolically, in 1868 when the Emperor Meiji was restored to the throne.

Despite recent scholarly controversies and revisions, the main features of the era continue to stand out in an unmistakable manner. In considering this period of somewhat over thirty years it is best to divide it into two segments: the years of transition from 1868 to perhaps 1885, and the years of initial modern economic growth beginning in the mid-1880s and ending with the turn of the century. Let us look at each one of these segments in turn.

The years of transition during which the initial shock of Western contact was absorbed were necessarily confused, full of false starts and experimentation. They were more important as years of institutional reform spearheaded by the government than as years of rapid economic growth. (Indeed, the available quantitative information is such that it is most difficult to establish aggregate economic growth rates before the middle of the 1880s.)

A brief look at the major reforms should make their significance obvious. Between 1869 and 1871, for example, the government entirely revamped the old feudal class structure. The official categories of court noble, warrior, peasant, merchant, and outcast were done away with and restructured into two new classes – a small nobility and everyone else. By 1876 the government had also succeeded in pensioning off all the former members of the warrior class – previously they had received stipends from Tokugawa or from their domains – at a cost of over 200 million yen. During this time, also, the new government abolished previously existing barriers to internal travel and opened the ports to external visitors. Of great importance also was the agricultural reform which occupied the new leaders during most of the 1870s. The land was formally turned over to the peasants (in feudal times ownership had been officially in the hands of the emperor), but they were now required to pay a heavy land tax to the central and local government. This tax was placed on the assessed valuation of the land (and not, as in the past, on the harvest) and was levied at nationally uniform levels. Currency and banking reforms also occupied the Meiji oligarchy in this period. It introduced order into the system of coinage, and by the end of the 1880s it had succeeded in creating a central bank (the Bank of Japan) and in establishing regulations for a growing private banking system. Other well-known activities of the public sector in this period might also be mentioned: the establishment of model factories, the hiring of foreign experts, and the dispatch of students abroad. All of these activities taken together added up to a most active era of institutional innovation.

During this transition the Japanese economy underwent some severe fluctuations. Until 1876 the situation remained relatively calm, but thereafter great shocks occurred in the form of a severe inflation lasting until 1881, followed by an intense deflation which ended only in 1885. The causes of these events are intricate, but they need not detain us for long. Briefly, throughout the transition years the government lacked sufficient revenue even for its ordinary needs. In the latter half of the 1870s, however, these needs were very much magnified by the desire to pension off the warrior class and by the outbreak of the Satsuma rebellion. The government and the banks turned to the printing press, and the resulting inflation – beneficial to no one but the farmers – endangered the stability of the new leadership. Its revenues – especially those relating to the land tax – were fixed, and they were being diminished in real terms by the rising prices. Economic order was restored by Finance Minister Matsukata, but it required four years of severe and officially sponsored deflation.[4]

Modern economic growth in Japan began during the next subperiod, that is to say some time after the middle of the 1880s. Clearly one must not imagine that Japanese industrialization was in any sense an accomplished fact by the time the twentieth century had started, but some very significant steps had been taken in the right direction. The

fifteen years following the Matsukata deflation represented a period of
virtually uninterrupted development of modern industry. Silk and
cotton-spinning were the main achievements of the private sector,
while road-building, railways, and public works in general were
carried out and encouraged by the government. By 1901 factory output
constituted nearly 10 per cent of net national product; gross domestic
fixed capital formation was over 10 per cent of GNP; and exports
were over 10 per cent of GNP. All these indicators showed sustained
increases over the preceding decades.

From our perspective, the most noteworthy element in initial
economic growth is its mechanism. As mentioned somewhat earlier,
we find it to be rather different from that which obtained in the
twentieth century. Ever since the Restoration, the Japanese economy
has contained a number of rather well-defined sectors. Usually these
have been labelled as 'modern' and 'traditional', and sometimes we
have added the category 'hybrid'. There is nothing new or surprising
about these categories; they are part of all dual-economy analyses. The
characteristics of the sectors are equally well known, and they obtain
as well in other countries. Modern sectors rely on imported Western
technology and organization and employ methods of relatively high
capital-intensity. By contrast, traditional production relies on more
indigenous technology and organization and on relatively low levels
of capital-intensity. Hybrid sectors fall in between, combining (say)
modern technique and traditional organization. The Asian peasant
cultivating his small field with hand tools is a perfect example of the
traditional economy. The large cotton-spinning establishment with its
machines and its wage workers is a perfect example of the modern
sector.

All of this is very familiar to students of economic development,
just as is the fact that modern economic growth is a process by which
traditional ways of doing things gradually yield to modern ways. What
is perhaps less familiar is the vividness of the contrast between modern and
traditional in the Japanese setting. There the traditional economy often
has a quaint and (at least for Westerners) an exotic appearance – one
need only think of the wonderful Japanese crafts and the range of
unusual services – and therefore the dichotomy is more readily identifiable. But in terms of economic analysis this added bit of colour makes
little difference.

Four simple propositions applied to modern economic growth in its
initial phase.

(1) In the absence of large capital imports, and with limited possibilities for redistributing an existing surplus, the initial establishment
and subsequent development of the modern economy depended on the

accelerated growth of the traditional economy – and also to some extent on the accelerated growth of the hybrid economy.

(2) The traditional economy was capable of accelerated growth.

(3) However, the growth potential of the traditional economy was limited. When its growth rate began to decline – approximately at the time of the First World War – the initial phase of modern economic growth came to an end.

(4) By the time the initial phase came to an end, the dependence of the modern economy on the traditional economy had greatly decreased – although it had not disappeared.

These propositions can be summarized as follows: the opportunities for initial economic modernization hinged on the more rapid growth of peasant agriculture, because this produced most of the needed surpluses for development (public revenues, private investment funds, foreign exchange, and labour force). When traditional agriculture faltered, a different model came into play.

This schematic presentation of nineteenth-century growth is not without its critics. The major problem undoubtedly relates to the rate of growth of traditional agriculture during the Meiji era. At one time it would have been easy to outline the main economic trends. If this is no longer so, it is because of a lively controversy concerning Meiji agricultural growth. This is not the place to cover this dispute in detail: it has been done in many places elsewhere, and all we need to do here is to state our conclusions.[5]

Many authorities seem to agree that Japanese agriculture during the relevant years (from the 1870s to the 1900s) grew at about 1·7 per cent per annum. Some would place this figure slightly lower (some very much lower), and some may select slightly higher figures; but 1·7 per cent seems to us an acceptable modal value. If this rate is approximately correct, it follows that the Meiji era witnessed a considerable acceleration over the older Tokugawa values, for no one has ever suggested that before the 1870s growth was of this magnitude. Undoubtedly Tokugawa agricultural output grew much more slowly than Meiji agricultural output, no matter what the actual rate may have been.

Various reasons can account for the acceleration of agricultural output in Meiji Japan. Of undoubted importance were the development and diffusion of improved agricultural techniques, partly the work of individual farmers and their organizations and partly the result of government sponsorship and research. For example, these activities led to improved seed selection and a wider and more rational use of fertilizers. The improved incentive structure for landowners must also be taken into account. In Tokugawa Japan, the peasant paid a heavy harvest tax, which fluctuated considerably from year to year and frequently depended on the specific short-term financial needs of the lords. Thus there was no guarantee that the agriculturist would be able to retain any of the increased output. Now the situation was entirely different, since the land tax was based on the value of land, and it was pretty well known that the assessments would remain fairly stable. Another element in explaining the acceleration of output is connected to the regional structure of the pre-modern Japanese economy. The agricultural economy of Tokugawa Japan – especially with respect to levels of productivity – was not at all uniform. There existed areas of relatively high and low productivity, and only in part could this be explained by differing qualities of soil or geography. In very broad terms, agriculture was more backward in northeastern Japan than in southwestern Japan. The Restoration provided an opportunity for exploiting these productivity gaps. Before the 1860s the transfer of know-how and technology had been impeded by Tokugawa theory and practice; now it became an aim of the Meiji government to spread useful knowledge throughout the entire country.

This type of expansion, however, has limited possibilities. Output grew in Meiji agriculture owing to the employment of techniques based on increased labour input combined with improvements in conventional inputs – seed, fertilizers, etc. All these were highly divisible and well suited to the peasant unit of production. But this could not go on indefinitely. Eventually, when these types of improvements had been fully exploited, maintaining the growth rate would have required major capital and land improvements. These did not have a significant effect until after the Second World War, and therefore shortly after 1914 the rate of growth of Japanese agriculture started to stagnate.[6]

Why were agriculture and other sectors in similar positions so crucial? This is easy to see when we consider the needs of modern economic growth. Fundamentally it is a matter of 'he who dances must pay the fiddler', at a time when the vast majority of dancers were in traditional occupations. In the beginning their productivity levels were low, but by raising them they could generate the necessary surpluses with which to begin industrialization. And, given the traditional techniques, this could be accomplished without heavy expenditures on fixed investment.

After all, what were the needs of modern economic growth at a time when reinvestment by a small sector of modern industry was tiny? and how were those needs met? First of all, Japan needed a growing food supply for a larger population in which the standards of diet were rising. Importing food was relatively expensive and diverted funds from productive investment possibilities. In large measure the increased food supplies were provided by the peasantry. Secondly, the new government required a rising flow of revenues for social overhead and other investment purposes, as well as for administrative modernization. Again the traditional economy played a key role here, through land-tax revenue and as a source of indirect taxation. Thirdly, foreign exchange was vital for the importation of modern producers' durables and to acquire the services of foreign experts. The Meiji economy secured foreign exchange largely through the export of tea and silk, both products closely linked to traditional agriculture. Finally, the Japanese economy needed to effect a labour transfer so as to provide the workers for the expanding modern sectors. These workers came almost entirely from the rural areas, and this transfer did not adversely affect the rate of growth of agricultural output.

Having outlined the mechanism of Meiji economic growth, let us now examine the character of pre-twentieth-century capital inputs. We can accomplish this most easily by attempting to sharpen the contrasts between the nineteenth and twentieth centuries.

By 1900, the proportion of gross fixed domestic investment to gross aggregate product in Japan had probably reached 12 per cent – by no means an insignificant level.[7] Yet the share of modern industry in the economy was very modest. Factory output accounted for some 8 per cent of net domestic product, and the definition of a factory – an establishment with five or more employees – meant that a great deal of handicraft production was included. We know that factory output grew rapidly during the thirty years before 1900 – in 1885 the proportion had been 4 per cent – but we also know that it continued to increase, reaching levels of over 30 per cent after the Second World War.

The output stream emanating from these factories underwent a considerable change during the Meiji era. In 1868, 66 per cent of gross output came from food-processing and kindred activities, and 28 per cent from textile-manufacturing, which was dominated by the silk industry. By 1905, the share of food-processing had dropped to 39 per cent, textiles had risen to 38 per cent – with cotton becoming more important – and chemicals, metals, and machines accounted for 23 per cent. However, it should be added that the representative units were small. At the turn of the century, 68 per cent of the workers in food-processing were engaged in establishments with fewer than fifty employees; for textiles and heavy industry this proportion stood at 37 per cent and 43 per cent respectively.

Once more, a glance at future developments can indicate the magnitude of change to come. Whereas Meiji industrial output was dominated by food-processing and textiles produced by rather small units, twentieth-century production – certainly by the 1930s – was dominated by heavier industry and larger units. For example, at the end of the 1930s, chemicals, metals, and machines accounted for about 70 per cent of gross industrial output, and nearly 50 per cent of the labour force in these industries was working in large factories.

The early and limited industrialization of Meiji Japan was supported by a specific pattern of capital formation. It can be described as follows:

(1) Public investment generally exceeded the level of private productive investment.

(2) Investment in construction outweighed investment in producers' durable equipment.

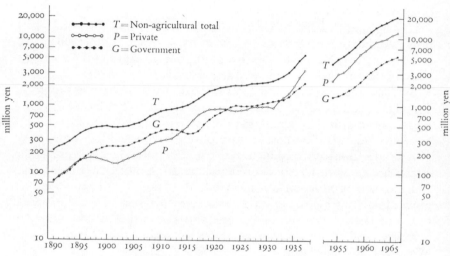

Fig. 9. Gross Domestic Fixed Investment (1934–6 prices).
SOURCE. Ohkawa and Rosovsky, *Japanese Economic Growth*, 32.

(3) Most of the investments represented the application of traditional techniques and therefore did not embody imported technological progress.

As Figure 9 shows, government investments generally exceeded those of the private sector until the First World War. This was undoubtedly due to a combination of two factors. First of all, the government was very active in improving the quantity and quality of social overheads; it was also very active in raising Japan's military capability. Indeed, during the Meiji era one can account for well over half of capital formation on the part of central government by summing up expenditures on public works (especially railways) and military investments. If one adds reconstruction expenditures related to periodic natural disasters such as earthquakes and typhoons, it is possible to account for over 70 per cent of government investment expenditures.

The second explanation of the government's large share in total investment simply relates to the small absolute size of private industry. Figure 9 indicates that private investments were gaining on those of the public sector, but during most of the Meiji era the types of industries which made extensive use of expensive capital equipment were still infants – though growing at a lusty pace.

At this time also – especially if we concentrate on productive investment – construction was the main form of national investment. This generalization is valid through the first decade of the twentieth century; at some time between 1911 and 1917, a sharp break occurred in the compositions of domestic capital formation, and from that time onward private producers' durable equipment absorbed the greatest share of resources.

In large measure the leading role of construction was merely a reflection of the overall primacy of public investments and their nature at this time. Road-building, port improvements, government buildings, etc. – all construction activities with high capital–output ratios – accounted for over two-thirds of public capital formation. Even in the private sector, investments were relatively equally divided between construction and durable equipment until the time of the First World War, when the latter category suddenly assumed a new level of significance. Factory and commercial construction, and also – before the nationalizations of the early twentieth century – private railway construction, represented expenditures that were nearly as great as those on machinery and equipment.

The last aspect of the Meiji investment pattern is, perhaps, the most unusual. In Japan at this time, capital goods were produced by two rather distinct methods: one can be called 'traditional' and the other 'modern'. When it came to the building of railways or waterworks, or the acquisition of producers' durables, all sorts of modern and imported techniques were necessarily involved. Roadbeds had to be scientifically surveyed and graded; steam pumps and iron pipes were needed for waterworks; producers' durables meant machines activated by steam engines and later by electricity. All these were ways of doing things which were largely unknown in Meiji Japan. But there was another side to the coin. Traditional techniques could also create capital goods, as in the case of residential and commercial construction (largely wooden structures), irrigation and land reclamation for agriculture, and even road and bridge construction. In these instances, pre-Meiji techniques of a highly labour-intensive nature retained their usefulness and supported the modernization process. It should be noted that in the circumstances of the times, these techniques were especially economical. They used labour, tools, and skills which were readily available; they did not require much capital or new skills which were relatively expensive.

According to this classification, in Meiji Japan roughly one-half of the capital goods were produced by traditional techniques. This was a unique characteristic of early Japanese industrialization, because in post-Meiji years the proportion of traditional investments declined sharply while, simultaneously, many of the older ways in (say) house- and road-building were abandoned in favour of imported methods. However, while it lasted, Japan provided a good example of what Joan Robinson has called 'walking on two legs'.

Perhaps we can now summarize the situation obtaining in the last third of the nineteenth century. Initial modern economic growth was in large measure based on the achievements of a traditional economy. This was the first step towards the accomplishment of industrialization. It was now time to take the second and much bigger step – perhaps one could call it the leap toward a semi-developed state – and for that we turn to an analysis of the period from 1900 to the present.

IV. *Twentieth-Century Japan: The Economics of Trend Acceleration*

A. THE HISTORICAL PATH OF INVESTMENT

We begin the analysis of the twentieth century by outlining some of the major quantitative aspects of investment. The primary focus will be on the rate of growth of private non-agricultural capital formation $(\Delta I/I)$.[8] This emphasis has a number of justifications. Most important, our intention is to argue (in an ensuing section) that private investment was the key dynamic element for rapid economic growth in this century. Secondly, the amplitude of private $\Delta I/I$ moves with great clarity. Finally, the measurement of private $\Delta I/I$ is direct and comparatively simple, and therefore statistically more accurate than competing measures.[9]

Quantitative analysis of Japanese capital formation covers a period of nearly one hundred years, from the present back to the 1870s. For this long period, the pattern has been remarkably stable. It consists of a steeply rising trend combined with wave-like movements of the growth rate. An investment wave or long swing consists of a period relatively rapid growth of capital formation followed by a number of years of lower growth.

Taking the broadest possible time span, it is possible to speak of three and one-half swings. The first consists of very high growth rates until the middle of the 1890s, followed by about six years of much slower capital formation. As Table 26 shows, a second upswing begins somewhat hesitantly during the Russo-Japanese War and falters a bit between 1909 and 1912, but then the expansion carries through the First World War. The latter half of this swing comprises the rather low investment growth rates prevailing throughout the 1920s. Then, beginning in the 1930s and continuing until the impact of the coming

Table 26. *Private Non-Agricultural Investment: Annual Rates of Growth (per cent) at Constant Prices*

	Growth rate		Growth rate		Growth rate
1901	−7·2(T)	1918	8·9	1935	20·3
1902	2·7	1919	6·3	1936	31·4
1903	14·5	1920	−0·4	1937	20·2(P)
1904	9·8	1921	−2·5		
1905	12·0	1922	−8·5		
1906	9·7	1923	−9·5		
1907	14·0	1924	−9·8	1956	12·1(T)
1908	19·3	1925	−4·2	1957	15·1
1909	6·1	1926	1·2	1958	25·3
1910	5·4	1927	8·0	1959	26·4
1911	6·1	1928	−2·1	1960	18·6
1912	2·6	1929	−4·7	1961	17·6
1913	9·1	1930	−2·0	1962	18·3(P)
1914	18·9	1931	5·0(T)	1963	9·0
1915	24·0	1932	12·0	1964	6·0
1916	23·9	1933	11·4	1965	11·4
1917	19·3(P)	1934	13·9	1966	16·0

NOTE. Investment in residential construction is excluded. Growth rates are based on series smoothed by a seven-year moving average before the Second World War. 'Constant prices': 1934–6 prices before the Second World War; 1960 prices after the Second World War.

SOURCE. K. Ohkawa and H. Rosovsky, *Japanese Economic Growth* (Stanford, Calif., 1973), 33.

war made itself felt directly, a sharp investment spurt is in evidence. This has to be considered a 'half-swing', because the period between the late 1930s and the early 1950s – some fifteen years – includes the destructive effects of the Second World War, the occupation, and the initial rehabilitation of Japan's economy. Normal economic analysis for this time span would make little sense; statistics are unavailable, and a great variety of distortions effectively prevent the fitting of these years into a consideration of long-run development. However, after the Second World War the familiar pattern appears again. Private investment expands at near-record rates somewhat beyond the 1950s; this upsurge is followed by considerably slower investment growth through 1966, when our period of analysis ends.

While a general identification of these long investment swings is a pretty simple matter, the selection of actual turning points (peaks and troughs) is inevitably more complicated and more debatable. For the twentieth century, we suggest the following dating:

	T	P	T
Swing I	1901	1917	1931
Swing II	1931	1937	
Swing III	1956	1962	1966

Perhaps some of these dates could be shifted one year in either direction, but this would not affect the conclusions. In any event, peaks and troughs are based on moving averages, and each individual year stands for the centre point of a band of seven (pre-war) or five (post-war) years. What should be unambiguous, especially after an inspection of Table 26, is that before and after each turning point (T or P) the annual rates of growth of private investment maintain – for a long time – very different levels.

Let us, however, take note of three specific problems of interpretation relating to the selection of turning points.

(1) In our periodization, 1901–17 is treated as a single upswing even though the smoothed growth rate of private capital formation falters from 1909 to 1912. Had the First World War not provided a strong stimulus to entrepreneurs during the decade 1910–19 – and we must always keep in mind that these are time series smoothed by a seven-year moving average – it is entirely possible that 1909–12 would have developed into a fully fledged downswing. As it is, we prefer to consider the period as a unified step forward containing a small stumble. There is no 'right' or 'wrong' in this sort of conclusion; it is largely a matter of taste.

(2) The post-war investment spurt is dated as beginning in 1956. This decision contains a measure of arbitrariness and is related to the aftermath of defeat in the Second World War. Nearly all authorities agree that around 1952–4 the Japanese economy returned to 'normalcy': the allied occupation had ended, and most indicators – capital–output ratio, employment, food production, etc. – were showing expected long-run levels. We accept this date, and since moving averages are employed we begin in 1956, which is the earliest available entry.

(3) Lastly, a word about the 1966 turning point. A new investment spurt may have begun at that time; alternatively, one may eventually wish to treat 1962–6 as a 'stumble' analogous to the earlier experience

of 1909–12. In any event, the data are as yet too sparse for making a long-range historical judgement.

Of the three spurts contained in the data, the second (1931–7) and third (1956–62) are much more powerful than the first (1901–17). In fact, the average level of annual growth rates of private non-agricultural investment was higher in each successive spurt.

One should also note the relationship between public and private capital formation. It is clear from Figure 9 that the gap between these types of investment changes in accordance with the historical periodization: it narrows during upswings and widens during downswings. In other words, whenever the Japanese economy experienced its most rapid secular expansions, private investment expanded more rapidly than public investment, and the reverse was true when the economy contracted.

B. THE CHANGING COMPOSITION OF INVESTMENT

Although investment spurts have recurred regularly in Japanese economic growth, their composition has changed, reflecting the increasing maturity of the industrial structure. Visual evidence is provided in Figure 10, where private capital formation has been divided into

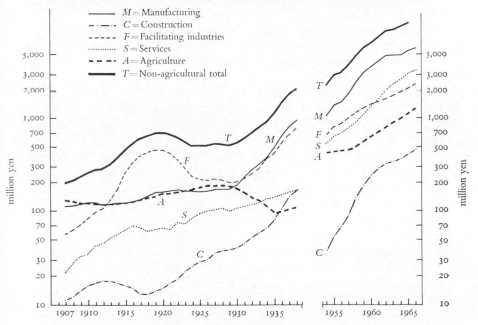

Fig. 10. Composition of Private Investment (1934–6 prices)
SOURCE. Table 27.

major industrial components: agriculture, manufacturing (including mining), construction, facilitating industries, and services.

The first investment spurt of this century was due most of all to the rapid increase of investments in private facilitating industries, which include transportation, communications, and public utilities. At the beginning of the twentieth century, total non-agricultural private capital formation in constant prices averaged approximately 200 million yen per annum (see Table 27). By the end of the First World

Table 27. *Average Private Non-Agricultural Investment by Industries: Selected Years (million yen, 1934–6 prices)*

	Manufacturing	Construction	Facilitating industries	Services[a]	Total
1907[b]	111	11	57	22	201
1917	135	13	402	69	619
1931	232	46	228	113	619
1937	820	143	682	161	1,806
1956	1,504	70	889	709	3,172
1962	4,830	336	1,680	2,065	8,911
1966	5,812	478	2,376	3,382	12,048

NOTE. Seven-year averages before Second World War; five-year averages after Second World War.

[a] Excludes residential construction.

[b] Investment by industrial sectors cannot be carried back further than 1907.

SOURCE. Ohkawa and Rosovsky, *Japanese Economic Growth*, 154.

War, this had risen to an average of over 600 million yen per annum. The level of investment flow rose by some 400 million yen, out of which about 350 million yen were accounted for by facilitating industries.

During the second investment spurt the lead was taken by manufacturing industries, with facilitating industries a close second. In the early 1930s, private capital formation averaged 600 million yen per annum; towards the end of that decade, yearly totals were in the neighbourhood of 1,800 million yen. The average annual flow had risen by 1,200 million yen, of which some 800 million yen originated in manufacturing, and 700 million in facilitating industries.

The post-war investment spurt (1956–62) produced sharp increases in capital-formation levels for all industries: a threefold increase in the total and in manufacturing and services, fivefold in construction, and twofold in facilitating industries – all accomplished in six years. However, when the weights of the industrial sectors are considered, it becomes apparent that manufacturing played an even stronger leading role than in the 1930s: it accounted for close to 60 per cent of the increases. Furthermore, capital formation in the service industries became a significant factor for the first time: its contribution (25 per cent) was larger than that of facilitating industries (14 per cent).[10]

Although these data classify investment by industrial origin, they can equally well confirm the growing significance of durable equipment as compared to construction. All industries engage in construction activities, but the proportion of this kind of investment is greatest for facilitating activities; it represents a much smaller part of manufacturing expenditures.

Finally, a brief look at the changing composition of investment during the two downswings. Clearly the periods in question were very different. In the former – 1917–31 – the average flow of private capital formation remained unchanged for well over a decade. In the latter – 1962–6 – private capital formation continued to rise, though at much lower rates. Nevertheless there are important similarities. With the exception of the decline in private investment in facilitating industries for 1917–31, all industries continued to raise their levels of investment. But a strong growth leader is missing. Compared to the preceding spurts, the growth rates are not only lower but also more nearly at similar levels for the various components.

C. THE GROWTH PATTERN

The years from 1901 to 1966 constitute an identifiable historical unit – or, to use a term previously employed, a growth phase[11] – because during this long period certain important characteristics of Japanese economic growth have persisted. In other words, this period established a specific growth pattern whose principal features we must attempt to outline.

(1) During the sixty-odd years with which we are concerned, the trend rate of growth of aggregate product has been very rapid, as indicated by the average annual growth rates shown in Table 28.[12] The expansion can be described as 'very rapid' because among the fifteen to twenty countries that have established a long-term record of modern economic growth, only the United States and Canada (and perhaps Sweden and the Soviet Union) have turned in achievements of similar magnitudes. Thus, in the overall distribution of historical growth rates, a conservative estimate of Japan's performance would place her in the top quartile.

(2) An inspection of the figures in Table 28 also shows that Japan's trend rate of growth of aggregate product has been accelerating during the period of analysis. Average growth rates, according to our period-

ization of the time series, alternate between periods of comparatively more rapid and less rapid growth, but the trend rate is clearly rising all the time: the economy developed more speedily in the 1930s than in the early part of the century, and the sharpest acceleration occurred after the Second World War.

(3) The more than sixty years between 1901 and 1966 have been subdivided into segments of unequal length, and each one of these segments represents an upswing or a downswing of a long swing. Long swings have been an enduring feature of Japanese growth, and they have been especially prominent in the rate of growth of private and

Table 28. *GNP: Average Annual Rates of Growth during Long Swings (smoothed series at constant prices; per cent)*

	Period	GNP[a]
(1)	1897 (Peak)–1901 (Trough)	1·96
(2)	1901 (T)–1917 (P)	2·88
(2')	1912–1917	4·56
(3)	1917 (P)–1931 (T)	2·75
(4)	1931 (T)–1937 (P)	5·71
(5)	1937 (P)–1956 (T)	1·83
(6)	1956 (T)–1962 (P)	10·72
(7)	1962–1969	11·91

NOTE. All series smoothed by a seven-year moving average before the Second World War, and by a five-year moving average thereafter, except for 1969, which represents a three-year centred average. Pre-war data in 1934–6 prices. Postwar data in lines 5 and 6 in 1960 prices; line 7 has been tentatively converted to 1960 prices by using the aggregate deflator. The values for 1937 (1934–6 prices) and 1956 (1960 prices) have been linked using the aggregate deflator for gross national expenditures: this was 321·6 in 1955 (1934–6 = 1).

[a] Average compound growth rates between successive trough and peak years of the smoothed series.

SOURCE. Ohkawa and Rosovsky, *Japanese Economic Growth*, 25.

total capital formation. Since 1901 there have been three periods of especially rapid growth of capital formation – 1901–17, 1931–7, and 1956–62 – and these have been designated as 'investment spurts' or upswings. The remaining years - 1917–31 and 1962–6 – were periods of much slower investment growth and have been designated as downswings.

(4) Long swings in the rate of growth of capital formation and aggregate product have had, between 1901 and 1966, certain systematic associations with some other standard measures of economic performance.

(a) From the figures cited previously, we already know that capital formation grew more rapidly than output, and therefore during the years under review the trend of I/Y (the investment ratio) rose substantially. However, the rise of this ratio was closely associated with investment spurts: when the rate of growth of capital formation spurted, the investment proportion went up sharply; when capital formation grew at more deliberate speeds, I/Y remained relatively stable, as Table 29 shows. The stability of I/Y during downswings – when a sharp decline might have been expected – is related to a persistent 'leader–follower' relationship between public and private investment. When the rate of expansion lies above the long-run trend

Table 29. *Investment Ratio* (I/Y) *and Related Terms* (*per cent*)

	I/Y: total	I/Y: private non-agricultural	K/Y: private non-agricultural
1907	12·75	5·68	1·29
1917	16·46	11·78	1·39
1931	15·13	6·47	1·83
1937	20·53	12·00	1·74
1956	29·74	17·38	1·88
1962	36·42	23·66	1·59
1964	35·68	21·98	1·61

I, gross domestic fixed investment; Y, gross domestic product; K, gross fixed capital stock.

NOTE. Smoothed series. Figures for 1907, 1956, and 1962 are five-year moving averages; those for 1917, 1931, and 1937 are seven-year moving averages; and those for 1964 are three-year averages.

SOURCE. Ohkawa and Rosovsky, *Japanese Economic Growth*, 47 and 148.

line, private investment grows more rapidly than public investment. The reverse is the case when output growth is below trend values. This pattern can be observed in the changing proportions of private and public investment (see Fig. 9).

(b) The proportion of total domestic savings to total product (S/Y) presents essentially the same pattern as the development of I/Y. As a trend, the domestic savings proportion rose steeply during this century, and the path of increase closely resembled that of the investment proportion: when capital-formation and output growth rates were in an upswing, domestic savings rates went up sharply; by contrast, savings rates declined during downswings. The figures in Table 30 tell the story.

(c) The relationship between long swings and the private non-agricultural capital–output ratio (K/Y) is somewhat complicated, and the historical pattern is most readily discernible in Table 29. These movements combine the divergent influences of trends and swings. During an upswing or investment spurt, the values of K/Y generally declined. In a trend sense, however, K/Y gradually increased from the beginning of this century until the first half of the 1930s. From then until the beginning of the 1960s, the values of K/Y generally declined.

(d) The trend and swing association of the relative income shares of capital (α) and labour (β) are also systematic. The trends of both shares

Table 30. *Composition of Domestic Savings (per cent)*

	Gross aggregate ratio[a]	Net ratio[b]	Proportion of private to total domestic savings[c]
1908	15·6	7·9	23·7
1917	32·6	22·4	57·8
1924	15·6	5·3	—14·5
1931	15·7	6·7	24·5
1937	24·5	16·3	50·4
1956	27·7	20·4	47·6
1962	33·9	25·6	45·9
1966	36·0	26·7	48·3

NOTE. Smoothed series. Figures for 1908, 1956, 1962, and 1966 are five-year moving averages; figures for 1917, 1924, and 1931 are seven-year averages; and figures for 1937 are three-year averages.
  [a] National savings/GNP.
  [b] Net savings/NNP.
  [c] Corporate savings are included.

SOURCE. Ohkawa and Rosovsky, *Japanese Economic Growth*, 167.

were rather steady in this century. For example, the values of α during the entire pre-war period ranged from a low of 33·7 per cent in 1924 to a high of 50·2 per cent in 1917. However, during investment upswings it was characteristic for α to rise and for β to decline, and the opposite was true for downswings. A very typical case was the expansion that peaked in 1917. From the beginning of the century until that year, α rose quite steadily from values in the neighbourhood of 40 per cent to above 50 per cent. During the 1920s, when the economy contracted, the average level of α was below 35 per cent.[13]

(e) The movements of K/Y and α also suggest certain systematic alterations in the expected rate of return on capital (r). Since $\alpha = Kr/Y$, during investment upswings the rate of return on capital must tend to rise, since K/Y rises less rapidly or declines while the income share of capital increases. During investment downswings, a reverse tendency must have existed. For trend values, we may assume that r was relatively steady.

(5) Another growth characteristic of this period is the steady and uninterrupted rise in the capital-intensity (K/L) of production of the non-primary private sector. The figures are as follows (in terms of average annual growth rates): [14]

For	1908–17, $G(K) - G(L) =$	4·27 per cent
	1917–31	3·25
	1931–8	2·69
	1955–61	4·67
	1962–4	8·44

Were it not for the unusually low rate of growth during the 1930s, one would conclude that $G(K/L)$ exhibits both trend acceleration and a close association with the investment spurt. In fact, this was undoubtedly the case; the failure of a strong upturn of $G(K/L)$ from 1931 to 1938 was obviously due to the abnormally heavy weight of military investments. If these were to be included, we can safely assume that the average annual growth rate of capital-intensity would have been well in excess of 4·5 per cent per annum. [15]

(6) Elsewhere we have characterized the Japanese economy of this period as being affected by a special type of dual economy called 'differential structure'. A dual economy implies the presence of two sectors – one traditional and the other modern – operating with different methods, techniques, and incentives. Differential structure includes the additional attribute of a growing gap between the modern and traditional sectors, and this can be most conveniently expressed in terms of relative partial productivity (Y/L) and wage levels. As a representative example for the modern sector, one can use manufacturing, with its imported and increasingly capital-intensive methods of production. As representative of the traditional sector, one can take agriculture, which at this time retained many indigenous features: small units, labour-intensive methods, etc. What happened to the relative positions of these two sectors in the twentieth century can be seen in Tables 31 and 32.

From the point of view of the partial productivity of labour, the gap between agriculture and non-agriculture widened both before the Second World War and again between 1956 and 1964. This is reflected in the movements of the ratio of agricultural to non-agricultural wages. It sustains two distinct levels: until the 1920s agricultural wages – though

Table 31. *Wage Differentials for Selected Years*

	Wa/Wm (per cent)
1905	67·4
1910	68·3
1915	71·9
1919	83·3
1925	79·7
1931	48·9
1935	47·9
1939	71·3
1954	36·5
1960	40·4
1965	51·1

Wa, wages of male daily-contract workers in agriculture; *Wm*, wages of regular male workers in manufacturing.

NOTE. Smoothed series: five-year moving averages (except 1965, three-year average).

SOURCE. Ohkawa and Rosovsky, *Japanese Economic Growth*, 126.

Table 32. *Productivity Differentials for Selected Years, 1897–1937 (yen, 1934–6 prices) and 1956–64 (hundred yen, 1960 prices)*

	Y/L Total	Y/L Non-agricultural	Y/L Agricultural
1897	231	464	120
1901	243	466	129
1917	404	711	171
1931	534	863	199
1937	850	1,069	229
1956	2,480	3,293	1,155
1962	4,607	5,880	1,584
1964	5,044	6,846	1,695

L, labour force; *Y*, output (gross of depreciation).

NOTE. Smoothed series: five-year averages centred on the indicated year.

SOURCE. Ohkawa and Rosovsky, *Japanese Economic Growth*, 36.

lower – did not suffer relatively. Since the 1930s, however, we can easily see the effect of the so-called differential structure.

(7) Finally, two characteristics of Japan's export growth pattern should be noted. During the entire period under review, the average annual rate of growth of exports (in constant prices) exceeded that of GNP. This can be seen in Table 33, where exports occupy an ever larger share of aggregate demand – with only a brief interruption

Table 33. *Exports: Prices and Proportion of Aggregate Demand*

	Indexes of relative prices		Exports/Aggregate demand (per cent)
	Exports	General expenditures prices	
1906	100·0	100·0	5·5
1912	69·5	120·5	7·7
1917	74·7	165·4	10·8
1924	70·6	250·0	—
1931	41·7	191·6	13·0
1938	43·5	249·8	17·0
1953	100·0	100·0	—
1955	86·3	105·1	9·4
1960	79·9	118·5	10·6
1965	57·9	149·1	12·6

NOTE. The original price indexes are three-year averages for the pre-war and single years for the post-war period. Individual indexes have been expressed as ratios of the general price index, and then converted to 1906 and 1953 comparison bases.

SOURCE. Ohkawa and Rosovsky, *Japanese Economic Growth*, 179 and 143.

during the Second World War. Furthermore, as shown in the same table, the prices of exports declined, relative to domestic prices, during the entire period.

V. *An Interpretation*

The main historical facts have been presented, and our last task will be to suggest how they might be interpreted. We are primarily interested in saying something about the overall significance of capital inputs in Japanese modern economic growth during the twentieth century. Specifically, we should like, if possible, to shed some light both on the rapidity of Japanese growth from 1900 to the present and also on what we have called trend acceleration. These are complicated issues, and within the confines of even a long chapter it is out of the question to deal with them in depth. Nevertheless, it would be even less satisfactory to ignore these issues, which are of wide interest.

We may begin by going back once more to the recurring swings in private investment. In terms of formal economic reasoning, they can be 'explained' without undue difficulty. Let us make four behavioural assumptions (based on standard economic theory):

(1) that private investment was the main agent of economic modernization as the carrier of new and largely imported technology;

(2) that the level of private investment is determined by profit expectations;

(3) that a simple aggregate production function of the type $G(Y) = G(R) + \alpha G(K) + \beta G(L)$ can describe the main trend of output growth for the private modern sector. $G(R)$ (R being the residual) refers to the rate of growth of technical and organizational progress (as is well known, this production function assumes the existence of neutral and disembodied technological progress);

(4) that there exists a personal savings function of the type $S_t = A + bY_t + cY_{t-1}$. This simply says that the savings ratio depends on a constant term, the level of income, and the rate of growth of income.

The historical record shows that the duration of upswings and down-swings varied considerably, and there is no doubt that *ad hoc* phenomena such as wars and a changing international political and economic climate played key roles in determining certain turning points. And yet these observed long swings do have significant common characteristics. Coupled with our standard assumptions, they can suggest a formal explanation.

It is most convenient to start with an investment spurt which can be outlined first as a simple or theoretical case; then we can turn to a less simple and more true-to-life version. In the simple case we rigorously retain the specifications of the production function in which α is held constant. Even with this restriction, the rate of return on capital (r) could rise owing to a fall in K/Y attributable to technological and organizational progress and rising demand. A rise in r would mean a greater amount of capital formation as well as a shift towards more capital-intensive production for private modern output. S/Y would also increase with a time lag – in accordance with the previously assumed savings function.

The simple case has been mentioned only to show that technological progress and demand alone could give rise to an investment spurt. But it is a much too simple-minded and unrealistic formulation. We have shown that α rises in the upswing, and this must have been so for two reasons: first, technological progress may be not neutral (as assumed by our long-run production function) but biased in favour of capital, especially in the upswing; secondly, there may be a wage lag behind increases in the partial productivity of labour. Both reasons would raise the rate of return on capital and intensify the investment spurt.

Whether technical change in Japan has or has not been biased – and in which direction – is a most difficult empirical problem. No one can render a valid historical judgement, and one can safely continue to think in terms of neutrality. At the same time it is clear that in Japan the wage lag was present, especially in earlier upswings, and that both technological influences (via K/Y) and lagging wages raised the rate of return on capital in the modern sector. Both were present at the same time, and they interacted with one another: this is the essence of the less simple and more empirical case.

Lagging wages or a flexible supply of labour are related to the differential structure. By a flexible supply of labour we mean simply that a small increase in modern wages produces a relatively large increase in the labour supply. The labour supply was flexible because of the productivity differentials which characterized the Japanese economy, and flexibility was additionally supported by a growing population and the comparatively small labour requirements of the modern sector.[16]

The end of the upswing and the ensuing downswing are harder to systematize because there are only two downturns in the record, each of which is strongly affected by different external events. Still, the common features stand out. Towards the end of the upswing, the expected rate of return on capital falls owing to a rise in K/Y caused by a slowdown in the rate of growth of technological progress, which has to be explained by considering specific historical circumstances. (Admittedly, all of the foregoing is stated in very 'ideal–typical' terms.)[17] At the same time, the labour supply will – temporarily – become less flexible as the pool of transferable workers shrinks. All these factors combine to pull down the growth of private capital formation, and during the downswing $\Delta I/I$ and $G(R)$ maintain lower average levels, while to some extent government activity helps to sustain the aggregate investment proportion (I/Y) at a new plateau. After some time, the rate of return on capital will rise again when – because of a renewed wave of technological or organizational opportunities – K/Y begins to decline, and another private investment spurt will have started.[18]

We come now to the heart of the matter: the relationship between long swings in the rate of growth of private capital formation and the trend acceleration of aggregate output. What happened during upswings or investment spurts has already been described: the very rapid expansion of private investment, declining capital–output ratios (especially in the leading expansion industries),[19] and a rising share of private as opposed to public capital formation. In addition, each investment spurt features an identifiable set of growth industries. Foods and textiles accounted for more than half of the growth of manufacturing between 1901 and 1917; in the 1930s, chemicals, metals, and machinery contributed over 60 per cent;[20] during the 1950s and 1960s one would have to assign leading roles to electronics and cars.

Taken together, all these factors establish the strong presumption for viewing investment spurts as periods of innovational changes – i.e.

periods during which technological and organizational progress was imported and introduced at especially rapid rates. Subject to the severe limitations of the previously used production function, this is apparently confirmed by the changing growth pattern of the residual. The measured residual invariably grew more rapidly during investment spurts, and never more rapidly than after the Second World War.[21]

The framework of the production function also suggests a relationship between the input of capital, the residual, and trend acceleration. A stable 'equilibrium' growth path for the private modern sector in the twentieth century can be described by the equation $G(R) = (1 - \alpha) [G(K) - G(L)]$. This equilibrium growth path is simply the production function used previously, where K/Y and α are taken as constants – which was in fact approximately true for the trends. Therefore, in this historical long run, we can reasonably assume a steady relationship between the growth of the residual (technological and organizational progress) and the rate of growth of capital-intensity. Of course, the equilibrium growth path also contains all the necessary ingredients of trend acceleration if – as was indeed the case – the rate of growth of K/L keeps rising over time. But that leaves open the central question: Why is a higher rate of growth of K/L associated with a higher rate of residual growth?

Relationships between $G(R)$ and $G(K/L)$ are not meant to be interpreted as simple causalities. On the contrary, to gain a realistic historical picture of this relationship requires the supposition of complicated interactions. By way of conclusion we should like to offer a few speculations concerning these interactions.

Periodic spurts in private investment of long duration must have had both a supply-production and demand effect. On the supply side, an investment spurt resulted in more rapid capital accumulation, a higher level of capital-intensity, and more output. It would also be reasonable to suppose that new investment, which served as a carrier for imported technology on which Japan depended, contributed towards raising $G(R)$. This is the most direct and simple explanation.

Investment spurts also affected demand because we can assume that the increases in output raised the level and rate of growth of per capita income, especially in an economy in which underemployment was a persistent characteristic; and the rate of growth of per capita income can also affect $G(R)$. To explain the reasoning behind this last assertion requires a much broader view of economic processes.

That Japan was a borrower of Western technology is a well-established fact. Furthermore, in acquiring foreign machinery and know-how Japan was not, in general, limited by the availability of suitable items. In a follower country there always existed room for introducing improvements of foreign origin, and this is why one can take the rate of growth of technological opportunities as given or as externally determined. There is, however, a very different side to this issue. Technology is developed in the most advanced countries, and it conforms most closely to the factor proportions and skills available in the United States or Western Europe. Almost by definition this makes technological emulation a most difficult task for a less-developed country like Japan, in which capital was relatively scarce and labour relatively plentiful. Thus, despite the manifold opportunities for borrowing, there existed also a set of limiting factors which we shall call the level of 'social capability' – those factors which constitute a country's ability to import or engage in technological and organizational progress.

A higher rate of growth of per capita income may raise social capability in two major ways. First, it would improve human capital (better schools, improved diet, etc.), thereby making labour more suitable for work with advanced methods. Second, rising per capita income would also widen the market, thereby improving the possibilities of exploiting economies of scale.[22]

This then is what we mean by the 'interaction' between $G(R)$ and $G(K/L)$. In the simple case one can move from increases in K to a higher level of R. But R can rise because income has risen, and this can lead to a higher level of K/L.

In this chapter we have, for obvious reasons, concentrated on the role of capital. One should not, however, overlook the importance of institutional developments in raising Japan's social capability to import increasing quantities of productive technology. Each investment spurt brought forth new institutions which enhanced this process. Between 1901 and 1917 there arose both the zaibatsu and permanent employment. Combines of the zaibatsu type created early and lasting opportunities for taking advantage of economies associated with large-scale, worldwide operations. Permanent employment led to a labour force which had no incentive to resist even labour-displacing innovations. During the 1930s an alliance between the zaibatsu and government, which centred on military needs, led to the development of heavy industries subsidized by public funds. After the Second World War, the newly created Ministry of International Trade and Industry and the new activities of private banks were both critical factors in furthering the rapid absorption of American and West German technology. Undoubtedly these institutions all contributed to a secular increase in the level of social capability. Furthermore, we believe that these advances were additive: an advance created in one era did not lose its effectiveness in later years. All these are aspects of Japan's trend acceleration in the twentieth century which deserve closer study.

CHAPTER IV

Factory Labour and the Industrial Revolution in Japan[1]

I. *Introduction*

An industrial revolution transforms a traditional society into an industrial one. The primary agent in this process is the factory system, which organizes capital and labour on a scale unheard of in traditional society, on the basis of technology and behaviour that are difficult for 'traditional man' to understand. By the logic of traditional social organization and according to the outlook of traditional man, the human dimension of a typical work place under the factory system is mysterious and fearsome: that is, a large number of workers, far exceeding the population of a typical traditional village, are organized into a work force in which tasks follow the dictates of the technologically determined division of labour but hang together at the same time in an interdependent framework administered by management. In other words, workers are divided and ruled by managers who derive their authority from technology and the market. Whether this new social structure, though limited to the workplace, is a boon or peril to traditional man depends very much upon the style and pace of industrialization. Eventually traditional man is transformed into 'industrial man', as he sheds the traditional outlook and work habits and acquires new personal qualities that enable him to manoeuvre rationally in the class structure of an industrial society. These concurrent transformations, societal and personal, are often fraught with lags and frictions requiring facilitating or regulatory interventions by the state. This chapter sets out to trace these developments in the course of Japanese industrialization. It covers such major aspects of the factory system as the hiring, training, structuring, and rewarding of the work force, the fashioning of principles, rules, and procedures of industrial relations, and the use of state power to regulate and resolve conflicts between workers and managers.

Japan made substantial progress in industrialization during the seven decades between the Meiji Restoration of 1868 and the Second World War, although even at the end of this period Japan was at best a semi-industrialized society. The fiasco of the Pacific war initiated by Japan herself demonstrated the dynastic and atavistic backwardness of her values and the uncontrollable irrationality of her institutional processes. Nevertheless, her transformation into a semi-industrial society was a historical reality of great significance. Although this transformation was not thorough enough to produce even a nineteenth-century equivalent of European liberalism, it at least represented a more or less unique case of industrial revolution in which a non-Western traditional society had managed to absorb the impact of Western industrialism without losing its own national identity or historical continuity. Because of the peculiar circumstances which governed Japan's participation in the worldwide spread of industrialism and the uniqueness of the cultural base on which she erected her industrial system, the expansion of her factory system and the formation of her industrial labour force produced many unusual features unknown in Western labour history.

While the topics of this chapter are limited to the factory sector of the Japanese economy, it is useful to take an aggregative view of Japan's economic growth before the factory sector is extracted from it for an intensive observation and analysis. Unlike post-war Japan's spectacular rate of economic growth, averaging about 10 per cent per annum (stopped by the oil shortage of 1973 and the ensuing 'stagflation'), economic growth in pre-war Japan was a rather leisurely affair. The most careful estimates ever made on Japan's long-term economic performance indicate that between 1887 and 1938 (on the basis of five-year averages centred at the indicated dates) the gross national product in constant prices increased at 3·16 per cent per annum in the aggregate and at 1·94 per cent per capita (the difference being the rate of population growth, 1·22 per cent).[2] The pace of economic growth represented by these figures is certainly moderate, even compared with the performance of average underdeveloped countries after the Second World War. But, historically, Japan's pre-war economic growth is still commendable by the standards that today's developed countries reached at comparable stages of development.

The moderate nature of Japan's pre-war growth comes to the fore when the growth of factors of production is considered along with the aggregate income growth. During the same period, between 1887 and 1938, Japan's labour force increased at 0·8 per cent per annum, while her gross capital stock increased at 3·6 per cent excluding residential stock (or at 2·6 per cent including residential stock).[3] On the basis of these rates of increase in capital and labour, and with the help of an assumption about the relative shares of factors in output – such as, for example, 40 per cent for capital and 60 per cent for labour – it can be calculated that the growth of factors of production alone would have brought about the growth of the gross national product at 1·80 per cent per annum excluding residential stock, or 1·40 per cent including residential stock.[4] Thus, the total growth rate of the gross national product

(3·16 per cent) was far higher than what was possible owing solely to the sheer quantitative growth of factors of production. This 'residual' growth rate, under the stated assumption about the relative shares, amounts to 43 per cent of the total growth rate excluding residential stock, or 56 per cent including residential stock. Different relative shares of factors would naturally produce different values of the residual rate, but it is clear that within conceivable limits of the relative shares the residual would still be quite substantial. What accounts for the residual is a complex issue, as it signifies everything other than the growth of labour or capital as measured in the usual quantitative manner (the number of gainfully occupied persons, and the value of all capital goods in constant prices). Therefore this at least suggests that qualitative aspects of Japan's socio-economic changes ('modernization' is a convenient catch-all term for these changes) were far more important than the mere increases in aggregates associated with capital accumulation and the growth of the work force. These qualitative changes certainly include changes in economic structure, such as the relative expansion of industry and the widening of markets for all kinds of goods and services, as well as improvements in the efficiency of factor use in each sector of the economy.

Now, to turn to the rise and expansion of the factory sector, it is generally accepted that in the early 1870s more than 80 per cent of the gainfully occupied population was in agriculture and less than 5 per cent in manufacturing.[5] The percentage for the factory labour force was infinitesimal. By 1940, the proportion of employment in agriculture had dropped below 50 per cent, enabling Japan at last to look like a non-agricultural society. At the same time, the proportion of employment in manufacturing rose to more than 20 per cent by 1940, but it was only during the 1930s that factories had begun to absorb more than 50 per cent of manufacturing employment.[6] Even so, the 'factory' was generously defined as a manufacturing establishment employing five or more operatives. In hindsight, the incursion of the factory system into pre-war Japan seems rather benign, absorbing only 12 or 13 per cent of the labour force at the end of seventy years of industrialization. Although this fact attests to the resilience and viability of non-factory manufacturing processes in the course of industrialization, as well as to the productivity of all sectors other than manufacturing, the growth of the factory labour force was phenomenal – from a few thousand in the 1870s to nearly four million in 1940, representing roughly a thousandfold increase over seventy years. The wedge relentlessly driven into the Japanese economy by the factory system during this period was the source of several major economic, political, and social convulsions, often shaking Japanese society to its foundations, as will be reviewed in this chapter.

A warning of a methodological nature may be noted in passing. In view of the small proportion of Japan's labour force in factory employment throughout the pre-war period, one may be tempted to conclude that Japan should have been in a state of 'unlimited supplies of labour', in Arthur Lewis's phrase, for her modern sector and that the recruitment of factory labour should have posed no problem at all. Had Japanese employers emerged with the foresight, courage, and calculation that generations of economists have attributed to the hypothetical entrepreneur, they would no doubt have succeeded in taking advantage of the demographic and economic conditions of Meiji Japan and thus ensured themselves unlimited supplies of labour through an appropriate manipulation of pay and working conditions. However, the Meiji employers were just as much a part of the society's traditional backwardness as all other Japanese. The problems related to the hiring, training, organization, and retention of a work force were as formidable to them as capital flotation, factory construction, and technical choice. Although capital was scarce, at least its use posed no problems once they obtained it. But hiring labour was just the beginning of problems of work-force management. In this sense, labour could have been a serious constraint on the rationality of technical choice, the scale of production, and ultimately the general rate of economic growth. Appropriate control over the size, skill, and quality of the work force as required by the expanding, and often fluctuating, output were acquired only after much trial and error. The great pains suffered by workers, employers, and society at large in order to generate an expanding, committed labour force for Japan's factory sector, as detailed in the subsequent pages, should serve as a warning against a cavalier acceptance of the hypothesis that labour is no problem when industrialization takes place in the setting of traditional backwardness.

II. *The Preconditions for Factory Labour, 1850–90*

One prerequisite for the expansion of factory employment is that employers and workers understand their relationship as trading work for wages. To borrow Polanyi's felicitous phrase, labour and land must become 'fictitious commodities' bought and sold in the market. But a transaction that treated land or labour as if they were no different from ordinary commodities was alien to the social organization and economic relations of feudal Japan, and the transformation of feudal into capitalist employment relations was a protracted and complicated process. Although the subject of this chapter is factory labour, changes in the use of labour in agriculture prior to Japan's industrialization are useful as an indicator of how feudal institutions were changing toward capitalist resource allocations and employment relations.

A. FROM SERVITUDE TO WAGE LABOUR IN AGRICULTURE

T. C. Smith describes the development of rural employment relations in feudal Japan as a progressive loosening of the bond between master and servant. It became easier for a servant (*hōkōnin*) to redeem his freedom. Smith notes three types of *hōkōnin* in this respect. 'Least free of the three types was a *hōkōnin* given to someone by his family for an indefinite period in return for a loan. He served as a kind of security on the loan and was compelled to work for the person with no compensation but his keep until the loan was repaid.'[7] However, the loan was usually too large for the borrower to repay, and the *hōkōnin* had no chance to redeem his freedom. The second type in Smith's classification was the *hōkōnin* who, like the first, was put in service for a loan but whose wages were computed and charged against the loan, so that when the loan was repaid the amount actually paid was smaller than what was due by the amount of accrued wages. The third type was the *hōkōnin* whose labour and period of service were reckoned in such a way as to write off the debt completely by the end of the loan period.[8]

So long as labour services were subsidiary to the transaction of loans, employment relations as transactions in wage labour were a remote possibility. However, the development of commercial agriculture gradually changed the situation. The worker customarily still received a lump sum at the beginning of the employment period. But its character changed from a loan to a partial advance payment of wages. The emergence of *hiwari-hōkōnin* (service reckoned on a daily basis), which was already in practice in the early nineteenth century, is a case in point. An employment 'contract' dated 1829 in the Osaka area specifies two years' service on the basis of twenty days per month and stipulates a certain sum of money as a 'wage immediately payable' (*sokkyūgin*).[9] The contract is signed by the *hōkōnin*'s father, the *hōkōnin* himself (aged thirty-three at the time), and two 'guarantors', in that order. It may be emphasized that the *hōkōnin* was not the principal party to the contract, although it was his labour service that was contracted. The contract was accompanied by an affidavit by his father and guarantors stating that in default of the specified service by the *hōkōnin* they would send a substitute or return the advance payment. Records surviving with another family in this area indicate that the number of *hiwari-hōkōnin* consistently fluctuated with the state of farm work between 1838 and 1868.[10]

Furthermore, according to the records of a leading peasant family in the Prefecture of Yamagata, wage-earning servants contracted for three to twelve months (*kyūdori-hōkōnin* or *nenki-hōkōnin*), and servants hired by the day are found together with Smith's second type as early as in 1777. For 1824, however, the debt-linked servants are no longer listed.[11] These examples, together with those mentioned in the preceding paragraph, indicate that many types of *hōkōnin* coexisted for a long time, and there was no neat succession of one type to another over time. But in terms of shifting importance, one can speak of an evolution in employment relations during the feudal period – that is, of an increasing number of shorter-term, debt-free servants, and ultimately of day labourers.

By the early 1870s, a substantial proportion of Japan's rural inhabitants had come to depend for livelihood on day labour (*hiyatoi*). In six villages in the Murayama area, Yamagata, this proportion rose to 12 per cent.[12] A close inspection of the data indicates that the *hiyatoi* in the early 1870 were largely peasants who no longer possessed enough land to fully occupy themselves. Many of them had lost their land completely.[13]

The surveys of agrarian conditions undertaken in 1890 in various prefectures (*nōji chōsa*) clearly indicated that employment relations in agriculture were no longer independent of expanding labour markets for rural and urban industries.[14] Four types of agricultural employment were noted in the survey for Osaka: daily, monthly, semi-annual, and long-term. The first two types of employment strictly depended upon the demand for labour during the busy seasons. The semi-annual employment applied to domestic servants. The long-term employment (*nenki yatoi*), usually from a period of five to seven years, was no doubt a direct descendant of the *nenki-bōkō* of the previous age. But no indication was found concerning the indebtedness of the *nenki* worker.[15] Farming, sericulture, and other by-employments in the countryside competed for the same labour. Weaving, silk-reeling, and cotton-spinning absorbed increasing numbers of women and girls from the farm households. Mining, industry, and construction drew away large numbers of men and boys from the villages. For example, the villages near Osaka lost their workers to Osaka's urban industries and replaced them by workers brought over from other parts of Japan through middlemen in the labour market. This geographical re-shuffling of the labour force was not always smooth. Consequently, complaints about a labour shortage were often heard among the richer farmers.

B. LABOUR SERVICES IN WEAVING

One of the oldest branches of manufacturing is weaving, which during the feudal period was an important by-employment of the peasant households. The hub of the fabric industry was the merchant–employer (clothier – *orimoto*), who put out work to weavers working in their homes. The clothier undertook major preparatory and finishing processes within his factory and trained weavers who would later work under the putting-out arrangement. The clothier also employed adult weavers, mostly women, to work on the looms set up in his factory. The development of the factory system and wage labour in the textile industry meant the expansion of the numbers of directly employed adult weavers. During the feudal period and through much of the Meiji Era, working for the clothier as an apprentice or a weaver was invariably called '*hōkō*' and the worker '*hōkōnin*'.

During the feudal period, it was usual for a peasant family to state in the service contract, as a reason for supplying a *hōkōnin*, that they were hard pressed with the tax burden, implying that *hōkō* was resorted to as a means of raising money for paying taxes. Among the eighty-three remnants of old employment contracts in the possession of two cotton clothiers in the Prefecture of Aichi, two contracts dated 1879 and 1884 indicate that the *hōkōnin* were sent into service precisely for this reason.[16] This kind of tax burden, which originated in the feudal lord's desire to keep the peasantry tied to the land – is no longer mentioned in contracts effected after 1887. The content of the typical contract followed a pattern that was characteristic of feudal employment relations. It specified that the purpose of service was learning how to weave, that the employer would supply clothing twice a year, that the employment period would be extended by the same number of days as were lost through the *hōkōnin*'s illness (if such were to occur), and that the *hōkōnin* and her family would return the cost of her keep, fees for her training, and the loan, principal, and interest, in case she should leave prior to the expiration of the contract. The service contract was signed by the *hōkōnin*, her parent or guardian, and a few guarantors.

Among ninety-four service contracts surviving from the period of 1849 to 1866 at a fabric factory in the Prefecture of Tochigi, a leading centre of fabrics, twenty-seven were renewals by the same workers.[17] For thirteen of these workers, the records indicate that each of them started as a young apprentice for a term of service well beyond five years and, after one or two renewals with successively shorter terms of service, ended up as a weaver hired by the day or by piece. Several young long-term *hōkōnin* returned home to take work put out by the clothier who had trained them. This leaves unexplained how so many other *hōkōnin*, older skilled weavers, had come to be employed by the clothier in question, or where other apprentices trained by him had gone. Perhaps many apprentices trained by this clothier became domestic weavers or *hōkōnin* for other clothiers, while he also used the existing pool of weavers (trained by other clothiers) for obtaining his own short-term *hōkōnin*. Thus, there was evidently something akin to a labour market in this area. Another interesting feature of the ninety-four surviving contracts under discussion is that they are for a wide variety of employment periods. Excepting four unclear cases, the remaining ninety are distributed as follows: thirty-seven for more than three years (fifteen of which are for five to six years), thirty-five for less than three years (of which twenty-one are for one to two years), and eighteen for day work or piece work. Many of the weavers contracted for day or piece work are free of the loans which characterize the other *hōkōnin*, and their wages are higher than those of others. Nevertheless, the *hōkōnin* was not yet a wage-earner. The unusual strength of the putting-out system in the fabric industry had long resisted the full proletarianization of the weavers. And although the custom of calling the employee '*hōkōnin*' tended to disappear in the 1880s, the terms of employment contracts largely remained the same as when she was a *hōkōnin*.[18] The terminology of the factory system was adopted in the fabric industry as in other industries during the 1890s.

C. THE LABOUR MARKET FOR THE RAW SILK INDUSTRY

The production of raw silk was an offshoot of agriculture. Factory-like establishments were fewer in silk-reeling than in weaving during the feudal period. After the Meiji Restoration, owing in part to the government encouragement, there was a remarkable increase in the factory production of raw silk. Because of the rapid transition to the factory system, labour recruitment in the raw silk industry was at first fairly free of the traditional procedure of recruiting *hōkōnin*; but it was not long before a reaction set in due to a tightening labour market. Employers discovered that a 'feudalistic' control of their workers was easier and more profitable than following the dictates of the labour market.

The Meiji Government in the early 1870s encouraged the modernization of raw silk production by introducing Western technology through model factories.[19] Particularly impressive was the silk filature at Tomioka, modelled on French silk-reeling techniques. The operatives trained in the Tomioka Filature were then employed by private mills in other parts of Japan to start operation of newly imported silk-reeling

machines. A private company, the Ono-gumi, had already experimented with less-mechanized Italian techniques in a mill built in
Tsukiji, Tokyo, in 1871. The Ono-gumi had also financed silk factories
adopting these techniques in the Nagano area. The Nagano silk manufacturers were also the first to try French techniques after the superiority
of the Tomioka Filature was demonstrated. Still, among more than
three thousand silk factories employing ten or more workers in 1893,
those using the traditional techniques (*zakuri*) amounted to nearly one-
fourth.[20] Nor do these figures capture the total picture of the silk
industry, since non-factory establishments were of equal importance
in this industry, though less so than in fabrics. According to data for
three relatively advanced counties (*gun*) of the Prefecture of Gunma,
technologically inferior to Nagano but far above the average for a silk-
producing area using Japanese techniques, there were only twenty
'mechanized' filatures among the 24,193 silk-reeling establishments in
1890, and the putting-out system was widespread.[21] This structure was
more representative of the Japanese raw silk industry as a whole. The
broad non-factory base of the raw silk industry implies that there were
large numbers of non-factory workers experienced in silk-reeling
whom the expanding factories could draw upon.

In the 1880s these workers were locally recruited and were paid
wages according to a peculiar combination of piece and time work.[22]
But the quality of silk thread reeled was also important. Therefore,
wages were eventually quoted as daily rates differentiated into several
steps according to the amount of cocoons used and the quality of silk
thread reeled. But once a worker was placed in a certain step indicating
her skill level, she enjoyed the wages appropriate to the step irrespective
of the quantity of work, which naturally varied from day to day,
principally owing to factors not directly under her control. The
identity of personal status and wage rank (*tōkyūbetsu chingin*) was a
general characteristic of wage administration in Japanese factories in
the 1880s.

In contrast to later developments in employment relations in the silk
industry, it is significant that the workers in the silk factories of the
1880s were local commuters and that many of them were married
women. The 'dormitory system', which became almost synonymous
with the factory system in textiles after 1890, did not exist during the
1880s. When lodging was needed near factories, workers found it on
their own. Also, many of the workers at the time of hiring were
already skilled in the sense that they had reeled silk at home. The
women of the farm households engaged in sericulture often worked
in the factories which bought their cocoons. Since the factory method
of reeling was not yet decisively superior to household reeling, there

was no urgency for farm families to send their women and children to the factories. Factory employment was a 'secondary' occupation (*kakei hojo teki rōdō*) in the true sense of the word. And since no mention was made of loans in the employment contracts in the raw silk industry of the 1880s, it may be supposed that the element of coercion over a worker by her employer was minimal. The working day was generally fourteen hours long. This was the normal length of a working day in peasant households, and workers did not object to it in the factories. However, when employers tried to lengthen the working day by half an hour in Kōfu, Yamanashi, in 1886, workers considered it unacceptable. A few spontaneous strikes not only restored the customary working day but shortened it by half an hour in some factories.[23] The fluid and relaxed employment relations in the raw silk industry would lead one to believe that a free labour market – with no disadvantages to the workers, remarkably enough – had finally emerged in rural Japan. Workers and their families were free of debt and of prior commitment to a fixed period of service as a condition of employment. The workers were free to leave any time they wanted to. Yet this kind of labour market frustrated and annoyed silk employers, since they did not know how to expand output and make profits while operating within such a tight labour market. The employers' feudalistic reaction set the stage for the next development in Japanese employment relations.

D. THE METAL AND ENGINEERING INDUSTRIES

In contrast to the predominantly female labour force of the textile industries, workers employed in metalworking and engineering factories were predominantly skilled adult males. They were originally traditional artisans but were drawn into factory employment when the government promoted metalworking and engineering industries.

After the visit of Commodore Perry in 1853, the Shogunate and provinces had reacted to the impact of the West largely through their military reflexes. These military and industrial efforts by the feudal governments were bequeathed to the Meiji Government as a substantial list of capital assets and industrial plants.[24] The Meiji Government itself added more but was forced to liquidate all non-military enterprises because of operational losses which caused tremendous treasury drains. Most of these enterprises were sold to private interests by 1885. The liquidation was completed when the Tomioka Silk Filature was transferred to Mitsui in 1893. Nevertheless, so far as the metal and engineering industries were concerned, throughout the Meiji Era (1868–

1912) the government was employing far more workers than private factories in similar lines.

Unlike weaving and silk-reeling, these government factories had two major problems due to their technology and size. Their scale was enormous by Meiji Japan's standards, creating a grave organizational problem. To this the government responded with traditional techniques of feudal administration. The other problem, far more serious, was to find the proper quantity of skilled labour to work with imported technology. The problems of organization and skills may be illustrated by the experience of government-operated shipyards at Yokosuka and Nagasaki. Although the Nagasaki shipyard passed to Mitsubishi in 1884, these problems did not disappear with the change to private ownership.[25]

The construction of the Yokosuka Shipyard was started in 1865 by the Shogunate and taken over by the Meiji Government. Initially, there were forty-five French engineers and mechanics; their number decreased to twenty-five by 1876, and to one or two by 1885. The activities at the shipyard covered the whole range from iron-smelting to the building and rigging of iron ships. The workers were essentially paid labour. Yet the work-force structure consistently followed the feudal pattern. In 1868 there were fifty-three Japanese officials and clerks and 705 Japanese workers. The officials and clerks were samurai, and the workers artisans and common labourers. There were 575 artisans, of whom sixty-five formed the privileged core (*kakae shokkō*), supported by 113 regular workers (*jōyatoi*) and 397 helpers (*shokkō tetsudai*). In addition, there were fifty-four common labourers. For launching and sailing ships, a similarly structured small group of seventy-six workers was maintained. The difference in status between leading and ordinary artisans followed the feudal pattern in which a small number of artisans (*okakae shokunin*) served the feudal lord directly and held power over the rest of the craft community in the castle town. At first, there were no Japanese engineers or mechanics. The sole function of the Japanese officials and clerks was to manage the work force. The technical organization and supervision of work were left to the Frenchmen. The skills were essentially traditional or adapted from what was then available in Japan, but the French engineers organized them into a system of interrelated processes for making modern products with modern techniques (tools, machines, materials, etc.). Thus the problem that lay ahead of the Yokosuka management was to transform this peculiar duality of modern technology and feudal social relations into a viable system which was Japanese both socially and technically.

Although traditional crafts were adapted to the requirements of modern shipbuilding to a remarkable extent, it was necessary to obtain a corps of Japanese engineers and technicians who could understand modern technology and take over the shipyard operation upon the departure of the French. The Shogunate had inaugurated two training schools, for engineers (*gishi*) and technicians (*gite*) respectively. Although discontinued for a while after the Meiji Restoration, these schools were later reopened under new names. Originally, engineering candidates were selected from among young samurai in Edo and Yokohama; the candidates for technicians were selected from among commoners in or near Yokosuka. In 1876, there were thirty-seven trainees in the 'engineering school' (now called *seisoku gakkō*), and more than fifty in the 'technical school' (called *hensoku gakkō*). The samurai–commoner division was no longer honoured. Young samurai who desired to 'rise in the world through industrial work' also enrolled in the 'technical school', and the presence of samurai in their midst seemed to stimulate the commoner–trainees enormously, so that the performance of all the trainees rose substantially.[26] The ordinary workers who did not go through the training schools learned their skills on the job from senior workers. They were a new breed of apprentices (*minarai shokkō* – trainees on the job). Since internal training alone fell far short of requirements, many were hired from the labour market. The fifteenth of each month was the day of hiring at the gate. Applicants had to be at least fifteen years old, and they were sent to different shops within the shipyard according to their qualifications and the labour needs of each shop. Simple tests were given to evaluate the skills of the experienced workers or the aptitude of novices, and each shop enjoyed substantial autonomy in hiring, training, assigning, promoting, retiring, or dismissing workers. In 1872, the working day in the summer was from 6.30 a.m. to 5.30 p.m., with an hour of lunch break; it was from 7.0 a.m. to 5.0 p.m. in the winter. There were no rest days except on a few traditional festive occasions.

After hiring, training, and assigning workers, one faced the problem of how to keep them as long as they were needed. The employment relations at the Yokosuka Shipyard were essentially 'capitalist'. Even before 1868, workers voluntarily applied for jobs and quit freely without fearing feudal sanctions. Because of competition from new factories after 1868, however, the Yokosuka authorities began to experiment on the method of retaining workers. In the late 1870s, the manual workers at Yokosuka were in three classes: regular craftsmen (*jōyatai*), daily employed craftsmen (*hiyatoi shokkō*), and common labourers (*jōninsoku*). The workers admitted to 'regular' status had to promise to stay for a given number of years (varying according to the worker's age), in return for certain amenities. In addition, the regular workers were exempted from military service. Further experiments were made during the 1880s, but these were largely changes in job titles and manipulations of related allowances and privileges. The frequency of these experiments reflected both the resourcefulness of the Yokosuka management and the difficulty of reducing labour turnover and stabilizing the work force.

A stable work force is meaningless, however, if management cannot use it efficiently. During the Meiji Era, management was largely ignorant concerning daily work performance on the factory floor. Effective work-force supervision was beyond their management techniques, since the feudalistic mentality of Meiji Japan barred interactions between management and workers except for commands and obedience from a distance. One curious result of this status difference and communication barrier was the high degree of autonomy enjoyed by the workers, who clustered around leaders of their own choice and formed informal groups to organize and execute work. The Yokosuka Shipyard authorities reluctantly recognized this fact and tried to co-opt the worker groups into the managerial structure. In 1882, confessing that the availability of manpower kept factory supervision at a minimum, and fearing (for no valid reason) that pilfering and other wasteful uses of materials might result from a lack of supervision, they proposed to create 'worker gangs' (*shokkō kumiai*) headed by gang leaders (*gochō*) appointed from among senior operatives. A gang included five to twenty workers, and each shop manager (*kōbachō*) was directed to organize his workers into such gangs. Gangs were then exhorted to display the *esprit de corps* through collective achievement. Each gang, when its work was slack, was expected to spontaneously help busy gangs. The gang leaders within a shop were directed to meet daily to discuss measures for co-ordination and mutual help. Each leader had responsibility for misdemeanours by his gang members if he failed to detect them early and report them to the shop manager for corrective action.

However, there is no evidence to suggest that the worker gangs ever worked in the way the Yokosuka management had intended. Informal worker groups had already existed and functioned as the basic operational units without management's meddling in their daily activities. By co-opting them into the formal structure and trying to mould them in some fashion by appointing leaders and setting down rules, the Yokosuka management may even have damaged the effectiveness of informal control and discipline among workers under their own arrangements. For example, at the Nagasaki Shipyard, which passed to Mitsubishi in 1884, the evolution of work-force management was not characterized by the formal rules of the official Yokosuka Shipyard.

Until work rules were elaborated for the first time in 1890, work-force management at Nagasaki was frankly admitted to be a system by 'craft masters' pushes and pulls' (*oyakata suiban hō*). The craft masters (formally '*kogashira*' in the managerial structure, informally '*oyakata*' among workers) recruited, trained, rewarded, and disciplined their workers at the Nagasaki Shipyard. The situation was about the same at Yokosuka, but the bureaucratic officials appointed to manage the shipyard cared more about structural neatness than about getting work done. Nevertheless, it is interesting that the naval bureaucracy of autocratic Meiji Japan, by its own admission, had to depend, for the daily work of iron-smelting and shipbuilding, upon the ingenuity and spontaneity of the craftsmen it looked down upon.

More generally, the social process leading to the emergence of a labour market was accompanied by government efforts at fashioning modern rules for Japanese life. A new state, still backward by the international standards of the day, was finally brought into being by the Imperial Constitution of 1889, which brought in its train the Civil Code (1890), the Commercial Code (1890 and drastically revised later), and many other laws and regulations designed for a capitalist system. The Civil Code, for example, envisaged capitalist employment relations by declaring the relationship between employer and worker to be a private contract freely entered into by the parties concerned. In anticipation of the worst cases that might arise under the pretext of a contract (like indentured labour or slavery dressed up as a voluntary agreement), the Civil Code prohibited employment contracts of more than five years and in such cases explicitly enabled either party to dissolve such contracts unilaterally at three months' notice. In most cases, employment relationships could be terminated by either party with notice equal to one-half of the accounting period for wage computation and payment. In emergencies, the contract could be dissolved immediately, though the injured party could contest the legitimacy of the 'emergency' and sue the other party for damages.

III. *Factory Labour, 1890–1910*

Large-scale factory production in the private sector spread rapidly in the late 1880s and the 1890s, led by the cotton textile industry. The factory scales in silk-reeling and weaving also expanded, though not to anything like the extent of cotton textiles. The metal and engineering industries were expanding faster than all textiles, but the latter still had a preponderance of factory employment (65 per cent in 1890 and 55 per cent in 1920). Textiles, metalworking, and engineering together maintained a roughly stable proportion of employment (around 70 per cent) through the decades before the Second World War. The prime characteristics of the labour market until about 1920 were the labour shortage in textiles and the backwardness of work-force management in the metal and engineering works. On account of these extraordinary circumstances, capitalist employment relations, either as an ideal or as a reality, had no chance to emerge.

A. LABOUR SHORTAGE IN TEXTILES

During its early years, the Meiji Government encouraged cotton-spinning by both direct investment and favourable credit to entrepreneurs. The mills were generally small, with 2,000 spindles at most, and were usually operated by water power. They used domestically produced cotton. This period of government encouragement (*shōrei jidai*) came to an end in the early 1880s, however, because of widespread bankruptcies stemming from excessive production costs, insufficiency and irregularity of raw materials, and the difficulties of marketing. These cotton-spinning mills also suffered from managerial difficulties on account of their character as workhouses (*jusanjo*) for the declassés created by the Meiji Restoration. But the failure was the father of innovation. Eiichi Shibusawa, one of the most celebrated 'community-centred' entrepreneurs of the Meiji Era, travelled in England and noted that most cotton-spinning mills had at least 10,000 spindles, five times as many as in the average Japanese mill. He then organized the Osaka Cotton Textile Company and in 1883 began the operation of the first large-scale modern cotton textile factory in the history of Japan.[27] This mill initially had 10,500 spindles, and in a few years more than 60,000. It used steam power and was located in the heart of urban Osaka. Its initial work force in 1833 was under three hundred workers, of whom 80 per cent were women and girls. By 1891 the Osaka Cotton Textile Company was employing nearly four thousand workers, of whom more than three thousand were women and girls. Stimulated by its success, many new mills arose in the late 1880s, and soon the cotton textile industry was heavily concentrated in Osaka.

Between 1887 and 1893, the number of cotton-spinning mills in Japan increased from nineteen to forty and the number of workers from 2,330 to 25,448 persons. Ordinarily one would not associate this situation with intense employer competition for labour. The large urban centres like Tokyo and Osaka could easily have supplied the required number of workers to these textile factories. But the average number of workers needed for starting the operation of a mill was very large, and it was difficult to assemble several hundreds of workers on short notice. Worse still, the new mills wanted workers who could tend the machines immediately. In the absence of advance work-force training, the only source of labour was workers employed by the established mills. Thus each new mill invariably 'stole' workers from older mills at least in numbers large enough to start its operation and train new recruits. Employer competition for labour eventually became general. Each firm, new or old, raided all other firms for experienced workers whenever possible, although while training large numbers of workers at the same time. Under the circumstances, workers themselves quickly learned to turn the state of the labour market to their advantage. The textile workers in the Osaka area frequently changed their jobs, sometimes for no other reason than a desire to see different places. The acute labour shortage turned the employer–worker relationship upside down: the employer had to kneel and beg for help, while the worker stood aloof and pondered the offer.[28]

Labour turnover in cotton textiles was very high during the 1890s. An annual hiring or dismissal rate of 100 to 120 per cent of the work force was common in many factories. At first, a considerable proportion of this labour turnover was voluntary job mobility on the part of the workers. Later, when labour-market intermediation became a flourishing business, much of the turnover was brought about by middlemen's machinations. But during the 1880s and early 1890s – before this complication arose – the fluid labour market was on the whole advantageous to the worker, though it was a woe to the employer. Unfortunately, popular opinion was not ready to accept job mobility as a normal feature of modern life. On the employment relations in cotton textiles during the days of government encouragement, a historian has observed approvingly: 'The wages were low and the period of employment was long. The workers found it a great shame to leave their jobs for whatever reasons. The employment relations were much like the lord–retainer relations of the feudal period.'[29] In the space of a little more than ten years, the traditional values seemed to have collapsed among the workers in cotton textiles. Public officials were alarmed by the new state of the labour market and, with their feudalist ethics, regarded the mobile workers as 'deserters' (tōsō shokkō). Employers, too, considered many possible measures to reduce labour turnover.

The employers' first response was a dormitory for factory workers. By erecting a fence around the dormitory and the factory and guarding the gates day and night, it seemed an easy matter to keep the workers from moving to other employers. In this way, the factory dormitory ceased to be a housing facility and took on different characteristics. Kazuo Okochi observes: 'The girl recruits were as a rule lodged in factory dormitories, which often had more in common with a prison than a welfare institution.'[30] The dormitory, to put it differently, was a storehouse for the human factor of production. The factory was run for twenty-four hours a day on two shifts, for the day and night, each working twelve hours. However, where there were absences, some workers were bound to their machines day and night until their replacements were found. The dormitory rooms ranged from ten to twenty *jō* in area (one *jō*, or one *tatami*, equals three by six feet), accommodating girls at the rate of one per *jō*, or two girls to every three *jō* in better places. It was like covering the entire floor of an unfurnished Western apartment with mattresses and accommodating lodgers at the rate of one person per mattress. Taking a walk outside the dormitory compound was a privilege granted only to those who were so faithful and diligent that the management did not fear their desertion. The same criteria applied to outings on Sundays or holidays. The area outside the dormitory compound was constantly patrolled by the factory's private police force. When attempted deserters were discovered (though many did succeed in deserting despite the careful policing), they were physically punished: slapped, kicked, or beaten. Subject to the whims of the dormitory management, the offenders were sometimes stripped of all their clothes and led stark naked around the dormitory halls carrying signs describing their offences. The predominant concern of the dormitory management was to keep workers from deserting and to ensure a maximum flow of work to the factory. There were also boarding houses operated under special contracts with factories (*shitei geshuku*). The owners made easy loans to their boarders and foreclosed their pay with the co-operation of the factory management. Many of these boarding-house owners were members of well-known gangster groups and had no scruples about scheming for exploiting the mill workers who were defenceless in the face of cold-blooded violence. The boarding-house owners were even more efficient in forcing workers to work and in keeping track of them than the dormitory management.

Three factors were responsible for turning the dormitory into a prison: (1) a fixed term of employment (three to five years), (2) the employers' preference for workers from faraway places, and (3) labour-market middlemen.

As the labour shortage had become more acute, employers in the Osaka area in 1892 agreed to regulate employer competition for labour by a variety of measures, including a fixed term of employment uniformly imposed on textile workers. Toward the end of the 1890s, in all but a few factories, a promise to stay on the job for three to five years was exacted from each worker when he or she was hired.[31] New workers from faraway places, before they knew whether or not they were fit for factory work, were thus 'sentenced' to a term of servitude within the factory–dormitory complex.

The employers' preference for workers from faraway places was a calculated policy. The cotton textile employers' association, *Dainippon Menshi Bōseki rengōkai*, in its 1898 report on the labour conditions in the industry compared the benefits and costs of hiring from local and distant areas.[32] It was observed that workers from faraway places tended to put up with the rigour of factory work and to honour the terms of employment more readily than local workers. The report noted that fifty mills had already extended their hiring areas to a radius of hundreds of *ri* (one *ri* equals roughly 4 km). Regional variations in workers' reputations were also carefully analysed. Workers from Osaka, where four-fifths of the cotton-spinning mills were concentrated, were said to be lazy, footloose, devoid of perseverance, and full of grievances. On the other hand, workers from Hiroshima (to take one favourite example) were lauded for their extreme perseverance, if at times they were slow in learning new skills. About half of the mills engaged in long-distance hiring mentioned Hiroshima as one of their major sources of labour. The Tokyo factory of the Kanegafuchi Cotton Textile Company, for example, at first recruited from Osaka, Aichi, and Niigata, but by 1894 it concentrated on Hiroshima.[33]

The third factor that turned factory dormitories into prisons was the employers' dependence on labour-market intermediaries for obtaining workers from faraway places.[34] The middlemen, interested only in the profit that the 'sale' of workers to factories brought to them, did not care about the well-being of their recruits so long as a minimum of willingness to try a factory job was observed. They used all kinds of tricks, not excluding outright lies, to talk country women and girls into taking factory jobs. Guided by considerations of the ease of persuasion, degree of credulity and need for money among peasant households, the labour-market middlemen focused their attention on the unsophisticated and poverty-stricken peasants in backward areas. A pittance of advance payment accompanied by some gifts, kind words, and a glowing picture of life, work, and pay in factories easily moved these poor inhabitants of the hinterland. Having 'bought' the workers at an exorbitant price, the factory tried to hold on to them as long as possible. The dormitory overseers saw to it that girls were kept at all costs. In this connection, it may be useful to remember that labour-market intermediation has always been a flourishing, if contemptible, business in Japan. Around the turn of the century, when total dependence on men was women's supreme virtue and any kind of independent dealings by women were frowned upon, it was customary that men – fathers, brothers, relatives, friends, or even strangers in acceptable guise – should stand as guarantors when women were involved in business contracts whether for sale of property or for employment. The social inferiority of women was abused in many aspects of Japanese life. Women had no place except essentially as servants in the very households where they were wives and mothers. Girls and unmarried women were 'sold' (that is, put in long-term service in return for a loan) to brothels or for domestic service. Labour-market intermediation for factory girls was only one aspect of a value system and social organization that held women in a grossly inferior position as objects fit for traffic.

Since there were monetary incentives involved, anyone with wits and guts could become a labour-market middleman. The male employees of a textile firm, who pirated workers from other firms, would soon put their skills to their own advantage as independent operators. Sometimes they obtained better positions in other firms by supplying a group of operatives whom they decoyed out of their former work place. Everywhere, the kidnapping of girls became something of a national sport. Labour-market middlemen even ambushed girls at railway stations, diverting them to different employers than those to whom they were originally going. Outlaws, gamblers, pimps, and hooligans in the towns were naturally extremely skilful labour-market intermediaries. The houses of ill repute were their principal customers. They also operated many cheap inns and boarding houses. Textile firms also employed these gangsters to guard the dormitories and to hijack workers from other firms. These middlemen saw little difference between factory employment and brothel service. Their labour-market manipulations included handing girls on from one middleman to another, leading to the large-scale degradation of factory girls. Kidnapping occurred everywhere, in shops, street-corners, playgrounds, and village squares. Ironically, Japan's progress in industrial urbanization threatened at first to bring about a reign of terror for women and girls throughout the country.

Because of the indiscriminate recruitment, many of the girls brought to factories by the labour-market middlemen were unfit for factory work. Nearly one-half of the recruits dropped out in the first six months; about half of the rest failed to reach the end of the contractual period; eventually, 20 to 30 per cent of the initial cohort fulfilled the contracts.[35] The survivors usually re-contracted with the same employer or became regular participants in the textile labour market for several more years. The typical work force of a cotton textile factory around the turn of the century was 80 per cent female. Of these female workers, 60 per cent were aged twenty or under.[36] Though the minimum age varied from factory to factory, about 10 to 20 per cent of all the female workers were fourteen years old or younger. More than half the female workers were accommodated in dormitories. But the commuters were not 'free' by any means. They had to give the same promise of a specified period's faithful work as dormitory inmates and had a fraction of their pay deducted as a surety. Many of them were boarders in the boarding houses which subcontracted dormitory functions under special arrangements. Yet labour turnover was still very high. In 1900, in one factory near Osaka, 1,112 male and 4,524 female workers were carried over from the previous year.[37] During the year, this factory dismissed 1,877 male workers and hired 1,323. The corresponding figures for female workers were 5,824 and 4,762 respectively. The normal dormitory population of this factory at the time was not revealed, but what happened to it in 1900 was reported as follows:

Dismissals:	400 persons
Desertions:	2,800
Discharges for illness:	225
Deaths:	31
Total:	3,456

If it is assumed that 60 per cent of the female workers of this factory at the beginning of 1900 were dormitory inmates, the total number of discharges can be said to have exceeded the dormitory population by 30 per cent. This was about the same as the turnover rate for the factory in question.

Another point of interest shown by the above figures is that the rate of illness and death per year in the dormitory population was 9 per cent. Deaths alone exceeded 1 per cent. By comparison, during the period of 1899 and 1903, the death rates of all Japanese girls in the age group of ten to nineteen ranged between 3·8 and 9·3 per thousand.[38] In 1909, in six northern prefectures (Niigata and others) of Japan known as sources of factory workers, there were 14,834 persons who emigrated for factory work and 5,358 persons who returned. Of the latter, 1,233 persons (23 per cent) were already ill, or fell critically ill after they returned, or died of illness at home. Deaths alone accounted for 5 per cent of those who returned from factory work.[39] As the health hazards of factory work would have been greater in 1900 than in 1909, one should add several dozens of deaths to those who died in the particular factory dormitory in 1900 as mentioned above to give a more complete picture of the fate of factory girls. It is known only that this factory was the Hyogo mill of some textile company, but it may have been the Hyogo branch of the Kanegafuchi Cotton Textile Company, one of the most progressive textile companies in work-force management at that time. Labour conditions in other companies must have been far worse. Indeed, well before 1900 there was a popular belief that factory girls were particularly liable to illness and death, and death was the factory girl's familiar neighbour in everyday life. One former factory girl interviewed by the officials of the Ministry of Agriculture and Commerce said that in her factory she saw people die of illness or accident at the rate of one person per month.[40] Another girl, asked how many had died in the dormitory where she stayed, said 'a considerable number' (*zuibun aru*). At the same time, factory managements failed to treat these dead in a way that would alleviate the fear and sorrow of their workers. One of the former operatives of a certain textile factory, who jumped the fence one night under cover of storm and darkness, recalled that her horror at the casual burials given to dead workers by her former employer had made her brave the dangers of desertion. But then, life in Meiji Japan was short, brutish, and miserable for most people. During the period from 1891 to 1913, life expectancy at birth was only forty-five years; and at the age of ten it was only forty-eight.[41] Far from being a forerunner of modernization, industrialism in Japan was a concentrated and condensed version of the general misery.

As for labour conditions in weaving and silk-reeling, a brief note suffices. During the period from 1890 to 1920, these indigenous industries shared fully in the general expansion of the Japanese economy, employing a large proportion of industrial labour. Large-scale factories were rare, however. The smallest modern cotton textile factories would easily have ranked among their largest. On the other hand, factory employment was larger in weaving or silk-reeling than in cotton-spinning. In 1909, there were 103,000 workers in cotton-spinning as against 155,000 in weaving and 192,000 in silk-reeling.[42] But the recruitment areas of these industries were not as extensive as in the case of cotton textiles and were largely limited to towns and villages within the prefectures where the factories were located, extending to neighbouring prefectures in certain cases.[43] Nevertheless, employer competition for labour and long-distance hiring brought into being the evils of labour-market intermediaries and factory dormitories. The working conditions and dormitory facilities were even poorer in silk and weaving than in cotton textiles. But the silk factories were closed during the winter, and the contracts were negotiated annually during the slack season. The working day was longer than in cotton textiles, ranging from twelve to seventeen hours, though the daily wages were slightly higher. There was some night work, but it was not universal as in cotton textiles. The statistics for length of employment in 205 factories in the Prefecture of Nagano around the turn of the century indicate that 34 per cent of workers had worked one year or less, while 29 per cent had worked three years or more.[44] Similar data for sixteen cotton textile factories in Osaka indicate that 48 per cent had worked one year or less and 21 per cent three years or more.[45] Thus, despite annual contracts and less favourable working conditions, the silk industry enjoyed a higher degree of worker retention than cotton textiles.

In the weaving industry during the period of Japan's 'take-off' in the 1890s, tradition still dominated life and work. The aggregate output of fabrics increased, but this was due principally to the multiplication of household workshops together with the widening of the merchant employers' marketing network. The traditional practice of taking in apprentices (*denshūjosei*) was continued in many weaving establishments. The initial loans and the promises of steady work for a period of years were still prevalent. The intrusion of the labour-market middlemen was accommodated by contracts between them and the parents of prospective workers, delegating to the middlemen all power and responsibility for negotiating with employers on the workers' behalf. The typical contract was couched in language which implied the unconditional subservience of the worker to her employer. But both parties knew that the words were only rhetoric, so that no litigation ever arose over the terms of the contract.[46]

B. MANAGERIAL BACKWARDNESS IN THE METAL AND ENGINEERING INDUSTRIES

Until the First World War, Japan's metal and engineering industries were in a primitive state. As late as in 1909, there was more employment in government-owned factories than in private enterprises, though the expansion of the private sector during the First World War remedied this situation. In 1920, therefore, employment in the private sector outweighed that in the public sector by a ratio of three to one. During the Meiji era, with the exception of basic metals, heavy machinery, and shipbuilding, small-scale workshops dominated the metal and engineering industries. The industrial revolution in these industries was small, but it was a social revolution – it provided an outlet for the manual aptitude of the Japanese and obliterated the status and privilege of the traditional artisans. The Meiji Government abolished the traditional craft guilds which had controlled access to manual trades, and under the stimulus of imported consumer goods, the variety of products that could be made or repaired in household workshops increased. In the mind of the public, the proud artisans were grouped together with all these domestic workers (*shokōgyōsha*) without allowing for their specialized skills and tradition. With the increased commercialization of the economy, the traditional crafts and new manual trades came under the control of merchant employers. Metalworkers (blacksmiths, casters, cutlers, pattern-makers, turners, and so on) went to work in factories or operated their workshops under subcontracting arrangements. Some of them expanded their workshops into small-scale factories, reducing the journeymen and apprentices to the position of hired hands. Thus the socio-economic forces inside and outside the craft community conspired to cheapen the social standing of the traditional crafts.[47]

The traditional apprenticeship, where it survived, was a grossly outmoded training technique. The apprentice was considered no better than a household servant. The master often lacked formal education and was not capable of explaining his trade systematically to his apprentice. Only the exceptional masters welcomed their youngsters' pursuit of formal education. Watching hands rather than reading books was their way of learning skills. In fact, before the Second World War – but especially before 1914 – acquiring skills was a kind of occult art akin to a personal religious experience. An objective analysis or explanation was considered vulgar. The skill was transmitted from master to apprentice through many years of close relationship and co-operation in all aspects of life and work. The union of minds (*ishin denshin*) was the basic principle of skill training. Of course, young men found this type of training highly frustrating, and the attrition rate among apprentices was very high. Remarkably, some youngsters did survive the period of frustration and uncertainty in traditional apprenticeship. These, together with craftsmen coming up from factory apprenticeships, became periodical additions to the supply of skilled workers for the metal and engineering industries. From among them, new craft masters emerged running their own workshops or supervising work teams in factories. They then took their turn in training the next generations of craftsmen.

In the factory, skill training was casual up until the end of the First World War, owing to a general backwardness of work-force management. Young workers in the age group susceptible to training (those in their teens) increased from less than 10 per cent of factory employment before 1890 to nearly 20 per cent on the eve of the First World War, in the metal and engineering industries.[48] Many of these young workers were in the process of learning skills, but in a majority of factories they were 'apprentices' (called *minaraisei* or *shūgyōsei*) only in name. They were not given the formal courses or work schedules necessary for systematic skill acquisition. Around 1900, there were two types of apprenticeship in the factory.[49] One was a variant of traditional apprenticeship in which a craft master came to work in the factory with his journeymen and apprentices and continued the workshop type of training. The other kind of training was a variant of on-the-job training which, it was hoped, would be acquired by youngsters while they were working in the midst of craftsmen as their helpers. No formal instruction was given to the young workers. They swept the floor, cleaned machines and tools, made tea, and ran errands for the craftsmen. If luck was with them, they received a few moments of guidance from this or that craftsman. The concept of a 'trade' tended to disappear from factory work. It was broken down into a series of specific tasks, and by knowing how to do one or another task, a worker could style himself a craftsman. By learning one task here and another there, alert workers were able to learn the whole 'trade'.

The absence of systematic skill training in Japanese factories before the First World War reflected the dearth of managerial talent required to organize, maintain, reward, and motivate a large number of workers as a single unit within the factory. An easy way around this impasse was to call in groups of craftsmen from outside and to form a work force via subcontracting relationships with these groups within the factory. The Japanese shipyards have been particularly adept at using such subcontracting groups. Adaptation of this type of decentralized work-force management was the method which the Yokosuka Shipyard formalized, owing to circumstances previously described. It was an arrangement under which group leaders were appointed, from among the workers hired by the factory, according to age, length of service, skill, or any other quality that would enable them to command the other workers' respect. They were then given a wide range of employer-like privileges, i.e. power and responsibility for managing their groups within broad guidelines laid down by the factory management. While the degree of autonomy of the group varied from factory to factory, this was the principal method of work-force management in Japanese factories before the First World War.

The group leader (called variously *kogashira*, *kumichō*, *gochō* (where the title of *kumichō* was not used), *joyaku*, *sewayaku*, etc.) hired, fired, and trained his underlings within broad limits in response to the fluctuating demand for labour in the factory. The management's function concerning the work force was thus reduced to keeping accounts of wage payments. The group leader was the *de facto* employer so far as the ordinary workers were concerned. He was seen as the *oyabun* or *oyakata* (parental role), while the workers perceived themselves as the *kobun* or *kokata* (filial role). In this way, the role structure in the factory was closely aligned with the prevailing social patterns and ethics. The factory was like a large village composed of many workshops, and each workshop was a kind of extended family anchored to the principle, ethos, and structure of the Japanese family. To society at large, the factory *oyakata*'s reputation was equivalent to that of a workshop-owner or craft master. Once his social standing was so fixed, he became the first point of contact for any worker seeking a job in the factory. The subdividing of the factory into workshops closely aligned to the general pattern of social organization reduced workers' fears and misgivings about the imposing size, strange appearance, and impersonal character of the factory. A worker was a member of his *oyakata–kokata* group, not an employee of the factory. Unlike the latter-day workers of Japan, a Meiji craftsman would rarely name the factory as his employer, nor would he derive any particular pride from mentioning its name. His pride was in his trade and in belonging to the circle of a respectable *oyakata*. The Meiji labour market for skilled metalworkers was a nexus of such social groups. Workers moved among factories by utilizing the network of references among the well-known *oyakata*.[50] The coveted goal for any worker was to establish himself as an *oyakata* with his own workshop and *kokata*.

The mobility of craftsmen during the Meiji Era was high, but it was less a strategy for economic gains than a cult or a step in the lives of craftsmen. When direct personal experience was practically the sole method for learning a trade, an aspiring journeyman had to travel widely in order to increase his knowledge of the world and to improve his skills so that he could be a respectable *oyakata* at a later stage. Since travelling was accepted as something fashionable, it was also practised by many workers as a cult without any other purpose. By practising it, however, the mobile workers became agents of technological diffusion because of their wide exposure to techniques and opportunities in different places. Therefore the mobile workers were generally considered more skilled and knowledgeable than those who stayed with the same employers for a long time. A report on the Nagasaki Shipyard explicitly recognized that workers who had travelled widely were often more skilled than workers who were trained and retained by the Shipyard.[51]

During the Meiji Era, the status of wage-earner was generally regarded as temporary. With age and experience, one hoped to rise to a supervisory position in the factory or to become a craft master on his own, with a concomitant rise in social standing. Because of this incomplete proletarianization of factory labour, the trade-union movement that arose among metalworkers toward the end of the nineteenth century proved to be far from a movement of wage-earners primarily interested in job security, wage increases, or improved working conditions. After having withdrawn legal status from all kinds of feudal guilds, the Meiji Government soon realized that free enterprise and occupational mobility tended to result in excessive competition in certain trades, coupled with a reduction in product quality. In 1885, the government therefore began to encourage the formation of trade associations (dōgyō kumiai) according to official guidelines defined in a series of regulations. A trade eligible for the formation of an association was broadly defined as a gainful activity in agriculture, industry or commerce. Craft associations, organized within the legal framework for dōgyō kumiai, were particularly successful among building trades. They regulated individualistic competition among members, endeavoured to secure favourable and uniform pay scales, policed the quality and standards of work, and contributed toward their members' moral uplift and educational development.[52] Since these were also some of the activities that trade unions would pursue, it seemed an easy matter to turn craft associations into craft unions. However, this process did not prove to be as simple as that.

The earliest attempt to organize a craft union was Dōmei Shinkō Gumi promoted in 1889 by craftsmen employed in the Ishikawajima Shipyard, the Army Arsenal, and other public and private engineering works in the Tokyo area. In addition to carrying on the activities of a trade union, the Dōmei Shinkō Gumi hoped to accumulate funds to build its own co-operative factory in order to employ its members and to train apprentices for the craft. This last hope was frustrated owing to an improper management of funds, and the union itself subsequently collapsed.[53]

The first trade union worthy of the name in Japanese labour history was Tekkō Kumiai (Metalworkers' Union), organized in December 1897 in Tokyo under the auspices of the Rōdō Kumiai Kiseikai (Society for the Promotion of Trade Unions).[54] Many of the workers related to the former Dōmei Shinkō Gumi joined the new Metalworkers' Union. The greatest attraction of the new union was its mutual-assistance scheme to pay benefits to dues-paying members in cases of work injury, sickness, and death. The union also organized co-operative stores. But the union's activities never reached the point of collective bargaining with any employer. In three years its failure was evident; the union rose and fell with the success and failure of its mutual-assistance scheme. The union had aspired to be a trade union but disappeared before it showed any signs of developing into one. There were many reasons for its failure. The main reason was that workers were not ready for a trade-union movement. The assistance scheme was an incentive for workers to join the union, but they wanted the benefits without paying for the costs. For example, although the union claimed a membership exceeding 5,000 in forty-two locals at its zenith three years after its organization, the dues-paying members were only one-fifth of the total membership. In addition, police harassment was constant, culminating in the Japanese Diet's hurried passing of a Public Peace Police Law in 1900. Although workers' organizations as such were not outlawed and the Metalworkers' Union was not officially dismantled, the trade-union movement could no longer exist under the regulations stipulated in the Public Peace Police Law. After 1907, no more was heard of the Metalworkers' Union.

The membership of the Metalworkers' Union largely consisted of craftsmen in supervisory positions and their close associates in various factories. Given the shortage of skilled workers in Japanese factories during this period and the high voluntary job mobility, job protection was not an issue for most metalworkers. Thus the principal factor which built and sustained labour movements in other countries, namely job scarcity, was absent in Meiji Japan. Furthermore, the shortening of the working day, which gave rise to a social movement at an early stage in other countries, was not among the objectives of the Japanese labour movement. Around the turn of the century, the working day ranged from ten to twelve hours, including a lunch break of thirty minutes or less, or sometimes none at all.[55] However, there were conflicting tendencies concerning the amount of work. Compared with the experience of Yokosuka and Nagasaki in the early Meiji years, the working day had become longer by an hour or more everywhere by 1900. But unlike the earlier period, two days of rest per month had become common. At a few factories, there were three days of rest. At the Nagasaki Shipyard and the Shibaura Engineering Works, weekly rest in the Western fashion was provided for. At the same time, given the autonomy of the *oyakata*-led worker groups, the intensity of work was no doubt adjusted to the level considered appropriate by them. Wages in the metal trades were fifty to eighty per cent higher than unskilled wages in cities or villages. However, the household economy was in difficulty, for the metalworkers' life style, with a heavy emphasis on the excellence of manual performance and magnanimity of heart, put a low value on careful pecuniary calculations such as savings and expenditure planning.[56] Under the circumstances, it was quite consistent with the reality of work and life that the Metalworkers' Union was more active in the organization of co-operative stores and mutual assistance than in fighting for economic ends within the factory. About thirty co-operative stores were built by locals of the Metalworkers' Union, and many continued to prosper independently of the union.

The Society for the Promotion of Trade Unions was also equally enthusiastic about the promotion of co-operatives of all kinds. In addition to co-operative stores, the Society proposed co-operative factories, housing co-operatives, and credit unions. These proposals were not realized, with the exception of one co-operative factory which enjoyed a brilliant, but short-lived, success. An affiliate of the Society, Kōgyō Dantai Dōmeikai (Federation of Industrial Organizations – a misleading title for workers' organizations), was a case in point. It was an association of metalworkers, drawing its membership, numbering 800, from the Army and Navy arsenals located in many parts of Japan and Formosa. In 1900, the Federation established a co-operative factory in Koishikawa, Tokyo, for the production of machines and tools. As might be expected of a co-operative venture of craft masters, the factory was keenly interested in enforcing rigorous apprenticeship. Heartened by the financial success of the factory, however, the members retired their original subscriptions, assuming that profits alone would ensure the continuation of the factory. It then terminated its status as a co-operative as of 1906 and continued to operate as a private business for a while longer, under the ownership and management of key figures in the Federation.[57]

There were other unsuccessful attempts at trade-union organization around the turn of the century. The basic reason for the failure of trade-union movements at this time was that the skilled workers, if they happened to be working for wages at a particular time, hardly saw themselves as permanent members of the wage-earning class. They envisaged their future as workshop-masters on their own account. Self-employment, not paid employment, was the idea, and it was reasonably within reach for many workers. The early trade-union movement would have fared better had the unions styled themselves craft associations. Indeed, a trade-union leader himself, Sen Katayama (1860–1933), spoke about sawyers' and plasterers' associations as examples of successful organizations of workers.[58] In the meantime, quite independently of the success or failure of the trade-union movement, the individual privilege and prestige of the *oyakata* in the factory continued unimpared. Some of the *oyakata* had acquired extensive influence over other *oyakata* and their underlings as a consequence of informal sociopolitical forces within the factory and community. The leading *oyakata* collected around themselves large groups of followers and took advantage of management's passivity in order to secure preferential treatment (i.e. better jobs, overtime, subcontracting, etc.). It was reported that some of these influential *oyakata* came to work leading large entourages, numbering tens or hundreds depending upon the factory size.[59] The workers who were not members of the powerful groups were saddled with the worst jobs and had little chance for better work or higher pay. Occasionally, their dissatisfaction erupted in disputes, quarrels, and even physical violence. It also showed up in quick labour turnover, high absenteeism, mass sabotage, and other outlets for grievances. The sudden increase in industrial conflicts which took place after the Sino-Japanese War (1894–5) was attributed in part to these ordinary workers' complaints about the disproportionate power and privilege of some *oyakata*. Ironically, the factory-owner, who was the true employer, was spared these complaints thanks to the protective layer of *oyakata* who faced and settled the disputes with workers. With time, this factory life changed as well as society as a whole. After the Russo-Japanese War (1904–5), the ordinary workers rose up against the factory management, and the *oyakata* workers acted merely as intermediaries between workers and management. These direct conflicts between management and workers indicate a change in the status and power of the *oyakata* and in work-force management.[60] This change will be reviewed in the next section.

Looking over the industrial scene of Meiji Japan, one feels that the adjustment of employment relations to the emerging industrialism was a difficult, often painful, process. Despite the belief of many Japanese to the contrary, the virtuous tradition anchored to the employer's absolute, though ideally benevolent, authority and reciprocated by the employee's good-natured and unconditional loyalty was not workable in large factories. But employers generally rejected a labour market based on wage incentives and the freedom of occupational choice as valid alternatives to traditional Japanese life. The prevailing labour shortage intensified their reactionary longing for the past pattern of employment relations, creating cruel despots in textile mills or effete feudal lords of a classic type in metal and engineering works. Dangers implicit in traditional authoritarianism spelled personal catastrophe for factory girls in textiles. Although the craft communities in the metal and engineering industries represented an ingenious interim synthesis of traditional life style and industrialization, they were a tremendous drag on efficiency and technological progress. The labour market at the time favoured the workers, but they were no more committed to market behaviour than were employers. Labour-market participation was only temporary, and early withdrawal into domestic life or self-employment was characteristic. Workers who remained in the market beyond a certain time were regarded as gross failures and were denied social status. In autocratic Meiji Japan the poor had no suffrage, and workers, as long as they depended on wages, had no chance to earn enough to vote. In the meantime, employment relations in the factory sank into chaos, inefficiency, and indignity.

IV. *The Emergence of Japanese-Style Management*

A contract is meaningless unless both parties can read and understand its terms; nor can it be equitable unless both parties are on an equal footing in negotiating its terms. The worker in particular is at a grave disadvantage unless he is free and knowledgeable about the rights and obligations stipulated or implied in the contract he concludes with his employer. These qualities, however, depend primarily upon education. Regrettably, one must recognize that Meiji workers were deficient in the qualities that would have made them the equals of their employers. Although the Meiji Government's sense of law and order easily turned into the oppression of the masses, atomistic but equitable contractual relations were recognized as the line of least resistance in the modernization of employment relations, as evidenced in the Civil Code. In addition, the Meiji Government did other things relating to industrialization and labour conditions, of which two most relevant to the issue at hand were universal elementary education, and measures to redress power imbalances between employer and worker. The latter finally took the form of the Factory Law of 1911 and its associated rules and regulations.

The Meiji Government's objectives in modernizing Japan were summarized in two slogans: '*bummei kaika*' ('civilization and enlightenment'), and '*fukoku kyōhei*' ('a rich country and a strong army'). The first slogan was comprehensive enough to gain support or acknowledgement from all classes. The second slogan, in the course of time, created a dilemma. Capitalism and private enterprise seemed eminently capable of delivering the goods to enrich the country. But a strong army needed sturdy and intelligent soldiers. Since youths tended to be overworked in their early years, their physical fitness for military service was very low. Factory girls grew up under circumstances hazardous to mind, health, and morals. Later, as wretched wives and mothers, they failed to rear their sons to be good soldiers. There was therefore a serious conflict between *fukoku* and *kyōhei*, which was resolved only when private business learned how to maximize profit while strengthening workers' health and intelligence. The Meiji Government's response to the conflict was the Factory Law, which business at first instinctively rejected. Faced with unusual firmness on the part of the government, business leaders then changed tactics by stalling the legislation and improving their conduct in the hope of obviating the legislative intervention. But in the course of time, business discovered that greater output and profit were not irreconcilable with better working conditions. Out of this discovery emerged a Japanese-style management, major features of which are now well known in the sociology of the Japanese factory.[61]

A. ELEMENTARY EDUCATION

At the beginning the Meiji Government entertained a grand dream about education.[62] The objective was universal literacy at short notice. According to the educational system instituted in 1872, the whole country was divided into eight university districts, each of which was in turn subdivided into thirty-two secondary-school districts, with 210 elementary schools for each secondary school. Elementary education had two cycles with four years in each, the first cycle being compulsory. Secondary education also had two cycles, of three years each. Finally, fourteen years of elementary and secondary education were to be crowned with four years of university. Various levels of special and technical schools were also envisaged, though not emphasized, for those who would not qualify for the course leading to university. This grand scheme was a great failure from the start. Since the government had no resources, the cost of elementary education had to be partly borne by the localities and families of the school-going children. To poor farmers, compulsory education appeared as an encouragement to the children to loaf in school when they could be helping on the farm. In some poorer parts of Japan there were a number of riots against compulsory education, in which hundreds of school buildings were destroyed.

Eventually, the government learned the lesson and experimented with more realistic principles and methods of education. Educational policy was very much in flux in the 1870s and 1880s. The Matsukata deflation of the 1880s reduced school attendance. The new school ordinances in 1886, the Imperial Constitution of 1889, and the Imperial Rescript on Education of 1890 finally stabilized the purpose and organization of education in Japan. The rapid economic expansion of the 1890s helped ease the economic burden of education for the government as well as for the common households of Japan. The Japanese school system during the first twenty years of the Meiji period was particularly deficient with respect to vocational and professional training. Remedies began with public subsidies to vocational schools in 1892 and became firmly established with the ordinance for vocational and professional schools issued in 1899.[63] The period of compulsory elementary education was extended to six years in 1907, while the second cycle of elementary education was cut to two years.

The spread of education and the emergence of an educated populace were a slow, often frustrating process. Only a modest accomplishment was made during the Meiji Era. At the end of the Edo period, according to Dore, the school attendance rate may have been 40 per cent for boys and 10 per cent for girls.[64] Allowing for the secular rise in school attendance which occurred during the Edo period, one may say that the literate were at most 30 per cent of the working-age population at the end of the Edo period. During the Meiji Era, the educational level of the Japanese population rose slowly, even haltingly, during its earlier years. In 1910, only 41 per cent of males and 23 per cent of females in Japan's working-age population had finished elementary or higher education.[65] If one-half of the rest were 'literate', the literacy rate of the working-age population in 1910 would be about 70 per cent. The rise in the literacy rate from 30 per cent to 70 per cent during the Meiji Era may appear to be an impressive accomplishment, but the qualitative content discounts the quantitative indicator.[66]

To the distress of many Japanese, the educational effectiveness of the time spent in school or in learning in general is reduced by the difficulty of the written language.[67] Western historians often identify literacy by the ability to sign one's name and have attempted to trace the development of literary at the pre-industrial stage of Western economies through marriage contracts signed by the marriage partners. This convenient yardstick of literacy is useless in Japan because the ability to write the specific symbols representing one's name does not imply that the person understands all the ideographs required for effective communication in daily life. There are two sets of forty-seven phonetic symbols each (kana) which in principle can be used to spell any word in Japanese. But a knowledge of these symbols alone does not constitute literacy in the Japanese culture: even the daily newspapers would be beyond the ability of anyone with that level of literacy. It is doubtful that the full four years of elementary education during the Meiji Era provided people with the ability to handle the number of ideographs necessary for effective communication. Several hundreds of these symbols would have been a bare minimum. On many occasions, thousands were necessary.

Due to the historical accident of cultural borrowing from China, ignorance was perpetuated in Japan by a barrier more formidable than in other countries. In 1894, deploring the absence of a labour movement in Japan, one of the first trade-union organizers, Fusataro Takano, pointed to ignorance as its principal cause. Without education, the working people lacked the motivation for a better life. Without this motivation, he concluded, there would be no labour movement.[68] A few years later, he was happily surprised to discover that his call for organization did reach thousands of workers. But it turned out to be a short-lived triumph, for the movement collapsed in a few years.

Takano's letter to workers urging them to organize – *Shokkō shokun ni yosu* (*To My Friends Who are Workers*) – was brilliant and heart-warming, written in excellent literary Japanese, as different from spoken Japanese as Shakespeare is from modern English. It employed more than five thousand different characters (*kana* and *kanji*), many of which required more than fifteen strokes to write.[69] A majority of today's university students, educated in simplified writing and more familiar with loan-words from Western languages than with those from Chinese, would fail to understand Takano's letter; the workers in 1897 would have been even more helpless. One reason for the failure of the labour movement to capture more workers and to sustain itself may thus very well have been the unwieldiness of written Japanese. Therefore, when the police suppressed public speech, mass rallies, group recreations, etc., workers' loss of control over the spread of ideas was almost total. The barrier to effective literacy created, on the one hand, a small group of radical intellectuals – the intelligentsia – who monopolized theory and, on the other, the lagging masses whose social values and economic behaviour perforce remained traditional and unimaginative. Workers' dissatisfaction and frustration at times exploded in a variety of collective protests; but ideals, principles, and logic, which alone can turn discontent and protest into a sustained social movement, were notably absent among workers of Meiji Japan.

Under these circumstances, it is not surprising that only 15 per cent of male and 8 per cent of female workers in six cotton textile factories in Osaka in 1898 had completed four years of compulsory elementary education. Those showing no signs of education amounted to 29 per cent of male and 42 per cent of female workers in these factories.[70] The rest were considered 'slightly educated', meaning that although they fell short of the standard of full elementary education they were not completely illiterate either. About this time, workers in an engineering works in Osaka showed a higher level of education; 25 per cent of them were graduates of elementary or higher schools.[71] Workers at the Nagasaki Shipyard were much better educated, nearly half of them having finished elementary or higher levels of education. Among the least educated were workers in cement factories. In one of these, female workers were 100 per cent illiterate – not even 'slightly educated'. Even among the males, total illiteracy amounted to 80 per cent in this factory. Workers in raw silk factories were comparable to those in cotton textiles, while workers in the fabric industry were inferior to the latter. The glass and match factories were the worst sweat-shops, exploiting workers from the most poverty-stricken and least educated segment of the population.

Deplorable though it was, the quality of factory workers described above was no worse than that of the general population. In 1905, only 30 per cent of men and 12 per cent of women in the working-age population were graduates of elementary or higher schools. By 1910, these proportions had increased to 41 per cent and 23 per cent respectively.[72] These were rather rapid changes for a period of five years. For the same reason, the level of formal education of the general population in the years before 1900 would have been far worse than in 1905 – perhaps as bad as that of factory workers quoted earlier. In contrast, a Home Ministry study of 344 factory workers in Tokyo in 1912 showed that of 312 married male workers nearly 75 per cent had at least completed elementary education, while 41 per cent of their wives had done so. Those who had 'no education' were only 7 per cent of the men and 33 per cent of the wives.[73] The workers of 1912 were thus far better educated than workers of 1900.

One may infer that factory workers of the 1910s were on the whole more knowledgeable and more self-assured than those of the 1890s. Despite this improvement over time, however, the perspective of factory workers at the end of the Meiji Era was still imprisoned in a negative self-image. In 1912, among the aforementioned 344 factory workers in Tokyo, those who claimed that they had become factory workers out of their own preference or volition were barely 10 per cent of the workers interviewed. Diverse involuntary factors, which suggest that one would not have taken a factory job had there been other choices, accounted for two-thirds of the stated motives or reasons for becoming factory workers. These factors were revealed by answers like 'having lost other jobs', 'compelled by family poverty', and 'persuaded by parents and friends'. Conviction, dignity, and pride were hardly visible among the answers given by these workers. On the eve of the First World War, Japanese workers had not yet acquired the fierce class-consciousness of European workers or the rugged individualism of Americans. Given the workers' passivity, employers were in a privileged position to experiment on various methods of work-force management for the avowed goal of profit maximization. Indeed, after the Russo-Japanese War (1904–5), an increasing number of employers initiated such experiments in search of better approaches in work-force management.

B. COTTON TEXTILES[74]

The employers' problem, when reduced to its essence, was simply how to attract and hold the quantity and quality of labour required for production and how to motivate the work force to perform in ways that would maximize their profits. When employers became aware that the 'know-how' of work-force management was considerably variable and subject to choice rather than being fixed in a single set of traditional behaviour patterns, they were beginning to acquire the much-needed analytical and rational outlook which later led to the improvement of work-force management. Certainly, such an outlook was not to be generated overnight. It also depended on education. After the turn of the century, however, the management of Japanese business was increasingly transferred to a new generation of business-men and managers who were highly educated in Japan and abroad. The modernization of management therefore started at the top and trickled down to the factory level.

The largest and most attractive employer for educated persons during the Meiji Era was the civil service. Due to large salary differen-tials between the civil service and private business, private business was not attractive to university graduates. The degree of attractiveness of the civil service was particularly high before 1890. When he entered Mitsui in 1891, Hikojiro Nakamigawa (1854–1901), one of the most highly educated persons of his day, initiated a managerial revolution by doubling the salaries of the directors by a profit-sharing device and raising those of managerial personnel in varying degrees all down the line. The effect of this reform was an influx of educated manpower into Mitsui concerns, demonstrating the obvious truth that the higher the pay, the larger and better the supply of labour. One reform led to another. Some years passed, and tension arose among salaried managers on the question of equitable salary scales. There had now developed wide income differentials between the directors (*jūyaku*) and the directors of departments or branch offices (*buchō* or *shitenchō*). The source of this gap was the distribution of 10 to 20 per cent of the net profit to the *jūyaku* class in the form of bonuses, which was a legacy of Nakamigawa's reform. In the early years of the twentieth century, Shigeaki Ikeda (1867–1950), who later rose to the highest position in the Mitsui zaibatsu, led a protest against the meagre rewards accorded to young executives. A further equalization of pay occurred, spreading the benefits of the House of Mitsui over a larger number of persons.

As salaried managers in time moved up to business directorships, the demand from below for greater equality and rationality was increas-ingly realized. As managing director of the Fuji Spinning Company in 1906, Toyoji Wada (1861–1924) – once one of Nakamigawa's lieuten-ants – reduced the directors' bonuses from the customary 15 per cent to 5 per cent of the net profit, using the other 10 per cent for bonuses, pensions, and benefits for other managers, staff employees, and factory operatives. Another business leader who grew up under Nakamigawa's influence, Sanji Mutō (1867–1934), became an evangelist for modern management and demonstrated his ideals through the Kanegafuchi Cotton Textile Company, with which he stayed for thirty years beginning in 1894.[75]

Examples of efforts observed in cotton textile firms after the Russo-Japanese War (1904–5) may now be summarized. There were three interrelated problems: absenteeism, labour turnover, and recruitment. The traditional technique of handling the problem of absenteeism was to attribute it to workers' sloth and to resort to punitive measures. The factory dormitory was particularly conducive to managerial despotism. The reluctant workers were hunted out and subjected to physical torture. Accrued wages were often confiscated. Medical facilities, the pride of Japanese textile firms in later years, were first brought into being for the necessity of checking upon the feigned illness of dormitory workers and of those who ended their day's work before the closing time. The modernization of work-force management was marked by a transition from punishment to inducement.

The first step in a constructive approach to the improvement of work-force management was to ascertain and analyse relevant data. Research and analysis were the first habits that management had to acquire before it could hope to do something useful about the organization and utilization of the work force. Upon researching their own records, some cotton textile firms discovered that the ups and downs in absenteeism within each month were found to be related to the method of wage computation prevalent in those days. At a spinning mill in Osaka, for example, the work records were closed on the twentieth day of each month, and the wages accrued during the month ending on this day were paid on the fifth of the next month. The daily attendance records showed that attendance fell drastically after the twentieth day, reached the bottom on the twenty-third, increased irregularly until the fifth of the following month, then fell drastically again until the ninth, after which attendance steadily improved until the twentieth. Some firms therefore made every day a payday for a certain group of workers, so that, given the rate of absenteeism following payday, there would at least be a stable, predictable level of absenteeism. More popular were a variety of bonuses, paid on an individual as well as on a group basis. Payments in addition to the regular daily wages were made to individuals or groups of individuals who worked without absence for a whole month. The bonus sometimes took the form of exemption from boarding charges for workers housed in the factory dormitory. Another form was a remittance of additional cash directly to the homes of the workers in the hope that parents might become instrumental in encouraging their children to cultivate regular work habits. A group bonus was also used; one form of it was to improve the facilities of the dormitory rooms for commendable groups of workers, so that they could share in an increase in comfort as the fruit of group effort.

In addition to the day-to-day instability of the work force, there was also the problem of high labour turnover. In some mills, labour turnover was seasonal, the difference between the peak of the work force (March and April) and the trough (August) often amounting to 30 per cent of the annual average. Given the regularity of the fluctuation, however, one counter-measure was to employ two groups of workers, so that when one group was falling below the normal level of work requirements, the other group could be called in to fill the gap. Temporary workers were often hired from the neighbouring communities. There were some ingenious and elaborate measures. One large establishment hired a number of girls of twelve to fourteen years of age, housed them in dormitories, taught them factory work part of the time after school, and used them as supplementary workers to fill vacancies due to seasonality or absenteeism. A few mills had a training course for the wives and daughters of the salaried employees for similar purposes. There were also attempts to reduce labour turnover by differential rewards for long and steady work records. These rewards were various in form but were always related to, or scaled upwards by, the length of service – e.g. periodic increments, bonuses, profit-sharing, company-paid recreational trips, advantages in company-sponsored lotteries, and company contributions to workers' savings. According to one example, the last device worked in this fashion: a worker was required to save 10 per cent of his wages from time to time at a rate of interest equal to 4·5 per cent per annum, and at the end of a year of steady work he received an extra payment equal to 35 per cent of the sum of the principal saved and interested earned. The worker's desire for recognition and prestige was also manipulated by measures like public announcements of merits (hyōshōsei), e.g. the fulfilment of a contractual period, unusual frugality as demonstrated in savings or remittances to parents, and so on.

Despite these efforts by the cotton textile firms, however, the length of service did not improve very much. In 1915, data on factory girls in Osaka indicated that 48·5 per cent of them were employed for less than a year and 18·4 per cent for three or more years. This situation was almost identical with what had prevailed in the industry fifteen years earlier.

The recruitment of labour for textile mills was the most difficult problem in work-force management. The problem of recruitment described previously could have been abolished by shifting the source of labour to nearby urban adult workers by raising wages enough to attract them. Textile mills did not consider this to be a major solution for their problems. Girls from the distant hinterland were preferable, but this source of supply was dwindling fast because even the poorest farm households wanted their daughters to survive and grow up to be good wives and mothers. It was not unusual for factory girls to return home sick or disabled for the rest of their lives. Many died away from home. It was common for girls to learn nothing during the period of factory employment that prepared them for their family and community roles later. For this reason, local communities one after another joined silent revolts against factory employment. This was known to the textile mills as the 'drying-up' of recruitment areas, which led to further increases in recruitment expenses. One obvious step for easing the labour supply to factories was the reform of living conditions within the factory dormitory. These had to be improved so that the period of employment would cease to be just one large hole in the personal and cultural development of young girls. Major textile firms did carry out such reforms. Educational, recreational, and cultural facilities were installed, and the hours of work were shortened, while holidays were increased to allow girls to utilize the new environmental amenities.

Then there was the problem of labour-market intermediaries. After many years of dependence on middlemen, some firms began to set up personnel departments in order to administer the procedure of recruitment, selection, hiring, and training of workers. Guidelines were set for hiring standards in terms of health, education, and aptitude. Recruitment methods were worked out as a step in the whole series of measures for rational work-force management. A new type of recruitment, which was approximated in varying degrees by different firms, was embodied in the notion of a 'recruitment territory', in which the firm's resident representative maintained direct personal contacts with the local families and kept a close watch over demographic developments in the area. The firm consciously co-ordinated its labour requirements within the demographic dynamics of the 'territory', so that as older workers withdrew from factory employment after several years of service, vacancies were filled by younger ones recruited from the area. When the growth of the firm required more labour than the area could supply, the firm used more capital per worker instead of enlarging the recruitment territory, which would surely have started 'colonial wars' with other firms. Since the security of the recruitment territory depended upon the working and living conditions of employees, the firm made continuous efforts to improve them at a rate that would enable it to maintain friendly relations with people in the recruitment territory. Concomitantly, therefore, public-relations activities were stepped up. It was generally believed that two sick girls from a given area would wipe it out as a recruitment territory. Given the strength of the local resistance, textile firms were compelled to devise better methods of work-force management and greater safety in factory life. Of course, one should not be too sanguine about the extent of the rationalization of work-force management in cotton textiles at the end of the Meiji Era. When the First World War brought about an unprecedented boom in Japan, the pattern of the 1890s returned to the textile labour market. It took the relative stability of labour requirements during the 1920s and sustained legislative efforts to produce a tolerable level of order in the textile industry's labour market and employment relations.

Nevertheless, there is no doubt that the quality of labour as well as the cultural level of textile workers improved greatly after 1910. To mention but one of the best-known cases in point, a substantial tome of 400 pages, entitled *Jokō aishi* [*The Tragic History of Female Factory Workers*], was published in 1925 by an ordinary factory hand, Wakizō Hosoi. Raised in a broken family and having lost his mother at the age of seven, Wakizō Hosoi (1896–1925) entered the world of work before he finished elementary school. Starting as an apprentice weaver at the age of twelve, Hosoi worked in the weaving departments of different cotton textile companies until his death in 1925, only a month after the first publication of *Jokō aishi*. He lost many jobs because of his trade-union activities, but his skills as a weaver and mechanic ensured him a series of brief spells of employment as long as employers failed to notice his name on the black list.

Jokō aishi was the fullest possible description of technology, management, life, and work in cotton textiles that had ever been attempted. As a work that contains detailed information on labour conditions in an important branch of Japanese industry, *Jokō aishi* takes its place in the stream of classics of labour history such as *Nihon no kasō shakai* [*The Lower-Class Society of Japan*] (1898), by Gennosuke Yokoyama, and *Shokkō jijō* [*The Conditions of Factory Labor*] (1903), prepared by the Ministry of Agriculture and Commerce.[76] But *Jokō aishi* is not only a classic from today's point of view. At the time of its publication, it was a sensation. By capturing the attention and arousing the conscience of the whole nation, it contributed in no small measure to a cultural enrichment of society and a further modernization of factory life. The weak and sorrowful found an understanding companion in *Jokō aishi*. The brave and active were stimulated to action in search of social justice. The rich and powerful were reminded that the society they controlled was devoid of humanity. Since Hosoi's death shortly after the publication of *Jokō aishi*, royalties from the book have been paid to an association called Hosoi Wakizō Ishikai (The Friends of Wakizō Hosoi), and used for the promotion of the labour movement and social work among textile workers.

C. METALWORKING AND ENGINEERING

The first task in the rationalization of work-force management in metalworking and engineering was the transfer of the *oyakata* functions to the firm, while changing the *oyakata* into a first-line supervisor akin to the foreman in the Western factory. There were two crucial questions in this process: (1) who – the employer or the *oyakata* – should enjoy the loyalty of workers, and (2) how workers should be trained. The contest between *oyakata* and employer over worker loyalty was a real power struggle which at times erupted into violent personal confrontations. In most cases, compromises were worked out much like the Meiji Restoration: just as the feudal lords handed their people over to the Emperor, the *oyakata* gave up their workers to the firm for its direct management. But as the ex-lords were assured of position, prestige, and income, the *oyakata* were offered a variety of comforts and inducements such as a status in the management structure, permanent tenure, higher pay, and regular increments. This comparison is more than heuristic; the Meiji Restoration, which was at first little different from a palace coup, permeated Japanese society and, at the end of the Meiji Era, began to touch the factory floor. The logic of the socio-political process was surprisingly identical at all levels of Japanese society. The principal instrument of reform was always a compromise. On the factory floor, there were technical and social reasons that made these compromises not only desirable but inevitable. At the stage of socio-economic modernization that characterized Japan at the end of the Meiji Era, the *oyakata* were after all the only people available for an effective management of workers in practical activities in the factory. Managers and engineers, university-educated and with privileged family backgrounds, scarcely knew how to mix with workers who were largely from the lower classes, with inferior education and different values about life and work. Managers and engineers had the basic scientific knowledge about broad outlines and designs of factory work; but they lacked skill or experience in the details of actual tasks in production. Since the status differences between management and workers were too great to bridge without intermediaries, someone like an *oyakata* was indispensable.[77]

A typically Japanese institutional reform which transformed the *oyakata* system into the employer's direct management took place at the Nagasaki Shipyard.[78] Two types of training were devised for different levels of skills and function. By the First World War, these were firmly established and were consciously perceived as indispensable elements in the modernization of work-force management. One was a vocational school (Mitsubishi kōgyō yobi gakkō) which gave three years of education and training to boys with elementary or higher education. The graduates of this school were then assigned to the *oyakata* at the shipyard as their assistants. These young workers, who were called *shūgyōsei* (student workers), were required to attend formal courses in the training school for four more years. With several years of practical experience after this, they were promoted to the position of *oyakata*. The second type of training was a type of apprenticeship called *minaraikō* (training on the job). Young workers aged twelve years or older were assigned to different shops and worker groups for unskilled tasks, receiving training for certain skills at the same time. The *minarai* period was five years. During this period, the *minarai* spent a few hours each day on formal course work in the vocational school mentioned above. Upon the completion of the *minarai* period, these young workers joined the ranks of ordinary workers (*futsū shokkō*).

The Mitsubishi Vocational School was inaugurated in 1899 with forty-two students. The enrolment fluctuated from year to year and remained most of the time well below 200 students, as against the planned capacity of 400. If at least five more years of practical experience were needed on top of the seven years of the full course of training before the graduates became mature enough to take over the *oyakata*'s functions, it would seem that the new *oyakata* from this source began to appear in 1912. This suggests that the process of replacing the traditional *oyakata* was a protracted battle. To make matters worse, the attrition rate at every stage of the trainees' progress was very high. Only a quarter of students admitted in a given year stayed in school until they were graduated. Although more than 90 per cent of the graduates went to the Nagasaki Shipyard as 'student workers', half of them resigned in five years, during the first ten years of this programme (1902 to 1912). Therefore, roughly one-tenth of the original cohort of students admitted to the vocational school ever reached the *oyakata* level. At this rate, the new *oyakata* would have numbered fewer than 200 in the middle of the 1920s, when the Nagasaki work force comprised 12,000 men. The *minarai* had reached 15 per cent of the work force of the Nagasaki Shipyard by 1910. If one-fifth of the recruits for *minarai* had stayed on to become ordinary workers and if there had been no further attrition, it should have taken ten years for the internally trained workers to reach one-half of the work force at Nagasaki. But given the cult of travelling journeymen, the commitment rate should have been lower. Of course, these calculations are merely heuristic, but they suggest that the efforts at the modernization of the work force which were started in the 1900s began to show some effects only in the 1920s. In the meantime, the traditional *oyakata* remained in large numbers and continued to play a vital role in the firm's work-force policy.

Upon a closer look, the Nagasaki Shipyard's policy for replacing the traditional *oyakata* was much more benign than is implied in the preceding paragraphs. The admissions policy at the vocational school preferred the children and relatives of the shipyard workers, while the *oyakata* recruited and selected the *minarai*. Between 1903 and 1912, 17 per cent of the vocational-school students were related to shipyard workers. Since the sons and relatives of the *oyakata* shared this privilege, when the older *oyakata* gave up their positions and retired they were in part doing so in favour of their sons and relatives. While formal control over personnel administration was centralized through a series of institutional reforms, the *oyakata* were still at the critical junctions between management and ordinary workers, holding the power to recommend action in all matters affecting the well-being of the workers.

During 1908–10 other institutional reforms appeared in rapid succession at the Nagasaki Shipyard. The customary practice of sub-letting work to the *oyakata* was abolished; hiring standards were specified and upgraded; piece-work and premium-wage systems were adopted; relief and assistance schemes were strengthened or newly established for injury, sickness, disablement, death, unemployment, retirement, and other inconveniences of workers. Within the frame-work of industrial bureaucracy under management's direct control, the *oyakata* were assured of their proper functions as employees of the firm. Indeed, given the size and sophistication of the structure, the complexity of work rules, the refinement of wage payment, the variety of incentives and benefits to workers, and the pace of change in all aspects of life and work, independent worker groups led by the *oyakata* under subcontracting arrangements would have failed to maximize the benefits which the shipyard made available to workers.

The example of the Nagasaki Shipyard was repeated in the experience of many other firms in varying forms and degrees. In a nutshell, management's direct grasp of the work force transferred to management three functions of the traditional *oyakata*: training, pay, and the provision of job and income security. An experienced observer of the industrial scene of Meiji Japan noted in 1910 that the traditional *oyakata* had disappeared from many engineering works and that their place was taken by younger supervisory personnel while the whole work force was brought under the firm's direct management.[79] Where firms found it difficult to have formal training schools independently as in Nagasaki, they jointly financed training schools for their workers.[80] Eventually, firms discovered the power of wages as a factor in keeping or losing their workers. Under the impact of an acute labour shortage during the First World War, large firms raised wages faster than the market, reversing the trend in which wages in large firms had lagged behind market wages before the war.[81] However, it was only after the mid-1920s that wages in large firms began to show a decisive superiority over market wages, partly aided by the downward pressure on wages in smaller firms in the course of deepening depression. As for income security, employers learned a lesson from the popularity of the Metal-workers' Union for its mutual-assistance scheme. At the same time, public and private research was turning up evidence on the physical hazards of industrial work, and not a few industrial conflicts had their origins in the workers' desire for safer working conditions.[82] Thus, after the Russo-Japanese War firms began to set up various compensation and benefit schemes, while the enactment of factory legislation at the state level was considered only a matter of time.

D. FACTORY LEGISLATION[83]

In the 1880s, the government repeatedly consulted representatives of industry and commerce on the draft statutes on labour. The consensus was hard to obtain, and these early attempts were duly abandoned. Nevertheless, the Bureau of Industry of the Ministry of Agriculture and Commerce continued to explore new avenues of thoughts and methods, while accumulating data on the conditions of industry and labour. In 1896, prefectural governors were sounded out as to the desirability of legislation for the 'protection and regulation' of factory labour. Twenty out of forty-six prefectures turned in their opinions, and fifteen of them roughly favoured the idea. The Minister of Agriculture and Commerce then appointed a council, consisting of representatives of industry and of the academic world, to discuss economic and industrial problems, including the question of factory legislation. It was called the Superior Council on Agriculture, Commerce, and Industry (Nōshōkō Kōtō Kaigi), and it met in three sessions to discuss the question of factory law. A draft factory law emerged from the conferences of this council. The cabinet crisis in 1898 destroyed the chances for the draft to reach the floor of the Diet.

A draft factory law actually reached the floor of the Diet in 1910, but the government voluntarily withdrew the bill. Further revisions were made, and copies of a new draft were sent to various ministries, prefectural governments, chambers of commerce and industry, textile manufacturers' associations, other industrial associations, and the Association for Social Policy, an academic organization which had recently come into being. In March 1910, a special commission called the Commission for Inquiry into Production (Seisan Chōsakai) was appointed by an Imperial Ordinance to examine the draft factory law. The draft that emerged from the Commission was approved by the Cabinet Council of Ministers (Kakugi) and sent to the Diet in 1911. The House of Commons quickly acted upon the bill and, within a month, passed it on to the House of Peers with certain modifications. The Upper House passed the bill within three weeks. The Factory Law was enacted on 20 March 1911; but as was usually the case with the pre-war legislative process in Japan, no date for the implementation of the Factory Law was specified in the Law itself.

The Factory Law proper was a short document of twenty-five articles and stipulated a minimum set of standards for employment, covering manufacturing establishments employing fifteen or more operatives (later amended to cover those employing ten or more) or establishments using processes of work dangerous to health. It prohibited the employment of persons below the age of twelve, the use of operatives between the ages of twelve and fifteen or of female operatives regardless of age for more than twelve hours a day, and night work for minors or women between 10.0 p.m. and 4.0 a.m. The law required at least two rest days per month for minors and women, at least four rest days per month for night-shift workers, and at least a thirty-minute rest period per day where a day's work exceeded ten hours. The law prohibited the employment of workers under fifteen years of age on certain dangerous or disagreeable jobs and obligated the factory-owner to support disabled workers and their families. Factory-owners who violated the provisions of the law or who did not co-operate with the factory inspectors were subject to fines.

For the specification of some vital matters the Factory Law depended upon the Imperial Ordinance for the Implementation of the Law, which was finally issued in August 1916 to put the law into effect beginning in September of that year. The ordinance elaborated the provisions of the Factory Law. It specified the frequency and methods of wage payment, though wage determination was largely left to free bargaining between the parties concerned. Each factory had to maintain the register of workers employed. Wages were to be paid in legal tender at least once a month. When the employer took charge of workers' deposits, he had to obtain the prior approval of the prefectural governor. No employment contract was allowed which obligated the worker in advance to compensate the employer for a possible breach of the contract or for damage to property.

Matters related to recruitment, hiring, and dismissal were elaborated to some extent. For example, where school-age youths were employed, the employer had to guarantee their continued schooling. Young workers and women employees who were discharged at the employer's discretion were entitled to travel expenses to return to their homes. In addition, certain formalities were prescribed for employing apprentices. Fines were stipulated for violations of the law and the ordinance as well as for fraudulent practices in the recruitment of workers by either employer or recruiter. Additional rules for the implementation of the Factory Law were simultaneously issued as a Ministerial Order of the Ministry of Agriculture and Commerce.

Unfortunately, two exceptions – on hours of work and night work – were written into the Factory Law for the duration of fifteen years. The first exception had to do with Article 3, which limited a day's work to twelve hours. The Minister of State was allowed to permit the extension of the working day by two more hours in certain industries. The other, more important, exception was to Article 4, which prohibited the night work of young workers or women. These exceptions were granted to factories where the production process required continuous work and where workers were organized in two or more shifts. The workers in the night shift, who were more numerous in the textile industries, fluctuated between 15 and 25 per cent of all workers in factories covered by the law during its first six years (1916–22). In the textile industries, it was the large concerns that took advantage of the night-shift exception: smaller ones did not have that much work to do. The number of workers in factories where the working day was allowed to exceed twelve hours was about one-tenth of 1 per cent of all the workers in the factories covered.

Other state actions relating to the labour market and employment relations during the inter-war period may now be quickly noted. The Factory Law was revised in 1926. By this time, a few important pieces of legislation had been enacted. In 1921, the Employment Exchange Law was enacted and set up public employment offices in several parts of the country to render services gratis and to subsidize job-seekers with transportation expenses, keeping an eye on the activities of private labour recruiters at the same time. In the following year the Health Insurance Law was enacted, to be implemented in 1927. In 1923, there were laws to define minimum ages for factory workers and seamen. Among the administrative ordinances issued during this period, the most important from the point of view of the labour market were the Ordinance to Regulate Labour Recruitment (1924) and the Rules to Regulate Private Labour Exchange Businesses (1925).

The revisions of the Code of Factory Law in 1926 postponed the life of the escape clauses on the use of women for night shifts for three more years (until 1929). An important innovation was added to the Code, however – two weeks' advance notice for the termination of employment when initiated by the employer or two weeks' pay in the case of an immediate dismissal. The benefits payable to the worker or his family were all upgraded substantially. Certain benefits which overlapped with the Health Insurance Scheme were transferred entirely to the jurisdiction of the latter. Modifications of certain provisions of the Code continued throughout the inter-war period, owing to the necessity for adjustments with other statutes. In 1931, the Law to Aid Injured Workers was passed to take care of workers not covered under the Factory Law or the Health Insurance Law. These were the workers employed in civil engineering, construction, quarries, transportation, docks, and warehouses. Because these industries were organized on the basis of complex subcontracting arrangements, there was a technical difficulty in pinning responsibility on any employer. The state therefore agreed to underwrite benefits paid, and primary responsibility was placed on the principal contractor for the workers in his employ and for those employed by his subcontractors. In 1936, the Law for Funding Retirement Allowances and Payments was enacted, requiring factories and mines employing more than fifty workers to pay allowances to retiring or dismissed workers. It may be useful to summarize the non-wage benefits provided for by the Code of Factory Law before and after 1926.

	1916–26	1926–40
1. Compensation for work injury		
i. Medical care	Facility or cost	Facility or cost
ii. Sickness benefit	50% of daily wage up to 3 months, $\frac{1}{3}$ of daily wage thereafter	60% of daily wage up to 180 days, 40% of daily wage thereafter
iii. Disability benefit		
a. Unable to care for self	170 days' wages	540 days' wages
b. Unable to work	150 days' wages	360 days' wages
c. Unable to do previous work	100 days' wages	180 days' wages
d. Temporary, able to return to previous work	30 days' wages	40 days' wages
iv. Death benefit	170 days' wages	360 days' wages
v. Funeral allowance	10 yen or more	30 days' wages but not less than 30 yen
vi. Terminal medical benefit after 3 years of medical care	170 days' wages	540 days' wages
2. Travel expenses for young workers, women, and disabled workers	Obligatory	Obligatory
3. Dismissal allowance	Not obligatory	Obligatory

	1916–26	1926–40
4. Health insurance premium	Not obligatory	Cost equally shared with employee, 3% of pay
5. Retirement allowance	Not obligatory	Obligatory, partly on a contributory basis

The thirties were the period of Japan's real industrialization. In manufacturing employment, the weight of textiles declined from more than 50 per cent in 1930 to about 25 per cent in 1940. The weight of 'heavy and chemical' industries rose from 25 per cent to 55 per cent during the decade. The coincidence of progress in social policy and heavy industrialization during the 1930s gave rise to an industrial relations system that was to develop more fully after the Second World War. In any age, however, it is only the least efficient employers who stay close to the legal minimum standards. Major firms had become far more 'paternalistic' than was implied in the above discussion of the Factory Law.

E. THE IMPACT OF THE LABOUR MOVEMENT[84]

The influence of the labour movement on the progress of social policy and work-force management has never been officially acknowledged, but one suspects that during the inter-war period the government and employers modernized industrial relations partly as a way of keeping trade unions at a distance. The labour movement was cautiously revived in 1912 by Bunji Suzuki (1885–1946), and his Yūaikai (Friendly Society) expanded rapidly during the First World War. In 1921, Yūaikai became Sōdōmei (General Federation of Trade Unions). Trade union membership reached 234,000 persons in 1925 and increased to 384,300 in 1930, attaining the inter-war peak of 420,600 in 1936. Although it never amounted to more than 8 per cent of all paid workers in Japan, its distribution varied from industry to industry – more than 80 per cent unionization in gas and electricity, about 30 per cent in transportation and communications, and a little more than 25 per cent in metalworking and engineering.[85] During the early years of the International Labour Organization, the Japanese government refused to recognize the right of trade unions to elect and send their representative to the International Labour Conference. Labour fought hard and succeeded in securing this right, starting to exercise it in 1924. Although the Japanese government continued its policy of non-recognition of trade unions in domestic industrial relations, it honoured – though selectively – the international conventions on labour standards in which the Japanese labour representative participated.

With the end of the First World War, massive unemployment appeared for the first time on the Japanese industrial scene. Workers protested, and strikes became a familiar feature of Japanese life during the 1920s and 1930s. Throughout Japanese society there was unmistakable enthusiasm for democracy, modern life, and ideological freedom, which found expression in diverse forms and activities. Under the pressure of popular demand, the government enacted universal manhood suffrage in 1925, enabling the whole adult male population, rich and poor, to vote. On the other hand, political leaders felt that too much democracy was bad for the country and cracked down on communists, anarchists, and suspects of like persuasions through the Public Peace Maintenance Law of 1926 (*Chian Iji Hō*). At the same time, the government and employers became more paternalistic in work places. The repression of progressive activities in national politics, combined with the provision of amenities in firms, corroded the labour movement, which in 1939–40 voluntarily dissolved itself and handed over workers to Sampō, the nationalist 'Movement in Service for the Country'. The unofficial war with China, started in 1937, developed into the total Pacific War in 1941, leading to the collapse of Imperial Japan in the atomic holocaust of 1945.

V. *Conclusion*

By the standards of the 1860s, when servants, labourers, and artisans were mostly illiterate, the factory workers of the 1930s were incomparably better educated and more sophisticated. All of them, save a small fraction (4 per cent in 1936),[86] had completed six years of elementary education, and many of them (two-thirds of male workers and one-third of female workers in 1936) had received at least two additional years of education. At the same time, the average worker in the 1930s was three times better off than the average Japanese of the 1860s. Unlike the commoners of the 1860s, the adult males of the 1930s had a share in government, though the effectiveness of the popular suffrage was debatable in many cases. Furthermore, in contrast to the hereditary status system of the 1860s, modern Japan had erected no barrier to social mobility, although there was much to be desired about the distribution of opportunities. In the mid-1930s, Japan had not yet acquired the sense of equality before God or law, but there was a homespun notion of equality before the Emperor. As the subjects of His Majesty, the Japanese equally took part in the political process, and in his name, they received fair trials at courts of law. But lacking the support of individual freedom and the sanctity of contracts between individuals, Japanese 'equality' before the Emperor quickly turned into unreserved loyalty to him, equally shared by all. In place of the individual pursuit of happiness in a growing economy, the Japanese bound themselves together and shared the discipline and toil for a better future which never became a reality. When Japan mobilized for the Second World War, even the freedom of occupational choice was obliterated, and finally 'all traces of individuality were submerged in service to the country' (*messhi hōkō*). Thus, with Japan's decision to enter the war, the history of Japanese workers had run full circle, from *hōkō* to *hōkō* – that is, from servitude to servitude.

CHAPTER V

Entrepreneurship, Ownership, and Management in Japan

I. *Introduction*

Because of its rapidity, sustained achievement, and initial low per capita income, the process of Japanese industrialization is a fascinating subject of study for economists and economic historians. An increasing number of Western students of Japan, after nearly two post-war decades of concerted work with their Japanese colleagues, are providing us with a substantial amount of quantitative evidence on the performance of the Japanese economy during the past hundred years. This evidence has been examined and re-examined, and we now have extremely useful sets of analyses and yet more refined data which compare favourably with those made for any other nation.

While these studies on Japan – analogous to those of Deane and Cole and others on England – were being made, another set of equally important questions for economic historians trying to understand Japan's industrialization suffered relative neglect. I refer to the set of questions which can be loosely classified under the heading of 'entrepreneurship and management in historical perspective'. More specifically, this is the whole spectrum of questions relating to the rise, recruitment, and composition of entrepreneurship; ownership and control; and the management of industrial firms in the process of Japan's industrialization and modernization.

During the past several years, increasing attention has been paid to these questions by Japanese and Western students alike. But the literature on these aspects of Japanese economic history is either inaccessible or fragmentary, or both. The inaccessibility is mostly due to the fact that the literature is available only in Japanese. Studies of Japanese entrepreneurship and management are fragmentary because each study deals in turn with a limited aspect of one of these questions or with only a sub-period of time, without providing a historical perspective and a cohesive analysis of all related issues.

The relative neglect suffered by this aspect of Japan's industrialization is not difficult to explain. One of the major reasons is undoubtedly that a majority of Japanese economic historians have been Marxists and have had little interest in analysing the functions of entrepreneurship and the evolution of the managerial system within a capitalist economy. They have their answers. Several Western students who attempted before the

Second World War to examine entrepreneurship and management questions became, perhaps unconsciously, merely transmitters of the Marxist view at worst, and at best they made the Japanese literature more palatable to Western readers. There were few exceptions.

Two important factors tended to perpetuate this uninspiring state of research. One was the severe linguistic barrier which made original research by Western scholars extremely difficult; and any competent research on Japanese entrepreneurship and the managerial system necessitates a wide use of Japanese sources. The other factor was the basic approach of Western students in analysing Japanese entrepreneurship and management. Because Japan was the only nation in Asia to industrialize, the Western student sought out what he thought to be unique in that country. Earlier Western students were predisposed to find what contrasted the Japanese case with the Chinese and the Western cases. When this approach was grafted on to the Japanese literature, which long lacked a comparative perspective, the end results were often explanations and descriptions which rarely provided anything more useful than the undefined 'spirit of samurai' and a tiresome emphasis on Confucian ethics.

This unsatisfactory state of affairs has changed rather dramatically since the end of the Second World War. Both the quantity and the quality of Japanese and Western studies in entrepreneurship and the managerial system have undergone significant changes. Along with the economists who are essentially interested in various quantitative analyses of Japanese growth, economic historians and others interested in entrepreneurship and the managerial system began to provide more searching, cohesive, and comparative analyses of these neglected aspects of the Japanese success story. Though a large part of the contribution is still being made in Japanese, the depth of understanding and the level of analyses achieved by Western scholars, especially during the past decade, have indeed been remarkable.

What appeared out of these pre-war and post-war endeavours is by now a widely accepted view – which we could perhaps call an 'orthodox' interpretation – of Japanese entrepreneurship, ownership, and control of industrial firms, and the Japanese managerial system. This, in effect, is a major thesis, well supported by leading students of these aspects of Japanese industrialization and modernization, and one which provides a persuasive set of explanations for Japan's singular accomplishment.

Thus, a major task of this chapter is to attempt to capture the salient tenets of the 'orthodoxy' in as concise a form as possible. Parts of this chapter therefore recapitulate certain basic arguments, and this I hope will be useful to those not specializing in Japanese economic history.

Also, an equally important task of this chapter is to attempt to present several recent suggestions for the revision of this orthodoxy. These reflect new sets of questions now being asked of established interpretations, and they also indicate the increased interest in questions relating to entrepreneurship, ownership, and control in Japanese economic growth. The new suggestions range from differences in emphasis to a relatively clear-cut challenge to the orthodoxy. As research in the area continues, these new suggestions may prove to be a difference in emphasis and may cause parts of the orthodoxy to be re-written, or they may force a basic revision of the orthodoxy. In dealing with such large and multi-faceted questions as entrepreneurship and management, and in attempting to summarize what is already a large volume of literature appearing in Japanese and in Western languages, this chapter cannot hope to cover all aspects of these large topics. For instance, the discussions on the managerial system and on the years after the Second World War are only outlines of what is required of fuller treatments.[1]

It should be pointed out before proceeding that the term 'entrepreneur' is used loosely in this chapter. Entrepreneurs are a group of individuals who precipitate changes in the method and manner of producing goods, and the group can include government officials, business leaders, bankers, and any other individual who is instrumental in effecting such changes. Also, even when I implicitly touch upon better-known general frameworks of analyses such as Gerschenkron's or Schumpeter's, or upon economic theory in general, I subsume these in the writing as they will be obvious to the reader.

II. *The Rise and Composition of Japanese Entrepreneurship*

Immediately following the Meiji Restoration of 1868, the government began vigorously to encourage industrialization by building pilot plants, hiring foreign experts, and granting various types of subsidies. Energetic and determined private entrepreneurs also appeared. By the turn of the century, it was obvious that Japan had successfully undertaken the important first step toward industrialization. Who supplied this initial entrepreneurial leadership, and why?

A large number of articles and books (mostly in Japanese) which attempted to answer this question appeared before the end of the Second World War. The answer, evolving as a common denominator out of this literature, is a thesis which stresses the uniqueness of Japanese entrepreneurship as a product of Japan's cultural and historical heritages, and one which emphasizes the overriding significance of the lateness of

Japan's entry into industrialization, in explaining the composition and motivations of the Japanese entrepreneurs. The essence of this thesis can be summarized as follows.

During the Tokugawa period, class distinctions between the samurai (the warriors) and the *heimin* (commoners consisting of peasants, merchants, and artisans) were formally established, and the barriers became increasingly rigid. The education, aspirations, and *Weltanschauung* in general of the samurai class and those of the *heimin* class differed significantly. Samurai, the moral and political elite of the Tokugawa society, were indoctrinated in Confucian ethics, which stressed dedication to duty and selfless devotion to the established order and authority. The prime virtue and obligation of the samurai class was to provide leadership in whatever task was assigned to them for the good of the total polity. The commoners, on the other hand, lacked – or rather were not required to possess – the samurai virtues; rather they were to obey, to be thrifty and to produce – virtues more fitting to their ordained station in life. The samurai leadership was not immediately challenged after the Restoration because it was the Shōgunate which was discredited by the events of 1868 and not the samurai class.

Thus, following the Restoration, the new government was manned by the samurai, who were expected to provide the leadership. The international circumstances of the mid nineteenth century only strengthened the samurai's relative position, as Japan hastened to 'enrich the nation and build a strong army' in order to ward off possible incursions by foreign powers on the Japanese sovereignty. This was the basic framework of analysis which was sufficient, for example, for Tsuchiya, who believed that 'in the case of Japan' it was 'inevitable' for the samurai to become entrepreneurs.[2]

The pre-war Japanese thesis argued that the samurai were destined to lead, while the *chōnin* (merchants) – the logical contenders for the entrepreneurship, if European histories are any guide – were expected to follow the samurai leadership and did so.[3] The merchant class was found to be passive, cautious, and conservative. In Sansom's words, they were 'too narrow, they had thrived under protection, and with a few exceptions they fell back on huckstering, while ambitious samurai of low and middle rank became bankers, merchants and manufacturers'.[4] Also, the *chōnin*, in addition to their unsuitability for innovative leadership, were thought to be financially incapable of assuming the role of entrepreneurship, as they had been ruined by the forced loans and general economic dislocation of the late Tokugawa period. Even the largest house, the House of Mitsui, was tottering. Thus, it was argued that they had neither the innovative leadership nor the capital necessary to venture into modern industry.

This, then, was the basic premise, and evidence to support the dominance of samurai–entrepreneurs was marshalled by two generations of Japanese economic historians. They richly documented the role of the former samurai as bureaucrat–entrepreneurs, as innovative industrialists, and as patriotic bankers. This literature stressed the importance of government-funded industrial undertakings as the path-breakers of Japanese industrialization.[5] The government-operated ventures, indeed, extended to numerous industries including silk filatures, shipyards, glass, cement, sugar-refining, paper, printing, minting, weaponry, and mining.

Examples of samurai–bureaucrats and samurai–entrepreneurs in establishing modern banking and the cotton textile industry are useful in capturing the main thesis of this pre-war literature. These writers credit the establishment of the modern banking system – an important step toward industrialization – well-nigh completely to samurai–bureaucrats and samurai–bankers. The pre-war literature argued as follows. The government, first showing its concern in providing sufficient credits to the economy, unsuccessfully attempted to launch the Commerce Bureau and then the Trade Bureau during the first few years of its existence. But after failing in these ventures, it succeeded in building four Western-type banks by the first Banking Act of 1872, and soon afterwards 153 banks based on the law of 1876. The first four depended on the capital supplied by large merchant houses, but it was the government which forced unwilling merchants to establish these banks. The 153 banks, which became the real foundation of Japanese modern banking, relied both on the initiative of the former samurai and on their capital in the form of commutation bonds which they received in exchange for their lost economic and social privileges.

The cotton textile industry has been cited by numerous writers as the prime example of government entrepreneurship. To develop the industry, the government established and operated pilot plants which trained workers and introduced new technology. The government also imported ten sets of spindles, 2,000 units each, and sold them mostly to samurai-turned-entrepreneurs on ten-year credit. These activities and subsidies provided by the government, it was argued, meant that the government assumed the initial risks of new ventures and played a major role in laying the foundation for the industry which by the end of the century had grown to lead Japanese industrialization.

These and numerous other examples of government–samurai entrepreneurship only make the well-known point that the economic development of Japan came from above, and this was 'inevitable' given the socio-economic heritages of Japan and the lateness of her entry to industrialization. To make the same point, the life of Eiichi Shibusawa –

the Meiji entrepreneur *par excellence* in the pre-war literature – has been told many times, and to devote a few paragraphs to him here is perhaps necessary to convey the image of the Meiji entrepreneur as seen by those early writers.

Shibusawa (1840–1931), the son of a rich farmer, became a low-ranking samurai at the end of the Tokugawa era, when he entered the service of the last Shōgun. He soon gained the confidence of the Shōgun and was even selected to accompany the Shōgun's brother to Paris, in 1867, as financial manager. After the fall of the Shōgunate, he found it equally easy to advance in the new Meiji government hierarchy, and he attained the second highest position in the Ministry of Finance before he left the post as a protest against militaristic and bureaucratic policies.

As a private individual, Shibusawa took the initiative in many 'modern', i.e. Western, ventures. He was a key promoter of the First National Bank (Daiichi Ginkō) in 1872 and was its first president. Again, as he had done in the case of the bank, he persuaded rich merchant houses to build the first large Western paper mill in Japan and was also instrumental in founding the giant – by the standard of the day – Osaka Cotton Spinning Company, which was to lead the cotton textile industry in the years to come. The list of his achievements is impressive.

What stood out in Shibusawa in the eyes of pre-war writers was his constant concern for the good of the nation – his efforts to strengthen the Japanese economy by reducing imports and increasing exports, and his role in advocating the necessity of carrying out Japanese industrial-ization based on the ethical doctrines of Confucianism. His voluminous writings and numerous speeches were a mine of quotable phrases and epigrams for those early economic historians intent on finding evidence to support the view that he was an ideal type of entrepreneur, evidence needed for their general thesis of Japan's rapid success. Shibusawa con-stantly wished to elevate the social status of business leaders, and to do this, he demanded that these men possess the samurai spirit and 'the Japanese spirit' (*yamatodamashii*), which honoured integrity, justice, magnanimity, chivalry, and courtesy. The first duty of the entrepreneur was to the public, and in discharging this duty the Japanese business elite could gain the respect of their fellow-countrymen and of the West. In short, the Meiji entrepreneurs were to conduct their affairs 'with the abacus and the Analects of Confucius'.[6]

The main thesis of these pre-war writers, who saw in Shibusawa an ideal entrepreneur, is clear. The government, along with active pro-grammes to provide social overhead capital (for example, capital invest-ment in telegraph and communications equipment), actively introduced Western technology, provided subsidies, and by the other means at its command promoted economic development from above. The government was manned by samurai bureaucrats who assumed the leadership role taken by the samurai in the pre-Restoration era. It provided the energizing force for the economy even when it had to pull and push unwilling merchant houses and commoners. In industrialization, government initiative was direct and pervasive, and modern banks too were initiated by the government and made possible because of the capital provided by samurai. Tsuchiya, compiling a list of leading Meiji entrepreneurs, found the samurai and the samurai spirit dominating the industrializing efforts during the Meiji years.[7] The main virtue of this pre-war thesis was that it seemed to offer a unique explanation for the rapidity of Japanese growth in terms of her culture, history, and traditions. This also was a general thesis which explained why the lateness of Japan's entry to industrialization was an important cause of her rapid achievement, and why Japan alone in Asia was able to accomplish the feat. Then, beginning about 1950, Japanese entrepreneurship began to receive the renewed attention of Western students. It was natural that the post-war interest in Japan as a case of successful industrialization should include studies of her entrepreneurship. These studies on Japanese entrepreneurship, however, were essentially a refined version of the pre-war thesis described above. Refinements came in the Schumpeterian framework, with comparative insights and often with generally higher standards of scholarship.

That these post-war writings were only refinements is obvious in their basic view of Japanese entrepreneurship. One writer called the Meiji entrepreneurs 'community-centered' and found them to lie 'somewhere between the innovating and profit-maximizing Schumpeterian entrepreneurs and bureaucrats' whose 'motivation is quasi-tribal, to further the ends of the community; the individual seeks to grow, not so much in reflection of his wealth, a private good, as in the prestige of the cohesive unit, a social good'.[8] Nearly ten years later, another author expressed the same view a little more directly:

An important characteristic of the samurai mentality was a sense of public consciousness, a concern for public welfare, and a strong nationalistic spirit. These attitudes were a product of the Bushidō tradition and Confucian philosophy. This spirit undoubtedly spurred those who shared samurai values to rise to meet national challenges at the time of the great crisis of the need for modernization.[9]

Perhaps the consensus of the post-war literature in English is best summarized by Hirschmeier, who contributed a significant book on the subject. He wrote:

The uniqueness of the Meiji experience is that the samurai were declassed by compeers who were extremely anxious to activate the best qualities of that elite class, and succeeded in doing so. Thus the samurai were able to generate a good deal of entrepreneurial dynamism and eventually provided the modern entrepreneurial elite with a new status image, based on the old vibrant 'spirit of samurai'.[10]

The Meiji entrepreneurs were seen as possessors of the samurai spirit, and in fact Hirschmeier and other post-war writers found, as had Tsuchiya before the war, that former samurai comprised the dominant part of Meiji business leaders. As had Tsuchiya, Hirschmeier too found Eiichi Shibusawa to be the Meiji entrepreneur *par excellence*, because 'in his career as a government official, banker, and industrialist, and in his life philosophy, we find reflected most of the basic characteristics of the Meiji elite'.[11]

The social origins of entrepreneurs and their motivations explained to their satisfaction, these post-war writers proceeded to find (as pre-war writers had found) the dominance of the samurai government in the process of industrialization, both in banking and in industry. Post-war writers' observations on banking differed only in the degree in which they emphasized the importance of the samurai's role in the establishment of modern banking. These post-war writers, represented in Hirschmeier's words below, in essence repeated the pre-war view by saying that 'The rush of the samurai to found banks stands out in striking contrast to the attitudes of the wealthy merchant houses, which had to be forced to establish the first four national banks in 1872. Correspondingly, in the early phase the merchants fell far behind the samurai as contributors of capital to the whole banking system.'[12] And in support of their view, the post-war writers often cited the following breakdown by class of the contribution made to the total capital of the banks in 1879: *kazoku* (nobility and former *daimyō*), 44·1 per cent; samurai, 31·9; merchants, 14·6; farmers, 3·5; artisans, 0·1; and others, 5·6.[13] The argument was straightforward: the nobility and samurai contributed initiative and three-fourths of the capital to found the first successful modern banks.

In discussing industrial development in general, the post-war writers, especially those Western writers who depended heavily on Japanese studies of a generation ago, followed the pre-war view in stressing the importance of the roles of the government and the samurai. Their evaluation gained depth, but their views ranged from mere restatements of the pre-war literature to carefully guarded and refined versions of the earlier assessments of the roles of the government and the samurai. But, as the few samples below show, these writings nevertheless were cut out of the same cloth from which the pre-war writers fashioned their views. T. C. Smith appraised the role of the government by saying that

The government mills had served as models for private enterprise, working out technical difficulties and problems of plant organization. But equally if not more important was the financial assistance government extended to private enterprises after 1878. It seems clear that without government help of both kinds, private capital would have been no more successful than it had been in the decade before.[14]

Also representative is the view expressed by Bronfenbrenner on the contribution of samurai and an assessment of *chōnin* in industrialization. He observed, like many Japanese scholars before him, that 'the *chōnin* were technologically conservative and generally unwilling to embark on innovation, or indeed on production (as distinguished from trade and finance), until the way had been shown by foreigners or by the Japanese government. For this reason, they were outstripped early in the Meiji period by rival entrepreneurs of samurai origin.'[15] The echoes of the pre-war literature are evident. What Moulton had to say in 1931 differed little in content:

The government has, in fact, performed in a large way the function of the entrepreneurs. We have already noted that because of old traditions and conditions, there were few experienced business entrepreneurs in Japan in the early part of the Meiji era and virtually no accumulation of capital, and that under these circumstances the government performed a very important function in setting the pace for private enterprise and furnishing funds required for development of economic resources.[16]

How accurate is this view? It is correct, I believe, to say that a re-evaluation of this view had begun to call into question its fundamental premises. The emerging revisions cannot yet be called a counter-thesis, but when these recent challenges to the established view are considered in their entirety, they appear to require a synthesis with the existing interpretation of Meiji entrepreneurship.

The challenge comes from many fronts. The new perspective argues in essence, however, that the roles of the government and the samurai have been overemphasized to a degree which seriously misinterprets the nature of Japanese entrepreneurship in the Meiji era. That is, the new perspective argues that the Meiji government did not initiate but rather aided the first steps, and in a manner much more analogous to that observed in the industrialization of the Western European nations during comparable stages of industrialization. This also means, as a corollary, that it was entrepreneurs and capitalists of various social origins who began the industrialization of Japan. An added advantage claimed for the new perspective is that it will enable us to evaluate the importance of the role of the Meiji government in performing the role which is more commonly associated with a government during the early stages of industrialization – the establishment of infrastructure and institutions to enhance industrialization.

The implicit theory of those who support the 'orthodox' view of the Meiji entrepreneur is, in effect, that (1) almost all of the leading Meiji business leaders were samurai or quasi-samurai; (2) the *Weltanschauung* of the samurai class is distinct from that of other classes because of the long tradition of the 'spirit of the samurai', which was cultivated and preserved by their education and mode of living: the spirit of the samurai, in the final analysis, was the ability to sacrifice self-interest, be it for one's feudal lord or for the 'enrichment of the nation'; thus (3) most of the leading Meiji entrepreneurs possessed *shikon shōsai* (spirit of the samurai, ability of the merchant) and were 'community-centered'.

The danger of this type of theorizing, however, is made evident when a closer scrutiny is made of the leading entrepreneurs of the Meiji years. To emphasize or to assume the meaningfulness of class distinction is the common and necessary weakness of the orthodox view. Those entrepreneurs often classified as 'of samurai origin' by writers from Tsuchiya to Hirschmeier reveal, upon closer examination of their respective biographies, that in many cases their class origins were at least doubtful and that they were often samurai only in name. Examples can be cited readily. Zenjiro Yasuda, 'the King of bankers', was technically a samurai, but his education and the pattern of his daily life differed little from those of peasants.[17] Yataro Iwasaki, the builder of the Mitsubishi Zaibatsu,[18] came from generations of peasant-merchants. He bought a *gōshi* (country samurai) share so that he could obtain a job with a *han* (domain) bureaucracy.[19] Rempei Kondō and Ryōhei Toyokawa, both of whom helped Iwasaki to build the Mitsubishi Zaibatsu, and who were leading businessmen in their own right, were commoners who became marginal samurai. The former was the son of a *han*-doctor who was given a quasi-samurai status, and the latter was the son of a country samurai who later became a *han*-doctor.[20] The great manager of the House of Sumitomo, Saihei Hirose, who had worked as an errand boy since the age of eleven, is known to have come 'from the farm': i.e., he was either of peasant or, at most, of *gōshi* origin.[21] Rizaemon Minomura, who almost single-handedly rebuilt the House of Mitsui, is known 'to have come from nowhere' and to have worked as a child. Tsuchiya ventured his opinion that Minomura's father was a *rōnin*, a masterless samurai.[22] Sōichiro Asano, who was called a 'demon of business' for his ruthless activities in the cement and shipping industries, was selling cloth at the age of fifteen, when 'he would have been going through a ceremony of *genpuku* [to mark his attainment of manhood] had he been a samurai'.[23]

These men, and others such as Tomiji Hirano, Takeo Yamabe, and Keiichiro Kawabe, were in fact *chōnin* or at best marginal samurai.[24] Coming from 'very poor families in which there was only one *kimono* for each person',[25] they rose to become leading entrepreneurs through their willingness to work 'for days without sleep'[26] and other qualities similar to those found in Iwasaki and Yasuda. In short, biographies of these men show that they simply were not the kind of samurai who, with the 'spirit of samurai' and a knowledge of Confucian ethics, dedicated themselves to great causes.[27] Noteworthy also in this context is a recent study which found that over three-fourths of a sample of 189 early Meiji entrepreneurs came from the commoner classes, and most of these commoner–entrepreneurs were drawn from the upper economic and social strata.[28]

Perhaps a more important point to be made is that the distinction between the samurai class and the *chōnin* class is of highly questionable validity. That the distinction had become unimportant by the late Tokugawa period has been noted often. Horie observed that 'many samurai had been reduced to supplementing their income by earning wages or by trading',[29] and Yui wrote that 'at the end of the Tokugawa period, one finds rich peasants and small-scale entrepreneurs in villages who begin to have thoughts and education akin to those of the samurai class, and class distinction became negligible'.[30] Many writers, Western and Japanese alike, would agree with the view that class distinctions had become, as Hirschmeier himself put it, 'blurred'[31] by the late Tokugawa period.

The importance of re-evaluating the current view lies in the fact that it encourages inaccurate evaluations of historical facts, which in turn are used to support the orthodoxy. A case in point is provided by the interpretations of the development of modern banking referred to earlier. Many authors, as we have seen, have long maintained that modern banking in Japan was developed by the samurai class under the guidance of the government. These sources also reiterated that the *chōnin* had to be pressured by the government and the samurai class to join in the establishment of the banks. Recently, empirical studies have shown that such a view is untenable.[32] Rather, the foundation of modern banking in Japan was laid in 1876 when the Banking Act of 1872 was amended to allow profitable banking operations for the first time. All earlier attempts by the government had failed, but once the profitability of modern banking was assured, banks were immediately established in large numbers. When close examinations of annual reports and bank histories are made, the only possible conclusion is that the initiative in establishing and operating these banks came from merchants and rich peasants who saw an opportunity for profit, rather than from the

samurai class who might have wished to serve the cause of the modernization of Japan.

The observation that the success of modern banking in Japan must
be attributed to the samurai class cannot be supported. The major
'evidence' that the samurai class contributed over three-quarters of the
initial capital is inadequate. The fact is that the samurai contributed the
commutation bonds they had just received to the establishment of these
banks more for lack of alternatives than for any more positive reasons.
While the participation of samurai in new banks was thus passive, the
commoner class participated actively in the majority of new banks
by supplying the necessary cash (20 per cent of the initial capital)
and the entrepreneurial energy in the form of directors and initiators
in obtaining charters. Even the nominal control of banks by the
samurai as majority shareholders shifted, in most cases, to the
hands of commoners a few years after the establishment of these
banks. Hugh T. Patrick, who has studied Japanese financial institutions, and who does not subscribe to the earlier view of the 'community-centered' entrepreneurs, aptly summarized the new view
when he wrote that 'it was mainly through the initiative of profit-
minded individuals that most Japanese financial institutions were
born'.[33]

More generally, how accurate is the prevailing view which stresses
the importance of the roles of the government and the samurai in the
development industries? Can the oft-cited examples of government
entrepreneurship be supported by facts and figures? Let us closely
examine a few cases of the most frequently cited examples of the
effectiveness of the government's – and therefore samurai's – contribution in the early phases of industrialization.

We can begin with the case of the Tomioka filature, one of the first
government-owned and government-operated plants and the one
which has been cited constantly as the best example of the entrepreneurial role of the Meiji government. Despite the stated objective of the
government – that it financed the plant in order to help develop the silk
industry – a close examination reveals how one could be misled in
interpreting the role of the government, and therefore the role of the
chōnin, if one takes such policy statements at face value. The records
reveal that the plant officials consistently refused permission to aspiring
entrepreneurs to see the machines and plant organization. For example,
Furushima found that 'the filature plant at Tomioka did not allow access
to those who wished to examine the machines at the plants so that they
could copy the machines'.[34] Existing records also show that a newly
organized company called Rokkō-sha had to learn the workings of the
plant's boiler from a fireman of the boiler and that a would-be silk-

reeler obtained access to the plant with the special aid of a cook at the plant.[35]

These actions of the plant officials are baffling when considered in the light of the declared goal of the government. But it is not difficult to understand these actions when we learn that 'these bureaucrats were more concerned with writing good reports to the Ministry which could influence their own advancement. Also, they were often ignorant of financial and technical matters.'[36] Understandably, they were afraid of exposing their own inefficiency, which could hinder their promotion. In fact, according to a study made by Kensō Hayami, the plant had much to hide, as it failed to live up to its billing as a 'model plant of silk-reeling'. The officials paid 'high prices for large quantities of cocoons, as they possessed no skill in bargaining; they were also plagued with a high turnover of female labour, which caused a shortage of skilled employees, and by unwise decision in the selection of the plant sites'.[37]

Hayami found the performance of the Tomioka filature extremely poor. When filatures were grouped into the six categories of superior, average, and inferior filatures using Western machines and superior, average, and inferior filatures using hand-operated machines, Hayami found that for a given scale of operation (450 employees each working 288 days per year) the yield of filature per yen of cocoon was lowest for the Tomioka filature. The Tomioka's yield was 21·42 *momme*, while all other categories of plants showed a yield of some 36–42 *momme*. Also the yield of filature per hand per day was the lowest for the Tomioka filature – slightly lower than 17 yen for the inferior plant using hand-operated machines. The figure for non-government machine-operated plants was as high as 26 yen. When it was operated on this 450-employee, 288-day scale – which was chosen for the Tomioka filature's technical requirements – Hayami found that the government plant lost 55,268 yen annually while all the others made profits ranging from 486 yen to 12,214 yen.[38]

More importantly, 'the rapid increase in the number of silk-reeling machines during the period 1878–86 was based on wooden machines which were not reproduced from the Tomioka model'.[39] The industry grew through the use of Italian and traditional models, either hand-operated or driven by water power, rather than by the engine-operated French model which the Tomioka plant used. The Italian model was introduced and popularized by the merchant house of Ono in Nagano, Fukushima, and Chikuma[40] prefectures, in which the industry grew most rapidly. Furthermore, Furushima noted that while Gumma prefecture supplied the largest number of apprentice–employees to the Tomioka plant in Fukushima (708 out of a total of 3,472), Gumma prefecture lagged in the development of the industry. Obviously the oft-stated benefit expected from the government plants – the training of future textile workers who would in turn work in privately built plants or establish more plants – was not obtained in the case of the Tomioka filature. This caused Furushima to observe that 'little relationship exists between the Tomioka filature and the growth of the industry'.[41]

As noted earlier, the ten sets of 2,000-spindle units imported by the government from England and sold on a ten-year credit basis to ten private individuals in 1880 have been cited frequently as a typical example of the Meiji government's role in stimulating the development of the cotton textile industry in Japan.[42] Even in this case, a close examination of the records reveals facts which many writers on Japanese economic development have failed to note or have chosen to ignore. Of the ten entrepreneurs, a few failed shortly after the operation of spindles began, while others remained in struggling and obscure establishments. The only successful case was that of Denhichi Itō, who went on from his 2,000 spindles to establish a leading cotton textile company. A study of his biography and company history, however, casts serious doubts on the importance of the government contribution to his success.

Inventive and mechanically adept, Itō had a long-standing interest in cotton-spinning.[43] He had been exposed to his cousin's interest in cotton-weaving and had heard the news of imported cotton-spinning 'machines' used by Satsuma-*han*. It is evident that by 1870 Itō had made up his mind to pursue cotton-spinning. A few of the major factors in his decision can be seen readily. First, Itō's *sake-kabu* (guild rights to *sake*-making) were abolished by the new government, and his village monopoly had begun to be threatened by increasing competition. Second, his cousin indicated that he was willing to help Itō's new venture financially. Last, but perhaps most important, the more Itō investigated the industry, the more he was fascinated by the mechanical aspects of the industry compared to the tradition-bound area of *sake*-making. One could, as has been done too frequently, quote Itō's biographer as to why Itō entered cotton-spinning: 'to stop the flood of foreign cotton goods' to Japan.[44] I am confident that for those who read Itō's biographies, this possibility is akin to imputing to early settlers in the American West the desire to spread the virtues of freedom of religion.

During the next several years, Itō visited the Sakai Bōseki-sho (Sakai Spinning and Weaving Plant, a former Satsuma-*han* plant which had just been taken over by the Meiji government), and in 1875 he and his cousin somehow managed to acquire a hand-operated American spinning machine. They studied it until it was 'completely mutilated'. By the late 1870s, Itō had reached the stage of designing his plant and was casting about for appropriate machines, as he already had financial resources, his own plus those of his cousin and other relatives. It was at this point that the government announced its plan to sell the ten sets of 2,000-spindle units on ten-year credit without interest. Itō applied immediately; and his application was successful, despite stiff competition from a group of samurai from the same Mie prefecture. His long-standing interest in the industry apparently was sufficient to overcome the officials' usual preference for samurai who were in need of a new livelihood. However, immediately after this success, his cousin suddenly decided to withdraw his financial backing. Although the reasons for this were not stated explicitly, it is evident from the carefully expressed resentment of Itō that his cousin found traditional weaving more to his liking than risking capital on foreign machines. To fill this gap, Itō managed, with considerable difficulty, to persuade a few friends to supply capital. A sum of 30,000 yen was raised, of which Itō contributed 55 per cent.

Itō's life for the next several years was a biographer's dream and Itō's nightmare. Itō and his son struggled through the designing and supervising of the building of the plant and the installation. 'During this period, Itō's life was hard. He worked with his employees and so did his family. He often forgot to eat and went without sleep.'[45] Technical and financial problems beset Itō from the beginning. The machines were larger than had been expected, and the plant had to be redesigned. A sum of 65,000 yen, more than twice that originally anticipated, had to be spent. This meant that, with minimum operating expenses of 10,000 yen, Itō was deeply in debt without even counting the 22,416 yen of government credit for spindles. His house had to be second-mortgaged and loans from friends and relatives increased rapidly; on occasion he had to sell his family's clothing to pay the wages.

Once the spindles began operation in 1883, it was evident that his problems had just begun. A 2,000-spindle unit was not economical in terms of making efficient use of inputs, labour, and ancillary machines. The river site selected on the advice of a government official yielded only one-third of the expected power, and to supplement this Itō had to buy a 25-h.p. steam engine at the cost of 4,078 yen, of which 4,000 yen was borrowed and 78 yen came out of the already meagre operating fund.

At the height of these disappointments, Itō died. This was in September 1883, at a time when he was writing to the government that 'the credit could be repaid if another 100 years were allowed'.[46] Itō's son, also named Denhichi Itō, then 34 years old, carried on for the next few years with no visible success. In 1886, he listed four major causes for his

difficulties. (1) The initial capital requirement was far larger than anticipated and critically affected all aspects of operation from the beginning.
(2) The 2,000-spindle unit was highly uneconomical because of its
'imbalance' for efficient uses of labour, inputs, and ancillary machines,
thus affecting the unit cost or even the quality of the product. (3) Little
guidance in the operating of imported spindles was available, and operations had to be executed on a costly trial-and-error basis. (4) For various
reasons, the use of water power, which had been recommended by the
government, was a mistake. Also, the site selected on the advice of
government officials was insufficient to operate 1,000 spindles, even in
seasons of maximum water supply.[47]

Convinced that there was no hope for the 2,000-spindle unit, and
seeing the successful example of the entirely privately financed and
operated Osaka Cotton Textile Company (Osaka Bōseki) – which had a
dividend rate of 18 per cent in 1885 – Itō's son decided to increase the
number of spindles to 10,000, the scale of Osaka Cotton Textiles. To
achieve this, he needed 170,000 yen. Itō himself could contribute in the
form of the physical assets and inventories of his failing plant. For the
remainder, he had to rely on public subscription; but, given the record
of Itō's plant, there were no subscribers to the shares. Fortunately for
Itō, however, the governor of the prefecture, who had known Itō's
father because of his long struggles in the venture, introduced Itō to
Shibusawa Eiichi, then the president of the First National Bank (Daiichi
Ginkō). Shibusawa instructed his branch office in Mie, where Itō's
plant was located, to purchase a portion of the shares. After this show of
confidence by the largest bank in Japan, the remaining shares were fully
subscribed by the public within a brief period. The total capital was
increased to 220,000 yen shortly afterwards, and Itō's Mie Cotton
Textiles began operation in November 1886. From then on, the company history of Mie Cotton Textiles was one of continued success. It
absorbed seven smaller firms before 1914, when Mie Cotton Textiles
merged with Osaka Cotton Textiles to create the giant Tōyō Cotton
Textiles. At the time of the merger, the Mie's paid-in capital stood at
7,768,450 yen, and it owned eleven plants and 306,376 spindles.[48]

Even in the case of the most successful of the ten recipients of government credit, it is difficult to conclude that the government had built a
foundation for the large Mie Cotton Textiles, let alone to support the
inference carelessly made by some writers that those ten sets of 2,000-
spindle units somehow became the foundation of the Japanese cotton
textile industry. We should recall that even in Itō's case the venture
became successful only after Itō's son decided to follow the example of
the successful, entirely private Osaka Cotton Textile Company and to
completely abandon the uneconomical 2,000-spindle plant, the use of

water power, and the site, all recommended by the government. The major ingredients in the success of the Mie Cotton Textile Company were the tenacity and drive of the men involved and the capital which became available in the form of subscribed shares. If the importance of the government contribution is to be stressed, one should recall that for this assistance Itō paid 55,000 yen and went through years of agonizing struggle.

In addition to these well known and frequently cited examples in the silk and cotton textile industries, the case of Tōsaburō Suzuki in sugar-refining is also a very revealing one. Because I believe that this case represents many Meiji *chōnin*–entrepreneurs who succeeded in establishing a firm in a 'Western' industry without the help of an influential banker, without the guidance of foreign experts, and with no direct help from the government, I shall sketch its bare outlines.[49]

Although an adopted son of a poor candy merchant, Suzuki did not want to 'end his life as a small merchant'. He was extremely ambitious, in the American 'get-rich-quick' sense of the term. Always on the lookout for new money-making schemes, he speculated in tea but was unsuccessful because of his meagre capital. He worked tirelessly in his small candy business but was reminded constantly that wealth could be gained only by beginning some new business. Although he did not yet know what that new business might be, he resolved to save as much and as fast as he could. A large amount of capital, he had decided, was necessary for success. For the next five years, he worked almost to the point of ruining his health. The hard work, along with extreme self-denial, increased his savings from 260 yen to 1,300 yen.

During the next five years, he became increasingly curious about the manufacture of what the Japanese call ice-sugar, or crystalline sugar; this interest deepened into a large commitment of time and effort. This was a natural evolution of events stemming from his daily use of brown sugar and inferior 'cloudy' ice-sugar, which was then imported mostly from China.

Suzuki's initial efforts were discouraging. His search yielded no books on sugar crystallization, and he found that only a few merchants on the island of Shikoku were producing 'cloudy' ice-sugar, refined by the traditional method. In 1877, modern refining was virtually unknown in Japan, and refined sugar was imported from Hawaii, Russia, and Europe. In 1878, the government imported the first machines from France, but they failed to produce sugar though they were operated in Hokkaidō, where European-type beets were grown. Machines repeatedly exploded when operated by the inexperienced Japanese. This was about the extent of the government's efforts until 1883, when two German experts arrived to operate the machines. Private groups, including a company called Hōraisha, had also imported machines from England and attempted to operate them, but all attempts were unsuccessful. The unrewarding efforts Suzuki made in 1887–8 were understandable when seen in this light. He, in effect, was attempting to start modern sugar-refining in a country which still practised the method it had been using since 1723, when the first sugar was refined from sugar cane imported from Okinawa.

From 1878 to 1882, Suzuki continued to experiment against the strenuous objections of his family. Since he had neither training nor scientific knowledge, his experiments consisted of boiling and cooling various sugar solutions under numerous combinations of heat, duration, and quantity. At one point, he used the ash of human bones, misinterpreting the advice of a local druggist who had recommended the use of a catalyst. This attempt failed to yield ice-sugar, though it produced sufficient stench to bring in the local police. An ordinary man would have given up, but Suzuki persisted.

It was in early 1883, when he was away at a university in Tokyo to learn more about possible catalysts, that ice-sugar was produced almost by accident. By a series of fortunate coincidences, the family unintentionally heated one sugar solution which Suzuki had left in an airtight container. It was then cooled over the period of Suzuki's absence. The quantity of ice-sugar yielded was small and not entirely pure; but Suzuki, now knowing the basic process of crystallization, plunged into a new series of experiments. He continued to improve the yield and purity during the next eleven months in a large furnace he built, and by the end of 1883 he finally succeeded in producing pure ice-sugar at a cost which would allow profitable marketing.

A merchant in Tokyo agreed to sell Suzuki's ice-sugar. The business was excellent from the beginning, and Suzuki soon wished to expand his output. The immediate problem he faced was capital. His savings spent, and his expenditures for new equipment not yet amortized by the profits of his current business, he tried his circle of friends, but to no avail. His guarantee of a return of 10 per cent failed to interest possible investors, who could earn more by making safe loans. Desperate, Suzuki decided to try a relative stranger, a retired second-hand-kimono dealer who was reputed to be wealthy. To Suzuki's surprise, the dealer agreed to lend him 2,000 yen.

But Suzuki was the kind of man who constantly thought of the next step before the first was completed. He now made the decision to relocate his business in Tokyo, for two reasons. The first was to increase his sales and profits by reducing transportation costs to Tokyo and by obtaining his inputs at lower cost. The second, equally important, was his new desire to refine his sugar according to Western methods. By this time Suzuki was confident of successfully competing against the imported Chinese ice-sugar and brown sugar. He now wanted to tackle modern refining itself.

This meant that he needed a large amount of capital to relocate and to begin refining. Suzuki had, however, little difficulty in persuading the kimono dealer – who had seen the results of his first investment – to invest another several thousand yen. For additional funds, Suzuki tried his sole agent in Tokyo, but the latter flatly refused any loan on the ground that earlier private attempts and 'even the government had failed' in sugar-refining. This was a bitter disappointment for Suzuki. He wanted to relocate in Tokyo but had to abandon the idea because of a lack of finances. With the capital provided by the kimono dealer, Suzuki built a second oven to increase his business. Though Suzuki's net profit was only 3·5 yen for the first six months of 1885, because of the costs of expansion and interest, the expansion paid off by the end of the year, and he showed a net profit of 3,000 yen for the last half of 1885. Throughout 1886 and 1887 sales of Suzuki's ice-sugar increased. The annual profit began to exceed 10,000 yen, and he completely eliminated his Chinese competition. His biggest problem during these two years was the constant attempts of others to copy his process.

A decisive moment came in April 1888 when his father, who had vigorously opposed his plans, died. With his accumulated and projected earnings, and with no one to object to the move, Suzuki decided to relocate. The new plant in Tokyo was completed early in 1889, and it proved much more profitable than he had anticipated. New ovens, which eliminated all the weaknesses of the former mud ovens, performed far better than had been expected. Savings owing to reduced costs of transportation and raw material were added to his profits. Following this success, Suzuki began to concentrate on refining. He worked all day at the new ice-sugar plant, and in the evenings he read – often till dawn – all the available scientific writings on the subject. He visited chemists and engineers and learned to read blueprints. He took copious notes from foreign books which were read to him by university students. This time he did not wish to waste several years for lack of a systematic and scientific approach.

Finally, Suzuki visited the Hokkaidō sugar plant before he embarked on a new large investment. This was the factory which had originally been begun by the government and was now operated by a group of former samurai. The operation Suzuki saw was badly run and hardly profitable; but there Suzuki confirmed what he had learned and made mental improvements on what he saw. He then began to build refining machines. To do this, he had to build a machine-tool shop of his own, since no one was able to produce what he needed. By June 1890, Suzuki succeeded in producing the first sugar-refining machines in Japan. The costs were huge and took all the reserves his successful ice-sugar plant could provide. For the next ten months, Suzuki had to improve the machines to increase the yield ratio of sugar to a profitable level, and this was accomplished by April 1891. Suzuki was now ready to conquer the refined-sugar market of Japan which imported 93 per cent of its needs.[50]

In lieu of more cases to prove the point I wish to make, let me merely add the following. The oft-cited government-owned glass factory was actually begun as a private firm, and success came only after the government sold the plant back to private entrepreneurs. Again, a careful reading of the five-volume history of the giant Oji Paper Company shows that it was merchant capital and entrepreneurship which made this firm a success in spite of occasional competition and interference from government officials. Even in shipbuilding, shipping, and electricity, a long list of cases can be compiled to demonstrate that the contribution of the government and the samurai class has indeed been overemphasized at the cost of an accurate appraisal of the role of merchant capital and entrepreneurship.

In the new perspective, the former *chōnin* and other non-samurai individuals play a much more important role as entrepreneurs and capitalists in Japan's industrialization than has been previously granted. For those students who have held the long-standing view, this is perhaps difficult to accept, and the difficulty is easily understandable. In a framework which stressed the leadership role performed by the government and the former samurai class in Japan's rapid industrialization, the former *chōnin* with their supposed lack of initiative had to be relegated to a minor position. This framework was readily acceptable to many students of Japan, since it provided them with a ready explanation of the rapid industrialization of Japan as a typical case of growth 'induced' from above, and because it accommodated a simple extrapolation of the behaviour and role of the Tokugawa *chōnin*, who are supposed to have lacked 'high ideals' or the 'spirit of samurai'.

Paraphrasing Keynes, if we are not to be enslaved by the theories of yesterday, all facts must be accommodated within a new framework. The facts of the cases we have examined above appear to suggest that Landes was quite right when he wrote:

In promoting economic growth, government spending is just one of several devices for mobilizing and allocating resources. For backward countries especially, it is linked closely as we have seen to import of capital from abroad, the one complementing the other. When one examines the Japanese experience in this light, one is less impressed by the contribution of the state;

one expects it to be higher to compensate for the lack of funds from outside. And one is struck by the high proportion of investment accounted for by private enterprise.[51]

Also, as Landes noted, the new perspective is not inconsistent with Rosovsky's findings that the government was responsible for an important share of gross domestic fixed capital. On the contrary, the new perspective adds strength to Rosovsky's view of the early Meiji years as a transition phase, in which the government provided the environment for rapid economic growth, and supports Crawcour's recent emphasis on the role of government as a builder of the infrastructure necessary for economic development.[52] These views of my colleagues and such observations as the one that the Japanese relied 'far less than Europeans on the skills, knowledge, and enterprise of foreigners' begin to fall into place in the framework of the new perspective. The Itōs and Suzukis who provided the sustaining force for rapid economic growth need not and cannot be neglected as we realize the necessity of a renewed evaluation of this Asian success story.

By the beginning of the new century, when the cotton textile industry was rapidly expanding, both the demand and supply of entrepreneurs – now gradually coming to include the executive-level personnel of the more rapidly expanding among the larger firms – underwent a visible change. Larger and more complex firms demanded a set of abilities akin to those required of corporate executives as we envision them today, rather than those personal qualities of successful managers of merchant houses or of zaibatsu-founders such as Iwasaki and Yasuda. Firms sought their top-level executives and managerial staff at the newly expanding universities and colleges. That the firms began to find their entrepreneurial recruits in the schools reflects the importance of education in Japanese society. As has been demonstrated by Dore, Jansen, and others,[53] learning historically commanded deep respect among the Japanese, and newly emerging schools, especially a few elite universities, were now looked upon as the source of the most able. Firms naturally relied, as did the bureaucracy, on this efficient filter of abilities. And the ability to learn, and mostly from books, was precisely the talent needed for a nation which was busily learning in all phases, but especially in industrial ones, from the West. Dependence on the universities was well-nigh complete by this time, and thus Dore was able to write: 'By the first decade of this century an individual's life chances were determined not so much by his family status in itself as by the income and amenities attaching to his father's occupational position – the pattern of occupational mobility became not so very different from that of western societies.'[54] This fact should not be underrated, inasmuch as it indicates the rapid adaptability of the Japanese in meeting the demands of a new age.

This transition can be seen quite well in the House of Mitsui. The last of the old-style *bantō*, Rizaemon Minomura, was a *chōnin*'s son with no formal education.[55] He was shrewd in the best tradition of the Tokugawa commercial world and adept at gaining favours from political leaders who were in a position to dispense substantial financial rewards. Thus, during the politically and economically turbulent years of the late Tokugawa and early Meiji periods, Minomura's talents were great assets to the House of Mitsui, which, on the eve of Restoration, was none too secure. But the new industrial age, with its more impersonal and complex requirements, was beyond his understanding and ability. When he died, Mitsui was facing numerous difficulties; compared to Mitsubishi it was slow to make the transition needed in building an industrial empire, and its bank was in grave difficulties because of large amounts of loans made, largely to high government officials, with little or no collateral.

Hikojiro Nakamigawa, who took over Minomura's position at Mitsui, was a product of the new age.[56] A graduate of Keiō University, he had taught at a college and had lived for three years in England. He was progressive and injected the economic rationality of the industrial age into Mitsui's management. The temporary frictions he caused were to be expected. To the chagrin of Buddhists all over the nation, he forced Higashi Honganji, one of the largest temples, to pay back its overdue loans immediately, thus compelling the abbot of the temple to launch a nationwide campaign to raise the money. He next required collateral for loans to high government officials, in order to maintain sound banking practices on Western standards. Well supported by able lieutenants, most of whom were college graduates, he acquired the government-owned Tomioka filature, won control of the Oji paper firm, and took over the Kanegafuchi Cotton Textile Company. When Nakamigawa gained control, even the money-losing Kanegafuchi was made profitable and was soon the most efficient textile mill in Japan.

The transition of Mitsui was dramatic; but in most other firms the same change from merchant business leaders to college-educated industrial entrepreneurs took place, though less dramatically and more gradually. It had to, if the firms were to survive and prosper. For each merchant house which failed at the beginning of Meiji, such as the house of Ono, scores of large and small firms made the transition successfully. And this pattern of using colleges and universities as the sources of business leaders became gradually more entrenched as Japanese industrialization continued. Dore wrote:

At any rate the existence of the trend [of placing emphasis on learning] is not hard to document. Of a sample of business leaders in a directory of 1915, only 15 per cent had been to a university. The figure was 83 per cent for a similar sample from the 1955 edition. In the latter year 48 per cent of the sample had spent all their working lives in salaried employment, compared with only 5 per cent in the earlier sample.[57]

In making a study of the inter-class mobility of Japanese elites, Abegglen and Mannari found that in the late 1950s the top-level business leaders' 'grandfathers were of two groups for the most part, merchants from an urban setting perhaps, and small businessmen and landowners from rural backgrounds, with movement to urban white-collar and business positions in the next generation'.[58] We can assume that the men examined by these writers were born about 1900 on the average, and it might be assumed that their fathers were born about 1870, while their grandfathers would have been born about 1840.

Leaving further observations on Japanese entrepreneurship in more recent times to the last section of this chapter, we might conclude here with the following caveat. Given the weight of the literature supporting the orthodox view, I am not contending here that the foregoing discussions and the limited evidence are sufficient to disprove the long-held view. Rather, the main aim of this section is to present those observations and evidence which are helpful in gaining a more complete, and I hope a more accurate, understanding of Japanese entrepreneurship. For some, the descriptions of the cases of Itō and Suzuki may have been too detailed, and the view expressed on the roles of the government and the samurai may have been too forceful. But these must be understood as attempts to counterbalance the accumulated evidence marshalled on behalf of the orthodox view.

Those who are familiar with the pre-war literature can easily recall Tomoatsu Godai, a samurai who became an industrial pioneer in many fields; Takashi Masuda, a former samurai entrepreneur who was a leader in mining and in international trade; and a dozen other former samurai entrepreneurs including Goichi Nakano, Heigoro Shoda, and Taizo Abe.[59] The once-giant Fifteenth National Bank, which played an important role in financing the first privately owned railways in Japan, among other industrial ventures, was established by former *daimyō* and nobility who provided entrepreneurship and capital.[60] A long list of significant contributions made by the government toward industrialization can also be easily compiled. It is an academic truism that the evidence gathered and the observations made by earlier generations of economic historians can no more be ignored than the evidence presented in this chapter.

An eminent British historian has written that 'the facts are really not at all like fish on the fishmonger's slab. They are like fish swimming in a vast and sometimes inaccessible ocean; and what the historian catches will depend partly on chance, but mainly on what part of the ocean he chooses to fish in and what tackle he chooses to use – those two factors being, of course, determined by the kind of fish he wants to catch.'[61] The fish we catch may appear to fit badly into the established scheme of classification which we hold dear, but when the ocean is searched more thoroughly and a new classification scheme is fully worked out, I am confident that all the fish will find their places, resulting in an increased knowledge of the sea.

III.   *Ownership and Control*

A small number of industrial undertakings during the late Tokugawa period were owned and operated by the Bakufu or *han* (domains). Wide-ranging commercial activities of large merchant houses were exclusively controlled by the respective families. *Bantō*, the chief managers, usually conducted the day-to-day business of these merchant houses, and in a few instances strong *bantō* made important entrepreneurial decisions. However, as a rule they were hired managers. The Meiji Restoration did not change this pattern immediately. The government plants were owned and operated by the government and managed by samurai-turned-bureaucrats. The ownership and control of merchant houses remained as before, and the emerging fortunes of Iwasaki, Yasuda, Asano, Furukawa, and other zaibatsu were strictly owned and controlled by the strong-willed founders. In fact, the law establishing *kabushiki kaisha* (share-issuing incorporated legal persons) was not enacted until 1890.

Though Japanese economic historians have not agreed as to when the first firm with share capital in the modern sense came into existence – in fact if not in name – one finds that a forerunner of the *kabushiki kaisha* had already appeared within a few years of the Restoration.[62] Mostly to supply credits and also to aid trading firms engaged in international trade, the government in 1869 established eight *kawase kaisha* on a share-capital basis in port cities. '*Kawase kaisha*' literally means 'bills-of-exchange companies', but this was meant to be a translation of the English word 'bank', for which there existed no exact equivalent in Japanese. *Kawase kaisha* had the 'characteristics of banks and were authorized to issue their own notes'.[63] The capital for these *kawase kaisha* was supplied by wealthy merchants, rich farmers, and money-exchangers who had established large houses during the late Tokugawa period, and by the government, which nearly matched the capital supplied from these private sources. Excessive and unwise control and interference by the government, and the generally unfavourable economic conditions of the time, caused these *kawase kaisha* to fail, save one in Yokohama.[64]

While the government financed its industrial undertakings, attempted to establish *kawase kaisha*, and enacted the banking acts, private firms faced the difficult task of obtaining sufficient capital to undertake ventures which were too large to be financed out of the individual resources of most entrepreneurs. How was the necessary capital for Japan's rapid industrialization obtained, and who controlled the firms? Although they must be accompanied with the usual proviso needed in making historical periodization, these questions can best be answered by examining the years from 1868 to 1940 in three periods. As will become evident, these are fairly distinct periods for the purpose of the analysis of the ownership and control of Japanese industrial firms.

The first period can be thought of as extending from the Restoration into the mid-1880s. This was a period of preparation for modern economic growth, and it continued to the eve of the visible spurt in investment activities in the cotton textile industry. Private industrial firms, such as those of Suzuki in sugar refining and Itō in cotton textiles, began in most instances with capital which the entrepreneurs accumulated themselves and/or borrowed from their friends and relatives. The Oji Paper Company, which was to grow into the largest in the industry, began in 1873 with capital shared by the House of Mitsui and a dozen other merchants.[65] The Tokyo Electric Light Company began construction of its plants in 1886 when, after four years of struggling to raise capital, it finally persuaded sixty-four individuals to invest 200,000 yen.[66] These were also the years during which Hirano Tomiji, who was to build one of the largest shipbuilding firms in Japan, laboured mightily to accumulate the necessary capital to start a shipyard and to make it sufficiently profitable to obtain a bank loan.[67] These were the years of the industrial pioneers whose meagre capital and abundant determination laid the foundations for the rapid growth to come.

The bankers, still groping for the fundamentals of sound modern banking practices in the new industrial age, were not yet ready to participate in industrial financing. An examination of bank records and recent empirical studies conducted by Japanese scholars make it clear that most bank funds tended to flow to agriculture and commerce.[68] I agree with Patrick's observation: 'It is clear that until the late 1880's most bank loans financed domestic and foreign trade, small-scale units of production in agriculture and processing industries, and, to some extent, the consumption of poor samurai and poor farmers (who, respectively, used pension bonds and land as collateral).'[69]

The zaibatsu, which were to become a dominant force in the economy, were still at the stage of recovering from the financial difficulties
which they had met from the forced loans and economic dislocation of
the past few decades and were occupied in building up their financial
strength. They were still merchant houses at the dawn of a new industrial era. The House of Mitsui, for example, was under the management
of Rizaemon Minomura, as described earlier. His forte was more in
cultivating the good will of political leaders than in assessing the profitability of industrial ventures. Minomura was successful in getting the
House of Mitsui appointed to the profitable position of 'Official
Agent' of the new government's *dajōkan-satsu* (Privy Councillor's
notes) and was a shrewd speculator in the new currency, taking the best
advantage of its fluctuating prices. Mitsui bought a trading company in
1875 from Mitsui's political benefactor, Kaoru Inoue, who entered the
new cabinet. Renamed the Mitsui Bussan (Trading Company), it grew
rapidly, to earn large profits from government contracts to market coal
produced by a government mine and from lucrative dealings in textile
goods and the importation of a large number of industrial goods from
the West.[70]

Then, in 1876, Mitsui established its own bank, capitalized at 2 million
yen. The bank, exclusively controlled by the Mitsui family, began its
business with thirty branches located all over the nation. From the
beginning this bank enjoyed the same political favours given to the
other Mitsui enterprises: namely, the bank received large government
deposits and benefited from the tax-collection services which all local
branches rendered to the Ministry of Finance. By 1882, the bank was
large enough to withstand a momentary crisis which was caused by the
establishment of the Bank of Japan, to which the Mitsui Bank immediately lost 6·8 million yen in government deposits.

The second period, from the mid-1880s to the First World War, saw
a few important developments which changed the ownership and control patterns of Japanese industrial firms. Most notable is the fact that the
largest merchant houses, now financially strong and equipped with
their respective thriving banks, took the first steps toward creating their
own industrial empires. Beginning in the early 1880s, the largest among
them, especially, began to acquire government plants. These acquisi-
tions – twenty industrial plants and mines in all – proved highly profitable. Thus they became an added impetus for these zaibatsu to establish,
acquire, and increase their financial control in industrial undertakings.
The industrial empires of these zaibatsu had not yet approached the
proportions they were to reach after the end of the First World War,
but by the first decade of the new century they had become the new
industrial economic powers within the nation. Mitsui formally organ-

ized a holding company, Mitsui Gōmei, in 1911 to exercise tight financial control over its bank, trading company, mining firms, real estate,
and warehousing activities, as well as the Oji Paper Company and a
dozen other enterprises. Mitsubishi, too, established its holding company, the Mitsubishi Gōshikaisha, in 1917 to increase the financial
control over its firms.[71]

Banks during this period began to make long- and short-term loans to
industrial firms, and their holdings of industrial shares increased. However, contrary to the long-maintained proposition that the banks,
especially the large ones, were a dominant factor in providing industrial
capital, a close examination of the data seems to reveal that the importance of large banks as owners of individual shares and as individual
financiers during this period has been significantly overstated. One can
show this in several ways.

Beginning with the oft-quoted aggregate data, we find for 1899–1902
that the loans made by all ordinary banks using shares as collateral were
in the neighbourhood of 25 per cent of all the loans made in each year;
when loans made on debentures are added, the figure rises to approximately 30 per cent. These data seem to show the importance of banks in
industrial financing, but a closer scrutiny reveals that this first impression is deceptive. In a more meaningful context, we find that the loans
made using shares as collateral amounted to about 22 per cent of the
total paid-in capital in 1899, 18 per cent in 1900, 12 per cent in 1901, and
11 per cent in 1902. These percentages, however, do not indicate the
degree of direct contribution by the banks to industrial financing. Even
assuming that all the loans made using shares as collateral were used for
financing industry, these percentages must be almost halved before we
can consider them as indicators of the degree of the direct contribution
of the banks to industrial financing, because only slightly more than
half of these loans and investments were for industrial firms. Not only
was nearly half of the total paid-up capital for non-industrial firms, but
the banks tended to prefer to finance other banks, insurance companies,
and established commercial firms.[72]

It is true that some portion of loans made using non-industrial shares
as collateral found their way to industry, and the total direct investment
by banks in industrial and non-industrial shares amounted to slightly
over half of those loans made using shares as collateral. But from what
can be observed of the aggregate data, direct bank financing in industrial
firms by means of loans and direct investment was limited. That is, as
the bank records of the period reveal, the industrial financing made by
these banks during the period 1899–1902 was limited in magnitude to
no more than 15 per cent of the total industrial paid-up capital – often
much less – and was not of an order of magnitude to justify the view

held by numerous earlier writers who, though differing in their choice
of phrases, observed in effect that 'the banks were the major source of
industrial financing by the turn of the century'.

Another set of data frequently used is the one calculated by the
Industrial Bank of Japan. Earlier authors often cited the data to show that
bank loans were the major source of industrial financing by the beginning of the twentieth century. According to these data the sources of 'a
total of 247 million yen in industrial funds supplied to industrial corporations between 1897 and 1913 were bank loans (57·7 per cent), new stock
issues (32·4 per cent), corporate debentures (6·5 per cent) and internal
reserves (3·6 per cent)'.[73] I believe these data are small in coverage and
are heavily biased to overemphasize bank loans; this can be seen easily.
The new stock issues increased by about 700 million yen during the
period 1897–1913. This means that the coverage of the Industrial Bank's
data was only slightly over 11 per cent of new stock issues. That is,
when the bank found that 32·4 per cent of the total industrial funds
(247 million) were financed by means of stock issues, the capital so
obtained was slightly over 80 million yen, which is 11·4 per cent of
700 million yen. It seems evident that the data covered only this small
fraction of all the bank loans made to industrial firms. Also, regardless
of the coverage and source, the figure of 3·6 per cent attributed to
internal reserves is hardly acceptable, as will be shown shortly. One
rather suspects that the data reflects much of the intra-zaibatsu financing,
i.e. from zaibatsu bank to zaibatsu-controlled firms.

It is evident from company and bank histories that many of the long-
term loans made by the largest banks went to a small number of firms
which were closely connected with these banks or ventures and which
were organized by the bankers themselves. These were the zaibatsu
industrial firms in mining, shipbuilding, and other industries, and they
were in many instances firms which were established from the former
government plants. The firms receiving long-term loans were small in
number compared to the large number of firms which lamented the
lack of long-term credit. The largest banks were, in fact, quite frank in
admitting such practices. The Bank of Mitsui noted that 'over 7
million yen', or nearly 40 per cent of the total amount lent, went to
several firms 'connected' with the bank. During the 1897–8 recession,
the bank 'curtailed loans as much as possible to general borrowers', and
large loans were confined to the firms in which Mitsui had a direct
interest.[74] The Mitsubishi Bank followed the same practice during the
period 'by lending only to those firms which are Mitsubishi-related',
while 'all branch offices sharply reduced loans to general [non-related]
borrowers'.[75] What percentage of the total amount in long-term loans
was borrowed by the minority of the zaibatsu firms is difficult to ascer-

tain. One conclusion which can be drawn safely is that it would be extremely difficult to show that a large number of industrial firms enjoyed long-term loans of any appreciable amount. This is especially true since it is well known that the smaller banks were even less willing to make long-term industrial loans.

That bank participation in industrial financing was not as important as has long been believed can be shown when we examine the cotton textile industry, which initiated the first industrial spurt of Japan. The Osaka Cotton Textile Company, the first large-scale firm (10,500 spindles), was established on private capital in 1882. This company, which by growth and the absorption of other firms was to become the giant Tōyō Textile Company, financed its growth by selling increasing amounts of shares and by ploughing back its profits. There is little evidence that bank loans played a significant role in its rapid expansion. The firm began with a capital of 25,000 yen in 1882; but in the following year this was increased to 280,000, and it was doing well enough to declare a dividend of 6 per cent. Over the next several years the firm gradually increased its capital to reach by 1888 the truly large sum – by the standards of the day – of 1·2 million yen, with cash reserves of 124,600 yen. The dividend rates for the years between 1884 and 1888 were 18, 11, 12, 30, and 33 per cent respectively. These rates undoubtedly aided shareholders in buying newly issued shares. By 1914, when the firm merged with Mie Cotton Textiles (Itō Denhichi's company) it had 13,009,225 yen of paid-in capital and 8,124,242 yen of reserve funds.[76]

Except for a few firms such as Kanegafuchi Cotton Textiles, which was taken over by Mitsui interests, the industry as a whole was relatively free of zaibatsu incursion and dependence on banks, and this is clearly seen in the industry-wide figures for 1905, at the height of the boom which followed the Russo-Japanese War. The industry's total assets were 51,469,000 yen with a paid-in capital of 34,332,000 yen, and the total internal reserve stood at 11,598,000 yen. Against this, outside loans of all types amounted to 5,565,000 yen, thus yielding a ratio of industry-wide total loans (short- and long-term) to total assets of 0·11, compared with a ratio of total reserve to owners' equity of 0·34, and one of total reserves to total assets of 0·23. The internal reserve was nearly twice the amount of outside loans.[77]

Behind this industrial expansion, and especially in view of the much less than dominant participation of the banks in such an important industry as the cotton textile industry, we must note the following oft-neglected figures. Even before the turn of the century, public participation in stock-buying had significantly increased. The total number of shareholders in Japan increased rapidly from 108,296 persons in 1886 to 244,585 persons in 1890 and then rose sharply to 684,070 persons by the end of 1898. When these figures are examined for different industries we find that the average number of shareholders per firm increased rapidly for 'modern' industries, while it declined visibly for other types of industries. Between 1893 and 1898, the average number of shareholders per firm rose from 136 to 457 in cotton-spinning, from 714 to 1,040 in railways, and from 4 to 124 in shipbuilding, while the same figure declined from 228 to 28 in cocoon-raising, from 410 to 45 in foreign trade, and from 361 to 93 in land development.[78]

During the third period, the inter-war years, we find that the ownership and control of Japanese industrial firms underwent significant changes. Most notable among them is the rapid rise of the financial control of, and increased ownership of, industrial firms by the zaibatsu banks. Concentration of product and capital markets continued at a rapid pace, and mutual shareholding and interlocking directorships continued to increase. It also was during this period that nearly a dozen holding companies, both large and small, appeared.

The First World War boom, which made Japan a fully fledged industrial power, profoundly changed banking practices. The largest banks, which were beginning to be called zaibatsu banks, began to advance significant sums in long-term loans to industrial firms in such capital-using industries as the heavy, chemical, and utility industries. More importantly, these new recipients of long-term bank loans were not, as earlier, a small number of firms which had close zaibatsu connections, either having been established partly by zaibatsu capital (such as the Oji Paper Company) or being one of the zaibatsu industrial ventures developed from plants bought by the zaibatsu interests from the Meiji government at the beginning of the 1880s. One could say that the zaibatsu banks became, during the 1920s, investment banks of the German type.

This transition was possible because the formerly bank-dependent zaibatsu-connected firms had by the end of the First World War become self-sufficient in terms of financing their own growth, and the banks themselves became large enough during the 1920s to make this transition possible in practice. The data indicate that these giant banks grew rapidly in strength, both in absolute and in relative terms, through increases in capital, deposits, and the number of mergers. It is well known that depositors sought these giant banks after a series of bank runs in the 1920s.

Facts to substantiate these observations can be found in numerous company histories and aggregate bank data. Preceding more general observations on the destinations of bank loans, several samples from the semi-annual financial reports of zaibatsu-connected firms will be useful in showing the transformation of the financial patterns of these firms, demonstrating that the rapidly growing zaibatsu banks no longer needed to concern themselves with supplying capital to their 'own' firms. These examples are 'representative' firms in that they were selected to reflect the financing patterns of zaibatsu firms during the Taisho and early Showa periods and were chosen from thirty-seven major zaibatsu-connected firms, for which these data are available.[79]

As early as 1907, the Shibaura Seisakusho (Shibaura Machine-Tool Industries) of the Mitsui group had stopped long-term borrowing from the Mitsui and other banks, and no long-term loan was made again until 1934. Neither does any short-term loan appear on the financial reports after 1908. The firm's capital was increased from 2 million yen to 5 million in 1912 before the investment boom of the First World War, and it was increased again to 20 million yen in 1920. A dividend rate in excess of 20 per cent was maintained between 1916 and 1921, and this fact enabled the company to sell its shares easily for the purpose of expansion.[80]

The Dainihon Seruroido KK (The Greater Japan Celluloid Company) of the Mitsui group ceased making short-term loans in 1921, and long-term loans disappeared from the reports in 1926. The long-term loans existing during the Taisho period (1912–25) never exceeded an amount equivalent to a small percentage of the total assets of the company. The firm increased the ratio of reserves to owners' equity (paid-in capital) from 5 per cent to 35 per cent during the period between 1921 and 1929. Share capital increased during the same time from 12·5 million yen in 1919 to 100 million in 1921.[81]

The Mitsui Kōzan KK (Mitsui Mining Company) issued no bonds during the Taisho or early Showa years. Its capital increased from 20 million yen in 1916 to 50 million in 1918, and then to 100 million yen in 1920 in order to finance the expansions of the boom years. Long-term loans were made from Mitsui Gōmei[82] until 1918, although the total amount was small – in the neighbourhood of 0·5 per cent of total assets. Between 1919 and 1929, only six loans were made from Mitsui Bussan (Trading Company) as extended advances to coal and other chemical by-products which the mining company sold to the Bussan. However, these loans from the Bussan did not exceed 1·5 per cent of the total assets of the firm, and steadily increasing reserves reached 12 million yen by 1929.[83]

Even the Oji Paper Company, which had borrowed from the Daiichi and Mitsui banks, became much more financially independent after the war. Short-term loans disappeared after 1919, and long-term loans amounted to no more than 10 per cent of the total assets except twice – once in 1922, when they came to just over 10 per cent, and in 1927, when they were 23 per cent. Most outside capital was obtained by means of bonds, which were issued in an amount equivalent to 23 per cent of the total assets in 1916, while during most of the 1920s the figure fluctuated within the range of 18–26 per cent of total assets. However, the firm's ratio of reserves to total assets was at a higher level (8–14 per cent) compared with the pre-war years, when it was only a small percentage of total assets. The ratio of reserves to owners' equity also increased, from 24 per cent to 44 per cent, during the period between 1917 and 1929.[84]

In the Mitsubishi group, the Mitsubishi Zōsen KK (Mitsubishi Ship-building Company) relied on bond financing to the magnitude of 10 million yen against a paid-in capital of 30 million yen in 1918. The bond obligation was gradually eliminated and stood at zero in 1927. No short-term loans were seen after 1919, and only one long-term loan of 0·5 million yen was made in 1930, against a reserve which increased from 2 million in 1919 to 5·8 million by 1930.[85] The Mitsubishi Kōgyō KK (Mitsubishi Mining Company) was even sounder: in 1918 it was capi-talized at 50 million yen, and no bonds were sold and no long-term loans made after 1919, while reserves rose from 0·3 million yen in 1918 to 3·2 million yen in 1929.[86]

The Nisshin Seifun KK (Nisshin Flour-Milling Company) stayed clear of long-term borrowing during the Taisho and the early Showa years; it borrowed only during 1922–5 and in an amount equivalent to 4·2 per cent of total assets. No explicit mention is made of short-term loans, and no bonds were sold before 1930. Capital steadily increased from 1·7 million in 1914 to 4 million in 1917, and then to 12·3 million in 1925. Since the dividend rate remained well above the floor of 15 per cent after 1916, with an exceptionally high 30 per cent at the height of the war boom, the firm had no difficulty in marketing its own shares for the purpose of acquiring capital for expansion.[87]

One could easily add many more examples to convey this changing pattern of financing in zaibatsu-connected firms. Suffice it to say that in addition to these firms, there were many more zaibatsu firms which depended only to a very limited extent on long-term loans from their respective zaibatsu banks. In fact, of the sample examined, fifteen firms in the Mitsui, Mitsubishi, Sumitomo, Asano, and Koga groups – including the Mitsui Kōzan and Mitsubishi Zōsen – made no long-term loans at all throughout the 1920s. It can be safely concluded that zaibatsu-related firms were financially secure by the beginning of the 1920s and required little long-term capital from their parent banks.[88]

In examining bank data, we can confirm the financial independence of zaibatsu firms. If we take the example of the Mitsui Bank, for which useful information is available, we find that by 1930 only 9·8 per cent of the total amount lent went to Mitsui-connected firms.[89] Although direct evidence is not available, one can conclude that all other major banks followed an essentially similar pattern. For example, loans to Sumitomo-related firms by the Sumitomo bank were even smaller because the group's major firms had no long-term loans by the late 1920s.[90]

Throughout the 1920s, the basic pattern was one in which the zaibatsu firms, because of past relationships, enjoyed a high degree of participation from the zaibatsu banks and families, even though these largest firms could easily sell shares to the public. For the subsidiary firms, zaibatsu participation in equity was limited, but these firms too were sufficiently sound to be able to float shares of their own and required few or no zaibatsu loans. By 1928, the share holdings of zaibatsu families, banks, and other zaibatsu firms within the same zaibatsu group were extensive. The percentages of the total paid-up capital supplied by the respective zaibatsu *honsha* (holding company and bank) of the four largest zaibatsu to the so-called zaibatsu firms which they controlled were: Mitsui, 90·2 per cent; Mitsubishi, 69·4; Sumitomo, 79·1; and Yasuda, 32·0. When the percentage of total paid-up capital supplied by other zaibatsu firms belonging to the same zaibatsu group is added, the respective figures rose to: Mitsui, 90·6 per cent; Mitsubishi, 77·6; Sumitomo, 80·5; and Yasuda, 48·0.[91]

That the zaibatsu banks provided during the 1920s an increasing amount of long-term capital to non-zaibatsu firms can be shown easily. First, bonds were a much more important means of obtaining capital than were long-term loans during the 1920s. Of the 352 largest firms examined by the Mitsubishi Economic Research Institute, bonds accounted for 21 per cent of the total capital, long-term loans 7 per cent, share capital 56 per cent, and short-term capital 15 per cent. Out of twenty-two industries examined by the Institute, thirteen industries depended more on bonds than on long-term loans. The total value of bonds sold during the period 1920–5 was 2,422 million yen, of which only 18·1 per cent was in bonds of zaibatsu-connected firms. The major share of the total, 41·3 per cent, was in bonds floated by utility firms, and 20·7 per cent was for electric railway companies. These were two industries in which zaibatsu interests were extremely small. By 1930, the total value of bonds floated was 2,927 million yen, of which zaibatsu-connected firms accounted for only 15·2 per cent. The zaibatsu firms floating the bonds were small subsidiaries and affiliates, and not major zaibatsu firms.[92]

An important point to be made is that the four largest zaibatsu banks held, by the end of 1929, 27·1 per cent of all outstanding bonds. If the insurance and credit companies of the zaibatsu groups are added, the bond holdings increase to 29·1 per cent of the total.[93] Among the zaibatsu banks, the ratio of bonds to the total negotiable paper ranged in 1924 from 41·7 per cent for the Mitsubishi Bank to 37·0 per cent for the Mitsui Bank.[94]

As noted earlier, the long-term loans made by the zaibatsu banks increased rapidly during the latter half of the 1920s. The Mitsui Bank's ratio of long-term loans to total assets rose from 0·24 in 1912 to 0·44 at the end of 1930. The ratio was somewhat lower during the period 1919–24, but the rising trend is unmistakable. The ratio of long-term loans to total loans rose steadily with no visible departure from the trend throughout the period 1912–30. These data for the Mitsui Bank show a clear departure from the bank's loan practices during the first 'spurt' from 1885 to 1905. The Mitsubishi Bank shows an even more distinct change in its loan practices between the first 'spurt' period and the First World War. The ratio of long-term loans to total assets rose sharply during the First World War, and it remained, in spite of the gradual decline from the peak of 0·65 in 1917, at a relatively high level throughout the 1920s. The ratio of long-term loans to total loans jumped distinctly during the war and remained at a high level with no visible sign of declining. It is also noteworthy that the Mitsubishi Bank began to purchase an increasingly large amount of negotiable papers (bonds and shares) throughout the period 1912–30, in clear contrast to the pattern observed before 1912. As the Mitsubishi Bank's holdings in shares of Mitsubishi-connected firms were smaller than any other zaibatsu bank's holdings in the shares of its respective group, the Mitsubishi Bank's high ratios of negotiable paper to total assets and of long-term loans to total assets reflect the bank's increased holdings in bonds and shares of non-zaibatsu firms. Since the Yasuda, Sumitomo, and Daiichi banks also showed similar increases in the importance of long-term loans *vis-à-vis* total assets and total loans, the conclusion that during the 1920s the zaibatsu banks were making long-term loans to non-zaibatsu firms in increasing amounts appears to be well founded.[95]

Banking was increasingly dominated by the zaibatsu banks during the 1920s. It is easy to show that there were significant changes in both the absolute and relative positions of the zaibatsu banks between 1919 and 1927. During those eight years, the zaibatsu banks increased their relative share of the total deposits from 25 per cent to 31 per cent, or from 5,700 million to 9,000 million in absolute amounts. The market share of loans remained virtually unchanged, but the total amount lent by these banks increased from 5,700 million yen to 8,200 million. These developments are especially significant when considered against the fact that the relative share of the paid-in capital of these banks decreased from 21·2 per cent to 19 per cent. Another way of appraising the financial power of the zaibatsu group is to note that eight zaibatsu (including banks, insurance companies, and credit companies) accounted for 45·7 per cent of the total capital plus deposits plus reserves of all private banks, insurance companies, and credit companies at the end of 1929.[96]

A few important factors contributed to this rapid concentration of the financial market. One of these was the sporadic bank runs which the banking industry experienced after the First World War and the nationwide bank runs of 1927 which resulted from the accumulated ills of the 'earthquake bills' and the practice of banks acting as 'organ banks'. 'Earthquake bills' were those notes which many borrowers were unable to pay because of the earthquake of 1923 and which were guaranteed to banks by the Bank of Japan. These bills resulted in limiting the freedom of the monetary policy of the Bank of Japan and also constrained the activities of banks because the banks had to depend on heel-dragging political decisions by the government as to the amount of loans to be made to banks holding these bills.[97]

The 'organ banks' were the many Japanese banks of the period which became 'organs' of their specific clients. This meant that banks were often forced into the position of making unsound loans to their clients, mostly industrial firms, who were facing financial difficulties. Since the banks were committed to their clients in the sense that large loans had already been made to these firms and their bankruptcy meant the end of the banks themselves, the banks were forced to make further unsound loans. Such a practice could and did lead to nationwide bank runs, as the Bank of Taiwan discovered in dealing with the Suzuki Shōten.[98]

The instability of the banking industry caused many savers to transfer their deposits to larger and better-established banks. The zaibatsu banks, which survived these crises with only an occasional run on their branch banks, naturally were the major beneficiaries of these transferred savings. Throughout the period, also, the government was anxious to stabilize the financial market and chose to actively promote mergers and unifications of weaker (small and/or local) banks. Beginning in 1924, the Ministry of Finance engaged in an active programme to reduce the number of banks in each prefecture, to extend assistance in the evaluation of assets at the time of a merger, and to help select the best-qualified managers for newly unified banks. This programme was carried on throughout the 1920s, and the Ministry's 'persuasion' was extremely effective in numerous instances.[99]

No less important in bringing about the highly oligopolistic structure of the banking industry were the aggressive merger and absorption measures adopted by the largest banks themselves. A typical case is that of the Yasuda Bank. In 1923, the Yasuda Bank absorbed ten other banks scattered throughout the country to create a giant bank.[100] It was common practice at that time for the larger city banks to absorb smaller local banks and make them into branch offices.

The expansion of financial power continued throughout the 1930s, and by 1942 the financial control of the four largest zaibatsu was indeed pervasive. In finance, the four zaibatsu accounted for 49·7 per cent of the total paid-in capital of the banking, insurance, and credit industries. In industry, the same four owned 32·4 per cent of the total paid-in capital of the heavy industries and 10·8 per cent of that in light industry. In addition, the four zaibatsu accounted for 12·9 per cent of the total paid-in capital of utility, transportation, real estate, and trading companies. In the aggregate, the holding companies of these four zaibatsu directly accounted for 24·5 per cent of the total paid-in capital of the industries listed above.[101]

The control exerted by these zaibatsu holding companies far exceeded that expressed by the above percentage figures for paid-in capital. The extent of their control of the various industrial sectors was significantly augmented by their power to grant loans, by the use of interlocking directorships, and by the numerous other leverages which these super-large financial empires had at their command. The extent of these powers can easily be surmised when we discover that by 1944 74·9 per cent of all loans made within Japan were made by the four zaibatsu banks,[102] and each zaibatsu had woven an elaborate net of interlocking directorships. For example Mitsui alone commanded the fate of nearly two hundred large firms, in which it placed key executive officers.[103]

The march toward the concentration of the ownership and control of Japanese industries became visible after the end of the First World War, and it continued at a rapid pace throughout the 1920s and 1930s. There are numerous indicators of a highly concentrated economy, but it is sufficient to note here that 2·59 per cent of all the shareholders in Japan at the end of the Second World War, or slightly over 40,000 individuals, owned over 64 per cent of the total outstanding shares, and less than 10 per cent of those individuals – 3,762 zaibatsu-connected or other extremely wealthy persons to be exact – owned 216 million shares or 48·74 per cent of the total outstanding shares.[104]

Our narrative on the years after the Second World War can be briefly summarized because much has been written in English.[105] The Allied Command, on encountering the highly concentrated ownership and control of Japanese industries, instituted a wide-ranging policy of 'economic democratization' to eliminate what it termed a 'cancerous' zaibatsu dominance. Holding companies were outlawed; giant firms which were virtual monopolists were dissolved, and in the place of each giant, two or more firms were created; the ownership of former zaibatsu banks was taken from the zaibatsu families; mutual share holdings among zaibatsu firms and between zaibatsu banks and zaibatsu firms were made illegal; zaibatsu families were forced to sell their shares through a commission which, in turn, made efforts to sell them to the public; and interlocking directorships were prohibited, and a large number of former officers of zaibatsu firms were purged from such positions.

This was, in fundamental ways, a revolution in the ownership and control patterns of the Japanese economy. The forced sales of their shares, plus the newly instituted capital levies and inheritance taxes, reduced the zaibatsu families' real wealth to about a twentieth of what it once had been before these policies were carried out. The distribution of share holdings was now much more widespread; neither large firms nor banks were owned by a few individuals. Rarely does anyone own more than 5 per cent of the total shares of a large firm or a bank, and majority owners, who were common before the end of the war, no longer exist.

Then, as is well known, the political effects of the Korean War began to dilute this thoroughgoing economic democratization policy, and after the return of sovereignty to Japan in 1952 the Japanese government began to reverse the occupation policies on the ground that these policies were detrimental to rapid economic recovery and growth. Each step need not be retraced here, but by the mid-1960s the ownership and control patterns of Japanese industrial firms certainly did not resemble the patterns which the Allied Command had once tried to establish.

When the twenty-five years of post-war history are reviewed, a few salient points emerge with regard to the ownership and control patterns of Japanese industries. Most obvious is the marked difference in the share-holding patterns of the mid-1960s compared with those observed during the pre-war years. It is true that the onetime ideal of the Allied Command – widely diffused share-holding by millions of 'little people' – has never been realized, that there has been a tendency for the share-holding pattern to concentrate in the hands of a decreasing number of individuals. However, compared to the heyday of the zaibatsu trust companies, the share-holding patterns of today are fundamentally different in that nearly 20 million people, or roughly one in five Japanese, are shareholders. Unlike the pre-war years, 11 million shares out of the total of 20 million shares outstanding are owned by persons owning between 1,000 and 5,000 shares. That is, there is a large number of middle-class shareholders today compared to the highly concentrated pre-war ownership of shares in the hands of zaibatsu interests and a limited number of individuals.

Dramatic examples of this change, which some Japanese economists called 'the revolution in share-holding', can be readily found. The Mitsubishi Heavy Industry Company, which was once owned and controlled by the Mitsubishi zaibatsu, now has 380,000 shareholders. The Yawata Iron and Steel Company, a firm jointly owned by the government and zaibatsu interests, is now owned by 400,000 shareholders. Hitachi Ltd, a diversified electric equipment and machinery manufacturer which was not controlled by any zaibatsu, has 420,000 shareholders. Also, we find that the present pattern of share-holding of the largest banks is even more diffused than for the giant firms. Gone completely is the family-trust ownership and/or control of these banks. Today, only rarely does the largest shareholder own more than 3 per cent of all the outstanding shares, and even legal persons, who jointly own the majority shares of these banks, usually own only from 1 to 3 per cent of all the outstanding shares.

Though the share-holding pattern is diffused, and the zaibatsu as they were known in the pre-war years have disappeared from the economy, the ownership and control patterns of the Japanese economy had, by the mid-1960s, regrouped themselves on various lines. To be sure, though the new groupings are different from the pre-war zaibatsu-controlled ones, there are many resemblances as well. The new groupings, often called *keiretsu* (literally 'lineage'), can be either vertical or horizontal. Vertical *keiretsu* is usually a grouping of smaller firms by a large firm. The large firm is usually in an industry which requires many subcontractors or subordinate firms capable of supplying various inputs to, or relying on the outputs of, the parent firm. The parent firm is often a majority shareholder and/or in a position to make changes in the upper executive levels of the 'child' companies (*kogaiska*). Also, parent companies are often able to secure necessary loans for child firms. In 1962, the Japan Fair Trade Commission found that the 256 largest firms had on the average 16 child companies each, which were defined as those firms of which 10 per cent or more of the shares were owned by the parent firm. The Matsushita Electric Co. headed the list with 193 subsidiary firms.

The horizontal *keiretsu* are groupings of large former zaibatsu-connected firms across industrial boundaries. The new groupings are loose 'community of interest' groups rather than the tightly knit groups dominated by the respective zaibatsu trust and bank. By the mid-1960s these groups were easily identifiable. The presidents of the respective groups have regularly scheduled meetings, and each group strives to have maximum dealings with those within the group instead of with those who are outsiders to the group. Intra-group mutual share holdings increased from the early 1950s to 1957, though the latest observation for 1965 indicated a levelling-off in this trend. The Mitsui group's mutual share holdings in 1951 were 6·2 per cent of the total outstanding shares of the group, and the figure reached 11·0 per cent in 1957, though it again fell to 10 per cent in 1965. For the Mitsubishi group, the figures were 1·3 per cent in 1951, 16·4 in 1957, and 17·0 in 1965; for the Sumitomo groups, the figures were 7·0 per cent, 14·0 per cent, and 19·0 per cent for the same three years.

It is not difficult to understand the rapid post-war development of vertical *keiretsu*, given the post-war economic conditions of Japan – wage differentials between large and small firms, constant investment activities with general credit shortages, and increasingly complex technological requirements. After all, subcontracting and subsidiary firms of various types are common in advanced industrial economies, and the Japanese case is perhaps no more than an accentuated version of Western models.

The horizontal *keiretsu* are much more difficult to interpret. They are products of the historical legacy and the economic rationale. The historical legacy led the former zaibatsu firms to seek out others within the respective confines of their former zaibatsu groupings. The former Mitsui firms tend to borrow from Mitsui banks, and these firms co-operate in investment, technological development, marketing, and many other aspects of their activities. Personal ties and the advantages of familiarity with former fellow zaibatsu-connected firms played a role no less important than the economic advantages which could be gained by belonging to each group.

The new horizontal *keiretsu* is a loose grouping. Unlike the pre-war zaibatsu groups, it is possible for a firm within a group to place its interests before that of the group, and a few have done so. Firms can, and at times do, do business with firms of other groups. Bank loans, for example, for a so-called Mitsui-group firm can and often do come from a Mitsubishi or Sumitomo bank. As among siblings, the new horizontal *keiretsu* is based on the past; and, again as among siblings, the exigencies of the present can and do lead some of the members of the new group to seek new associations or new attachments. Many economists seek the reasons for this new horizontal grouping in purely economic terms. Their efforts, however, cannot be successful unless it is realized that, in the final analysis, these *keiretsu* are based on Japanese group-orientation and the need to identify themselves within a group. After the parents are gone – the dissolution of the zaibatsu holding companies – siblings work together for common causes because of their common lineage. A sibling might for his own interest ignore the interest of the family, but this is much rarer in Japan than in most other societies. In the same way, a Mitsui-*keiretsu* firm, although a rigid code to bind together firms is no longer in force, is quite unlikely to disregard the interests of the group:

most workers, whether blue- or white-collar, work for the Mitsui Shipbuilding Company with the emphasis on 'Mitsui' rather than on 'Shipbuilding Company'.

The powerful and pervasive zaibatsu of the pre-war years are gone; the ownership and control patterns of post-war Japan differ fundamentally from those of pre-war years. The same name, the same trademark, and even the same senior officers, along with the new *keiretsu*, may give the impression that the difference is deceptive. But we know that the difference is real. On the other hand, behind these names, trademarks, and senior officers, we discover a living legacy of years past. Economic historians can somehow sense the handiwork of history which makes the ownership and control patterns of today's Japan so very Japanese. This discovery is not contradictory to the fundamental difference in those patterns between pre-war and post-war years, because changes, however fundamental, take place within the confines of a nation's culture and tradition.

IV. *The Managerial System*

As economic historians we ask, What are the most significant features of the Japanese managerial system, and how did it evolve as Japan's industrialization proceeded? If one is to briefly highlight the major characteristics of the Japanese managerial system, one might select two as being among the most important: these are industrial paternalism and an emphasis on group harmony and co-operation, as manifested in the so-called *ringi* system of decision-making. We shall thus discuss each in turn, and with these two as the basic building blocks, we shall examine related aspects of the Japanese managerial system in historical perspective.

A highly structured hierarchical society emerged during the Tokugawa period. Apprenticeship in the crafts during this period was rigid and highly formalized. Each apprentice had to observe a long apprenticeship, one which often lasted for nearly a decade or even fifteen years. The relationship between master and apprentice was rigorously defined and highly personal. A master exercised full authority over the persons of his apprentices and expected to receive complete loyalty and obedience from them. Apprentices, in return, received training in the craft, full maintenance, and aid when starting out as new masters. Japanese literature and folklore richly document that the master–apprentice relationships were nearly as absolute as those observed between a lord and his samurai.

The institution of *ie* (house) which developed among the Tokugawa merchants is another example of the hierarchically structured society. An *ie* was a functionally simulated kinship organization built around the head of an *ie*. The relationship between the head of the house and his employees was similar to that between a master and his apprentice. However, for an *ie*, there was another dimension which did not exist in the master–apprentice relationship.[106] That is, an *ie* was an entity, a name to be honoured by all and protected by all at all costs. For well-established and large *ie*, such as the House of Mitsui or Sumitomo, rules which governed their respective *ie* were minutely codified. These rules defined the intra-*ie* personal relationships, schedules of advancements, and above all the duties and obligations of the head of the house and all its employees.

These examples typify the rigidly hierarchical, group-oriented social structure of Tokugawa Japan.[107] As in the world of samurai, the hierarchy was founded on the principle that the superiors in these social classes were under an obligation to provide for the economic security of their inferiors in exchange for the latter's total loyalty and obedience. Ability and aggressiveness could advance status, but only within a class, and the social position of an individual, determined by birth, allowed virtually no inter-class mobility except in the late Tokugawa period, when the rigid class barriers could no longer be maintained. This was the world of Tokugawa Japan into which modern industry intruded. Larger, more complex human organizations were demanded by the new industries, and the Tokugawa institutions were forced to adapt themselves.

But, the Tokugawa institutions yielded only grudgingly. For the first two decades or so of the Meiji years, or before the coming of the cotton textile boom, we find a period of institutional disorientation. During these politically and economically turbulent years the government built pilot plants, recruited needed labour from the ranks of commoners, and depended on samurai-turned-bureaucrats to manage its plants. Although class distinctions were abolished shortly after the Restoration, they persisted during these decades, preserving much of the Tokugawa hierarchical relationship between management and labour. Case studies show that the government plants were managed as if they belonged to a feudal lord.

The few private firms which began to emerge differed little from the government plants. Private firms had to be concerned with profits, but the adjustments which they made to the requirements of their new industries were too small and few to be considered a first step toward modern industrial management practices. True, a few men like Iwasaki, the founder of the Mitsubishi Zaibatsu, adopted daring modern policies while samurai-turned-managers groped painfully for a *modus operandi* in industrial management. But Iwasaki and his kind were still a small minority.[108]

During the early 1880s, the government, as we have seen, sold most of its plants, and the appearance of the private firms in the cotton textile and other industries heralded the first industrial spurt in Japan. This was the beginning of a period which Hazama called the 'primitive' period,[109] which extended into the First World War years. These were the years of rapid increases in industrial output based on newly imported technologies; they were also the years of laissez-faire, the years during which new entrepreneurs pursued profits and exploited western technology while the workers were exposed to the fate of the English workers of a few generations before.

The problems which the new industrial entrepreneurs faced were many, and obtaining a sufficient amount of the desired kind of labour was no less a problem than finding the necessary capital and technology. Skilled workers – those able to operate the Western machines – were few, and the unskilled and semi-skilled had to be coerced into the irksome disciplines of factory work. A new generation of managerial staff, equipped with or willing to learn the necessary administrative and technical skills, had to be found.

Generally speaking, the entrepreneurs found their managerial personnel from the new universities, as was discussed in section I. For the bulk of unskilled labour, the surplus labour of the agricultural sector and poverty-stricken and unemployed lower-class samurai were employed. The new employees – reflecting their past social status – were docile and disciplined to the long hours and often substandard working and living conditions. The management could exert maximum authority over them with a minimum of restraint. The abject condition of the female hands in the cotton textile industry and the miners' working conditions, which were found less desirable than prison life by the journalists of the day, characterized this 'primitive' period.

A large proportion of skilled workers and often semi-skilled workers were employed by the now-familiar method of contracting through an *oyabun*. He was, in most cases, a skilled workman himself who had from several to as many as several hundred *kobun*, the skilled workers who worked under the protection and command of the *oyabun*. The *oyabun* contracted to supply his *kobun* to a firm and functioned as a foreman. The contract was signed usually on a short-term basis, and the wages were paid through the *oyabun*. The system of *oyabun–kobun* was a replica of the master–apprentice system of the Tokugawa period, and the relationship between the *oyabun* and *kobun* was equally pre-industrial in many respects.

Before the First World War, Japanese management enjoyed a period of freedom in dealing with its employees. Still free of social legislation which was soon to constrain managerial freedom, employers pursued profit as had their English counterparts a century earlier. Because the Meiji Restoration destroyed those delicately balanced, perhaps more human, relationships of Tokugawa society, unprotected workers were now exposed to the anonymous and often ruthless air of the new industrial age. The shocking documentaries of the operatives of cotton textile factories of the period are a legacy of this transition.

With the new constitution and an increased franchise, the first Factory Act of 1911 was to be expected. Industrial firms, which were now employing most of their labour directly, dispensing with the *oyabun–kobun* system to meet the rapidly increasing needs of skilled personnel for its exclusive employment, opposed the Act. Employers argued that the Act and any other Western-style factory laws were unsuitable for Japan because Japanese society functioned best not on impersonal contractual relationships but on more human, personal, and group relationships. Although a few acknowledged the detrimental effects which these restrictions on the authority of the management might have on rapid capital accumulation and on Japan's ability to be internationally competitive, many argued – and sincerely, if the eloquence of their arguments is to be believed – that Japanese management could more than adequately accomplish what these acts intended.

This was the period during which industrial paternalism – 'a company is a family' – became explicit. The management, under the threat of further laws and leftist ideology, and also to appease the critics of huge profits earned during the First World War, instituted numerous welfare and fringe-benefit programmes. This industrial paternalism was to cushion the sharpening edge of economic and social discontent of the years following the First World War. During the Taisho years (1911–25), punctuated by the rice riots of 1918 and the formation of the Japanese Communist Party in 1922, industrial firms – especially zaibatsu-related giant firms – appealed to the importance of the Japanese tradition of family and widened the scope of employee benefits and welfare programmes of various types.

We have noted earlier that today's employees of the Mitsui Shipbuilding Company identify themselves with Mitsui and are highly conscious of belonging to the Mitsui group, as other employees of any large firm do with their own firms. Between the First World War and the present much has intervened, not the least being the rise of strong, politically oriented labour unions. Despite all these changes, the Mitsui employee's identification with the Mitsui group and the development of the horizontal *keiretsu* of today somehow attest to the fact that management's continued insistence on the importance of 'a company is

a family' is not a totally baseless ploy to stave off the political and economic criticisms which it has received. One must not misread the facts of a
capitalist economy to the point of believing that warm words and a
small contribution to the dowry of a departing female employee are a
substitute for shorter hours and higher wages. But, at the same time,
cynicism can misread the intentions and practices of Japanese management if carried to the point of ignoring Japan's historical and cultural
heritage.

Specialists agree that industrial paternalism continues to be practised
in Japan to a degree not found in Western economies. From the first
decade of the century, the nature of paternalism changed. It is now
much less crude, less offensive – even apologetic. But it is still observable,
and Japanese accept the practice of daily exhortations from the company president and compulsory Zen camps for new employees, as their
parents accepted their president's concern for the taste of the pickles in
an employees' canteen, with gratitude. This was and is possible because
the Japanese find a strong need to identify themselves with a group, and
they appear to function most effectively within one. To most Japanese,
post-war labour unions and active political party activities seem poor
substitutes for group identification with a firm, because it is on the job
that they spend most of their waking hours, and they find a need to be a
part of a co-operative effort. The fact that firms, in recruiting their future
executives, seem to favour applicants from one university as opposed to
those from others is also an indication that the firms place a premium on
cohesiveness and intra-firm harmony, which such a policy can help
foster. To this day, some firms are known to be biased toward Tokyo
University, while others favour Keio, Hitotsubashi, or other elite
universities.

The nature and the extent to which group orientation is ingrained in
Japanese culture can best be seen in the *ringi* system of decision-making
in Japanese firms. '*Ringi*' is one of those compound words in Japanese
which are most difficult to translate literally; '*rin*' means the act of
submitting a proposal to one's superior for his sanction, and '*gi*' means
to discuss or to deliberate. Thus, the *ringi* system is a system of decision-
making within a group by means of sanctioning proposals originating
from one's subordinates.[110]

This system, which has well-developed roots in the Tokugawa
bakufu and its local offices, was formalized and widely used by the
bureaucrats of the Meiji period, and private firms adopted the procedure
at the beginning of industrialization. Typically, a small group of office
workers within a section propose a particular measure after extensive
discussion among themselves. Then, the proposal is submitted to the
section chief in charge. The section chief, before making his decision,

consults other section chiefs who may be affected or who have an interest in the proposal. If any part of the proposal is objected to, the proposal is returned to the section members for re-examination or is rejected. If the proposal is approved by the section, it will be submitted to a higher group of managerial personnel, who in most cases will be bureau chiefs working under the executive officers of the firm. If the proposal is accepted at this level, it then goes to the executive board and, with its approval, to the president for final sanction.

There can, of course, be variations in this pattern. A section chief might suggest that a proposal be prepared on a specific problem, or on rare occasions a bureau chief or even an executive officer might suggest that a section chief draw up a proposal. However, in such cases, these suggestions, which in fact are orders, do not come to the lower level as orders, because if an order is issued the person who does so will be personally responsible for the proposal. Personal responsibility and identification with a specific proposal must be avoided at all costs, because if the proposal is disapproved the loss of prestige results in the worst social disgrace for any administrator of any rank, and if the proposal is accepted it is socially unacceptable to personally receive credit for the success.

The attraction of such a system within the Japanese social context is obvious. Decisions are made anonymously. No one is either blamed for or credited with the failure or success of a proposal, and all is done in the name of collectivity. Thus, infinite care is taken from the first step so that consensus is obtained within the group which is involved in the deliberation of a proposal. Then, when the proposal is finally approved for execution, it is a decision of the entire firm, and all are expected to do their best in order that the proposal accomplish its intended aim.

The shortcomings of such a system are also evident. To begin with, it is cumbersome and slow. Innovative ideas can be stifled at the discussion stage and bold approaches tend to be shelved in the name of consensus, even before they reach the higher-echelon executives. It is, of course, unthinkable to ignore the chain of command within a firm. The high-level decision-makers are forced into the position of viewing a proposal with a strong presumption for approval, and they rarely have access to the facts or the minority opinions necessary to counter-balance the weight of the proposal. Many company presidents, rather than risk prestige, tend to accept all proposals after a few perfunctory questions – the practice which Japanese call 'mekura-ban', literally 'blind seal'. Most Japanese firms have apparently found that these shortcomings are a bearable price compared to the great merits of the system, the anonymity of decision-making and the rule of consensus. Few prices are too high in Japan for intra-group harmony.

What has been described above is a realistic model of the *ringi* system. Though the basic ingredients of the system – consensus, anonymity, and harmony – are guarded carefully, an increasingly large number of firms have begun to introduce significant variations to this model, and there were always exceptions even during the pre-war years. The reaction time to economic and sometimes political events must now be much shorter than before. Increasing government participation in economic affairs, especially with long-range growth plans, makes it necessary for firms to have long-range plans. The *ringi* system, which is generally sufficient for short-run policy-making and problem-solving, is no longer adequate. Decisions in today's industrial economy must come quickly, and long-run and short-run decisions must be co-ordinated if both are to be effective.

For these reasons, a majority of firms now have a planning department which specializes in long-run planning, and the decision-making process has been increasingly decentralized to increase autonomy and the speed of decisions. But it is nevertheless true that these innovations are not replacing the *ringi* system but rather are grafted on to it. It is the observation of students specializing in the management system that many of the key decisions are still made on a consensus basis using the *ringi* system, while recent additions such as the planning department and the decentralized decision-making process are more confined to questions which are basically technical in nature. Post-war Japan has experienced periodic revivals of emphasis on the Japanese way of management, alternating with periods of eager adoption of American managerial methods. But on balance the *ringi* system is far from being made obsolete, and it is most likely that as long as the Japanese value consensus, anonymity, and harmony in their corporate life, the system will continue to be used.

V. *Conclusion*

Japanese industrialization continues to fascinate economists and economic historians because of its rapidity and the uniqueness of its Asian setting. Few economies have accomplished as much in so short a time, and Japan's modernization, accompanying the process of industrialization, profoundly transformed the society during the past century. Thus, it was natural that attempts were and are being made to understand and to explain this feat. These attempts have yielded a set of interpretations and views which try to explain why this Asian nation succeeded in industrializing so rapidly.

The orthodox view explains the success of Japan's industrialization by emphasizing its distinct social and historical uniqueness and its lateness of entry to industrialization. The vision of dedicated and selfless bureaucrats and entrepreneurs, former samurai and those motivated by samurai spirit, battling to industrialize from above to bring the late-comer to the industrial age as rapidly as possible was presented persuasively. And as this view was strengthened and refined during the course of nearly a half-century of its development, it became increasingly difficult to deny its validity.

Another part of this orthodoxy firmly holds to the view that the banks, originally established under government–samurai initiative, played the crucial role of industrial financier, and that by the beginning of the twentieth century they had become the dominant suppliers of industrial capital. The Japanese pattern, it has long been argued, was like that of nineteenth-century Germany, which had also industrialized as a latecomer and which found it needed to mobilize its capital by means of highly oligopolistic banks. But after two generations and two world wars, this orthodoxy too appears to be faced with the necessity of making an accommodation to a series of recent challenges. The students who suggest re-evaluation of the current view are questioning its interpretation and views with findings obtained by more thorough examinations of data and other evidence. These challenges need to be further evaluated; they can, however, no longer be neglected, because they question the fundamental building blocks of the accepted view.

In many respects, the recent wave of explicit questions raised of the existing view has long been overdue. In Japan, the militarism which stifled the freedom of academic pursuits, and the futile *Methodenstreit* on the economic nature of the Meiji Restoration and the Second World War, perhaps retarded a more natural course of re-examination and evolution of these views. For Westerners Japan was long a quaint subject of curiosity, and only after the Second World War was full-scale research begun. And even then, this research was deeply coloured by earlier Japanese works and hampered by a formidable linguistic barrier. In these circumstances, more empirically oriented historical research by both Japanese and Westerners has been delayed.

Thus, the recent re-examinations of the established views have not been surprises for most specialists in Japanese economic history. When the role of the government and the samurai was de-emphasized and put in a new perspective, and when the role of commoners and their profit motivations was given its due place, it appeared that we had merely confirmed what had long been expected. Thus, if the continued re-evaluation of the process of Japanese industrialization can indeed demonstrate that the long-held view must now undergo a fundamental reappraisal and that the suggested new interpretations are to replace the old, one may find Dore's words on Japanese modernization equally applicable to Japan's industrialization:

In sum, it was important that the Japanese populace was not just a sack of potatoes. The modernization of Japan was not simply a matter of top-level changes. It was also a cumulation of a mass of small initiatives by large numbers of people who could appreciate new possibilities, make new choices, or at the very least allow themselves to be pursuaded to do for the first time something they had never done before.[111]

For an economy to industrialize successfully, it requires efforts from the broad spectrum of its people. Industrialization, like modernization, cannot be achieved if the government is compelled to try to motivate 'a sack of potatoes' while the populace remains passive and conservative and clings to its old ways.

However, as parts of pre-Keynesian economic theory found a niche in post-Keynesian economics, some aspects of the orthodox view of Japanese industrialization can and must be accommodated within the new framework which is to be established on the strength of continued research. The tasks involved in establishing a new set of coherent interpretations on the nature and roles of entrepreneurship, government, banks, and management will necessarily be those of synthesis, as all such endeavours must be.

When these tasks are successfully accomplished, we should be better able to explain the rapid industrialization of Japan. The role of government can then be evaluated more accurately, and the roles accorded to various social classes can then be seen in a more meaningful light. The story of Japanese economic growth can be told not just with Shibusawa and the zaibatsu but with a full cast including the Suzukis, Itōs, Yasudas, Iwasakis, Minomuras, and Nakamigawas. The role played by the banks and the changing patterns of ownership and control of Japanese industrial firms can also be appraised and understood much more accurately with the use of more detailed data. If further research supports the basic findings expressed in this chapter, then true industrial banking began only in the 1920s, and the earlier patterns of financing approximated to the English pattern rather than that of Germany. This, if established, is an important insight in understanding the development of labour-intensive industries, especially the cotton textile industry, which appears to have depended mostly on share capital and ploughed-back profits rather than on industrial bank loans. In this new perspective, it becomes possible to evaluate much more accurately the evolution of ownership and control patterns in general and the zaibatsu's economic significance.

For a general framework to emerge benefiting from the strength of both the old and the new views, one should recognize the most salient point arising from both views on Japanese entrepreneurship, ownership and control, and the managerial system. That is, Japan was able to industrialize because she was able to adapt her society and culture to the requirements of industrialization. It is a mistake to argue that the early Japanese entrepreneurs were not basically Western in outlook, and therefore that they did not modernize but depended on the 'old vibrant spirit of samurai'. It is a serious error to conclude that the Japanese *ringi* system is not modern because it is not Western. It is also fallacious to say that the new *keiretsu* groupings find no counterparts in the West, and therefore that the emergence of these groupings is a reversion to the pre-war form of economic organization. Many writers tended to emphasize the Japaneseness of the Japanese industrialization or were inclined to stress the Japanese ability to Westernize in order to achieve industrialization. To emphasize Japaneseness while equating modernization and Westernization is to overemphasize the traditional at the cost of ignoring the ability of Japanese society to modernize itself in its own way. To argue that Japan Westernized and sought replicas of Western models is to misjudge the scope and depth of Japanese modernization.

Given the history, culture, and traditions of Japan, her task for industrialization was dual. She had to produce goods by using Western technology while at the same time transforming her society to make it capable of meeting the needs of industrialization. This transformation of society was carried out at two levels. One was in form and the other in substance. Changes in form included the codification of commercial laws following the Western model, the enactment of the Factory Acts, the establishment of planning departments within corporations, and a series of laws enacted under the Allied Command.

But the transformation in substance was accomplished much less visibly and much more continuously. This transformation was profound. The *ie* gradually adopted the interpersonal relationships of the new era, and industrial paternalism emerged. The industrial paternalism of the 1920s was significantly different from the education- and welfare-oriented programmes of today's corporations. But the *ie* still exists. Group identification, the values placed on co-operation and harmony, an assiduous observation of rank differentials, and a premium placed on personal rather than legal relationships – all are transformed characteristics of the *ie*. And, as we have seen, the *ringi* system still continues to be used along with computers in the decision-making process in post-war Japanese firms. The *keiretsu* groupings of the 1960s resemble the pre-war zaibatsu, and some have even spoken of a zaibatsu revival. But neither the *ringi* system of today nor the *keiretsu* groupings are what they appear to be in form. These living institutions change and do not remain what they once were. These changes in substance are the process of Japanese modernization, and it is crucial to realize this fact before we can gain a better understanding of Japanese economic history.

That Japan is a modern nation and that Japan is an Asian nation cannot be disputed. Thus, the only logical conclusion we can reach is that Japan modernized in a Japanese way. A *kimono* made of a synthetic fibre conjures up both a vision of a *kimono*-clad samurai and a vision of a gigantic and highly complex chemical plant. But we need not call a *kimono* a suit, or a chemical process Western magic. The Japanese economy, like the rayon *kimono*, is a product of industrialization, but the modernization which accompanied it has not Westernized Japan to the point of emasculating those distinct historical and cultural heritages of its past. And this is the source of the fascination which Japan's economic history holds for us, and this ability to modernize within the Japanese heritage is the secret of Japan's successful industrialization.

Capital Formation during the Period of Early Industrialization in Russia, 1890–1913[1]

I. General Characteristics

Economic historians commonly describe the period from the late 1880s until the First World War as a period of intensive industrialization in Russia, during which a number of structural changes in the economy and society took place. It was a period marked by rapid population growth and advances in agriculture: the growth of the planted area and of crop yields, the increased commercialization of agricultural production, and a rise in the mobility of the agricultural labour force. It was accompanied by a rapid increase of capital overhead, chiefly railways, built with the assistance of foreign capital and government subsidies. But it was also a period of accelerated urbanization, an expansion of the market economy which stimulated the growth in the size of the capital stock of industry as the fastest-growing sector of the Russian economy. The increase of industrial production was also due to the formation of an industrial labour force, growing both in numbers and quality of its industrial skills. To be sure, all these changes were not sufficient to transform Russia from a backward agricultural economy into a modern industrial one; nevertheless, much was achieved during this particular period that facilitated the subsequent efforts to industrialize Russia.

It is, therefore, to the chief elements of change – the economic and social forces that harnessed Russia to the chariot of industrialization – that this chapter addresses itself. The task is a difficult one for a number of reasons. First, one must forgo for the time being the temptation to dwell on the fascinating problems of the pre-industrialization period and to re-examine some of the assumptions and allegations made about the origins and causes of early industrialization. Second, the availability of statistical data declines and their quality deteriorates at a rapid rate as the period is extended further back beyond 1890. Third, even for the period under investigation many of the most general and conventionally accepted measures, such as the size of GNP or national income, are not as yet available for Russia. This constitutes a serious drawback, because it deprives an analyst of the possibility of testing empirically some significant hypotheses for the reconstruction of basic economic relationships, and it forces him to resort to descriptive materials, which give too free rein to impressionistic conclusions which, although seemingly plausible, nevertheless harbour the danger of substantial error.

Although the main emphasis in this essay is upon the formation of capital and its financing within the private economy, by households and business firms, to keep government policies out of the range of our considerations and discussion would amount to an ahistorical bias toward the economic development of Russia. A balanced, realistic view of the respective roles of foreign and domestic, private and public, elements in the process of capital formation will provide a more thorough understanding of the period of industrialization covered in this chapter.

We may start with an overview of the Russian economy at the beginning and end of the period.

In 1861 Russia joined the civilized world by abolishing serfdom and emancipating the serf peasants of the private serf-owners. However, the economic structure of Russian agriculture did not change overnight when personal freedom was bestowed upon the serfs. In fact, it took decades for the changes to become discernible. The large landowners of the Russian nobility retained their lands – in some areas perhaps even enlarged their holdings at the expense of land previously tilled by the serfs – and were handsomely paid for the land apportioned to the peasantry. But most important, the land was given to the peasants in communal holding and excluded from the land market, the traditional three-field system was maintained, and the peasants' immobility was enforced by the institutions of collective fiscal responsibility and by the system of redemption payments. It took about two decades to complete the process of land apportionment, during which time the peasants bore the obligations of rendering labour services on the estates until they (as collective bodies) received title to their lands. The slowness of this process provided the large landowners with ample time to adjust to the conditions of the market for hired labour, to sell some of their lands and lease some, and to organize production on their estates. The results were the transformation of some large farm units into market-oriented ones, using hired farm labour, and the continuation of farm units which derived their incomes from leasing their lands to peasants whose land–labour ratio was far from optimal.

In the 1880s Russian agriculture had to face a challenge from abroad, marked by a sharp downward trend in world grain prices, that made the production of grain – the mainstay of Russian agricultural exports – less competitive in the world market. A drop in internal grain prices was followed by a decrease in land prices and decreased profitability of grain production. Agricultural incomes did not rise, capital accumulation in the agricultural sector shrank, and both landowners and peasants avoided investing their diminished savings in agricultural production. While such conditions prevailed for a number of years, the depressed state of Russian agriculture demanded a search for solutions.

The solutions varied between agricultural regions and between the various categories of agricultural producers and in terms of their short- or long-run effects. The peasants within the non-blacksoil region of Central Russia reacted to the declining prices by expanding grain production by ploughing up the meadows and contracting the fallow land, thus undermining in the long run the prevailing three-field system, upon which they depended for restoration of soil fertility. Such practices weakened the feed base of their livestock herd, which in turn affected soil fertility and diminished their incomes. It was not until a later period that improved foreign and domestic demand for livestock products restored the livestock economy in this region.

The expansion of the area planted under wheat in the Eastern and Southeastern regions was a response of landowners and peasants, but one which was not an unmixed blessing since in the long run it adversely affected sheep-breeding in those regions. In some areas of the blacksoil region, the agricultural adjustment resulted in a shift toward the production of industrial crops, notably sugar beet, especially in areas with a labour supply sufficient to produce this labour-intensive crop.

The agricultural problem became more serious in view of the rapidly growing agricultural population, which meant an increase in the labour force without an increase in per capita income, and so a demand for more land and the formation of new farms in the absence of new sources for investment. Thus, sharecropping arrangements between estates and peasants became more frequent – a measure which was probably a substitute for investment by landed estates in agricultural machinery and workstock. Such arrangements, although they saved expenditures in agricultural capital for the estates, were inferior in the long run to an increase in the capital-intensity of the estates. In addition, given the differential in the grain yield between peasant farms and estates, share-cropping probably adversely affected the level of grain production. The government also sought to aid agriculture. So, for example, the government-constructed and subsidized railways' granting of preferential rates to grain exporters was a measure designed to improve the competitive position of Russian grain in the world market (and to improve the trade balance of Russia). But this measure, like other policies of the Russian government during this period, was only a palliative which did not get at the heart of the real problems.[2]

Even the drought in 1891 and the following epidemic of cholera in 1892–3, which reached the dimensions of a serious calamity, did not produce any serious reforms on the part of the government. Thus the economic conditions of the agricultural population began to improve only during the second half of the 1890s, when the trend of world grain prices reversed itself. Russian agriculture became imbued with a certain sense of dynamics, which can be traced to the development of a growing market economy and the increased commercialization of agricultural production.

The pattern of development of the manufacturing industries differed from that of agriculture. The Russian government had not entirely forgotten the lesson of the Crimean War (1855–6), when Russia was defeated by the industrially advanced countries of Western Europe and attributed its defeat to the backwardness of its industry and its transportation network. If time, and the effects of building some strategic railways, had erased the shock of 1855–6, then Russia was reminded at the Berlin Congress (1878) that political victory could elude an industrially backward country even if it had 'big battalions'. Thus, while certain realities kept reminding the Russian government about the urgency of industrialization, political inertia and fiscal and internal social considerations precluded a more decisive policy. The need to support an existing huge bureaucracy, the strain upon the budget from military spending, the difficulties in raising revenues from an already heavily taxed population, and the fear of the growth of an urban proletariat prevented the government from making a commitment to industrial expansion. This, coupled with the resistance of the nobility to raising the tariff to a level that would assure protection to Russian domestic industry, made for an indecisive and ineffective industrial policy. The distrust of the soundness of industrial investments and the lack of trained personnel and managerial talent were additional obstacles to industrial development.

Governmental monetary policies, oscillating between inflationary (especially during periods of war like 1877–8) and clearly deflationary, tended at times to aggravate the impact of the business cycle and did very little to stabilize the market or stimulate demand for industrial goods. Thus, the internal market grew slowly, and Russian industry could not compete effectively with foreign industrial goods, especially capital goods. The major exception among branches of industry, and the one in which the government played an active role, was railway equipment. The railways, built with the help of foreign capital and technology, were of such political significance that the government decided that Russia should become self-sufficient in the production of its major inputs (rails, rolling stock, fuel, etc.). Government contracts and subsidies, together with foreign capital, were instrumental in the development of this particular industry. It was a development which later accelerated the creation of a new industrial region in the South of Russia, a large concentration of metallurgy and machine-building based upon the coal and iron-ore deposits there. In other branches of industry, relying upon both domestic capital investment and market demand in the private sector, the pace of development was relatively slow, with the textile industry – particularly cotton – acting as the pace-setter.

Prior to the 1890s, industrial enterprises were generally dispersed, many of them serving local rather than major regional markets or the national market. The majority of the enterprises and of the work force were located in the countryside rather than in the cities proper, and the contours of major industrial regions were only slowly emerging.

It was left for the period 1890–1913 to achieve a much higher degree of regional concentration of industrial enterprises, which also allowed for a higher degree of specialization between and within the regions. The growing density of the transportation network connected the southern region of ferrous metallurgy not only with the competing Polish region bordering on Silesia but, most important, with the St Petersburg concentration of metalworking and machinery industry. The central region of Moscow and Vladimir developed as the chief concentration of textile-manufacturing, challenged only by the Polish textile region of Łódź. The highly concentrated region of oil production (the oilfields of Baku in the Caucasus) did not have to face competition from the Groznyi oilfields until shortly before the First World War, although as a producer of fuel it had to compete with coal in many markets inside Russia.

Thus, in industry even more than in agriculture, the years around 1890 marked an acceleration of activity, a quickening of the pace of development in many areas – in the growth of the labour force, in the increase of tangible assets, in the size and variety of production and in its organizational structure, and in the shift from privately owned firms to corporate or joint-stock companies.

To express in capsule form the multi-faceted development of Russia's economy during the period 1890–1913 is difficult, and to select quantitative indicators reflecting the process of change in its complexity is reduction without justice. Therefore, the following indicators are presented primarily for illustrative purposes.

The growth rates of the indicators enumerated in Table 34 bear witness to the dynamics of the growth process in the Russian economy. However, in addition, the indicators point to some structural changes as indicated by the quantitative measures of the activities represented in the table.

The increased share of commercial output in total output was one of the most important changes during this period, especially since this was a change in which the agricultural sector of the economy participated together with the industrial sector. Allowing for changes in the popula-

tion size, the trade turnover increased (according to the available estimates) by almost 123 per cent,[3] and the marketability of agricultural
products accounted for a sizeable share of the total.

When Russian agriculture emerged from the difficult period of the
1880s and early 1890s, the share of its marketable output began to rise
faster than the growth of total agricultural production. The marketable
share increased both under the impact of foreign demand and of
domestic demand stimulated by urban population growth and under

Table 34. *Selected Economic Indicators, 1890 and 1913*

	1890	1913	% change
Population	117,787,000	161,723,000	37·3
Urban population	11,774,000	18,604,000	68·9
Per capita grain output[a] (1913 roubles)	20·60	27·88	35·3
Per capita gross industrial output (1913 roubles)	19·16	42·91	124·0
Per capita trade turnover (current roubles)	34·24	72·68	122·66
Per capita exports (current roubles)	5·84	9·06	55·14
Wholesale price index (113 = 100)	76·7	100·0	30·4
Employment in manufacturing, mining, and railways	1,682,100	3,844,000	128·5
Length of railway network (km)	30,596	70,990	132·0
Per capita currency in circulation (roubles)	7·88	13·88	76·1
Per capita expenditures of state budget (roubles)	8·97	20·92	133·2
Per capita government-guaranteed securities (roubles)	50·14[b]	77·18	53·9

[a] Per capita grain output is determined by the size of the harvest, which fluctuated
greatly in Russia. The 1913 harvest was one of the best on record, and the 1890 estimate was calculated as per capita production in only sixty districts of Russia. The
actual five-year average of grain production indicated a lower per capita growth rate.
[b] Figure for 1 January 1893 instead of 1890.

the impact of increasing regional specialization within the rural population. The exports of a selected group of agricultural commodities[4]
increased, on a per capita basis, by 41·1 per cent. In view of the fact that
the export trade in agricultural commodities represented a declining
share of the marketable agricultural production, the increase in marketability of agriculture was significant. It was significant not only because
it increased the share of monetized income in the total income of the
agricultural population but also because it made for closer ties between
farming and the market and strengthened the impact of the market

mechanism upon the behaviour of the agricultural producers. The growth of commercial agriculture from the late 1880s to 1913 was causing and intensifying income differentiation within the peasantry. While the process of income differentiation was to some extent hindered by institutional arrangements (peasant commune, tax structure, etc.) and by traditional attitudes within the peasant milieu; it could not be prevented from proceeding, in spite of the additional costs imposed by these impediments. When some of the institutional impediments were removed by the Stolypin reforms of 1906–10, the process of the commercialization of agriculture and of income differentiation among the peasants received a strong boost.

Another important structural change during this period was the growth of the share of the industrial and service sectors in employment and production. The increase of the labour force in mining, manufacturing, and railways was impressive. Employment in those branches increased from 1,682 thousand in 1890 to 3,844 thousand in 1913, a rise of 128·5 per cent. But most important, apart from the quantitative growth of the non-agricultural labour force, was its increased mobility, reflected in the growth of urbanization, the migration from rural to the urban areas, to a large extent motivated by employment opportunities.[5]

Although one could not ascribe most of the growth of the urban population to the impact of industrial employment, industrialization was exerting a powerful influence upon the mobility of the urban labour force and the growth of the city population.[6]

The growth of industrial production in Russia during the period 1890–1913 has been widely discussed by a succession of Russian and foreign scholars. According to Raymond Goldsmith's recalculation of the so-called 'Kondratiev Index' of physical output of large-scale industry, the annual growth rate for 1888–1913 was about 5 per cent, with about 7 per cent for 1888–1900 and about 4 per cent for 1900–13.[7] By international standards the growth rates compare favourably with most other countries during a similar stage in the industrialization process. To the extent that the growth of industrial production (of large-scale industry) is relatively well known, some other characteristics of economic activity were largely left outside the spectrum of public attention or scholarly study and therefore warrant mentioning.

The growth of Russian exports was a significant element of economic activity, reflecting to some extent the increased commercialization of agricultural production, since agricultural products constituted the largest component of Russian export trade. To the extent that the need to balance foreign trade, in the absence of a major influx of foreign capital, imposes constraints upon economic growth, the increased value of exports not only had to maintain a surplus in the trade balance but also had to achieve a balance of payments not unfavourable to Russia. This was a difficult task in view of the pattern of government spending, with its emphasis upon the priority of the military budget and the costs of preserving public order, as well as the payments of interest on the national debt, which was incurred to a considerable degree to finance the expansionist foreign policies pursued by the government. The large sums spent abroad, not only by the government but also by Russian citizens, apparently added to the burden of meeting foreign claims. Thus, the government tried to stimulate exports and, through a high tariff policy, to discourage the growth of imports. But the increase of exports was insufficient to provide the government and the country with the necessary surplus. Therefore the monetary policy of the government was directed toward the achievement of a foreign-exchange surplus and to facilitate an influx of foreign capital.

The introduction of convertibility of the currency into gold was the main achievement of Russian monetary policy during the 1890s. By accepting the gold standard the Russian government tried to achieve two objectives. First, it sanctioned the *de facto* devaluation of the currency and, by preventing its fluctuations, made certain that Russian goods would not become more expensive in terms of foreign currencies. This had the beneficial effect of introducing some stabilizers in the foreign trade area. Second, the government hoped to diminish the risks which a fluctuating currency created for prospective foreign lenders and investors. The convertibility of the currency into gold followed years of a ruthless policy of accumulation of a gold reserve and the deflationary pressures associated with it. The government's efforts to maintain a convertible currency were not achieved without further costs borne by some sectors of the economy, but the adherence to the gold standard helped to increase the flow of foreign capital into Russia.

Was Russia's monetary policy a deflationary or an inflationary one? It is difficult to answer the question without going into a detailed analysis of the monetary and credit policy. The most plausible answer is that the policy was not a consistent one. When peacetime inflationary pressures were building up, the Russian ministry of finance, through the State Bank, tried to contract the money supply; but when wartime expenditures were necessary or when budgetary deficits were large, the printing presses would work overtime. Thus, we find the oscillations between monetary expansion and contraction, often leading to economic instability. There is, however, no doubt that by the standards of other countries the phase of rapid growth of industry in the 1890s did not receive sufficient support from the monetary authorities, and the relative stagnation during 1900–8 was not counteracted by a more vigorous monetary expansion.[8] It was not, however, until the beginning of this century that the banks in Russia gained a measure of independence from the government that made them more responsive to the demand of the market for loanable funds. During the 1890s the banks were so closely following the precepts of governmental policy that it was impossible to expect on their part a restoration of the equilibrium destroyed by governmental policy measures. On balance, if one is to use the change in the price level as a yardstick for the effects of monetary policies, the price level in Russia did not rise much above the increase in the level of English prices during 1890–1913. Whether this could be considered optimal for a rapidly industrializing country is a matter of debate that is outside of the scope of this chapter.

The period 1890–1913 was marked by a substantial increase in the national debt. Both components of the national debt, foreign borrowing and domestic borrowing, increased simultaneously. A disproportionate share of the increase in foreign borrowing was devoted to the increase of the gold reserve[9] and to the budget financing of railway construction.[10] But a better understanding of the role of the national debt in the Russian economy could be gained by measuring the change in the amounts of government and government-guaranteed loans and bonds,[11] for which consecutive data are available since January 1893. The data indicate an increase from 6,090 million roubles in January 1893 to 12,745 million in January 1914. During this period the total debt held by foreigners increased from 3,818 million roubles to 6,507 million roubles, and the share held by Russian citizens, officially estimated, rose from 2,273 million roubles to 6,238 million. Thus the share held by Russian citizens increased from 37·3 per cent to 43·9 per cent.

The increase in foreign holdings of Russian securities was brought about in part by the prospect of higher yields than those available in Western Europe and in part by political considerations based upon the *entente cordiale* between France and Russia, which made France the largest creditor of Russia.

The doubling of the per capita holdings of interest-bearing government or government-guaranteed securities within Russia itself indicates the growth of internal capital accumulation, and although the participation of financial institutions like savings banks or commercial banks was significant, the direct subscription by individuals was constantly increasing. Thus, the money market in Russia was growing during the period under consideration, and government securities, railway bonds, and mortgage bonds occupied the commanding positions in the market.[12] Therefore, one could perhaps conclude that the government was, by and large, successful in its policies of mobilizing the savings of the population into the areas of major concern of its economic policies, namely the creation of capital overhead and the support of its agricultural endeavours.

It was against this background that the growth of the volume of corporate industrial firms had to compete with the 'safe' types of securities to gain the capital necessary for growth. Although the major St Petersburg banks participated in the financing of industry and the floating of industrial corporate securities as early as the 1890s, the investing public considered them highly speculative. Since the first seven or eight years of this century witnessed little expansion of bank financing of industry, the change in attitudes among bankers and investors took place during the years of economic recovery and industrial boom which preceded the First World War.

It was basically during the years 1909–13 that the securities of Russian industrial enterprises firmly took their place in the foreign and internal money markets.[13] The growth of the volume of borrowings by industrial enterprises in the money markets exhibited a pattern similar to that of government borrowing, namely an increase in both foreign and domestic markets, with the domestic market exceeding the foreign one.[14]

It would be a gross omission to ignore the development of railways in Russia in this short review of the major changes in the Russian economy during 1890–1913. However, it is difficult to be definite about the role of the railways in the absence of a fundamental study of this industry. Many of the questions most crucial for economic analysis and historical evaluation are as yet unexplored and unanswered. For our purposes it might be sufficient to point out that the period of the 1890s was one of unexcelled expansion of the railway network, which assisted in the process of commercialization of agriculture, facilitated the mobility of labour, contributed to the expansion of production of mining and manufacturing, and stimulated trade. The railways were important in providing employment and the inculcation of technical skills. The railways absorbed a sizeable portion of both foreign borrowings and domestic investment funds, channelled primarily by the state. In terms of the state's policies, railway transportation was given top priority among industry branches, for economic as well as political reasons. During the period 1890–1913 the state directly assumed much of the cost of railway construction and relied less upon the floating of railway bonds in the foreign and domestic money markets than before.[15]

Nevertheless, in comparison with the earlier period of intensive railway construction of the 1860s and 1870s, railway construction during 1890–1913 played a considerably less important role in the total growth of capital in Russia. To some extent this was to be expected, it is implied in the definition of industrialization. That a great many historians and economists studying the period have missed the point is easy to understand: their attention was habitually fixed on the public sector of the Russian economy, because of their conviction that the exclusive, active agent of economic development in Russia was the government. To disagree with the extremity of such a notion is not consonant with the view that in the 1890s or later Russia entered a period of classical laissez-faire, or that the railways ceased to play an important economic role. It is only to suggest that unless the railways are put in the perspective of a comparison either with the growth of industrial capital or with changes in the capital stock of agriculture, our notions of existing proportions about this period will remain impressionistic or actually distorted.

The comparison between railway construction and industrial capital is a particularly instructive one. In both instances the components of building construction were significant, the components of machinery (or rolling stock for railways) very important. According to our preliminary inquiries, no matter whether the increments of the capital stock were measured in current prices or in stable prices, and regardless of the most minimal assumed depreciation rates for railways, the result of the comparison was an unequivocal one – namely, that the growth of the railway stock during this period did not exceed the absolute increase in the stock of industrial capital. Starting with a considerably larger stock of capital (approximately twice the capital stock of industry), the railways continued their lead in accretions to the capital stock during the 1890s and until about 1907–8, when the decisive turning point occurred. It was sufficient during the remaining few years to change the proportions decisively.[16]

II. *Some Empirical Results*

The objective of this chapter is not to duplicate previous productive efforts to review the achievements of the Russian economy, but rather to inquire about the process of capital formation. In order that the examination of capital formation should be intelligible for international comparisons at some future date, the national accounting methodology of Professor Simon Kuznets is adopted.[17] Kuznets's definition of capital, 'the stock of means, separable from human beings and legally disposable in economic transactions, intended for use in producing goods or income', is followed. The coverage of capital formation in our empirical study is far from being complete; it does not even exhaust the private sector of the economy. However, there are reasons to believe that the pattern of capital formation presented in the following pages approximates the composition and growth pattern of the entire capital stock,[18] except perhaps in underestimating the share of equipment. In deriving our estimates, sources of Russian insurance companies and governmental insurance agencies, whenever they were available, were used, following the example of the Russian statistician Albert Vainshtein.[19] The following results of the empirical study are viewed as prolegomena to a more definitive study of capital formation in Russia.

A. CAPITAL IN AGRICULTURE

Capital formation in agriculture, regardless of various policies to stimulate capital investments in other sectors of the economy, was still very important in terms of size.

The burden of taxation in Russia limited the rate and scope of capital formation, particularly that of the peasants. An example of the most conspicuous, but by no means the most significant, part of the tax burden was the continuity of the redemption payments for forty-five years following the Emancipation of the serfs.[20]

The tax system imposed upon the peasants shifted increasingly toward indirect taxation of a regressive nature. Indirect taxes were levied on such items as alcohol, sugar, kerosene, tobacco, and matches – all products used in peasants' households.[21] In addition, the import duties on tea were high. The consumption costs of high tariffs on textiles and metal goods amounted to a shift of resources from agriculture to other branches of the economy. Even in the area of services like railway passenger traffic and commodity shipments, discrimination against the peasant helped the government to subsidize other social groups. Thus, the government policy of excise taxes and discriminatory pricing affected the value of the peasants' savings and reduced the investments which might have been forthcoming out of their incomes.

Capital investment in agriculture on the part of the peasant population was limited because of the substantial land purchases of the peasants.

Apart from population pressure on land, the conditions of the prevailing short-term land leases apparently did not encourage the peasants to make investments in the land available for leases.[22] In other words, the peasants considered proprietary rights a precondition for capital improvements. In addition, the rising land prices and rents stimulated the demand for land and resulted in purchases on the part of the peasants. All the factors combined resulted in an impressive transfer of land ownership from the nobility to the peasantry. According to avail-

able data, during the period of 1890–1913 the land holdings of the
nobility in forty-five districts of European Russia declined by over
35 per cent, from 65·2 million *dessiatiny* to at least 42·2 million *dessiatiny*.[23] And although not all of this land was transferred to the peasants,
the bulk of it was acquired by the peasants, either individually or
collectively (through the village communes or local voluntary
associations).

Having tied up their savings and future income in the purchase of
land – with limited access to the credit markets, at least until 1906–7 –
there was not much left that the peasants could invest in their farming
operations. Thus, while the period witnessed a growth in savings on the
part of the Russian peasantry, they actually made relatively little in the
way of capital investments which would yield high returns in the short
run.

In view of the relatively heavy burden of taxation and relatively large
expenditures for the acquisition of land and for investment in such
durables as farm dwellings, the residual for other types of farm investment was relatively limited. For most of the period investment in livestock and workstock, in agricultural machinery, in irrigation and drainage, or in such current inputs as improved fertilizers, higher-yielding
seed varieties, etc. ought to be considered a competitive alternative to
land acquisition and farm construction rather than a set of complementary investments. There is little doubt that the choice of the alternatives
played an important role in the pattern of growth of Russian agriculture
during this period and helps to explain the backwardness of this sector.

In order to follow the conventional distribution of capital in agriculture, it would be necessary to distinguish capital as represented by usable
land, capital in farm dwellings and farm buildings, and capital in the
form of equipment, machinery, workstock, and productive livestock.[24]
As far as land is concerned, the data on the area of usable land are not
uniform in their coverage for the whole period; and some land price
data which are needed in order to construct continuous series reflecting
capital formation in land are not available. Instead, the additions to
the planted area will be used as a proxy for the growth of capital in
agricultural land.[25]

There are two official series of data on the growth of the planted
area under grains and potatoes: one for fifty districts of European
Russia for 1893–1913, and another for seventy-two districts of Russia
for 1895–1913.

According to the first series (in fifty districts), the planted area grew
from 62·3 million *dessiatiny* in 1893 to 72·4 million in 1904 and 76·0
million in 1913, or by 22 per cent from 1893–1913. According to the
second series (in seventy-two districts), the area increased from 72·9

million *dessiatiny* in 1895 to 86·7 million in 1904 and 102·1 million in 1913, or by 40·1 per cent from 1895 to 1913. For the total territory of Russia the total increase in the planted area appears to be even higher and could be estimated at about 43 per cent for the period 1895–1913. A change in the crop pattern was also discernible.

The increase in the planted area reflected to a considerable extent the growth of the area under wheat and barley.[26] Since these crops required better land than crops such as rye and oats, it would be justifiable to assume that the shift in the crop pattern which accompanied the expansion of the planted area involved additional land improvement, thus causing an increase in the amount of capital represented by land.

A preliminary calculation of the value of land improvements for the years 1896–1913, based solely on the data of the increase of the planted area, yielded a sum of about 870 million roubles in terms of current prices.[27] Although the sum is significant in comparison with the growth of capital in agriculture, it was not included in the results of the study since it covers neither the value of land nor that of irrigation and drainage facilities. This estimate is used primarily for illustrative purposes.

Except for land, farm dwellings and farm buildings constitute the greatest component of capital in agriculture. The change in the size of this component is directly related to the growth in the number of farm units, whereas the number of farm units is a function of population growth and rise in incomes.

In view of the growth of the farm population the growth of the number of farm units was an almost foregone conclusion, given the existing social distribution of farm ownership between the peasantry and the large landowners, especially since institutional arrangements such as primogeniture were alien to the traditional concepts of inheritance and ownership.[28] Thus, given the preponderance of peasant farms, the focus of formation of new farm units was almost exclusively concentrated in the peasant sector. As was pointed out earlier, the numerical growth of farm units was supported by intensification of agricultural production on the existing area on the one hand, and by an expansion of the planted area within a colonization movement and government-sponsored migration from the densely populated areas of Central Russia to the Southeast, to Siberia and to the steppe regions of Asiatic Russia. It was this internal migration which compensated for the decline of the per capita planted area in European Russia and helped to maintain the formation of new farm units.

Although further research will undoubtedly improve the present estimates of the growth in the number of farm units, they can nevertheless be used as a first approximation for the task of estimating the capital stock in farm structures.[29]

According to our calculations the capital stock in farm dwellings increased in 1913 prices from 5,244 million roubles in 1890 to 7,005 million in 1913, or by 33·6 per cent – somewhat less than the growth rate of the rural population.

Farm buildings increased at a similar pace to that of farm dwellings:[30] their value increased from 2,595 million roubles to 3,482 million, or by 34·2 per cent. Thus the total stock of farm structures increased from 7,839 million roubles to 10,487 million, or by 33·8 per cent.[31] Nevertheless, in view of the scarcity of funds in Russian agriculture and the various impediments to investment, this was an impressive record.

Transportation equipment, other farm equipment, and machinery represent a separate component of the capital stock in agriculture, whose most striking feature was the relatively high share of transportation equipment in comparison with other categories of equipment and farm machinery.

Transportation equipment, in the form of horse-drawn wagons, sleighs, etc., was important for the farm economy for a number of reasons. Given the prevailing system of strip cultivation in some regions of the country, and the considerable distances from the fields to the farm buildings in other regions, there was an obvious need for transportation equipment both for seasonal agricultural work and for bringing the marketable output to the nearest markets. But in a country with a sparsely developed transportation network there existed a demand for transportation services by the non-agricultural sector, and such demand could at least in part be satisfied by the transportation facilities of the farm population, thus providing additional income, especially during periods free from work in the fields.

The growth of capital in transportation equipment was most closely related to the formation of new farms and to the state of workstock ownership by the peasants, since no major effects of substitution for this form of capital emerged during the period. One is therefore inclined to assume a stable demand for services by the non-agricultural sector[32] and an increasing demand for services by the agricultural sector. Perhaps a not very spectacular, but certainly the most dynamic, component of the capital stock in agriculture was farm machinery and equipment. It consisted of at least four sub-components: (1) farm implements produced in the villages by the peasants or local rural craftsmen; (2) farm implements produced by small-scale industry and craft shops specializing in the production of certain implements and farm equipment; (3) farm equipment and machinery domestically produced in large-scale industrial enterprises; and (4) farm machinery and equipment imported from abroad, most of which was technologically rather advanced in comparison with domestic production.

The chief characteristic of the farm equipment and machinery component of the capital stock in agriculture during the period under consideration was the gradual substitution of domestically produced and imported machinery, produced by large-scale industry, for the more primitive equipment, previously produced by small-scale industry, artisans, and rural craftsmen. It thus represented one of the few modernizing inputs in Russian agriculture, leading both to savings of labour and improvement in cultivation, which presumably affected both the size of output and the cost structure of agricultural production. Within the area of agricultural machinery of industrial origin, we find during this period not only a rapid pace of growth but also the increasing adoption by Russian industry of types of machinery previously produced abroad, and a rapid rise in the share of domestically produced agricultural machinery relative to imported machinery. What the sketchy data on agricultural machinery do not convey is the territorial distribution of the increase in capital and its distribution among farms of various sizes. Such data are available from the railway transportation statistics and from the only census of agricultural machinery and equipment, conducted in 1910. The available data indicate a heavy concentration of harvesting machinery, especially for the areas of commercial grain production (in the South and Southeast of European Russia and in the Steppe regions of Asiatic Russia). As far as farm implements for tillage and planting are concerned, the areas of commercial agriculture were setting the pace but were also followed by the grain-importing non-blacksoil areas. While the small peasant farms were still engaged in the transition from wooden to iron ploughs, the larger-scale farms were forging ahead in their demand for more complex agricultural machinery. The rising costs of agricultural labour were an accompanying determinant in the decision to substitute machinery for men. As the data make clear, the machinery and equipment input in the agricultural production process was only starting to have an effect by the end of the period under consideration. If the progress of mechanization in crop production was slow, it was even worse in livestock production, whether in the preparation of feed or in the processing of products. Except in cases when the products entered the channels of international or interregional trade and required uniform standards (like butter, eggs, and some meat products), the availability of labour in the farm households and the lack in many cases of alternative employment opportunities mitigated against the more intensive use of capital in livestock production.

Of all the components of capital in agriculture estimated in this study, the most puzzling and controversial is livestock and workstock. The behaviour of this capital series is puzzling for at least the following reasons. (1) The official data are extremely inaccurate and do not indicate a consistent definable pattern of behaviour. (2) The crop data point to an expansion of grains, but no apparent substitution of feed grains at the expense of food grains is discernible; the impression is thus created of a contraction of the livestock and workstock herd. (3) The increase in commercial output of livestock products gives the impression of an expanding livestock sector in agriculture. Out of this contradiction one has to find an approximation to the economic reality of the period with respect to livestock and workstock. It is possible to resolve the apparent contradiction by considering the following phenomena. (1) The livestock herd in Russia was exposed to the impact of frequent droughts, which affected not only the food supply but also to a large extent the supply of feed, thus causing a contraction of the size of the herd which would ordinarily require a number of years to bring it back to the pre-drought level. In addition, the livestock herd was continuously exposed to diseases that diminished the ability of the herd to expand within a relatively short period. (2) Russian agriculture, given its institutional features, demonstrated its inability to develop specialized breeds of livestock (e.g. dairy cattle as against beef cattle) and could not benefit from specialization and gains in productivity to the same extent as other countries. (3) During most of the period under consideration, the price differential between livestock products and grains was insufficient to move resources into livestock on a scale that would visibly counteract the adverse effects of climatic calamities, cattle diseases, and low productivity per farm animal.

The increase in commercial output of livestock products could be explained – apart from foreign demand and the growth of the urban population – by the process of economic differentiation of the Russian peasantry, the growth of production on larger, market-oriented farms, and the probable contraction of livestock consumption on the poorer farms. The formation of specialized regions of livestock production was still in its infancy.

A pattern similar to the one for productive livestock appears for the workstock. In spite of the growth of the number of farms, the differentiation of workstock ownership was progressing, and interregional as well as inter-group differentials of workstock holdings were increasing, while the total grew very slowly – on balance.

Anyone familiar with an agricultural economy would recognize the importance of stocks of farm commodities for both the production and the consumption of the agricultural producers. To the extent that stocks represent a form of capital (like inventories and stores in the industrial sector), it would have been desirable to include them in the volume of capital employed in the agricultural sector. However, the nature of the data makes it impossible to include this important item of capital in our continuous yearly estimates.[33] Nevertheless, a few characteristics of the behaviour of stocks could be reconstructed from the scattered evidence. Since our evidence pertains to the date of the lowest level of grain stocks, the stock information has to be treated as representing a minimum of reserves maintained by the farms. One of the most striking features of this reserve is the great degree of fluctuation, which is primarily a function of the size of the harvest. For the four major grains, the 15 July stocks on farms in the territory of sixty-four districts of Russia fluctuated between about 475 million roubles (in 1913 prices) for 1897 and 173 million roubles for 1908, at an average of 300 million roubles. The yearly changes in the level of the stocks were within the range of minus 180 million roubles for 1898 and plus 117 million roubles for 1910, with an average for 1897–1913 of minus 100 million

Table 35. *Estimates of the Capital Stock in the Farm Sector*

(1913 prices, million roubles)

	1890	1913	Increase	Increase (%)
Farm dwellings	5,244·0	7,005·1	1,761·1	33·6
Farm buildings	2,594·6	3,481·8	887·2	34·2
Productive livestock	3,782·7	4,003·2	220·5	5·8
Workstock	2,719·3	2,872·8	153·5	5·6
Transportation equipment	1,063·9	1,445·1	381·2	35·8
Farm equipment and machinery	366·4	1,053·0	686·6	87·4
Total accounted for	15,770·9	19,861·0	4,090·1	25·9

and plus 53 million roubles. The secular trend was for stocks on the farms to decline, which can be attributed not only to the weather conditions but also to the growth of commercialization of agriculture and perhaps to improvement in transportation facilities. The above observations are based upon incomplete data and upon minimum levels of stocks on the farms, and they are therefore subject to revision when more accurate data become available. They indicate, however, that the estimated values of capital in agriculture and its changes will have to be corrected in the future by the inclusion of changes in the volume of the stocks of agricultural commodities on the farms.

The changes in the capital stock of the farm sector during the period 1890–1913 are represented in Table 35, a summary of the major components of the capital which were included in our research effort.

It might be interesting to note that if we remove the category of farm dwellings from the total, and view the residual capital as an input in the production process of agriculture, its growth amounted to 22·1 per cent, while the composition of this residual capital stock did not change in any drastic form. The most notable change is accounted for by the increase of farm equipment and machinery, and some smaller change in the growth of farm buildings. The growth of those components was at the expense of the decline in the share of livestock and workstock on the farms. As will become clear from the discussion that follows, the share of agriculture (excluding land) in the capital stock of the non-government sector of the Russian economy declined during the period 1890–1913.

In the preceding discussion an attempt was made to estimate the changes in the amount of private capital in agriculture (outside of land, perennial crops, irrigation works, and stocks). The available sources do not, however, permit an estimate of the financial assets that participated in the process of capital formation. In the case of the peasant population, one can estimate the bulk of capital formation in farm construction or use estimates of many of their current expenditures (like taxes, rent payments, savings in savings banks), but it is difficult to document the sources of their capital investment in the absence of reliable income data. There is no doubt that some of the peasants' investments contained a substantial element of their own labour inputs, which does not make the task easier.

The situation with regard to the large landowners is quite different. For example, we know that during 1890–1913 they received approximately two thousand million roubles from the sales of their lands. We also know that during the same period the mortgage debt of landed private proprietors (excluding peasants) increased by at least 1,275 million roubles. Yet the data on the increasing indebtedness of the landed proprietors and the cash receipts from the sale of land seem to exceed by a wide margin the increases in the capital stock of the estimates. Thus, one would have to assume that the proceeds (or a substantial portion thereof) from land sale and the mortgaging of estates were diverted into other areas of capital investment (possible agricultural processing industries, urban real estate, and the purchase of government bonds and industrial shares) or into consumption expenditures. Obviously, without additional research one cannot resolve this problem.

B. CAPITAL IN STRUCTURES

In Russia, as in many other countries, the early phase of the industrialization process was marked by the phenomenon of allocating a large share of reproducible capital to construction. It is useful and methodologically necessary to distinguish between two types of construction: residential construction, and construction which 'participates' in the production process.

In view of the growth of population, it is not surprising that residential construction was quantitatively the more important of the two types. In terms of the changes in the value of the capital stock of structures between 1890–1913 – which rose from 12,167 million roubles to 18,167 million, or by 49·3 per cent – the share of residential capital in the increase was 4,317 million roubles, and the share of productive buildings 1,676 million roubles.

The services provided by residential construction, although not participating directly in the process of production, affect the long-term process of economic growth through their impact upon the health of the population, their support of labour mobility, etc. In addition, vigorous residential construction helps the development of the construction industry, creates a more efficient use of raw materials and manufactured goods used as inputs into the industry, and provides incomes for workers and entrepreneurs in the construction field. Its secondary effects of creating a demand for public utilities, transportation networks, and other services are also important in developing an infrastructure necessary for economic growth.

The total increase of residential structures in 1913 prices was from 9,007 million roubles to 13,324 million roubles, or 47.9 per cent, or on a per capita basis 7·74 per cent. This total can be divided between 1,761 million roubles' increase in farm dwellings and 2,556 million roubles' increase in the stock of urban dwellings. Thus, the share of urban dwellings in the total increase of the stock of residential structures was 59·2 per cent.[34]

One could not fail to note that the stock of urban residential structures increased by a larger percentage than the stock of rural dwellings (67·9 per cent as against 33·6 per cent), while on a per capita basis urban residential construction did not exceed the growth of the population, nor did the stock of rural dwellings quite keep pace with the population increase. The data might also indicate that the incomes of the urban population rose relatively faster than the incomes of the rural population, or that the income elasticity for housing was higher within the urban areas than in the rural ones.

The total capital stock of structures in productive use was estimated to have grown from 3,160 million roubles in 1890 to 4,836 million roubles in 1913, or by 53 per cent. Of this increase of 1,676 million roubles, 897 million were attributed to the growth of the stock of farm buildings, and 789 million to that of industrial buildings, although the growth rate of industrial buildings was considerably higher than that of farm buildings.

In summarizing our observations on the growth of the capital stock of privately owned structures in Russia for the period 1890–1913, perhaps a distribution between farm and non-farm structures might be in order. Farm structures increased from 7,839 million roubles (in 1913 prices) to 10,487 million roubles, or by 33·8 per cent. At the same time non-farm structures increased from 4,328 million roubles to 7,673 million, or by 77·3 per cent. Thus, the 5,993 million roubles' increase of capital stock in structures contains 3,345 million roubles of non-farm structures and 2,648 million of farm structures, and their relative shares in the total increase are 55·8 per cent for non-farm structures and 44·2 per cent for farm structures.[35]

The stock of capital in urban housing in terms of 1913 prices increased from 3,763 million roubles to 6,319 million, or by 67·9 per cent.

How can one explain the growth of capital embodied in urban housing? One of the explanations is the growth of the demand for urban housing, which was related to the numerical growth of the urban population. The only continuing yearly series of data on urban population growth pertains to the territory of the fifty provinces of European Russia.[36] The data indicate an increase of 68·9 per cent during the period 1890–1913. The growth rate was not even for various years, since during the first decade of the period the urban population grew only by 22·4 per cent.

If we were to use the urban population data for the whole Empire (available for 1897, and for consecutive years from 1904 onward) to obtain a figure for per capita growth, we should find that the per capita increase during 1897–1913 constituted a mere 4·97 per cent.

It is also important to note that, in addition to the numerical growth of the urban population, supporting evidence for the existence of a strong demand for urban housing is provided by the index of urban rents, which was rising during the decade of the 1890s faster than any other component of the consumer price index. The pressure of a strong demand for urban housing presumably provided an incentive to build urban houses and apartments.

The available data about the capital market show a generally favourable response to the demand for housing construction, as represented by the change in the supply of mortgage funds, which increased by 1,139 million roubles during 1890–1913. The long-term debt arising from urban real estate increased by 583 million roubles from 1890 to 1901, from 484 million roubles to 1,067 million. Out of this total, 357 million was provided by land mortgage banks and 226 million by urban credit associations. However, government policy, which by and large preferred to support land mortgages as against urban real estate, and consequently restricted the activities of the land banks to the extent that they could lend only up to one-third of their long-term loans against urban real estate, put a lid upon further expansion by land banks in the urban real estate market. Thus, for all practical purposes, the urban credit associations assumed the major role as a source of mortgage capital for urban housing. This had a number of detrimental effects upon the financing of investment in urban real estate.

There was a heavy concentration of capital in the urban credit associations in four major cities (St Petersburg, Moscow, Odessa, and Warsaw), and although the four major cities accounted for a sizeable share in the growth of the urban population, their share in mortgage capital was disproportionately larger. Thus, this would indicate that many urban centres of the country experienced difficulties in their access to the organized capital market and had to rely upon other types of loans or upon local savings to provide the means of financing housing construction. In addition, the urban credit associations were forced to pay higher interest rates on their mortgage capital, while competing with the government-sponsored and government-controlled land mortgage banks, which in turn made mortgage loans more expensive to home-builders and buyers. Relatively little new capital was directly provided by the banks for urban real estate during the period between 1901–9 (the net increase was only 136 million roubles, from 1,067 million to 1,203 million roubles). The general acceleration of economic activity and the continuous growth of the urban population were the basic stimuli for an increased flow of mortgage capital into urban construction during 1909–13, when 420 million roubles was lent on urban real estate mortgages, of which 344 million was provided by the urban credit associations. There are also indications, based upon the study of the investment behaviour of the owners of large estates, that some fraction of the mortgage capital supplied to agricultural holdings, or proceeds from the sale of landed estates, found its way directly or indirectly into the urban real estate market. Thus seepage of land mortgage loans, combined with the growth of savings by the urban population, might help to explain the rise of capital embodied in urban housing for periods during which the net flow of mortgage capital was insufficient to account for the observed growth.[37]

C. INDUSTRIAL CAPITAL

To the extent that the period under investigation is characterized as the period of early industrialization, the data reflecting the changes in the size and composition of industrial capital occupy a central place in our considerations.

The basic data underlying our calculations are the reports of the fire insurance companies, which reported the insured value of industrial plants. It was assumed that by and large the reported magnitudes represented the current value of the assets actually in use.[38]

In accordance with conventional practice, industrial capital was calculated by its main components, two of which (structures and equipment) represented fixed capital and the third the level of inventories.

Apart from its growth pattern in current and in stable prices the most interesting characteristic of the composition of industrial capital during this period is the secular trend of inventories to grow as a component of the total (measured in current prices) and the trend of the share of fixed capital to decline. Although one would expect the decline of the share of structures in total capital, the slight decline of equipment as a share in total capital is somewhat surprising. It is possible that the maintenance of a higher level of inventories was dictated by the conditions of the market, the inadequacy of the transportation network, and the problems of supply and distribution. It is also plausible to assume, on the basis of Russian banking policies, that credits were more abundant for short-term investment in inventories, rather than for long-term investments in fixed assets.

It is rather difficult to obtain reliable information on the financing of industrial capital from primary data, even to the extent that it is possible to derive estimates on the changes and composition of industrial capital. Quite often economists and historians have tried to obtain such information from data about the capital of joint-stock companies, naively assuming that the formation of a joint-stock company reporting its basic capital assets was equivalent to a net addition to the capital stock. The process of transformation of privately owned firms into joint-stock companies was an uninterrupted one during our whole period, but we have no information about the transformation of ownership status prior to 1900.[39] Therefore, the employment of data about the capital of industrial corporations as a surrogate for the total of industrial enterprises would distort not only the composition but also the growth pattern of industrial capital. There are, however, some behavioural characteristics of the industrial corporations which can be generalized as a pattern followed by all industrial entrepreneurs. One of them is the increase of capital by existing enterprises. If one accepts the data on the increase of capital by corporations, the following pattern emerges. Out of a total increase in the capital of all corporations during 1901–13,[40] 23·5 per cent was added by newly established firms, 26·3 per cent was added by private firms being converted into corporations, and 50·2 per cent was added by existing corporations. Thus the largest share in the financing of the corporate sector was achieved as a result of the growth of the enterprises themselves, whether by investment from profits or by borrowing against an increasing value of assets.

The borrowings of industrial enterprises cannot be traced for most of the period, given our present state of knowledge.[41] The data for the flotation of industrial shares and bonds are available for 1908–13 only, and they reflect the conditions of the industrial boom in Russia preceding the First World War. There is a strong presumption that some portion of the total floated shares and bonds did not reach the investing public but remained in the portfolios of the banks themselves. This would indicate that the attitude of the banking community toward industrial borrowings underwent considerable change from the time of the 1890s and early 1900s, when the banks by and large followed the preferences of the Russian public for stable, high-yielding state-guaranteed loans or mortgage bonds and themselves hesitated to provide industry with long term capital funds. Thus while during the early stage of our period industry encountered considerable difficulties in raising capital, during the later one borrowing was facilitated. In addition, internal accumulation was increasing within the firms, and when it coincided with a decline in the interest rate, it provided an incentive for enterprises to expand their capital investments.

A comparison of the time pattern of changes in the size of industrial capital with the changes in production of large-scale industry in Russia is revealing in a number of ways. During the 1890s the rate of growth of industrial capital (in 1913 prices) was rising more rapidly than the growth in value of industrial output (in 1913 prices), thereby causing the capital–output ratio to increase. However, during the period 1901–8, this trend was reversed, thus causing the capital–output ratio to decline. During the period 1909–13, both industrial capital and industrial production were growing at relatively high rates.

The discrepancy between the growth rates of capital and production during the period of the slump in the Russian economy of 1901–8 would suggest that the growth pattern and growth rates of industrial production cannot be fully explained by changes in the labour force and capital inputs alone. The residual to be explained was due to technological change – both technological borrowing and advancement in Russia proper.

Preliminary investigation comparing the growth patterns of industrial capital and the capital stock in railways (which is outside our main concern in this chapter) yields – despite certain discrepancies – additional insight into the relative size of the industrial capital stock. During the period 1893–1912, the sub-periods of highest growth of the capital stock in railways were 1897–1900 and 1901–4 (the latter not because of new investment, but presumably because of the gestation period of previous investment). For industrial capital, 1897–1900 and 1909–12 were the periods of highest growth rates. It is clear that the complementarity between the patterns of growth of the industrial capital and of the capital stock in railways created in the second half of the 1890s conditions favourable to a broadly based industrialization process. The divergence of the patterns of growth in the two sectors of capital formation during the period 1901–9, apart from the relative decline in the growth rates of both, was in part responsible for the duration of the slump in economic activity.

As far as the relative size of the growth of the capital stock in industry and in railways is concerned, the data indicate that until roughly 1905–6 the yearly additions to the capital stock in railways exceeded the additions to the industrial stock. Beginning in 1908, however, the growth of the industrial capital stock outdistanced the railways to such an extent that during the closing years of our period the railway investments were relegated to a supporting but not decisive position in the growth of capital in Russia.

Anyone interested in the growth of industrial capital in Russia during the period before the First World War cannot and ought not to ignore the role played by the state. At least three types of state activities have to be taken into account. First, the direct and induced investment in capital overhead, notably in the development of the railway network, which apart from cheapening transportation costs became a source of demand for industrial production; second, the policies which provided a protectionist umbrella for numerous branches of Russian industry; and third, the direct subsidies and government guarantees granted to various industrial enterprises. All of these, together with governmental policies designed to assure industrial peace, were important 'environmental' measures which favoured the growth of industrial capital. By comparison with industry in other countries, both the size of the enterprises and the capital per enterprise were relatively high. Whether this last phenomenon resulted in economies of scale is still a debatable problem. One thing, however, is clear: in the area of industrial capital, the lag between the Russian economy and the more advanced industrial nations was shorter than in other areas of economic activity.

III. *Summary*

A few tables will serve to summarize briefly the quantitative results of our inquiry into the process of capital formation in Russia during the period 1890–1913.

For the classification of the capital stock in terms of industry branches, we might divide the assembled data as in Table 36. Although the data indicate a growth rate of 48·7 per cent for the measured capital stock, it is necessary to keep in mind that the population of Russia increased by 37·3 per cent during the same period, which reduces the per capita

Table 36. *Capital Stock, Classification by Industry*
(1913 prices, million roubles)

	1890	1913	Increase
Construction	12,167	18,160	5,993
Agriculture	7,932	9,374	1,442
Manufacturing and mining	1,143	4,059	2,916
Total	21,242	31,593	10,351

growth of capital to a fraction of the above-mentioned growth rate. Concerning the distribution of the capital between the farm sector and the non-farm sector – a distribution which is crucial for the economy of a developing country – the data in Table 37 are indicative.

Table 37. *Distribution of Capital Stock between Farm and Non-Farm Sectors*
(1913 prices, million roubles)

	1890	1913	Increase	Increase (%)
Farm sector	15,771	19,861	4,090	25·6
Non-farm sector	5,471	11,732	6,261	114·4

Finally, in order to separate the residential structures, the changes in the capital stock can be presented in the form shown in Table 38.

Table 38. *Capital Stock in Agriculture, Industry, and Residential Structures*
(1913 prices, million roubles)

	1890	1913	Increase	Increase (%)
Agriculture	10,527	12,856	2,329	22·1
Industry	1,709	5,413	3,704	216·7
Residential structures	9,006	13,324	4,318	47·9

IV. *Postscript*

Since our calculations of capital – primarily in the private sector of the economy – have left out a number of important areas of capital formation, a glance at the amount of capital not accounted for in our calculations is in order. Of major interest is the amount of capital classified as social capital. The best estimates for this category can be derived from the calculations of the statistician Albert Vainshtein.[42] Vainshtein provides the basis for estimates of capital overhead for the year 1913 (1 January 1914) as presented in Table 39.

This table indicates that from the measured components of the social capital of Russia 6,837 million roubles, or 78·3 per cent, belonged to the public sector. Actually the public sector was even larger, since we have not included here the public share of irrigation facilities in agriculture (of a magnitude of over 500 million roubles) and the value of military installations, facilities and equipment (which exceeded two thousand million roubles).[43]

Table 39. *Components of Capital Overhead, 1913*
(million roubles)

Components	Total value	Share of private capital
Railroads	4,996	
Water transportation	687	
Roads	754	
Total transportation	6,437	1,625
Communication	127	45
Municipal services and amenities	1,485	222
Public buildings[a]	680	
Total	8,729	1,892

[a] Houses of worship are excluded: their value was estimated at about a thousand million roubles.

Do other available data about the economic development of Russia support or contradict the capital estimates presented in this chapter?

Unfortunately there are no GNP estimates for frequent intervals, with which one could compare the results reported above and against which one could test the findings. Of the data in circulation and known to most students of the Russian economy, those that could come closest to representing a major segment of the GNP are the estimates of crop production (in physical terms) and estimates of the gross output of large-scale industry. Both of those measures, representing incomplete estimates of the production of two sectors of the economy, would hardly meet the requirements of a test of capital estimates as against GNP estimates.[44]

The data that come closest to representing a series at the macro-economic level that could perhaps serve as a substitute for a GNP measure were constructed by the Russian statistician V. E. Varzar as a general consumption index of a basket of thirty-five commodities, both agricultural and industrial, which make up the bulk of final consumption.[45] A closer examination of the Varzar index reveals that by not wholly eliminating intermediate goods it contained elements of both production and consumption indexes.

The increase in the volume of the consumption basket in 1913 prices calculated by V. E. Varzar is represented in abridged form in Table 40. The data indicate, among other things, the limits imposed upon the volume of per capita consumption by population growth, which might

Table 40. *Index of Growth of Varzar Consumption Basket*
(1890 = 100)[a]

	Absolute growth	Per capita growth
1900	139·5	120·1
1910	177·3	128·9
1913	207·2	142·0

[a] The figures underlying the above table are the following:

	Absolute volume (million roubles)	Per capita volume (roubles)
1890	4,279·9	45·58
1900	5,971·7	54·74
1910	7,589·9	58·75
1913	8,866·6	64·72

SOURCE. P. P. Maslow, *Kriticheskii analiz burzhuaznykh statisticheskich publikatsii* (Moscow, 1955), 458–60.

also have hindered the process of capital accumulation. The published fragments of the Varzar index (data for 1887, 1900, and 1910) indicate that during 1887–1900 the growth rates of the agricultural and industrial goods included in the index were 154·8 per cent for industry and 13·9 per cent for agriculture, while during 1900–10 they were 24·7 per cent for industry and 28·3 per cent for agriculture.

The implication is that the per capita consumption of agricultural products in 1900 was below the 1887 level but that it recovered by 1910, while the share of agricultural products in total consumption declined substantially during 1887–1900 and remained at the same level during 1900–10. This appears to be consistent with physical production data for the period.

To the extent that the Varzar index included exports – and the volume of agricultural exports was rising almost without interruption since the second half of the 1890s – the decline of the share of domestic agricultural consumption in the total domestic consumption might in fact have been greater than the share reflected in the index. But, regardless of any refinements which have to be introduced into the index to reflect domestic consumption more precisely, the message is clear: namely, that during the period of intensive industrialization, 1887–1900, the shift from consumption of agricultural products toward consumption of industrial goods was more pronounced than during the period 1900–10. Thus the Varzar index helps to substantiate the observation that the substitution of industrial goods for agricultural ones in total consumption was an accompanying element of the industrialization process in Russia, and perhaps even a precondition for the continuity of industrialization. At the most general level, Varzar's Consumption Basket grows much faster than what we would expect of output, given our capital data.[46]

A question, therefore, arises as to the causes of the discrepancy. In our view there are three basic reasons which ought to be considered. One is undoubtedly the growth of the labour force. The second and perhaps most important factor is technological change, which is not necessarily fully reflected in the prices of capital goods and to which a large fraction of increased output can be attributed. The third factor is the improvement of the quality of the labour force, a subject which will be mentioned further. Until we calculate the economic impact of these three factors upon the volume of production, one cannot pass judgement about the degree of compatibility between the Varzar index and our capital-formation estimates. In one respect, both support the contention that the highest rates of growth are to be found during the period 1910–13. That the congruence of the two measures is much less for the earlier periods can perhaps be attributed not only to the factors listed above but also to the movements of the price indexes that were used to deflate the current value of the capital stock into the 1913 price series.

Capital formation embodied in physical assets had to compete with, but was also complementary with, the improvement in education and technical skills embodied in the labour force.[47]

The assumption for Russia, as for many developing countries, that literacy is a significant threshold in education and the acquisition of skills has to be made in the absence of detailed educational data. For the agricultural labour force, the growth of literacy was approximately the following: for males, an increase from about 22 per cent in 1890 to about 42 per cent by 1913; for females, from about 12 per cent to about 25 per cent for the same period.[48]

During this period, the relatively rapid increase in the education level of the younger age cohorts helped to accelerate the process of commercialization of farming and adoption of improved methods of farming. The introduction of planted grasses in crop rotation or of new crop varieties, irrigation and drainage, use of more modern farm implements, etc. – all these measures depended upon the ability to communicate, an understanding of the new opportunities, and a willingness to experiment. Ultimately such 'modernizing' measures were related to increasing incomes and education. There is no doubt that without the increased schooling the Russian peasantry would have been unable to exhibit the feverish drive to organize its collective and individual activities, especially during the years preceding the First World War, such as the network of rural co-operatives and rural credit associations. These were institutions requiring literacy; business acumen and the rudiments of managerial skills and education were the key elements for their presence within the peasant milieu. Thus one could conclude even on the basis of circumstantial evidence that the public and private investment in rural schooling was yielding high returns.

A considerable increase in literacy took place among factory workers. Literacy among male factory workers in European Russia increased from 56·5 per cent in 1897 to about 80 per cent in 1913; and among female workers, from 20 per cent to about 44 per cent.[49] Thus a major contribution to the increase in literacy of the factory labour force was made by investment in the education of women.

The main instrument for the achievement of literacy was the school system in primary education. The school enrolment data for the two largest elementary-school networks (those of the Ministry of Education and of the Greek Orthodox Church) indicate an increase from 2,283 thousand in 1890 to 7,570 thousand in 1913, or almost 232 per cent, as against a total population increase of 37·3 per cent (see Table 52 below). Although still small by the standards of developed countries, elementary-school enrolment in the two major networks increased from 1·94 per cent of the total population in 1890 to 4·68 per cent in 1913.

Although we do not have exact data on the cost of education in Russia, the existing estimates probably do not deviate from the actual direct costs (except for income forgone). According to the estimates by Strumilin, the yearly costs of education in 1913 were 21 roubles per pupil in primary schools, 116 roubles in secondary schools, and 261 roubles at the university level. Obviously we should have to compare the costs with some general yardstick in the economy, and if we were to assume about 110 roubles as the per capita GNP in Russia in 1913 we should gain some perspective on the order of magnitude represented by the cost of education.

While investment in primary education was largely borne by the state (or its central and local government institutions) out of the taxes levied upon the population, investment in secondary education represented – to a larger extent than primary education – the direct investment decisions of individuals, as well as a larger proportion of forgone incomes. But the enrolment in secondary schools increased from about 130 thousand in 1890 to 535·8 thousand in 1913, with females accounting for the larger share of the growth (the enrolment of girls increased from about 60 thousand to 303·7 thousand).

Thus, while leaving aside the problem of higher education as a source of skill acquisition, the expansion of elementary and secondary education in Russia during this period was making a significant contribution to the quality of the labour force and to the growth of the Russian economy.

Some insight into the effectiveness of education could be gained by a glance at some data on white-collar employment derived from the population census of 1897 and shown in Table 41. The lack of comparable data for 1913–14 is deplorable. Nevertheless, we know that the

Table 41. *Number of White-Collar Workers Employed in the Non-Agricultural Sector, 1897*

Category	Employment (thousands)
Civilian bureaucracy	151,345
Military	52,471
Education	172,842
Industry, railways, trade, and Banking	298,623
Free professions	52,825
Total	728,106

number of teachers in 1914 was over 280,000 (in the present territory of the USSR, which is less than in the Empire); that the number of physicians increased from 13,344 in 1905 to over 22,000 in 1913; and that while in 1897 the total number of engineers employed in Russia was 4,010, by 1913 the yearly number of graduates of engineering schools was about 1,500. There is no doubt that in such areas as industry, transportation, communication, and trade the number of white-collar workers increased substantially between 1897 and 1913, and the level of education of the employed grew alongside their numerical growth. The sheer fact of an enrolment of about 130,000 students in institutions of higher learning in 1913 is indicative of the growth of human capital, especially during the period preceding the First World War.

STATISTICAL APPENDIX

Tables 42–52

Table 42. *Estimates of Total Private Capital*
(1913 prices, million roubles)

	Total	Three-year moving average
1890	21,242·4	
1891	21,040·0	21,046·2
1892	20,856·2	20,949·3
1893	20,951·7	21,112·1
1894	21,528·3	21,483·5
1895	21,970·6	22,019·6
1896	22,559·8	22,597·3
1897	23,261·5	23,120·3
1898	23,539·6	23,558·2
1899	23,873·6	23,957·8
1900	24,460·3	24,560·4
1901	25,347·2	25,321·4
1902	26,156·7	25,950·1
1903	26,346·5	26,431·3
1904	26,790·7	26,848·9
1905	27,409·4	27,121·8
1906	27,165·3	27,306·5
1907	27,324·9	27,498·7
1908	27,985·9	28,085·1
1909	28,924·7	28,930·2
1910	29,880·1	29,760·6
1911	30,476·9	30,363·9
1912	30,734·7	30,934·9
1913	31,593·2	

Table 43. *Capital Stock in Structures (1913 prices, million roubles)*

	Farm dwellings	Urban dwellings	Farm buildings	Industrial buildings	Total
1890	5,244·0	3,762·9	2,594·6	565·2	12,166·7
1891	5,309·6	3,807·4	2,631·0	563·0	12,311·0
1892	5,303·1	3,774·2	2,628·4	582·4	12,288·1
1893	5,351·5	3,731·9	2,652·1	608·7	12,344·2
1894	5,455·5	3,848·0	2,700·0	617·2	12,620·7
1895	5,538·7	3,958·6	2,738·9	655·4	12,891·0
1896	5,598·6	4,037·0	2,769·0	680·3	13,084·9
1897	5,712·0	4,200·1	2,821·1	743·5	13,476·7
1898	5,728·1	4,274·8	2,834·4	772·1	13,609·4
1899	5,784·0	4,259·3	2,863·9	830·0	13,737·2
1900	5,905·4	4,396·2	2,919·3	898·4	14,119·3
1901	5,951·1	4,753·4	2,944·8	928·2	14,577·5
1902	6,004·3	5,055·4	2,973·2	902·6	14,935·5
1903	6,110·3	5,204·7	3,006·0	896·9	15,217·9
1904	6,172·7	5,479·1	3,055·0	925·8	15,632·6
1905	6,240·6	5,762·1	3,089·5	998·7	16,090·9
1906	6,324·8	5,822·3	3,130·6	950·1	16,227·8
1907	6,360·1	5,890·1	3,152·5	961·8	16,364·5
1908	6,453·8	5,991·7	3,199·4	997·9	16,642·8
1909	6,534·6	6,312·3	3,242·1	1,026·4	17,116·4
1910	6,646·1	6,704·0	3,296·9	1,071·0	17,718·0
1911	6,818·6	6,628·3	3,360·5	1,182·0	17,989·4
1912	6,851·1	6,326·4	3,401·0	1,274·0	17,852·5
1913	7,005·1	6,319·1	3,481·8	1,353·7	18,159·7

Table 44. *Capital Stock in Structures: Three-Year Moving Averages*
(*1913 prices, million roubles*)

	Total dwellings	Total productive buildings	Total structures
1891	9,067·1	3,188·2	12,255·3
1892	9,092·6	3,221·8	12,314·4
1893	9,154·4	3,262·9	12,417·3
1894	9,294·4	3,324·1	12,618·5
1895	9,478·5	3,386·9	12,865·4
1896	9,681·7	3,469·4	13,151·1
1897	9,850·2	3,540·0	13,390·3
1898	9,986·1	3,621·7	13,607·8
1899	10,115·9	3,706·1	13,822·0
1900	10,349·8	3,794·9	14,144·7
1901	10,688·6	3,855·5	14,544·1
1902	11,026·4	3,883·9	14,910·3
1903	11,342·2	3,919·8	15,262·0
1904	11,656·5	3,990·6	15,647·1
1905	11,933·9	4,049·9	15,983·8
1906	12,133·3	4,094·4	16,227·7
1907	12,280·9	4,130·8	16,411·7
1908	12,514·2	4,193·7	16,707·9
1909	12,880·8	4,278·3	17,159·1
1910	13,214·6	4,393·3	17,607·9
1911	13,324·8	4,528·5	17,853·3
1912	13,316·2	4,684·3	18,000·5

Table 45. *Capital Stock in Farm Structures*
(*1913 prices, million roubles*)

	Farm dwellings	Farm buildings	Total farm structures
1890	5,244·0	2,594·6	7,838·6
1891	5,309·6	2,631·0	7,940·6
1892	5,330·1	2,628·4	7,931·5
1893	5,351·5	1,652·1	8,003·7
1894	5,455·5	2,700·0	8,155·5
1895	5,538·7	2,738·9	8,277·6
1896	5,598·6	2,769·0	8,367·6
1897	5,712·0	2,821·1	8,533·1
1898	5,728·1	2,834·4	8,562·5
1899	5,784·0	2,863·9	8,647·9
1900	5,905·4	2,919·3	8,824·8
1901	5,951·1	2,944·8	8,895·9
1902	6,004·3	2,973·2	8,977·5
1903	6,110·3	3,006·0	9,116·3
1904	6,172·7	3,055·0	9,227·7
1905	6,240·6	3,089·5	9,330·1
1906	6,324·8	3,130·6	9,455·4
1907	6,360·1	3,152·5	9,512·6
1908	6,453·8	3,199·4	9,653·2
1909	6,534·6	3,242·1	9,776·7
1910	6,646·1	3,296·9	9,943·0
1911	6,818·6	3,360·5	10,179·1
1912	6,851·1	3,401·0	10,252·0
1913	7,005·1	3,481·8	10,486·9

Table 46. *Capital Stock in Agriculture, except for Farm Buildings*
(1913 prices, million roubles)

	Equipment and machinery	Transportation equipment	Workstock	Livestock	Total
1890	366·4	1,063·9	2,294·4	3,470·2	7,194·9
1891	375·4	1,085·2	2,038·7	3,298·1	6,797·4
1892	379·1	1,085·6	1,969·5	3,245·5	6,679·7
1893	387·0	1,094·9	1,975·0	3,230·6	6,687·5
1894	399·9	1,108·2	1,977·7	3,218·2	6,704·0
1895	421·0	1,120·7	2,024·2	3,297·8	6,863·7
1896	440·5	1,133·9	2,034·9	3,370·7	6,980·0
1897	456·9	1,148·6	2,071·4	3,433·1	7,110·0
1898	470·1	1,163·0	2,092·1	3,397·2	7,122·4
1899	487·6	1,177·7	2,148·9	3,439·9	7,254·1
1900	507·3	1,192·9	2,171·4	3,536·9	7,408·5
1901	525·6	1,208·0	2,209·9	3,495·4	7,438·9
1902	551·8	1,223·2	2,244·4	3,639·4	7,658·8
1903	584·4	1,238·4	2,232·2	3,597·6	7,652·6
1904	628·1	1,254·3	2,262·5	3,603·9	7,748·8
1905	657·0	1,269·8	2,257·0	3,536·2	7,720·0
1906	681·3	1,285·8	2,220·7	3,446·8	7,634·6
1907	701·3	1,302·3	2,207·8	3,377·4	7,588·8
1908	725·3	1,322·5	2,221·3	3,391·3	7,660·4
1909	773·6	1,344·4	2,292·6	3,464·0	7,874·6
1910	833·3	1,366·0	2,351·7	3,570·9	8,021·9
1911	903·7	1,394·2	2,345·0	3,572·4	8,215·3
1912	983·0	1,412·1	2,374·3	3,580·8	8,350·2
1913	1,053·0	1,445·1	2,429·3	3,710·8	8,638·2

Table 47. *Components of the Capital Stock in Agriculture:*
Three-Year Moving Averages (1913 prices, million roubles)

	Farm buildings	Transportation equipment	Equipment and machinery	Workstock	Livestock	Total
1891	2,618·0	1,078·2	373·6	2,488·5	3,609·1	10,167·5
1892	2,637·2	1,088·6	380·5	2,359·3	3,496·7	9,962·3
1893	2,660·2	1,096·2	388·7	2,331·8	3,446·1	9,922·9
1894	2,697·0	1,107·9	402·6	2,298·0	3,458·2	9,963·8
1895	2,736·0	1,120·9	420·5	2,330·4	3,510·6	10,118·3
1896	2,776·3	1,344·4	439·5	2,367·3	3,590·9	10,308·3
1897	2,808·2	1,148·5	455·8	2,449·0	3,638·2	10,499·7
1898	2,839·8	1,163·1	471·5	2,485·7	3,668·8	10,628·9
1899	2,872·5	1,177·9	488·3	2,524·9	3,710·4	10,774·0
1900	2,909·3	1,192·9	506·8	2,571·4	3,751·2	10,931·6
1901	2,945·8	1,208·0	528·2	2,608·9	3,821·2	11,112·1
1902	2,974·7	1,223·2	553·9	2,633·2	3,844·7	11,229·7
1903	3,011·4	1,238·6	588·1	2,653·9	3,881·4	11,373·4
1904	3,050·2	1,254·2	623·2	2,659·0	3,847·8	11,434·3
1905	3,091·7	1,270·0	655·5	2,654·6	3,794·2	11,465·9
1906	3,124·2	1,286·0	679·9	2,633·4	3,714·1	11,437·5
1907	3,160·8	1,303·5	702·6	2,619·3	3,662·7	11,449·0
1908	3,198·0	1,323·1	733·4	2,647·9	3,671·6	11,573·9
1909	3,246·1	1,344·3	777·4	2,704·0	3,742·7	11,814·5
1910	3,299·8	1,368·2	836·9	2,753·0	3,806·5	12,064·4
1911	3,352·8	1,390·8	906·7	2,785·1	3,846·0	12,281·4
1912	3,414·4	1,417·1	979·9	2,816·8	3,898·8	12,527·0

Table 48. *Capital Stock in Industry* (*1913 prices, million roubles*)

	Structures	Equipment	Inventories	Total
1890	565·2	598·0	545·3	1,708·6
1891	563·0	648·0	618·2	1,829·2
1892	582·4	676·2	638·6	1,897·1
1893	608·7	653·1	695·3	1,957·1
1894	617·2	772·2	858·8	2,248·2
1895	655·4	868·6	945·0	2,468·9
1896	680·3	886·4	982·8	2,549·5
1897	743·5	979·0	1,081·0	2,803·5
1898	772·1	1,025·9	1,160·3	2,958·3
1899	(830·0)	(1,057·9)	(1,174·1)	(3,062·0)
1900	898·4	1,090·5	1,188·5	3,177·4
1901	928·2	1,258·7	1,404·6	3,591·5
1902	902·6	1,417·2	1,473·3	3,793·1
1903	896·9	1,265·0	1,535·7	3,697·6
1904	925·8	1,209·9	1,520·8	3,656·5
1905	998·7	1,313·5	1,607·7	3,919·9
1906	950·1	1,166·2	1,473·4	3,589·7
1907	961·8	1,138·8	1,576·9	3,677·5
1908	997·9	1,283·4	1,737·7	4,019·0
1909	1,026·4	1,384·6	1,863·6	4,274·5
1910	1,071·0	1,348·0	1,992·1	4,411·1
1911	1,182·0	1,504·1	2,073·0	4,759·1
1912	1,274·0	1,675·4	2,153·6	5,103·0
1913	1,353·7	1,785·4	2,274·0	5,413·1

Table 49. *Capital Stock in Industry: Three-Year Moving Averages*
(1913 prices, million roubles)

	Structures	Equipment	Inventories	Total
1891	570·2	640·7	600·7	1,811·6
1892	584·7	659·1	650·7	1,894·5
1893	602·8	700·5	730·9	2,034·2
1894	627·1	764·6	733·0	2,124·8
1895	651·0	843·1	828·9	2,322·9
1896	693·1	912·0	902·9	2,508·0
1897	732·0	964·4	1,074·7	2,771·1
1898	781·9	1,021·0	1,138·4	2,941·3
1899	833·5	1,058·1	1,174·3	3,065·9
1900	885·5	1,135·7	1,255·7	3,277·0
1901	909·7	1,255·5	1,355·5	3,520·7
1902	909·2	1,313·6	1,471·2	3,694·0
1903	908·4	1,297·4	1,509·9	3,715·7
1904	940·5	1,262·8	1,554·7	3,758·0
1905	958·2	1,229·9	1,534·7	3,722·0
1906	970·2	1,208·9	1,552·7	3,729·0
1907	969·9	1,196·1	1,596·0	3,762·0
1908	995·4	1,268·9	1,726·1	3,990·4
1909	1,031·8	1,338·7	1,864·5	4,234·9
1910	1,093·1	1,412·2	1,976·2	4,481·6
1911	1,175·7	1,509·2	2,072·9	4,757·7
1912	1,269·9	1,655·0	2,166·9	5,091·7

Table 50. *Money Stocks in Russia,*

State Bank

Year (1 Jan.)	Currency in circulation				Private deposits and current accounts		
	Banknotes	Gold	Silver	Total	Deposits	Current accounts	Total
1890	928·4	—	—	—	161·1	63·5	224·6
1891	907·4	—	—	—	158·4	75·5	233·9
1892	1,054·8	—	—	—	148·4	83·4	231·8
1893	1,074·1	—	—	—	159·8	66·7	226·5
1894	1,071·9	—	—	—	135·3	72·0	207·3
1895	1,047·1	—	—	—	128·7	69·0	197·7
1896	1,055·3	—	—	—	117·6	68·2	185·8
1897	1,067·9	30·0	129·9	1,133·8	109·6	89·7	192·3
1898	901·0	147·8	78·9	1,127·7	91·8	114·0	205·8
1899	661·8	451·4	121·5	1,234·7	86·6	117·6	204·2
1900	491·2	641·3	145·3	1,277·8	83·3	112·3	195·6
1901	555·0	683·1	145·7	1,383·8	72·6	95·0	167·6
1902	542·4	694·2	140·3	1,376·9	68·3	115·6	183·9
1903	553·5	731·9	137·5	1,422·9	58·9	198·6	257·5
1904	578·4	774·3	133·2	1,485·4	52·7	178·3	231·0
1905	853·7	683·6	123·0	1,660·3	53·0	202·1	255·1
1906	1,207·5	837·8	133·4	2,178·7	59·5	204·3	263·8
1907	1,194·6	641·9	119·8	1,956·3	66·2	183·0	249·2
1908	1,154·7	622·4	119·6	1,896·7	64·1	167·0	231·1
1909	1,087·1	561·1	110·5	1,758·7	57·5	252·2	309·7
1910	1,173·8	580·9	112·5	1,867·2	55·9	217·8	273·7
1911	1,234·5	641·7	115·9	1,992·1	48·9	212·4	261·3
1912	1,326·5	655·8	117·6	2,099·9	38·6	219·7	258·3
1913	1,494·8	628·7	120·6	2,244·0	33·9	232·1	266·0
1914	1,664·7	494·2	122·7	2,281·6	28·5	234·6	263·1

Year (1 Jan.)	Exchange banks			Other	Total private banks			Total private banks and state bank		
	Deposits	Current accounts	Total		Deposits	Current accounts	Total	Deposits	Current accounts	Total
1890	—	—	—	—	—	—	—	—	—	—
1891	—	—	—	—	—	—	—	—	—	—
1892	—	—	—	—	—	—	—	—	—	—
1893	12·5	3·1	15·6	—	263·8	242·2	506·0	423·6	308·9	732·5
1894	11·1	2·5	13·6	—	249·7	222·3	472·0	385·0	294·3	679·3
1895	11·0	1·7	12·7	—	264·0	253·2	517·2	392·7	322·2	714·9
1896	13·6	2·2	15·8	--	292·4	231·1	523·5	410·0	299·3	709·3
1897	13·6	2·2	15·8	—	317·3	265·3	582·6	426·9	335·0	781·9
1898	19·1	3·8	19·9	—	345·8	354·7	704·5	437·6	468·7	910·3
1899	17·9	3·8	21·7	—	430·6	403·2	842·6	517·2	520·8	1,046·8
1900	17·7	3·6	21·3	—	447·2	387·1	849·7	530·5	499·4	1,045·3
1901	19·1	3·3	22·4	—	441·3	392·4	850·4	513·9	487·4	1,018·0
1902	20·5	4·7	25·2	3·9	439·2	405·7	872·1	507·5	524·3	1,056·0
1903	19·5	6·1	25·6	8·8	458·6	482·4	972·9	517·5	681·0	1,230·4
1904	19·6	5·9	25·5	15·4	486·0	581·8	1,105·1	538·7	760·1	1,336·1
1905	19·5	6·6	26·4	16·7	472·1	653·2	1,160·0	525·1	855·3	1,415·1
1906	18·0	6·2	24·2	24·2	414·5	579·5	1,048·7	474·0	783·8	1,312·5
1907	19·8	7·9	27·7	31·9	414·7	685·5	1,170·5	480·9	868·5	1,419·7
1908	18·0	8·0	26·0	37·3	453·5	731·0	1,235·8	517·6	898·0	1,466·9
1909	20·9	9·5	30·4	34·7	524·2	868·9	1,445·6	581·7	1,121·1	1,755·3
1910	22·8	9·4	32·2	54·7	592·7	1,159·5	1,851·5	648·6	1,377·3	2,125·2
1911	23·1	11·2	34·3	70·3	724·0	1,537·1	2,261·1	772·9	1,749·5	2,522·4
1912	24·2	11·5	35·7	51·3	884·0	1,622·3	2,506·3	922·6	1,842·0	2,764·6
1913	24·5	11·1	35·6	52·5	1,051·9	2,006·6	3,058·4	1,083·8	2,238·6	3,324·4
1914	22·7	9·2	31·9	99·3	1,173·7	2,190·8	3,364·5	1,202·2	2,425·4	3,627·6

Joint-stock commercial banks					Municipal banks			Mutal credit associations		
Deposits			Current			Current			Current	
Demand	Time	Total	accounts	Total	Deposits	accounts	Total	Deposits	accounts	Total
11·0	88 6	99·6	130·5	230·1	—	—	—	—	—	—
18·8	101·1	114·9	172·8	287·7	—	—	—	—	—	—
16·9	112·8	127·7	191·8	319·5	—	—	—	—	—	—
18·0	97·8	110·8	174·6	285·4	81·9	8·9	89·9	59·5	55·6	115·1
11·4	91·4	102·8	165·0	267·8	78·0	8·7	86·7	57·8	46·1	103·9
11·0	104·3	115·3	192·4	307·7	78·0	9·2	87·2	59·7	49·9	109·6
12·1	121·5	133·6	171·6	305·2	78·8	8·4	87·2	66·4	48·9	115·3
12·9	137·5	140·4	203·6	354·0	78·8	8·4	87·2	74·5	51·1	125·6
13·1	155·3	168·4	279·7	448·1	78·8	10·0	88·8	82·5	61·2	143·7
16·2	215·0	231·2	320·1	551·3	83·0	11·5	94·5	98·5	67·8	166·3
13·0	227·6	245·6	302·3	547·9	84·0	13·0	97·0	99·9	68·2	168·1
17·0	218·2	235·2	300·9	536·1	84·1	13·2	97·3	102·9	75·0	177·9
15·4	214·5	229·9	315·0	544·9	84·0	14·0	98·0	104·8	75·0	179·8
17·1	218·9	236·0	377·3	613·3	87·9	16·0	103·9	115·2	83·0	198·2
18·2	246·4	264·6	457·5	722·1	88·2	18·4	106·6	113·6	100·0	213·6
17·6	236·8	254·4	521·2	775·6	87·3	21·4	108·7	110·6	104·0	214·6
14·1	200·1	214·2	457·2	671·4	84·3	24·1	108·4	98·0	92·0	190·0
70·4	196·6	217·0	543·9	760·9	83·1	25·7	108·8	94·8	108·0	202·8
21·8	218·0	239·8	578·3	818·1	82·6	26·8	111·4	111·1	117·8	228·9
28·0	262·1	290·1	686·7	976·8	89·7	30·1	115·8	127·5	142·6	270·1
24·8	309·2	334·0	928·2	1,262·2	88·3	40·0	128·3	147·6	181·9	329·5
40·1	382·8	422·9	1,252·1	1,675·1	97·2	48·9	146·1	180·8	224·9	405·7
50·3	478·6	528·9	1,288·4	1,817·3	110·2	55·8	166·0	220·7	266·6	487·3
64·4	603·3	657·7	1,635·6	2,293·3	121·7	61·8	183·5	247·0	298·0	545·0
69·6	683·3	752·9	1,786·1	2,539·0	130·1	68·2	198·3	268·0	327·3	395·3

Money stock (1)			Money Stock (2)		State Bank			
	Total deposits and current		State Bank deposits and			Treasury special	Treasury	
Currency in circulation	accounts of private banks	Total	current accounts	Total	Saving institution deposits	funds and deposits	current accounts	Treasury total
928·4	—	—	224·6	—	2·7	92·1	69·9	162·0
907·4	—	—	233·9	—	3·7	135·9	63·7	199·6
1,054·8	—	—	231·8	—	17·9	175·3	28·8	204·1
1,074·1	506·0	1,580·1	226·5	1,806·6	52·4	108·6	39·1	167·7
1,071·9	472·0	1,543·9	207·3	1,751·2	74·3	110·7	61·3	172·0
1,047·7	517·2	1,564·9	197·7	1,762·6	50·7	154·6	176·6	331·2
1,055·3	523·5	1,578·8	185·8	1,746·6	46·7	171·9	131·7	323·6
1,133·8	387·6	1,716·4	199·3	1,915·7	27·9	89·6	242·8	332·4
1,227·7	704·5	1,832·3	205·8	2,038·0	73·0	130·4	288·7	419·1
1,234·7	842·6	2,077·3	204·2	2,281·5	8·3	141·4	330·2	471·3
1,277·8	849·7	2,126·5	195·6	2,322·1	23·0	144·6	449·5	594·0
1,383·8	850·4	2,234·2	167·6	2,401·8	23·9	146·2	333·6	479·8
1,376·9	872·1	2,248·1	183·9	2,431·9	54·4	156·9	342·4	439·3
1,422·9	972·9	2,395·8	257·5	2,653·3	114·5	167·1	186·9	354·0
1,485·4	1,305·1	2,590·5	231·0	2,821·5	69·7	179·2	374·5	353·6
1,660·3	1,160·0	2,820·3	255·1	3,075·4	43·7	177·0	174·2	351·2
2,178·7	1,048·2	3,227·4	263·8	3,491·2	—	169·9	99·9	259·7
1,956·3	1,170·5	3,126·8	249·2	3,375·0	36·6	202·8	98·3	301·2
1,896·7	3,235·8	3,132·5	231·1	3,353·6	51·3	206·0	151·4	357·4
1,758·7	1,445·6	3,204·3	309·7	3,514·0	52·0	211·5	211·8	432·4
1,867·2	1,851·5	3,718·7	273·7	3,992·4	37·7	252·8	174·2	427·2
1,992·1	2,261·1	4,253·2	261·3	4,514·5	24·0	275·3	375·9	652·2
2,099·9	2,306·3	4,606·2	258·3	4,864·5	18·3	303·1	553·9	857·0
2,244·0	3,058·4	5,302·4	266·0	5,568·4	15·1	344·6	528·4	572·9
2,281·6	3,364·5	3,646·1	263·1	5,909·2	13·9	343·3	607·9	951·8

Table 51. *Domestic Holdings of Government-Guaranteed Securities*
(nominal value, million roubles)

Date (1 Jan.)	State bonds	Railway bonds	Nobility and Peasant Banks	Total
1893	1,735·2	346·6	190·9	2,272·7
1894	1,774·2	380·3	197·7	2,352·1
1895	1,877·9	419·4	215·3	2,512·6
1896	1,922·4	437·2	249·9	2,609·5
1897	2,046·4	407·3	314·8	2,768·5
1898	2,066·1	439·9	346·2	2,852·2
1899	2,121·1	457·0	359·6	2,937·7
1900	2,146·5	468·6	403·0	3,018·1
1901	2,223·7	555·6	433·2	3,212·0
1902	2,254·0	596·8	531·2	3,382·0
1903	2,259·2	554·2	620·9	3,434·3
1904	2,319·0	612·4	721·8	3,653·2
1905	2,457·4	668·9	786·0	3,912·3
1906	2,963·7	653·5	844·6	4,461·8
1907	3,100·5	301·8	936·6	4,738·9
1908	3,224·8	710·1	971·3	4,906·2
1909	3,347·4	726·0	1,078·0	5,151·4
1910	3,483·2	722·2	1,148·8	5,354·2
1911	3,516·0	755·5	1,233·3	5,504·8
1912	3,622·2	759·8	1,400·5	5,782·5
1913	3,583·5	767·0	1,676·3	6,026·8
1914	3,442·2	787·3	2,008·1	6,237·6

Table 52. *Enrolment in Elementary Schools of the Ministry of Education and Parochial Schools of the Greek Orthodox Synod, 1890–1914*

	Number of schools	Number of pupils (thousands)
1890	46,092	2,282·6
1891	49,333	2,454·5
1892	52,992	2,654·7
1893	55,384	2,776·1
1894	58,933	2,854·3
1895	61,745	2,959·5
1896	64,268	3,202·1
1897	71,876	3,656·7
1898	76,869	3,910·2
1899	79,872	4,091·6
1900	79,433	4,227·1
1901	81,180	4,414·7
1902	83,261	4,632·9
1903	85,202	4,949·4
1904	87,269	5,125·7
1905	86,437	5,340·7
1906	87,309	5,618·0
1907	88,033	5,722·4
1908	90,025	5,831·9
1909	93,169	6,130·5
1910	97,226	6,490·8
1911	102,050	6,837·2
1912	106,984	7,124·4
1913	114,006	7,569·9
1914	118,329	8,022·0

CHAPTER VII
Labour and Industrialization in Russia

I. *Introduction*

By 'industrialization', for the purpose of this study, is understood a process of change in time at the centre of which is a switch from manufacture of commodities by hand to that using machinery and mechanical motive power. It marks the rise of 'modern industry', absorbing increasing proportions of fixed capital relative to circulating capital. Its corollary is the factory system, entailing the problems of recruiting, training, and managing a spatially concentrated labour force and of apportioning resources between various factors of production in accordance with the nature of the individual enterprise and its ultimate aim of maximizing profit.

In the long run, and at a pace and in patterns differing with individual economies, industrialization releases processes of change in the nature of society, in the composition of the labour force, in the structure of the GNP, and in incomes per head.

In Russia 'modern industry' of any significance dates from the 1830s, when it was confined by and large to the cotton-spinning and beet-sugar industries. By 1861, a date conventionally regarded as the watershed separating modern from traditional Russia, about 85 per cent of sugar and about 90 per cent of cotton yarn was produced in factories by mechanical means.[1] In these two industries there was undoubtedly continuity across the watershed of the Emancipation of serfs in 1861. Other industries, however, were only marginally affected by the new methods of manufacture: cotton-weaving remained at the handicraft stage, and mining, metallurgy, and metal-processing in particular remained backward and traditional. It was only during the 1880s and 1890s that mechanical methods of manufacture became significantly diffused and that a modern mining and metallurgical region sprang up in South Russia. However, even by 1913, although Russia was by then the fourth largest industrial nation in Europe and although she had a substantial industrial sector in absolute terms, in which the majority of 'modern' manufacturing branches were represented and which included an embryonic indigenous aviation industry, the structure of society, of the labour force, and of the GNP remained characteristic of a pre-industrial, or at best a semi-industrial, economy. Though average annual growth rates in the value of industrial output were high in terms of nineteenth- and early-twentieth-century European experience and during the late 1890s and between 1910 and 1914 were comparable with the highest, industrial growth was not fast enough to make up for the backlog of backwardness and to do more than nibble at the giant agricultural sector.

The latter grew at a much slower pace than industry. Although the average annual growth rate of just under 2 per cent during 1860–1914[2] was quite respectable even in comparison with countries whose performance in the agrarian sector is commonly rated highly – e.g. Japan – the sheer bulk of the agrarian sector and its weight in the GNP tended to erode the dynamic effect of high industrial growth rates upon aggregate growth, while the rise in population kept incomes per head among the lowest in Europe.

Russia's industrial performance, high rates notwithstanding, remained uneven and distinctly patchy, the latter in a literal sense when looked at geographically. Areas such as the Baku oil-producing region, Piotrkow in the Kingdom of Poland, and Moscow and St Petersburg provinces had industrial output values per head of population and proportions of factory workers relative to the population which were comparable with the averages in some advanced countries of the time. These areas, however, were lost in a vast expanse of a traditional or semi-traditional economy.

In 1908 the average value of factory output per head of population was not more than 30 roubles, or just over £3 sterling, and the weight of factory workers in the total population not more than 1·43 per cent.[3] However, while in the Baku province the value of industrial output was 239 roubles per head, in Moscow 212, in Piotrkow 172, and in St Petersburg 164, it was under 10 roubles in Voronezh and under 5 roubles in a very large number of regions. The proportion of factory workers in the population was as high as 11 per cent in Moscow province, but only in three regions – the Baltic region including St Petersburg, the central industrial region including Moscow and Vladimir, and the Vistula region of the Kingdom of Poland – were the value of industrial output per head of population and the share of factory work in the population above the average for the country at large. In terms of active population – i.e. those aged 15 to 60, who according to the population census of 1897 made up 48·5 per cent of the total – factory workers accounted in 1900 for some 3 per cent of the active population and in 1913 for not more than 5 per cent of the total.[4] In Moscow province, however, 22 per cent of the active population, or more than one in five, were factory workers. On the other hand, male factory workers in Moscow province made up about 40 per cent of the active male population.[5] Unevenness and patchiness are of course features of all developing countries, but in Russia the underdevelopment of backward regions was of such depth, the dimensions of the territory so vast, that the few advanced regions made only a slight impact upon aggregates.

II. *Industrial Labour in the 'Proto-Industrial' Age*[6]

A. THE SEVENTEENTH CENTURY AND BEFORE

Though industrialization in the sense of a massive development of modern industry was in Russia essentially a development of the last three and a half decades before 1914, any study of the formation of an industrial labour force, which requires recruitment, training in skills, and discipline may reasonably go beyond the stage at which factory production based on machinery became a mass phenomenon. It may go back to the *pre-modern*, the so-called *proto-industrial*, phase of economic development, to the manufacturing establishments of the seventeenth, eighteenth, and early nineteenth centuries. Large industrial establishments, commonly referred to as 'manufactories', reported to have existed in the seventeenth century numbered at least twenty-one, and according to a recent study by an American scholar even as many as fifty-seven. Another 118 (or 233) made their appearance under Peter the Great, and some 1,200 are estimated to have existed by 1804.[7]

The majority of the large manufactories of the seventeenth century were situated in areas where population was relatively dense, and recruitment by hire from among urban or semi-urban elements was the predominant feature of labour supply. However, this was not hired labour in the modern sense. There is evidence of hire of casual day labourers for building, carting, loading, and unloading at river ports and for river haulage. Some payment in cash was involved, but the main form of remuneration was subsistence and issues in kind – a cut of salt, a measure of grain, or a cut of meat. Where skilled workers were retained for any length of time, a garden plot and even arable would be allotted as part of the remuneration. Often, as in the production of salt, the ostensible wage was more in the nature of a share in output. In river haulage, subcontracting to an *artel'* (i.e. an association of haulers under an elder), rather than hire, was prevalent.[8]

Whenever the sources speak of hire of labour by contract, more often than not a debt bondage was involved, entered into either voluntarily or of necessity when an advance received could not be repaid. More often than not such bondage did not end with the life of the bondsman but extended to his family and offspring, though contracts stipulating termination of bondage with the life of the debtor or creditor were also known. In the countryside debt bondage was a common occurrence, resulting from the hazards and uncertainties of subsistence agriculture and from the increasing pressure of local and state taxes since the beginning of the sixteenth century.[9]

However, Russian manufactories required a large supplementary force for activities such as wood-cutting, charcoal-burning, loading, and hauling, as well as for provisioning the main labour force. This was specifically the case in metallurgy and metal-processing but was also important in the manufacture of gunpowder, potash, and glass. The Dutch founders of manufactories in seventeenth-century Russia, A. Vinius and F. Akema, and, following them, Russian entrepreneurs, had whole villages and even districts settled by Crown peasants 'ascribed' to them with the obligation to provide ancillary services in lieu of tax payments for which the employer had become responsible. This development, albeit on a small scale relative to subsequent applications of this method of securing labour, antedated the formal introduction of serfdom by the Code of Laws of 1649. The state often attained two aims: it secured a labour force for industries considered desirable for military or mercantilist reasons, and it made sure of a more certain and prompt tax yield, which was not the case when local authorities were responsible for tax collection.[10]

Skilled labour was provided by foreign craftsmen, by Russian craftsmen, such as the Tula weapon-makers, and state-registered blacksmiths and carpenters trained in building fortifications and in the Tsar's own workshops. Workmen who acquired skills in manufactories in one part of the country were transferred to new areas to impart them to others.[11] Some rural labour out of season was also employed, but as yet not on a large scale.

The formal introduction of serfdom in 1649 does not seem to have made any difference to the pattern described above. Industry's demand for labour was still limited, and the various floating elements seem to have sufficed as casual labour. Furthermore the location of industries in the north central areas, where landlordism was less well represented, made for the availability of 'ascribed' labour from Crown villages over which the state had direct authority.

B. FROM PETER THE GREAT TO THE EMANCIPATION

The vast programme of planting large-scale enterprises under Peter the Great dramatically changed the scale and pace at which an industrial labour force had to be recruited and trained. Moreover, the creation of the Ural metallurgical complex at an appreciable distance from existing population centres and transportation routes made it well-nigh impossible to attract by way of the market a labour force of the size required. Peter's military ventures and the building of the St Petersburg dock, of the Petersburg–Moscow Road, and of canals made vast demands on labour supply and exacted an enormous toll in men. The need for manpower could be met only partly by criminals, prostitutes, illegitimate children, orphans, and retired soldiers.[12]

Peter's fiscal policy, in particular the introduction of the Poll Tax in 1718, still further compounded the difficulty of labour recruitment. First, a fortuitous consequence of a poll tax levied per head, as distinct from a tax on arable, was that it encouraged the extension of the culti- vated area and consequently stimulated demand for more labour input in agriculture. Secondly, by tightening the taxation net to include floating elements, Peter cut off the very source from which labour requirements had hitherto been met, as there was no longer any tax advantage in remaining outside the agrarian commune. More import- antly, the rigour with which the tax was enforced made landowners and the government agencies in charge of Crown villages much more zealous than hitherto in their surveillance over the whereabouts of their 'souls' (the name given to males subject to tax). In 1727 landlords were made responsible for collecting Poll Tax, thus becoming tax-collectors and policemen on behalf of the state. As they were subject to joint responsibility for taxes and military recruits, the communes, whether rural or urban, on private estates or on Crown land, were anxious to retain the full complement of taxpayers specified in tax-census returns.[13]

In consequence, recourse to obligatory labour, first and foremost 'ascription' of Crown peasants to factories, became the most important single means of assuring labour for Peter's vast industrial projects. In construction, where seasonal labour was needed, mixed types of labour recruitment could be resorted to, but whenever all-year-round regular work was required, ascription of Crown peasants was again resorted to. In 1724 there were 1,049,287 male Crown peasants, and they repre- sented the basic reservoir of factory labour.[14] The other source of labour was 'possessional peasants', a special category created in 1721 by the right given to non-nobles to purchase villages with serfs for 'possessional factories'. This right, though sporadically suspended, was not finally revoked until 1816.

Even in individual cases of so-called 'freely hired labour', the employer's undertaking to pay the worker's Poll Tax played a consider- able part in securing labour. There is also evidence that such an arrangement led to abuse, in that it led to a worker's being entered on the Poll Tax register under his employer's name, which deprived him of freedom of departure. Altogether, in conditions of bureaucratic chaos, arbitrariness, and scant respect for the rights of the individual, many a 'free hire' turned into compulsory attachment to an enterprise.[15] This even happened to foreign specialists, whom the government was very careful not to antagonize. Of course chaos and disregard for law could and did work in the opposite direction too, allowing for employment of runaway serfs on the basis of free hire and for various other labour arrangements, especially in privately owned works in which monetary and similar incentives were used to entice labour, especially skilled labour.

With regard to runaway peasants the government pursued an ambivalent policy. While the authorities were loath to encourage flights which meant loss of taxpayers and recruits in central areas, they were eager to man the Urals works. They hit on a compromise whereby refugee serfs in the Urals could not be returned to their masters if they had in the meantime acquired industrial skill. This gave management all the latitude they wished for.

By the decree of 1736 the skilled labour force as distinct from ancillary workers was 'for ever attached' to the works (*vechno-otdannyye*), and as late as 1807 a proportion of the ascribed peasants from the Crown villages in the Urals, at the ratio of 58 per thousand, were turned into workers 'for ever attached' to the plant. A tendency in this direction had made itself felt from the start, the main reasons being a shortage of fully skilled workers ('masters'), their tendency to float, fierce competition between enterprises for skilled men, leading to friction and litigation, and the very high cost of such labour.[16]

Owners of works complained that it took about ten years to amortize the cost of training up a single worker and complained bitterly at the loss sustained when such a man left. State-owned enterprises were often at a disadvantage in that private owners were usually successful in enticing 'masters' trained in state-owned works or state mining schools by offering them higher wages. The director of the Mines Board (*Gornaya Kollegya*), Tatishchev, tried to standardize wage rates to prevent the loss of trained men to private owners, but the latter, while agreeing to respect the maxima and minima laid down for attached workers, insisted on their right to pay 'free' workers according to contract. Wages in privately owned works in the Urals were on average about 25 per cent higher than in state enterprises. It is not surprising, therefore, that the celebrated Demidov, one of a dynasty of Urals entrepreneurs, could boast that for every man he had lost through flight he had enticed four trained masters from state-owned works.[17]

Scarcity of labour relative to demand – especially of skilled labour – made it very expensive. The easiest remedy against the scarcity and high wages seemed to be to round up craftsmen and to pressgang them into work on terms stipulated by the authorities.

Even as late as the 1760s, when labour for hire was becoming increasingly available from among serfs and Crown peasants on furlough from their communes, the problem of securing all-year-round labour remained as acute as ever. Ivan Zatrapeznov, a manufacturer from the Yaroslav textile district, complained in 1764 that hired workers 'melted away into villages and river ports as soon as the ice broke on the rivers'.[18] A factory worker became in the summer a field hand or barge haulier. It is not surprising, therefore, that manufacturers were at pains to acquire populated villages as a reliable source of cheap labour.

By and large, throughout the eighteenth century various forms of compulsory labour predominated. In metallurgy, especially in the Urals and western Siberia, coercion was a *conditio sine qua non* of success. Inhabited villages were at a considerable distance from works. Moreover, as land was plentiful and fertile, their inhabitants 'living in abundance' would not hire themselves out 'voluntarily'. In 1722 the director of the Mines Board, Von Hennin, could recruit only seventeen men from various settlements at an appreciable distance from the works. The difficulty in this region was compounded by the very high manpower requirements: according to Tatishchev in 1734 over a thousand workers were needed to serve one furnace and six forge hammers, of whom 910 were required for the extraction and delivery of the iron ore to the works, for the cutting, burning, and delivery of fuel, for the extraction and delivery of limestone, and for similar jobs. In addition large numbers were needed for the provisioning of the work force. Growing foreign demand for Russian iron was also among the factors making for resort to compulsory labour, as the supply of labour lagged behind the expanding market for iron.[19]

Skilled labour was provided by the importation of foreigners and by sending Russians abroad, especially to Sweden, to acquire skills. This was very costly, often very difficult, and on occasion counterproductive. The importation of foreign workers was often impeded by the hostility of Sweden, which refused transit. The Saxon court also made difficulties for recruitment by Russians because 'these people would not be allowed to come back'. Special difficulties in procuring skilled labour were encountered by new branches of industry, such as copper, where dependence on foreign skills was very real. In 1720 twenty-nine foreign specialists were imported from abroad, but most of them were used in management or as interpreters.[20]

Many of the highly paid foreigners were completely ignorant of the skills they undertook to impart, or jealously guarded their secrets and failed to train the Russians as required in the contracts, a tendency reported to be particularly pronounced among foreign master-dyers. On the other hand, foreign masters were resented by the Russians, especially Russian manufacturers, who found the insistence of the authorities that they employ foreign specialists irksome and expensive.[21]

At first there was very strict regulation and control by the relevant government authorities over foreign specialists, and an attempt was made to use them as stipulated in contracts and in accordance with the needs of a particular branch of industry or to terminate the contracts when the aim was attained. Under the Empress Anna, during 1736–8, there was a large influx of foreigners, reportedly seeking out means of speedy enrichment and conferring no benefit upon the economy. Saxon artisans were being imported whose skills were said to be not in short supply. However, the evidence does not support this contention, and there is little doubt about the positive contribution of and need for foreign skills during this period, as indeed long afterwards. The Soviet historian Pavlenko maintains that by the 1730s in metallurgy there were enough people with technical skills and managerial ability among Russians and russified foreigners. A few years earlier, according to the same authority, in the Olonetz metallurgical industry during 1720–8 foreign specialists accounted only for 3·5 per cent of the total labour force. This, however, may have represented a much higher proportion of the labour force directly employed at the plant, because the total was inflated by the use of large numbers of workers for ancillary jobs.[22]

By the 1730s the mining schools and the apprenticeship system were making their contribution to the supply of skilled labour. By 1736 there were fourteen schools with 744 pupils. Although originally the aim was to attract children of gentry and officials, in fact recruitment was more democratic. Between a quarter and one-half were workers' children, who tended to become skilled masters and were forced to stay in the works 'for ever'. Sons of gentry went into management or administration.[23]

Trained workmen and master craftsmen transferred from other regions were another important source of skilled labour. In metallurgy, specialists from the central metallurgical region around Tula and Kashira were instrumental in setting up works in the Olonetz and Ural regions at the beginning of the eighteenth century. Olonetz in its turn performed the same role with respect to the Urals in the 1720s. From the 1730s onwards, the Urals were becoming the centre from which most advanced technology was being disseminated. Such transfers were possible and on the whole successful because of the high degree of administrative centralization in metallurgy.[24]

The most important source of skills, however, was learning on the job. In state-owned metallurgical works, bonuses were offered to workers who acquired the desired skills. Though privately owned works could often boast of a larger contingent of skilled labour, it would appear that both technical and managerial personnel, as well as skilled workers of these enterprises, were usually trained in the government-owned enterprises.

The combined supply from all these sources may have proved adequate for the needs of this industry. At least one historian argues that the question of the supply of specialists in metallurgy was successfully solved by the end of the first quarter of the eighteenth century.[25] In textiles, however, difficulties seem to have continued. Although the craft of linen and cloth manufacture was of long standing in Russia, under Peter a whole range of new fabrics was introduced. The complexity of operations meant that large numbers of hands had to be employed, and given the newness of many of the products and processes, it was not easy to entrust them to out-workers. Even a small textile mill in the first half of the eighteenth century had apparently a labour force of not less than a hundred hands. As technology was static throughout most of the eighteenth century, increase in output depended mainly on increase in numbers, and quality on the skill, versatility, powers of concentration, and precision of the individual worker.[26]

The Russian manufactories of the eighteenth century were not successful in solving the problem of labour quality. The difficulty lay in the underdevelopment of urban life. By the end of Catherine II's reign in 1796, the urban population accounted for 4·1 per cent, much of it from the newly conquered or annexed Baltic and Polish territories. Furthermore, excepting the Western provinces where craft guilds had some roots, urban craftsmanship had never reached the levels it had attained in Western Europe. Peter the Great ascribed the low standing of urban craftsmanship to the lack of craftsmen's guilds in Russia. Artisan guilds before Peter existed only in embryonic form and were confined to a few localities, since most of the towns which were founded during the Muscovite period, especially in the newly colonized areas, were more in the nature of military and administrative settlements. Peter's regulations of 1721, and associated enactments during 1720–3, provided for corporations of artisans by trades (*tsekhi*) based on the Western European pattern with masters entitled to run their own shops (*mastyera*), journeymen (*podmaster'ya*), and apprentices (*uchenniki*). Each *tsekh* was headed by an elected elder as well as an elected corporate assembly. The elders were incorporated into the municipal structure of the towns in an advisory capacity on matters relating to artisans.

Within each *tsekh* the elder supervised internal regulations and standards and the collection of taxes. This function of the guilds as administrative and fiscal agents of the government played from the earliest times a larger part than their specifically corporate functions. Moreover the Russian *tsekh* has never become a truly closed corporation; its membership was neither restricted numerically nor made obligatory to all local artisans. Finally, there were no limitations upon the goods produced in each *tsekh*. Thus the *tsekh* did not exercise a craft monopoly; at the same time its control over quality and over training and qualifications was ephemeral.

This was one of the reasons for poor-quality output for which the evidence is overwhelming. In 1740 a special commission was set up to investigate the reasons for the poor quality of the cloth for uniforms. In 1744 the Manufactures Board investigated complaints of foreign merchants that Russian sailcloth was below the required standard of strength and whiteness. The report of the inspectors disclosed that apprentices in one of the largest linen manufactories had not mastered the art of burning ashes for bleaching. It became necessary to dispatch Russian linen to Holland for bleaching. In 1765 Volkov, the Chairman of the Manufactures Board, reported to the Empress that not a single factory produced fine cloth. In linen, as late as 1799 the proportion of fine linen fabrics relative to the total production was infinitesimal (88,000 *arshins* only as against 8 million *arshins* of *ravenduck*, 4·5 million of coarse Flemish cloth, and over 1·6 million of sailcloth).[27]

However, the poor quality of Russian manufacturing output was due not only to the inadequacy of the Russian worker and the primitive techniques used but also to the nature of demand. The silk manufactories, though set up under Peter to produce expensive sorts, soon turned to production of cheap articles such as ribbons and kerchiefs, especially after the Tariff of 1731, which made foreign silk imports more competitive. In metallurgy, foreign demand for crude iron and the narrowness of internal demand were among the reasons why the manufacture of metal wares did not develop near the main centre of metallurgy.

In general it can be said that Russia was able to create in the eighteenth century a labour force of a type best suited to the output of crude, semi-finished goods for which there was large demand either from the state or from abroad, even though she had succeeded in doing so over a fairly short time. The fact that a vast proportion of the labour force was *drafted* into industry was less important in affecting its productivity than the generally low level of skills and the character of the market. Indeed without compulsion and without the concentrated effort by the state it is unlikely that anything approaching the scale of output actually achieved would have proved possible.

The effect of Peter's policies in general and of his economic measures in particular upon Russia's destinies have long been the centre of intellectual and ideological controversy. It has been argued that by *artificially* planting factory industry and by enforcing specific techniques,

Peter destroyed or distorted the economy's *organic* evolution. More specifically, from the point of view of this study, it was argued that Peter damaged Russia's indigenous industry, i.e. the so-called 'kustar' or seasonal rural industry, by his attempts to impose upon it specific regulations as to quality etc. and by the competition of the state-subsidized factories. However, although there have been cases of peasant industries declining in some areas, as in Archangel for instance, Peter's policies made a positive contribution to economic activity in the countryside.[28] The factories created under Peter and his successors became schools of skills and disseminators of techniques among rural artisans, some of whom had become founders of factories themselves, the so-called merchant or peasant manufactories (*kupecheskaya* or *krest'yanskaya manufaktura*). The economic developments under Peter also led to greater specialization of regions and a widening of markets. In consequence, once population growth became stabilized and then accelerated, as happened after 1740, the supply of labour for hire grew both among Crown peasants and among privately owned serfs. These were the so-called *otkhodniki* or off-farm workers, who were allowed to pay their rents out of their off-farm earnings (*promysly*).[29]

This development was concentrated in regions where the vegetation period in agriculture was very short, land was poor, population was relatively dense, and above all transport and access to markets were better than elsewhere. It is for these reasons that both factories and kustar industry developed in Moscow and the neighbouring provinces, which subsequently became the 'central industrial region'. It should be added that serf densities in this region were among the highest in the country, indicating that where other circumstances favoured industrial growth the institutional constraints were ineffective.[30]

In addition to peasants plying their trades, factories were being founded by estate-owners (*votchinnaya manufaktura*) as adjuncts to their estates, as supplementary sources of cash income, and as a means of using their own produce – as in distilling, in cloth and linen manufacture, and later in sugar-refining – and of using the estate's labour force. The fall in grain prices after the Napoleonic Wars, the high prices commanded by cloth for uniforms, and the destruction or the winding-up of the sumptuous town establishments in the course of Napoleon's invasion, which rendered idle large numbers of household serfs, stimulated the formation of estate factories after 1815. In many cases estate factories became the main source of income of gentry landowners, a feature most pronounced in the Ukraine in sugar-refining after 1840.

At first only household serfs or serfs working off their rents were employed; subsequently, however, workers of estate factories were in the majority of cases paid wages, out of which they met their rents and tax payments. There was a great variety in the patterns of employment. Where a landlord, in setting up a factory, used only household serfs or uprooted existing farming serfs from their farms and transferred them to a factory for all-year-round work, he thereby created a genuine proletarian divorced from other sources of income and trained from infancy in a particular craft in the factory where his parents were also employed.

V. A. Pogozhev, the author of a monumental statistical study of the Russian factory labour force as it existed in 1903, maintained that the pre-Emancipation estate factory had produced a true, hereditary factory worker, whose descendants continued to work in post-1861 factories. Descendants of these former factory household serfs pop up in various studies of the work forces of individual plants during the 1890s and surface again as late as 1910 in regions where estate factories were wound up after the Emancipation. During the pre-1914 boom, when conditions again favoured small rural factories, employers were able to tap the labour potential of the sometime estate factories.[31]

Privately owned serfs or Crown peasants on furlough were – from the employers' viewpoint – freely hired wage labour, though there were many instances of peasants being handed over to factories by their landlords or by the communes to work off arrears in rents or taxes or debts in general. In such cases the element of free hire was absent, the workers being no better than bonded labour. The practice persisted though forbidden by law in 1825, the worker's family being prevailed upon to act on behalf of the landlord or the commune.[32]

Labour which was in the main 'bonded' also characterized enterprises established and managed by serfs. The successful rise of serf-entrepreneurs, founders of industrial dynasties which survived till 1917, had started in the late eighteenth century and was a distinctive feature of industrial development in the first half of the nineteenth century, excelling in success all other forms of factory enterprise. Although they were serfs themselves, these entrepreneurs often owned whole villages of serfs in the name of their landlords. To a greater extent than in other forms of industrial enterprise, they tended to rely on bonded labour (*kabal'nyye*) – other serfs handed over by the landlords or, after 1825, by communes to work off arrears in rents or taxes. Indeed, access to such labour in the formative stages of their businesses might have been one of the causes of the serf-entrepreneur's success.

Given collective responsibility for rents and taxes, the serf-entrepreneur was often called upon to advance payments of rents and taxes for the less fortunate or more improvident members of his commune. This gave him the right to lay claim to the time and labour of such debtors. The prestige he enjoyed with communal authorities in the village as its

richest member and its source of income and credit, his personal knowledge of the circumstances and personalities of his bonded labourers, and
his own and his family's direct participation in the business (often side
by side with his workers) enabled him to wring from his bonded
labourers a productivity denied to other employers.

However, though the serf–entrepreneur might have had preferential
access to labour, it would appear that the greatest advances in rates of
output and in technological progress were in industries turning out goods
for which there was rising demand irrespective of what type of labour
they used. Even as early as 1790–3 a glance at Russian imports would
show that the very two industries which became technologically most
modern offered the greatest scope for import substitution. Sugar and
cotton fabrics together accounted for 22 per cent of the value of Russian
imports. But whereas in cotton mills the workers were mainly 'hired',
in the sugar mills they were estate serfs working in lieu of labour
services – an arrangement not dissimilar to that obtaining in metallurgy,
the stagnation of which has been commonly ascribed to the servile
nature of its labour force.[33]

Hired labour began to be increasingly important from the last third of
the eighteenth century, especially in manufacturing. Though compulsory labour continued to grow in absolute numbers, there was a widening of the labour market which reduced the need to resort to such
labour, especially in enterprises located near cities. That such a widening
of the labour market actually occurred is evident from the fact that
when, in 1816, Alexander I finally revoked the law originally introduced by Peter which granted the right to buy populated villages for
factories, it transpired that in nineteen years this right had been resorted
to in only six individual instances. Moreover, owners of possessional
factories had begun to find ownership of an attached labour force a
doubtful privilege. They were unable to adjust the size and composition
of their labour force to the needs of business and to demand, and they
were obliged to maintain the old and the sick among their workers and
provide them with food at subsidized prices. Furthermore, because freely
hired workers – whose money wages tended to be higher – worked side
by side with the possessional workers, the latter felt aggrieved and were
in constant state of discontent. Possessional workers had become a
liability which their owners in the majority of cases were ready to shed.
By a law of June 1840 the release of the bulk of possessional workers
was permitted.

Of the 14,441 possessional workers released by the decree of 1840
who were investigated by Tugan-Baranovsky, as many as 43 per cent
had opted to become Crown peasants, which may indicate that they
had not fully severed their ties with agriculture or that they had hoped

to work as kustars in Crown villages. Of the 8,000 who had opted to become burghers (*meshchane*), most must have lost the habit of agricultural work. Tugan-Baranovsky also showed that large groups of former possessional workers had become entirely dependent on wage payments and long after their release were found not to possess any land, not even houses of their own.[34]

On the eve of the abolition of serfdom, there still existed fifty-two possessional factories in manufacturing, with over 27,000 males employed mainly in paper, sailcloth and crystal glass. In mining and metallurgy, where some of the works had possessional status, various forms of compulsory labour still accounted for 70 per cent of the labour force employed, and there is no evidence of any pressure from employers for change. Undoubtedly conditions were different in those industries located mainly on the geographical periphery of the country. In manufacturing, compulsory labour accounted for only 18 per cent of the total.[35]

By 1860 the factory labour force in mining, metallurgy, and manufacturing, as recalculated from official data by M. Zlotnikov, stood at just under 860,000, of whom 565,000 were in manufacturing alone. They were employed in 2,818 establishments (not in the 14,388 units given in statistics), according to Zlotnikov, who used Lenin's criterion of a factory establishment as a unit employing a minimum of sixteen. In 1804 the total labour force was about 225,000, in 1825 over 340,000. On the first date 75 per cent of the labour force was servile, in 1825 two-thirds were in this category, while by 1860 two-thirds were freely hired.[36]

How relevant was the proto-industrialization period for subsequent development? Serious authorities such as Tugan-Baranovsky, Dementyev, Schultze-Gaevernitz, and Pogozhev were in no doubt that the eighteenth- and early-nineteenth-century factories paved the way for the modern factory. Of the factories which existed in 1903, nearly one-seventh were founded before 1861, and they accounted for the highest proportion of the largest firms by 1903. Tugan-Baranovsky saw in these factories 'technical schools of the modern industrial worker'.[37] The role played in the labour force after 1861 by the former estate factories and by some possessional factories has already been alluded to. Among the ironmasters of the Urals, cadres of hereditary workers had been formed for generations, as is evident from the registers of personnel in the archives of individual works.[38]

The indirect way in which the pre-modern factory prepared the labour force for the post-Emancipation factory was probably more significant. In his brilliant study Tugan-Baranovsky has described the manner in which the eighteenth- and early-nineteenth-century factory contributed to the dissemination of skills among kustars, skills which had little to do with ancient rural crafts but owed their very existence to the factories. 'The kustar industry,' Tugan-Baranovsky maintained, 'was the legitimate offspring of the factory and the large workshop.'[39] In its turn the kustar cottage or workshop was the environment which bred both entrepreneurs and workers for the mechanized factory or provided a link with it through the putting-out system.

Much criticism has been levelled at Tugan-Baranovsky for his account of the victory of the kustar over the factory in the second quarter of the nineteenth century. But allowing for exaggeration, there is no doubt that he rightly diagnosed the formidable competitive powers of rural industry, which operated with very low fixed costs and small overheads and with ability to withstand heavy downward pressures on wages. With these competitive advantages the kustars could undercut factory industry, which had grown up over-protected, and the quality of whose production was not significantly different from that turned out by kustars. It is a fact that most of the growth in manufacturing output in the first half of the nineteenth century was to be accounted for by growth of small kustar and kustar-type industry. By 1850 the value of large-scale manufacture was only half that of cottage industry.[40]

On the other hand some of the legacies of the pre-modern factories were entirely negative. The adaptation of existing plant and organization to new conditions of technology and methods of production often proved more difficult than starting anew. Above all, workers and employers alike had grown up in an environment in which factory production was looked upon as a form of service to the state, and the maintenance of the labour force as a duty which the employer undertook at the behest of the state.

It was this mentality which kept the workers of the Urals ensconced in their houses amidst the forests expecting employment from metallurgical works as of right. The same sentiments were voiced by workers in textile mills, as reported by a factory inspector in 1911.[41] The workers believed that the government forced men with money to open factories and to provide barracks for the workers. They believed that the employer had no right to close the factory and that if the workers fared badly the government would take over the factory. Such a mentality was bred by the actual practice of the possessional factories, which was still within the living memory of the generation of the 1890s take-off. In the Urals the possessional rights of the state, however modified, were still maintained in some plants right up to 1914.

Looked at from the Marxist point of view, the men employed in Russian factories of the proto-industrialization period were factory workers but not proletarians. The process of 'expropriation' of the primary producer, which forms an essential feature of Marxist theory, can be said to have affected only a few categories of workers. Moreover, those affected remained potential agriculturalists and small owners, since the process of expropriation was not an irreversible one. The labourer, though often 'obliged to offer for sale as a commodity that very labour power which exists only in his living self', was also in a position to sell commodities in which 'his labour . . . [was] incorporated' either as an agriculturalist or as a kustar.

Neither did the pre-Emancipation factory worker satisfy the Marxian definition that he be 'the untrammelled owner of his capacity for labour, i.e. of his person'.[42] From the legal point of view the bulk of the labour force in Russian factories before 1861 were not 'untrammelled owners' of their persons, though by a law of 24 May 1835 they could no longer be arbitrarily recalled by their owners before their contracts expired.[43]

In both these aspects there was continuity between developments before 1861 and those subsequently. The factory worker in many cases continued to be a small owner who had at his disposal alternative means of earning or supplementing his living. Like his serf predecessor he was subject to certain institutional constraints, which, however, gave way under pressure of economic circumstance, as they did under serfdom.

C. THE GROWTH OF LABOUR SUPPLY AFTER EMANCIPATION

Much has been said about the defects of the Emancipation Act from the point of view of industrialization. In particular, its provisions for communal ownership and for collective fiscal responsibility with regard to redemption payments and direct taxation have been considered as a major constraint upon peasant mobility and *ipso facto* upon the supply of labour to industry. There is no denying that taken in isolation these provisions detracted from the peasant's newly won freedom. But life has a way of bypassing laws where conditions are favourable. We have seen that even serfdom did not succeed in inhibiting labour supply to factory industry, as is clear from a more than fivefold rise in the factory labour force between 1804 and 1860. What then were the facts about labour supply after the Emancipation Act?

Its provisions for the communal ownership of land did not prevent pockets of landless peasants from appearing. They may have represented a tiny fraction of the landowning peasant mass but were nevertheless large enough in absolute numbers to be of significance in industrial employment. The Act made no provision for household serfs, retired soldiers, serfs without arable who before 1861 lived on a monthly subsistence (*messyatsniki*), serfs from certain estate factories, serfs of petty nobles, and others. It has been estimated that 2·6 million male peasants were landless on the morrow of the Emancipation, a number more than sufficient to continue to meet the needs of manufacturing as late as 1897.[44]

Furthermore, contrary to common assumptions that under periodic land re-allocation the communal ownership of land made sure that changes in family composition, population growth, and splitting of households were automatically taken care of, many communes practised no land redistribution at all. By 1910, about three million households – about one-quarter of the total – were occupying holdings which had not been repartitioned since 1861.[45]

In a great many communes where land partition was practised, the actual number of households was not taken into account in reallocating land. Land tended to be apportioned in accordance with the distribution pattern of the last pre-Emancipation census of 1858. Consequently, there was no automatic adjustment to take account of the multiplication of households in the commune, due to the growing self-assertion of younger members no longer willing to accept subservience to heads of households upon marriage.[46]

Splitting of households often created two weak farms in the place of one viable one and was among the factors which made resort to wage labour essential. If splitting occurred against the wishes of the head of the household, it often compelled the head of the new household to employment outside the village. Where increased family membership was accommodated without splitting households, the result was an imbalance between the available arable, the supply of labour, and the subsistence needs of the family.

On the whole, peasants' attitudes to the land allotted to them differed from region to region and depended on the quality of the land, on the relative costs of redemption payments, increasingly on the purchase price for land, on the cost of renting land, and on the availability and security of earning opportunities outside agriculture. In general it can be said that where the quality of the land was good, much value was attached to it, and a peasant desirous of pursuing a full-time occupation outside had no difficulty in finding a tenant who would take over his redemption payments and tax commitments and would usually pay a rent into the bargain. Where land was of poor quality and redemption payments high, it was more difficult to find tenants to take over financial commitments, especially as in such regions holdings tended to be larger and more land was usually available for renting from estates or the Crown. A peasant entering full-time occupation could, however, abandon his holding; the latter would then be disposed of by the commune, and financial liabilities connected with it would be apportioned among commune members. But as will be shown repeatedly elsewhere, peasants, however long involved in occupations outside the village, preferred to retain their land in the commune. Many kept up the family farms which continued to be cultivated by the members of their families remaining in the village.[47]

Thus, communal ownership and collective responsibility *per se* need not have inhibited the supply of labour to industry. What then were the other factors? Among those factors which encouraged labour supply were population growth, the splitting of households, financial commitments stemming from the Emancipation, and inadequate holdings in general. Among the factors which inhibited labour supply were the expansion of peasant agriculture by taking up slack in old areas, by colonizing new ones, by purchasing land, or by selling produce rather than labour; employment on large estates, and local employment as self-employed or own-account kustars, further reduced the availability of wage labour. In addition there were certain long-term factors which affected not so much the supply of labour as its character. The seasonal character of Russian agriculture was one such factor. In most of the territory of European Russia, except for its southernmost fringes, the agricultural season lasted only five months. It generated peak demand for labour both on the peasants' own farms and on estates and contributed to the availability of labour on a large scale in the remaining seven months of the year. The high seasonality of agriculture was compounded by its uniformity over most of the country and by the underdevelopment of mixed farming. The effect was to put a premium on activities which could be combined with farming: hence the growth of local artisan industry on a seasonal basis, the kustar industry often referred to, and the prevalence of such jobs as carting, hawking, storekeeping, domestic service, etc.

So far the transfer of labour from the rural sector has been approached from the supply side. On the demand side there were such factors as the local availability of employment outside the agrarian sector, the power and speed with which industrial employment grew, and the level of wages and social security provisions offered by the industrial sector. In the short term, cyclical fluctuations in business activity could affect the movement of labour from the rural sector.

Some of these factors will be considered in more detail later in this study. What needs to be emphasized at this stage is that there was not simply a choice between subsistence farming and wage-earning activity. Russian agriculture was dual: both estate and peasant. A peasant, when faced with the alternatives of producing agricultural goods for the market, of producing goods as a self-employed kustar, or of working for wages in or outside agriculture, tended to move back and forth between these alternatives in response to changes in their relative profitability. The tendency of the wage-earning labour force to move to and from the peasant sector was undoubtedly the greatest obstacle to the creation of a stable labour force, especially in factory industry. Purely institutional factors had nothing to do with this. That 'compulsory' land ownership did not weigh heavily upon the majority of peasants is evident from peasant behaviour after 1906, when compulsory communal ownership was abolished by Stolypin's legislation and allotment land was made a marketable commodity. Collective responsibility for taxation had gone two years earlier, in 1903. Yet there was no stampede of reluctant owners to sell their lands. Fewer than half a million peasants engaged in sales of land, but almost the same number of landless and near-landless were willing to buy. It is also not quite clear whether those selling were not also buying elsewhere or emigrating to Siberia to acquire land there. Professor Strumilin noted the relatively small increase in so-called proletarian elements in the countryside during the two decades between 1897 and 1917. Even in the predominantly industrial areas peasants bought over half a million *dessyatinas* of land, which represented about one-fifth of the net increase in peasant ownership by purchase in European Russia at large.[48]

From the moment at which economic development proceeded on a scale at which it could be influenced by economic forces in the country as a whole, these forces – rather than the exceptional acts of governments and entrepreneurs – began to affect the formation of the labour force. Of these fundamental economic factors by far the most important was population growth. Population growth revealed itself most clearly not so much in the overall supply of labour across the country as in regional differences.

Roughly the whole area of European Russia running northwards from a line drawn horizontally to the south of Moscow was the main source of labour supply to factory industry, to kustar enterprise, and to other forms of employment outside farming. Farming in this region could no longer provide a livelihood for the majority of the peasant population at the existing levels of agricultural productivity.

South of this line was an area consisting of some thirteen provinces in which agriculture was the main source of livelihood of the majority of the population, but in which population pressure had resulted in a proliferation of farms which could satisfy the subsistence needs of their members only in times of good harvests. In poor years, and during the 1880s and 1890s even in years of good harvests, many peasants had to eke out a living as seasonal agricultural labourers or as casual or common labourers in the winter season. Often resort to agricultural wage-earning in this area was prompted not by subsistence needs only: young members of viable farms sought migratory earnings in the steppes of Southeastern Russia to earn cash to enable the family to expand its production for the market by buying or renting more land. N. F. Rudnev estimated that about one-quarter of all peasants of working age in this area hired themselves out as agricultural labourers.[49]

Finally, in the Southeast of European Russia, the source of the bulk of Russia's export wheat, local labour was not sufficient to cope with peak seasonal demand. This area therefore drew migratory agricultural labour from the overcrowded areas to the north. Parts of this area – the Don Territory, Ekaternislav province, and Kherson – were also areas where industrial employment was rapidly being created in mining and metallurgy. The result was keen competition for labour, especially in the summer, and particularly in mining, which tended to rely on the same type of labour as estate farming. It has been noted that, while in the majority of areas which employed hired agricultural labour wages were largely determined by the previous year's harvest, in the three localities mentioned the competition of industry for labour added a new factor to the determination of wage levels.[50]

Population growth in the country as a whole had been sustained since 1724, largely owing to high birth rates and continuous internal colonization of new areas, where birth rates were above the average. Between 1724 and 1796 European Russia had, to judge by poll-tax returns, an average rate of population growth of 8·1 per thousand. This was a high rate for the eighteenth century and compares favourably with a rate of 5 per thousand for Europe. During the period from 1796 to 1851 the rate was only 7 per thousand, mainly on account of high death rates during the 1830s and 1840s owing to cholera outbreaks and harvest failures and on account of emigration to areas which escaped poll tax registration. Between 1867 and 1897 population grew on the average annually at 13·9 per thousand and reached 16·8 per thousand between 1897 and 1916.[51]

The non-European areas of the Russian Empire grew faster than European Russia proper (Finland and Poland are not included). If the population in 1863 is reckoned as 100, by 1913 it had become 222 in the Empire and 199·3 in European Russia. The share of European Russia in the total fell from 95·7 in 1861 to 78·4 in 1913.[52]

A large proportion of the population increase in Asiatic Russia was due to emigration from European Russia, which became intensive from the 1880s onwards and reached its peak during 1905–10. Till the 1880s emigration was more intensive in the direction of the sparsely populated areas to the north of the Caucasus and Black Sea (sometimes referred to as New Russia), and the Lower Volga valley.

Altogether, about 5·5 million Russians emigrated to Asiatic Russia between 1861 and 1915. Most of this emigration was rural in character and entailed expansion of areas under cultivation and seed. The bulk of emigrants came from the congested central agricultural provinces and from some parts of the Ukraine. These areas sent more than three-quarters of all emigrants during 1896–1910.[53]

However, even during periods of greatest intensity, emigration absorbed no more than one-quarter of the natural population growth, and on the average not more than 14 per cent of the population increase during this period, in European Russia. However, in a few congested provinces – i.e. Poltava, Chernigov, and Kharkov – emigration made a greater impact, absorbing between 37 and 51 per cent of their natural population growth. The industrial central provinces made up only 1·8 per cent of all emigrants, and the four northern provinces (of which St Petersburg was one) contributed only one-half of 1 per cent of all emigrants to Siberia. This figure suggests that where there were employment opportunities outside agriculture, emigration was not much of an attraction. Moreover, in these regions population growth might have been the effect rather than the cause of large-scale involvement in non-agricultural employment.[54]

Though overall population growth exceeded that of the rural population, the latter still grew significantly for a country in the throes of industrialization. Thus, between 1863 and 1897 the rural population increased by 43 per cent, and between 1897 and 1913 by a further 26 per cent, as against an overall increase of 51 and 30 per cent respectively. Even if one makes adjustments for the understatement of the urban element caused by classifying as rural some industrial settlements and industrial suburbs of big cities, the substantial growth of the rural population shows that transfers from the rural sector had not made much of an impact upon numbers, and that rural areas were a vast reservoir of labour.[55]

Unfortunately, official data about numbers employed in farming are not available except for 1897. I. Chernyshev used the data of the 1897 census for his draft on the law of franchise and estimated that out of a population of 125,640,000 fewer than one-tenth derived their income from industry and seven-tenths from farming. Of the 94 million persons in agriculture, 88 million were in cereal cultivation. In terms of active population, agriculture accounted for 72 per cent.[56]

Precise information on labour productivity in agriculture is also lacking. It has been estimated that national income from farming had grown by nearly 2 per cent on the average annually during the period 1860–1913, and that half of this growth was on account of area extension, the other half being due to higher yields.[57] We possess no accurate data on output values per person employed in agriculture. The character of the agricultural labour force, the importance of female and child labour, the part-time employment of adult male workers, and in general the lack of precision as to the time and numbers employed in agricultural work proper as distinct from activities of a managerial, commercial, and industrial kind make accurate calculation very difficult if not impossible. Raymond Goldsmith reckoned that agriculture still accounted for about two-thirds of the population and for about 45 per cent of the national income by 1913. Malcolm Falkus calculated the weight of agriculture in the national income as over 48 per cent, and as much as 55 per cent if forestry, fishing, and hunting were included.[58]

Much has been said about hidden unemployment in Russian agriculture and about the very low, even negative, marginal productivity of agricultural labour. It can be asserted, however, that there was in Russia no general disguised unemployment as postulated by W. A. Lewis in his 'Economic Development with Unlimited Supply of Labour'. There was periodic disguised unemployment, especially of male labour, in the sense that individual members of family farms could be withdrawn for parts of the year without any sacrifice to agricultural output. More accurately it could be said that in many regions of Russia population was underemployed, underemployment being defined as a surplus stock of man-hours relative to labour requirements over large parts of the year and in some areas throughout the year. The surplus rural manpower has been variously estimated at 30 per cent of the total for Imperial Russia, at between 38 and 50 per cent at the beginning of the First Five-year Plan, but at only 8–9 million persons by Strumilin for the late twenties. The latter figure was probably nearer reality in terms of net surpluses over the whole year.[59]

If at times less labour time was sold on the labour market than was warranted by manpower surpluses, it was because peasants often found the effort of earning cash as agricultural producers or as kustars less than that of earning it as labourers. On occasion there was an interdependence between these two sets of factors, in that participation in the labour market was often necessary if a peasant wanted to participate in the produce market, i.e. in order to earn cash for land purchase and to keep up mortgage repayments.

III.   *Wage Employment*

A. RURAL WAGE-EARNERS

The evolution of wage-earning employment and of the factory labour force reflects the interaction of various factors upon labour supply. These factors make it extremely difficult to determine exactly the numbers and proportions of those whose sole means of livelihood was from wage earnings, and who were employed all through the year outside the family farm. With the exceptions of workers in factories and mines subject to inspection (where an all-year-round commitment gradually developed), of the railway workers, and of urban artisans, most of our information is based on peasants' declarations as to their 'earnings from trades' (*zarabotki ot promyslov*), usually conceived of as supplementary to income from farms.

Rashin estimated the total number of wage-earners in 1860 at just under four million, which represented roughly 6·5 per cent of the population of European Russia. This figure is somewhat arbitrary, since it includes groups for whom wage earnings must have been the sole or main means of livelihood and those for whom it was a supplementary and seasonal source of income. Furthermore, the figure of only 800,000 for rural and urban artisans together was based on the narrowest definition of the term. On the whole, in a society where the vast majority of the population was not, even by 1914, enrolled in an organized wage economy, an attempt to isolate wage-earners for 1860 is somewhat questionable.[60] Nevertheless, the figure is a convenient point of departure for assessing changes in the numbers of wage-earners over time, as follows:[61]

1860	3,960,000	(index 100)
1897	9,156,620	(index 231)
1900	10,375,080	(index 262)
	(non-agricultural)	
1913	17,815,000	(index 450)

The figures for 1897 and subsequent dates are based on more reliable data than those for 1860 but present similar difficulties with regard to full-time, seasonal, or casual and sporadic wage-earning activities. The data for 1897 are based on Russia's first population census. However, Russian peasants – conditioned by past experience to associating censuses with new taxation, stricter assessment, or punishment for evasion – refused to complete, or gave inaccurate answers to, question 4 on the census form, which concerned sources of income other than the family farm. The most frequent answer was that the family farm was the one and only source of livelihood. Only about one in every fifteen of the seventy-million-strong peasant population of European Russia declared subsidiary earnings, a proportion which would have to be doubled for the active population and increased still further for adult males, as women took outside employment less frequently. In six provinces the percentage of those who declared subsidiary earnings was twice the national average.

Data collected over a long period by the local councils (*zemstva*), though not systematized and differing in quality from province to province, yielded a much higher percentage of the rural population who derived incomes from sources other than the family farm. Using *zemstva* data, N. F. Rudnev estimated that in the 1880s, in 148 districts of the twenty-three provinces out of a total of fifty for European Russia, 55 per cent of the active male population had subsidiary earnings. The proportion was as low as 20 per cent in the southern provinces of Kherson and Taurida, where the seasonality of agriculture was much less marked than on the average in Russia, and where harvests were on the average high and population densities relatively low. It was as high as 91 per cent in Smolensk, 83 per cent in St Petersburg, and 80 per cent in the Moscow province, all areas with relatively poor-quality soil, short growing season, and high population densities.[62]

For the period from 1890 to 1913 an investigation based on a slightly larger spread of districts of the same provinces yielded nearly 60 per cent of males of working age taking off-farm employment. The available data suggest 1·77 off-farm workers per household on the average, the highest figure being 2·62, in Moscow province, and the most frequently mentioned figures lying between 1·60 and 1·90 workers per household.[63]

The proportion of women of working age following off-farm occupations was much lower than that of men: overall, in twenty-one provinces, it was around one-fifth of the off-farm workers investigated. The main reason for the relatively low weight of female labour in off-farm employment lay in the fact that women tended to replace men on the farms. It was reported that in Vladimir province, where over 81 per cent of active male workers sought off-farm earnings, women were undertaking such specifically male jobs as ploughing and hay-cutting; children and older members of the household coped with the remaining work.[64]

The wage-earning pursuits of the rural population could be entirely local or could involve migration, sometimes within the borders of a province, sometimes to neighbouring provinces, and often across country. Passport statistics are commonly used to gauge the degree of peasant departure for outside earnings. They are not a perfect measure; nevertheless, given their mass character, they are a vital statistical source for observing movements in search of work. If we take the number of passports issued for a year or less, on the average annually, we get the following growth:[65]

1861–70	index 100
1871–80	287
1881–90	384
1891–1900	533
1901–10	698

The rise in the number of passports for 'going-away' work (*otkhod*) was much steeper than was the rise in wage-earning occupations at large, and steeper still than the growth in factory employment. During the period from 1906 to 1910, 9,399,400 passports for up to one year were issued annually on the average in European Russia. This entailed 94 passports per thousand inhabitants, as against 83 per thousand during 1891–1900 and 24 per thousand during 1861–70. The proportion of

Table 53. *Distribution of Workers in Different Forms of Employment*

	Number of persons (thousands)			Index (1860 = 100)	
Groups	1860	1913	1917	1913	1917
I. Industrial workers					
(a) in factories and mines	860	3,100	3,643	360·5	423·6
(b) employed in their own homes, in rural or urban industry not under (a)	800	3,000	3,500	375·0	437·5
Total industrial	1,660	6,100	7,143	367·4	430·3
II. Employed in building	350	1,500	1,500	428·6	428·6
III. Transport					
(a) water	500	500⎫	1,857	100·0⎫	363·4
(b) railways	11	815⎭		7,409·1⎭	
Total transport (approx.)	511	1,315	1,857	257·3	363·4
IV. Agricultural wage-earners	700	4,500	5,000	642·8	714·3
V. Other persons working for wages (urban unskilled and day labourers, and apprentices in commerce, restaurants, and domestic service)	800	4,065	4,465	508·1	558·1
Total non-industrial wage-earners (total II–V)	2,361	11,380	12,822	482·0	543·0
Overall total	4,021	17,480	19,965	434·7	496·5

those taking out passports would be doubled if calculated on the basis of active workers only, and increased still further if men's passports are measured as a proportion of men in the active population.[66]

Table 53 gives the approximate distribution of wage-earners between different forms of employment at three benchmark dates. Data for 1917 are given here not for the purpose of indicating shifts in employment during the 1914 war but mainly because the 1917 data include certain categories of labour not taken into account by Rashin, from whose tables the bulk of the data, with minor adjustments, have been taken.

For 1900, the estimates of the Imperial Commission give a different breakdown into various forms of employment. They give much more weight to kustar and '*remeslo*' employment, i.e. to item I(b) of Table 53. On the basis of the Imperial Commission's estimates, the breakdown of non-agricultural employment of the active population of the fifty provinces of European Russia in 1900 was as follows:[67]

	Millions	Per cent of total
Total active population	44·6	—
Total in non-agricultural employment	10·4	23·3

Of which:

	Millions	Per cent	
In factories and mines	1·9	18·2	4·4
Kustar and remeslo	4·6	44·2	10·3
Miscellaneous off-farm employment	3·7	35·5	8·3

Agriculture accounted for the highest proportion of wage-earners, making up about one-quarter of the total except in 1860.[68] For a country where according to the census of 1897 more than 74 per cent of the total population, and about 72 per cent of all persons aged fifteen and over, were occupied in agriculture, even five million wage-earners is a relatively small number. However, the majority of farms were family units relying almost entirely on family labour.

Only in a few areas such as the Baltic and some former Polish regions, and on some estates in New Russia, was all-year-round agricultural labour employed. In Central Russia, even large estates employed a small nucleus of permanent labourers, more in the nature of servants, and hired local peasants for seasonal work either for a daily wage or for an agreed payment for a particular job, or on the basis of crop-sharing or working off rents. An advance in cash or kind was nearly always made, and the labourer's draft animals and implements were used.

This arrangement, undoubtedly deleterious in its effects upon the productivity of estate farming, was due in part to shortage of capital among estate-owners for equipping their farms, but mainly to the relative cheapness of labour in the congested parts of the central agricultural region and of the Southwest. It was also due to rising prices for land, which made land purchase or renting by peasants more difficult, though peasant purchases were in fact rising steeply. The often-referred-to highly seasonal character of agriculture and the prevalence of monoculture made resort to all-year-round farm labour uneconomical even for estate-owners whose capital resources were adequate.[69]

The 1897 census recorded only 2·7 million agricultural labourers. This was undoubtedly an underestimate. Strumilin believes that the figure was nearer 4·5 million. The Imperial Commission of November 1901 estimated the number of agricultural labourers in 1900 as around 3·8 million. If Strumilin is right, then it would have to be accepted that, though the agricultural population of Russia had grown by 26 per cent in twenty years between 1897 and 1917, hired labour in agriculture had increased by only 8 per cent. Strumilin ascribes the discrepancy entirely to the increased use of agricultural machinery. While the latter did undoubtedly have a significant effect, the increase in the contribution of self-employed peasant agriculture relative to estate farming and improved terms of trade, as well as good harvests after 1900, which increased peasant incomes in agricultural provinces, undoubtedly played a part. Improved credit facilities for peasants and the abolition of redemption payments in 1906 also reduced peasant need to resort to agricultural wage labour. Finally, assisted emigration somewhat eased the pressure of the weakest households in the most congested areas.

It seems certain that 'going-away' work as well as all those forms of employment which were by their nature seasonal were resorted to by members of peasant families in agricultural provinces as a means of supporting their agricultural economy. In a typical agricultural province such as Kursk in 1910, one-third of those employed for wages worked in agriculture, 29 per cent were engaged in casual work, i.e. digging, quarrying, carting, 18 per cent in carpentering and masonry work, and 5 per cent in the mines. On the other hand, in such a non-agricultural province as Tver, sandwiched between Moscow and St Petersburg, where migration for non-agricultural earnings was significant already in the eighteenth century, about 50 per cent of the 128,000 labourers who took out passports in 1896 went to occupations which were by their nature seasonal, building taking pride of place with 39 per cent of the total. At 13 per cent, building was the third largest occupational group among non-agricultural labourers in the 1897 census, after textile-processing and metalworking. In Russian climatic conditions building was essentially a summer trade, one most frequently requiring migration to cities and also one most exposed to the effects of the trade cycle.[70]

In the view of some investigators, the prevalence of seasonal or short-term earnings seems to explain why the connection with land was valued, even in areas where a farm could no longer provide a livelihood even at the best of times, for in its turn seasonal work outside the farm could not provide enough income for the whole year. 'The fact that it is not possible to subsist on the wage alone', wrote S. Vikhlayev, 'is in itself a powerful tie binding the worker to the land.' The prevalence of short-term off-farm employment, most of it of a seasonal nature, seems to have been a matter not so much of choice as of opportunity. It was the greater availability of employment in building, quarrying, railway construction, haulage, hawking, etc. relative to other forms of employment, rather than choice, which determined their greater weight in wage employment. Railway transport also provided a fast-growing and regular form of employment and, moreover, one in which the workers enjoyed the benefits of a social security scheme since the 1880s. Workers in railway transport and communications had undoubtedly become an all-year-round labour force, with relatively longer work records than those in other occupations.[71]

The extent to which wage earnings were divided between local and migratory work cannot be exactly ascertained. Whereas some of the investigations considered as migratory those trades which involved work in another province, others considered work in another parish or even village as migratory. The majority, however, considered trades within the boundaries of the same district as local. Given the size of individual districts and the distances involved, such a classification in fact understates the migratory element in various trades. Of the three million wage-earners investigated in fifteen provinces from data for the period roughly covering 1894 to 1913, the proportion of local workers was 53·5 per cent, fluctuating between 79 per cent in Vologda and 27 per cent in Vitebsk. The more industrially or commercially developed a region was, and the more local the supplies of raw materials for processing (such as timber or hides) were, the greater were the opportunities for local employment. The greater the weight of the migratory element was in the employment structure of a given locality, the less was the weight of women in off-farm employment.[72]

B. KUSTAR INDUSTRY

Among local trades kustar industry held a prominent position. Here as elsewhere, the term 'kustar' is used rather loosely to describe 'small', 'cottage', or 'family' industry. The definition which best describes the ideal type is a small-scale family organization, manufacturing for a market (not for a specific customer), pursued by peasants as subsidiary to their main farming activity. There were of course departures from the ideal type, in that a few hands were sometimes hired to work side by side with the family; income from subsidiary occupations could exceed that from farming; some members of the family might continue working throughout the year and not just during the off-farm season.

It was from among successful kustars that some of Russia's greatest entrepreneurs like the Morozovs or Grachevs had emerged at the end of the eighteenth century and the early nineteenth. An independent, own-account kustar planned his production and marketed it himself; nevertheless, there is some justification for considering the majority of those employed as kustars as wage-earners in terms of the size of their earnings, the toil involved, and the life-style. Wherever this was no longer the case, the occupation was not strictly 'kustar', though the term was sometimes applied to primitive small factory establishments. One comes across terms such as 'kustar-like' mines etc.

Kustar industries developed most intensively in areas where the seasonal nature of agriculture was most pronounced, where the quality of the land was relatively poor, where raw materials such as timber, flax, hemp, wool, and hides were available, and most importantly where there was good access to markets. The central industrial region (often referred to), consisting of nine provinces, where all the above conditions existed, was among the most important areas of kustar activity. Here factory industry was grafted on to existing rural industries; at the same time it was factory industry which gave a massive impetus to rural industries by disseminating new skills and by creating opportunities for kustar activities which complemented those of the factory.

Access to markets determined widespread development of kustar industries in regions closest to the two capitals and to the large commercial centre on the Volga, Nizhny Novgorod. Availability of timber determined the development of kustar trades in Vyatka, Vologda, and Nizhny Novgorod; access to ores and minerals encouraged kustar trades in Perm and Tula; sheep-rearing and cattle-breeding in the Volga regions encouraged the trades of tanners, furriers, saddlers, and bootmakers. Over fifty different kustar trades have been identified, ranging from the simplest, roughest articles for use by peasant masses to artistic objects for export and even precision instruments such as thermometers, barometers, and scales. Whole villages were known to specialize in certain trades. In the central provinces, fibre-processing from flax, hemp, and wool were most prominent.

The attraction of kustar activity lay in the fact that it did not necessitate severance from farming; it was a family activity in which the old and young alike could participate, thereby increasing the aggregate productivity of labour of the whole household over the whole year. In such a trade as the making of wooden spoons, every member of the family had a specific function, well adjusted to his age and capabilities. The youngest children would sort out pieces of wood according to size. Those aged ten to fifteen would shape them roughly. The adult men would give them their final shape with knife and chisel. The women and the old would smooth and polish them; and the daughters of the family would apply patterns and lacquer. It was this family co-operation which kept costs low and made for prices accessible to the poorest, and also made for great resilience and ability to withstand competition, often also factory competition. This explains why even in the Moscow province, where factory industry was more advanced than elsewhere in Russia, there were in 1896 181,500 kustars (men, women, and children) earning an estimated 11·5 million roubles from their various trades a year, while in factory industry there were only 40,463 persons earning 4·3 million roubles annually. Even in 1909, there were still in the Moscow province over 360,000 kustars and only 314,476 factory workers.[73]

On the average, kustar earnings were very low, often lower than the wages in the same industry in a factory or medium-sized workshop, though there were periods when the kustar did earn more than his equivalent in a factory. Professor A. A. Isayev estimated the average weekly income of a kustar in the 1880s at three roubles. It fluctuated between 1·5 to 2 roubles in nail-making and 7 to 8 roubles in furniture-making. The annual earnings in trades in which predominantly women were employed – weaving and lace-making – fluctuated between 25 and 30 roubles and could be as low as 12 to 15 roubles. In other industries the annual average was between 50 and 70 roubles, though in some it reached 125 to 200 and even 300 roubles.

A comparison with the average factory wage in 1897, which was 185 roubles annually, and 167 roubles annually in workshops employing fewer than sixteen hands, would explain both the attraction and the resilience of kustar industry. It must be remembered, moreover, that while there were kustars who worked for most of the year except during the height of the harvest, on the whole these earnings applied to a maximum of seven months and often only four, and in some cases (as in the carding of wool) to only a few weeks. On the other hand the working day of fifteen to sixteen hours, and often all-night work as in the making of rugs or before the annual fair, were not uncommon.[74]

In certain industries, especially those in which giant-size factories were prominent, kustars were connected with the factory through the putting-out system. This system showed great resilience despite the technological changes in Russian factory industry. It made it possible for manufacturers to cope with increased demand without adding to capacity. In its turn the factory often accepted kustar-produced fabrics for dyeing and finishing or entrusted the winding and carding to kustars. Most often, however, this function of intermediaries was performed by special distributing offices (*razdatochniye kontory*) or even petty traders (*torgovki*), who peddled the goods produced by kustars.

The resilience and tenacity of kustar industry was due to the fact that in many areas of activity the factory was still absent, especially in consumer-goods industries, and, where present, it was often technologically backward and therefore not able to reduce unit costs significantly enough to squeeze out the kustar. Furthermore, even technologically advanced factories had high fixed costs and large overheads, and consequently higher unit costs, than small workshops and could overcome competition only by their control over credit or raw materials.

Kustar industry as a *genre* was flexible, adaptable, and ready to meet demand left unsatisfied by the factory sector. It was of course sensitive to a variety of adverse factors, such as rising costs of raw materials and fuel or the fall of agricultural prices, which affected the rural market. By comparison the growth of modern industry did not always damage it, since technological advance sometimes aided the kustar, in that simple power tools, the sewing machine, and later even small electric stations for a whole kustar village, could be used. Factory competition, where it existed (a factory of rubber overshoes in distant Riga could ruin a kustar bootmaker in Arzamas on the Volga or in Kimry of Tver province, if he was not quick enough to switch to making felt boots; residues from Baku oil could kill kustar production of tar in Vologda or Archangel province), and similar difficulties led to the tendency for the kustar enterprise to diminish in size; to rely more or entirely on family labour; to use the family house or shed instead of a special workshop; to work longer hours; to undertake arduous journeys often on foot to 'earn' raw material or sell it in a better market; to work off credit and interest in various ways; etc. Only when all else failed would a kustar seek work 'on the side' (*na storone*), eventually in the factory and even then not directly. He would first try a variety of trades and occupations in the hope of restoring his independence. 'Going-away work' was, according to most observers, the most frequent route to the factory, usually for seasonal work at first.[75]

Yet in spite of the constant transfer to factory employment from this and other rural sources, the extent to which the bulk of the potential labour force was still unspecialized and not yet enrolled in an organized wage economy is evident from the family budgets of peasant households in the most industrialized regions of Russia such as Moscow or Vladimir provinces. A few examples will suffice. In Zagor, an area of widespread metalworking activities, a family consisting of two able-bodied male workers, successfully and efficiently running a family farm, in the 1890s derived 43 per cent of its income from the family farm, another 43 per cent from carting and carrying trades, and the balance from miscellaneous small-scale semi-industrial activities performed by the male and female members of the family, old and young alike. In a region where bristle-making was a widespread activity, a family with only one male worker, an allotment of about 16 acres, and one horse derived 40 per cent of its income from the farm, 22 per cent from agricultural hire and carting, 25 per cent from bristle-making over six and a half months, with husband, wife, and young children all working, and 13 per cent from casual earnings.[76]

The above examples bear out the view held by H. Myint that the tendency to describe developing economies in terms of strictly defined sectors, one a traditional subsistence sector and the other a modern market sector, does not reflect reality. There was a much greater blurring and overlapping of market-type activities and subsistence activities, both between households and within households, at least for the bulk of the population.[77]

C. URBAN HANDICRAFTS (REMESLO)

By 'remeslo' is usually meant non-factory artisan *urban* industry. It differed from rural crafts not only in its location but also in its non-seasonal character. Furthermore, it was usually the main source of livelihood and not supplementary to farming.

In 1858 there were in European Russia (excluding Poland and Finland) 355,508 artisans, including journeymen and apprentices. Moscow and St Petersburg provinces accounted for nearly one-quarter of the total.[78]

During the 1850s there was a tendency on the part of the municipal crafts authorities (*remeslennyye upravlenya*), especially in the two capitals, to class as remeslo various small workshops which had been mushrooming since the 1830s. This ran counter to the views of the Finance Ministry, which was inclined to widen the concept of 'factory' to include the broadest possible spectrum of manufacturing units. In the event, the demarcation line between urban artisan workshops and factories was never firmly drawn, thereby creating problems for the historian and the statistician.

For this and other reasons institutional criteria for separating remeslo from small-scale factory industry cannot be applied with any accuracy. Nor were the numbers of journeymen and apprentices known exactly either, because of frequent transfers from master to master, waves of migrations, and general fluidity of numbers. Most of the figures therefore underestimate the actual employment in remeslo activities.

In 1910, according to an inquiry conducted by the Ministry of Commerce and Industry, there were in the 82 provinces of Russia 103,469 artisan workshops. This was undoubtedly an underestimate, as the inquiry was confined mainly to large towns with populations of over thirty thousand each. Over 83 per cent of all workshops were very small, employing two to four hands. Over 14 per cent of all workshops employed between five and fifteen hands; those employing between sixteen and twenty-five and over twenty-five made up only 1·2 and 0·9 per cent respectively of all workshops.[79]

The number of artisans working as a rule without any hired hands or with one only amounted, according to the registry, to 110,642 persons. The registry recorded 89,324 apprentices. They were mainly to be found in larger workshops, on the average two per workshop employing over twenty-five hands, but less than one (0·8) on the average in the workshops employing two to four hands.[80]

The overall estimate of urban craftsmen fluctuates between 1·2 and 2·5 million people for 1913. The numbers were decidedly less than for rural craftsmen and reflected the relative weakness of Russian towns, most of which were administrative and military centres rather than leaders in the economic life of the country. On the other hand, most rural artisans were only seasonally employed. Neither was urban craftsmanship of very high quality despite the efforts to raise it made by Peter the Great and Catherine II and by Count Kankrin in Nicholas I's reign. Given the poverty of the general public, urban artisan industry was not able to compete with kustar industry in catering to mass demand, while the sophisticated tastes of the small circle of the rich could best be satisfied by imports. The fiscal policy of the government also had an inhibiting effect upon urban artisan industry by reducing its competitiveness as against peasant artisans. Despite pressure from urban elements, successive governments refused to interfere with rural manufacturing and trading. Paradoxical though this may sound, within a highly restrictive political and bureaucratic system, a particular social class met with fewer official obstacles in undertaking commercial or industrial activity than existed elsewhere in Europe, except Britain. The effect of this policy was detrimental to the growth of urban craftsmanship.[81]

Urban craftsmanship was most successful in areas which were not ethnically Russian, as in the Baltic or Vistula Region, or in regions which developed partly under Polish influence and where large numbers of Jews were concentrated in towns, mainly because of the legal restraint on Jewish ownership of land. It was also successful in the South, where the seasonal nature of agriculture was less pronounced, as in Taurida, and generally in the southeastern parts of Russia, where the descendants of German colonists settled by Catherine II and Alexander I practised their crafts in the cities.[82]

All in all, remeslo as defined institutionally did not constitute an important element in the industrial structure in Russia. With the development of large-scale factory industry it was losing, except in a few regions, whatever importance it ever had, becoming subsidiary to large-scale industry or retaining the character of petty industry in those branches where factory industry had not yet developed. However, there were still many spheres in which urban craftsmanship was significant: in luxury, fashion, and precision trades in large cities, in repairs and alterations, and in all kinds of tinkering, making, and mending in a society still very poor and expecting long service from articles in use.

Although it is also not always easy to separate rural from urban small-artisan industry, it is clear that the rural element decisively predominated. S. N. Prokopovich, in his study of the Russian National Income in 1900 and 1913, estimates the value of remeslo at 338 million roubles in 1900 and at 612 million roubles in 1913, which was much higher than his estimate for kustar industry. But then Prokopovich classed under remeslo most workshops and small factories in non-mechanical trades, and under kustar mainly the seasonal output from cottage workers only. The two forms of industry taken together accounted for a formidable share of the labour force and for a sizeable share of industrial output. In terms of the share of the mass consumer market, except in textiles, small industry was leading.[83]

D. EMPLOYMENT IN FACTORIES AND MINES

Measurement of the growth of the industrial labour force in pre-revolutionary Russia is made particularly difficult by the fact that the available statistical material is incomplete and is not easily comparable from year to year. Above all it tends to overestimate the employment in large industrial units. Furthermore, an additional difficulty is the absence of reliable measurements of urban and rural artisan industries, which were such a significant element of the industrial structure of Russia right up to 1917 and beyond, till the beginning of planning in the USSR. In pre-Revolutionary Russia the term 'industry' comprised all physical output other than agriculture, forestry, and construction. It consisted of four main components. The first was factory industry, defined as including all enterprises which had more than a small number of workers or which were provided with mechanical power. The term 'small' was never clearly defined. Lenin used sixteen as a minimum number of employed separating a factory from a workshop. Before 1897, official sources took output value of not less than 1,000 roubles as qualifying a plant as a factory. The Industrial Census of 1900 gave the use of either mechanical power or a labour force of sixteen or more as the criteria for classification as a factory, but in fact the minimum employed was higher. For statistical purposes 'factory industry' was generally divided into industries subject to excise taxes (principally alcoholic beverages, tobacco, sugar, yeast, and matches) and the bulk of industries not subject to them. Of the latter, the main component were industries subject to the Factory Inspectorate, introduced in 1884. The second main component was mining, subject to the Administration of Mines of the Ministry of State Domains. Urban artisan workshops (remeslo) constituted the third component. The fourth component of industry, *rural* artisan industry (kustar) conducted to a large extent on a part-time basis, was not recorded officially at all. More often than not government-owned factories and works were not included in the official statistics of the labour force. In general the reliability of the sources is marred by constant shifts in coverage of plants subject to inspection and by an imprecise definition of what constitutes a factory, as well as by incomplete or unsystematic registration. Although the tendency throughout was to omit smaller units, sometimes quite large units were also dropped from the registry either upon the intervention of employers or for other reasons. There was also no systematic geographical coverage, since sometimes different criteria were used for political reasons in certain provinces. For example, in the Western Provinces, where many of the employers were Jewish, artisan-type workshops were registered, while elsewhere bakeries employing 400 hands were left out. Pogozhev estimated that official statistics for 1902 missed out 9,000 units with 175,000 workers.[84]

These defects of the Russian statistics are a serious impediment to an objective study of the structure of industry, and they largely account for the widely accepted view as to the prevalence of large industrial units. Neither the population census of 1897 – the first and only census not conducted for taxation purposes – nor the two partial industrial censuses of 1887 and 1897 nor finally the two comprehensive industrial censuses of 1900 and 1908 are free from these defects. The statistician Pogozhev maintained that official publications underestimated employment in small and medium units. He compared the business directory *Vsya Rossiya* (edited by A. S. Suvorin and published in St Petersburg in 1901), covering the period 1898–1900, which cited 142,000 firms with

1,695,000 workmen, giving an average of 12 per firm, with the Report of the Inspectorate for 1900, citing 18,000 firms, which gave an average of 93·6 workers per enterprise.[85] The explanatory notes to the 1908 industrial census throw light on this tendency to neglect smaller units. 4,691 firms with 184,857 workers recorded in the 1900 census did not enter the 1908 census. This number represented 23·5 per cent of the total number of workers recorded in the census. More than half of this number – 2,794 firms with 153,068 workers – went out of operation for various reasons of an economic nature. They accounted for 13·9 per cent of the factories in the 1908 census and for 7 per cent of the total labour force. However, they were dismissed by the compilers of the census as insignificant and 'very small' in that their labour force was on the average *only* 55 workers per plant and the output value *only* 1,575 roubles per worker, as against the average of 112 workers and 2,064 roubles output per worker of the plants actually recorded. Similarly dismissed as insignificant were the 445 firms employing 12,893 workers or 29 per plant, which had been freed from factory inspection since the 1900 census, and the 1,452 plants with 18,896 workers or an average of 13 workers each, excluded from the register on account of size.[86]

Further difficulties arise because of the differences between industries with regard to the definition of the labour force. Some included white-collar workers; others excluded supplementary workers because they were not directly connected with the main manufacturing operations or were not employed on a permanent basis.

The statistical data make it particularly difficult to study changes in productivity over time, because statistics give us the average number of workers employed in a given plant or industry over the year but not the actual number of man-hours worked, or how many men actually worked during the year. In many plants, especially in the Urals, a short three-to-four-day week was worked during recessions to avoid laying off workers. In the Urals, workers often worked alternate fortnights. In the central industrial region, employers were reluctant to dismiss workers, especially during the winter months when no alternative employment was available. Last but not least, the tendency for the largest enterprises to function as conglomerate units, combining multifarious activities, created serious statistical problems. Sometimes, as in the Urals, management sent in only one form for a whole mining district consisting of well-known separate works (i.e. the Urals–Demidov works) but refused to allocate the labour force, wages, and cost of fuel and raw materials to individual plants. Obviously, such information makes it utterly impossible to calculate the number of workers for each individual plant and renders the numbers of factories in industrial statistics purely nominal.[87]

While this does not affect the numbers of workers in industry at large, it tends to give a misleading picture of the industrial structure, implying much greater concentration of workers and resources per plant than was actually the case. At the risk of repetition it must be emphasized that the picture of Russia's industrial structure implying large concentration of workers, a feature from which important political implications were drawn, is misleading not only because of the inadequate registration of small units but also because many units which were in fact quite small were included in the large conglomerates.

The dynamics of factory formation and the evolution of the factory labour force between 1861 and the turn of the century was calculated by A. V. Pogozhev on the basis of a list of factories and works compiled by the Ministry of Finance from 1900 and published in 1903. The 14,464 industrial units which operated in the fifty provinces of European Russia in 1903 were distributed by dates of foundation as in Table 54.[88]

Table 54. *Number of Industrial Firms in 1903,*
by Date of Foundation

Date	Number of firms	Per cent of total
Before 1861	2,177	15·1
1861–70	1,285	8·9
1871–80	2,100	14·5
1881–90	3,036	21·0
1891–1900	5,788	40·0
1901–3	78	0·5
Total	14,464	100·0

This table gives a very neat picture of post-Emancipation developments. It shows that during the decade of the sixties relatively few new firms were being founded. It was a decade during which much of the growth of the secondary sector came from kustar industry. During the sixties, and to a large extent during the next two decades, effort went into providing at least a rudimentary infrastructure in transport, banks, education, and law. Moreover, the abolition of serfdom led to the liquidation or contraction of the labour force in those branches of industry in which forced or serf labour was still applied by 1860. Most severely affected were the woollen cloth mills owned by estate-owners in purely agricultural regions such as Tambov, Simbirsk, Poltava, Voronezh, Penza, and the Ukraine.

In the same situation were those possessional factories which were not dissolved following the law of 1840 and the state-owned factories where compulsory labour was the rule before 1861. Except where dealt with individually, the freeing of the labour force in military and naval establishments took place in the late sixties. The mining and metallurgical industries of the Urals were significantly affected and suffered an overall fall in the number of workers of about 25 per cent (about 37 per cent in state-owned works) by 1863. In Perm province, the works belonging to the heirs of Yakovlev, which before 1861 employed 15,743 workers, were left in 1862 with only 9,352; the Demidov works suffered a reduction from 25,585 to 9,147. In manufacturing, the labour force contracted by about 200,000, from an estimated 565,000 in 1860 to 363,600 in 1863. However, these two figures are not strictly comparable, as the data for 1863 did not include a number of plants in distilling and sugar and tobacco production, accounting for nearly a hundred thousand workers.[89]

Not all the downward trend in factory industry is to be attributed to the effects of the release of the serfs. Many long-established factory workers 'collected their saved-up kopecks' to return to the villages in order to claim their allotments and to attempt to use their skills as independent kustars. The Emancipation occurred during a cyclical downturn in industrial activity which retarded the adaptation to the changed situation of those industries and plants which hitherto used forced labour. Labour-saving technology was introduced very gradually, and this made it easier for the rural artisan to enter the market. Furthermore, the upheaval due to Emancipation was accompanied by an upheaval due to the cotton famine connected with the American Civil War. Total imports of cotton by weight represented only about one-third of the 1860 imports. The number of factory workers in cotton-spinning fell from 119,100 in 1860 to 58,100 in 1863, and only in 1866 was the 1860 level restored. Rashin claims that in manufacturing only a net contraction of some 40,000 can be directly ascribed to the effects of Emancipation upon the factory labour force. Lenin calculated that by 1865 the labour force was 509,000 in manufacturing and 165,000 in mining and metallurgy, or a total of 674,000. This is still considerably less than the 860,000 estimated by Zlotnikov for 1860. On the whole the reduction was mainly on account of the fall in the number of workers in mining and metallurgy, mainly consequent upon the reduction in the number of supplementary workers who had been drawn before from among Crown peasants. This was the beginning of a long-term development connected partly with the growth of railway transport and partly with technological change within the industry. To some extent the reduction in the labour force in mining and metallurgy reflected a change in methods of recording, especially in the Urals. However, output indices during the sixties also show very little growth and in some branches even a fall in output of factory industry. By 1870 the size of the work force in factories and mines was still some 7 per cent below the estimated number for 1860.[90]

Table 55. *Factory Industry in 1903: Date of Foundation, distributed by Size of Factory (per cent)*

Number of workers per unit	Year of foundation						As % of all factories in 1903
	Before 1861	1861–70	1871–80	1881–90	1891–1900	1901–3	
Under 50	56·6	63·3	64·5	70·9	75·2	79·5	68·9
50–99	13·2	13·9	15·9	13·7	13·4	15·4	13·8
100–499	20·7	16·3	14·4	12·4	9·7	5·1	13·2
500–999	5·5	3·9	3·3	1·9	1·3	—	2·6
1,000 and over	4·0	2·6	1·9	1·1	0·4	—	1·5
Total	100·0	100·0	100·0	100·0	100·0	100·0	100·0

Table 56. *Factory Industry in 1903: Size of Factory, distributed by Date of Foundation (per cent)*

Year of foundation	Number of workers per unit					As % of all factories in 1903
	Under 50	50–99	100–499	500–999	1,000 and over	
Before 1861	12·3	14·4	23·6	32·6	39·7	15·1
1861–70	8·2	8·9	11·3	13·5	15·1	8·9
1871–80	13·6	16·6	15·8	18·6	18·7	14·5
1881–90	21·6	20·7	19·7	15·4	15·5	21·0
1891–1900	43·7	38·8	29·4	19·9	11·0	40·0
1901–3	0·6	0·6	0·2	—	—	0·5
Total	100·0	100·0	100·0	100·0	100·0	100·0

The data on factory formation as given in Tables 55 and 56 emphasize the strategic two decades of the eighties and nineties, the latter in particular. Nearly two-thirds of all plants in existence at the start of the twentieth century came into being during these two decades. It is interesting that nearly 70 per cent of all firms extant in 1903 had a labour force under fifty each. More than two-thirds of these small units were created during the decades of the eighties and nineties, a period commonly associated with the technological transformation of Russian industry and the formation of large joint-stock industrial companies. The highest proportion of the largest units extant by 1903 – those of 500 upwards – traced their beginnings to the days of serfdom, which is further evidence of continuity between the two periods; 75 per cent of all the plants founded during the nineties were in the under-fifty category.[91]

Though Pogozhev took into account smaller units not as a rule entered into the Summary Reports of the Factory Inspectorate, there is no evidence that he gave undue emphasis to very small firms. Indeed, the 14,500-odd units which he examined for 1903 constituted less than one-half of the number of factories and mines recorded in the official statistics of the Finance Ministry for the whole Empire excluding Finland (i.e. 30,888 in 1887, 30,333 in 1893, 39,029 in 1897, and 24,460 in 1900). In 1900 the Summary Report specifically stated that just under 14,000 smaller units were excluded. The Factory Inspectorate, which from 1903 recorded only units with a labour force of twenty and above, registered 16,173 units in 1903.[92]

The number of workers in factories and works in the fifty provinces of European Russia during 1861–1900 evolved as follows:[93]

1861–70	797,649	(index 100)
1871–80	945,597	(index 118·5)
1881–90	1,160,771	(index 145·5)
1891–1900	1,637,595	(index 205·3)

The labour force in factories and works in European Russia more than doubled, on the average, during four decades; the largest increase had occurred in the decade of the nineties. Lenin, using data for thirty-four industries and taking 1865 as base year, arrived at a 70 per cent rise in the labour force by 1890. Most of the growth in his calculation had occurred between 1865 and 1879, especially during the seventies. His figures imply a fall in the labour force of about 6·4 per cent during the early eighties (which tallies with our information about return of workers to the villages) and a slow rise during the second half of the eighties.[94]

For the Empire the official data from censuses suggest the following figures (Finland is not included):[95]

1887	1,318,048	(index 100)
1893	1,582,904	(index 120·1)
1897	2,098,262	(index 159·2)
1900	2,277,652	(index 172·8)

Using data for the labour force in the Empire (excluding however the Kingdom of Poland and Finland) and taking 1887 as base year, the index of the labour force 1887–1900 stood at 121 in 1895 and at 166·6 in 1900. If we compare the growth of the labour force between 1865 and 1887 from Lenin's data with the above, we find that it took twelve years after 1887 for the labour force to grow by the same percentage as it did in twenty-one years after 1865. On the other hand, the growth of the labour force in the four decades after Emancipation was much slower than it had been between 1804 and 1860, for which we have year-to-year figures (from the Manufactures Board) for manufacturing only. During the pre-Emancipation period the labour force in manufacturing had grown sixfold in forty-nine years, as against just over twofold growth in the forty years following the Emancipation. Particularly striking was the growth of the pre-Emancipation labour force in the two industries which had been described as 'modern'. In cotton, the work force rose from 8,000 at the start of the century to 152,200 in 1860, and in sugar from only 108 workmen to 64,763, and all this in spite of the so-called 'institutional constraint' of serfdom which has been charged with the responsibility for the under-achievement of the Russian economy.[96]

For the period from 1900 to 1914 there are figures (as of the beginning of each year) of the labour force in manufacturing in the factories and works subject to factory inspection, as given in Table 57.[97] In mining and metallurgy (the latter exclusive of supplementary workers), the labour force increased from 506,500 in 1900 to 647,700 in 1913, an increase of 141,200 or 27·9 per cent.[98]

These figures indicate a much slower rate of growth of the labour force than was the case during the preceding thirteen years (1887–1900) – indeed, half the average annual rate, if the labour force in the works under the Administration of Mines is added. Most of the increase of the labour force occurred in the four years toward the end of the period, in connection with the pre-1914 boom after nearly a decade of slump and depression, prolonged on account of defeat in the war with Japan and the 1905 Revolution.

If we add the labour force in mining and metallurgy under the Administration of Mines and a few categories such as supplementary

Table 57. *Labour Force Subject to Factory Inspection, 1901–14*

	Workers (thousands)	Index (1901 = 100)
1901	1,692·3	100
1902	1,691·4	100
1903	1,640·4	96·9
1904	1,684·3	99·5
1905	1,660·7	98·1
1906	1,684·6	99·5
1907	1,718·1	101·5
1908	1,768·7	104·5
1909	1,762·2	104·1
1910	1,793·4	106·0
1911	1,922·6	113·6
1912	2,024·2	119·6
1913	2,120·8	125·3
1914	2,282·1	134·9

workers in mining and workers employed by the Ministries of War and Navy as recorded in the Industrial Census of 1908, we get the state of the labour force at the end of 1913 as shown in Table 58.[99] As neither factories belonging to municipal authorities (work force not known) nor repair workshops of the Ministry of Communications (85,400

Table 58. *Industrial Labour Force, 1900–13*

Factories and mines	Number of workers (thousands)		Increase 1900 to 1913	
	1900	1913	thousands	per cent
A. Subject to factory inspection	1,692·3	2,282·1	589·8	34·9
B. Subject to inspection of mines	506·5	647·7	141·2	27·9
Subtotal A + B	2,198·8	2,929·8	731·0	33·2
C. Supplementary workers in mining and metallurgy, not recorded in B (1911)	—	72·0	—	—
D. Work force in works under Naval authorities (1908)	—	22·4	—	—
E. Work force in works under War Ministry (1908)	—	37·3	—	—
Overall total	—	3,061·5	—	—

workers) have been included in the table, a round figure of 3·1 million workers in large-scale industry, as given by Rashin, is probably accurate.[100]

Over three million workers in large-scale factory industry is undoubtedly a respectable indicator of the industrial strength of a country at the beginning of the twentieth century. However, these three million represented only a minute fraction of the total labour force of the country. Relative to the total ascertainable number of wage-earners, factory and mine workers represented nearly 18 per cent. Nevertheless, a comparison of Table 58 with Table 53 above (tracing the evolution of the whole population of wage-earners: see p. 332) suggests the employment structure of a still relatively underdeveloped country.

Between 1860 and 1913 non-industrial wage-earners increased at a faster rate than industrial ones. The overall index for wage-earners in 1913 stood at 434·7 relative to 1860, but only at 367·4 for industrial wage-earners and at 482·0 for various categories of non-industrial labourers. If one excludes railway workers, who were a new category, the index stood at its highest for agricultural labourers (642·8) and for various categories of unskilled and casual labourers and for domestic and similar services (508·1). If only factory workers are considered, it will appear that for every man or woman at the factory bench there were six employed either in small-scale non-factory industry or in a variety of employments only marginally related to the modern industrial structure. Finally, looking only at the industrial labour force, one notes that the work force in factories and mines grew more slowly between 1860 and 1913 than did that of small industry, mainly kustar and remeslo. The weight of small industry (which was almost entirely in manufacturing) in the total labour force employed in manufacturing was about 56 per cent in 1913. If one adds the roughly 10 per cent of the workers employed by 1914 in units with fewer than fifty workers each, one arrives at an industrial structure in which about 66 per cent of the work force was in small units. This conclusion is at variance with the orthodox interpretation of Russia's industrial structure.[101]

The relatively more rapid growth of the non-industrial labour force as well as of smaller units is easily explicable by the fact that the growth of modern industry was only one, and not the most important, aspect of development in Russia. Another aspect – the most significant – was the erosion of the self-sufficiency of peasant households and the growth of a money economy both in terms of new areas of activity and in geographical areas hitherto barely drawn into the exchange circuit. If the industrial revolution in Western European countries occurred when the economies of these countries had already become significantly market economies, this was not the case in Russia, where the development of a market was part of the process of industrialization.

IV. *Changes in the Structure and Distribution of Labour*

A. DISTRIBUTION BY INDUSTRY

The story of the labour force in factories and mines between the Emancipation and 1914 as told here so far does not reveal the changes within the labour force, its distribution by industries and regions and its composition by age and sex. Changes in the labour forces of individual industries mirrored a variety of processes. The main ones were connected with expansion or contraction of production owing to cyclical factors, capital investment, and technological change.

In 1854, out of 9,751 firms in manufacturing with an estimated output value of 151·7 million roubles and a labour force of over 460,000, textiles accounted for about 22 per cent of the number of firms, for over half of the value of output, and for 57 per cent of the labour force. Cotton alone accounted for 8·5 per cent of the number of firms (indicating the relatively large size of individual firms), 27 per cent of the value of output, and 26 per cent of the labour force.[102] The metalworking industry accounted for 7 per cent of the number of firms, 9 per cent of the value of output, and 14 per cent of the labour force.[103]

Between 1865 and 1890 there was a net fall of 26 per cent in the labour force in woollen-cloth-manufacturing. In all other branches of manufacturing the labour force rose, highest of all in ceramics and cement (275 per cent), followed by the cotton and chemical industries (180 per cent). The boom of the late seventies undoubtedly contributed to an increase in the labour force. V. P. Bezobrazov reported sky-high prices for goods and labour and feverish attempts to expand production and recruit more labour. In the autumn of 1879 manufacturers retained summer rates for wages in order to attract labour. Especially pronounced was the boom in the cotton industry where all goods sold a year ahead. The factory founded by Zakhary Savvich Morozov in 1845 (Bogorodsk Glukhovsk Cotton and Mechanical Weaving Mill) had a labour force of 465 in 1856 and of 2,269 in 1871, and in 1884 it reached 8,500.[104]

In the woollen industry the fall in the labour force was accompanied by substantial increases in productivity, largely because of technical improvements and the taking-up of slack. In the cotton industry development took the form of substituting factory work for the putting-out system. Domestic workers, who in 1866 accounted for 70 per cent of employed in factories, were not more than 8 per cent in 1894–5. The most rapid transfer of domestic weavers to the factory occurred in the 1880s and early 1890s. Observers wrote that in Suzdal in Vladimir province in the 1850s the entire population – from the youngest to the oldest, man, woman, and child – were engaged in weaving. At the time of the investigation in 1899, not more than two to three thousand hand-loom weavers remained, of whom not more than a hundred were males. In some villages not a single hand loom was to be found. The main reason for the decline, investigators reported, was the inability to withstand the competition of the mechanical factory loom, not only in terms of price but also in quality. As late as 1869, local people reported, a hand-loom weaver could easily earn between 80 kopecks and 1 rouble for a piece of cloth; now (in 1899) 30 to 40 kopecks was the maximum he could command. Such a price was considered insufficient remuneration even for female labour in the winter season. It did not compensate the family for the inconvenience connected with weaving: the constant din of the loom, the crowding of space in the peasant hut, and the dampness collecting in the corner behind the loom.[105]

The historian of the famous Ivanovo district, the birthplace of serf–entrepreneurs, noted the rise in the factory work force and the drop in the number of out-workers in Ivanovo roughly between 1869 and 1895, parallel with an almost ninefold increase in the number of mechanical looms and a two-thirds decline in the number of hand looms. Nevertheless, in the woollen and linen industries the process of substitution of factory workers for home workers was far from complete even by 1914. Even in the cotton industry there were still in 1908 at least 21,000 out-workers. They formed only 4·2 per cent of the factory labour force in cotton, which was then over 492,000. However, these 21,000 did not exhaust the numbers of self-employed or those working in small workshops.[106]

It is not certain whether it was the competition of the mechanical loom which forced the hand-loom weaver out of the market, so much as the rising price of yarn on account of tariffs and the domination of the market by a few powerful mills. By withholding the yarn or by whipping up the price of it and refusing credit, they could lower the competitiveness of the self-employed weaver or of the small workshop and force them to work on their terms. This was still the case during the pre-1914 boom. Large firms with high fixed costs in the Vladimir province had found that they were being undercut by small rural workshops which, because of their lower wage costs and overheads, offered goods at prices 20 to 25 per cent lower than the factory prices. By withholding yarn or credit they forced these small producers to work for them.[107]

In metalworking and machine construction the factory work force began to grow significantly in the 1850s, especially in St Petersburg, in connection with the Crimean War, and continued in connection with railway construction and the re-equipment of military and similar establishments which used compulsory labour till the sixties. Between 1866 and 1897 the number of firms increased more than sixfold, while the value of output and of the labour force registered more than twentyfold and tenfold increases respectively. However, after 1878 tariffs had raised the price of raw materials – especially iron – and of machines, so that the productivity gain was much less than these figures seem to imply. Productivity gains had undoubtedly been made in this industry, dominated as it was by foreign capital, management, and technical personnel. So great was that domination that the names of owners or managers of machine plants in Russia look as if they all came straight from a London directory. Russian names were sprinkled thinly among the mainly Anglo-Saxon names of plant-owners, especially in St Petersburg and the Baltic area, but also in the Moscow region.[108]

In mining and metallurgy, including salt-mining, there were in 1865 around 200,000 workers. By 1887 the numbers had again risen, to nearly 400,000. In the iron industry alone, a threefold rise in output was connected with railway construction. The railway network grew sevenfold during this period. Between 1887 and 1900 the labour force in mining and metallurgy grew by 68 per cent, which was less than the average for industry. However, in South Russia, where several modern metallurgical works were founded by foreigners, the work force in metallurgy grew by a factor of twelve between 1882 and 1900. Especially rapid was the growth of the labour force in the three years after 1896, when it more than doubled. In the coal industry the labour force grew by a factor of 3·3, but in the Donetz Basin alone four and a half times, the rise being again most pronounced after 1896. In the oil industry the number of workers had increased from 1,300 in 1883 to 25,200 in 1891.[109]

As a result of these changes, the relative weight of South Russia in the work force in metallurgy rose from 12·6 per cent in 1887 to 26·7 in 1900, while the weight of the Urals, where the labour force in metallurgy grew only by 16·7 per cent, fell from nearly 60 per cent in 1887 to 41 per cent in 1900.[110]

Table 59 gives the structure of industry and employment in 1897 and 1908 in terms of the relative importance of different industries.[111] By 1914 the textile group was still in the lead. It accounted for 28 per cent of the value of gross output and 30 per cent of the labour force in industry. It showed remarkable steadiness in its relative position, notwithstanding the very considerable expansion of metallurgy in the 1890s. Food and connected industries accounted by 1914 for 22 per cent of the value of output and 13 per cent of the labour force employed.

Thus the two industries working for a mass consumer market and unconnected with government demand or subsidy made up half the gross value of industrial output and 43 per cent of the labour force.[112] Mining and metallurgy accounted only for under one-seventh of the value of gross output of industry, and for less still if the output of *small* industry (which was mainly in manufacturing) is added to the total. The relatively low weight of heavy industry in terms of output value was in contrast to the amount of capital sunk in this industry. Mining, metallurgy, metalworking, and machine construction had absorbed more than half of the total nominal capital invested in industrial joint-stock companies by 1914.[113]

Table 59. *Shares of Different Industries in Employment and Production, 1897 and 1908 (per cent)*

Group of industries	Number of workers		Gross value of production	
	1897	1908	1897	1908
Textiles	30·6	36·5	33·3	29·8
(Cotton)	—[a]	(22·7)	—[a]	(21·0)
Foodstuffs	12·2	17·1	22·8	33·9
Mining and metallurgy	25·9	24·5	13·9	16·4
Metal goods and machinery	10·2		10·9	
Timber-processing	4·1	4·1	3·6	3·7
Livestock products	3·1	2·8	4·7	3·5
Ceramics (including building materials)	6·8	n.a.	2·9	n.a.
Chemicals	1·7	2·9	2·1	3·8
Paper	2·2	3·9	1·6	2·8
Others	3·2	8·2	4·2	6·1
	100·0	100·0	100·0	100·0

[a] No separate figures for cotton in 1897 data.

Only in St Petersburg and in Riga was the structure of industry, as measured by factory employment, closer to that of a more mature economy. In St Petersburg the importance of textiles, which in 1852 still made up half of the factory labour force, fell to 35 per cent relatively in 1897, to sink finally to only one-fifth of the labour force by 1914, while the share of metalworking rose to 40 per cent. St Petersburg accounted for one-third of the country's output of machinery by value. Paper and printing and chemicals also made up a higher share of factory employment in St Petersburg than was the case in the country at large.[114] In Riga, which in 1913 employed nearly 88,000 workers, one-third were in metalworking, machine construction, and the electricity industry, 17·5 per cent in rubber goods, and 11·3 per cent in textiles.[115]

The growth of industries catering for the mass consumer market between 1900 and 1908 – a period of slump and depression – shows that the commonly accepted interpretation of the slump needs revising. It is usually represented as the result of the impoverishment of the peasantry, owing among other things to government policies designed to further the growth of heavy industries. In actual fact the depression affected mainly the metal industries. Their output value grew by only 14 per cent in eight years, as against an average of 50 per cent for the twelve main industries, 68 per cent for cotton fibres, and 77 per cent for food-stuffs.[116] On the eve of the war, machine-construction industries (military establishments included) accounted for around 14 per cent of the labour force and for just over 11 per cent of the gross output value of industry. Their output value grew by 40 per cent between 1900 and 1912, mainly because of the increased output of agricultural machinery and shipbuilding.[117]

B. GEOGRAPHICAL DISTRIBUTION OF THE LABOUR FORCE

In 1913 the labour force in manufacturing and mining employed in factories and mines in fifty provinces of European Russia was 2,557,400. Between 1861–70 and 1913 the changes shown in Table 60 took place in the numbers and regional distribution of employment.

Table 60. *Number of Workers in Manufacturing and Mining, 1861–1913*

Regions	1861–70 Thousands	%	1891–1900 Thousands	%	1913 Thousands	%
Moscow industrial	260·3	32·6	513·0	31·3	818·2	32·0
New Russia	23·1	2·9	150·6	9·2	391·6	15·3
Lakes (*Priozerny*)	63·8	8·0	149·3	9·1	305·2	12·0
Urals	121·3	15·2	285·8	17·5	261·5	10·2
Central agricultural	110·0	13·8	169·7	[10·4][a]	191·4	7·5
Baltic	20·0	2·5	55·6	3·4	143·9	5·6
Southwest	66·9	8·4	92·1	5·6	142·5	5·6
Little Russia	57·0	7·2	56·3	3·4	103·0	4·0
Lower Volga	41·0	5·2	78·2	4·8	89·0	3·5
Byelorussia	12·1	1·5	29·3	1·8	46·7	1·8
Others	22·2	2·8	56·7	3·5	64·4	2·5
Total	797·7	100·0	1,636·6	100·0	2,557·4	100·0

a 16·4 in the source (see note 118): presumably a printer's error.

Of the total labour force, 77 per cent was concentrated in the first five regions. Throughout the period, the Moscow industrial region retained its relative weight of nearly one-third of the total. Most striking was the growth of the labour force in New Russia, where in connection with the high rates of growth of mining and metallurgy (which absorbed over 79 per cent of the labour force of this region) the number of workers in the province of Ekaterinoslav alone grew from 5,200 in 1861–70 to 64,300 in 1891–1900 and to 211,000 in 1913, affording more than a fortyfold rise. In the Territory of the Don Army the labour force grew from 1,500 to 35,200 and to 91,700 respectively.[118]

Machine construction was concentrated, to the extent of over 75 per cent of the output value and of the labour force, in three areas – St Petersburg, the Central Industrial Region, and what is now the Ukraine. In the Empire at large (Poland included), the total number of workers in this industry was around 175,000, and the value of output just over 292 million roubles, in 1912. The central industrial region was leading, followed by St Petersburg and the Ukraine. However, the data for St Petersburg are probably an underestimate in that the labour force in military establishments was not taken into account.[119]

In contrast to all industry, in mining and metallurgy non-European areas made up 46 per cent of all firms, and accounted for 46·4 per cent of the value of output and for 27·3 per cent of the labour force employed.[120]

C. COMPOSITION OF THE LABOUR FORCE BY SEX AND AGE

The proportion of female labour within the factory labour force fluctuated at around not more than a quarter of the total, mainly because of the importance of migratory labour in the formation of the factory labour force and the more limited mobility of women. Only in certain trades – fibre-processing, clothing, tobacco, and rubber – was the proportion of women more pronounced. Another factor which helped to reduce the use of female labour was factory legislation, limiting night labour by women in 1885. This affected precisely those industries where the proportion of women workers was above average, e.g. fibre-processing, where night shifts were the practice. The greater share of mining and metallurgy in the labour force after 1890 and the low cost of male labour during cyclical downturns reduced the resort to female labour. Before 1905 greater use of women workers was made only during boom periods when labour was in short supply. The substitution of mechanical looms for hand looms in fibre-processing had the effect, from the 1880s, of increasing the share of women in fibre-processing. At various dates, female workers were represented in the labour force in manufacturing as follows:

1887	24·4 per cent, of which	38·3 per cent in fibre-processing
1894–5	25·8 per cent	40·1 per cent
1900	27·1 per cent	44·3 per cent
1914	31·1 per cent	56·2 per cent

In all factory industry – i.e., including mining and metallurgy – women were represented as follows:[121]

1897	15·0 per cent
1900	18·0 per cent
1914	26·7 per cent

After 1900, the number of women workers in firms subject to factory inspection grew as follows:[122]

1901	441,000	(index 100)
1905	457,900	(index 103·8)
1910	565,200	(index 128·1)
1914	723,900	(index 164·1)

Thus the number of women employed in manufacturing firms subject to inspection rose at a much higher rate than the labour force as a whole. By 1913 the share of women in manufacturing employment was 31·1 per cent. This share falls to 26·7 per cent if establishments subject to mining inspection are added.[123] In the latter, women made up only 3·8 per cent of the labour force. Nevertheless, women were now employed in a wider range of industries, i.e. sugar, tobacco, matches, glass, cement, brickyards, and the metal trades. In the industries connected with metal wares, specifically the making of tools and machines, the share of women in employment rose from 2·9 in 1901 to 5·9 per cent in 1913 – in absolute numbers, from 7,000 to nearly 23,000. In Ekaterinoslav, where the employment of women rose by 18 per cent, women workers were engaged in the making of hinges, loops, spikes, wire sieves, and bolts.[124]

Above all, the number of women continued to grow in fibre-processing industries, where factory inspectors reported that retired or fired men were being replaced by women. In 1907, for example, the number of male workers rose by only 0·85 per cent but that of women by 9·25 per cent. Most pronounced was the substitution of female for male labour in cotton-weaving. Between 1902 and 1914 the number of women in the cotton industry rose from 195,000 to just over 318,000 – an increase of 63·4 per cent – and as a proportion of the total from 47·8 to 56·2 per cent.[125]

Women workers had always been valued by employers on account of their 'moral qualities': 'greater application, concentration, and restraint (do not drink or smoke)'; they were valued as being 'more submissive and less demanding as regards pay'. A German observer noted that at first more intensive use of female labour was made in 1904 when some men were called up for the Russo-Japanese War and economic activity increased. When the Revolutionary events came, it was discovered that women were much less given to disturbances and agitation.[126]

After 1905, therefore, preference for a more 'pacific' labour force became a very pronounced feature of employment policy, a feature which even determined choice of plant location. The increased cost of labour as a result of the Revolution, especially the reduction of the length of the working day and the pressure for higher wages and other concessions to the newly authorized trade unions, combined with the downturn in economic activity which followed the Russo-Japanese War and the Revolution, made it more than ever necessary for employers to try to cut labour costs by employing women, who were much cheaper and less militant. This was made easier by the fact that buoyant peasant demand owing to excellent harvests ensured that textile industries, unlike the others, were not thrown into depression. Expansion of the labour force in these industries could only proceed by engaging women.

By 1913 there were about 800,000 women workers in factory industry. We possess no figures for the proportion of female labour in the overall labour force of the country by 1913. In peasant farms, as is known, the proportion of women undoubtedly exceeded that of males, especially if all-year-round averages are taken into account. Women were also employed in domestic, hotel, and restaurant service in larger proportions than was the case in factory industry. In the 1897 population census, the relative proportion of women to total wage-earners was just under 31 per cent, which was more than double their relative weight in manufacturing and mining. Most female workers were in domestic service (47·3 per cent) and in hired agricultural work (nearly 27 per cent).[127]

In the two big cities the relative proportion of women workers did not grow substantially – in St Petersburg only from 19 per cent in 1881 to 20·3 per cent in 1910 – a fact which reflects the share in the labour force of immigrant male workers without families. In Moscow the proportion of women in wage employment grew only from 17·3 in 1882 to 19·2 in 1902 and to 21·6 per cent in 1912. In railway transport the percentage of women employed was under 9 in 1913, and remained more or less stationary relative to the total between 1904 to 1914 though absolutely the number grew from 31,000 to 39,000.[128]

Among agricultural labourers young women predominated, probably indicating the employment of unmarried daughters of farmers. In 1898 over 80 per cent of all women agricultural workers in the Kherson province were under twenty-five years of age; of these, 74 per cent were aged between sixteen and twenty-five. Female labour was substituted for male labour because of its relative cheapness and greater submissiveness. But the most important inducement for the increased use of female labour in the steppe areas of Southern Russia was the growing resort to agricultural machinery, which pushed out or reduced the employment of adult male workers. Particularly in threshing, adult male labour became wholly redundant. A South Russian estate-owner explained that before machines began to be used the contingent of hired workers for the season consisted entirely of men, so-called 'full workers'. 'Now of every thirty fixed-term workers whom we always hire for the period from 9 May to 1 October, only four are full workers, while the rest ... are only half workers, women and boys. With this number of workers we accomplish all the summer work, except the hay-cutting.' The workers themselves complained that 'before the introduction of reapers, we scythe-men were the best-paid workers; now we cannot even get work for half the previous rates. If only these harvesting machines had never been invented! ... They are to blame that people die of hunger.'[129]

There was undoubtedly some exaggeration in these laments about the squeezing-out of male labour by machinery. Although the use of machines increased very substantially, especially with the improvement in grain prices after 1900, followed by a series of good harvests and government assistance after 1906, on the whole mechanization was not yet far advanced in Russia relative to the area under plough.

Female labour was also more frequently employed in kustar industry than in factories. The Factory Inspectorate had no jurisdiction over kustar workshops, and consequently night hours or much longer hours in general could be worked. However, more important probably was the greater flexibility which kustar work afforded, its seasonal character, and the possibility it gave to the female of working side by side with her children, to whom factory legislation also did not apply. In Vladimir province in 1897–1900, the percentage of women among the 49,000 kustar workers investigated was 45 per cent, which was much higher than for factories in the region. In the processing of fibres the proportion of women among kustar workers was nearly 70 per cent.

More interesting, in that it throws some light on the age structure of the labour force in factory industry and among kustars, is the much higher share of the lowest and highest age groups among kustar workers. Thus, the large-scale investigation of household in Moscow province during 1898–1900 had disclosed that 75 to 81 per cent of women factory workers were in the age groups from eighteen to forty-five, as against only 65 to 66 per cent among kustar women. The age group up to seventeen represented only 15 to 17 per cent of the factory labour force, as against 19 to 23 per cent in kustar industry. Finally, groups aged above forty-five were represented in the factory labour force by only 4·5 to 8 per cent of the total, as against 11 to 16 per cent of the total among kustar women.[130]

These differences, though less sharply emphasized, apply also to male workers in both types of industry and may indicate another reason for both the attraction and the relative profitability of kustar industry.

By comparison, the employment of child labour became an issue in the first half of the nineteenth century in connection with 'bonded' workers handed over to factories by estate-owners or communal authorities to work off their rents or debts. Children constituted a high proportion of such workers. An inquiry into the conditions of factory industry in Moscow province, prompted by disturbances at Voznessensk in 1844, revealed the employment of 3,000 child labourers, most of them bonded, of whom 1,000 did night work. The inquiry led to the law of 7 August 1845 prohibiting night labour, defined as between midnight and 6 a.m., for children under the age of twelve. However, the law was never incorporated in the Law Code, and child labour continued unregulated.[131]

Nevertheless the question of child labour, like that of night labour, was almost continuously on the agenda. It was prominent in the discussions of various commissions in the 1860s and 1870s, partly for humanitarian considerations, partly in connection with the educational reforms then in progress, and partly under the influence of foreign legislation. No legislation regulating child labour was implemented before the 1880s because the question was tied up with those of night labour in general, the length of the working day, and the degree of permissible government intervention in the relations between employers and labour.[132]

The employment of children in Russian factory industry began to be significantly affected by the factory legislation of June 1882, 1884, and 1885, which prohibited work in factories for children under twelve altogether; limited the working day of children aged between twelve and fifteen to eight hours, of which not more than four could be without a break; prohibited night work for children aged twelve to fifteen from 9 p.m. to 5 a.m., and night work for adolescents aged fifteen to seventeen in the cotton, woollen, and linen industries.[133]

However, even before 1885 child labour did not constitute a significant element in the employment structure. In 1882–3 the under-twelves made up not more than 1·3 per cent of the labour force. Those aged over twelve represented 9·17 per cent of the labour force of over 540,000 workers in the 3,316 firms investigated. In some industries such as printing and allied trades, children represented nearly 18 per cent of the labour force, and in the processing of fibres about 13 per cent. The use of child labour was most widespread in match factories, in glass and crystal factories, and in wool-spinning.[134]

The consequence of the laws relating to child labour was mass release by employers not only of children under twelve but also of those under fifteen years of age. The reasons were manifold. Many employers did not fully understand the law and in any case distrusted and wished to avoid the supervision involved. Employers feared that inspectors would be 'giving workers ideas' and would see discontent where none existed. Many were worried about the law's provision concerning the employer's responsibility for schooling for young workers. Especially perturbed were small factory-owners in rural areas where there were no council or church schools in the vicinity, and where the employer feared that the law would require him to set up a school. Most importantly, however, the law coincided with a downturn in economic activity, and enough adult labour was available at low rates. Dr Peskov, the factory inspector of the Vladimir district, found that the number of youths under fifteen in the forty factories he visited fell from 4,595 in 1883 to 1,371 in 1885. Simultaneously, however, the total number of workers fell by 2,302.[135]

In 1894–5 the proportion of juveniles aged twelve to fifteen was only 1·87 per cent, and of those aged fifteen to seventeen less than 9 per cent – a total of just over 10 per cent in a labour force of over one million. The highest percentage relative to the total labour force was in the paper industry, followed by fibre-processing and minerals, at 17·4, 17·1, and 15 per cent respectively. Nearly one-half of all workers under eighteen were employed in the textile industry.[136]

After 1900 the number of adolescent workers in factories subject to inspection fluctuated around 180,000, and only after 1910, in connection with the pre-1914 boom, was there a fairly steep increase in numbers. At this time, the number of adolescents in the labour force rose to 148·1 per cent of the 1901 figure, which is a higher growth rate than for the total labour force but less than the rate for women workers.[137]

In 1913 the proportion of those under eighteen in plants subject to factory inspection was 11·1 per cent; with mining and metallurgy added, the proportion of adolescents falls to 10·4 per cent of the total. In absolute numbers there were 273,000 young workers of whom 39 per cent were girls – the latter a percentage which exceeded that of women workers in the total force. The proportion of young girls to all adolescent labourers was about 60 per cent in textiles and the chemical industry.[138]

Official data may have somewhat underestimated the number of juveniles in employment. This was certainly the case in small factories; children were allegedly being hidden whenever the inspector made an appearance. Labour inspectors and foreign observers claimed that many workers concealed their real age. An elder of a rural commune would usually put on the family passport the age given by the parents. This age would be entered by the employer without further checking even though the youngster before him could not possibly be the age he claimed to be. Because of many frauds of this kind, inspectors began to demand extracts from parish registers. Parish priests found in these certificates a good source of income and pitched their fees high. Certificates belonging to older sisters or brothers or even of strangers were produced, and though inspectors had their doubts about the true age of the young workers, there was not much they could do about it. Nevertheless, it is not likely that the number of such workers was very large.[139]

The number of young workers was more significant in the kustar industries and in small-scale industry in general. The descriptions of the horrors of child labour usually referred to small factories not subject to inspection, where whole families were usually working day and night, especially before the great holidays. Such exhausting work was possible because after a few months of intensive work they could 'sleep it off' on the proverbial Russian stove.[140]

The relatively limited use of child labour must be accounted for by the high proportion of immigrant workers without families; the availability of cheap adult labour for jobs done elsewhere by children; the relative underdevelopment of sophisticated industries in which long apprenticeship was needed; and the prevalence of jobs requiring physical strength and endurance.

Though child labour was never much above 10 per cent of the labour force, there is evidence of a very early starting age in industry. Most of this evidence relates to Moscow and Vladimir provinces and mainly to the textile industry. This usually indicates not the factory but the kustar workshop, which often acted as a preparatory school for the factory labour force.[141]

V. Rural Origins and Affiliations

A. URBAN IMMIGRATION FROM VILLAGES

The foregoing story of Russian industrial labour since Peter the Great has so far been concerned with the sheer dimensions of the process, the stages through which it passed, and the changes in geographical and industrial distribution. But this story will also account for its predominantly – almost exclusively – rural origins and for the persistency of its peasant characteristics and of its links with village society. These peasant origins and rural links were so characteristic a feature of the Russian labour force that they will require looking into more closely.

Russia's economy being what it was, it is not surprising that the village should have provided by far the most important source of industrial labour. In considering the possible sources of labour supply to industry it is necessary to keep in mind the relative underdevelopment of city life at the start of modern industrial development, and hence the very limited contribution which the urban population could make to it in numbers or above all in skills, especially in view of the very low standing of urban craftsmanship. Therefore only the village could serve as the major reservoir of labour for factory industry. Within the village, kustar workers, both those working independently and those involved in the putting-out system or as hired hands in rural workshops, were a major source of labour supply, with some skills and occasionally with some discipline.

Above all it must be borne in mind that the time-span over which the labour force could develop was relatively short. Industrial growth on any appreciable scale was a matter of not more than three decades, which was not more than a life-span of one generation. Consequently it would not be reasonable to expect that within so short a time there could have developed a class of industrial workers with a working-class ancestry, specialized skill, and a mentality all its own.

Even though eventually in a few large industrial centres – especially in the cities of St Petersburg, partly in Moscow, and even more in Łódź, Piotrkow, and Sosnowice of the Kingdom of Poland, or in Riga – a core of factory workers made its appearance whose life-style and expectations were entirely shaped by the factory, they were constantly swamped by masses of new arrivals from the countryside as industry expanded.

Moreover, even though the evidence is strong that a proportion of workers with a fairly long record of factory work had made its appearance by around 1900, and though there were many workers whose parents were also workers, there is still much uncertainty as to the extent to which a typical Russian worker actually ended his life in the working-class environment or how often his son started his life there. There is evidence (as will be shown) that workers, even of the most industrialized cities, resumed their life in the village, often from the age of forty and usually by the age of fifty, and that many of their offspring tended to spend their childhood, usually up to the age of fifteen, in the village, usually with their paternal grandparents, even when they happened to be born in factory maternity wards, and even though their mothers might have continued working in the factory.

B. VILLAGE TIES

Although a labour force of sorts with continuous commitment to factory employment was taking shape, it was not clearly divorced from village life. There is no certainty about where the balance of its commitment lay, on the side of industry and the factory or on that of agriculture and the village. Furthermore, by a strange paradox, precisely in those regions where labour historians can provide evidence for stability of industrial employment and for the hereditary nature of the labour force, the rural character of industry and its proximity to and connection with the village were much more to the fore. The Ural worker who came from a long line of industrial workers was still a countryman with his horse and his piece of meadow, who took a break from work during the haymaking season. Similarly, in the Central Industrial Region, in the provinces of Vladimir, Kostroma, and even Moscow, the rural atmosphere of the industrial settlements was unmistakable despite the smoking chimneys

The worker in the city, even though he might be a new arrival, and though he still had a farm which was being worked by his family, nevertheless came into a new environment which required much more drastic adjustment than was the case elsewhere. On the other hand, the tendency of factory workers to congregate in special suburbs, and the constant influx of villagers, had the effect of imposing upon the city a distinctly non-urban character.

Most of the evidence from urban censuses, from the population census of 1897, and from the studies of individual plants points to the overwhelming weight of the peasant element – usually an immigrant peasant element – in the urban population in general and in the labouring population in particular. In 1869 in St Petersburg 31 per cent of the population were classed as peasants. In six years the number of peasants increased by nearly 30 per cent. In 1881 in St Petersburg the proportion of mostly peasant immigrants was over 70 per cent. The proportion of those born outside the city continued to be high in subsequent censuses – over 68 per cent in 1890 and 1900 and just under 68 per cent in 1910.[142] In Moscow in 1882, 74 per cent of the population was born outside the city. Nearly one-fifth had lived there only one year at the time of the census; only about a third had arrived there within five years of the 1882 census. In 1902 the proportion of those born outside the city was still 72·3 per cent, and in 1912 it was 68 per cent. Nearly two-thirds of all the newcomers in Moscow were classed as peasants, while the proportion of peasants born in the city grew from 7·4 per cent in 1902 to only 10·1 per cent in 1912.[143]

Given the constant influx of rural immigrants and the negative natural

growth till the 1880s, the proportion of those who had lived in the city
for less than one year increased from 14·3 per cent in 1890 to 15·1 in
1910, while the proportion of those who had lived longer than ten years
fell from 43 to 35 per cent. Nevertheless, there were now in the main
cities substantial numbers of peasants who had lived there more than
five years; and as many as 142,000 peasants in St Petersburg and more
than 95,000 in Moscow by 1910 and 1902 respectively had lived in the
city for more than twenty years.[144] In other industrial cities the situation
was identical. The 1903 Baku census recorded only 5 per cent of workers
in the oil industry as having been born in the Baku factory district. In
Kharkov, Baku, and Riga in 1912 more than two-thirds of residents
were born in rural areas.

Odessa, one of the fastest-growing cities of Russia, had a different
structure. Only 54 per cent of its inhabitants were of rural birth. However, Odessa was not an industrial centre but had large contingents of
craftsmen and wage-earners in service industries, who tended to settle
with their families. The large Jewish element probably also contributed
to the different pattern in Odessa.[145]

The high proportion of immigrants of working age in the cities was
reflected in the age structure. For every thousand persons in Moscow,
there were only 124 aged ten and under, 221 aged from eleven to
twenty, and as many as 263 aged from twenty-one to thirty. Furthermore, the age groups from fifteen to fifty were much better-represented
than were those under fifteen and over fifty. The age distribution (in
persons per thousand) in European cities compared with Moscow and
St Petersburg emphasizes this feature of Russia's industrial cities, as
follows:[146]

	Per thousand persons			
Age group	Central Europe	Berlin	Moscow	St Petersburg
0–15	329	279	221	217
16–30	253	318	387	396
31–50	248	277	286	282
51 and over	170	125	115	104

This age structure finds confirmation in the 1897 population census
and in all available studies relating to individual industries or plants.
According to the 1897 population census, the proportion of factory
workers in the under-fifteen age group was only 3·9 per cent; nearly
77 per cent were in the age group fifteen to thirty-nine, and 55 per cent
were aged between twenty and thirty-nine. Only 19·3 per cent were
over forty years old.[147]

In Moscow in 1902, only 0·9 per cent were under fifteen, 20 per cent under twenty, 60 per cent in the age group twenty to thirty-nine, 19 per cent over forty, and only five per cent were over fifty.[148]

In the Zindel model textile mill, out of a labour force of nearly 1,600 in the late 1890s only 3·4 per cent of the workers were over fifty, only 13 per cent were over forty, and 71 per cent were under thirty. Over 87 per cent of the labour force were in the age group sixteen to forty. In Sormovo, a metal-goods and machine-working plant on the Volga, out of a labour force of nearly 6,000 in 1896, 78 per cent were in the age group sixteen to thirty-five, and two-thirds were aged between twenty-one and thirty-five. Here many of the factory shops required workers of considerable physical strength – hence the emphasis on the younger age groups. This was also reflected in the age composition of Krivoy Rog iron-ore miners, where 74 per cent of the labour force were in the age group twenty-one to thirty, and nearly 90 per cent in the group eighteen to thirty. Only 11 per cent were in age groups over thirty.[149]

The data for thirteen industries in St Petersburg in 1900 conform to the general pattern, i.e. a thick wedge of around 60 per cent in the middle for the age groups between twenty and forty, around 20–25 per cent in age groups under twenty, and between 7·6 and 16 per cent for age groups over forty. The St Petersburg data are significant in that they conform to pattern even in those trades where one would have expected higher percentages in the older age groups, because of the more specialized and physically less strenuous nature of the work. Similarly, in printing in Moscow, investigated in 1907, the same pattern is discernible though this was an industry where one would also have expected more importance attached to the older age groups. Only one-eighth of the labour force investigated were over forty, 78·3 per cent were under thirty years old, and only 2·7 per cent were over fifty.[150]

The investigator of the Zindel plant, P. M. Shostakov, believed that the age structure of the labour force reflected its persistent connection with the village and farming. It reflected the tendency of young members of peasant families to enter employment early and of workers over thirty-five or forty to return to the village, upon the death or retirement through old age or illness of the head of the household, to take his place. This conclusion finds confirmation in the evidence relating to Moscow printers, where in some specializations the proportion of workers of urban origin was higher than elsewhere. 12,100 workers in printing, binding, etc. investigated in the Moscow census of 1902 were of urban origin, but among typesetters the proportion was 65 per cent. While among the workers of rural origin the proportion of those aged forty and over was only 10 per cent, it was nearly 18 per cent among those of urban birth. Similarly, the proportion of younger workers under twenty-one years of age was lower among the printers of urban origin, i.e. 8 per cent only, as against 13 per cent for those who hailed from the villages.[151]

The emphasis on the younger and young–middle age groups was in part a reflection of low life expectancy and the early ageing of Russian workers. However, the structure of the labour force in the countryside, or among other wage-earning occupations or among kustars, does not exhibit the same tapering-off in higher age groups. A comparison of the age structure of the labour force at the Glukhovsk factory, in the Bogo-rodsk district of the Moscow province, with the structure of the population of the district as a whole shows almost identical groupings for ages from nine to forty. For ages above forty, the proportions were 14·5 per cent for workers and 25·3 per cent for the population of the district. In the over-fifty group, the percentages were 5·5 for workers and 15·2 per cent for the population.[152]

The main factor behind the relatively small numbers in the older age groups was the tendency of industrial workers to retire to their native villages in later life. However, this early retirement was not motivated solely by the call of the farm. Employers' preference for particular age groups as specified in contracts, with factory agents commissioned to recruit workers, undoubtedly played a part.

Another factor in early retirement was the very low wage of workers in older age groups. This is partly accounted for by the high proportion of lower-paid workers, such as store-keepers and guards, and of semi-invalids or retired soldiers among the older age groups. Finally, literacy levels among older workers were much lower than the average. The correlation between literacy and wages was not always a close one, since in some trades physical strength was more important than literacy in determining wage levels, while in others experience and length of stay on the same job were worth more to the employer than literacy. But by and large, most studies show a high correlation between literacy and wages and, presumably, productivity.

Early retirement to the village was also due to the fact that by and large the farm or the house in the village was the only form of security that was available to the old, sick, and infirm. The Act of 1903 provided only for injury sustained directly at the job, and only if it could be proved that it was not due to the negligence of the worker. The largest firms and state-owned enterprises made quite enlightened provision for injury and illness, but even the best preferred to avoid responsibility for older workers. The tendency was to give the injured a lump sum and send him off to the village, a procedure which was also applied to workers who were considered trouble-makers. Workers themselves tended to opt for a lump sum as compensation. In spite of hard work and conditions of life in the factories, most of returning workers were sound in body and mind and were able to resume their places on the family farm while younger members of the family took their places in the factory.[153]

The influx of males of working age from the countryside was reflected not only in the age structure of the workers but also in their sex structure as well as their marital status, i.e. the proportion of men with families as seen in the urban censuses. In 1869 in St Petersburg there were 830 women to a thousand men in the population at large. Among peasants, there were 454 women to each thousand men; and among peasants following industrial employment in the two most industrialized quarters of the city, the ratio of women to men was as low as 250 per thousand. In the artisan occupational group there was practically a perfect balance between the sexes, while in all other classes (except for the military) the balance tipped in favour of women.[154]

Similarly, in Moscow in 1882 there were only 740 women to every thousand men. Relating sex and age structure shows that the prevalence of men started just above the age of ten and persisted until fifty, and the imbalance was greatest between twenty and twenty-five, at which ages there were almost twice as many men as women. This reflected the immigration of young male members of peasant families for industrial or similar work. In the age group fifty to fifty-five, the sexes were in balance; in the age groups over fifty-five women exceeded men in number, probably because of greater longevity and because of the practice among male workers of peasant origin of returning to the villages.

If from the data of the 1882 Moscow census we exclude the group classed as peasants the balance tips in the opposite direction, there being 1,040 women to a thousand men. If we take peasants separately, we arrive at a ratio of 480 women to a thousand men. If we look at the classification by occupation, we find that in the group described as 'industrial wage-earners' there were only 160 women to a thousand men. This conforms to the sex structure of the factory labour force in the Empire in the 1897 census, where the proportion of women workers was only 150 per thousand men.[155]

The high proportion of males among workers of relatively recent peasant origin clearly reflects the large numbers of workers living away from their families. The 1897 population census indicated that nearly 60 per cent of all wage-earners in the Empire were without families, the proportion for St Petersburg being as high as 86·5 per cent. The proportion of members of families (i.e. *not* heads of households) living with their families was only 25 per cent for the Empire and only 6·8 per cent for St Petersburg. Of the married wage-earners, only 48 per cent lived with their families in the country at large, as against only 18·8 per cent in St Petersburg. Finally, only 24·9 per cent of heads of families lived with their families (8·2 per cent in St Petersburg).[156]

The data for the decade or so before 1914 are not as explicit as those for the preceding period. An investigation among metalworkers in St Petersburg in 1908 and 1909 still showed a very high proportion of workers living singly – in age groups in which it was normal for Russians to be married – as well as a very low number of dependants. In the oil industry in Baku in 1911, out of the 32,600 all-year-round workers and employees over 79 per cent were in Baku without families. Since among the employee group those without families accounted only for 23 per cent, the weight of workers without families must have been higher than 79 per cent. Nevertheless, this denoted some progress compared with 1903. The urban census of that year in the city of Baku and its suburbs recorded only 9·4 per cent of all workers in oil extraction whose families lived in Baku. In 1911 the proportion was 20·4 per cent. The proportion of refinery workers living with their families rose from 33·5 to 49 per cent.[157]

The prevalence of workers without families was in some part accounted for by the housing conditions in towns and industrial settlements. The picture of factory barracks or corners in cellars and attics, with their rows of wooden cots in which single workers were crowded, sometimes using the sleeping accommodation in turn, is too well-worn to dwell on here. But it confirms that the worker of peasant origin did not often live with his family. Employers in the best firms began to provide family accommodation. It was still in barracks but was provided with partitions for families or with special rooms for three to four families together. There was still no room for children or for separate cooking arrangements, though the most enlightened employers were providing crèches, schools, and maternity homes. In many of the family barrack rooms Schultze-Gaevernitz found cradles suspended from ceilings and children playing in the corridors.[158]

The most satisfactory means of enabling the worker's family to live together was the construction of special housing for families. This problem was solved successfully, at least for a proportion of workers, in the mining and metallurgical industries of South Russia, where employers provided housing for clerical and technical staff first and for workers later. The effect was to create in a relatively short time a reliable labour force in what had been a steppe.[159]

Many firms in Central Russia also provided special accommodation. In St Petersburg the St Galli firm had model accommodation for its 600 workers. In 1914, the British firm of Vickers was planning a workers' colony with family houses, gardens, and shops in Tsaritsyn on the Volga. Nevertheless, in most cases it was still barrack accommodation, which gave industrial areas the appearance of an army camp. In areas such as Baku and especially on the mining sites in Eastern Siberia very primitive forms of housing for workers persisted.[160]

C. RURAL CONNECTIONS OF FACTORY WORKERS

Distribution by age, sex, and family status were all indirect indications of the recent peasant origin of industrial labour. There is, however, much direct evidence of its peasant derivation. A study of one textile plant, covering the period from 1881 to 1917, showed that in the initial phase during 1881–2 less than 60 per cent of the labour force were peasants by origin, 26·2 per cent being burghers (meshchane). In 1889–90 the weight of peasants in the labour force had grown to 80 per cent. In 1914, on the eve of the war, peasants made up 93·4 per cent of the labour force. The total labour force had grown in the meantime by a factor of 8·5, but the urban element by not more than a factor of 2. The number of workers with a work record of ten years and more was only 9·5 per cent in 1900. On the other hand, the percentage of workers with a work record of over five years was nearly 28 per cent in 1905 and grew to 48 per cent in 1913.[161]

However, the authors of a family history of the owners of this firm, published in 1915, believed that about half the workers were only nominally connected with the village by way of the passport which they continued to order from the rural communal authorities. This highlights an important point, namely the tendency of the authorities to classify the population by juridical categories or estates (soslov'ye), which could give a misleading idea as to the real social or occupational position, which coincided less and less with juridical status – and not only where peasants were concerned.[162]

More important is the fact that factory workers referred to themselves as peasants. Though the late L. M. Ivanov may be right that they did so by force of habit, one cannot help wondering whether this 'weight of tradition' (to use Ivanov's own words) was not also a reflection of the worker's self-identification, and even a pointer to the degree of prestige attached to the respective statuses of peasant or worker.[163]

In the Zindel textile mill in 1896, less than 6 per cent of the labour force were not classed as peasants. Only 9 per cent of all peasant workers did not own an allotment; most of them were former household serfs, retired soldiers, and the like, who did not receive land upon emancipation. Half of those who had no allotment, had a house and garden plot in the village, so that in the final count only about 5 per cent had no property connection with the village (as far as is known, for the investigator had no information about land acquired by purchase).

Only 0·5 per cent of the workers with allotments on the Zindel plant had given up their holdings altogether, and 14 per cent let theirs to tenants. About 78 per cent cultivated their land with the help of their families, and over 7 per cent even hired workers to do it for them. This confirms the observations made by *zemstvo* officials that they had not come across peasants who had found their farms a burden which they would have been glad to shed. In the Zindel plant the more than 82 per cent of the workers were not just 'proletarians with allotments', as Lenin would have it: they did not just *reluctantly own* land but *worked* it, despite the fact that more than half of the worker–owners had fathers who were factory workers.[164]

In as urban an industry as printing, in Moscow in 1907, 65 per cent of the labour force was rural by birth. About half of all the workers still maintained their farms in operation. More than half of those of peasant birth did not have their families with them, and nearly 90 per cent of these sent money to the village – nearly 100 roubles each, which represented about 23 per cent of their earnings. Over one-sixth still owned land and a house or only a house and a garden plot, though their immediate families no longer lived in the village. However, nearly one-third of these also sent money to their relatives in the village.[165]

The findings for St Petersburg printers for the same year indicate a less close but nevertheless quite substantial connection with the village, if not always with farming. More than half still maintained ties with the village, but only one-fifth operated their farms with the help of their families; another one-fifth still owned land and a house, and 14 per cent still sent money to their relatives in the village, though they no longer had land there.[166]

On the other hand, only 12·6 per cent of the workers of the Zindel plant left the factory for farm work in the summer. In the country at large by 1900, counting only firms with over fifty workers, those leaving for farm work represented not more than 9 per cent of the work force. The percentage of those leaving was as low as 3 per cent in the metal industries and as high as 24 per cent in the mineral-processing industries. In the largest cotton industry it was only 5 per cent.[167]

These figures indicate that by the end of the century in the larger plants and in the more specialized and technologically advanced trades an all-year-round labour force had come into existence. However, given the weight of smaller plants in the industrial structure, and considering the industrial labour force as a whole, the worker was still – as the Soviet historian Pankratova assessed him to be by 1905 – at a stage of transition between peasant and worker. Theodore H. von Laue expressed it more graphically: the Russian factory worker around 1900 was a peasant caught midway between the factory and the field.[168] From the point of view of his self-identification he was probably closer to the field. For more than half the labour force, the ties with the village were not only juridical tie or ties of ownership but those of dependence on the farm, in the last resort, for survival. The factory was for the 'meantime', it meant 'plying trades on the side', and even when factory work turned out much more than that, the intention was that it should be no more, and subjectively it was no more.[169]

D. RURAL TIES IN THE TWENTIETH CENTURY

This was the situation around 1900. How did it change between 1900 and 1914? Traditionally 1905–6 is considered a demarcation line between two stages, first because in 1905 the proletariat appeared as a political force, and secondly because Stolypin's reform cut what was considered to be an imposed connection between worker and village by dissolving the compulsory commune and by making peasant allotment land marketable.

This is not the place to consider the political aspect of Stolypin's reform, but as regards its effects on the ties with the village and farming the evidence is, to say the least, inconclusive. The interval between 1906 and the outbreak of the war was too short for the effects to make themselves obvious. A. I. Tyumenev, who studied the records of the Ministry of the Interior, noted that among peasants selling land after 1906 there were to be found workers in the provinces nearest to the industrialized centres. This makes sense and was to be expected. There were undoubtedly many whose connection with the village was nominal; and where land values were good, as they undoubtedly were in the areas referred to by Tyumenev, it made good economic sense for these men to try and sell.[170]

L. M. Ivanov, who maintained that the rural connections and antecedents of the Russian factory worker had been overplayed, used a 1929 Soviet survey which applied to less than 10 per cent of the pre-1914 labour force to show that before 1905 58 per cent of factory workers had come from working-class families, i.e. were at least second-generation workers. Only 37 per cent had come from peasant families. During the period 1906–13 the proportion of workers of working-class descent grew to 59 per cent, and the percentage of workers of peasant descent fell to 35·4 per cent.[171] Thus according to this survey there was no indication of a dramatic change after 1905. However, not only is the survey based on a sample, but it was conducted at a sensitive moment politically, at a time when a peasant with a reasonably viable farm was branded as *kulak* and every kustar as a capitalist. It is unlikely, therefore, that workers would have given truthful answers to questions about the size of their pre-Revolutionary farm economy or parental status.

A census carried out by the Soviet government in 1918, which related to fewer than a million workers and did not include the Ukraine and the Urals, indicated that nearly one-third of the total recorded owned land before the Revolution and that over one-fifth possessed a working farm run with the help of the family. As the census took place in the autumn, workers with closer rural connections were likely to have left the factories and cities. Moreover, by then War Communism was in full swing, the cities were starving, and everyone who could left for the country. Therefore, the proportion of those with land and farms in the census is beyond doubt an underestimate.[172]

Nevertheless, though no dramatic changes in the origins and nature of the labour force appear to have occurred as a result of Stolypin's reforms, the period 1900–13 saw important changes. The slump at the turn of the century and the long depression which followed had the effect of stabilizing the labour force. The weight of new recruits from the villages had somewhat lessened, at least before 1910; the precariousness of industrial employment imposed a certain discipline and circumspection upon those for whom factory employment had become a vital source of livelihood, while the influx of casual workers was checked by the improvement in the countryside owing to better harvests, improved terms of trade, and the 'face to the village' policy of the government. There was also a much more sober assessment on the part of employers of the potentialities of the Russian worker and of the kind of management needed to use him to best advantage.

Potentially, a comprehensive scheme of social security would have done most to reduce the worker's dependence on his rural connections. However, although the 1912 Social Insurance Act provided for more comprehensive coverage for workers in all firms subject to factory inspection as from 1 January 1913, it did not go far enough. It replaced employers' individual responsibility for accident insurance by a collective liability through their organization of insurance associations. This was a step forward. In the past, compensation or pension had not always been recoverable at law, and individual firms – not being insured against claims themselves – had every incentive to prolong adjudication proceedings. The worker therefore was inclined to accept anything that was offered to him, or else he gave up and departed for the village.[173]

The Medical Act of the same year, providing for sick funds (*bol'nichnyye kassy*), is considered by some to be a step backwards from previous legislation and a dilution of the services provided. However, the

law had significant bearing on future prospects in that it extended
health-service provisions to firms which would not offer them before
and, on the whole, placed the system on a less discretionary basis. But
there was as yet no provision for permanent disability not due to injury
at work and no obligatory pension scheme for men in old age or for
dependants. The existing state and private pension schemes probably
covered not more than one-third of the labour force. For this reason the
worker was likely to continue to depend on his farm, or even his garden
patch and house, especially as long as the employment-creating power
of Russian industry remained as unimpressive as it was and was
punctuated by prolonged periods of recession.[174]

The discussion of the Stolypin reform in its relation to industrial
employment has been affected by the tendency of historians to approach
the question of the supply of labour to industry from the viewpoint of
the countryside, that is from the supply side only. Moreover, the historians approach it either from the institutional point of view, i.e. from
the angle of likely constraints on mobility by legal disabilities, or from
the viewpoint of peasant ownership of land, i.e. the adequacy or otherwise of the land allotments provided by the Emancipation Act. They
have entirely ignored the special features of Russian agriculture which
affect the elasticity of labour supply to factory industry, above all its
high seasonal nature and the availability of alternative sources of cash
more compatible with farming than factory employment. These special
features continued to operate whatever government policy might be.
On the other hand, fast population growth and low levels of agricultural incomes sustained a supply of labour from the countryside for
factory employment, a supply which was larger than factories could
absorb, and not only in the winter. Vikhlyayev's contention that the
prevalence of short-term, seasonal, and casual forms of employment
among peasants was a matter not always of choice but sometimes of
necessity finds confirmation in the large numbers of labouring poor
which had become a feature of Russian cities and of factory settlements.
The large number of men filling low-paid and unproductive jobs in
various forms of service, and the persistence of manual and labour-
intensive techniques in industry, were indicative of abundant overall
labour supply, as was the relatively lower weight of female and child
labour than existed in other countries during the same stage of development. Still, looking at the problem from the factory end, there was also
the question of wage levels. These may have been (as will be shown)
high from the employer's viewpoint in that in addition to the direct
wage he had to provide various services which raised the share of labour
in his total costs and also added significantly to his overheads. In addition, productivity of labour was low, which meant that in the last

instance labour unit costs were not lower than in other countries. But from the worker's end, the individual wage was on average too low to provide for himself and his family and to compensate him for the income and the security of his farm.[175]

It is for all these reasons that the factory worker remained, even by 1913, suspended midway between factory and farm. When the boom came in 1910 – accompanied, unlike the boom of the 1890s, by high food prices and bumper harvests – a director of one of the largest cotton mills could complain that the factory worker still had the itch to move on as soon as the ice melted and that he was but a peasant who had to compensate his family for his absence on the family farm. The ability of factory workers to sustain themselves during long periods of unemployment during the early years of Soviet power, as well as the almost total emptying of the cities of Russia during the Civil War, point also to the close connection between the townsman and the village after several decades of intensive industrialization.[176]

VI.   The Adaptation of Labour in Industry

A. THE PROBLEM OF ADAPTATION

The overwhelmingly peasant origin of the labour force made the task of recruiting and organizing a truly disciplined labour force a formidable challenge.

In the ability to adapt to factory work the kustar was ahead of the peasant cultivator, whose range of activities in wholly primitive agriculture was determined by the cycle of nature, and whose timing of individual operations and decision-making in general conformed to traditional patterns determined by the collective. The Russian peasant, however, was much more than a primitive cultivator. He had to be very versatile and handy with the axe, hammer, and chisel. More often than not he had to be a house-builder, thatcher, and joiner; he had to fell trees for timber and fuel, dig wells, assemble carts, and do a multitude of jobs to pay for the things he acquired on the market. This versatility vastly added to the productivity of his labour and indicates that in calculations of underemployment in the village the opportunity costs of non-agricultural activities were not sufficiently allowed for. Most foreign observers stressed peasant versatility and skill with tools. The German writer Otto Goebel even maintained that from this point of view the Russian worker of peasant origin was superior to his German counterpart.[177]

What he lacked was power to sustain his effort, to work systematically with concentration and in disciplined fashion. Agricultural work,

with its concentration of back-breaking effort within some five months
of the year, had conditioned the Russian peasant into an irregular
'shock' rhythm of work. Russian literature is replete with terms
relating to harvest time such as the 'critical time' or, even more appro-
priately, '*strada*', which implies both suffering and passion. This capacity for concentrated effort over a limited period of time could be
utilized in industry as long as the rhythm of economic life conformed to
the cycle of nature. Most of the marketing of industrial produce was
done once a year through annual fairs and utilized transport which was
also conditioned by the seasons of the year. But the introduction of
railways and the use of steam and in general of power-driven machinery
required a worker able to spread his effort uniformly over the whole
year and concentrate on one or a few specific operations instead of on
the variety of activities which rural work entailed. It required years of
training and a whole series of measures of the stick-and-carrot variety to
turn him into a disciplined worker. A great deal more was needed to
impart to him the qualities of concentration and precision for working
with sophisticated machines and turning out complicated high-quality
manufactured articles.

On the other hand the kustar had the opportunity to acquire skills in
one particular field. He had to plan and pace his work independently of
the collective. The element of 'shock' work was still present in the
timing of his work, as sometimes he worked with special intensity, often
day and night, to have his merchandise ready for the annual fair or
before big holidays. He would not necessarily behave in this way if he
happened to be employed in a workshop on the putting-out system, but
even there work could intensify over a limited period with slack time
to follow.

B. COLLECTIVE RECRUITMENT AND EMPLOYMENT

Peasants were usually recruited at their place of residence by agents of
firms and private subcontractors. In the early stages this was done with
the active participation of communal authorities. The labour inspector
of the Kiev factory district reported in the 1880s that this was still the
case, especially with regard to sugar-mill workers. The contract was
signed at the communal offices, the elder of the commune appended his
signature, and often the workers also bound themselves by mutual
guarantee to respect it. Such contracts were often a means whereby the
communal authorities secured wage attachment for tax or redemption
payments or even for private debts, a procedure made illegal in the
1880s.[178]

The agents or subcontractors paid advances to enable workers to meet their outstanding commitments, and journey money which was usually less than was needed to travel by rail. The latter was only one-way: a return fare was paid only if the contract was faithfully met. The workers from a given locality would arrive as informally organized groups (*arteli*) under an elder, who sometimes acted as the subcontractor. He was paid the same wage as members of his group, though not working himself. The elder usually acted on behalf of the members of his *artel'* in their dealings with the factory administration. Workers from the same locality would usually be lodged as a group, in the barracks provided by the employers, and would feed communally; the elder or someone assigned by him took the responsibility for catering and cooking.[179] Sometimes the *artel'* also formed a work group, in which case the elder was responsible for all assignments and apportionment of work. This was usually the case in coal mines and in all those jobs limited to specific periods, as in sugar mills. The elder of the *artel'* was in charge of the Works Books (where used), in which particulars of the rules and each worker's earnings and duties were entered. He was ultimately in charge of distributing the net earnings of workers.[180]

It is clear that in such an arrangement the ties with the village and the insulation from new influences remained as strong as ever. On the other hand, the *artel'* helped the worker to adjust to a new way of life and discipline more gently than he would have done otherwise. A self-taught foreman (*steiger*) of the Donets Basin believed that the *artel'* was an excellent way of organizing people for work in mines. He regretted that by 1906 complements of workers for particular assignments were, as a rule, formed either by agents of the firm or by private subcontractors, who assembled people from different localities. Discipline – so the *steiger* thought – was much worse; there was a great deal of friction in the dormitories. There was also much more wastefulness and loose living, especially as groups were now paid weekly instead of upon completion of a job. The *steiger* believed that an *artel'* of men from the same locality under a respected elder made for more careful living and ultimately for larger net earnings to bring back home.[181]

However, it seems that if the *artel'* of people from the same locality was breaking up in some areas it was due to the growing individualism of the workers themselves and probably to the 'exploitative proclivities' of some *artel'* elders. The Moscow Factory Inspector, Yanzhul, described vividly how these village entrepreneurs were filling their pockets at the expense of the workers, how they were usurping for their private benefit the discounts offered by shops for the food and other merchandise purchased for the *artel'*, how they were lending money to workers at high interest (money which was not theirs in the first place), and so on and so forth. There was some hysteria in the way members of the

Russian intelligentsia tended to denounce any initiative and business enterprise as exploitation, and there was undoubtedly some exaggeration in this account. More to the point was the fact that peasants, especially young ones who could read and write, soon discovered that they could 'go it alone' and live more cheaply.[182]

C. CONTINUITY OF EMPLOYMENT

The employers, seeing that the authority of the *artel'* elder did not prevent contracts from being broken, and that peasants disappeared without paying back the advances they received, preferred different methods. Moreover, in those industries and regions where employers began to provide accommodation and facilities for families, a different pattern of life and labour organization was making its appearance. This was also the case where local labour was becoming more important. Here, employment of individuals as distinct from groups was becoming the rule. Nevertheless, large *arteli* of people from the same locality still existed in most large plants in Central Russia. The role of their elders with respect to the administration was still very important and presumably useful from the employer's point of view.

During the 1880s, to judge from the very detailed and often chatty reports of the first factory inspectors, employers seemed to prefer immigrant labour over local labour, as being more dependable. Hundreds of miles away from his home where the family were expecting his earnings, the immigrant worker (the Vladimir factory inspector noted in 1884) had to stick it out whatever the conditions, if only in order to earn enough money for the return journey.[183]

By and large, local labour was used in the winter season. In the summer local labour seemed to be in short supply in the coal-mining region of the Don Basin, although all sorts of riff-raff would be made to assemble to keep the mines going. A subcontractor would round up men in the market place from among the 'barefoot ones' (*bossyaki*) many of them retired soldiers, the work-shy, the dossers, etc., and would attempt to fashion them into some sort of work gang. In the summer season in the 1880s and early 1890s it was decidedly a seller's labour market in the steppe areas of South Russia, which may explain, among other things, the capital-intensity of some of the industry there. There were even suggestions from the Congress of the Mining and Metallurgical Industries of South Russia that the government should take administrative measures to transfer peasants to these regions for settlement in order to ease the supply of labour to industry. A later Congress wanted the government to organize labour exchanges at each major railway station in Central Russia, with a central bureau in

Moscow which would provide information about the availability of employment and would assist with the recruitment of peasants from the overcrowded rural areas. During the pre-1914 boom, the works in these areas used the *zemstva* as channels for informing peasants about employment opportunities.[184]

There is little doubt that certain areas had special problems of labour recruitment. However, as time went on, the question was not so much of absolute shortages as it was of the penalties of an unorganized labour market. As the mines and sugar mills attracted a similar type of labour (and from the same areas) as the estates and farms of South Russia, the problems were very much the same. The sugar producers in the Ukraine claimed and were granted exemption from the provision of the 1886 legislation which forbade advance payment of wages on the grounds that advances were the only means of assuring a timely start and completion of work in the sugar mills. They claimed that failure to do so might ruin the sugar-beet crop, and that in a sense their position was similar to that of agricultural producers who used advances to secure labour for the harvest season.

The problem of securing labour in the summer and preventing fluidity of the labour force throughout the year was reflected in the terms of the contracts. Employers stipulated long-term contracts in which they fixed very high fines for leaving work between April and September or October. Some offered bonuses to workers who stayed in the factory over the summer season. Nearly all employers gave the workers the right to leave in the winter before expiry of contract at Easter. Some contracts stipulated that a worker leaving during the summer must provide a replacement. Wages offered for the summer were higher than for the winter. On the other hand, employers had difficulty in laying off labour or reducing wages in the winter because this was usually connected with a certain risk of 'unpleasantness' with workers (and sometimes also with the authorities). If a worker was made redundant in the winter, he not only could not find anywhere to work but usually had nowhere to live.[185]

In larger plants workers were given individual Works Books, in which were entered extracts from the factory rules, the terms of the contract, and particulars of jobs done and pay due. Management also posted rules of internal discipline and safety regulations on the walls of the factory shops. A worker had to pay a fee for the book, and a double fee for a duplicate if he lost it. He also had to pay for another book if he happened to be transferred to another job or section which entailed a change in the terms of work. According to the employers, the aim of these fees was to inculcate in the workers respect for regulations. Workers tended to plead ignorance of the regulations in justification of misdemeanours or when complaining to the authorities about unfair treatment. Contracts usually specified that no official complaint or judicial proceedings could be made or instituted without presentation of the Works Book.[186]

The truck system of payment was widely used. Workers received ration books which specified the amounts of food issued and records of credits opened in the factory or specified local stores. Food and other goods provided by management or bought in shops which had arrangements with employers were as a rule 10 to 20 per cent dearer than on the open market. Some employers explained to factory inspectors that the store compensated them for the losses on the advances to workers. This applied especially to industries where workers were hired for specific periods and could abscond without working off the advance, the more so as the advance was usually higher than the monthly wage. On the other hand, workers usually spent the advance partly to pay for the journey to the place of work. Payment for work was usually at the end of the season or upon carrying out a particular assignment, and they had no cash in the meantime. The food rations were therefore not always consumed in full but were exchanged for cash. However, the rations appeared to be very high in the Kiev factory district, where each worker was provided with one pound of meat per day and a double ration of fish during Orthodox fast-days.[187]

The method of payment at the end of the agreed term led also to much stealing. Many absented themselves to make money on the side or absconded. Of the 400 workers in one of the plants visited by the Kiev Factory Inspector, seventy-four had left within a month of having received an advance greater than the monthly wage. Often the ostensible reason for departure was the intention to lodge a complaint with the authorities for unfair treatment or demands. Employers stipulated that workers must not leave work if they had a grievance but elect two or three representatives among themselves to seek redress. In the Vladimir factory district, management held back part of the workers' pay as surety. But the deductions from pay for a variety of reasons were very high and could, as in the case of the advances, exceed the actual pay and aggravate the workers' indebtedness to employers, which in turn was the common cause of their flight.[188]

Though by 1900 there was in most technologically advanced industries an all-year-round labour force, the actual working year was still very fluid. There was an enormous variety of feast-days: major and minor saints, local and national saints, historical and royal anniversaries and occasions were being celebrated, not to count the 'St Mondays' etc. It is possible to calculate the number of working days in the year for the Kolomna machine-construction plant from the period from 1878 to 1901. The number of working days fluctuated between 239 in 1979 and 271 in 1892 and then stabilized at around 261 days during the 1890s. Pogozhev estimated the average length of the working year in factory industry for the country around 1900 at 264 days, which compared with 283·3 days for Massachusetts, in the USA in 1897. It was 284 days in chemicals, 261 in metalworking, and 256 in cotton-processing. In individual firms the working year fluctuated between 117 and 355 days.[189]

In 1913 the average length of the working year in factories in the Empire was 257·4 days. However, by 1913, the length of the working year was affected not only by the tendency to celebrate too many feast-days and by the shutting-down of some plants for the summer, but also by the loss of working days through strikes and industrial unrest. In fibre-processing the working year was 295 days in Piotrkov province in the Kingdom of Poland, 282 days in Moscow and Vladimir provinces, and 280 days in Kostroma. In St Petersburg before 1900 the working year was already much longer than in other industrial regions, which was among the reason for the alleged willingness of St Petersburg firms to limit night work and in general to reduce the length of the working day.[190]

However, although by 1900 factory chimneys were smoking for about three-quarters of the calendar year, the length of stay of individual workers in each plant was still extremely low owing to the turnover of the labour force. A German professor from Hanover, Otto Goebel, who visited Russian industrial firms in 1904 and 1905, saw many factories in which the whole labour force changed on the average once a year. He believed that at best not more than one-tenth formed a permanent core. He thought that the degree of permanency depended on the age at which a worker started factory employment – that is, the younger he had started the longer he was likely to stay in the same factory – and on the type of work he did. The more his job was connected with machines and the more qualifications it required, the less likely the workman was to move from one factory to another or from one industry to another. The high rate of actual turnover of the labour force therefore reflects the high proportion of common labourers without qualifications in the labour force even by 1905.[191]

Employers tried to ensure greater stability by stipulating long-term contracts. However, this made it more difficult to adjust the labour force to the short-term requirements of the market, and moreover it was not always enforceable. The tendency to recruit more labour than was actually needed was another way of coping with high labour turnover, which was also prompted by an uncertainty as to the actual number of arrivals. Employers tended to hold back passports and Works

Books to prevent workers from leaving. However, workers left without waiting for settlement, forfeiting pay and forgoing passport or reference.[192]

Goebel estimated that in the metal factories he visited in St Petersburg in 1904, between 10 and 25 per cent of those who left the previous year did so without giving notice. From 30 to 50 per cent left 'upon request' or 'by mutual agreement'. Between 10 and 45 per cent were dismissed because of idleness, loafing, bad work, refusing assignments, refractoriness, and drunkenness. The rest were called up for military service, left on account of illness, or died. 1903 was not a typical year as demand for labour in metal factories increased in connection with rumours of war, and this could have contributed to greater labour turnover than usual. Individual plants or industries for which data are available suggest greater permanency of employment than Goebel's observations suggest. In the Zindel plant the average was 5·4 years. In the Baku oil industry, where there was considerable fluidity, the permanent core – i.e. those who had worked five years or longer – was about 22 per cent. In Sormovo the average length of work in the same plant was four years.[193]

In 1910, which was the first year of the pre-1914 boom, employers' complaints to factory inspectors were mostly concerned with workers leaving work, and this continued to be a constant refrain in employers' complaints right up to 1914. On the other hand, to judge by fines, absenteeism was no longer significant among the large employers in factory districts of St Petersburg, Moscow, and Warsaw. In 1909, 1911, 1912, and 1913 fines for absenteeism accounted for only 15 per cent of all fines, and those for breaking works rules for around 10 per cent. The majority of fines, 75 to 80 per cent, were imposed for bad work. In other factory districts, however, and in smaller plants, fines for absenteeism and rule-breaking were in the majority, indicating that the process of adaptation in these areas was still far from complete.[194]

D. FACTORY DISCIPLINE

The regulations introduced by employers were in the main designed to enforce respect for the time contract, to prevent departure from work without due notice, and to enforce prompt daily arrival at work. Gates were installed at the entrances to the actual factory buildings to prevent workers from just clocking in at the entrance to the site and then whiling their time away before actually starting work. But hair-raising tales were told about workers who sustained injuries trying to climb or jump over the high factory gates.

The rules stipulated fines for failure to appear promptly on the day specified in the contract; contracts even named the day of the workers' departure from the village to forestall delays and to make sure they would arrive in time. Fines for absenteeism were usually a loss of two (or sometimes three) days' pay for each day missed. Other fines were for refusal to carry out a particular job, substituting another worker for oneself without permission, for 'contradicting', disobedience, insolence, bad language, immoral behaviour, 'bad character', dissoluteness, drunkenness, etc. In practice, management did not always enforce the rules or impose fines. In the best firms proceeds from fines were used for the benefit of workers long before this was required by law.[195]

Stealing was a real scourge, and orthodox means of combating it were of little avail. Some employers instituted comrades' courts, which usually ended with a good thrashing of the thief. Management kept its distance, and the punishment could be ascribed to the moral indignation of the fellow-workers. It was more effective than money fines. Nevertheless, as late as 1910 searches upon leaving the factory were still the practice even in such advanced regions as St Petersburg.[196]

The problems which management encountered in trying to 'break in' former hand-loom weavers and make them accept factory discipline were clearly reflected in the factory rules. 'There is not an industry,' wrote the Vladimir Factory Inspector Peskov, 'where workers are so much burdened with all kinds of rules and regulations, relating mainly to technical defects of work, and where the failure to comply brings with it as many fines and deductions, as in weaving.' The rules also mirrored well the attempt to train workers to look after machines and parts and to avoid waste; 'not to clean machines while in operation', 'not to sit on the machine', 'not to doze at the machine', 'keep fabrics away from machine grease . . . from gas light', etc.[197]

Employers were also using positive means of influencing the labour force in the desired direction. A system of bonuses and awards was applied to encourage workers in the best practices. Term-contract workers were paid the return fare and an additional bonus if they stayed to the end of the stipulated term without major misdemeanour. Extra payments were made each month for work considered exceptionally difficult or urgent, and bonuses were paid to each shift which had exceeded the quotas for particular jobs. In some plants whole *arteli* were given specified sums at the end of the year as a reward. These sums, while amounting only to 1·5 to 5·5 roubles per worker, ran into thousands for individual plants.

In the famous Nikol'sk Manufactory of Savva Morozov in Vladimir district, the whole work force received at the end of a stipulated term a 10 per cent bonus in addition to their wages if they had respected the rules laid down by management. Morozov issued special instructions

which specified under what circumstances workers could absent themselves without forfeiting the bonus. These instructions show that there
were in Russia enlightened employers whose practices were much
ahead of factory legislation. They give a very good indication of the
kinds of problems employers were facing in attempting to turn peasants
into a factory work force, to detach them from the connection with the
village, and to inculcate in them a sense of priority of work commitment over family and social obligations. It was clear to the employer
that where women workers were concerned family and social obligations were more likely to take the upper hand over work commitment –
hence rules directed at them specifically. However, the employer was
concerned to employ women not only as workers but also as a means
of stabilizing the labour force in general. Schultze-Gaevernitz set great
store by the role which female labour played in the evolution of a true
factory labour force. Where both husband and wife worked in industry
their commitment to the factory was likely to begin to dominate that to
the village, especially as it also added to the family income and reduced
the role of farming in the total. Unfortunately, data for the employment
of wives as distinct from female labour in general are not available, and
the indirect information relating to the proportion of workers living as
members of families shows that the evolution had not gone very far
except in some regions.[198]

The Morozov factory rules point to another feature of the labour
force, namely the attention to rituals, to wedding, christening, and
funeral feasts, which were such an important part of rural life and which
involved not just the family but the whole community. These were an
important cause of absenteeism, as were the many feast-days and the
days immediately following them. They entailed not only loss of time
and hence of production but also – because the large quantities of vodka
consumed on such occasions caused accidents – waste of material, loss of
tools, and many fires.

In most of these respects labour regulations in Russian factories
resembled the disciplinary codes in other countries in the early phases of
industrialization.[199] But the problem facing Russian employers differed
in at least two respects from that which had faced employers in England
and France. One was connected with the attitudes of government and
society to the business classes; the other was the persistence of rural ties.

E. GOVERNMENT ATTITUDES

In most countries during early industrialization, certainly in Britain, the
employer could be certain that he had the law and the authorities on his
side; he could also enlist the prevailing business ethos of the middle

classes for his task. In Russia the government, ambivalent and indecisive in its policies though it was, had throughout given higher priority to maintaining stability and order and to endeavouring not to forfeit the assumed loyalty of the masses than to purely economic considerations in general and to employers' interests in particular. In part this reflected the weakness of the business classes as well as the generally anti-capitalist ethos of the public. The fear of West-European-type radicalism pushed the government into a defensive position, towards attempts to antici-pate class conflict of the West European type by trying to organize the workers themselves. Hence the ill-fated 'Police Socialism' which so tragically misfired and ended in Bloody Sunday on 9 January 1905, and which defeated the government in the very purpose it had set itself, of securing the loyalty of the masses.

Although strikes and workers' organizations were a criminal offence till 1906 (as they were everywhere during the early period of industrial-ization), employers in Russia did not have the freedom of action and the certainty of support of the law and of the public that mattered as did employers in Western Europe at the equivalent stage of industrializa-tion. Gerschenkron argued that it did not matter if society at large did not share the business ethos as long as government policy was commit-ted to industrialization. However, assuming that – even though Russia did not possess a cabinet capable of coordinating policies – there was such a thing as a government industrialization policy, in matters of labour the government did not speak with one voice. The voice which sounded loudest and was the most effective was the one which reflected the anti-capitalist ethos of society at large and widespread fears about disorder.

Tsarist and Soviet labour historians have dwelt with relish on the police functions sometimes undertaken by the factory inspectors, or their subservience to provincial governors or the Interior Ministry. However, although the various government pressures upon factory inspectors might have influenced their mode of action at certain stages in favour of individual employers, most of them shared the anti-business ethos of society at large and the intelligentsia's preoccupation with welfare rather than efficiency and growth. Their instinctive sym-pathy was with the workers, while their relations with employers were governed by an implicit mistrust of their intentions and professions and an almost aristocratic distaste for the profit motive. This mistrust and disdain found most expression in their dealings with Jewish and foreign management or with any foreigner in a position of authority in an individual firm. While the substitution of Russian for foreign personnel in management and technical supervisory posts was prompted by a variety of motives, the desire to ensure more equitable treatment and to avoid friction with factory inspectors played an important part in it. The ultimate outcome of government policy was to have neither the trust of the employers nor that of the workers.[200]

Most Russian labour historians approach the question of factory legislation and of labour policy in general from the political angle, i.e. from the point of view of its failure to forestall the participation of the workers in the October Revolution, or else from the point of view of welfare. Nevertheless, whatever they did or failed to do, the factory acts and the various provisions made by large employers were very much in advance of what was done in most other countries at an equivalent stage of development. On the whole, however grim the conditions of the early factories as depicted in the reports of the first factory inspectors, they were positively rosy compared with what is known about conditions elsewhere during early industrialization. The Russian employer had to tread very carefully when it came to redundancies and had to bear high costs of provision of social capital, a major part of which was expected to come from him rather than from the state or the municipalities.

F. RURAL TIES

The behaviour of labour – its stability and industrial discipline – was bound to be affected by the persistent connection of industrial workers with their villages of origin. This connection gave them a certain degree of independence. The ultimate deterrent of dismissal was therefore less effective than in countries where the worker owned no land, however little. In any case an employer desirous of building up a stable work force and in conditions of competition for labour in the same locality would use the deterrent of dismissal only sparingly.

Most firms accepted these limitations of the peasant labour force and adapted themselves to them. It would appear that management, even foreign management, as late as 1909 took calmly the possibility of having to shut down plant to allow workers to attend to their fields, as was the case in the plants in the Urals which a representative of the American firm of International Harvester was visiting with a view to acquiring it. A laconic 'account will have to be taken of this feature' was all the representative of the firm had to say on the matter. So perhaps after all, good management could take features of this kind in its stride.

Most firms accepted the necessity for higher wages in the summer months and tended to concentrate the bulk of their labour-intensive operations during the winter months. This created problems of stock-piling and higher interest costs and added to costs of raw materials, and it may explain the difference of 20 per cent in the cost of raw materials which International Harvester reckoned existed between Russia and the USA, though tariffs, transport costs, and similar factors played a larger role in this differential.[201]

VII. *The Role of Education*

A. LITERACY AND THE FORMATION OF THE INDUSTRIAL LABOUR FORCE

It is generally assumed that the formation of the industrial labour force and the ease and speed of its adaptation to industrial employment – and hence also the progress of industrialization itself – required a relatively high standard of literacy. Hence the correlation which sociologists or historians have been trying to establish between industrialization and rising levels of literacy, and hence also the tendency to regard literacy as one of the preconditions of an industrial 'take-off'.[202] How, it will be asked, did the Russian labour force fare in this respect?

Throughout our period standards of literacy were rising, more particularly after 1900, and were reflected in the literacy of the labour force and its quality. The extent to which employers actually exercised a preference for workers who were literate is not absolutely clear. The relatively high weight of lower age groups in the labour force may indicate such preference, though the references in sources stress the advantage to a plant of 'training up boys' and the greater adaptability and flexibility of younger workers in adopting modern practices. Schultze-Gaevernitz believed that educated workers were more stable, less prone to accidents, and less wasteful of material and time.[203]

The few studies which attempt to examine the correlation between literacy and earnings show a good correlation except in trades where physical strength was the primary consideration. A large-scale study carried out by Koz'nminykh-Lanin in 1908 in the Moscow province involved some 70,000 workers. He found that the average level of earnings of literate workers was some 13 per cent higher than that of illiterates, but he stressed that the average was strongly affected by the age structure, i.e. the relatively smaller numbers of older workers in the work force, who also tended to have a lower literacy rate. The differential in favour of literates was highest in machine construction (23 per cent). Among Baku workers the wage differential in favour of literate workers was, on the average, 12 per cent in 1908. It was higher among Armenians and higher still among workers of other nationalities than it was for Russians, which may indicate that factors other than simple literacy were involved. There seems to be some evidence that in the first year of employment the wage differential between literate and illiterate workers was fairly high but that it gradually decreased, which may indicate that the initial wage may well have depended on literacy.[204]

Only one study attempted to correlate length of stay at school with earnings for some 1,500 workers of three factories in machine construction in 1895 and concluded that it was positive – i.e. the longer the course the higher the earnings – and that an informal education equalled two years of school education. Strumilin estimated that four years of schooling raised the average productivity of a worker by 40 per cent.[205]

Tugan-Baranovsky believed that the educational facilities provided by the *zemstva* and the government met an already existing demand for literacy connected with general economic development. According to him, seasonal migrations of peasants for commercial and similar employment stimulated peasant awareness of the advantages of literacy. There was a positive correlation between the percentage of passports issued and the rates of literacy among military recruits in the same district. This was particularly in evidence in the provinces of Yaroslav and Tver: both these provinces supplied large proportions of workers to St Petersburg factories.[206]

Acquisition of literacy, in Tugan-Baranovsky's view, tended also to affect negatively the supply of labour to kustar industry, as the literate workers 'prefer[red] the more easily earned money' in St Petersburg, since the city offered other attractions as well. The little data we possess seem to bear out the view that the factory worker was likely to be more literate than his equivalent in kustar industry. However, only in one of the three districts of the Moscow province examined during 1898–1900 was there a large difference between literacy rates of kustar and factory weavers (28 per cent among male workers: the difference for the women workers was very small).[207]

In actual fact the industrial workers were *ab initio* more literate than the rest of the population and were becoming still more literate with time. In 1913 the overall level of literacy in the country was not more than 30 per cent, and around 38 per cent if the under-nine age groups are left out. This was a much lower rate than for mid-eighteenth-century England.[208] Detailed aggregate figures for literacy rates are available only for 1897. For other dates regional studies, studies of city populations, and data from individual plants have to be used to fill in gaps. Literacy data for military recruits have been available since the military reforms of 1874, thereby affording a time series for literacy growth among males aged twenty to twenty-four. The industrial census carried out by the Soviet government in the winter of 1918, though incomplete in that it omits the Ukraine and the Urals, is nevertheless the only aggregate information available for comparative purposes, though it contains a smaller proportion of workers of rural descent than existed in the labour force at large.

Table 61 gives levels of literacy in the population at large and in certain population groups, on the basis of the 1897 census.[209]

Table 61. *Literacy Rates, 1897 (per cent of total)*

	Total	Men	Women
Whole population	21·1	29·3	13·1
Urban	45·3	54·0	35·6
Rural	17·4	25·2	9·8
Wage-earners[a]	40·2	47·2	25·8
Workers[b]	53·6	57·8	28·4
Factory workers	50·3	56·5	21·3

  [a] All wage-earners, including agricultural labourers.
  [b] Workers in industry, transport, and commerce.

The highest literacy rate was among male workers. Among factory workers it was highest in printing and allied trades, followed by metal-workers, who had a literacy level of 66·2 per cent. Among textile workers the percentage was only 39 per cent, on account of the high proportion of women textile workers, whose literacy rate was only 12·2 per cent. The lowest literacy rates were among miners (32 per cent) and smelters (38 per cent).[210]

By age groups, the highest levels of literacy were in the age groups thirteen to thirty-nine, with a sharp drop after the age of forty conforming to the age structure of the factory labour force. In the population at large, although there was also a fall in literacy levels in the older age groups, the drop was much less pronounced.[211]

By 1897, when the census was compiled, Russia was at the height of her industrial take-off, and about three decades had passed since the educational reforms of Alexander II and the introduction of elementary education in 1864. Unfortunately, there are no aggregate data for the period before 1897, but the studies for particular groups of workers or regions indicate a very gradual rise of levels of literacy.

A survey among textile workers in Moscow in the early 1880s disclosed that only 29 per cent were literate – 36·3 per cent of men workers and only 2·2 per cent of women workers. The lowest level of literacy was among cotton-weavers – only 21 per cent. Among engravers and draughtsmen in textiles, the literacy rate was 92 per cent. In St Petersburg in 1869, the literacy level among workers was 38 per cent; by 1897 it had risen to 63 per cent.[212] In Moscow province, literacy rates were lower than in the city: the average for factory workers was 23·1 per cent – 33 per cent for men and nearly 5 per cent for women, a higher rate than for women workers in Moscow city.[213]

The growth in the number of pupils and students in lower, secondary, and higher education was also relatively slow until the mid-nineties, as is evident from the following figures. If the total number of pupils and students in 1865 is taken as 100, and again in 1895, the index growth at ten-year intervals was as follows:[214]

	Index 1865	Index 1895
1865:	100	
1875:	150	
1885:	237	
1895:	350	1895: 100
1905:	700	1905: 200
1914:	1,187	1914: 339

Similarly, literacy rates of military recruits show a rapid acceleration only after 1894, as indicated by the following figures at ten-year intervals:[215]

1874:	21·4 per cent
1884:	25·5 per cent
1894:	37·8 per cent
1904:	55·5 per cent
1913:	67·8 per cent

Data for urban literacy rates in the two main cities, based on urban censuses, confirm the trend, as seen in Table 62.[216]

In Moscow factories in 1908, literacy levels of 95 to 97 per cent had been reached by age groups fifteen to twenty-five, with well over 80

Table 62. *Literacy Rates in the Two Main Cities, 1869–1912 (per cent)*

	St Petersburg (over 6 years of age)			Moscow (over 5 years of age)	
	Total average	Men		Total average	Men
1869	59·5	66·3	1871	45·7	52·0
1881	64·4	71·8	1882	49·8	58·0
1890	64·8	74·3	1897	60·7	71·4
1900	70·5	79·7	1902	66·0	74·2
1910	76·6	86·3	1912	70·0	81·1

per cent for higher age groups up to forty, and of 84·6 per cent among all workers in machine-construction plants. In cotton-spinning and -weaving mills the overall level of literacy was still under 50 per cent, though it reached 72 per cent for men. There was a significant drop in literacy levels in this group after the age of forty-five, reflecting the

recentness of the improvements as well as the rural origins and connections of these industries and the weight of female labour in them. In
1902 the overall literacy levels of workers were just under 70 per cent,
but the rate for women workers was less than 20 per cent.[217]

The 1918 survey by the Soviet government disclosed an average
literacy level of 64 per cent among the nearly one million workers
investigated. The highest levels of literacy were among printers (95 per
cent) and among workers in machine plants (84 per cent). The lowest
rates were among cotton-mill workers (52·2 per cent), where the
proportion of women workers in the survey was two-thirds of the
total. Literacy rates for male cotton-mill workers were below average
but not significantly so (76·4 per cent, as against 79·2 for all men
workers). As was the case among workers of Moscow province in
1908, the level of literacy was lowest among textile workers, especially
among women, in the older age groups – an age differential which was
less pronounced among metalworkers. Among women workers, the
literacy rate of 63 per cent among those aged fifteen to nineteen, fell to
11 per cent for those aged forty-five to forty-nine and 8 per cent for
those aged fifty to fifty-four, giving an overall rate of only 37·5 per
cent.[218]

Thus, on the basis of the 1897 and 1918 data, the following changes
took place in the literacy rates of factory workers:

	1897	1918
Average total	50·3	64·0
Men	57·8	79·2
Women	21·3	44·2

In 1918 about two-thirds of the factory labour force were literate, as
against only 38–9 per cent in the population at large.

For several comparable trades the change between 1897 and 1918 was
as shown in Table 63. It is not clear whether the heading 'machines,
instruments, etc.' applies to the same group of trades at both dates; in
1897 it applied specifically to precision instruments, watches, etc., and
it is possible that machine construction as such was included under
metalworking.

The much higher levels of literacy in the factory work force compared with the average suggests that data on primary-school enrolment
ratios are only part of the story of education in Imperial Russia. Indeed,
during the period of Russia's most intensive development between 1885
and 1913, when the average growth of national income was 2·8 per cent
per annum, the primary-school enrolment ratio (as shown by Michael
Kaser) was only 2 per cent. It was much lower than in other countries at

Table 63. *Literacy Rates of Factory Workers, 1897 and 1918*

	Average total		Men		Women	
Trade	1897	1918	1897	1918	1897	1918
Mining	31·8⎫	70·0	33·5⎫	74·0	12·2⎫	42·6
Metallurgy	38·2⎭		39·3⎭		12·5⎭	
Metalworking	66·2	76·5	66·8	81·4	32·1	50·0
Machines, instruments, and apparatus	82·9	83·6	85·1	86·7	57·9	59·0
Processing of timber	58·4	69·6	59·6	84·3	28·6	46·6
Chemicals	49·7	70·0	55·8	78·7	30·3	54·7
Food and drink	49·7	66·0	52·6	75·0	28·9	48·3
Printing and allied trades	82·6	94·7	87·4	96·6	44·2	89·4
Textiles	38·9		53·9		12·2	
cotton		52·2		76·4		37·9
woollens		52·2		68·2		37·1
linen		55·5		78·3		40·3

SOURCE. Data for 1897 based on N. A. Troynitsky (ed.), *Chislennost' i sostav rab-ochikh v Rossii na osnovanii dannykh pervoy vseobshchey perepisi naseleniya rossiyskoy imperii 1897 g.* (St Petersburg, 1906); for 1918, on Russia, Tsentral'noye Statistiche-skoye Upravleniye SSSR, *Fabrichno-zavodskaya promyshlennost' v period 1913–1918 gg.* (Moscow, 1922).

a comparable stage of economic growth and much lower than the rate considered to be one of the conditions for an industrial take-off.[219]

Only 49 per cent of children aged between eight and eleven were attending school on 1 January 1915, while the percentage of pupils in rural elementary schools relative to the total number of children aged seven to fourteen was only as follows:

> 1880:   8·7 per cent (14·6 per cent of male children)
> 1894:   15·6 per cent (15·6 per cent)
> 1911:   23·8 per cent (33·3 per cent)

Moreover, a very small percentage of children who entered elementary schools actually completed the course: in 1908 the ratio was only 10·2 per cent in rural and urban elementary schools and 10·5 per cent in parish schools.[220]

The above figures indicate that those in industrial employment had differential access to education either because more of it was available to them or because those with schooling obtained in rural areas were more likely to choose the path to the factory or because employment in industry demonstrated the need for at least literacy. The higher literacy rates among factory workers could also have been due to the better opportunity they had, relative to other population groups, for adult education. All these factors undoubtedly played their part, though it is not possible to rank them in order of importance. I. M. Koz'minykh-Lanin demonstrated that in 1908 the literacy rates among workers in Moscow province whose parents were workers were on average 52·5 per cent, as against 39 per cent for those who were first-generation workers. Among men the rates were 80·5 per cent for the first category against 66·4 for the second; among women, 34·4 and 20·2 per cent respectively.[221]

Studies of individual plants confirm the higher levels of literacy among factory workers. In the metalworking and machine-construction plant in Sormovo, the average level of literacy was 62·4 per cent in 1902, out of a labour force of nearly 6,000, which came mainly from the surrounding rural areas. The highest level (77 per cent) was for mechanics, the lowest (45 per cent) for common labourers (*chorno-rabochiye*). Those in the age range fifteen to twenty had a literacy level of over 75 per cent. In the age groups from 21 to 35 it was over 60 per cent and it dipped to 41·6 per cent in the age group 45 to 50 and to 30 per cent for those fifty and over.[222]

At Zindel, literacy among workers who were classified as peasants in the autumn of 1895 was 66 per cent, which was lower than the average for the plant's labour force (with a level of literacy of over 67 per cent) but was higher than the average for workers in Moscow province (56 per cent), where the plant was situated. As elsewhere, the degree of literacy was in inverse ratio to age, with a steep decline in literacy after age forty to forty-five. As elsewhere, nearly one-quarter of all literates had acquired their education informally, and only one-fifth had actually finished elementary school.[223]

A comparison with standards of literacy in the provinces of their origin showed that the workers of the Zindel plant had a rate of literacy above the average for the localities they came from. In the Bogorodsk district of Moscow province in 1883-4, an inquiry among workers as to the sources of their literacy showed that 36 per cent had taught themselves or had acquired literacy in informal ways; 9·5 per cent learned to read and write in factory schools, 7 per cent while doing military service and 9 per cent from local priests. Thus about 60 per cent of all the workers in question had learnt to read and write outside the formal educational channels.[224]

It is difficult to judge the quality of literacy achieved. It is not quite certain how literacy was defined and whether it meant in all cases ability to write as well as to read. In the individual studies it usually meant full literacy, as the investigators took the trouble to check and usually provided sets of data separately for those who had only reading ability. In mass surveys, such as the population census of 1897, the issue is much less certain.[225]

Implicit in most studies was the realization that the worker was more likely to maintain his effective literacy because of the greater opportunity he had of using it. Given equal educational facilities, the person who stayed in agriculture was likely to fall behind in his reading ability, to say nothing of his writing skills. Strumilin estimated the average length of schooling of factory workers as three to four years.[226] This estimate is difficult to check, but considering the relatively late entry to work for the majority of children, and the vocational and general education provided in factory schools (often as high as secondary level), it may well be right. What is beyond doubt is that during this period literacy was increasing very rapidly in the younger age groups in the labour force and that in some trades it had almost reached 100 per cent levels in these age groups. It was also growing fast among women workers in the youngest age groups (65 per cent in 1918 among cotton-mill workers in the age group fifteen to nineteen), which may have been either one of the causes or one of the effects of increased employment for women. The latter is more likely, to judge by the reasons given by employers as to the desirability of employing women. The increase in the number of literate women workers was also undoubtedly due to the increased enrolment of girls in elementary schools, relative to the total number of pupils, as follows:[227]

$$
\begin{array}{ll}
1880: & 21 \quad \text{per cent} \\
1896: & 24 \cdot 2 \text{ per cent} \\
1906: & 29 \cdot 2 \text{ per cent} \\
1911: & 32 \cdot 1 \text{ per cent}
\end{array}
$$

B. TECHNICAL EDUCATION AND TRAINING

There was a great deal of discussion in Russia during the 1880s and 1890s as to the advantages or otherwise of general versus specialized education from the point of view of the needs of the economy. Official policy, though ambivalent at times, on the whole supported general education, with a tendency to shift on to the employer the task of providing specialized education, except at the level of higher education. Even where general education was concerned there was much pressure on the part of government during the discussions on factory legislation of the 1880s and 1890s to make the education of young workers and of the children of workers entirely the responsibility of employers. The latter insisted that this was the responsibility of government. In practice, however, the largest firms provided schooling to a lesser extent to juvenile workers, who often did not have the energy to benefit by it, than to children of workers and even to local children whose parents did not work in the factory. This feature had already been observed by the first factory inspectors in the early 1880s.[228]

Russia was on the whole fairly well catered for as regards formal technical education. W. Blackwell, a student of Russia's pre-Emancipation industrialization, believed that the Russian universities and engineering schools, with substantial state encouragement, were able by 1860 to provide comprehensive and up-to-date training in the main branches of applied science and technology, but that the practical application of technology was 'at best partial'. The Russian Technical Society founded in 1866 in St Petersburg, which subsequently set up branches in most industrial cities, devoted itself to the development and dissemination of the most advanced technology and was prominent throughout the period in its criticism of backward technology and practice. Russian diploma engineers enjoyed a high reputation as regards their theoretical standing and their knowledge of modern practice, but they were thought to be given to abstract thinking and less effective on the shop floor.[229]

By 1912–13 there were in Russia 661 institutes for commercial and technical education, under the auspices of the Ministry of Industry and Trade, of which twelve were higher educational establishments. Among these, the St Petersburg Polytechnic Institute (opened in 1902) and the Mining Department of the Warsaw Polytechnic took pride of place. Of the twelve, six were specifically technical. The number of students in the higher technical and mining institutes was 11,559 in 1912–13. Another 8,000 were in higher business schools.[230]

Of greater interest from the point of view of the factory labour force were the middle and lower technical and trade schools, under the auspices of the Ministry of Industry and Trade, of which there were only 649 with about 104,000 pupils and students in 1912–13, an increase of about 13 per cent in one year. Forty-four of the schools were specifically for training in industrial design, first introduced in 1903 under the Ministry of Finance. Zemstva, municipalities, local organizations, and industrial firms were called upon to organize schools, model workshops, courses, museums, and exhibitions, to promote good taste in the population, to teach industrial drawing, and in general to try to overcome the inferiority of Russian design and patterns compared with foreign ones. Many firms responded and instituted special classes and courses of industrial drawing and design in factory schools.[231]

Of the schools, fifty-eight were technical and trade schools, seven were mining schools, and forty-four were rural artisan training schools. The latter, set up in order to raise the standards of kustar craftsmanship, were subsidized by the government, unlike the technical and commercial schools.

To judge by enrolments, there occurred a fourfold increase in technical education and a twelvefold increase in commercial education.
Nevertheless, most of the learning was done by doing. A machine-
construction firm such as the Singer Sewing Machines plant built its
entire labour force by using common labourers with Russian foremen
trained from among them; it was obviously possible to do so in most
industries.[232]

As most of the training was by doing, the availability of technical
personnel capable of imposing higher skills and, above all, of skilled
foremen and middle technical personnel and management from abroad
was of immeasurable significance. Unfortunately their number cannot
be estimated with any certainty since in our data it is not always easy to
separate skilled foreign workmen and foremen from other foreign
personnel employed. They were, however, undoubtedly numerous. In
the French-owned Huta Bankowa Company in Russian Poland, only
4 per cent of all workers and employees in 1897 were Frenchmen. In
1911 this proportion fell to 2 per cent of the total. However, the proportion of foreign foremen remained high, there being thirty-seven
French foremen to twenty Russian ones. The Donets–Yur'yev Company, which was an entirely Russian-owned enterprise, employed
mostly foreign foremen, on the grounds that Russians with the right
qualifications were not coming forward: this was in 1900.[233]

The Russian Providence Steel Company still had in 1913 twenty-
three foreign foremen, out of a total of thirty-two. The twenty-three
French-financed companies operating in Russia, recorded in 1918,
employed at least 328 Frenchmen, of whom some were managers and
engineers – i.e. fourteen Frenchmen per company. German-owned
firms in engineering, chemicals, and electrical goods, which were
usually subsidiaries of home-based firms, tended to a much greater
extent than other foreign firms to use entirely German personnel as
foremen. In the oil industry foreign personnel were most prominent in
the administration and among foremen. In 1909 there were 704
foreigners, or 1·8 per cent of the total labour force: over 47 per cent of
the foreigners were foremen, and 22·4 and 15·5 per cent respectively
were in administrative or clerical positions.[234]

On the other hand, American-owned firms in the Moscow region
seemed to have been fairly successful in training Russian personnel as
foremen and supervisors. Managers of the Singer Sewing Machine
Company, one of the most successful foreign companies in Russia, and
of the Westinghouse Air Brake Company advised in 1909 that it 'was
best to Russianize the factory using supervisors and foremen who at
least spoke Russian, though native Russians were preferable'. This
advice was partly prompted by the desire to avoid unpleasantness with

the authorities. 'The system of factory inspection would cause less trouble if the officials found Russians in most places of authority.' This was not the only reason, however. The Westinghouse Air Brake Company, which brought in twenty foremen from America, found them a failure: there were heavy losses through poor-quality work. However, after they 'broke in Russian foremen, the workers turned out better work than in the U.S.'. The higher technical personnel in this firm were also Russian. The two Russian-educated engineers had received training at the Company's factories in the USA, one for three months and the other for ten months.[235] In the Singer Podolsk Plant in Moscow district, all the foremen were Russians, trained by the company. In the beginning they had a few American foremen, but not for more than six months, and only to train the Russians. The entire labour force – from 1,800 to 2,000 on average – was drawn from the surrounding villages, and except for a handful working on the finished parts of sewing machines it was entirely made up of common labourers. The Singer Podolsk Plant had reached '100 per cent foundry efficiency of America'; in other departments 75 to 80 per cent efficiency was reached within some seven years. Similarly, in the Lyubertsy Air Brakes Plant 'workmen [were] fine and fast' but 'organization less good'.[236]

The Americans had no doubt that the Russian worker was as good and as intelligent as any, given 'a good organization', by which they meant not only day-to-day management but a proper strategy, because the cost of setting up a good organization was high. It required at least six years with good management to put an organization into shape, but most likely between seven and nine years. They thought that during this preparatory period it was advisable to have one profitable line of production, capable of carrying the losses, and gradually to add to the buildings and to the assortment of goods to the extent that the labour force is trained and 'as rapidly as they are able to educate men to modern practice'. Americans working in Russia had preferential access to capital and, indeed, were concerned that they might lose some of their competitive advantage as against Russian firms should the Russian government advance cheap credits to Russian machine-construction plants, as it was rumoured they might.[237]

If this strategy, based on 'best American experience', was the right one for Russia, one might argue that most French and Belgian entrepreneurs in South Russia in the 1890s had plunged into high-technology investment and only subsequently set about putting the organization into shape. If the 'pioneers' reaped handsome profits, it was due to special circumstances: preferential access to capital, guaranteed demand by government (often at subsidized prices), tariff-free importing of equipment, and the stimulus of the boom of the 1890s connected with the railway expansion programme.[238] In general, South Russia – though handicapped in the recruitment of a labour force because of the lower population densities – was not as badly placed as is commonly argued in the matter of skilled labour. Undoubtedly, firms setting up in the 1890s had considerable problems because of the rapid pace of development and because they were anxious to cash in on the boom and on government orders for railway equipment and competed with each other for labour. However, by then John Hughes of Merthyr Tydfil had been operating his New Russia Iron and Steel Plant for over twenty years. Although he and his colony of Welshmen (of whom there were still at least seventy as late as 1896) had an uphill struggle for some years after 1869, when the company was incorporated, Yuzovka (i.e. 'Hughesovka'), as the factory settlement he had created came to be known, had gathered a sizeable population which provided skilled labour for the French and Belgian companies setting up in the 1880s and 1890s.[239]

A better-than-average supply of managerial and technical talent – more often than not foreign – was to be found in St Petersburg. On occasion that led to friction and resentment, but it turned St Petersburg factory industry into a school of skills and a filter for advanced foreign technology and practice. The Estonian and Finnish workers in St Petersburg, though less docile and more expensive than the Russian ones, were allegedly better learners of skills because of their generally higher educational standards. The same was said to apply to workers in Riga. Some labour historians maintain, however, that too much has been made of the ostensible differences in productivity and teachability between workers in the Western border territories, including Poland, and the indigenous Russian worker. The difference, they argue, is largely to be ascribed to the urban character of much of the industry in the Western border regions.[240]

If by 1909 many firms in well-established areas could dispense with foreign personnel, it was due to the fact that by then new firms could draw upon the skills of workers trained up by the pioneers. The extent to which there was continuity in the transfer of skills is illustrated by the fact that the often-mentioned Zindel plant – the origins of which go back to 1825, when many French prisoners from Alsace were employed in Russian textile mills as dyers – in the late 1890s still had workers who could read French and were illiterate in Russian, though they had Russian names. The many Polish foremen and other personnel in positions of responsibility in South Russia transmitted skills which they themselves had originally acquired from German or French foremen, managers and engineers in the Polish industrial region.[241]

Nevertheless, though there is evidence of replacement of foreign foremen by Russian personnel trained on the job, foreigners continued to be employed right up to 1914. Even in such a long-established and thoroughly russified industry as cotton, employers complained in 1913 of the shortage of foremen with specialized technical qualifications and of the fact that they had to accept men with general secondary education and train them on the shop floor. Similarly, the shipping and armaments programme before 1913 was being held up by shortages of foremen, and foreign foremen had to be sought abroad.[242]

To sum up, skills whether acquired through formal educational channels or through contacts from foreman to learner were still very thinly spread and were not usually of the highest level. The fault, however, was not all on the side of labour. Spreading literacy and general education undoubtedly helped to speed up the process.

VIII. *Changes in the Productivity of Labour*

As shown above by the employment data, estimates of productivity gains measured by output per worker are vitiated by the fact that annual figures of employment are not always a true indication of the effective number of workers employed throughout the year, and also by changes in the length of the working day. Therefore the data on output per worker for certain years (especially years of depression), for certain regions, and for seasonal industries tend to underestimate the real changes in productivity.

The annual rate of growth of industrial production including small industry was around 5 per cent between 1860 and 1913; per capita growth was about 3·5 per cent. The peaks of growth were during the 1890s and during 1910–1913.[243] At a rough estimate, gross output per worker in mining and manufacturing, not taking into account price changes, grew two and a half to three times between the early 1860s and 1913. For the period from 1887 to 1913 annual figures of the gross output value per worker, at current prices, are available. Data for output per worker are given below at four intervals:[244]

> 1887: 1,158 roubles
> 1897: 1,441 roubles
> 1907: 2,059 roubles
> 1913: 2,291 roubles

Table 64 presents the index growth of the labour force, gross value of output, and gross output value per worker, from 1887 to 1913. According to these data the labour force grew two and a half times, the gross value of output grew nearly fivefold, and the output per worker nearly doubled.[245]

If 1900 is taken as the base year, one finds that in thirteen years the labour force grew by 56·5 per cent, the gross value of output (at current

Table 64. *Index Growth of Labour Force, Gross Value of Output, and Output Value per Worker (current prices), 1887–1913 (1887 = 100)*

Year	Number of workers	Gross value of output	Gross output per worker
1887	100	100	100
1888	104·8	110·0	105·7
1889	106·9	113·4	106·0
1890	107·6	112·8	105·7
1891	108·5	115·1	106·6
1892	112·3	122·1	108·8
1893	120·9	130·1	107·6
1894	120·2	135·4	113·2
1895	121·3	140·4	115·8
1896	137·0	175·3	127·9
1897	155·7	193·9	125·3
1898	158·6	208·9	131·6
1899	162·9	218·2	133·9
1900	166·6	228·7	137·3
1901	175·3	240·4	137·1
1902	172·3	243·2	141·1
1903	173·9	259·6	149·2
1904	173·8	278·7	160·2
1905	175·1	273·2	156·0
1906	179·0	298·2	166·4
1907	185·1	329·1	177·7
1908	191·4	328·7	171·6
1909	190·2	341·0	179·2
1910	200·1	388·5	194·1
1911	212·9	422·1	198·1
1912	222·2	461·0	207·4
1913	250·3	495·2	197·8

prices) by 116 per cent, and output per worker by 43·3 per cent. However, in real terms the productivity gain during the period 1900–13 was much less because of the rise in prices. Table 65 gives the index of the gross output value per worker at current prices during 1900–13, the wholesale index of prices and output value per worker in real terms.[246]

The index of wholesale prices may have unduly depressed the real value of output, as much of the rise in prices was due to higher food prices and (to a much lesser extent) to higher industrial prices, especially before 1910. By 1908 the index of industrial prices stood at 110 relative to 1900. Moreover, the price index used here – recalculated from Podtyagin's index, which took 1913 as the base year – seems to be somewhat inflated. N. K. Prokopovich, in his study of the Russian national income, reckoned the index of wholesale prices in 1913 to have stood at 128·7 relative to 1900: on this basis the index of the output per worker in real terms in 1913 would stand at 111·3 relative to 1900.[247]

Table 65. *Index Growth in Productivity per Worker,*
1900–13 (1900 = 100)

Date	Output value per worker at current prices	Index of wholesale prices	Output value per worker in real terms
1900	100	100	100
1901	99·9	102·0	98·0
1902	102·7	103·5	99·9
1903	108·6	102·0	106·4
1904	116·6	104·9	110·0
1905	116·0	110·8	104·0
1906	121·1	119·2	101·5
1907	129·4	134·5	96·2
1908	124·9	135·3	81·2
1909	130·4	129·2	100·0
1910	141·2	123·6	114·3
1911	144·2	123·9	116·3
1912	150·9	132·9	113·5
1913	143·3	131·0	109·3

Of individual industries, the largest productivity gain between 1900 and 1908 was in the food industry, which stood at 145·4 per cent of the 1900 output value per worker, followed by the paper and printing industry, which stood at 136·8 per cent, and the cotton and chemical industries, at 132·6 per cent. In 1900 as in 1908, the highest output value per worker at current prices was in the food industry, followed by the chemical and animal-processing industries (i.e. leather, leather goods, etc.); cotton-processing came fourth and the metalworking industry fifth.[248]

In some industries there was in fact a fall in the value of output per worker in physical terms. This was the case in the oil industry, especially during the period 1900–8, mainly on account of the deterioration in the natural conditions of oil extraction, which necessitated greater expenditure of labour. The extraction of a ton of oil took six hours in 1889, nine hours in 1903, and eleven hours in 1913. The better technical equipment only partly compensated for the need for deeper drilling and the falling proportion of fountain oil to the total. The Russian oil industry, which in the 1880s and 1890s had higher productivity than that of the USA, was rapidly falling behind the latter after 1900.[249]

In the coal industry, similarly, there was a slight fall in the physical output per worker between 1899 and 1911, though relative to 1884 the index stood at 110·4 in 1911. The average output per worker in the main industrial countries was as follows:

Russia:	153 tons per worker
France:	203 tons
Great Britain:	264 tons
Germany:	287 tons
USA:	759 tons

The output per worker in the Dombrowa and Sosnowice areas of the Kingdom of Poland was substantially higher than in the Donets Basin, but the great weight of the latter in total output reduced the average for the country.[250] In this industry, too, deterioration in the conditions of extraction, i.e. exhaustion of the more accessible coal seams, was the cause of relatively stationary productivity. Moreover, technological change was rather slow. The pick-axe and shovel methods and a seasonal labour force were widely used; modern technology was in the main applied to subsidiary processes.[251]

Likewise, very little progress was made with regard to productivity in other branches of extractive industry. In gold-mining there was practically no increase in physical output per worker. Here, too, natural conditions played their part, but there was very little technological change because of the use of cheap unskilled labour. Dredgers began to be used only in 1901, and even by 1913 they were not yet employed to a large extent. Nevertheless, in most branches of mining energy equipment grew at a much higher rate than labour productivity.[252]

In metallurgy, capacity remained under-utilized in 1901 to the extent of 47, 39, and 46 per cent in 1901, 1904, and 1908 respectively. Even during the pre-1914 boom, the degree of under-utilization of capacity was 37 per cent in 1911 and 29 per cent in 1912.[253] During 1900 to 1909 there was very little increase in output per worker. Nevertheless, taking the whole period into account, physical output per worker grew more than fourfold between 1863 and 1913, though Russia still remained very much behind other industrial countries in terms of annual output of pig iron per worker, as seen below:[254]

Russia:	205 tons per worker
France:	239 tons
Great Britain:	356 tons
Germany:	404 tons
USA:	811 tons

In the cotton industry, output per worker by 1913 was about half of that in Great Britain and about a quarter of that in the USA.[255] Comparisons of productivity between countries in the cotton industry are somewhat difficult, because Russia tended to concentrate on lower counts of yarn and rougher and narrower types of fabric, and because before the 1890s Russian industry worked two shifts of twelve hours each, while in the United Kingdom one nine-hour shift prevailed. Nevertheless, with a twelve-hour shift even in the model Ramenskaya manufactory in Ivanovo, the weekly output of no. 32 twist was forty-two hanks as against forty to fifty hanks in Oldham with only a nine-hour shift (in the late 1880s).[256]

Schultze-Gaevernitz argued that the poorer quality of Russian labour made it impossible to utilize the largest machines. Self-acting mules with 1,500 spindles were only rarely met with, while in the United Kingdom those with 2,000 spindles were quite common. In Russia, according to official figures, 16·6 workers were employed per thousand spindles (the figure included supplementary workers) as against 3 per thousand in the United Kingdom. However, according to Schultze-Gaevernitz's own observations in Moscow and Vladimir, there were not more than 10 to 12 workers per thousand spindles, and in the Krenholm plant on the Narva the ratio was 6 per thousand spindles, which was better than in Germany. In the 1870s, output per worker in the Krenholm spinning mill was 402 roubles, as against 146 roubles in Moscow and 141 roubles in Vladimir.[257]

In fine weaving there were in Russia four to six workers per self-actor as against two to three in the United Kingdom. A similar disadvantage – roughly half the British output per worker – obtained in intermediate weaving. In weaving plants in Vladimir producing ordinary fabrics, there was one worker per 0·8 looms in good mills. In the United Kingdom there was one worker per 2·8 looms, and often one per 3–4 looms. If one excludes preparatory workers and counts only weavers, the ratio was one weaver per two looms in Russia as against four to six looms in the United Kingdom.[258]

In Russia many jobs, even in the technically advanced cotton mills, were still done by hand, especially in the preparation and in carding.

Similarly, much manual labour was used to make good defective work by picking up threads etc. This in its turn was partly due to the inferior quality of labour, partly to the ignorance of the manufacturers, who tended to select the cheapest varieties of raw materials, and partly to the faster run of machines and longer shifts per worker. The degree of wastage was 40 per cent in Vladimir as against 20 per cent in Germany and 10 per cent in the United Kingdom. However, in the most advanced mills the coefficient of defective work was much less than the average for Vladimir province. Machines worked faster than in Germany and Switzerland and almost as fast as in Oldham; this applied especially to lower counts of thread and rougher fabrics. But in the manufacture of finer fabrics, machines worked slower than in Western Europe. For higher counts of twist, labour unit costs were higher in Russia than in the UK. The average working day in the cotton industry during the 1880s and early 1890s was twelve hours; nevertheless, the daily output per spindle in Moscow was allegedly only just a little more than in Bolton, with a nine-hour working day, for the same count of twist.[259]

Schultze-Gaevernitz had ascribed the relatively lower output per worker in the cotton industry in Russia to the large number of overseers, supervisors, and controllers, which added between 21 and 23 per cent to running costs, and to the generally low value of the final output because Russia concentrated on lower counts of thread and rougher types of fabrics.[260] This type of output was best adapted to the nature of the market and to factor proportions in the economy, i.e. the high cost of capital relative to labour, at least in the short term, and made for relatively lower labour unit costs than was the case with finer fabrics. But in 1908, in an industry whose products were of the modern and sophisticated kind and in which the quality of labour was probably more important than elsewhere, e.g. in the Moscow area in machine-construction plants owned by Americans, labour productivity was probably about one-third of that obtaining in the USA. This undoubtedly marked an improvement compared with the 1880s and 1890s and was probably the best – rather than standard – experience.[261]

IX.   Wages and Earnings

Though the average wage per worker was low in Russia, labour unit costs were on the average not lower there than in advanced countries. The lower average output per worker was one reason for this; higher fixed and running costs of labour, such as provision of barracks or housing, schools, hospitals, etc., and extra supervisory and administrative costs, were another.

Though industry's expenditure in 1908 on the maintenance of housing, medical aid, workers' insurance, maintenance of schools, and other services amounted only to just about 31 million roubles and accounted only for 5·58 per cent of industry's total wage bill of 556 million roubles, this proportion was relatively much higher for the largest firms and for such industries as South Russian metallurgy or Baku oil. Moreover, that figure does not take into account amortization costs on the capital outlay for these services.[262]

It has been calculated that the provision of barracks for workers in the cotton industry added 25 per cent to the fixed costs per spindle in 1895. In the Baku oil industry in 1909, various fringe benefits – mainly housing, lighting, heating, water, and soap provision for workers – amounted to 37 per cent of the annual earnings of master workmen with families, 43·3 per cent for assistant master workers (*podmaster'ya*), and 43·3 per cent for ordinary labourers with families; for single workers in the three grades, these benefits amounted to 28·2, 27, and 32 per cent of their annual earnings respectively. Because of these fringe benefits workers in Baku with particular qualifications earned much more than their counterparts in Moscow metalworking industries, though not as much as St Petersburg metalworkers, who were the highest-paid in the country. In South Russian metallurgy around 1904, indirect expenditure on labour amounted to between 10 and 15 per cent of cash earnings.[263]

According to the industrial census of 1908 the average expenditure per worker in addition to wages was 14 roubles. In Baku it was 37·2 roubles; in the cotton industry and in metallurgy it was 20 roubles on the average. Between 1900 and 1908, while the cost of direct wages increased by 20·5 per cent, expenditure for the benefit of workers rose by over 63 per cent.[264] In 1913, annual expenditure by employers on the maintenance of schools, crèches, hospitals, theatres, and similar institutions constituted 3·66 per cent of the money wages of the firms recorded; workers' insurance, medical services, housing, and subsistence added another 4·5 per cent – a total of around 8 per cent of the money wages.[265]

When Baron Haxthausen visited Russia in the 1840s he was struck by the high level of wages in Russia. He thought that, making allowances for lower productivity of the Russian worker, wage rates were higher in Russia than in Germany. It was thought at the time that high wage levels were due to the inelastic supply of labour because of serfdom. Schultze-Gaevernitz, writing in 1899, believed that Baron Haxthausen's assessment of the cost of labour still held true in his time. He argued that if the nominal money wage only was taken into account, the average English wage was about three to five times higher than the Russian. But labour costs per unit of output were only a little less than in the United Kingdom. They were lower only in the largest Moscow mills which had adopted a nine-hour shift. However, this differential in favour of Moscow was more than offset by costs of accommodation and similar expenditure on the labour force, as well as costs of supervision and administration, which were higher in Russia than elsewhere.[266] International Harvester reckoned these additional costs to constitute 175 per cent of labour costs in 1909.[267]

Aggregate nominal wages of factory workers were recorded only from 1900 and only by those firms subject to factory inspection, which imposed fines. Although only one-quarter of all firms subject to inspection recorded wages in this way, they accounted for between one-half and three-quarters of the labour force. Their average annual money wage in current roubles in manufacturing (excluding the Warsaw factory district) – the index of the change in the money wage and in the wage in real terms – is given in Table 66.[268] Between 1900 and 1913, the level of average wages grew by 37·3 per cent. This was a period of industrial slump, which lasted till 1903 and was followed by depression compounded by the war and the Revolution. Nominal wages rose in 1906 as a result of strikes, but price rises – due partly to inflationary wage rises but largely to the change in terms of trade, which had an upward effect upon internal food prices – depressed wages in real terms below their 1900 level. Strikes and the financial crisis of 1907 affected industrial activity, with a downward effect upon real wages until the return of the boom in 1910. All in all, real money wages did not grow significantly during this period, and they certainly lagged behind productivity except in 1901 and 1902.[269]

On the other hand, during this period there was much substitution of female and juvenile labour for male labour, which depressed the average wage, especially in the textile industry, which was the largest employer and where employment of women was most common.

According to Strumilin, who made adjustments for seasonal employment in occupations such as the sugar industry and for the lower wages of women and juvenile workers, the average annual money earnings of an adult male worker were as follows (exclusive of the Warsaw factory district):[270]

	Nominal	Real
1900–4	240·8 roubles	308·2 roubles
1905–9	275·9 roubles	287·6 roubles
1910–14	311·5 roubles	312·4 roubles

The average wage of a woman worker was about half that of a male worker.

The highest level of wages in manufacturing was in the St Petersburg factory district, followed by the Warsaw and Kharkov factory districts. Moscow took fifth place after the Volga factory district, which included the Urals; the Kiev district came last. Although the cost of living in these regions significantly affected the wage levels, regional wage levels were also affected by such factors as the relative importance of industries, the structure of the labour force, and the length of the working year.

The average wage in individual manufacturing industries in 1913 was highest for metalworkers (417 roubles in 1913). The lowest wage was in the food and tobacco industry (169·4 roubles), followed by textiles (221·4 roubles). Within the textile group the lowest wage was in the

Table 66. *Average Money Wage in Manufacturing, 1900–13*

Year	Average wage at current prices (roubles)	Index of average wage (1900 = 100)	Index of average wage in real terms (1900 = 100)
1900	187·3	100	100
1901	196·0	104·6	102·5
1902	196·5	104·9	101·0
1903	203·5	108·6	106·4
1904	207·7	110·9	101·8
1905	199·0	106·2	95·8
1906	222·7	118·9	99·7
1907	233·1	124·5	92·4
1908	236·2	126·1	93·2
1909	228·5	122·0	94·2
1910	232·0	123·9	100·0
1911	241·5	128·9	104·0
1912	246·5	131·6	99·0
1913	257·2	137·3	104·8

processing of flax, hemp, and jute. In mining and metallurgy the average wage was 347 roubles annually, the highest being in the iron and steel industry (380 roubles), followed by the oil industry (374 roubles). The higher average wage in these industries was partly due to the fact that, almost entirely, male adult workers in the prime of life were employed. Making adjustment for the seasonal nature of some industries, Strumilin calculated the average money wage in 1913 in the factories and mines at 283 roubles, which – given the length of the working year of 257 days – suggests a daily wage of 1 rouble 10 kopecks on average.[271]

Though annual data for wage levels in factory industry are available only from 1900 onwards, we possess data for daily wages of seven categories of workers in St Petersburg for the whole period from 1853 to 1910. We also possess data for the same period for the prices of rye and wheat flour in St Petersburg. This gives us the possibility of following the course of real wages in terms of flour prices, from the Emancipation onwards, and enables us to assess the changes relative to the eight years preceding the abolition of serfdom.[272]

If the period 1853–60 is taken as 100 for the average wage and for the average prices of wheat and rye flour, we obtain the index of change at ten-year intervals which is set out in Table 67.

Thus, the amount of flour which a St Petersburg wage-earner could purchase with his money fell drastically in the two post-Emancipation decades – a fall which was even more pronounced in rye flour, which was the staple diet of the worker. Only during the 1890s was there a decisive upward movement, followed by a drop during the first decade

Table 67. *Indices of Wages and Flour Prices, 1853–1910 (1853–60 = 100)*

Years	Index of average wages, seven categories (1)	Index of average prices of wheat and rye flour (2)	Index of real wages (1:2)
1853–60	100	100	100
1861–70	110	131	84
1871–80	115	144	80
1881–90	129	145	89
1891–1900	151	137	110
1901–10	175	163	107

of the twentieth century. During the pre-Emancipation years an un-skilled labourer could buy with his daily wage 33 pounds of rye and 21 pounds of wheat flour; in the first decade of the twentieth century he could buy 34 pounds and 23 pounds respectively: a gain, but not a very striking one.

The relatively slow rise in the average nominal wage during the 1860s and 1870s tallies well with the indexes of growth of the labour force and of industrial growth, while the jump in the 1890s well reflects the boom of that decade. The averages for the ten-year periods do not fully reflect the rise in the nominal wage in the last three years of the nineties.

Of the seven categories of workers mentioned above, five were connected with the building trade (masons, house-painters, carpenters, joiners, and plasterers), one was locksmiths, and one common labourers. Of these, only carpenters and plasterers substantially improved their purchasing power (in terms of flour) by the 1900s, the first by 19 per cent and the second by 14 per cent. The money wage of the common labourer at current prices rose substantially during the first decade after Emancipation (by 30 per cent) and more or less closely followed the average index for all seven categories. The locksmiths' wages at current prices fell in the 1860s to 92 per cent of the pre-Emancipation wage, which may explain the flight of qualified factory workers to the villages recorded by Tugan-Baranovsky.[273] During the seventies the locksmiths' daily wages were still only 95 per cent of their wages during the 1850s. During the decade of the eighties, the wages of common labourers hardly grew compared with the decade of the sixties, while all other trades, especially those connected with building, registered a substantial upward swing in their daily wages. Nevertheless, with the exception of the wages of carpenters, joiners, and plasterers, the index of the money wages for the other categories of workers in the 1900s stood below the average. As building was by and large a seasonal trade in Russia, these wages may not be typical, though they are a good barometer of economic activity.

A feature of the movement of real wages was that the differentials between individual wages were less pronounced from period to period than was the case with money wages. Another feature was the relative stability of the wages of common labourers; the average amount of flour they could buy fluctuated much less from period to period than did the purchasing power in terms of flour of other categories of workers.

There has been a great preoccupation in Russian historiography with the connection between harvests and economic activity. It has been argued that, paradoxically as it may sound for a country where the majority of the population were farmers, low prices for food were advantageous for Russia because a large proportion of agricultural producers were forced to purchase food on the market. The best combination, it was argued, lay in good harvests and low prices. Years when the two coincided were known as 'peasant years', as this suited both the subsistence farmers and deficit farmers, considered to be in the majority. Moreover, it was argued that city labourers gained from good harvests of rye and low prices because of rises in wages owing to the reduced supply of labour from the countryside.

This was the burden of a large study commissioned by S. Witte and edited by A. I. Chuprov and A. S. Posnikov.[274] V. N. Grigor'yev, using data for 1883 to 1892 for ten categories of Moscow workers, came to the conclusion that wages rose sharply in Moscow during 1887–9 – i.e. during the two years of good harvests and the year following – and subsequently fell during three years, reaching their nadir in 1892 – i.e. after the famine of 1891 and the successive poor harvest of 1892.

Schultze-Gaevernitz, too, stressed the paradoxical situation in Russia whereby wages rose when food prices were low on account of good harvests, because of the reduced supply of labour from the villages and vice versa.[275]

The data on St Petersburg wage and price movements do not, however, confirm this view. If we consider all indicators of rise and fall of daily wages in St Petersburg in good harvest years following good harvest years, and in poor harvest years following poor harvest years, we find that in both cases the average index of wages rose more often than it fell. Only following successive harvest failures during 1875–6 and 1879–80 was there a substantial fall in daily wages. But nothing of the kind occurred following the hungry years 1891–2, nor after three bad harvests 1906–8. On the other hand, two excellent years, 1902–3, did not prevent a fall in wages in 1904, which was even more of a bumper harvest year, just as the 1870 harvest, which was the peak harvest for twenty-five years and followed a good harvest in 1869, did not prevent a fall in average wages in 1871.[276]

If, instead of the index of average wages of the labour force in the aggregate, we consider the movement of the wage of the common labourer, we can find a slight correlation between poor harvests and wages. The wage of an unskilled labourer also rose more often than it fell in bad harvest years; but in years following a bad harvest year the wage of an unskilled worker fell more often than it rose. However, the correlation even in this case is not consistent. The wage of unskilled labour rose, for instance, in 1890 after a poor harvest in 1889; it also rose after the harvest failures of 1875 and 1879, despite the fact that the years which followed them, 1876 and 1880, were also poor harvest years.[277]

Grigor'yev's data for Moscow are based on too short a time-span to be significant, and even if his findings were true for Moscow, where the connection between industry and farming was much closer, in St Petersburg the inverse relationship observed between food prices and wages did not manifest itself. The labour market in St Petersburg seemed to be much less sensitive to harvest fluctuations than the one in Moscow.

Years of war, 1854, 1855, 1877, 1878, and 1904, were marked by falls in the average wage level; but in 1905, as a result of Revolutionary pressures, the nominal wage rose sharply. There was throughout a remarkable correlation between wages and the trade cycle, which was already evident in 1858, when the wage index fell to its lowest level. The correlation was consistent during the second half of the seventies, the wage ups and downs following the behaviour of trade and output data. All three cases of maximum wage falls coincided with slump years, 1878, 1886, and 1900. All three most pronounced upswings in wages coincided with the known boom years, 1878–80, 1886–90, and 1897–9.[278]

Tugan-Baranovsky used data of transactions at the Nizhny Novgorod fair and of British exports to demonstrate the cyclical development of Russian industry after the Emancipation. Despite the entirely different nature of the statistical data used by Tugan-Baranovsky, the periods of greatest falls in the average daily wage in St Petersburg coincided with the lowest value of transactions at Nizhny Novgorod and the lowest value of United Kingdom exports.[279]

The average daily wage in St Petersburg at current prices for an unskilled labourer and for a skilled locksmith was as follows:[280]

	Wages (kopecks)	
	Common labourer	Locksmith
1853–60	52	113
1861–70	68	104
1871–80	69	107
1881–90	70	127
1891–1900	78	145
1901–10	91	186

This compares with average daily wages in 1913 of 110 kopecks in manufacturing and mining and 82·5 kopecks for an agricultural labourer.[281] Agricultural wages remained almost stationary at around 48 kopecks during the period from 1885 to 1900. In real terms, average daily agricultural wages, as calculated by Strumilin, grew by about 5 per cent during 1885–1900 and by about 20 per cent during 1900–13, in contrast to the industrial wage, which grew by only about 5 per cent. On the other hand, agricultural earnings were mainly seasonal.[282]

If we assume that the wages of common labourers in St Petersburg were the equivalent of a subsistence wage of a single worker, then the average daily money wage in factory industry in 1913 was not far removed from this level, and this may explain why the majority of workers did not sever their connections with farming. Even if we assume that a firm's average annual expenditure per worker in addition to wages was 20 roubles in 1913, this would still provide an average wage which was very low relative to the cost of maintaining a family outside the village.

N. K. Prokopovich argued that a worker earning on the average 200 roubles a year was too poor to raise a family. One who earned between 400 and 600 roubles could just maintain a wife but could not afford to rear his children in a city like St Petersburg because of the high cost of rents. S. Koehler pointed out that in 1910 a good working-class accommodation in Berlin cost the equivalent of 150 to 170 roubles annually, but in St Petersburg as much as 300 roubles. A basement 'hole' was said to cost 75 roubles in 1909. The wage which made it possible to maintain a family in the city was almost three times the average annual wage for the country during 1905–9.[283] Undoubtedly the wages reflected the relative productivity of the workers concerned, but they also explain why the proportion of those workers who transferred their families from the villages was so relatively low. Tugan-Baranovsky viewed this question as one of the vicious circles inherent in backwardness: the wages of the peasant workers in factories were low because their productivity was low; their productivity was low because they had not fully committed themselves to factory work; they did not fully commit themselves to a factory future because they could not afford to do so.[284]

This is not the place to enter into a detailed discussion of workers' budgets. The above is mentioned in order to emphasize the paradox that while, from the employer's viewpoint, labour unit costs were on the average not lower than in Western Europe, which (given higher costs of capital, raw materials, transport, etc.) made for lower profit margins on manufacturing in Russia, the wages the workers received were only between one-quarter and one-third of the average in Western Europe.[285]

There were, nevertheless, categories of workers in machine construction, metalworking, paper and printing, and metallurgy whose daily wages were much higher than the average. In large firms this was combined with various provisions for the benefit of workers and their families to make reliance on income from factory work for the maintenance of the worker and his family more practicable, especially where wives and other members of the family could enter employment as well. An analysis of the largest firms, which in 1907 employed 80 per cent of the labour force subject to factory inspection, suggests that family members who lived on the premises provided by employers made up around 16 per cent of the labour force. Another 16 per cent probably lived in the vicinity of factories, though not in accommodation provided by the employers.[286]

The question suggests itself whether the availability of other sources of income affected the level of average wages favourably because of the workers' greater bargaining power, or whether wages were kept down by that amount which the worker earned as a farmer. The question can only be answered tentatively and in a general way by suggesting that the farming connection influenced average wages negatively because of the low productivity of labour and positively because, with the supply of labour exceeding demand, a much lower average wage was more appropriate to the conditions of Russia's manufacturing with its high cost structure and marketing problems.

X. *Conclusion*

Though the process of industrialization had its dramatic interludes, as in the reign of Peter I in the first quarter of the eighteenth century, under Witte's administration in the 1890s, and in the four years before 1914, it was on the whole a picture in slow motion. It was a development in which elements of continuity were very strong and all-pervading. There was the same continuity also in the formation of the labour force in industry. The largest single break in continuity was the emergence of a labour market among peasants in the North Central provinces of European Russia roughly around the middle of the eighteenth century, which made possible a gradual shift from compulsory to voluntary forms of industrial employment.

By and large, the use of compulsory forms of labour by Peter the Great and his successors was the only means by which – in conditions of a largely natural economy – a labour force could be provided in a fairly short time for large-scale industrial production prompted by military needs and mercantilist preoccupations. With the emergence of a labour market, the supply of labour from the agrarian sector was not always perfectly elastic, but the imperfections owed little to institutional constraints or sociological rigidities.

The main factors affecting transfers of labour from the rural sector were, on the supply side, the strongly seasonal character of agriculture, which favoured forms of employment most easily combined with farming and penalized total severance from the village, and, on the demand side, the inadequate compensation which factory industry offered for the effort cost of such severance. This favoured growth of seasonal rural industries. It also accounted, among other things, for the rural location of much factory industry, especially in textiles, which was often grafted on to 'rural centred pre-modern growth'.[287]

Another factor affecting labour transfers was the relatively slow and discontinuous employment-creating capacity of factory industry. Although labour productivity in agriculture did not rise significantly, although labour inputs in agriculture grew as cultivated area expanded, and although the weight of peasant agriculture relative to large estates increased and more labour-intensive crops were grown, under-employment in agriculture emerged as a result of population growth and the splitting of households. This underemployment, defined as 'a surplus stock of man-hours and measured by subtracting labour requirements from availabilities', seems to have existed in many regions of Russia over large parts of the year and to have persisted in some throughout the year.[288] Consequently the supply of labour to industry usually exceeded demand, as is evident from a curious phenomenon sometimes described as 'hidden unemployment of expansion'. During cyclical upturns, when demand for labour rose, the numbers of peasants entering the labour market rose even faster, so that hidden unemployment appeared to increase simultaneously with a rise in visible employment.[289]

Probably not more than one-third of the factory labour force, even by 1913, was fully committed to industrial employment in the sense of total severance from farming and a corresponding social self-identification. One of the effects of such imperfect commitment to factory employment was the low productivity of labour and increased expenditure by large firms on housing and various social security provisions in an effort to attract and hold labour, which made for high labour unit costs.

The character of the labour force also encouraged the persistence of manual processes requiring little skill as complementary to the mechanized ones. The nature of demand, which was mainly for unsophisticated low-quality articles or for heavy goods as in metallurgy, and the high cost of capital reinforced this tendency. Even employers with preferential access to capital, mainly foreign entrepreneurs, tended to practise a kind of dualism in their business strategy, complementing capital-intensive processes with resort to unskilled, often seasonal, forms of labour.

Productivity gains from technology and organization in factory industry were often offset by the high fixed costs and overheads, so that workshop and individual artisan industry had a competitive edge over large-scale factory industry. This led to a tendency on the part of large firms to force smaller units out of the market by gaining control over the supply of raw materials or of credit, which favoured the emergence of huge firms usually combining all the processes within an industry. While this made it possible to spread fixed costs over a larger volume of output and reduced the costs of intermediate transactions, it also made for unwieldiness and high overheads. The consequence was a dualism in the industrial structure, in which the growth of industrial giants was matched by the tenacity of the small shop, which, even in 1913, accounted for the major share of the labour force in manufacturing.[290]

Though conventional wisdom has it otherwise, and allowing for some exaggeration, one must agree with the manager of International

Harvester that 'manufacturing interests in Russia on an average pay the lowest percentage of profit of any manufacturing interests in the world'.[291] High costs of raw materials, high marketing and debt-collecting costs, the high cost of capital not compensated by lower labour unit costs, high overheads, a still fairly restricted domestic market, limited prospects for exports, and the competition of better-quality and cheaper foreign goods were all responsible for low profit margins. In these circumstances only the very large and the very small firms had high survival ratings. The former could survive because they were able to distribute costs over a larger volume of output, and because they enjoyed easier-than-average access to capital and credit, better means of securing labour, and greater control over markets. The smallest firms, as a class, could survive because of the infinite flexibility of their cost structure, their lower profit expectations, and their adaptability to circumstances.

Industrialization in Russia was accompanied by a gradual erosion of the subsistence sector, but the majority of the population was not yet enrolled in an organized wage economy but was, to quote Myint, still in the 'vast intermediate zone of economic activity with a very low degree of economic specialisation, devoting varying parts of time and resources to subsistence activities and to cash earning activities'.[292]

Non-industrial forms of employment grew faster between 1860 and 1913 than industrial employment, and within the latter artisan forms of employment grew faster than factory employment. Productivity gains from the transfer of labour and resources to the industrial sector were not very high because of the still relatively unsophisticated nature of the final product, in which the cost of raw materials loomed large. In 1908 raw materials accounted for 58 per cent of the net value of manufacturing and mining output, and in the cotton industry for 69 per cent, while wages accounted only for 12 per cent of the total. Only in metallurgy and metalworking was the wages component more than 25 per cent of the total.[293]

In 1913 the factory labour force, which accounted for about one-twentieth of the active population, produced between one-fifth and one-quarter of the national income. The agrarian sector, which employed about two-thirds of the population, produced between 45 and 55 per cent of the national income.[294] Looked at from this angle, productivity gains from labour transfers appear very much more substantial, and the potential gain from future transfers to industry from the agrarian sector even more so.

CHAPTER VIII

Russian Entrepreneurship

I. *Entrepreneur or Manager?*

Regulation has been the substitute for entrepreneurship in Russia during the thousand years of its recorded economic history, and in the past five decades regulation has eliminated entrepreneurship altogether. The state cannot be considered to be the entrepreneur because this function can be exercised only by its citizens: Peter the Great established a framework of controls and incentives which induced the freemen among his subjects (and a very few foreigners) to act – and to continue to act – in new ways; Stalin's system, by contrast, prevented anyone from departing from the path which he or his officials defined as progressive. Since the First Five-year Plan, personal autonomy in the taking of economic decisions – a necessary feature of entrepreneurship – has not been permitted, but in the quarter-century before that deprivation every citizen had had the right to become an entrepreneur. In both earlier and subsequent times, however, the farm worker had much less liberty than the rest of the population. The serfs had been emancipated in 1861, but for another hundred years the country remained a predominantly rural society; townsmen, less than one-sixth of the total at the start of the century, came in 1961 exactly to equal the number of villagers, whose history had been one of uninterrupted restriction until the reform of 1906 and the Revolution of 1917. By determining the actions of those in their service, both Tsarist and Soviet governments have imposed the productive dynamism they desired. It has been their feat of discriminatory administration to have modernized some sectors while elsewhere maintaining traditional modes of production (or encouraging certain classes while repressing others). Under Soviet rule, control could be entrusted to those who were themselves being monitored.

Save at a few peripheral points where transactions are at least partly at the discretion of the agents,[1] the Soviet economy today is administered without scope for entrepreneurship. It is difficult indeed to identify the substitute: 'the administrative economy seems an intractable problem for economics in its present form'.[2] Such a task in any event is not the subject of this chapter, but the passage to a non-market, non-entrepreneurial system lends especial interest to the analysis of the preceding millennium of restriction upon economic choice.

Serfdom – the dates 1649–1861 are legal and precise – bound nine-tenths of the population to the soil and bondage labour at the time of the industrial revolutions of Western Europe and North America. Only for a short period in the subsequent century – again, 1906 and 1932 are benchmarks defined by legislation – did the peasant have the right to an identity card authorizing him to live outside his village of registration. A residential, and hence in large measure an occupational, tie does not degrade as serfdom did; a socialist administration honours and rewards labour which Tsarist officials and gentry despised and exploited; and of late no Soviet citizen has been threatened by poverty, pestilence, or famine, as was the common lot of Russians till the turn of this century. The reward of the worker for achieving his norm and of the manager for fulfilling his plan reflects, nevertheless, a social structure where conformism is prized and dissent penalized: enterprise outside the patterns drawn by the officials of the Party or the state is not merely discouraged but proscribed. Article 4 of the Soviet Constitution –

The economic foundation of the USSR is the socialist system of economy and the socialist ownership of the instruments and means of production, firmly established as a result of the liquidation of the capitalist system of economy, the abolition of private ownership of the means of production and the elimination of the exploitation of man by man

– enshrines a monopoly both to prosecute 'speculators', 'parasites', and others who seek personal, unauthorized gain and to muster the entire resources of the country by plan and regulation. The objective on which restriction and mobilization should converge was formulated by Stalin in his *Economic Problems of Socialism in the USSR* (1952): 'the provision of maximum satisfaction of the constantly growing material and cultural needs of all society by means of a constant increase and perfection of socialist production on the basis of the highest technique'.

Russian history also shows a correlation between peasant mobility and entrepreneurship of the Western type during the 1890s and the ensuing three decades. The genesis of both developments, for the Russia of Witte and for the Soviet Union under Lenin's NEP, was the state's acceptance of the market as its partner in economic development. Although Witte's leading sector and Lenin's commanding heights focused on coal and metals, their immediate objectives were market supplies to the individual consumer. The Bolshevik overturn of proprietorship was a political revolution, involving a temporary loss of the market (1919–20), but the economic pattern persisted until 1930. To draw a line at the date of collectivization and the First Five-year Plan is thus to underscore the economic ambiguity of the Socialist Revolution of 1917 and 1930. Signs of a possible third radical change may perhaps be found in the coincidental discussions of the mid-1960s about the abolition of restrictions on the peasant and a possible reform of Stalin's directive economy by readmitting a wholesale market among state enterprises. The views then aired did result (1976) in liberalization for the farmer, and in some measures for wholesaling. Some observers, both in the USSR and abroad, go further and interpret the Soviet manager of the 1970s as

more of a demand-oriented businessman and less of a supply-oriented production engineer ... The possibility of the development of comprehensive optimal planning and management based on a market-like system seems to be accepted by many Soviet economists and by some Western economic specialists, including the authors of this paper. It is both theoretically possible and rational in the context of the Soviet system.[3]

Hungarian economists have generalized from their own country's recent experience and anticipate the possibilities, in a planned economy, of market relations for small- and medium-scale producers, whose decisions are integrated 'into the socialist order of the economy by applying various legal regulators'.[4]

The market which could thereby be admitted into the Soviet economy would be under the shadow of oligopoly, for the industrial unit which can trace the longest continuous history is the horizontal cartel, which proliferated before the First World War, was transmuted into the *glavk* within Lenin's New Economic Policy (NEP), and became the *ob"edineniya* in 1973. All embody the product-specialized interest groups whom Stalin harnessed, Khrushchev dissolved, and Brezhnev and Kosygin revived. Witte's decade saw the culmination of de-control of entrepreneurs but no positive measures to establish competition among them. Their reaction was in restraint of a free market, the first major cartel dating from 1892. But that was also the decade when peasants – owing to a liberalization of the issue of identity cards to them (1894) – could begin to ignore the constraint from above, the compulsory commune. Later, 1932 – the terminal year of the First Five-year Plan – was to mark the end both of the market, imperfect though it had been, and of the villager's liberty to migrate.

The economic mechanism introduced with the five-year plans thus eclipsed an entrepreneurship which had lived under restriction for a millennium; the regulations by which it operated were, however, not wholly novel, for some can be traced far back into Russia's history of restrictions on entrepreneurship. The fact that the degree of mercantilization in the Russian economy was always lower than in Western Europe does not by itself exclude a search for entrepreneurship. An earlier contributor to this *History* has applied the term 'entrepreneur' to capital dealers in a predominantly unmercantilized Slav economy,[5] while another, examining current transactions in Western Europe during the fifth to the tenth centuries, has concluded that

not all payments in kind are symptoms of natural economy, nor is natural economy incompatible with the existence of trade. The key to the understanding of early medieval commerce does not lie in such broad formulae as 'natural economy' or, conversely, 'money economy', but in a patient investigation of specific branches of trade. Long-distance commerce commands the greatest attention because it requires the investment of considerable capital and it can be practised only by professional merchants.[6]

The characteristics of professional status and of the laying-out of capital are those of the Russian *gosti*, who appear in recorded history in the tenth century and with whom this account begins (section II below). Specialized ability and the willingness to risk even a modest capital are the marks of a Marshallian entrepreneur[7] and the essence of the defence of capitalism in W. W. Rostow's concept of the 'take-off'. Yet the functions found in the *gost'* trading between Kiev and Constantinople are also appropriate in the non-entrepreneurial perspectives of Marx and Hicks. In slave-owning or feudal societies, Marx saw the productive relations inherent in 'merchant's' (or 'commercial') capitalism prefiguring, and dialectically anticipating, the capitalist mode of production.[8] For Hicks, handicraft industries and trade are 'barely distinguishable economically'[9] – the *kustar'* as well as the subsistence peasant supplied the *gost'* with tradeables – but modern industry emerged when the proportion of fixed capital employed in businesses exceeded that of turnover capital; the concept is Marx's 'organic composition of capital', but with the impetus to change coming not from increasing exploitation but from scientific discovery and technical progress.[10]

While this argument would be sufficient to show the accumulative role of *gosti*, or to identify other prototypes, Hicksian analysis is especially relevant to Russia in three aspects of organization. Firstly, Hicks examines 'two pure types' of the non-market economy: 'the customary economy with its complete "belowness" and the command economy with its complete "aboveness" ... Under the pressure of what Toynbee would call a "challenge" the system may swing in the command direction, but in the absence of challenge there is a law of inertia ... which has the opposite effect.'[11] In Hicks's system of production as a 'structure of rules and understandings', both Petrine and Soviet Russia are dominated by 'aboveness'; the nature of serfdom – or, after the Emancipation, occupational restriction upon the mass of the population – almost eliminate 'belowness', viz, 'the power to take decisions, even over a limited field ... on which the normal person sets considerable value'.[12] Restrictions from above could obviate those from below: a study of industrialization in St Petersburg concludes that 'real economic gains were all too easily lost to demands for increased *obrok*' (quit-rent);[13] the 'serf–entrepreneur' had patently to struggle against far greater legal, social, and material pressures than any worker or peasant in other industrial revolutions. As to the 'aboveness', compulsion for the restricted subjects and motivation for the officials had to be induced by regulation. When a vacuum of managerial initiative again prevailed, after 1930, the interplay of personal self-interest and publicly regulated motivation established cumulation of commands, for the response to the application of a rule inconsistently with the objective as seen from above was to add more rules, which in turn engendered abuse or evasion and counter-measures in a new cycle.

Secondly, Hicks differentiates the modern working class by the regularity of its employment: 'it was casual labour that was the typical condition of the pre-industrial proletariat'.[14] The Russian townsman by contrast suffered from permanent employment: *gosti* and members of the two trading 'hundreds' (see below, p. 426) were alone able to change towns or occupations, and only *gosti* could become landowners. The artisan 'hundreds' and the yet lower urban orders were bound to the obligation of collective taxation, as serfs were to their gentry. Crisp relates this feature of Russia in the sixteenth to eighteenth centuries to Hicks's paradigm of

the 'Bureaucratic Revenue State', which existed in embryo elsewhere but which reached in Russia the dimensions and duration unique in Europe, because there was, or the rulers could claim that there was, ... almost a continuous state of emergency and because a market and autonomous centres of power within society were slow in forming to enable the state to relax its hold and leave certain functions to autonomous forces.[15]

A third organizational feature evolved from the tie of serfdom itself. Hicks is not alone in seeing its influence in the controlled maintenance of Soviet labour on the land until urban jobs are made available; Kalecki called it 'keeping unemployment behind the farm gate'. Such control was the easier to effect in the absence of urbanization; the low ratio of townsmen to villagers has already been noted, while in 1900 only fourteen towns of the Empire (Poland excluded) had populations exceeding 100,000.[16] When 41 million serfs were emancipated in 1861 there were only 860,000 industrial workers throughout the country (including those in Poland and the Baltic States, where there had been no serfs to liberate), but 520,000 of these were factory serfs.[17]

Three instances may be cited of the survival in Soviet management of attitudes formed under serfdom. The first has a personal aspect, when the worker makes free with the property or products of a collective farm or state factory, and an institutional one, i.e. the implication of zero price for assets or materials supplied under the state plan but a high barter price for those obtained outside the plan. Under bondage, the gentry's forests, orchards, and grazing

were generally regarded by the serfs as *res nullius* . . . [under] a moral code . . . far from obsolete half a century after the reform . . . labour services themselves presented plentiful and fully utilized opportunity to practise deceit and evasion of orders and regulations. It took a long time for Russian industrial labourers of serf origins to shed [such] attitudes . . . and the beliefs or behaviour of businessmen – artisans, merchants and industrialists – were not dissimilar.[18]

Another author has explicitly drawn a second parallel in 'The habits of perfunctory labour for others, formed in the fields of the *pomeshchik* . . . Even today the Russian factories are still plagued by *shturmovshchina*, the mad rush at the end of each plan period after its earlier parts had been spent in laxity and indifference.'[19] A third correspondence is to be found between the *skvoznaya barshchina*, whereby the proprietor set his serf tasks for all his working time and the *skvoznoy pokazatel'*, whereby the plan target formulated by a supervising ministry is incorporated directly as the target of the subordinate enterprise. In each case it is assumed that the executant is wholly dependent and is allowed no leeway.

The theme of this chapter is hence the constraint of trade in its widest sense. Some parallels are drawn between the limitations of choice in economic organization after the 1917 Revolution, but, as an introduction, five sets of constraints may be listed which hindered entrepreneurship for long periods over the preceding centuries.

First, ownership of productive factors was limited. 'Settled territory', the factor of land, and non-reproducible resources could only be owned by a hereditary class and, among traders, by only one small specified group. There was virtually no free manpower available after the introduction of serfdom, and for long periods factory serf-labour could be purchased only by designated groups. With respect to property in reproducible capital, the Petrine preference was for government managers or concessionaires. The same causes affected the second of the limitations – those on the mobility of factors of production – but there were in addition the legal ties of the peasant to the land and of the urban craftsman and trader to his *posad*. The levy of collective dues of a feudal kind inhibited migration, since the recipients prevented losses of tributaries, who in turn feared higher per capita imposts if any of their number left.

If money is an option held over resources, the third limitation – that of finance – is associated with the foregoing; but two further hindrances to productive accumulation must be considered. The few serfs who gained their freedom by entrepreneurship had to amass vast sums to purchase their liberty. Such funds, which otherwise could have been used for capital formation, generally contributed to the personal consumption of the serf-owner and his household. The primitive banks established in the eighteenth century largely served to make donations to the same gentry, and a financial system to mobilize savings (banks, joint-stock companies, and stock exchanges) arrived only in the second half of the nineteenth century. The limitation of risk-taking – a fourth set of impediments – was considerable before such institutions were established. Mistrust in commercial or fiscal obligations was rooted in a tradition of arbitrary regulation of economic activity 'from above' and by the inadequacy of legal recourse to violations of contract.[20]

Finally, since risk is usually associated with innovation, there must be noted the Russian practice of copying and the achievements of scale by the multiplication of units rather than by progress to a new level of technology.[21]

Passing from the conceptual to the chronological structure of this chapter, the next two sections (II and III) are defined by the beginning and end of feudalism, although its traces were not eliminated from farm tenure, taxation, and manpower mobility until the Stolypin reforms of 1906. Leaving aside the much more fundamental controversy over the similarity of Russian to West European feudalism, note may be taken of the somewhat differing views of Soviet historians over its dating. Marx's dialectic endows the conditions of transition from one system of productive relations to another with a greater significance than attaches to periodization in other frameworks of history.

Lyashchenko's pre-war classic sees development during the sixth to eighth centuries only as the replacement of primitive clans by a territorial society;[22] the collective work of a team led by Golubnichy, which first appeared in 1963, finds in that period the emergence of classes as the 'preconditions of feudalism',[23] which Lyashchenko reserves for the ninth and tenth centuries. Khromov[24] aligns himself more with Lenin in seeing the tenth century as the start of Russian feudalism;[25] and all are at one, firstly in finding no significant slave-owning period intervening before feudalism, and secondly in seeking to refute pre-revolutionary Russian historians, who considered the medieval epoch as a characteristically Russian system, unlike Western European feudalism.[26]

Lyashchenko finds 'the rudiments of capitalistic relations' as early as

the fifteenth century,[27] although Golubnichy *et al.* date these two
centuries later.[28] Khromov believes that it is impossible precisely to
define the genesis of capitalism in Russia, though the significant
turning point was the eighteenth century.[29] Tugan-Baranovsky accepts
the latter for 'industrial capitalism' but emphasizes the role of commercial capitalism in the pre-Petrine period;[30] Khromov defers the start
of industrial capitalism to the mid nineteenth century, which is for the
Golubnichy team the dividing line for the more evolved form of 'pre-
monopoly capitalism'. The first decade of the twentieth century began
'monopoly capitalism' for Khromov and 'imperialism' (Lenin's
'highest stage of capitalism') for Golubnichy *et al.*

If entrepreneurship had necessarily to be associated with capitalist
or post-capitalist societies, this chapter would have no more than a
century to cover. The roles of trader and state official under Russian
feudalism are, as has already been indicated, sufficiently entrepreneurial
to justify starting a millennium earlier.

II. *Limits to Enterprise in Pre-Petrine Russia*

A. CO-OPERATIVE ORGANIZATION AND INVESTMENT

Russia's first entrepreneurs, the *gosti*, appear in history in Prince Igor
of Kiev's treaty with Byzantium (944) and can be classified as merchants
in so far as they took the goods of others for sale 'to the Greeks', as
opposed to the chieftains who crossed the Black Sea to dispose of spoils.
Three features are relevant to their role in economic organization.
Yakovtsevsky, in the first place, regards the Kievan foreign-traders as
intermediaries for the disposal of the outcomes of pillage or slave
labour and hence as serving no function which could be considered
market-based.[31] The facts seem, however, to lie on the side of free
transactions, from the evidence of extensive crafts (*remeslo*) in Kievan
towns, as distinct from simpler processing within the village (*kustar'*),
as early as the eighth century in Khromov[32] or at least the eleventh
century according to Rybakov.[33] The second characteristic is the
detailed and sophisticated content of the treaty itself as evidence of the
gost's negotiating technique. One of the commercial clauses imposed
the first-ever import quota on Russia in a limitation of exports of
Byzantine silk,[34] but this was a concession from an embargo negotiated by the Kievans.[35] Finally, some authorities do not concede that
such process of foreign trade modified the domestic natural economy
on the grounds that all traded goods would have been obtained 'by
class domination through meta-economic duress, such as tribute [*dan'*],

corvée [*barshchina*], or quit-rent [*obrok*] – that is, by feudal exploitation of direct production'.[36] But they ignore the imports which constituted the counter-flow of the exchange economy. Some *gosti* formed themselves into groups according to their source of imports – the *Setichniki* trading with Stettin – while foreigners brought their products to, and collected their purchases at, their own yards (*dvory*) – the *Gotlandsky dvor*[37] of Novgorod or those for Saxon, Swedish, and Greek merchants in Moscow.

The literal translation of '*gosti*' – 'guests' – implies not alien nationality but the extraneity of entrepreneurship in the primitive Russian economy. Some foreigners were later assimilated as *gosti*, but for the centuries during which the group were recognized as a class, it was a stratum of Russian, not of expatriate, society. The pattern of their relations among themselves, moreover, throws light on a second characteristic of Russian business,[38] a propensity to co-operate as equals rather than to merge identities into a corporation. The present writer has elsewhere put forward the view 'that the instrumentality of the state, as the chief characteristic of Russian and Soviet economic development, is traceable to the weakness of the spirit of organization and enterprise as basic motivation for change. Russian communalism engendered fatalistic mutual reliance rather than forward-looking co-operation.'[39] The delineation of land ownership under Roman law in Western Europe showed marked contrasts with the indefiniteness of property rights in Russia:

Even chattels were of indefinite ownership within the kinship group, as is indicated by the joint derivation of the familiar *tovarishch* (comrade) and *tovarishchestvo* (association) from *tovar*, commodity or goods. The commune . . . was merely an instrument for the periodic re-partition of land in accordance with the varying needs and abilities of the constituent households . . . Communities of forest dwellers are rendered self-sufficient by their remoteness from others, but this independence of their neighbours is accompanied by indifference to possibilities of gain through exchange with others.[40]

Russian society traditionally valued *sobornost'* (collegiality) in decision and *partiinost'* (Party spirit) in execution: those who separated themselves by undertaking an independent commercial function were welcome but transmuted themselves into strangers, a sense which it is possible to read into the name of *gosti*.

The *gosti* were entrepreneurs neither in having 'the desire and the capacity to apply accumulated wealth to profit-making by organization of industrial enterprise' (a spirit Hobson saw as among the five essential conditions for modern capitalism)[41] nor in the Schumpeterian role of innovator,[42] but they were for very long alone in Russian society in making collective fixed investments and enjoying full property rights.

The *gostiny dvor* has some significance beyond co-operative capital formation, though this was substantial for its day: it was almost invariably a two- or three-storey rectangle of stone (in a land of much timber but remote quarries); that at Archangel was of three such rectangles. In their day they were the major buildings of Kostroma, Vladimir, Kaluga, Tambov, Yaroslavl, Pskov, Chernigov, and other towns, and the vast *Gostiny Dvor* of Moscow, built in 1790, has a lineage dating back to the twelfth century. Inside, however, they were multiples of individual warehouses.[43] The contrast is that of the Western capitalist, whose firm expanded by establishing bigger units, against Russian venturers, who multiplied an existing unit: many of the country's early factories were no more than colonies of cottage industry. It was for someone above them – a Peter the Great, a Witte, or a Stalin – to identify the new opportunities, create the markets, and forge the new structure of manufacturing capacity.

Turnover capital was invested in stocks of goods in store or transit, and a high degree of organization was needed to bring such items as pelts a thousand miles or more to the *dvory* or direct to ports (Archangel) or fairs (Novgorod). Capital which was surplus to such needs was reinvested in other productive assets, through the ownership of land. A title to populated land, otherwise limited to grant by the Tsar for service[44] in fee (*pomest'e*) or (from the fifteenth century) in hereditament (*votchina*), also conferred the economic freedom and the socio-political status fundamental to the exercise of entrepreneurship obtaining before the accession of Peter the Great. The Strogonov family is the outstanding example of this group, notably in opening Siberia to commerce and colonization from the sixteenth century onward. Given for this purpose the right (in 1572) to raise a private army (*druzhina*), they were formidably associated with Volga Tatars (notably Ermak) in expeditions in developing the river and portage routes across Siberia for regular trade.[45] The distinction accorded the Strogonov *gosti* at that time in being allowed to bear a patronymic,[46] *imenitye lyudi* (literally, 'named men'), foreshadowed Catherine the Great's definition of substantial merchants as *imenitiye grazhdane* (by then translatable as 'distinguished citizen'). Under the rules of 1785, entry to that group was confined, for example, to bankers with over 100,000 roubles of capital and factory-owners with over 50,000 roubles. It embraced also the liberal professions, who kept this status after 1807 when businessmen were assimilated with 'guild merchants' (*gil'denskoe kupechestvo*).[47]

B. GROUPINGS AT THE START OF MERCANTILIZATION

It is enough to point out that the introduction of the alien form of association was contemporary with the French Revolution, i.e. during the final phase of the guild's obsolescence in its lands of origin. The comparative delay in the Russian time-scale of economic organization compared to that of Western Europe is attributable to repressive Tatar rule in the thirteenth to fifteenth centuries; every Russian historian emphasizes the economic retardation under the *tatarskoe igo*.

The 'Tatar yoke' made its imprint upon entrepreneurship by its fiscal imposts (many of the terms for which in present-day Russian are of Tatar origin).[48] The form of taxation fostered the local stratification of producers and traders into groups collectively responsible for the tribute and at the same time promoted mercantilization. Both trends continued under the autocracy of the Muscovite Tsar, until progress toward a monetized economy was reversed by the imposition of serfdom (effectively by the *Ulozhenie* of 1649).

Under serfdom the functions of the village commune (*mir*) were both external (tax payment) and internal (resource allocation),[49] but, because the village was itself a chattel, neither role could be entrepreneurial. For occupations outside farming, the degree of authorized initiative was directly related to the legal possession of property rights. Since a title to the ownership of serfs was legally limited to gentry or certain *gosti*, Peter's decree of 1721 allowing the purchase of peasants for factories 'both by gentry and merchant persons' was to be of capital importance for entrepreneurs. Until then non-farm profits could essentially be ploughed back only into circulating capital (Marx's 'merchant capital'); the groupings which generated and distributed such profit comprised two which were continuous in nature, the *kupecheskie* and the *posadskie sotni*, and two which were episodic, the *skladnichestva* and the *arteli*.

The 'merchants' hundreds' (*kupecheskie sotni*)[50] were composed of three levels: of these the *gosti* were unequivocally superior to the other two, *gostinaya sotnya* and *sukonnaya sotnya*.[51] Those in Moscow (the earliest was the *Moskovskoe sto*) were often brought together by the destination or origin of their trade – e.g. the *Surozhane*, who traded with the Near East,[52] and the *sukonniki*, trading with Western Europe – as were those in Novgorod. Admission was regulated by fees: the group trading with Hanseatic merchants, the *Ivanovskoe sto*, was named the 'Hundred of St John' because every entrant (or son of a member seeking admission) had to contribute five silver roubles to St John's church; by contrast, members of the same city's *gostinaya sokha*[53] had each to finance a soldier. In smaller towns the geographic link was less specific.

The *posadskie sotni* grouped craftsmen (the skilled urban *remeslennik*, not – as noted above, p. 423 – the humbler rural artisan, the *kustar'*) who inhabited the *posad*, the commercial and workshop suburb of a Russian town. The *posadskie lyudi*, registered as such through their organization or through their kin, could not leave the town lest the tax burden be transferred to those remaining.[54] Though their members were legally forbidden to migrate to other towns[55] or to own land or serfs, the scale of operations of a *sotnya*, though modest, was greater than that of the poorer shopkeepers, stallholders, and artisans of the *posad*, who united on the territorial basis of the street (*ulitsa*) or the *ryad* (row of shops and work-places) or on that of the craft in a *tsekh*.[56] As in usual medieval practice, a street would often comprise those in a single trade, and features of a monopolist guild could arise in their organization.[57] Outside a town's *posad*,[58] freedom of self-administration was open only to those in the *slobody*[59] – state-owned suburbs and villages – where trade corporations also emerged.[60] The absolutism of the state was used to check local monopolies – Ivan the Terrible created a *sloboda* at the gates of Novgorod, free of taxes for five years, to limit the power of the town's existing corporations – but the *sotni* were more concerned to exclude the foreigner. They had their greatest success in mercantile trade, by retaining in native hands the trade between the interior and the ports of Archangel and Astrakhan.[61] In comparison with Western and Central European guilds, both *sotni* and *tsekhi* failed to evolve professional organization (e.g. to train apprentices, restrict entry, accumulate funds). Instead of developing a structured entity of their own, they concentrated on 'external' group activities, represented by the drafting of petitions, the organization of public processions, the veneration of a patronal saint (SS. Cosmas and Damian for the Moscow metalworkers, for example), or congregation in a chosen church.[62] In analysing their memorials to city authorities, Sergeevich found strong monopolistic pressures among the Moscow *sotni*,[63] whereas Tugan-Baranovsky characterized them as contributing significantly to commercial capitalism and considered that the New Trade Statute (*Novotorgovy Ustav*) of 1667 – issued (as its text states) at the petition of the *gosti*, *sotni*, and *slobody* – 'is permeated with the spirit of free trade'.[64] They made scant use of the concessions of civil liberties which elsewhere engendered capitalism,[65] and when industrialists' associations were established in the Western pattern at the beginning of the twentieth century, a persistent attitude of 'petitioning' was one of the criticisms levelled by the organizations of Moscow against those of St Petersburg (see below, p. 479). If anything, the 'episodic' groups manifested more of a proto-capitalist attitude. The *skladichestvo* ('pooling') is reportedly found as early as the late thirteenth century,[66] although examples were very rare in the next two centuries. Often associated with a 'fraternity' (*bratchina*) of merchant venturers, the 'pool' of funds could be for a single voyage or for repeated projects. The narrative of Afanasi Nikitin, a leading Tver' merchant who organized such *skladichestva*, has survived, but similar associations are not encountered after the seventeenth century. The *artel'* (team), on the other hand, has survived to the present time. It was and is the equivalent of an associated enterprise for those with only their labour to pool, the Volga boatmen (*burlaki*) in the past, and collective farmers, itinerant gangs of gold prospectors or woodcutters today.

C. ECONOMIC ORGANIZATION ON THE EVE OF THE PETRINE REFORMS

The shortcomings of the groups established by the seventeenth century were their smallness[67] and the separation of function between producer and distributor. An eighteenth-century German traveller remarked how, 'Except in the large cities, Russian artisans accept no work on order. They produce everything for sale – shoes, slippers, boots, coats and other garments, fur coats, beds, blankets, tables, chairs, in short all kinds of wares. The artisans deliver all these items at set prices to merchants, who sell them in their shops.'[68] Tugan-Baranovsky cites with approval the somewhat superficial reasons for this separation advanced by his predecessors – sparseness of population with an insignificant number of cities, and a sheer predilection for trade.[69] Three weightier factors may, however, be noted: first, the persistence of fairs as exchange points of transaction; secondly, the penetration of foreigners into trade but not into production; and thirdly, the difficulty of bridging the division between serfdom, to which craftsmen were subject, and the liberties available to merchants.

As late as the nineteenth century the fairs regularly numbered more than six thousand, and some were of national significance. It is reckoned that one-quarter of the total turnover was made at Nizhny Novgorod (now Gorky), a mart closed only with the introduction of Soviet central planning in 1929.[70] Whereas the importance of the *Jahrmarkt* beyond the local region dates from the twelfth century in Western Europe, the *yarmarka* (the Russian derivative) became significant only in the sixteenth. The fair hindered the penetration of the trader into production, and the penetration of the artisan into commerce was similarly limited, over wide regions, to another medieval relic, the itinerant craftsman.[71]

While the fair dominated overland trade, much seaborne traffic was in the hands of foreigners. Yakovtsevsky gives the lack of a Russian merchant fleet as the principal reason why the withdrawal of privileges in 1649 from the Muscovy Company[72] failed to force the foreigner out of the market. But he adds that the gentry preferred to have foreigners dispose abroad of the produce of serf labour,[73] because in towns such as Vyatka and Ufa the merchants were already politically more important than the *pomeshchiki* (who as a class were dominant above all in the South). Furthermore, Russian merchants engaged in overseas trade often entered into partnerships with foreigners in order to share in the higher profits.[74] It was as late as 1681 that the first foreigner was attracted into domestic production – Zacharias Paulsen, under privilege from the Tsar Alexei Romanov, founded a silk and velvet factory, which was, however, soon taken over by the state.[75]

For the mass of the population – the serf peasantry – access to external opportunity and the right to autonomous organization were legally precluded, from the sixteenth century until 1861. Their traditional grouping, the *artel'*, was a co-operative of equals, spontaneously formed for sharing out tasks or rewards.[76]

Although this is the subject of much controversy, it may be suggested that the urban groupings, as much as the rural ones, exemplify the natural co-operativeness of the Russians not against outsiders – as in a medieval corporation – but simply for mutual support. They may, moveover, represent a stoic acceptance of adversity on condition that its weight is equally distributed.

The serf's form of spontaneous organization reflected the preference for self-sufficiency induced by serfdom itself,[77] but it may throw light on the contrast between the peasant–landlord relationship in Eastern and in Western Europe. Shonfield's interpretation of Hicks's analysis is that, in an extreme bargaining situation, the Western landlord's reaction to the fall in the ratio of labour to land,

faced with the prospect of the destruction of property and the risk to life, would be to do a deal with the peasants which in practice conceded greater freedom to the latter in the disposition of their labour ... When the same model is applied to the East European situation, the rational judgement of the landlords in the face of equal threats and equal risks would be to refuse any compromise which favoured the peasants – the reason being simply that they could not afford to do otherwise.[78]

Hicks's theory presumes that the Eastern European landlord would, in an extreme case, have to choose 'between monopsony and annihilation. He therefore set about creating a new political and social framework which consolidated his power as the sole buyer of labour.'[79] The monopsony status of the Russian gentry was facilitated by the retrogression of a money economy, whereas – as Hicks points out – when the ratio of labour to land fell in the wake of the Black Death, 'In most parts of Western Europe, even in the fourteenth century, the mercantilization of agriculture had gone too far for the road to serfdom to be open.'[80] Just as in Hungary at the same time,[81] a substantial degree of rural monetization had been attained by the end of the fifteenth century, the chief agents of which were in Hungary the tenant farmer who paid some half of his rents and dues in cash and in Russia the hereditament craftsman (*votchinny remeslennik*) selling his artefacts.[82] In each country in the later sixteenth century the political ability of the landlords reversed the trend by sharply increasing the proportion of *corvée*.[83] Although there was a further cause in Hungary – the Turkish occupation and the militarization of the remaining areas which pre-empted peasant opposition – the retreat of the market economy in rural areas is found at that time not only in those countries but also in Poland and eastern Germany. In Russia, an additional factor in this trend may have been the inclination of the peasantry to consort together not for a positive objective but rather with the negative purpose of equalizing sacrifice.

A Russian ethos of egalitarian collectivism – as has already been briefly suggested in discussing *sobornost'* – in place of self-interested corporativeness may explain the failure of the medieval guild to take root: the pre-Petrine guild *tsekh* (a word taken from the German '*Zeche*', and hence implying no more than a 'band' or 'company') is on this assertion not a forerunner of the *tsunft*, imported later, which was quite specifically modelled on the German *Zunft*. The economic historian of Novgorod, Nikitinsky, affirms that in that city 'there was never any trace whatever of western European guilds',[84] a view supported for other Russian cities by his contemporaries.[85] The leading economic historian of the Soviet period concludes that 'during those centuries when craft guild organizations flourished in western Europe, they made no progress whatsoever in Moscow', though Pazhitnov finds the evidence weak.[86] At least one historian declares that the *tsekhi* were in restraint of trade,[87] but it is more commonly held that they concerted action directed against serf craftsmen working either for themselves on quit-rent or for their lord.[88]

The genesis of the East–West bifurcation in non-farm organization is to be found earlier than that which led the Eastern villager to serfdom and the Western to free peasant status: the dividing line is the capture of Suzdal' (to which the capital had moved from Kiev in 1169), Vladimir, and Moscow by the Tatars in 1238.

There is little significance in the signs of townsmen's organization in restraint of trade before that date.[89] Indeed, similarities with the West in urbanization would lead one to expect parallel development. Kiev, occupied by the Tatars in 1240, was 'one of the largest trade centres of the world',[90] the 'equal of Italian cities of that day',[91] a 'Ravenna of the North'.[92]

That development was abruptly terminated by the Tatar invasion. As Olga Crisp observes, 'The Russians became reduced to a most primitive form of existence, with a marked decline in commerce... agriculture and... population... The consequence was a savage concentration on the search for resources to ensure security... From the sixteenth to the late eighteenth century the Russians were almost constantly in a state of emergency.'[93] Even when Moscow had 'gathered the Russian lands', unrest continued through the Time of Troubles (1584–1613) to the uprising of Stepan Razin, a mere decade before Peter's accession. 'Where distance and internecine war made trade as precious as it was precarious, those who were enterprising enough to undertake it were accorded an esteem which they retained... however prostrate the condition to which the wars... reduced the economy'; but, concludes Leroy-Beaulieu, there was no one 'who deserved to be called a bourgeois'.[94]

Kaufmann-Rochard assigns one-half of 1 per cent to the bourgeoisie before the Petrine era – not quite 'nothing' – and a century later, for 1766, Yakovtsevsky puts the bourgeoisie at $2\frac{1}{2}$ per cent, though he includes serf–merchants. Leroy-Beaulieu cites the Strogonov concern as being as intricate as any contemporary European firm and finds in the hands of the native bourgeoisie of the seventeenth century many complex enterprises 'in which the master (who continued to keep his own close watch on the state of the firm and even to direct the business in person whenever the need arose) already had at his disposal an established network of managers, factors, relatives, or stewards who acted for him whenever needed and who, supervising the *dvory*, collected and shipped the merchandise'.[95]

Lyashchenko[96] and Kafengauz[97] date capitalism in Russia from the mid seventeenth century, when at least thirty factories were in operation. In 1650 the Moscow printing house employed 165 and the potash and saltworks of the Strogonovs and Pankratevs at Solikamsk 4,000. The armaments plant at Tula was substantial, and the Kadashev textile mill was founded in 1614. Both Kafengauz and Strumilin[98] find some of these plants employing hired labour rather than serfs and therefore consider them indubitably capitalist. Yakovtsevsky believes that pre-Petrine merchants' capital indicates to the Marxist the existence of other conditions for the genesis of capitalism – the exploitation of the smaller producers by the greater traders and the introduction of indirect production (with its consequent alienation).[99] Other Soviet economic historians would not accept that capitalist relations had emerged before the early nineteenth century,[100] but there can be no disagreement that in Russian economic organization the reign of Peter was a major turning point.

III.   *The Impetus from Peter the Great*[101]

It was the state, through the Petrine reforms, which at length compensated for the paucity of entrepreneurs and the constraints on their activity. At the start of this chapter it was pointed out that the embodiment of the institution is its officials and the regulations and motivations which they establish. To focus attention on the groups of persons for whom entrepreneurial conditions were created, or on whom regulations were imposed, facilitates comparison between governmental intervention under Peter and under Stalin, the differentiation of social classes by the one corresponding to the fostering of interest groups by the other. In the course of describing the various entrepreneurial classes which emerged after (or were greatly developed by) the Petrine reforms, comparisons can be made with techniques of man-management which were again promoted under the five-year plans.

The analysis by groups can most conveniently follow Sombart,[102] who distinguished seven in Western European experience. In descending order of social status, evidently the 'Prince' stood first, followed by his nobility (*adelige Grundherren*)[103] and the bourgeoisie (*Bürger*). The social origin of his fourth group, the 'innovators' (*Gründer, Projektemacher*), is so to speak accidental ('*vom Himmel gefallen*'), but they instigated ambitious schemes at home or overseas, discovered unorthodox ways to accumulate wealth and property, and engaged in financial speculations. The *donneurs d'avis* or *brasseurs d'affaires* were particularly numerous in France, and Frenchmen seem to have originated some of the more fantastic plans of the Tsarist era – the railway through Siberia to the Bering Strait, for example. Sombart put considerable emphasis on the role of religious heretics (*Ketzer*), as Weber did in the *Berufsethik* of Calvinism; Weber, though he did make comparisons with some extra-European sects, referred only briefly to the Russian Old Believers,[104] whose importance has been stressed by Gerschenkron.[105] The Jews occupy an intermediate position between religious dissidents and foreigners, who are in turn separated as entrepreneurs, as individuals, and as collective migrants.

With one addition (the serf–entrepreneur, peculiar to the era) and one extension (an official class, the nobility), Russian entrepreneurs can be classified within these groups but might be rearranged according to their origins: first, the creatures of the state, the Reformer–Tsar (*Tsar-*

Preobrazovatel') himself, administrative and technical innovator (learning his shipbuilding at Zaandam and Deptford), and his officials (managers of state factories, shipyards, and eventually railways); second, the native entrepreneurs – gentry, merchants, and serfs; third, the religious (and hence cultural) dissenters – *raskol'niki*, *skoptsy*, Jews, Tatars, and (later) Armenians; and last the foreigners – some who assimilated themselves and others, generally later, who remained expatriates.

A. INCENTIVES AND CONTROLS IN THE STATE SECTOR

Peter was, like other leaders of his kind, obsessed with the need to transform Russia within his lifetime into a great power, militarily and diplomatically. As his mobilization of resources was fundamentally for a non-economic end, his economic process had no exact parallel in the mercantilist era. Accumulation was sharply increased, and economic growth was rapid over a short period of time; the microeconomic maxim was not profit, nor the macroeconomic one a favourable balance of trade. Few state factories were established for consumer goods, unlike the French *manufactures royales* for porcelain, tapestries, furniture, etc.; and entrepreneurs participated in economic development more as instruments of the Tsar's will than as independent agents seeking their own industrial or commercial gain. The requirements of a 200,000-strong standing army and a 150-ship navy not only assured a demand for industrial products but also put their formulation into the hands of a civil and military bureaucracy, whose acts could be regulated by law and not left to the vagaries of the business climate.

Factories operated by, or under concessions from, state officials were thus producing goods according to a schedule formulated by state officials. The circle of decisions on resource allocation was confined to the bureaucracy, both in the provision of capital (establishing new plants or transferring existing ones to the private sector) and in current outlays (subsidization, product mix, etc.). The exercise of entrepreneurship lay in the control over those decisions by a combination of general regulation and personal incentive. The basis for Peter's model of microeconomic decision-making[106] was the Table of Ranks (*Tabel' o rangakh*) instituted in 1722. All of its fourteen classes (*klassy*) gave gentry status for life; membership of the eighth or a higher class conferred hereditary gentry status; and the individual ranks (*chiny*) were aligned for civil, military, and court service. Promotion in gentry status was as potent an incentive to state service as placement in the ascending steps of the Communist Party *nomenklatura* in the USSR today or as after-tax remuneration in a capitalist economy.

Under market regulation, however, it is open to the individual not to seek remuneration in employment but to live on unearned income in a status ranging from beggar to rentier. Within a serf-owning natural economy, Peter could not in practice eradicate all idle rentier existence (*oblomovshchina*),[107] but in principle the Tsar demanded service to the state for all not bound to serfdom. The symmetry of duties – of serf to the gentry, of gentry to the state – was to be ruptured as early as 1762 with respect to personal gentry service[108] and in 1785 with respect to fiscal obligations by the exemption of gentry from personal taxation – both of which obligations were retained for the peasantry. Though by then in disuse, the criterion of efficient service was formally in operation until 1900, when promotion within the 14th to 8th classes was made automatic after three years' service in each; appointment in the top four classes remained at the will of the Tsar.[109]

The bureaucracy which Peter shaped may be defined as 'mechanical' rather than 'organic',[110] in contrast to Weber's assertion that 'Bureaucracy as such is a precision instrument which can be put at the disposal of quite varied interests – purely political, purely economic or any other sort.'[111] Although allowing that there could be conflict between the 'expert bureaucrats' and the ruler,[112] his concept of bureaucracy can be refined according to the locus of initiative for innovation. It was Peter himself who learned abroad (adopting as his motto 'I am among the pupils and seek those who can teach me'),[113] who returned from Amsterdam with a thousand technicians,[114] and who laid down practical details for his projects ranging from the curriculum of the new schools to the process of exploiting peat and potash. Under him the bureaucracy was 'mechanical' in following such orders and in applying regulations by analogy; it was not 'organic' in generating innovation itself. The introduction of technical change – the ruler excepted – largely fell to foreigners (see below, p. 455), and some cause can be found in the type of individual recruited to the post-Petrine government service.

What is important is that the state's civil administration, even at the upper levels, was staffed with men who were committed to that career and no other and who seldom had any other significant source of income. The competence, efficiency, and honesty of the civil service were undoubtedly very low, and therefore its ability to accomplish things was strictly limited.[115]

Raeff notes that 'The government also strictly regulated the standards of production: the negative effect of this policy was that it undermined, and in some cases even destroyed, important crafts that might have served as a solid foundation for new industrial development.'[116] To the extent that such over-regulation deterred entrepreneurship, it pre-figured the exclusion of the entrepreneur in Stalin's five-year plans (see below, p. 492).

The provision of technology from 'above' (specific instructions from the Tsar) or 'outside' (foreigners) reflects an underlying dichotomy between administrative control and financial motivation at least in the state factories (*kazennye fabriki*) but relevant also to policy concerning the private sector.[117] The Petrine government shared some mercantilist attitudes but no particular concern for an active balance of trade: foreign earnings were needed to pay for expatriate skills or to bribe allies in the Swedish wars but scarcely to pay for competitive imports of final goods (and certainly not for primary materials of which the country was an exporter). Pressure for profitability in state enterprises was therefore weak from this quarter, and little pressure was exerted by domestic purchasers. Much of the output was invoiced to state officials; by 1750 ordnance orders were being placed at seventy-five metals plants, and those for uniforms, sail-cloth, etc. at fifty textile mills, of which 'only the third-ranking silk mills were specifically for private consumption'.[118] Since there were no dealers in money – subsequent state support for banking was slow and unsuccessful, and the first joint-stock bank was not to be formed until 1864 – there was no going discount rate to influence officials' investment decisions, and state loans were only a minor source of funds. Virtually all the structural decisions of the Petrine economy could be taken within the governmental circle, and in physical rather than monetary terms – that is, on the construction of particular factories and on the mobilization of current resources through the assurance of demand, the supply of managers, and the provision of serf labour. The predominance of physical over financial planning was to be inherited in the second half of the twentieth century by Ministers of Planning in countries as dissimilar as France ('finance is the handmaiden of the plan') and the USSR ('the budget follows the plan'), although the extent to which Stalin demonetized the economy remains a matter of controversy.[119] Some of the similarity between his administrative and financial controls and those of Peter (though not, of course, those of the French Commissariat du Plan) can be traced to their common concern with military objectives. The Tsar

could organize anything; but military necessities he put before all others ... Reading his letters one finds little that is brilliant or out of the way, but an absolute directness, a terseness which dispenses with all delays in the process of thought ... Peter was no theorist but an opportunist; each of his actions was dictated by a present necessity. All this vigour he threw into the work of military organization. His tremendous will was applied with the same nervous impact to every detail of military preparation . . . Reform, like every other activity of Peter the Great, grew out of the needs of his army.[120]

Lange's dictum that the Soviet system was '*sui generis* a war economy' would thus equally apply to the Petrine. At the level of central government Peter re-established the traditional (and haphazardly created) departments of state, *Prikazy*, on a systematic basis, vesting authority in the senior officials of each department as the *kollegiya* (an intra-departmental practice also adopted by Stalin's people's commissariats). Verification that departmental measures complied with regulations was in the hands of an Institute of Fiscals (*Institut fiskalov*),[121] at the head of which stood an *Ober-fiskal* responsible directly to the nine-man Senate, or council of ministers.

The pattern of economic departments set up in 1721–2 indicated the aversion to unified finance, because the *Kamer-kollegiya* for revenue was separate from the *Shtats-kontor-kollegiya* for expenditure. A *Kommerts-kollegiya* was established for foreign trade, a *Berg-kollegiya* for mining, and a *Manufaktur-kollegiya* for other industry.[122] The titles were German in inspiration as well as in form; their nationwide competence was absolutist in the service of the Tsar, paralleled in their enforcement process by the Secret Chancellery (*Tainaya Kantselariya*), 'whose prime task it was to investigate everyone conspiring against Peter'.[123]

Although as part of a general reorganization of provincial administration, urban self-government was permitted to the *grande bourgeoisie* in 1721 (through the chief magistracy, composed of 'men of consequence, worthy and well-endowed'),[124] it was not until 1826 that a similar representation was assured at the centre, with the creation of a Council for Manufactures. That Council was to advise the government more on industrial technology and patents than on economic policy as a whole,[125] a function which had then not been partly prised from the Ministry of Finance by the creation in 1810 of a Department of State Economy of the State Council. It may be claimed that the Soviet economic organization at the start of the First Five-year Plan was, in its central institutions, most fully prefigured at the time of Alexander I. The Ministry of Finance, set up in 1803, had to share power with other departments – the State Treasury, and the Department of Manufactures and Domestic Trade of the Ministry of Internal Affairs – just as under the Soviet NEP it was to be counter-checked by agencies for macroeconomic management (Gosplan and Vesenkha). In both governments, the ministry responsible for the livelihood of the overwhelming majority – Alexander's Ministry of State Economy (later termed 'of Agriculture') and the People's Commissariat of Agriculture – had little political force. Gosplan took nineteen years to establish its dominance,[126] as against the eighteen which Alexander's Finance Ministry took to absorb, in 1821, both the Treasury and the Department of Manufactures.

B. MOBILIZATION OF FINANCIAL AND MANPOWER RESOURCES

The subordinate role of finance in the Petrine administration should not diminish respect for the Tsar–Reformer's creation of a fiscal infrastructure to support industrialization. The collection of taxes and the disbursement of revenue were far easier for a 'mechanical' bureaucracy than the nuanced attraction of private savings and their profitable investment, even had Western experience been available and transferable. Capital expenditure from tax revenue was of three forms: for constructing factories to be run by state officials (e.g. the Admiralty Shipyard in St Petersburg),[127] for setting up plant for sale to private owners (e.g. the Nev'yansk Metal Works, built in the Urals in 1700 for Demidov), or as interest-free loans to industrial companies (e.g. the *Sukonny dvor* of Moscow, comprising fourteen merchants from that city, St Petersburg, Simbirsk, Serpukhov, etc.[128]). The first budget was drawn up in 1710,[129] and just after Peter's death (1725) a *Manufakturnaya kontora* (Office of Manufactures, 1727–79) unified the provision of credit for factory-building.

The rapid enlargement of tax assessment and the floating of state loans[130] supplanted the entrepreneur's initiative in raising capital for productive assets.[131] Tax revenue quintupled during Peter's reign, the new imposts including not only a conventional poll tax (*podushnaya podat'* or 'soul tax') after the country's first census (the 'First Revision' begun in 1718 and completed in 1724)[132] and salt excise, but also levies on such varied activities as the wearing of beards (primarily of course to Westernize the gentry), the sale of oak coffins or gherkins, beekeeping, and the grinding of knives and axes.[133] The proliferation of taxes was partly due to the harnessing of entrepreneurial talent into tax-collecting. The *pribil'shchik* or tax farmer was no novelty in Europe, and Peter employed this method extensively. Its disadvantages were the high diversion of revenue into private consumption – one estimate has it that only 30 per cent of the yield got as far as the Treasury.[134]

The tax revenues which reached the Treasury financed direct state investment and subsidies to private capital formation. The complement of state-supported investment banking was slow to come.

The history of Russian banking from the beginning of organised banking in
the 1750s to the 1860s is an uninspiring recital of the vicissitudes of a small
variety of government-organized and government-operated banking
institutions which in the main confined their activities to granting long-term
credit on mortgages of landed estates, or rather their serf working force . . .
Borrowers had to comply with bureaucratic supervision and a multiplicity
of regulations.[135]

Under Peter, Treasury grants or loans had been made direct to the
enterprise, through the appropriate *Kollegiya*, just as under the 'War
Communism' of 1918–21 funds were to be distributed by the People's
Commissariat of Finance direct to the *glavki* (chief administrations of
nationalized industry). It was Peter's female successors who considered
it more efficient for such capital to be disbursed by specialized state
financial institutions, which were termed 'banks', though they were
different from the capitalist banks then flourishing in the West.

The government of Tsarina Elizabeth established the Nobility
(*Dvoryansky*) and Merchants' (*Kupechesky*) Loan Banks (*Zaemnye Banki*)
in 1754, funded solely by state monies; but the former largely concerned itself with bailing out the gentry (who more often than not
neither repaid nor serviced the so-called loan), while the latter exhausted
its stocks in a single year. Replenished by more government capital[136]
almost annually, the first was liquidated in 1786 and the second in 1782.
The successor of the former was in practice just as ineffective in capital
formation – the landowning borrowers on the State Loan Bank
(*Gosudarstvenny Zaemny Bank*) 'considered loans to be in fact non-
repayable grants'[137] – but a foreign trade bank in Astrakhan (the
Astrakhansky Bank, 1764–1821) was a more successful pioneer than the
others; a third state-owned discount bank in St Petersburg had only a
short life. Catherine the Great, in her historic *Nakaz* (Instruction) of
1767, explicitly recognized the need for commercial banks, the importance of which may be judged by the inclusion of a bank in Potemkin's
town-plan for the capital of the newly acquired Ukraine, Ekaterinoslav
(now Dniepropetrovsk): in 1797, a few months after her death, the
government opened a number of local discount offices 'in an effort to
render the Russian merchants more independent of foreign lenders'.[138]
Garvy goes on:

The control over the distribution of short-term credit – in the earlier period
directly through the official banks and later as a result of the dominant
position of the state bank, as a direct lender and of the power exercised by the
Ministry of Finance in supervising and directing the credit activities of the
private banks – constitutes a remarkable antecedent for the ultimate centralization of the issuance of all short-term credit in the Soviet monobank.[139]

Alexander's economic reformer, Speransky, also unified control over government investment in the Superior Council of Imperial Credit Institutions of 1817, before authorizing the first Commercial Bank (so named), which broke with precedent in having businessmen on its Board. A similar inclination toward the private sector was reflected in the admission of businessmen to the Council for Manufactures. The Superior Council remained until 1894 the controller of the Russian banking system.

Under conditions of serfdom the state's possession of its own man-power – the Crown serfs[140] – represented a major command over resources which in labour-mobile societies would have had to be achieved by taxation. The supply by the state of both finance and man-power was especially important for the opening-up of the Urals.[141] The nine mining establishments created in the Perm region employed 25,000 serfs, and the development at Ekaterinburg (now Sverdlorsk) comprised two blast furnaces, three large forges, a foundry, a works for naval cannons and anchors, administrative buildings, warehouses, a technical school, and – to keep the serfs in order – a military garrison. Two men may properly be seen as entrepreneurs on behalf of the bureaucracy in the Urals of Peter's time – a Dutchman, Hennin, and a Russian, Tatishchev. The latter perceived the talents of the Old Believers (see below, pp. 452–3) as workers and supervisors.[142] But after the death of the Tsar the controlling managerial posts came to be mere sinecures, available for courtiers and adventurers. Urals industry in the second half of the eighteenth century underwent a rebirth under private entrepreneurs, who nevertheless failed adequately to invest in its modernization, a necessary condition for offsetting its higher delivery costs to consuming centres.

The inmates of prisons were also allocated to work in state as well as in private plant.[143] The agency of the state was used to draft apprentices for training and to keep them compulsorily employed for a substantial period in the master's factory (for instance, according to a decree of 1720 for the Tames factory, seven years as apprentice and three as skilled worker). Compulsory apprenticeship was used in the USSR between 1940 and 1953, and compulsory postings for university students for two years after graduation are still in force.

Of greater significance was the state's authorization, by a decree of 1721, of the purchase of serfs 'both by gentry and by merchant persons' for work in industrial and mining enterprises.[144] Although castigated by Soviet historians as 'unprogressive and wholly noncapitalist'[145] or 'capitalist manufacturing deformed into serfdom',[146] it opened the way for the merchant class to take up large-scale enterprise and for the gentry to utilize serf labour in non-farm employment away from their estates. Factories established in this fashion came to be known as 'possessional' (*posessionnaya*), though this did not become a legal term until the early nineteenth century, and some writers have confused them with those factories (described below) of which, in return for the provision of serfs, some or all of the output had to be delivered to the state.[147]

C. THE COMPLEMENT OF PRIVATE MOTIVATION

The institution of the 'obligated factory' (*obyazannaya fabrika*), in conformity with a decree of 1712, made use of personal incentives in a way to be used in Soviet practice two centuries later. A private or state enterprise with both 'obligated' and 'possessional' status in private ownership was required to fulfil a certain production quota for delivery to the state at a fixed price, any surplus to be disposable freely at the owner's own price.[148] The owner of a possessional factory, besides enjoying certain exemptions from state service and taxation and customs privileges, most importantly could buy from the Crown a regular quota of serfs. The obligations to the state with regard to outputs and inputs were by no means as satisfactory as they might seem. Until 1810, the Ministry of the Interior directly specified production volume and qualities in obligated factories; serf labour, which was used exclusively until 1840 in possessional factories (and predominantly until 1861), was often seasonal, being made available to the factory for 200 days a year and allocated to field work on Crown lands for the other 100 days.[149]

Serf-staffed industry (still 97 per cent of Urals manpower at the end of the eighteenth century)[150] would find a recent parallel in Stalin's forced labour camps.[151] The Urals developments were run on quasi-military lines under a Mining Commander (*gorny nachal'nik*), a combination of foreman and police officer, who had army detachments in lieu of a payroll. As late as the first decade of the nineteenth century, serfs petitioning for improvement could be killed on the spot or thrown into a blast furnace,[152] and insubordination might be punished by running the gauntlet.[153]

Given the security of the labour force and of order-books, the risk element in the capital invested in buying a possessional and/or obligated enterprise was not large; the technology was provided with the plant. It is a commentary on the paucity of entrepreneurship in such respects that investment in Urals industry was virtually confined to five families (the Gubins and the Yakovlevs ranked after the Demidovs, who employed over 30,000 serfs there by 1760): between them, they owned fifty-six establishments. Demidov, as already mentioned, accumulated the funds to buy into the Urals from his munitions profits at Tula; Gubin made his money as a Moscow merchant to buy six Urals plants from the state and to build one on his own.

The General Order of 1723 authorizing the sale of state enterprises to persons or companies, whether merchants, gentry, or foreigners, can be seen as a culmination of Peter's opening of trade to all classes except soldiers in 1699, as well as being a component of a newly adopted mercantilism.[154] However, the law of 1714 forbidding the transfer of mines to private persons remained in force, although some notable violations were later recorded. Thus, under the Tsarina Anna (1730–40) Count Shemberg, himself the Director General of Mining, was illegally leased mines and accorded monopoly privileges which yielded vast profits to be shared with the Empress and her favourite, Biron. When he absconded at her death (Biron was abducted to Siberia), he left unpaid debts to the Treasury of 370,000 roubles.

It would be wrong to generalize about such speculation and extortion under Anna, whose reign Pares called 'the gloomiest of all the period . . . The Court was five times more costly to the nation than it had been under Peter . . . The country was traversed by punitive columns [levying] impossibly heavy taxes.'[155] The experience did, however, eventually convince the Tsarina Catherine to abjure the grant of monopolies to individuals.

Merchants, rather than gentry or the state, were the principal contributors to the investment of the first half of the eighteenth century. Tugan-Baranovsky contends that merchants' capital formed the basis of large-scale 'industrial capital' in Russia but could not have done so without the infrastructure and organizational measures of the state.[156] He finds that only one in five of the factories founded in Peter's reign received state subsidies, and he concludes from his published list of entrepreneurs that native merchants, some gentry, and a few *razno-chintsy* (non-serf commoners) created the necessary capital. The foreign contribution was not of capital (as is noted below, p. 455, foreign owners were under disabilities until 1785) but of technology. Tugan-Baranovsky lists a very few foreign-owned works, usually small or with only a minority holding by an alien.[157]

Even before the general authorization some state factories were transferred to private owners: the merchants Turchaninov and Tsymbal'shchikov took over a line mill from the Foreign Office (*Posol'sky prikaz*) in 1711 together with its serf workers,[158] and wool and sailcloth mills were similarly transferred in 1720. The biggest beneficiary of the takeovers was in fact a foreigner, Tames (890 workers at his 443 Moscow looms and 180 at 172 looms in Yaroslavl'), but he held only one-tenth of the company's capital, the other partners being Russian merchants. Three Russian nobles – Counts Apraksin, Shefirov, and Tolstoy – obtained all the silk mills, but they soon had to admit merchants and were later forced to withdraw entirely.

Although the main school of Russian economic historians argue that commercial capitalists were the main entrepreneurs and financiers in the later Petrine period,[159] Kulischer contends that the state interest remained paramount even after 1723: he terms the new entrepreneurs 'caretakers' (*Inhaber*) rather than owners (*Eigentümer*), even though they operated the plants – often unprofitable at the time of transfer – at their own expense. Indeed, some went bankrupt in the process, and in these cases, to assure continuity of production, plants were taken back by the Treasury.[160] Following Kulischer, Falkus emphasizes that 'some of the big enterprises were in reality more like colonies of domestic handicraft workers, working for a single employer, than large-scale factories',[161] though this characteristic seems particularly true of the possessional and 'manorial' factories.

This latter category (*votchinnaya*) and the handicrafts sector were those which enjoyed no specific favour during the Petrine industrialization. The product of manorial, i.e. serf, crafts had been marketed from as early as the fifteenth century (see above, p. 430), but the employment of serfs in industrial enterprises on gentry estates began only after Peter's death. The second half of the eighteenth century was the golden age of the noble entrepreneur. The industrial activities concerned were chiefly in consumer goods. The Shuvalovs, the Vorontsovs, the Apraksins, and the Chernyshevs established distilleries – sale of spirits was one of the most profitable monopolies acquired by the gentry in 1765. In 1769 gentry owned 46 per cent of cloth factories, mainly producing material for army uniforms, and in 1809 they owned seventy-four out of ninety-eight such factories. Princess Potemkin had a woollen mill employing 9,000 serfs in 1825. Sugar refineries were later to be founded by noblemen on their estates, using locally grown beet. Experience with serf employment on the spot incited some of the gentry to go further afield and enter heavy industry. In the Urals four mining and iron works were purchased by Counts Vorontsov, Tsherin-shev, Jagushinsky, and Guryev; and by the end of the eighteenth century, gentry operated twenty-three of the seventy-one metallurgical plants in the private sector. A consequence of this trend was the *de facto* restriction of the term 'possessional factory' to those owned by non-gentry, although possessional serfs transferred from merchant to gentry ownership retained that status and did not become hereditament (*votchinnye*) serfs.[162]

The industrial activities of the gentry were greatly encouraged by the 1762 decrees of Peter III and Catherine II whereby purchase of serfs with or without lands for factory works became reserved to the gentry, a right extended to foreigners in the following year. A government report of 1773 on the 328 factories which were accounted at the time found sixty-six belonging to the gentry and forty-six to foreigners, but of 305 factories for which output was known, the fifty-seven gentry-owned plants accounted for nearly one-third.

The gentry's monopsonization of serfs for factory work after 1762, though not complete (*raznochintsy* – i.e. men risen from other classes – as well as foreigners could also buy such manpower), was of course only one of the many privileges which they won from the weak Peter III. Four months before his overthrow by his wife in June 1762, he had granted the Manifesto of the Rights of the Gentry; within six weeks of taking power Catherine confirmed her late husband's reservation of serf ownership and she followed his secularization of church estates by prohibiting two years later ecclesiastical ownership of serfs for gain (their so-called 'economic peasantry'); the privileges of 'authorized manufacturers' (*ukaznye fabrikantov*) were withdrawn in 1762–3, in effect to allow access by the gentry. The decree depriving serfs of the right to sign promissory notes (1761) was a particular blow to the few serf–entrepreneurs (see below), because banking offices to transfer such notes had opened only four years earlier; the power of the owner to exact profits from his quit-rent serfs in general was increased by his authority to exile serfs to hard labour after 1765 and by the non-admissibility in law of serf complaints against their owners two years later.

The situation in political terms, with the violent events of the Pugachev uprising and brutal supression (1773–5), is to be contrasted with a certain liberalism in economic policy. Tugan-Baranovsky cites the memorials which the gentry submitted to Catherine urging that merchant factories be restricted to freely hired labour: it would force merchants to turn out products 'as good as those made abroad'[163] and to pay higher wages to the gentry's quit-rent serfs.

The system of manorial manufactures offered certain advantages within the framework of the serf system: its own supply of large quantities of raw materials (flax, hemp, wool, hides, grain), tools, and labour, which did not have to be reckoned in money. Manufacturing was usually performed only during the long winters, thus leaving the summer months for field work. There was no question of wages, since the estate peasants were merely performing *corvée*.

On the other hand, the short-term expansion of manorial industry, developed during a period of intensified protectionism on the part of the nobility, sowed the seeds of its own decline in forcing non-gentry to hire free labour, which in the long run was much more productive.

Most serf manpower was entirely unsuitable for skilled jobs, and with no wage incentives output was excessively labour-intensive; escapes and uprisings among the serfs were frequent. Consequently, the gentry neither diversified into more advanced types of production requiring new techniques and materials (e.g. continuing to use wool rather than imported cotton) nor gained entrepreneurial experience which would encourage them into other private enterprise: their names were to be conspicuously lacking from the lists of investors in the early Russian joint-stock companies.

In another way also the manorial enterprise generated its own undoing. The gentry needed money to pay their growing bills for the amenities of the Westernized way of life, and while protection increased their incomes, only quite inadequate productive investment was undertaken because of extravagant consumption and interest on rising indebtedness.[164] The case may be instanced of the Yusupovs, who in 1806 owned 198 villages comprising 9,034 square miles of property, where 17,239 serfs lived. This large agro-industrial complex was in administrative terms well run through two administrative centres in Moscow and St Petersburg and numerous regional offices. Inspectors commuted between the two central and the regional offices, of which that controlling Yusupov enterprises in the Ukraine was 'a town of 2,320 inhabitants with shops, warehouses, factories, mills, barracks, administrative buildings, a tavern and a hospital'.[165] 25 to 30 per cent of the Yusupov income came from entrepreneurial activities in running manorial factories, primarily cloth mills for state orders and silk factories for the market. But the cost of the family's personal expenses was even higher than the maintenance of its estate; at the time of the death of N. B. Yusupov in 1831, half of his serfs were mortgaged and he owed 2·5 million roubles.

The Sheremetevs – the greatest of the landlords, apart from the Tsar – made little attempt to industrialize their holdings. On the eve of the manumission of their serfs, D. N. Sheremetev received a mere 18,400 roubles from sale of products (including farm produce), out of a total (1859) income of 702,000 roubles. His father and he trained serfs to perform opera but disdained to set them up in factories. Their income was chiefly gained from the enterprise of their serfs, whom they allowed to earn their own livings on payment of quit-rent; such payments amounted to 589,000 roubles in 1859.[166]

D. SERF—ENTREPRENEURS

Although Sheremetev's quit-rents were trivial on a per capita basis (3 roubles per serf in 1859), the principle was one which permitted the emergence of a category unique among capitalist elements in Russian society, the serf–entrepreneur.

Manorial industries, in Turgenev's phrase, were feared 'like the plague' by the peasants and evidently did not provide the necessary stimulus for genuine capitalist production. The most unhappy category among the peasants were the 'bondage workers' (*kabalnye rabochie*), who were lent to factories or hired for state public works by the landowner for a fixed charge paid directly to him.[167] They were recruited from among gentry-owned serfs but not on the basis of quit-rent, which endowed the serf with a certain mobility and motivation. The serf's legal status was a major obstacle in achieving an entrepreneurial position: by a law of 1730 he was prohibited from acquiring estates, the following year he was excluded from participation in state contracts, and from 1761 (as already noted) he could no longer sign promissory notes without the written consent of his owner.[168] The business partner of a serf undertook transactions on the understanding that at all times the serf's owner might nullify any contract. Although it was eventually enacted that an owner could not separate a 'serf–merchant' from his business for the purpose of sending him to the army or deporting him to Siberia, the serf was unprotected from other arbitrary interventions by his owner.

From the middle of the eighteenth century the peasant population in Russia, in particular the serf peasants, began to increase owing to the incorporation of new territories and the forcible enserfment of former Crown peasants and free peasants. According to the results of the Fifth Revision (1794–6), the recorded serf population reached 9·9 million males out of the total population of 36 million; thereafter, as Table 68 shows, serf numbers remained almost constant despite the rapid increase of the population as a whole.

The Sheremetev family derived its quit-rents largely from serf–entrepreneurs. The textile industry of Ivanovo, still the leading producer in the USSR, was established in such a fashion: in 1789, 188 serf workshops (the term '*izba*', 'hut', was used) and twenty larger factories were recorded for textile printing.

Serf–entrepreneurs were, furthermore, readier to introduce new technology than were manorial factories. Profits in the Ivanovo region – which underwent a boom when Moscow competitors were burned down in the conflagration of 1812 – were invested, e.g. in spinning jennies. Although the first jenny had been introduced in a state mill in St Petersburg in 1798, its first installer in Ivanovo, Grachev, was a serf.[169] Crown serfs, too, launched themselves into industry – in the later eighteenth century they were found among Moscow leather manufacturers (Zaitsev), haberdashery makers (Kusnetsov), and linen-

Table 68. *Population of Russia[a] (millions), 1722–1897*

		In original area	In annexed territories	Total	Rural		Serfs	
					millions	%	millions	%
1st Revision	1722	14	—	14	13·5	96·4	—	—
3rd Revision	1762	19	—	19	14·5[b]	—	7·6	52·4[c]
5th Revision	1796	29	7	36	34·7	96·4	20·0	55·5
7th Revision	1815	30·5	14·5	45	43·3	96·2	20·8	46·2
9th Revision	1851	39	28	67	63·6	95·0	21·7	31·5
10th Revision	1859	45	29	74	69·8	94·3	22·7	30·7
1st Census	1897	65	64	129	112·7	87·4	0·0	0·0

[a] Including population of Poland, the Baltic, and Finland.
[b] Great Russia and Siberia only.
[c] Among rural population only.

SOURCE. The source for the returns is Lyashchenko (*History*, 1st edn, 273, as amended in *Istoriya*, 2nd edn, 403), who selects modal dates for each revision. The periods over which returns were actually collected (*BSE2*, xxxvi, 175) were: 1st 1718–24, 3rd 1761–7, 5th 1794–1808, 7th 1815–25, and 10th 1857–9; the 9th was intended to be taken in 1850.

weavers (Luknovsky). In St Petersburg, a Sheremetev serf operated a fruit market on the Nevsky Prospekt with a capital of 3 m. roubles. In the rapidly expanding construction industry of St Petersburg, peasant contractors were especially prominent. A model career of a Russian 'self-made' entrepreneur can be illustrated in the persons of Savva Yakovlev and Savva Morozov, both quit-rent serfs. The former came to St Petersburg 'with a half-rouble piece in his pocket and his parents' blessings'; he was manumitted, and by 1762 he was ennobled; at the end of the century, his mill in St Petersburg employed nearly 3,000 workers. Later, he bought a total of twenty-two mining enterprises in the Urals.[170] Morozov opened a silk-ribbon workshop in Moscow in 1797, and by 1820 – when he was employing forty workers on twenty looms – he bought his freedom for 17,000 roubles and was enrolled in the merchant guild. He took advantage of the heavily protective tariff of 1822 to open a cotton-weaving mill, and with the help of Ludwig Knop, a tycoon of German birth but a Russian subject, the Morozovs acquired the latest English cotton machines, smuggled into Russia despite the export ban (lasting until 1842). By the 1840s his sons' factories employed over 2,500 workers, used nine steam engines, twenty-four mechanical looms, and 456 hand looms, and had an annual turnover of 1·9 m. roubles. Garelin, a calico manufacturer in Ivanovo, although owning the third largest factory in Ivanovo (1,407 workers by 1817), was unable to buy his freedom from Sheremetev until 1828. Other former serfs among the Moscow textile entrepreneurs were Alekseev, Naidenov, Konovalov, and Prokhorov; the Kondrat'ev brothers became prominent among the Moscow silk merchants, as did Malyshev, Fomin, the Nosov brothers, Grigor'ev, and Ushkov in other industrial or commercial pursuits.[171] The biographies of men like these show that while the gentry were encouraging the entrepreneurial talents of their serfs with the words later used by Bukharin to the Soviet peasantry – 'Enrichissez-vous!' – they never ceased to see the serfs as geese who laid golden eggs; they rarely agreed to release them, despite the large sums offered. To conceal their bondage, serfs would, for instance, buy houses and other property under false names, thus causing trouble to their landlords. And though a law of 1848 permitted serfs to purchase and sell landed properties in their own names (still with the written consent of their owner), such opportunities either affected only very large estates alone or remained largely unknown to the peasants.

E. ORGANIZATION OF THE MERCHANT CLASS

The merchants who stood between the serfs and the gentry had been accorded duties and privileges by analogy with, or by exemption from, those of the two principal classes. Thus, some merchants classified as *gosti* early acceded to the right to landed property, while others in the category of *posadskie lyudi* were bound in the manner of serfs. Their organization under law awaited the systematizations of Peter and Catherine, but already in the mid seventeenth century they had sufficient influence as a group to cause the withdrawal of privileges from the English Muscovy Company (1649). The measure served a political aim in expressing Tsar Alexei Mikhailovich's disapproval of the regicide by the English Parliament that January; 'it was also the result of the struggle of Russian merchants for their market and aimed at encouraging the merchant class'.[172] Yakovtsevsky finds the merchants then unable to follow up their gains partly because they were not strong enough to displace the gentry entrenched in trade (see, further, p. 455 below) and partly because they had virtually no mercantile marine.[173]

Peter seems to have been more concerned to regularize than to promote those economic activities of his subjects which were outside the control of the gentry (i.e. landowners and serfs). For his chosen organizational form, the medieval guild and the grant of monopoly, he looked both westward and backward. The Empress Catherine, while elaborating the guild, took the counsel of Adam Smith in abrogating monopoly; her *Nakaz* of 1767 was inspired by the ideas later published in *The Wealth of Nations*.

Regulations of the Chief Magistracy in 1721, implemented by decree the following year, required all 'regular' residents of commercial or industrial townships (*posady*) to join one of two guilds. The first was for large-scale merchants and the free professions (physicians and apothecaries, goldsmiths, painters, etc.), while the second was for the petty tradesman and artisan. The terms were Germanic: the small businessman's guild (*gil'diya*) was divided, according to occupation, into *tsunfty*, the derivation of which has already been mentioned (p. 430). The 'non-regular' (*neregularnye*) free wage-earners – the *chernorabochie*, 'black (i.e. taxable) labourers', and *obretayushchiesya v naimakh*, 'those seeking hire' – were not to be enrolled.[174] The guilds were duly set up and their existence reported to St Petersburg, but no attempt was made to activate them. The three 'ratings' – the word '*stat'ya*' in this meaning is now used in a nautical context – of the first guild were mere property classifications without any connotation of 'estate' (*soslovie*); the purely notional existence of the second guild can be measured from the Second Revision (1743–7), which reported membership as 709 in St Petersburg and a mere 117 in Moscow.

For handicrafts, guilds remained paper institutions. In 1799, Paul I issued a Corporative Code (*Ustav o tsekhakh*) concerning labourers, but only the first of three *tsekhi*, that for artisans, was ever set up; another would have been for the service sector (domestics, laundries, dressmaking) and a third for general labourers. Catherine's Craft Regulations (*Remeslennoe polozhenie*) of 1785, part of wider Urban Regulations (*Gorodovoe polozhenie*), prohibited work by a skilled craftsman not enrolled in the town's appropriate guild (if such had been established); training provisions were the only real reflection of a medieval guild – a journeyman should serve for three to five years – but there was neither self government (save among journeymen) nor control of working methods.

The crucial date for merchants and eventual capitalists was 1775, when a Manifesto on the Merchants' Estate, by declaring industrial enterprise open to all and abolishing all monopolies, opened access to entrepreneurship not to chosen beneficiaries but to candidates impersonally classified on the basis of capital ownership.

Minimum assets were not prescribed for the lower of the two formal groupings, the shopkeepers and the like of the *meshchanstvo*[175] (the term came to be applied not only to the whole lower middle class, including minor officials, but to the philistinism and vulgarity for which they were criticized by the intelligentsia). Three thresholds were applied to define the propertied guildsmen: membership of the First Guild was for those with a capital of at least 10,000 roubles (as already noted, a higher division, the *imenity grazhdan*, was soon introduced); of the Second Guild, a capital of at least 1,000; and of the Third, just 500 roubles. The rights accorded included graduated tax concessions and exemption from military service but chiefly related to diversification. Thus, by the mid nineteenth century (when inflation had pushed up the property qualification to 15,000 roubles) a member of the First Guild could engage in foreign trade and wholesaling anywhere in the Empire and in retailing in his own town, and he could own ships, banks, insurance companies, and large factories. One in the Second could undertake domestic wholesaling anywhere in Russia, as well as foreign non-financial transactions. The Third Guild (which in 1851 had 90 per cent of the three Guilds' total membership) was allowed to engage in smaller-scale commerce and industry.[176]

On the eve of the establishment of guilds and the abrogation of personal monopolies, only 2 per cent of Moscow merchants owned industrial undertakings, but by 1850 90 per cent of the membership of the First Guild, 59 per cent of the Second, and 10 per cent of the Third possessed industrial assets.[177] As early as 1821 half of the factories in St Petersburg were owned by merchants, and in 1843 over half of Third Guild members in that city had come up from the *meshchanstvo*.[178]

Citing these transformations of trading into industrial capital, Blackwell finds no reliable evidence on the process of change, partly because of the indiscriminate contemporary use of the word *'kupets'* for all engaged in banking and manufacture as well as in buying and selling.[179] Usage changed after, rather than during, the transformation, which can be seen either as a Marxian evolution from 'merchants' capitalism' into capitalism or as a Hicksian shift in productive assets from the preponderance of working to that of fixed capital. A legal barrier to the further intermingling of commercial and industrial capital was lifted in 1842, when factory-owners were allowed to open retail outlets at fairs and in cities other than their own. The opening-up of business opportunities encouraged by Catherine had meanwhile continued: in 1807 gentry were permitted to join any of the three guilds; by a series of regulations of 1810–12 a category of 'commercial peasants' was set up; and in 1818 peasants were allowed to establish factories. The Sixth Revision (1811) showed the urban population of Russia almost equally divided between the *kupechestvo–meshchanstvo* (42·5 per cent) and the peasantry (37·6 per cent including some minor social groups), with one-fifth (19·9 per cent) represented by gentry and other privileged classes.[180] However, the pace of liberalization proved too fast for the privileged classes and for the members of the two upper guilds: in 1816–22 new registrations in the guilds had declined by a quarter, while registrations as commercial peasants increased in the same proportion. Count Kankrin's reactionary tenure of the Ministry of Finance brought the Supplementary Regulation of the Guild System (1824) which imposed new levies on the Third Guild and the *mesh-chanstvo*, defined more restrictively the functions which each category of commercial peasant could undertake, and increased the latter's taxation. The Regulation also introduced a division within the *mesh-chanstvo*: the upper ('commercial') could own small trading, catering, or industrial establishments and employ up to eight workers; the lower (*posadskie*) could employ no more than three and – by exclusion from shop-owning or a stall at the *gostiny dvor* – was, as Blackwell remarks, 'severely limited to open-air peddling'.[181] In 1818 foreigners were precluded from membership of any guild.

If Kankrin had not in that year put forward a plan for emancipating the serfs and making peasant proprietors of them (in vain, given the determination of Alexander I not to exert compulsion on the gentry), his influence could have been considered uniformly retrograde. Falkus terms him 'conservative by nature and interested primarily in fiscal matters. He viewed with suspicion proposals for state-sponsored industrial projects, while the Director of Transport, Tol', opposed the introduction of railways in the 1830's.'[182] Kankrin himself called railways 'the injurious disease of our century'[183] and delayed until 1839 the implementation of Speransky's 'Finance Plan' of 1810, replacing the devalued paper *assignatsiya* by a silver rouble. When he retired in 1844, a century and a half had passed since Peter had described to his Swiss companion Lefort the urgent need to develop industry, trade, and the marine in Russia.[184]

F. THE GRANT OF MONOPOLIES

The private sector was, however, early able to free itself from the restriction of state-imposed monopoly or monopolistic price-regulation. Article 590 of Catherine's principal policy document (Second Supplement to her *Nakaz*, 1767) is one of a number owed to Adam Smith: 'in all circumstances monopolies should be avoided; that is, a privilege should not be given to anyone exclusively to trade in this or that commodity.'[185] This followed the words of Semyon Desnitsky, recently returned from Glasgow University, in 'A Proposal on the Establishment of Legislative, Judicial and Executive Authorities in the Russian Empire',[186] which the Russian pupil took down from Adam Smith's lectures of 1762–3 and which was eventually to figure in *The Wealth of Nations* (vol. II, book 5) in 1776.[187]

As one of the first acts of Catherine's reign, the foreign-trade monopolies established by Peter were replaced by privileged private companies. The Company for Trade with Spain, established (with obligatory participation by designated Russian merchants) in the last year of Peter's life, failed quickly, as did the three state corporations set up under the Tsarina Elizabeth. The Russian Commercial Company in Constantinople (1757), the Company for Persian Trade (1758), and the Commercial Company in Bukhara and Khiva (1760) were endowed with a monopoly at each entrepôt; but in the end local opposition led to the liquidation of all three companies in 1762. Private companies for foreign and domestic wholesale trade were thereafter encouraged with interest-free loans. The Company for Trade on the Mediterranean was created on this basis in 1763 and was followed on the home market by companies for the grain trade – at Nizhny Novgorod in 1766 and at Voronezh in 1772. Rather later, the White Sea Trading Company (1803) embraced also an organization of local handicraft production.

Many of these private companies were themselves accorded an appropriate monopoly, and Catherine's prompt confirmation at her accession of a monopsony to the gentry in the market for industrial serfs (see above, p. 443) made clear that her Smithian economics would be half-hearted. But her government did not resume the mercantilist policies which private manufacturers had forced the Empress Anna Ivanovna (1730–40) to abandon.

The episode of the discussions in 1734–6 between Urals proprietors and the government over a draft code of operation for the iron industry has been singled out by Kahan as evidence of two emergent features of Russian entrepreneurship. Firstly, 'During the post-Petrine period, dialogues between the entrepreneurs and the government become more frequent. It is possible to reconstruct some of the opinions and attitudes of the entrepreneurs and representatives of the government and to delineate and distinguish meaningful differences between their respective positions.'[188] Secondly, 'The position of the private entrepreneurs, exhibited in the bargaining about the proposed code, bears witness, at least for the iron producers, to the relatively high degree of consciousness about their real interests and potential economic power.'[189] The proportion of ironmasters from the merchant class had been rapidly rising: of the thirty-seven new entrants into large-scale iron- and copper-mining and smelting in 1701–30, all save one were merchants, although from then until 1760 nineteen new works were set up by gentry as against forty-eight by merchants.[190] They successfully resisted the introduction into private ironworks of state-appointed 'furnace charge masters' (*shikhtmeister*) for both quality and financial control. They declined to furnish the government (which had military and export requirements in mind) with metal of uniformly high quality, arguing that some of the output had to be cheap to be saleable. Consistently with this attitude, they rejected official price-setting, reaffirming the authority they had gained in 1719 to select their own product-mix.[191]

G. ENTREPRENEURSHIP AS A CHANNEL FOR RELIGIOUS DISSENT

The ironmasters who resisted further state intervention were motivated by capitalist self-interest; entrepreneurship may also manifest itself by rejection of the state's regulated scheme of life.

The intimate connection of the Orthodox Church with the Imperial authority and the latter's identification of revolution with heresy and schism set the environment in which the religious dissenter was 'excluded from the normal avenues of advancement, power and privilege in early nineteenth-century Russia. The professions were for the most part closed to him, as were the military and civil services. And so his energies were turned into the economic and particularly commercial spheres in an agrarian society.'[192] The reference was primarily to Jews and secondly to the Old Believers, the schismatics of 1666. Both had been excluded from the centres of early industrialization: the Old Believers lived in banishment or as fugitives until invited to return to towns by Catherine; Jews were confined to the Pale of Settlement (which had been annexed to the Empire in the partitions of Poland[193]) until the middle of the ensuing century.[194] As entrepreneurs, both have been the subject of special study. Gerschenkron chose the case of the Old Believers 'to test the plausibility of the causal connection between a theological doctrine and economic activities by exploring an area far removed from the West and in the case of a religious persuasion altogether alien to the doctrines of Calvin and Calvinist theologists.'[195] Blackwell accords entrepreneurial importance to their return to the ancient capital and, above all, their development of its textile industry of the early nineteenth century. 'Here the peculiar beliefs, way of life and organization of the larger communities of the schismatics seemed admirably suited to the accumulation of industrial capital, the provision of incentive for master and worker alike, and the mobilization of the lower strata of Moscow and the surrounding countryside into a factory labour force.'[196] Habits engendered by defensive isolation from a secularized Church – frugality, honesty, reliability, industry, and thrift – were a sound foundation for the community enterprises which they undertook, while literacy – necessary for apologetic exegesis, especially among congregations without priests (*bespopovtsy*) – facilitated commercial transactions. Among the schismatics who pooled property and banned inheritance, the propensity to save was far above that which might have been anticipated from current income levels; the elders of these communities chose to invest in modern techniques[197] to maximize the return on communal capital.[198] The communities with priests (*popovtsy*) needed funds for their survival and for training and ordaining ministers abroad, while both groups needed to bribe, or pay for representation before, unsympathetic or persecuting officials.

The fact that entrepreneurial activities actually yielded wealth far in excess of what was needed, or at least used, for the defence of the group and that fortunes of many millions were accumulated, should indicate the complexity of the relations between motivation and vindication. But it can be argued that vindication was not just a light veneer spread over crudely materialistic interests and aspirations.[199]

However, the impetus from the Old Believers did not go much beyond the industrial spurt before the Emancipation of the serfs. The entrepreneurs themselves were in the main attracted into the conventional way of life and assimilated themselves into the rest of the business community.

The fanatical Skoptsy, who castrated themselves (often after founding, and then deserting, a family), used their conspiratorial congregations for a variety of money-making pursuits from counterfeiting and smuggling to usury and gold-working. Pooling labour and wealth in their so-called 'ships', the sect enjoyed a brief period of toleration under Alexander I but by mid-century were largely eliminated by the police from European Russia. When the remainder, mostly withdrawn to Siberia, were dealt with by the Soviet authorities, three of the defendants at the 'Skoptsy Trial' of 1930 were ex-millionaires. Those who fled to Romania were of more modest substance – the cab trade was their calling – and were broken up a decade later.

Alexander I was also relatively more liberal toward the Jews, encouraging them to tender for state contracts, though his concern may chiefly have been aroused by a desire to remove disabilities which might unsettle the recently acquired Western territories. Within three years of his death, Jews owned seventy-five woollen mills in Russian Poland, while in neighbouring Volhynia one Jew, Joseph Bernstein, alone possessed twelve factories employing 740. In the 1840s Israel Brodsky helped to found Ukrainian sugar-refining, importing equipment and technicians from Germany; by 1872, one-quarter of the rapidly expanding sugar industry was in Jewish hands. Also in the 1840s, the Jews of the Pale developed a network of banks which underpinned Ukrainian industrialization generally – there were eight Jewish-controlled banks in Berdichev in 1849 – and the Warsaw banker Herman Epstein became one of the first railway magnates of the Empire. However, as already mentioned, economic restrictions on the Jews were not relaxed until the very eve of serf Emancipation; the persistence of anti-Semitism in the Pale (culminating in the pogroms of 1905) considerably reduced the scope for Jews in Russian entrepreneurship. The vast majority remained in poverty-stricken ghettos or emigrated.[200]

H. FOREIGN ENTREPRENEURS

Because virtually the entire Jewish population was brought into the Empire by annexation – the Pale, the Caucasus, and Central Asia – there would be some ground for equating them with foreigners engaging in entrepreneurship as a means to assimilation. Sombart saw this as the role of Jews as 'newcomers [who] must concentrate their thoughts to obtain a foothold, and all their economic activities will be dictated by this desire'.[201] The facts, however, indicate that the majority of foreign settlers in Tsarist Russia were inconspicuously assimilated into agriculture,[202] notably the German settlers brought in by Catherine, and Serbs fleeing to an Orthodox refuge from Turkish repression. The ruling class of the Baltic States, annexed in the eighteenth century, was predominantly German and spread its influence in industry and the crafts and professions, at first into Petersburg and later throughout the Empire. The German-language university of Tartu (Dorpat), founded by Gustavus Adolphus in 1632, had been closed for nearly a century when it was re-opened by Alexander I in 1802, to become a centre for the transmission of Western technology and education generally.

The capitalist enterprise of foreigners in Russia came, however, not through settlers but rather in line of descent from expatriates, who came to Russia to take up occupations – British, French, or Americans at various times – and who were ready to leave when conditions deteriorated – not one Dane remained after the October Revolution. The line begins with the Hanseatic Peterhof, and it is significant that the expulsion of the Muscovy Company did not lead to any significant reduction of foreign participation on the Russian market. As already indicated (p. 429), the nobility (*dvoryanstvo*) opposed their replacement by native merchants, who would have driven harder bargains with the gentry, and even many merchants preferred profit-sharing with foreigners to independent action.[203] Peter had sought to reassure the native merchant class of the security of their enterprise, by guaranteeing their title to industrial property even in the event of bankruptcy.[204]

The foreign technicians who furnished the technology for Peter's state-run factories rarely entered management at a point which could be termed entrepreneurial, since legally they could neither establish nor operate factories until Catherine's Urban Statute of 1785. Soviet historians have tended in the past to play down the role of foreigners in Petrine industrialization,[205] and Blackwell concludes that 'as with so many of Peter's reforms, the developments in science and technology during his reign were not spontaneous growths nourished by a receptive Russian culture, but were artificial creations stimulated into being by the will of the Tsar and shaped by state decree'.[206]

Catherine's authorization of foreign enterprise was largely annulled by Paul I, who restricted foreigners to Moscow and Petersburg. His son, Alexander, required (1807) such foreigners to register as 'foreign merchants' (*inostrannie gosti*), with a semi-permanent right to residence and eventually citizenship, or as 'visiting businessmen' (*zaezhnye kuptsi*), on a temporary basis. Those with 'incomplete citizenship' could register only in coastal and border towns and were obliged to pay a tax on assets exceeding 50,000 roubles. But they were permitted to hire labour and operate factories. In 1824, however, an *ukaz* forbade them to trade not only with the peasantry but also with all levels of the urban population below the Second Guild. Two years later this was relaxed by allowing a foreign factory-owner to register in the

Second or Third Guild for a period of ten years without having to become a Russian subject: at the end of this period, if he refused to do so, he had to sell his enterprise. Police surveillance, bureaucratic harassment, and heavy taxation limited the appeal of Nicolaian Russia to foreigners. It was not until June 1860 that restrictions on foreigners were abolished and the privileges granted by Catherine restored.

By mid-century (1850), at least 60,000 foreigners (over half of them Germans) resided in Petersburg, constituting more than one in ten of the city's population. Foreigners – most of whom had dual citizenship – dominated foreign trade in the first half of the nineteenth century but did not generally invest their profits in domestic industry, which remained overwhelmingly Russian. As is noted below, entrepreneurs from abroad tended to go directly into home manufacturing, generally in association with the introduction of new technology. By the time of Emancipation, the share of foreign holdings in joint-stock companies was, on one estimate, 14 per cent.

By contrast, the provision of foreign funds to government loans was substantial. A score of loans were floated abroad between 1798 and 1864, amounting to the equivalent of £92 m., but only a few brought entrepreneurial involvement. The railways loans might be considered, at least indirectly, among the latter. The main foreign bankers for Russia – the London house of Baring, and Hope & Co. of Amsterdam – collaborated in the loan of £5·5 m. for the St Petersburg–Moscow railway in 1849. Baring and Hope & Co. were associated with the Péreire brothers (founders of the Crédit Mobilier of Paris) and a Paris consortium headed by the Hottingers in outmanoeuvring the Rothschilds in 1856 in creating the Grande Société des Chemins de Fer Russes; the Rothschilds themselves provided only two loans in this period (43 m. roubles in 1822 and £15 m. in 1862). The German bankers Mendelssohn and Bleichröder also undertook the extensive financing of railways. On the other hand, the two Hope & Co. loans of 1831 and 1832 (20 m. roubles each) seem to have been used to finance the suppression of the Polish uprising.

The mobility of domestic capital and the transfer of foreign funds within the country should have been enhanced by the Statute on Joint-Stock Companies, which received the Imperial Assent on 6 December 1836.

The creation of the minimum of legal conditions necessary for the development of joint-stock institutions in the country, while keeping in the hands of the government the effective means of influencing the activity of those institutions – that, in brief, was the concept of the law of 1836.[207]

In the first Yearbook (1869) of the Ministry of Finance, only 28 companies figured in a list of all those established between 1799 and 1868, including those which had merged or ceased trading.[208] It is a measure of the subsequent pace of change that, as shown by a new list published in the fifth Yearbook (1874), 554 companies were created in 1869–73. Of the seventy-four companies established by 1856 under the provisions of the 1836 Statute, with an aggregate share capital of 65·6 m. roubles, five (with 3·7 m. roubles capital) had never been activated and twenty-two (16·9 m. roubles capital) had been liquidated.[209]

Foreigners in the Petrine scheme had been brought for their technological skills rather than their finance; but it was not long before the roles began to merge, by the association of a technical innovation with risk capital and management. In 1753, the Englishmen Chamberlain and Cuzzins founded near St Petersburg the first cotton-weaving and cotton-printing factory in Russia. They seem to have risked little in view of the remarkable concessions they were granted, namely a monopoly on calico production, tariff protection, the right to duty-free imports, 300 state serfs, and a loan of 30,000 roubles. Lyashchenko maintains that no similar privileges were granted prior to the protectionist tariff of 1822.[210] A Scot, Charles Baird, who originally went to Russia as an engineer from the Carron Works to modernize Russian foundry plant, soon set up wholly on his own account, in one of the 'very few private ventures', as a recent history of the city observes.[211] With a Welshman named Morgan, he produced Russia's first steam engines and other steam-powered equipment. He obtained a ten-year monopoly for a shipping line between Kronstadt and St Petersburg when his plant launched Russia's first steamship in 1815. Under his son Francis, the Baird Engineering Works was the largest in Russia, with an annual output (in 1860) of 0·5 m. roubles. In 1883 a Frenchman, Philippe Henri Girard, set up a mechanized linen mill on the outskirts of Warsaw (his name is perpetuated in the town district of Żyrardów) and a German, Louis Geyer, established the first cotton-spinning mill with steam machinery near Łódź in 1833.[212]

The ban on imports of machinery from Great Britain (until 1842) inhibited similar penetration from that country, although the German Ludwig Knop – who was a combination of John D. Rockefeller and Richard Arkwright, according to Schulze-Gaevernitz[213] – founded his industrial empire in Russia by the clandestine importing of such machinery. After the repeal, the inflow of technology and management from the UK was considerable. Blackwell lists five major British entrepreneur–innovators in the St Petersburg textile industry in the 1840s, three in engineering there, and seven in Moscow engineering. The three largest engineering works in the capital by mid-century were foreign-owned, those of a Swede (Nobel), a Bavarian (the Duke of

Lichtenberg, son-in-law of Nicholas I), and Americans (Harrison and the Winan brothers). More typical of them – Lichtenberg was a scientist and a senior scientific administrator to boot – were German entrepreneurs, chiefly from Hanseatic ports, who moved from trade to industry, notably textiles and sugar refining, e.g. Brandt, Knop, and Ludwig Stieglitz. The latter founded the first insurance company in 1827, which developed into Russia's leading commercial bank, and his son Alexander became Director of the State Bank on its creation in 1860.[214]

Finally, an impetus from those who may be termed both native and foreign is to be identified in Poland. The economic regime under which the 'Congress Kingdom' operated until the rising of 1830 was quasi-extraterritorial. The Imperial authorities allowed the Kingdom of Poland its own economic policy, including tariff protection. However, tariffs were intended to promote the growth of economic relations with the Russian Empire and to diminish those with the Prussian and Austrian Empires. The consequences for trade were dramatic. Whereas 21 per cent of Congress Poland's exports had gone to Austria in 1823, a mere 1 per cent was sold in 1830; Polish exports to the Russian Empire rose 74 per cent between 1821 and 1829, and at the latter date two-fifths of Polish cloth production was being delivered to Russian buyers.[215] The latter illuminates the significant development: from the Polish territories which partition had yielded to Prussia and Austria, Poles, Jews, and some German textile manufacturers migrated to the relatively more polonized administration of the Congress Kingdom in the 1820s and established themselves in Łódź.[216] They had their origin mainly in former Polish Silesia, whose export trade to the territory which had come under Russian administration had been stifled: 'the Russian tariff of 1821 constituted a virtual prohibition of imports of foreign textiles'.[217] The industrialization, subsidized by the Congress Kingdom, converted a trade deficit in 1820 equivalent to 66 per cent of turnover (66·3 m. złp imports, 13·7 m. złp exports) to a virtually balanced trade in 1830 (47·7 m. złp imports and 45·1 m. złp exports).[218]

The crushing of the Polish revolt of 1830 was followed by the erection of the 1831 tariff wall between Russia and Poland which led to a further entrepreneurial migration of textile manufacturers to the Polish–Jewish town of Białystok, which was just within the Russian tariff boundary.[219]

The decade beginning in the mid-forties was one of rapid development of Łódź industry: the Kingdom's output of cotton yarn rose three and one-half times between 1845 and 1851, when 40 per cent derived from the Geyer mills; half of the cotton cloth production in the Kingdom by length, and 70 per cent by value, came from Łódź itself;

but while the spinning and printing processes were extensively mechanized during this period, only the three major weaving establishments, those of foreign entrepreneurs, were mechanized: *viz.* Geyer (1839), Krusche at Pabianice (1849), and K. Scheibler (1857–8).[220]

The abolition of the tariff on the manufactures of the former Kingdom of Poland, as one of the measures of economic consolidation after the Russian defeat in the Crimean War, did not in the event injure either the Łódź or the Białystok industrialists, who came to a *de facto* agreement on the division of their Russian and Polish markets; the specialization soon extended to the Moscow manufacturers. Among the latter, Knop innovated in a different direction by contracting with cotton planters in Russian Turkestan: his scheme of advancing funds to growers for food, seed, and equipment was described by Chayanov as 'the first path for the penetration of capitalist relations into the countryside'.[221] He was citing the case to demonstrate how 'bringing agriculture into the general capitalist system need by no means involve the creation of very large, capitalistically organized production units based on hired labor. Repeating the stages in the development of industrial capitalism, agriculture comes out of its semi-natural existence and becomes subject to trading capitalism.'[222] For such relations to operate in rural European Russia, serfdom had to be abolished, and for this reason (and for many others), the Emancipation of 1861 is one of the crucial turning points in Russian history.

IV. *State-Led and State-Run Capitalism*

A. THE PROBLEM OF CREATING A MARKET

The momentum of Peter's industrialization by military demand and regulated supply expired with defeat on the Crimean battlefields, as the then Minister of War was among the first to recognize.[223] Cumbersome military procurement from inefficient producers epitomized the lag of the Russian economy behind the dynamic capitalism of the West. The 'Westernizers' attained their prime objective – the Great Reforms centring upon serf emancipation – in 1861, but the essentially negative policy of abandoning restrictions was not complemented by positive measures to create a competitive market.

Proof that Russia was not to be endowed with a free-market mechanism came with the new century; but the combination of small-scale peasant proprietorship, partially capitalistic, and large-scale industry, mostly monopolistic, was potentially stable. A market in non-farm labour was the elemental constituent of the changes which began the transitional period 1861–1905. The terms of the Emancipation of the serfs, allowing free choice of jobs for those who gained authorization to leave the land, provided a market in Russia's most abundant resource; by the promotion of infrastructure ahead of demand, the Russian government opened up and stabilized a market of great physical and financial magnitude. Railway construction, with a minimum return guaranteed by the government, encouraged the mobilization of capital at home and abroad to furnish the communications and to exploit those resources, and for a time it attracted the sort of entrepreneur who had contested, rather than conforming to, the restrictions of the previous system. But the colourful eccentrics who were representative of the early railway kings yielded to more sober company directors with the establishment of markets in financial assets and the ordering of public finance. The Bourse, however, never became as active a mart for the burgeoning joint-stock companies, which, rather, grew with debt capital from the new commercial banks. The lower proportion of risk capital to total corporate capital may have fostered cartelization, which was favourably regarded by the government as an antidote to the 1900 depression. The cartel certainly served to strengthen the hand of domestic entrepreneurs, who increasingly displaced the foreigner in the early years of the present century.

B. THE MARKET IN MANPOWER AND SPACE

On the eve of Emancipation, the industrial labour force included 386,000 Crown serfs in state factories, 230,000 Crown serfs in state mines, 519,000 possessional serfs, and 59,000 manorial serfs; serfs working as artisans or in business, even big business, on their own account were subject to recall by their owner. The methods of recruitment and of management went together – coercion and brutality rather than labour bargaining and incentives. Although limited until 1906 by the collectively payable redemption dues and the residence obligation, a market for manpower was created in 1861.[224] The reform was, as the Tsar explained, 'from above rather than from below', and all Soviet historians insist on its character as a precondition to capitalist industrialization or agricultural expansion.[225] Even if before the reform the peasantry was dividing itself, as Lenin suggested, into rural bourgeoisie and agricultural proletariat,[226] such proto-capitalism was heavily constrained. Before 1861, also, employers – state managers or private owners – had become accustomed to hiring a segment of their labour, but when faced with manpower that could withhold its labour and hold out or go elsewhere for more pay, they had to consider with far more scrutiny whether to replace manpower by capital, and in short they had to learn to become capitalists.

Among the small but growing band of intellectuals, the power of the state to operate directly within the production process was regarded with the same hostility as the power of the police or the provincial governor in political and social life. Herzen in 1857 equated a state-run economy with 'Ghengis Khan with railways and telegraphs'. The government, disenchanted with its Petrine role of economic management after military defeat had exposed the chaos of its supply services and industries, sought to foster a market which could co-ordinate its activities with those of independent entrepreneurs.

As the discussion of Peter's strategy has shown, the state itself had previously compensated for the lack of a unifying and stable market demand which apportioned capitalists' allocation in the Western industrial revolutions. Enterprises outside state sponsorship were in forms least conducive to encouraging this sort of market, namely of bespoke handicrafts and customary fairs. Mention has already been made of the isolation of producers from distributors and the prevalence of fairs (p. 428)[227], but both deserve further emphasis. The six thousand fairs to which reference was made in a medieval context were the antithesis of the capitalist counterpart, the specialized commodity exchange, and inhibited the promotion of regular wholesaling. Both that and retailing were stunted by the continuance of a large subsistence sector in food and simple consumer goods and – away from a few big centres – by the isolated and modest extent of urban commerce and industry. Such demand as was generated by cash crops and food-marketing by a basically subsistence peasantry was subject to wide fluctuation by region and by year, dictated by the vagaries of the climate. As late as 1891–2, the agricultural market and transport were sufficiently undeveloped for famine to decimate whole regions while surpluses were being traded elsewhere.[228]

This was also the time when the Tsarist Empire reached its greatest territorial extent. The significance of incorporating Poland in fostering the textile industry and the opening of capitalist relations in Turkestan cotton fields has been noted; but the annexations of the second half of the century were of virgin land – from the Far Eastern territories taken from Chinese suzerainty and the mountains of Svanetia wrested from Georgian chieftains (both in 1858) to the Pamir frontier of 1895.

C. STATE INFRASTRUCTURE

The unification and articulation of the immense potential within one-sixth of the world's land surface could serve military–political as well as domestic–economic ends. The construction of railways – Moscow and St Petersburg had already been linked in 1851 – was hence a prime concern of the government. They would draw the market together, facilitate access to the frontier as much for troops as for exports, and disperse the population. A more widely diffused economy was desirable not only to exploit remote mines and farms but also to minimize concentrations of workers who were a threat, by revolution or otherwise, to the autocracy. The Trans-Siberian and the Orenburg and Tashkent railways created ribbons of peasant settlement wherever the terrain allowed. The further the now-emancipated peasant was from urban settlement, the less would he rely on traditional cartage to the market town and fair and the more would he market by rail, thus offering room for capitalist intermediaries and enlarging exports. The transformation of transport structure for the grain trade was in itself significant in generating capitalist commerce: procurement, marketing, and export required heavier investment to cope with the greater volume of turnover and the greater distances involved. Moreover, new transport broke the hold of the old merchant class who had dominated the river wharves. Exports themselves were promoted by graduated railway tariffs to the Black Sea and Baltic ports.

The state provision of transport routes was not of course new. Peter had had the *Gosudareva doroga* built between the White Sea and Lake Onega in 1702 and linked the Baltic with the Caspian–Volga waterway by the Vyshy Volochok canal; the Russian government's guarantee of interest on the capital of private railway companies was already standard European practice outside the UK. Count Witte, the Minister of Finance whose imprint on the economic system was the greatest in the centuries between Peter and Stalin, made it a cardinal feature of his policy that railways be controlled – though by no means financed – by the state as instruments of industrialization and trade.[229] A certain clash occurred between the government's political desire to have railways built to link cities and the higher profit that could have been derived from a more intensive network in the industrializing areas (the Donbas or the Baltic states). Non-economic priorities were also evident in the financial provision made for such railways as Tiflis–Erevan and Kislovodsk–Tashkent – which served the same political and military purposes as the Georgian Military Highway earlier in the century.

It needs no reiteration that state and state-guaranteed railway construction furnished the flow of orders for large-scale industry to which private entrepreneurs responded in the second half of the nineteenth century.[230] Its 'backward linkage' was into an industrial revolution of coal, steel, and engineering, and its 'forward linkage' – through a freight network well ahead of demand – united and stabilized the market for consumer goods. The government also endeavoured to improve communications other than transport. These were needed to give substance to a market as a system of information and signals for action. The post office was reorganized (the first postage stamp appeared in 1858) and a telegraph network started. A Central Statistical Committee was established in the Ministry of Internal Affairs in 1858; its precursor (since 1811), the Statistical Department in the Ministry of Police, testifies to the prominence of political motives in such documentation, and even after 1863 (when the Statistical Council was created) data collection by provincial statistical committees was effected locally by the police and the *volost'* administration. Thereafter the annual reports of provincial governors had to include statements on land holdings and area, the grain crop, population, and other statistics. But because of their police origin, the figures were often incomplete or inadequately verified,[231] and the new elected local authorities of the *zemstvo* (1864) established their own statistical services. The first population census was conducted in 1897, and by the end of the century the government's annual abstract of statistics looked much like contemporary abstracts in Western Europe. Private publishing furnished the business directories and advertising which by that date were, at least for Moscow, St Petersburg, and Odessa, up to the standards of presentation and content set in towns of similar economic importance in the West.

D. RAILWAY MAGNATES

The Nikolaevskaya railway from Moscow to St Petersburg was built by the state, but its very high cost and the delays in its construction (1843–51) induced the government to prefer private initiative until after 1870. Reutern's tenure of the Ministry of Finance (1862–78) opened an unparalleled era of railway speculation. The beneficiaries of the railway boom, however – apart from their flair as entrepreneurs – exhibited no clear similarities. P. G. Derviz, who received his railway concessions from Reutern as an old schoolmate, retired (in 1868) at the age of 42, after only a few years of activity, to devote himself to the enjoyment of his wealth in ostentatious idleness and dissipation. Samuel Polyakov was a complete contrast – a hard-working Jewish entrepreneur who began as a modest post-office employee in Kharkov, and built, in four years and at half the cost, the Kozlov–Rostov and Kursk–Taganrog lines, each of them longer than the St Petersburg–Moscow railway, and connecting the grain-growing central regions with the Black Sea ports. He gave away a large portion of his fortune for educational and charitable purposes. Karl von Meck, of German stock, started under von Derviz's direction on the Moscow–Kozlov line and became a magnate on his own account. After his early death, his wife Nadezhda became the benefactress of Russian artists and supported the composer Tchaikovsky.

Ivan S. Bliokh devoted twenty years to railway-building and was in charge of the line connecting the Baltic with the grain centres of the Ukraine (Libau–Romny line) and Odessa with Brest. Bliokh was a fine example of a self-made entrepreneur of Jewish extraction, totally untutored, who started his career as a small railway contractor. When he prospered he had the bold intelligence to withdraw from his job and attend a German university. Thereupon he returned to Russia and made his way into high society by successful marriage and conversion to Christianity. He founded the Corporation of Southwestern Railways, where two later Ministers of Finance, Vyshnegradsky and Witte, were employed. At the summit of his career Bliokh decided to devote the rest of his life to scholarly pursuits and wrote a book, *The Influence of Railways on the Economic Life of Russia* (1878), of which a congenial parallel in the Anglo-Saxon literature may be found in the works of Admiral Mahan. At the end of his life Bliokh became a philanthropist and a pacifist; he died in 1901.

Savva Mamontov was a rather different type of entrepreneur. Coming from a very rich family of liquor salesmen (in 1850 the liquor monopoly was still in private hands), he appears to be typical of the late Russian entrepreneur, who, after achieving outstanding business success, would devote the rest of his life to non-commercial activities and leisure. In 1885 Mamontov founded a private opera company in Moscow to promote the works of Russian composers such as Mussorgsky, Rimsky-Korsakov, and Tchaikovsky, and he was the patron of Fedor Chalyapin. As a railway constructor, Mamontov developed the communications network north of Moscow connecting the capital with Yaroslavl', Vologda, and Archangel, but he went bankrupt in the financial crisis of 1900–3. He was imprisoned on the grounds of embezzling government loans but used his term for sculpture and the writing of opera librettos.

Under the Finance Ministry of Bunge (1881–6), the government resumed its rôle of chief promoter of industrialization. Instead of merely guaranteeing a return on capital, the Treasury started to purchase railway shares, so that by 1912 67 per cent of railway lines were owned by the state; the total amount of capital invested in railways amounted to 4,700 m. roubles in 1900, of which state participation was between 3,500 and 3,600 m. roubles. During 1890–1900 the Treasury contributed 120 m. roubles annually, foreign loans provided 341 m., and the rest came from various domestic credit institutions. On the first day of 1901, the current deposits of savings banks totalled 752 m. roubles, of which 637 m. were placed in securities, with the state using 37 per cent of these securities for direct investment in railways.[232]

E. PROVISION OF A FINANCIAL FRAMEWORK

As the government intended, railway construction attracted both domestic and foreign capital into other sectors. A previous volume of this *History* has already stressed the need to complement entrepreneurial risk-taking by the foundation of a capital market,[233] along with which may be noted measures to protect the rewards of risk-taking and to spread risks more widely. The Judicial Reform of November 1864 initiated changes in the legal framework for economic activity which were only in part a modernization.[234] Re-strengthening governmental control of the judiciary from 1885 was contrary to such a trend, but at least business began to be afforded 'a legal system capable of dealing with modern commercial relationships and institutions impartially, flexibly, swiftly and predictably'.[235]

The availability and protection of a market for long-term contracts (and an equity share can be regarded as a contract without a terminal date) helped to mobilize domestic savings. Whereas the bulk of the 178 m. roubles which flowed into railway joint-stock companies between 1851 and 1860 came from abroad (100 m. for the Grande Société de Chemins de Fer Russes alone), the nearly 700 m. raised in the ensuing decade contained a substantial domestic element.

Modern financial institutions appeared in the 1860s: a central bank of issue was founded in 1860 and the first private commercial bank in 1864, and the state bank was authorized to issue industrial bonds in 1894. In 1875 the assets of the five major banks totalled 247 m. roubles, and there were a total of twenty-five banks in St Petersburg and five in Moscow. By 1914 the assets of the big five were 2,255 m. roubles, and there were 567 banks in the capital and 153 in Moscow.[236] Mutual credit unions and urban communal banks sprang up throughout the country – in 1875 there were eighty-four of the former and 235 of the latter; aggregate holdings of financial assets rose from 1,600 m. roubles in 1861 – nearly all in state bonds, shares being a mere 5 per cent – to just under 5,000 m. in 1876, predominantly railway stocks and mortgage bonds of the agricultural banks.[237] The mobilization of small savings was promoted by the creation of the Peasant Land Bank in 1883 and by a new Savings Bank Statute in 1895.[238]

A revision of the 1836 Statute on Joint-Stock Companies consistent with the spirit of reform was slow to emerge. A draft was prepared within the Ministry of Finance in February–April 1861, but it took exactly five years (to February 1866) to pass through other departments and out of the Private Chancellery, and a further four years, mainly in the Ministry of Justice, before receiving the Imperial Assent on 17 February 1870.[239] Brokerage and jobbing were authorized in 1874, and an equity market appropriate to an industrial market economy was established.

The St Petersburg Bourse had been opened in 1703 and magnificently housed since 1816, but it stood almost alone in Russia until the second half of the nineteenth century. By 1914 there were 115 commodity and stock exchanges throughout the country, and shares quoted on the St Petersburg *Birzha* were valued at 2,000 m. roubles. The St Petersburg Bourse Committee and other regional committees were raised after 1870 to semi-official status as representative bodies facilitating relations between the Ministry of Finance and the main contributors of private savings,[240] and the taxation system was modernized – though not to contemporary Western European standards. The process began with tax reform and the unification of the state budget (1862) and continued with Bunge's abolition of the poll tax (1885), but neither he nor Witte succeeded in introducing income tax, which eventually came as a war-time measure in 1916: Witte, as Chairman of the Council of Ministers, included an income tax in his proposals of April 1906 to present to the First Duma, but he was dismissed even before the Tsar read the draft.[241]

Nor was Witte able to abolish collective tax liability. Redemption dues were levied on the village *obshchina*, and the retention of residence control was intended, in the age-old tradition of *mir* and *posad*, both to equalize and to safeguard tax payments. The Chairman of the Council of Ministers, Bunge, succeeded, while Witte was Finance Minister, in relaxing the regulations governing the issue of identity cards permitting settlement outside the taxable village. From 1894 such identity cards could be issued for five years (instead of one year) even though dues were in arrears.[242] The requirement of the consent of the *mir* if there were arrears, and of that of the head of household in any case, remained a barrier to peasant migration, a barrier which was not removed until the Stolypin reform of 1906.[243] Witte confessed to doubting 'whether the man can be found to carry through the change from the *obshchina* to the basis of individual farms which is so necessary for economic progress'.[244] In a letter to Nicholas II in 1898 he argued further for a 'capitalist peasantry' and against the multiplicity of authorities to whom he was subject – the rural chief,[245] the police, the *feldsher* (medical assistant paid by the *zemstvo* and hence the latter's local agent), the elders of the *volost* (rural district) and of his *obshchina*, as well as the squire (*barin*).[246] The rural chief himself was responsible for tax collection to the Ministry of the Interior, which the Ministry of Finance supervised.[247] The responsibility for tax collection was transferred from communes to the rural chief in 1899, but the reform required his 'unceasing coercion' to extract the taxes, and the only concession made was in allowing individual responsibility in hamlets.[248]

The modest relaxation of the constraints on peasant migration in the 1890s would not have ended so soon in complete repeal without the 1905 Revolution. What Soviet historians call the Stolypin reaction, and others his reforms or the 'Great Volte-face',[249] recalled the peasant proprietor to the Russian scene after an absence of two and a half centuries. The term 'reaction' correctly denotes the Stolypin policy of ignoring the revolutionary demands for agrarian reform, which were fulfilled only in 1917 by Lenin's famous first decree 'On Land'. From 1906 until Stalin's collectivization drive of 1930, small peasant farms were to remain the mainstay of agriculture. When the peasantry were brought together again into collective farms, the prohibition against migration and the collective responsibility toward state dues were resumed. After 1932, collective farmers could leave only with the permission of the board of the farm;[250] the compulsory delivery of produce at nominal prices between 1933 and 1958[251] (and continuing subsequently as 'state purchases' at cost-related prices) echoed the communal responsibility of the old *mir*.

If the institutions which distinguish the first three decades of the twentieth century from previous and later periods were to be characterized in a single phrase, it might be 'small farms and large cartels'. The peasantry began to take the opportunity of liberation from an enforced communalism to embrace small-scale capitalism, whereas the industrial capitalists merged their autonomy into national and occasionally international syndicates. After the October Revolution of 1917 farmers revived the *mir* or tried other co-operatives – the TOZ and the *kommuna* – all on a voluntary basis, while industry exchanged the capitalist cartel for the socialist *glavk*.

F. FINANCE CAPITAL

Lyashchenko believes that the 'preponderance of big-corporation capital, particularly foreign capital' was inherently monopolistic;[252] an earlier contribution to this *History* tentatively concluded that the cartels held production below a level which contemporary conditions would have reached because 'financially they were partially dependent on foreign support'. Cartelization itself led, in Portal's views, to an increasing dependence on banks for finance.[253]

Clearly it is no part of the present chapter to evaluate the decisions that entrepreneurs actually took; but the extent of domestic corporate involvement with banks and with foreign investors, and especially

with foreign banks, is of major significance for the development of
capitalism in what proved to be its terminal phase in Russia. Vanag
computes (see Table 69) that in 1913 75·0 per cent of coal-mining firms
in Russia drew on bank capital and that 75·8 per cent of these were
Franco-Belgian banks, 10·5 per cent Franco-German banks, 13·4 per
cent German, and 0·3 per cent British; the situation was similar in coal-
mining in the Polish region.

Table 69. *Bank Participation in Joint-Stock Coal-Mining Companies
in 1913 (million roubles)*

	Russia	Polish region
French banks	113·3[a]	7·3
Franco-German banks	15·8	9·8
German	20·0	11·9
British	0·5	—
Total capital	199·3	39·6

[a] Including Franco-Belgian.

SOURCE. N. Vanag, *Finansovy kapital v Rossii* (Moscow, 1925), 123 and 125.

Gerschenkron, in a well-known proposition, has termed the investment role of the banking system one of the many substitutes within the
process of industrial development which obviate an explanation in
terms of standard 'prerequisites' in the manner of Marx or Rostow.
The inadequacy of entrepreneurial ability may be compensated for by
increasing the unit size of plant above what would otherwise be optimal, by dividing the entrepreneurial function (the investment bank
was 'a powerful invention comparable in economic effect to that of
the steam engine'), or by importation.[254]

So far as domestic capital mobilization is concerned, Gerschenkron's
proposition illuminates the differences between Moscow and St Petersburg.[255] The founders of the Moscow banks were mostly textile manufacturers. The Moscow Merchant Bank, founded in 1856 and one of the
largest in the country (see Table 70, which also shows the limited

Table 70. *Distribution of Joint-Stock Banks in 1873 (million roubles
of deposits)*

St Petersburg area	
SPB Discount and Loan Bank	193
SPB International Commercial Bank	192
SPB Volga–Kama Bank	119
SPB Private Commercial Bank	112
SPB branch of the Warsaw Commercial Bank	69
Russian Bank for Foreign Trade	0
Area total	684

Table 70 (*cont.*).

Moscow area

Moscow Merchant Bank	129
Moscow Discount Bank	127
Moscow Volga–Kama Bank	93
Moscow Commercial Loan Bank	44
Moscow Trade Bank	40
Moscow Industrial	11
	——
Area total	443

Southern area

Odessa Commercial Bank	132
Kiev Private Bank	41
Azov–Don Bank[a]	39
Kharkov Trade Bank	15
Kiev Industrial Bank[a]	15
Nikolaev Bank	12
Tiflis Commercial Bank	10
Kishinev Bank	8
Ekaterinoslav Bank	8
Kremenchug Commercial Bank[a]	5
	——
Area total	304

East Central area

Volga–Kama Bank[a]	140
Simbirsk Trade Bank	15
Orel Commercial Bank	8
Nizhegorod Merchant Bank	7
Kostroma Commercial Bank	3
Ryazan Trade Bank	2
	——
Area total	175

Western area

Warsaw Commercial Bank	25
Riga Commercial Bank[a]	12
Warsaw Discount Bank	9
Reval Commercial Bank	7
Vilno Private Bank[a]	7
Kronshtad Commercial Bank	2
Łódź Bank	1
	——
Area total	63
	——
Grand total	1,670

[a] With branches.

SOURCE. *Statistichesky vremennik Rossiskoi Imperii*, 2nd ser., XI, 146–55.

extent of the network on the eve of development), had among its fifty shareholders such leading industrialists as Baranov, Bardygin, Bakhrushin, Prokhorov, and Yakunchikov. The Moscow Discount Bank, its close rival, founded in 1870, included among its shareholders Abrikosov, Bakhrushin, Guchkov, Karzinkin, Knop, and Morozov, while the Moscow Trade Bank also had Knop and Karzinkin as well as Konshin, Prokhorov, and Naidenov. Although the process was one of industrial profits being put into banking (the reverse of Gerschenkron's circuit), bank lending followed the British banking practice of mainly short-term advances, not exceeding nine months. The textile and sugar industries principally attracted the Moscow banks because of the higher ratio of working to fixed capital and the shorter recoupment period.

There were a few exceptions. The adventurous bank entrepreneur Lazar S. Polyakov (brother of S. S. Polyakov, the railway magnate) accumulated from successful railway-contracting during the 1870s enough capital to launch in the 1890s a wide range of speculative projects, some abroad (mainly building, railway, and tramway companies). During the financial crisis of 1900–3, at the time when Savva Mamontov went bankrupt, the state Inspectorate discovered a substantial deficit of 34 m. roubles in Polyakov's financial operations, but the government was dissuaded from rescuing him by an outburst of anti-Semitism led by the Black Hundreds, so that the State Bank took the bank over. Polyakov retired to Paris, where he died in 1914, leaving debts of 30·3 m. roubles. A minority holding by the Banque de l'Union Parisienne was later converted (early in 1914) into a majority interest, but the Bank returned to Russian control in 1917 under the Moscow financier Stakheev. Private holdings lasted only until the nationalization of banks at the end of that year. A more successful example of the financing of an investment bank by domestic capital is provided by the financial group of the Ryabushinsky brothers and N. A. Vtorov. The first Ryabushinsky opened a small shop in Moscow by 1802 and a factory by 1846. In 1887 his descendants had a textile firm with a capital of 2·4 m. roubles (5 m. by 1914). They bought up the Kharkov Agricultural Bank in 1900 and in 1902 opened their own banking house, Ryabushinsky and Brothers, with an initial capital of 5 m. roubles; between 1903 and 1911 they were able to increase their credit advances from 33·6 m. roubles to 1,423 m., after which they went public as the Bank of Moscow (1912) with an initial capital of 20 m. roubles. In addition to the Ryabushinskys, the main shareholders included the wealthiest Moscow textile manufacturers – Bardygin, Morozov, Karzinkin, Konovalov, Krestovnikov, Tretyakov, and others. The Ryabushinskys also diversified into food, glass, linen, and printing, and they started to build a motor-car factory in 1916. N. A. Vtorov acquired controlling shares in the Azov–Don Bank and in the Yunker & Co. Bank in 1916, having effected a series of mergers of Moscow firms in collaboration with the Ryabushinskys and the German firm Bogau; the latter controlled the Med' group, which in 1913 accounted for 94 per cent of Russia's total copper output.

The St Petersburg banks conformed to Gerschenkron's pattern of long-term investment, chiefly in mining and metals, effected by non-debenture securities. Their function in long-term lending involved them more closely than their Moscow counterparts with the Ministry of Finance.[256] In times of crisis, the State Bank (reformed in 1897) shared this collaboration as financial manager. The Polyakov rescue has been mentioned; another example was the Bank's replacement of short-term credits when foreign lenders withdrew funds at the onset of recession in 1899. Foreign investment, seeing this support, moved into Russian

Table 71. *Distribution of Russian Banks by Capital Assets (per cent),*
1900 and 1912

	1900	1912
Up to 9·9 m. roubles	30	24
10 to 19·9 m. roubles	6	11
20 to 29·9 m. roubles	2	4
30 and over m. roubles	0	7

SOURCE. Lyashchenko, *History*, 1st edn, 704.

bank shares increasingly after 1908, and by 1916 foreign holdings in the ten largest joint-stock banks were 45 per cent of a total capital of 420 m. roubles.[257] The inflow from abroad undoubtedly supported the increase in the average size of banks (see Table 71), which Lyashchenko adduces as evidence of 'bank concentration'. The rise in the average capital assets per bank and the diminishing importance of small banks may not be conclusive evidence of this change but are sufficient to indicate that bigger cartels could rely on bigger banks, which had expanded with foreign funds.

G. THE FOREIGN INFUSION

Gerschenkron comments that 'few things are more surprising than the great change in values, attitudes and standards experienced by the Russian entrepreneurs over just one generation between the 1880's and the years preceding World War I. An astonishing process of modernization took place, not before but in the very course – and as a consequence – of a spurt of industrialization.'[258] In the last decade of the nineteenth century, the number of joint-stock companies rose from 504 (1889) to 1,181 (1899) with an aggregate capital of 1,737 m. roubles. Foreign shareholders, who had invested a mere 27 m. roubles in 1870, had holdings of 911 m. in 1900.[259] In terms of new incorporations (as Table 72 shows), foreign companies represented just over one-third of this inflow; checked by the subsequent recession, new foreign registrations did not regain the end-of-century level until 1911–12. Metals, engineering, and chemicals were most affected by the decline, during which – after about 1908, according to McKay[260] – Russian banks took the lead in financing domestic joint-stock companies while the latter began also to offer their stocks and shares abroad. The recent

Table 72. *New Joint-Stock Companies Incorporated in Russia, 1899–1913*

Year	Total number of companies	Number of foreign companies	Total capital of foreign companies (million roubles)
1899	325	69	363
1900	202	40	251
1901	135	23	108
1902	78	13	73
1903	76	15	68
1904	94	13	119
1905	75	10	72
1906	115	10	105
1907	131	12	156
1908	120	12	113
1909	131	15	109
1910	198	17	224
1911	262	40	321
1912	342	20	402
1913	372	29	545

SOURCE. Lyashchenko, *History*, 1st edn, 655, 661, 713.

winding-up[261] of a Russian firm incorporated in the UK provides a random cross-section of the investors. Of the 121 shareholders, seven were Russian companies incorporated in the UK, thirteen were other companies (including the big Skorokhod Mechanical Footwear Production Co.), seven were partnerships, two were heirs to the estates of deceased persons, and the remainder were individuals, all with Russian surnames. 'In short, the ultimate tribute to foreign entrepreneurs was that they forced and encouraged imitation and brought their own relative decline.'[262]

Witte's confidential memorandum of 1899 to the Tsar observed that

The influx of foreign capital is, in the considered opinion of the Minister of Finance, the only way by which our industry will be able to supply our country quickly with abundant and cheap products. Each new wave of capital, rolling in from abroad, knocks down the excessively high level of profits to which our monopolistic businessmen are accustomed and forces them to seek equal profits through technical improvements which lead to price reductions.[263]

He was anxious to promote not merely the supply of funds – portfolio investment from abroad or foreign subscriptions to government bonds – but also the entrepreneurial presence arising from direct investment, which 'must educate, change attitudes and infuse a missing dynamism'.[264]

The extent of that infusion is difficult to quantify. As McKay points out, not all foreign companies incorporated in Russia were wholly

Table 73. *Foreign-Held Shares and Debentures in Russian Joint-Stock Companies (millions of 1897 gold roubles)*

	Foreign-held		Total foreign capital	Total capital issued	Share of capital held by foreigners (per cent)
	Shares	Debentures			
1860	10	—	10	—	—
1870	27	—	27	—	—
1880	92	6	98	—	—
1890	186	29	215	734	25
1900	762	149	911	2,030	37
1910	1,126	232	1,358	2,983	38
1914	1,856	269	2,125	4,311	43

SOURCE. McKay, *Pioneers*, 26–7, citing P. V. Ol', *Inostrannye kapitaly v narodnom khozyaistve dovoennoi Rossii* (Leningrad, 1925), pp. 12–13, and L. Ya. Eventov, *Inostrannye kapitaly v russkom promyshlennosti* (Moscow, 1931), p. 17.

foreign-owned, although such companies (as shown in Table 72) represent the direct investment which Witte was seeking. It is also impossible to distinguish (within the first column of Table 73) those foreigners who, either through a majority holding or by managerial interest, associated their shareholding with entrepreneurship.[265]

By promoting or financing infrastructure investment alone, Witte left the remainder of productive opportunities open to the private entrepreneur. By 1901 two-thirds of the railway network was government-owned, but 'only a minute part of budget expenditure went directly for the purposes of developing the industrial sector'.[266] The state undertook occasional rescue operations – the term 'Red Cross intervention' was used: the Polyakov debacle has been mentioned, and there was at about the same time the rescue of the Kerch Metallurgical

Company, and earlier that of the Putilov Works. McKay observes that the state undertook the salvage 'reluctantly and returned such plants to private owners as soon as possible'.[267] Thus the government offered two risk-averting incentives to foreigners: first the establishment of transport and communications which would not be withdrawn in time of recession,[268] and secondly willingness to limit the multiplier effect of major individual business failures.

In sum, McKay finds four counts on which foreign entrepreneurs contributed to the Russian economy.[269] First, they provided or mobilized capital which would otherwise not have been available – perhaps one-half of all new investment in industrial companies in 1881–1913. Secondly – though the extent cannot be gauged – they mobilized domestic capital for ventures conceived abroad. Thirdly, they implanted advanced technology ('at the heart of the foreign investment strategy') which was well in advance of that being adopted by Russian firms, especially in mining, metals and metalworking, and the electrical and chemicals industries; in such sectors they achieved cost levels in line with those of Western Europe. Finally, they contributed to a revision of domestic entrepreneurial attitudes, notably in the systematic reinvestment of profits,[270] training of workers, and the lowering of barriers to the recruitment of Jews and Poles at managerial level.

The integration of non-Russian nationals into management by foreign companies indifferent to the ethnic origin of their staff is to be seen in the context of conflicting political trends influencing the role in the economy of those other than Great Russians. On the one hand, the Polish and Jewish communities were seeking to engage themselves much more significantly in the economic life of the territory lying beyond the boundaries of the old Polish and Lithuanian kingdoms. On the other hand, the government in St Petersburg was subject to strong pressures by vocal groups of Russians to russify industrial control: this was directed particularly toward Jewish and German entrepreneurs, and toward any foreigner in frontier or politically delicate regions, but scarcely toward others (as an example of which the invitations to Danish entrepreneurs are examined below).

The russification of Poland after suppression of the 1863 rising – e.g. the re-abolition of the Polish Council of State and the prohibition of Polish language teaching in secondary schools – was countered among some Polish patriots by a policy of what was called 'colonizing Russia', that is, increasing the influence of Poles through economic power. Such an objective coincided with the attraction of the growing and tariff-protected Russian market to the new Polish industrial and professional classes. 'The keen activity of Polish technicians tended to give them inside this empire a position not unlike that of the Scots in the empire of Great Britain.'[271] The industrial base of Poland itself expanded rapidly during the nineteenth century, with the help of German entrepreneurs and capital, who found that business and man-power conditions similar to their own, and the proximity of the frontier regions, presented them with attractive sites within the Imperial tariff boundary. The establishment of the textile industry in the early part of the century (see above, p. 457) was accompanied by mining and metallurgy in the southern borderlands of Silesia, at Dąbrowa and Sosnowiec. A beginning had been made as early as the 1820s by the works owned by the Polish Minister of Finance, Drucki-Lubecki, but the principal subsequent development was by the German firms of Plater, Renar, and Donnersmarck.[272] Poland, too, had earlier possessed an investment banking system (developed mainly by Jewish finan-ciers): the Bank of Poland dates from 1828 and, as Table 70 shows, the biggest Warsaw bank established itself in St Petersburg (and was the sole provincial bank there) before any St Petersburg bank set itself up in Warsaw. At the date of the capital returns in Table 70 (1873), the turnovers of the bank's two offices were about equal, viz. 414 m. roubles at Warsaw and 521 m. roubles at St Petersburg, but within three years the latter was nearly three times the former (668 m. as against 234 m.).[273] The position was reversed by the end of the century as competition sharpened in Russia and banking needs increased in Poland: by 1900, a turnover of 1,105 m. roubles was recorded in Warsaw (and 423 m. by the branches it had opened elsewhere in Poland after 1895) as against 307 m. in the Russian capital.[274]

That bank was a substantial lender to Ukrainian metallurgy, but Polish entrepreneurship was especially significant in two other spheres: establishing the contractual relations for the cycle of cotton-planting, ginning, and spinning in Central Asia, and in various industries along the Trans-Siberian railway as it opened up new territory. The govern-ment's encouragement of industrial settlement along the new transport route, notably under Stolypin, had – in addition to the obvious economic reasons – the motive already noted of dispersing an industrial base which would otherwise be the focus of proletarian revolution. To this end Stolypin, whose policy was 'the repression of revolution and the reform programme worked out in the bureaucracy under Witte', revived the Council for Affairs of the Local Economy (instituted by the Minister of the Interior, Pleve, in 1903).[275] Stolypin's fostering of proprietorial farms in Siberia, after his agrarian reform, was com-plemented by local industrialization.

At the same time Russian industrial interests were making a reverse impact, notably in the Polish metals sector; the new cartels of the 1900s, Prodamet and Prodvagon, took in a large share of metallurgy and heavy engineering. Nevertheless the situation was no more than oligopolistic, though highly concentrated, for the number of production groupings in Poland was never reduced below seven.[276]

Polish and Ukrainian entrepreneurs were instrumental in the rapid expansion of sugar refining in the South in the second half of the nineteenth century, but the considerable contribution of Jews to finance and management was largely restricted in this sector to that within the area in the old Polono-Lithuanian frontier, particularly after 1881, when Jewish settlement outside the Pale was prohibited. In 1886 all Jews were dismissed from judicial appointments and excluded from most government and professional posts; the notorious *numerus clausus* limited their university entry to 10 per cent locally and 5 per cent in St Petersburg and Moscow (and still fewer under Nicholas I). Although Jewish merchants of the First and Second Guilds were permitted to reside outside the Pale, there were expulsions of Jewish businessmen from Moscow under further measures in 1891.

Such exclusion from participation in Russian economic expansion not only robbed the territory outside the Pale of entrepreneurial talent but ran counter to the sentiments of russification which many Jews of the younger generation had embraced after determining not to side with the Poles in the 1863 uprising.[277] Bezobrazov, the founder of the East Asiatic Company (to promote the exploitation of Korea), was typical of a segment of Russian entrepreneurs in claiming that his interests were 'truly Russian' in contrast to 'the Jews and Poles whom Sergei Yulevich [Witte] had commissioned to be our standard-bearers in Manchuria'.[278]

A corresponding sentiment of xenophobia, with some veneer of military *raison d'état*, lay behind the prohibition of the installation of firms with controlling foreign equity in numerous regions (subject to exception by special decree), and behind various obstacles placed by local authorities on 'foreign and Jewish capital'; but russification was the chief consideration behind the requirement that foreign citizens could not be in a majority on the board of a Russian company.[279]

It is significant that the first strike arranged by the 'police unionism' (*Zubatovshchina*) of 1903 was directed against a foreign firm. The Moscow police chief, who instigated the scheme for government-inspired trade unions, had launched his recruitment drive with a mass 'patriotic demonstration' in which 50,000 workers, peasants, and their families had taken part.[280]

Patriotic, and in the circumstances anti-German, sentiment played a major role in pressure for russification on the eve of the First World War. Ziv's arguments for the 'assimilation' of German-run enterprises were published in the journals *Torgovo-promyshlennaya gazeta* and *Vestnik finansov* in 1913 but appeared as a book during the war.[281] He was prepared to accept German capital after the war and claimed that, separately, the provision of finance and the services of expatriates were compatible with Russian national interests; it was the two in conjunction – effectively, entrepreneurship – which he sought to check. He was particularly concerned to trace German majority holdings in firms registered in other countries (e.g. in the Belgian companies owning tramways) a more careful evaluation of which was made after the Revolution by P. V. Ol'.[282] Ziv also criticized the expansion of the export of Russian iron ore to Germany in substitution for sales to the UK and Austro-Hungary.[283] Margaret Miller, in a contemporary work, converted Ziv's estimate at £150 m. for the total capital inflow into private business from all countries in the quarter-century before the war but also noted other very much higher figures – one by J. M. Keynes for the same twenty-five years is £1,000 to £1,500 m., which included foreign holdings of the Russian public debt.[284] When such widely varying estimates were being put about, Ziv's possible exaggerations are understandable.

The case of Danish expatriates in Russia presents a contrast to that of the Germans in a pattern of uniformly welcome entrepreneurship: the attitude is of course partly attributable to political factors – Denmark earned sympathy by its loss of Schleswig–Holstein to Bismarck's Germany in 1866 – and was small in impact on Russian foreign policy and domestic oligopolistic affairs. It was the Store Nordisk Telegrafselskab which obtained the concession to lay the first telegraph line to Nikolaevsk (1869), later extended to Vladivostok. The Sibiko (Det Sibirske Kompagni) and the Dansk–Sibirsk Exportselskab employed many Danes in various Siberian developments, and in 1895 the Russian government invited Danish butter-makers to establish a butter industry in Siberia.[285]

The role of John Hughes, director of a Welsh ironworks, is particularly important. He took over an unexploited concession from Prince Kochubei in the Southern Ukraine and not only saw to the smelting of the first Donbas iron in 1870 but 'was notable too in that the interests of south Russian metallurgy were as important to him as the success of his own particular company. He encouraged other entrepreneurs to move their operations south, and by the time of his death, the New Russia Company was only one among several metallurgical companies active in the area.'[286]

H. CARTELS AS AN ALTERNATIVE GOVERNMENT

The industrial and commercial depression of 1900 instigated a trend toward the cartelization of industry, the origins of which can be traced to the preceding decade. The petroleum syndicate (1892) was brought together with the blessing of the government, which translated a market-sharing agreement among sugar-refiners (1887) into a state-registered cartel (1895). The government also created a monopoly in spirits for itself, based partly on the French *régie de tabacs* and the Prussian system of licensed farm distillers.[287] Witte 'saw no drastic conflict between the state and private enterprise, so long as each worked in the spheres where they proved to be the most efficient'.[288] He tried to co-ordinate the activity of the two by joint committee discussion, e.g. at the Economic Conference of 1896, and encouraged the national and local associations of manufacturers, traders, and officials. In a secret memorandum to the Tsar (1899) he called for 'a definite plan . . . a carefully planned system'.[289] His government took the recession at least as a pretext, declaring that 'it would interpose no obstacles' should industry 'find it useful to combine its efforts in order to seek egress from existing difficulties'.[290]

Lyashchenko's argument (p. 467 above), which owes much to Lenin's analysis of capital concentration, may be complemented by considering the likelihood that cartelization was undertaken in order to capture the advantages of certain external economies. Being at an earlier stage of industrialization and with virgin resources to exploit, Russian firms would have found external economies very significant. Moreover, these firms tended to import the most advanced technology from the West – Russian steel-making led the world in the early twentieth century – and to apply it in bigger units – again, the Don Basin boasted the world's largest metallurgical works. The disparity between internal economies of scale and the external economies available by combination would have exercised particular force. The *glavk*, the post-Revolutionary cartel, was still more appropriate for internalizing externalities because factory executives were predominantly engineers, who, having displaced commercially minded managers or proprietors, concerned themselves (as Lenin's directives on planning to Krzhizhanovsky implied) with physical supplies and outputs. Ignoring valuations for exchanges within the production group – the 'deviation' termed glavkism – the directors of the *glavk* needed all the more an administrative mechanism which could ensure access to the external economies of scale. Soviet central planning can be seen as an attempt to internalize every economic activity, which was self-defeating because of the 'sheer scale of the task'.[291] Lenin, characterizing the capitalist business crisis as due to 'planlessness', commented on Plekhanov's draft of the Party's first programme of 1902 – which called for 'the application of the planned organization of the socialist productive process' – that 'organization of that kind will perhaps be provided even by the trusts'.[292]

The oil and sugar cartels which were somewhat loosely formed before the end of the century have already been mentioned; the tighter combinations in cement (1901) and metallurgy (1902) had appeared earlier in Poland.[293] The oil syndicate of 1892 was limited to the export trade and had been established with government co-operation to compete with the Standard Oil Company in foreign markets. The Baku oilfields were exploited partly by a multitude of small producers, of Tatar and Armenian origin, and partly by a few large companies, led by Nobel Brothers. The first stage in close control of production in the domestic market was consultation within producers' associations, and a Council of Congresses of Baku Oil Industrialists was subsequently set up. Groups with similar titles convened for the coal and ore fields, for 'South Russia', for the Urals, and for the 'Polish Region'. It was the first of these which established a joint selling agency, Prodamet, in 1902, which by 1908 controlled around 70 per cent of national production. Two selling agencies were established for certain metal products, Truboprodazha (1902) and Prodvagon (1904), respectively for pipes and railway wagons, the latter monopsonizing all but 3 per cent of supplies. Produgol (1906), the Donets coal syndicate, which controlled 75 per cent of the basin's output, was by contrast dominated by foreign companies, mostly French and Belgian. Smaller syndicates were set up in the following two years for the smaller Siberian fields, Cheremkhovo and Trans-Baikal. The looser Committee for Urals Ore and Metals Products (1904) and the Congress of Farm Machinery Manufacturers (1907) were concerned with about three-quarters of their respective outputs. A higher level for policy discussion was established for metallurgy as a whole in the Permanent Consultative Office of Iron Industrialists. The Cotton Manufacturers' Association was, by contrast, created by the Moscow manufacturers as a reply to the Łódź Cotton Syndicate (1908), but it never embraced a majority of the looms of the Central Region (3·7 m. spindles out of a total capacity of 8·8 m.). A Corporation of Woollen Manufacturers followed in 1910 and one of Linen Manufacturers in 1912.

The hierarchy of consultative organizations was capped by the *S"ezd s"ezdov prestavitelyi torgovlya i promyshlennosti* (1906), the Congress of Congresses of Trade and Industrial Representatives, which acted as the spokesman of industry to the government.[294] Its function was in this respect marred, according to its contemporary critics, by a long-standing and over-close association of St Petersburg industrialists with the ministries: 'through perpetual contact with the ossified bureaucracy, the commercial–industrial representation became itself a kind of industrial bureaucracy'.[295] Moscow interests eventually established (under the Provisional Government of 1917) their own counterweight, the *Vserossisky soyuz torgovli i promyshlennosti*, All-Russian Union of Trade and Industry. There is some controversy about whether the St Petersburg Congress of Congresses ever had more than token support from Moscow industrialists.[296]

In each city there were two local industrialists' associations, the *Obshchestvo fabrikantov i zavodshchikov* (Society of Mill and Factory Owners) and the long-established Bourse Committees. Although the latter represented the traditional Moscow *kupechestvo*, while the former was more for the *nouveaux riches*, both joined the Congress of Congresses. In St Petersburg only the Society adhered; the Bourse Committee stood aloof.[297]

The Societies, which had corresponding groups in other regions, fostered social approval of entrepreneurs, the absence of which two centuries earlier had – according to Gerschenkron's argument – required a state apparatus as a substitute.[298]

The public approbation of the entrepreneur reached its zenith during the First World War, when entrepreneurs' organizations virtually took over the management of the war economy. For the first eight months of the war both government and general public assumed a policy of 'business as usual', but in April 1915 the defeat on the Galician front and the enemy advance into Russian territory demonstrated the inferiority of the Russian industrial and supply systems. An economic conference of the 'Union of Cities', the spokesmen for municipalities and commerce, then initiated a series of consultations which – launching a new slogan, 'mobilize industry' – raised an outcry against the laxity and corruption of the Ministry of War in contracts for munitions. The government's first reaction – to establish a committee on army-supply contracts, including members of the Duma, under the chairmanship of the Minister of War – was judged insufficient, and the Union of Zemstvos, the spokesmen of district elective bodies, agriculture, and craft industry, declared the war effort to be 'beyond the unaided strength of the government officials. We must mobilize our forces: all Russia must be welded into one military organization.'[299]

The committee was thereupon replaced by a Special Council for the Co-ordination of War Supply (June 1915), responsible to the Tsar, but this in turn was rejected by the Duma, which established a quadripartite set of Special Councils attached to each key ministry, namely War, Trade and Industry, Agriculture, and Transport. Although intended by the Duma to co-ordinate the war economy, these four councils, in the two years of their existence, met 'in a casual way, not regularly, and the work of each was quite independent of the others'.[300]

The Congress of Congresses took matters into its own hands and established, at a conference in Petrograd in May 1915, its own Central

War Industries Committee: of its nineteen departments, fourteen dealt with individual industries and five were functional co-ordinators. A corresponding Moscow committee, created in the suspicion that Petrograd industrialists were scheming to corner war contracts, was absorbed into – or, as Roosa claims, took over – the Central Committee, which by the end of the year had twenty-eight provincial and seventy-four municipal committees.[301] 'It was hoped that the co-ordinated activity of unofficial organizations would mitigate the consequences of official ineptitude'.[302] Both the Petrograd and Moscow provincial committees included representatives elected by factory workers, but by May 1916 such delegates constituted only 3 per cent of all members of provincial committees. The biggest group was that of industrialists and merchants (36 per cent), followed by professional and technical associations (21 per cent) and local elective bodies (17 per cent); the small representation of government departments (11 per cent) and co-operative societies (2 per cent)[303] revealed their insignificance in the eyes of businessmen.

The Central War Industries Committee effected its own co-ordination partly by sitting on the government's committees.[304] It had four places on the reconstituted Special Council for Defence (August 1915) as against five members from government departments, and its local committees took not less than three places, as against four officials, on the territorial 'factory boards' (*zavodskoe soveshchanie*) which distributed and supervised the fulfilment of governmental contracts on the spot. The government was uneasy about this relationship, and on the grounds that the workers' element was a political threat it even tried to abolish all the war industries committees. This reflected a deeper division between the civil service and the industrialists, which resulted in stalemate rather than a *modus vivendi* of the type reached in Britain or France at the same time.[305]

Industrialists soon went beyond the co-ordination of munitions contracts to formalize the syndicate system for other sectors, though they did not simply seek monopsony for their own agencies. Thus, confronted by the failure of the Ministry of Trade and Industry to control iron and steel prices, they succeeded in establishing Rasmeko, a committee for metals supply (November 1915), with equal representation of officials and of the War Industries Committee, plus one delegate apiece from the Union of Cities and the Union of Zemstvos. The new statutory syndicates, with titles which were to persist into the era of 'War Communism', embraced the main raw materials: the autumn of 1916 saw the creation of Tsentrougol for coal, Tsentrokhlopok for cotton, Tsentrosherst' for wool; Tsentroles for timber was formed in March 1917.[306] The Union of Zemstvos was made the monopsonist for hides at abattoirs in July 1916, and the Union of Towns gave the lead in organizing urban food supplies.

The industrialists' agencies remained formally in existence between the February and October Revolutions of 1917 but were in practice superseded by local 'committees of supply', overseen from July 1917 by a central Procurement Committee (*Zagotovitel'ny Komitet*) and an Economic Council with a Supreme Economic Committee as its executive arm [307] A further move away from reliance on the cartels came with the institution of state monopolies of agricultural machinery and leather in April 1917, and of Donets coal in July.

I. THE REVOLUTIONARY ORDER

The all-embracing nationalization of non-farm enterprise which was eventually to be the mark of the Soviet system was the least likely of the three options which the Bolsheviks might have taken on the morrow of the October Revolution. These options (which would not have included collaboration with foreign interests, for the bond obligations of the Imperial and Provisional governments held at home or abroad were annulled on 28 January 1918) were firstly, an extension of the consortium with private enterprise; secondly, an acceptance of the syndicalism already overwhelming some factories and fully established on the railways; and thirdly, the creation of another hierarchy, based upon local economic authorities, as a parallel to the Soviet political hierarchy.

In the period from the October Revolution of 1917 to the first major round of nationalizations in the following July, Carr observes that

a certain tacit community of interests could be detected between the government and the more sensible and moderate of the industrialists in bringing about a return to some kind of orderly production. Extensive nationalization of industry was thus no part of the initial Bolshevik programme . . . The nationalization of industry was treated at the outset not as a desirable end in itself but as a response to special conditions.[308]

Most early takeovers were of individual factories[309] and were categorized either as 'punitive' – e.g. the Putilov Works in Leningrad, because of its 'indebtedness to the Treasury' – or as 'spontaneous' – e.g. the Turkestan Soviet takeover of the local cotton industry without any reference to Moscow; but a few branches were expropriated in their entirety – banks on grounds of a deadlocked strike of bank employees, water transport because of the peculiar situation (described below) on the railways, and sugar-refining owing to the German occupation of the Ukraine.

A fear of beleaguerment pressed the young Soviet administration into further control of distribution under the Supreme Economic Council (Vesenkha) which, from 1 December 1917, replaced the previous government's Supreme Economic Committee. Venediktov begins his monumental history of Soviet industrial organization with the assertion that Vesenkha was seen from the first as 'an organ of planning and regulation of the national economy as a whole', and considers its monopolies quite distinct from their predecessors.[310] Carr's stress on continuity, on the other hand, is part of the view that Lenin began by writing down (without, however, writing off) the wartime collaboration with industrialists' own agencies while enhancing the power of central government exercised through a committee structure. A contemporary source evokes a resolution of the Third Trade Union Conference of 20–8 June 1917 calling on the Provisional Government 'to introduce state syndicates or trusts in a range of industries, except where this would be inappropriate because of a low level of technology or lack of national financial support, and above all to put the coal industry under such a trust, since it is both the most concentrated and the most fundamental for all other industries.'[311] It stresses (in the edition of 1920) the validity of the cartelization experience for nationalized industry.[312]

The Prodamet and Krovlya syndicates (for ferrous metal products and roofing iron respectively) were transformed by a decree of Vesenkha of 22 January 1918 into 'state administrations for the regulation of the ferrous products industry supervised by the Met.llurgy Department of Vesenkha'.[313] To the *tsentra* for wool and cotton were added syndicates for textiles (Tsentrotekstil' of March 1918 — run by representatives of workers, employers, managers, and government offices), soap, and tea; a monopoly of various *Kolonialwaren* led to the incidental expropriation of match and candle factories, but they were put not under the state but under the retail co-operative union, Tsentrosoyuz.[314] *Glavki* (chief committees, but later chief administrations) were invested with the co-ordinating functions of pre-Revolutionary agencies, such as Glavkozh for leather or Glavkhim (whose antecedent was a chemicals committee of the Imperial Ministry of War).[315]

A syndicalist movement, embodied in factory committees (*fabzavkomy*), had been manifest since the February Revolution and was both a threat and a support to the victors of October. The threat was epitomized in Vikzhel, the All-Russian Executive Committee of the Railwaymen, in an industry which, already predominantly state-owned (the few private lines were soon expropriated), had no capitalists to displace. 'It played the role of a mammoth factory committee exercising "workers' control". It recognized no political authority and no interest other than the professional interest of the railwaymen.'[316] Vikzhel, which 'adopted a negative attitude to the seizure of power by any one political party',[317] was soon destroyed, and the Decree on Workers' Control of 14 November 1917 merely accorded workers' committees 'the right to supervise management' and 'to determine a minimum of production' (to counter managerial sabotage), explicitly forbidding them 'to take possession of the enterprise or to direct it'.

The other major Soviet historian of economic organization in this period, Gladkov, attributes the initiation of local planning and regulation to the *fabzavkomy*.[318] Venediktov, however, discerns it in the local councils of national economy (*guberniya sovnarkhozy*): he cites their terms of reference (when authorized on 23 December 1918) as being to take decisions 'based on principled judgement and valid for their entire area on reconversion to civilian orders, to verify inventories, and to operate the previously established monopolies'. Although 'the idea of economic Soviets was still-born',[319] Lenin was seriously considering a 'network of producer–consumer co-operatives conscientiously accounting for their production and consumption'.[320]

Gladkov's 'Introduction' to a collection of documents on the 1917–20 nationalizations is typical of a present school of Soviet historians who fail to recognize the complexities of the options on entrepreneurship open to Lenin. He confidently asserts, for example, that

the nationalization of fixed and circulating productive assets was of a planned character. The affirmations of bourgeois economists and opportunists that there was a 'spontaneous–chaotic proletarian nationalization', or that the movement for nationalization comprised 'unconnected actions of separate workers' groups', are both completely groundless and calumnious. Soviet power, breaking the resistance of the bourgeoisie and its servants – Mensheviks, SRs [Socialist Revolutionaries], Trotskyists and Bukharinists, Nationalists, and others – steadfastly and consistently realized nationalization according to the economic platform of the Communist Party.[321]

In another work Gladkov dates Lenin's determination to see Soviet political power protected by economic expropriation from 'the start of 1918', quoting Lenin's call of 22 February 1918 to seize 'land from the landlords and factories from the banks'.[322]

Venediktov considers the period up to mid-1918 rather as one of 'respite', while Dobb sees it as one of 'transitional state capitalism'.[323] Both are convinced that Lenin held for some time to the view, which he expressed in his draft for the decree on workers' control of November 1917, that private owners be retained as technical administrators and as a countervailing power to the *fabzavkomy*. As he subsequently explained, 'our work in organizing, accounting and control lagged considerably behind'.[324] It was in such circumstances that Lenin put his rhetorical question to workers' delegations – 'can you take the organization into your own hands?' – and that he published 'The Principal Tasks of Our Day: Left-Wing Childishness and Petit-Bourgeois Mentality' in May 1918.[325] 'State Capitalism' in the period of transition to socialism would contain elements of both economic systems. Collaboration would be possible with those 'cultured capital-ists who agree to State Capitalism, who are capable of putting it into practice and who are useful to the proletariat as intelligent and experi-enced organisers of the largest types of enterprises, which actually supply products to tens of millions of people'.[326] Lenin was then still much influenced by his analysis of the mixed economy of the German *Kriegswirtschaft*,[327] and Nove points out that the 'Declaration of the Rights of the Working and Exploited People' (17 January 1918) set no timetable for 'conversion of the factories and other means of production . . . into the property of the workers' and peasants' state'. After commenting on the inclusion of private employers in Tsentro-textil' in April 1918, he cites Samokhvalov's assessment that 'Lenin took a positive view of attempts to make agreements with capitalists on definite conditions favourable to the working class'.[328] Lenin enumerated five forms of economic relationships coexisting in Russia just after the Revolution: 'patriarchal (i.e. to a considerable extent natural, peasant farming), small commodity production, private capitalism, state capitalism, and socialism'. He feared that 'the shell of our state capitalism (grain monopoly, state-controlled entrepreneurs and traders, bourgeois co-operators) is pierced now in one place, now in another by profiteers, the chief object of profiteering being grain . . . The profiteer, the commercial racketeer, the disrupter of monopoly, these are . . . the enemies of the economic measures of Soviet power.'[329] His 'Basic Propositions on Economic and Especially on Banking Policy', written in April 1918 (though not published until 1933), is headed with 'completion of nationalization of industry and exchange'.[330]

Events compelling him to introduce his longer-run objective came rapidly. Anxiety to control foreign trade had already brought export and import licensing in December 1917, the nationalization of merchant shipping in January 1918, and the state monopoly of foreign trade in April. The measures were, however, more to limit the influence of external forces than to regulate the internal ones. As Krasin put it, 'The foreign trade monopoly must repulse all economic and financial inter-vention from abroad.' Putting the causes the other way round, the latest Soviet standard history, the twelve-volume *Istoriya SSSR*, attributes to the German military threat Lenin's postponement of a scheme of compulsory share transfers to the state which he advanced to

Vesenkha just before the New Year: 'the plan was realistic but difficult to execute in the circumstances of a large-scale German offensive'.[331]

The decree of 28 June 1918 which expropriated all companies with a capital exceeding 1 m. roubles in eight key industries[332] marked the rapid closure of the experiment of shared control with capitalist entrepreneurs and the opening of the period known in retrospect as War Communism, which saw the completion of nationalization. A decree of 29 November 1920 expropriated without compensation all enterprises employing more than five workers if mechanical power was used and more than ten if the work was entirely manual.

J. LIMITED ENTREPRENEURSHIP UNDER NEP

Following the definitive decree on nationalization of November 1920, only small-scale enterprises could remain in private hands. This exception was not without importance, though difficult to quantify, since the statistical boundary dividing 'small' from 'large' was set higher than that for nationalization.[333] In 1913 small enterprises according to statistical returns produced just over half (51 per cent) of all industrial output;[334] workshops (*izby*) making products for local farm or domestic use were eventually absorbed into collective farms, but those with a provincial or national market[335] were made to form artisan co-operatives during the farm collectivization of the thirties and were nationalized in 1960. Apart from the period of the New Economic Policy (1921–8), the limitations upon the exiguous private sector which remained outside farming were such – on accumulation, expansion, or diversification – that their management cannot be defined as entrepreneurship, nor can the tilling of a small plot of land by a collective-farm household, although this private sector of agriculture continues up to the present time to furnish a large share of the public marketing of vegetables, fruit, meat, and dairy produce.

But under NEP, when the peasant had full rights to choose and dispose of his production, to save or to consume, to quit agriculture or to remain, and to choose his form of organization,[336] small industry was entrepreneurial. The decree of August 1921 of the Council of People's Commissars (Sovnarkom) extending NEP to industry allowed enterprises not scheduled by the government for closure or for retention in the nationalized sector to be leased to individuals or to co-operatives or other social entities. The many small enterprises which had not actually been taken over under the decree of November 1920 would not be nationalized. By a supplementary decree of 10 December 1921 the criterion for nationalization was raised to twenty employees, and in both categories regional economic councils (*sovnarkhozy*) were authorized to grant applications by former owners to regain proprietorship.[337]

As a consequence, only 8·5 per cent of industrial enterprises remained nationalized, 3·1 per cent remaining in co-operatives and 88·5 per cent in private concerns. But these latter employed a mere 12·4 per cent of the labour force, whereas 84·1 per cent was in the state sector. Each state enterprise employed on average 155 workers, but the co-operatives and private units employed fifteen and two respectively.[338]

The Soviet Academy of Science's standard economic history describes the mixed trading companies established at this time – there were twenty-four in 1923, and their importance can be gauged from Table 74 – as 'the use of some elements of state capitalism which were of secondary importance and did not transgress the principles of the foreign-trade monopoly'.[339]

Table 74. *Share of Soviet Foreign Trade by Form of Enterprise, 1924–5 (per cent)*

	Export	Import
State agencies, trusts, and enterprises	47·3	86·6
Limited companies wholly owned by the state	31·6	6·4
Co-operatives	12·5	3·8
Mixed companies with foreign capital	5·5	1·3
Foreign firms	1·1	1·3
Private enterprises	0·7	0·3
Others	1·3	0·3

SOURCE. Archives of the People's Commissariat of Foreign Trade, reproduced in Akademiya nauk SSSR, Institut ekonomiki, *Sovietskoe narodnoe khozyaistvo*, 515.

More significant in readmitting external entrepreneurship were the domestic concessions. Little attention is paid to them by Soviet economic historians,[340] and Sutton's study in English is the most comprehensive.[341]

Foreigners and foreign corporations were permitted to lease or participate in state-owned enterprises by a decree of 8 March 1923, replaced by a law of 21 August. A Soviet agency, the Chief Concessions Committee (Glavkontsesskom), conducted negotiations with foreigners for exploiting or leasing state economic property under 'usufruct' arrangements or by participating in a jointly owned company (at first equally but later only as minority shareholders). By October 1926, 330 such agreements had been concluded; there were additionally 134 technical-assistance agreements, including those signed up to the end of the decade.[342] Some companies leased back plants that had been theirs before nationalization, saw their concessions terminated and, after the USSR–US agreement of October 1972, returned to the Soviet Union yet again under industrial co-operation contracts (e.g. International Harvester). One notable entrepreneur, Armand Hammer, took over an asbestos concession at Alapaevsk and a pencil factory in Moscow.[343] These concessions were withdrawn in a variety of ways in the late twenties, usually under a clause according the Soviet partner the option to buy out at an agreed valuation. The Hammer concession was ended in this manner in December 1929 'and accepted without the usual protest'.[344] The last concession to be signed was made the same month, whereby the Gillette Safety Razor Co. undertook to build a razor-blade factory in the USSR. No further action took place until Gillette renegotiated in October 1973 the construction of such plants in Moscow and Leningrad.

Baykov judges a regulation of Sovnarkom of 15 September 1928 announcing a list of new concessions on which Glavkontsesskom was authorized to negotiate 'the last attempt of the so-called Right-Wing of the Party to attract foreign capital for large-scale investment in industry and so to diminish the strain of domestic accumulation in the forthcoming years covered by the Five-year Plan'.[345] The Party Directives on the First Five-year Plan had been published in December 1927, and the Right Opposition were compelled by Stalin to renounce their criticism in a letter to the Party Central Committee of November 1929. The external symbol of the change of policy was perhaps the termination of convertibility of the rouble in March 1928,[346] initiating the era of the isolation of state economic decisions from those of the rest of the world. The Five-year Plan officially began on 1 October 1928.

In 1925–6, at the height of NEP and of the activity of its entrepreneurs (the '*nepmeni*'), private plants produced 3·5 per cent of the output of 'census industry', and foreign concessions 0·4 per cent. By 1928–9 the respective shares were 0·3 and 0·6 per cent.[347] Small-scale industry below the *tsenz* was either co-operative or private, but private firms employed (in 1925–6) only 74,000 out of the 3·5 m. in small-scale industry as a whole. The private sector was, as already indicated, in very small units; although because much of it was concentrated in certain areas ('clustered' (*gnezdovaya*), in the official phrase), it benefited from some economies of scale. Regulations made in July 1923 bringing those working at home on a putting-out system into the classification of employed labour, and hence subject to the wage and other controls of the RSFSR Labour Code, led many of these petty entrepreneurs to designate their artisans as licensees (*patentshchiki*) and hence, formally, self-employed.[348] 'The legislation restricting capitalist forms of organization thus led to a reversal of the pre-revolutionary process by which the putting-out system was replaced by workshops.'[349]

As in the case of concessions, the Sovnarkom in May 1928 urged the 'great importance' of artisan and craft industries and listed various measures for their encouragement, but the Vesenkha draft of the Five-year Plan in the previous year had already stated that 'it was unsuitable in modern conditions of technology to preserve small enterprises using primitive tools'.[350] The government's concurrent campaign against private trade made it difficult for private industry to obtain materials, because the state sector supplied itself on preferential terms. Thus by the end of 1930 the individual entrepreneur had all but disappeared from the Soviet scene.

K. SETTLEMENT ON THE GLAVK

The extinction of entrepreneurship had by no means been a certain conclusion from the patterns of economic organization which Lenin was considering in the early days of his administration. In a 'rough outline' of the Party Programme (eventually approved in 1919 without such remarks), he set out his economic order as 'close (and direct) connection with occupations and with productive–economic units (elections based on factories and on local peasant and handicraft areas). This close connection makes it possible to carry out profound socialist changes, such as (partly, if not wholly, covered by the preceding) the possibility of getting rid of bureaucracy.'[351]

The decision to centralize control of the productive sector of the economy through branch-specialized agencies was taken at the first meeting of the Economic Council, Vesenkha, on 5 January 1918.[352] It forthwith created the *glavk*, the agency which – alone in the Soviet economic system – has persisted until the present. Twice transformed into the *ob"edineniya* ('association') in December 1929 and in April 1973, it is still, after the most recent of those changes, more than ever the focal point of industrial management.

The statute drafted by the Second All-Russian Congress of *Sovnar-khozy* in December 1918 reflected the rapid phasing-out of regional industrial administration in favour of the *glavk*,[353] and at the culmination of War Communism at the end of 1920 Vesenkha operated thirteen production divisions (viz. those with *glavki*, without *glavki*, and with *glavki* in direct subordination to the Council), eight 'mixed divisions', of which three were *glavki* controlling entire sectors,[354] and various 'functional divisions', of which one was for retail supply and one for wholesale.[355] There was also a 'GOELRO Division' to run the State Plan for the Electrification of Russia, which on 22 February 1921 was superseded by a State General Planning Commission, Gosplan.

NEP brought reorganization with a view to concentrating Lenin's 'commanding heights of industry': Vesenkha established a 'Concentration Commission' to arrange industrial mergers,[356] and the lowest tier of production unit – the variously and inconsistently titled *fabrika*, *manufaktura*, and *predpriyatiya* – for a time lost juridical and accounting identity. The latter term 'enterprise' was then applied to the trust (*trest*), an integrated union of producers, which rivalled the *glavk* as the key agent of state industry.

The true successor to the cartel, the *sindikat*, operated as sales agent for trusts throughout NEP: the first and most powerful, the All-Union Textile Syndicate, was established by Vesenkha in February 1922. The fifteen syndicates established in the twelve months after February 1922 were state entrepreneurs in that they operated on a profit basis within a market and distributed a dividend (after a Treasury share) to their members.[357] The syndicate was the chief instrument for bringing trade in intermediate and capital goods under public control, a function exercised by the *torg* or consumer-goods wholesaler with respect to retail trade. When the end of NEP terminated that function, the trade agencies were assimilated into the administration (the syndicates as the *sbyty* of production ministries and the *torgi* into the ministry for internal trade).

The NEP period is of significance not only because it was the last in which entrepreneurship could be exercised but also because of the evolution of policy on the autonomy and control of the basic productive unit.

By September 1922 the process of concentration had left 430 trusts operating 4,144 enterprises (with 977,000 workers). Of these, 172 trusts were subordinated to Vesenkha or to an associated industrial office (*promburo*), but their 2,281 enterprises occupied 83·5 per cent of workers in the 'trust sector'. The 258 trusts under the *gubsovnarkhozy* employed the remaining 16·5 per cent of personnel in their 1,863 enterprises.[358] The regulations identifying the trust as the basic unit of enterprise (by a decree of 10 April 1923), to which brief reference was made above, were broken within a few months: from 2 January 1924 selected plants could be separated from the trust and designated 'All-Union Enterprises', while a few others were granted autonomy from their trusts.[359]

The return to the plant as the basic unit of organization and accountability was propounded at senior level by Felix Dzherzhinsky, then Chairman of Vesenkha, in a speech of 21 November 1924 but was generally adopted only after May 1926, when it was decided that all Yugostal' enterprises should be put on an autonomous financial basis (perhaps the most suitable translation of '*khozrashet*') from the following October. Thereafter, for the closing years of NEP, the factory was becoming the principal unit with which Vesenkha was to deal. The trust lost its powers to the *glavk* and syndicates on the one hand and to the factory on the other.[360]

Vesenkha itself was soon to be divided into industrial commissariats. In turn, the ministries, as they were renamed after the Second World War, were temporarily replaced under Khrushchev by regional councils of the national economy, *sovnarkhozy*. When NEP was terminated, the peasant farms established throughout agriculture by Lenin's master-stroke, the decree 'On Land', were either collectivized or incorporated into state farms. All banks, even the State Bank itself, were liquidated under War Communism, in measures consistent with the virtual abolition of money.

The loss of the *numéraire* of money under War Communism took away the conventional price mechanism but not then the market.[361] As Table 75 shows, even in the last year of War Communism a few

Table 75. *Markets of State Enterprises under War Communism* (*number of enterprises*)

	1918	1920
Working on individual orders	751	248
Working for free market	242	19
Working for own requirements	42	49
Working for *glavki*	1,506	2,471
Not reporting	394	148
Total	2,935	2,935

SOURCE. A. V. Venediktov, *Organizatsiya*, I, 617.

enterprises were still working for the open market and many others accepted individual orders rather than just orders from the *glavki*. It may indeed have been an eventual aim of some Soviet leaders to abandon the market,[362] and it is possible to argue that this has been an overriding objective of the Soviet government ever since.[363] It was certainly achieved by 1930–2 in the closure of all markets save petty confrontations of individual producers and households. The control of prices and the virtual withdrawal of money valuations from planning decisions followed.

The imposition of central planning did not displace the progress of the second of the two policies in controversy during NEP, namely the adoption of autonomous financing at enterprise level,[364] but the entre-preneurial connotation was withdrawn *pari passu* with the function of the prices forming the basis of those accounts. For the two years that autonomous finance for enterprises operated within a market environment, prices were active signals to managers for the appropriate combination of factors of production.[365] The realistic role of prices of the fiscal year 1926/7 was implicitly recognized in their long retention for Soviet planning and accounting. Although increasingly out of line with the rapidly altering pattern of factor proportions, they remained in use until 1949.[366] Resolution of a third notable debate of the time – between functional and 'line' management – in favour of 'one-man control' (*edinonachalie*) paved the way for the hierarchical structure of industrial administration under the Five-year Plan.

A necessary condition for the 'administrative economy' was the elimination of private ownership of productive assets. At least one of the railway magnates who remained in Russia after the October Revolution recognized that there was still scope for him under conditions of a large, though not exclusive, public sector. 'I am by no means frightened and embarrassed at the Soviet Government nationalizing a large proportion of the country's economy,' he wrote. 'Under the Tsarist regime, very large branches of the economy were owned by the State.'[367] The only novelty was that 'nationalization does not seem to have been practised to such a large extent in any other country'.

The twilight of NEP, symbolized by the extinction of private capital, begins at the earliest in February 1926[368] and ends at the latest in March 1931.[369]

It is worth restating that an economy with explicit money prices is not a necessary condition for entrepreneurship (p. 419). The power to choose among factors for productive ends is, however, such a condition, and the regulations of the state under the Five-year Plans left no opportunity for entrepreneurial selection outside the modest interstices it chose to allow, more often by tolerance or indifference than as deliberate policy.

The zone of managerial freedom is largely *extra legem* . . . At the level of each individual enterprise a managerial sally into greater independence is followed by a retreat towards greater obedience . . . Yet as managerial disobedience is eliminated, so is his free initiative . . . It is very often not recognized that dictatorial power requires incessant exercise. It is maintained and asserted by ruling and regulating.[370]

Though many substantive changes were made, the framework of rules for economic, political, and social life constructed in Stalin's day was not dismantled by his successors. They have, up to now, retained enough of his centralization to limit the use of 'entrepreneurship' to the fringe of managerial action and the penumbra of the private sector beyond.

The extent to which those who formulate the microeconomic rules and plan the macroeconomic allocations can be called entrepreneurs is a matter of controversy. McAuley criticizes 'a tendency among western observers to look at economic administration in eastern Europe through the eyes of enterprise managers and to see the intervention of central planners as petty interference by bureaucrats jealous of their political power and privileges'.[371] He rightly stresses the interdependence of managerial autonomy and the market determination of prices: if entrepreneurs are to bring together factors of production for the satisfaction of demand as heads or managers of separate firms, they must have information (which the market affords through prices) on which to take decisions. The expectations placed upon the application of mathematical techniques and the provision of computerized data in the Soviet Union in the 1970s could permit the planners justly to be termed entrepreneurs. But until such schemes are realized, as the 1980s may well see, no judgement can be made upon the degree of real choice that would be permitted. It is, above all, the control by those in authority of each other that has driven entrepreneurship from the USSR for nearly half a century. Peter the Great regulated and motivated his subjects but did not monopolize entrepreneurial decision-making. The long history of Russian economic regulation before and after Peter has shaped many of the institutions and activities characterizing Soviet economic management, but that management allows no scope formally for the entrepreneur.

NOTES

CHAPTER I

Capital Formation in the United States during the Nineteenth Century

1 This chapter was drafted in 1972 and early 1973 and was submitted to the editors in May 1973. Late in 1975, and again in the summer of 1976, the authors were given brief opportunities to revise but were unable to carry out a thorough revision. Thus only a few works published since mid-1973 could be taken into account, and these, unfortunately, receive only passing notice.

2 W. W. Rostow, *The Stages of Economic Growth*, 2nd edn (Cambridge, 1971), especially 37–40 and 189–93; W. A. Lewis, *The Theory of Economic Growth* (London, 1955), especially 201–8. For a good brief treatment of the relevant aspects of the Harrod–Domar models, see Y. S. Brenner, *Theories of Economic Development and Growth* (London, 1966), 179–85. While both Lewis and Rostow refer to the national income, investment, and capital stock – i.e. income earned by nationals, investment made by nationals, capital owned by nationals – they may actually have in mind domestic income, investment, and capital – i.e. income earned by factors of production located within the borders of the nation, and investment and capital located within the borders of the nation. See, for example, Lewis, p. 200, and Rostow's treatment of foreign borrowing. For present purposes, the distinctions between national and domestic income, investment, and capital are unimportant, since the quantitative differences between the relevant pairs of aggregates are slight, in the case of the US in the nineteenth century. (See, e.g., Table 11 below.)

3 Robert M. Solow, 'A Contribution to the Theory of Economic Growth', *Quarterly Journal of Economics*, LXX (1956). See also Peter Temin, 'General Equilibrium Models in Economic History', *Journal of Economic History*, XXXI, 1 (March 1971).

4 These and similar calculations in this section depend upon the derivation of the marginal capital–output ratio as the net investment share divided by the rate of growth of output, and the calculations rest on the assumption that the marginal capital–output ratio is stable. Thus, given the capital–output ratio and the investment share, the rate of growth can be computed by dividing the latter by the former; and given the capital–output ratio and the rate of growth of output, the investment share can be computed by multiplication. The calculations in the text were made as follows:

(a) $0.05/3.0 = 0.0167$; $0.05/3.5 = 0.0143$; $(0.0167 + 0.0143)/2.0 = 0.0155$.

(b) $0.10/3.0 = 0.0333$; $0.10/3.5 = 0.0286$; $(0.0333 + 0.0286)/2.0 = 0.0310$.

5 Calculated as follows: $0.062/3.5 = 0.018$; $0.070/3.0 = 0.023$; $0.197/3.5 = 0.056$; $0.197/3.0 = 0.066$. The investment shares (0.062, 0.070, 0.197) are taken from Table 1 above.

6 Paul A. David, 'The Growth of Real Product in the United States before 1840: New Evidence and Controlled Conjectures', *Journal of Economic History*, XXVII, 2 (June 1967), 155. See also Robert E. Gallman, 'The Statistical Approach: Fundamental Concepts as Applied to History', in George Rogers Taylor and Lucius F. Ellsworth, *Approaches to American Economic History* (Charlottesville, Virginia, 1971), and R. E. Gallman, 'The Agricultural Sector and the Pace of Economic Growth: U.S. Experience in the Nineteenth Century', in D. C. Klingaman and R. K. Vedder (eds.), *Essays in Nineteenth Century Economic History* (Athens, Ohio, 1975). David is dealing with gross domestic product, not net national product; but the average rates of growth of real GDP and real NNP could not have differed by much in the period 1800–1840.

7 See Edward F. Denison, *The Sources of Economic Growth in the United States* (New York, 1962), chap. 4, especially pp. 30–1. Scale effects are treated as part of productivity change.

The underlying model is one that treats the economy as a single plant using homogeneous factors of production to produce an output of which all units are the same. Of course the Rostow model can be described in the same way. The difference between the two models is that the production function of the latter involves fixed proportions – such that the elasticity of output with respect to capital takes a value of 1 – while the production function of the former involves variable proportions.

The assumption of a single plant can be dropped without posing theoretical difficulties. Heterogeneous outputs can also be accommodated, since they can be combined in value terms, but this procedure raises index number problems that must be borne in mind when the model is used to interpret historical events (see below).

With heterogeneous outputs, production functions may vary from one industry to another, but this raises no special theoretical problems. As will appear, our analysis of the forces responsible for the increase of the investment share exploits the fact that production functions did vary, historically, from one part of the economy to another.

Problems of measurement of the input – capital – are taken up in section III.

The literature on empirical applications of aggregate production functions is extensive. See Conference on Research in Income and Wealth, *Output, Input, and Productivity Measurement*, Studies in Income and Wealth, 25 (Princeton, 1961); and Murray Brown (ed.), *The Theory and Empirical Analysis of Production*, Studies in Income and Wealth, 31 (New York, 1967), especially the paper by Nerlove in the latter.

8 See L. E. Davis *et al.*, *American Economic Growth*, 35–40. Most of the figures used in this section were taken from chap. 2 of this book or from the worksheets underlying the chapter. Figures given without citation in the rest of this section should be understood to come from this source.

9 We thank Albert Fishlow for helpful discussions on these points.

10 See the sources described in Davis *et al., op. cit.* See, also, Davis and Gallman, 'Share of Savings and Investment'; and Dorothy S. Brady, 'Price Deflators for Final Product Estimates', in Brady (ed.), *Output, Employment, and Productivity*.

11 Brady, 'Price Deflators', 91–100.

12 Davis and Gallman, 'Share of Savings and Investment'.

13 On the relatively conservative assumption that capital consumption took between 4 and 5 per cent of the depreciable capital stock each year and 5 per cent of the stock of machinery and equipment.

14 Denison, *Sources of Economic Growth*, 266.

15 See Davis and Gallman, 'Share of Savings and Investment', 461 and 462.

16 Derived from worksheets underlying Robert E. Gallman and Thomas J. Weiss, 'The Service Industries in the 19th Century', in Victor R. Fuchs (ed.), *Production and Productivity in the Service Industries*, Studies in Income and Wealth, 34 (New York, National Bureau, 1969), 288, 289, and 292. The rates of growth were calculated from 'Variant I' estimates; use of 'Variant II' estimates (including the price index from line 12 of Table 3) would raise the rate of growth of services output to 5·0 per cent. 'Industry' includes mining, manufacturing, and construction. 'Services' include all activities except agriculture and industry.

17 Daniel Creamer, Sergei P. Dobrovolsky, and Israel Borenstein, *Capital in Manufacturing and Mining* (Princeton, 1960), 53. See the text, above, for the capital concept involved.

18 See Davis and Gallman, 'Share of Savings and Investment'.

19 We thank John Flemming for suggesting this possibility to us.

20 Dorothy S. Brady (ed.), *Output, Employment, and Productivity in the United States after 1800*, Studies in Income and Wealth, 30 (New York, 1966), 110 and 111.

21 See Nathan Rosenberg, 'Technological Change in the Machine Tool Industry, 1840–1910', *Journal of Economic History*, XXIII, 4 (December 1963), 418.

Jeffrey Williamson argues that the Civil War tariff operated to raise the price index of national product relative to the price index of capital goods and therefore contributed to the relative price decline of producers' durables ('Watersheds and Turning Points: Conjectures on the Long-Term Impact of Civil War Financing', *Journal of Economic History*, XXXIV, 3 (September 1974)). While this may be so, the quantitative effect of the tariff along these lines is unlikely to have been large. The value of American imports of finished goods (the variable relevant to the Williamson analysis) was apparently less than 4 per cent as large as the value of national product in each of the decades 1834–43, 1839–48, and 1849–58 (Simon Kuznets, 'Quantitative Aspects of the Economic Growth of Nations, Part X', *Economic Development and Cultural Change*, XV, 2 (January 1967), 113; and Davis *et al.*, *American Economic Growth*, 568). Perhaps more to the point, a large fraction of American final output consisted of non-traded goods, and another large fraction was of goods in which the US maintained a strong export balance. Thus it is difficult to believe that the tariff could have had a major impact on the relative movements of price indexes referring to the large aggregates, 'capital formation' and 'national product'.

22 It is actually a cost index, rather than a true price index. Therefore it makes no allowance for substitutions among materials or between materials and labour due to shifts in the structure of prices. Thus the rate of change described by the index is necessarily biased in an upward direction.

23 See also the discussion in Davis and Gallman, 'Share of Savings and Investment', part I and the Appendix. In the language of national-income accounting, the concept of savings underlying the calculations in the table *excludes* 'inventory valuation adjustment', while the concept underlying the calculations in the text *includes* 'inventory valuation adjustment'.

24 Gallman, 'Gross National Product', 11, 34–5, and 71–4.

25 Compare column 2 (alternative II) of Table 1 with column 1 of Table 2 in Davis and Gallman, 'Share of Savings and Investment'.

26 F. T. Juster and R. Lipsey, 'A Note on Consumer Asset Formation in the United States', *Economic Journal*, LXXVII, 308 (December 1967).

27 In principle, if consumer durables are to be counted as investment, the services obtained from durables should be counted as part of national product. Such a set of adjustments to the national product would be unlikely, however, to alter the conclusions reached in the text.

28 Albert Fishlow, 'Levels of Nineteenth-Century American Investment in Education', *Journal of Economic History*, XXVI, 4 (December 1966). A substantial part of the value of American human capital represented a gift (in the form of immigration) from other countries. Paul Uselding argues that in the last few decades before the Civil War the gift was of greater value than was the whole of conventional investment. Uselding, 'Conjectural Estimates of Gross Human Capital Inflows to the American Economy, 1790–1860', *Explorations in Economic History*, IX, 1 (Fall 1971).

29 Davis *et al.*, *American Economic Growth*, 55 and 57.

30 To put it another way, the savings rate for the nation averaged about 15 per cent in the 1840s and 1850s and 20 per cent in the two decades centred on 1880 (Table 14). If the rise in the national rate had been occasioned by Southern efforts to replace lost slave capital, then we may place the value of such savings at 5 per cent of the national product. But Southern income accounted for only 15 per cent of

national income and almost certainly a smaller share of the gross national product (since short-lived depreciable capital was concentrated in the North). Thus if the rise in the savings rate had been due to Southern efforts to replace the value of their slaves, Southerners would have had to save over one-third of their income for this purpose alone, in addition to maintaining their pre-existing savings rate. It is highly doubtful that post-war Southern savings rates reached anything like this level.

31 Davis *et al.*, *American Economic Growth*, 38. Two series are given, one averaging about 32 per cent, the other a little higher. We are concerned here with long-term phenomena. It may well be that the Civil War altered the functional distribution of income in the short run, with temporary consequences for the savings rate. See Stanley Engerman, 'The Economic Impact of the Civil War', *Explorations in Entrepreneurial History*, 2nd ser., III, 3 (Spring/Summer 1966), reprinted in Ralph Andreano (ed.), *The Economic Impact of the American Civil War*, rev. edn (Cambridge, Mass., 1967); Williamson, 'Watersheds and Turning-Points'; and Stephen J. De Canio and Joel Mokyr, 'Inflation and the Wage Lag during the American Civil War', Yale University Department of Economics Discussion Paper no. 32, October 1975 (mimeographed). Williamson also argues that Civil War finance sharply repressed capital formation during the period of the war, while post-war federal debt management operated to augment capital formation. On this reading of the evidence, the marked increase in the investment rate after the war reflected, as it were, a temporal displacement of investment from the war period to the post-war period. But, again, presumably this was a short-term phenomenon and does not explain the continuing high rates of savings and investment to the end of the century.

32 This is because we have made use of data on the share of capital consumption in real domestic investment as proxies for data on the share of capital consumption in current-price national investment. The latter almost certainly increased more slowly than did the former over the relevant period.

33 Moses Abramovitz and Paul David, 'Economic Growth in America: Historical Realities and Neoclassical Parables', *De Economist*, CXXI, 3 (1973), 255.

34 Imagine the following case. The economy consists of two sectors, A and B, which produce equal amounts of income in the base period. Property income composes 50 per cent of total income in sector A and 20 per cent in sector B. Between the base year and some subsequent year, the real income of sector A doubles but the price level of the sector drops by 50 per cent. Sector B experiences no change in output or in price level. In real terms, then, the share of property income in the total income of the economy rises from 35 per cent to 40 per cent, while in nominal terms it remains unchanged at 35 per cent. A development of this type may account for the differences between the direct estimates and the production function estimates described in the text. For example, we know that the railroad industry grew rapidly over the relevant period, that a large fraction of the income of the industry consisted of property income, and that the prices of the services offered by the sector fell dramatically, as compared with the general price index. See Gallman and Weiss, 'Service Industries', 292.

35 See Lance E. Davis, 'Stock Ownership in the Early New England Textile Industry', *Business History Review*, XXXII, 2 (Summer 1958).

36 See, for example, B. H. Meyer, C. MacGill, *et al.*, *History of Transportation in the United States before 1860*, Carnegie Institution of Washington publication no. 215C (reprinted, Forge Village, Mass., 1948), and A. M. Johnson and B. E. Supple, *Boston Capitalists and Western Railroads* (Cambridge, Mass., 1967).

37 J. G. Martin, *Seventy-Three Years' History of the Boston Stock Market* (Boston, 1871). T. Navin and M. Sears, 'The Rise of the Market for Industrial Securities, 1887–1902', *Business History Review*, XXX (1955).

38 Minutes of the Joint Finance Committee, Sun Fire and Life Insurance Companies, 6 March 1893.

39 In such a thin market, reinvestment costs must have been substantial, and a shareholder might well have preferred to leave his earnings in an activity of lower return, rather than being forced to pay a high initial cost in order to move them to a more profitable activity.

40 Evans, *Business Incorporations*.

41 See Paul F. McGouldrick, *New England Textiles in the Nineteenth Century: Profits and Investment*, Harvard Economic Studies, 131 (Cambridge, Mass., 1968), and Lance E. Davis, 'Sources of Industrial Finance: The American Textile Industry – A Case Study', *Explorations in Entrepreneurial History*, IX, 4 (April 1957).

42 'If it be the wish of the people that the construction of roads and canals should be conducted by the Federal Government, it is not only highly expedient, but indispensably necessary, that a previous amendment of the Constitution, delegating the necessary power and defining and restricting its exercise with reference to the sovereignty of the States, should be made. Without it nothing extensively useful can be effected.' (27 May 1830.)

43 *US Statutes at Large*, XII, p. 503 (Act of 2 July 1862).

44 The Ordinance reads, '. . . and the means of education shall be forever encouraged.' (13 July 1787.) The 'section sixteen provision' was first incorporated in the act that brought Ohio into the Union in 1802.

45 A. C. True, *A History of Agricultural Experimentation and Research in the United States, 1607–1925, including a History of the United States Department of Agriculture*, USDA Miscellaneous Publication no. 251 (Washington, 1937). On the question of productivity, Zvi Griliches estimates that the total return to investment in hybrid corn (both public and private) was about 700 per cent (Griliches, 'Research Cost and Social Returns: Hybrid Corn and Related Innovations', *Journal of Political Economy*, LXVI, 5 (October 1958).

46 Albert Fishlow has estimated that total public expenditures on education rose from $7·6 million in 1840 to $229·6 million in 1900 – an increase on a per capita basis from $0·33 to $3·01 (Fishlow, 'Levels of Investment in Education').

47 We assume that a potential investor will invest if:

$$PV \geq C$$

where:

$$PV = R_1/(1 + r) + R_2/(1 + r)^2 + R_3/(1 + r)^3 + \ldots + R_n/(1 + r)^n.$$

PV represents the discounted flow of future net income that the investor expects to realize from the investment; C is the cost to the investor of the investment; R_n is the net return that the investor expects to realize from the investment in year n; and r is the rate of interest at which the investor can borrow and lend. Clearly, the higher the value of r is, the more future returns are discounted, and – other things being equal – the less attractive investment with long-delayed returns will be.

48 Carter Goodrich, *Government Promotion of American Canals and Railroads, 1800–1890* (New York, 1960). Goodrich estimates that in the ante-bellum period all levels of government financed about 70 per cent of canal construction and between 25 and 30 per cent of railroad construction.

49 Federal land grants totalled over 131 million acres, and states granted an additional 49 million acres between 1850 and 1880. Grants were made in almost every Western state (Texas, Oklahoma, and South Dakota were the exceptions) and in Illinois, Michigan, Wisconsin, Florida, Alabama, and Mississippi.

50 Incorporation by special act of the state legislature was typical in the United States until the middle of the nineteenth century. Although there were some earlier

partial laws, the first laws requiring general incorporation were passed in the 1840s, and by 1875 most states had some provision for general incorporation. See Evans, *Business Incorporations*.

51 Much of the monetary history of the middle fifty years of the nineteenth century can be written in terms of the demands of business and agriculture for more credit – and thus from the economist's view probably more growth – and the demands of other sectors of the economy for more stability (but probably slower growth). Bray Hammond has rewritten the history of the Bank War in this context, and recent work shows that the growth of state regulation probably can be viewed as a victory for the forces of greater stability over those that wanted faster growth. The Forestall system, innovated in Louisiana in 1842, is a perfect example of a regulatory system that greatly increased stability but that reduced the state rate of growth equally spectacularly. See Bray Hammond, *Banks and Politics in America from the Revolution to the Civil War* (Princeton, 1957), and G. Green, *Finance and Economic Development in the Old South: Louisiana Banking, 1804–1861* (Palo Alto, Calif., 1972).

52 Between 1870 and 1900 the proportion of the five-to-seventeen-year age group enrolled in public schools rose from 57 to 72 per cent, while the average number of days attended increased from seventy-eight to ninety-nine. Lewis Solmon, in his study of capital formation in education, has estimated earnings forgone in 1890 and shows that by that time the sums were not inconsiderable. The total per capita expenditure on education was $8·37 in that year, and of that sum 57 per cent ($4·77) represented forgone earnings. For rural areas the numbers were only 45 per cent of $3·28 ($1·48), but in urban areas forgone income represented 69 per cent of the $12·62 per capita cost, or $8·71 (L. C. Solmon, 'Capital Formation and Expenditures on Education, 1880 and 1890' (unpublished Ph.D. dissertation, University of Chicago, 1969)).

53 The total for Champaign County rose from $400,000 in 1865 to $1,500,000 in 1876. For Tippecanoe County the figures were $590,000 and $810,000. R. F. Severson, Jr, 'The Source of Mortgage Credit for Champaign County, 1865–1880', *Agricultural History*, XXXVI (July 1962); and J. Ladin, 'Mortgage Credit in Tippecanoe County, Indiana, 1865–1880', *Agricultural History*, XLI (1967).

54 See G. K. Holmes and J. S. Lord, 'Report on Real Estate Mortgages in the United States', US Census Office, issued as Final Census Report, vol. XII, the 11th Census [1890].

55 See, for example, S. J. Buck, *The Granger Movement* (Cambridge, Mass., 1913), and J. D. Hicks, *The Populist Revolt* (Minneapolis, Minn., 1931).

56 See, for example, A. Bogue, *Money at Interest* (Ithaca, N.Y., 1955); C. S. Popple, *The Development of Two Bank Groups in the Central Northwest* (Cambridge, Mass., 1944); and D. M. Frederiksen, 'Mortgage Banking in America', *Journal of Political Economy*, II (1894). By 1890 there appear to have been at least 167 mortgage companies operating in the United States.

57 R. Goldsmith, *A Study of Savings in the United States*, 3 vols. (Princeton, 1955), I, p. 749. Since funds borrowed and used to acquire land at higher price show up as subtractions from the stream of savings, and since losses of initial investments are handled in the same fashion, over the last quarter of the nineteenth century the shift out of the farm sector probably helped underwrite a portion of the increase in the national savings–income ratio.

58 The indirect evidence with respect to income distribution has been appraised by Simon Kuznets ('Economic Growth and Income Inequality', *American Economic Review*, XLV, 1 (March 1955)), who concludes that the distribution may have grown more unequal between 1840 and 1890 (especially in the sub-period 1870–90), but he gives the conclusion the character of a hunch rather than a firmly based finding. Robert Gallman carried out a somewhat similar analysis with wealth data, concluding

that structural factors exerted a modest pressure toward a widening of wealth in-equalities in the period 1810–60 and a stronger pressure in the same direction in 1860–1900 (Gallman, 'Trends in the Size Distribution of Wealth in the Nineteenth Century: Some Speculations', in Lee Soltow (ed.), *Six Papers on the Size Distribution of Wealth and Income*, Studies in Income and Wealth, 33 (New York, 1969)). The same paper contains rough estimates of the share of total wealth held by the very rich in 1840, 1850, 1860, and 1890. Lee Soltow analysed trends in the distribution of wealth from 1790 to 1860 through data on slave holdings, concluding that the evidence was against any significant change over that period – a finding roughly consistent with the indirect evidence on structure (Soltow, 'Economic Inequalities in the United States in the Period from 1790 to 1860', *Journal of Economic History*, XXXI, 4 (December 1971)). Soltow is also responsible for the most recent treatment of the income-tax data ('Evidence on Income Inequalities in the United States, 1866–1965', *Journal of Economic History*, XXIX, 2 (June 1969)). Chap. 2 of Davis *et al.*, *American Economic Growth* contains a general treatment of these issues, but it is flawed by an overemphasis on the importance of relative per capita income levels by sectors and regions, and by a failure to take adequately into account shifts in the relative importance of regions and sectors.

59 Martin Primack, in his study of investment in nineteenth-century agriculture, has concluded that '(*a*) Land clearing was an important and time consuming part of the farmer's working life – at least in the forested regions; (*b*) Its burden was much less for farms formed on the prairie and plains; (*c*) Both in forests and in grass and arid lands, improved techniques after 1850 also contributed to reduce clearing labor.' His estimate suggests that in 1850 about 12 per cent of the farm labour time was engaged in land-clearing, while by 1900 that fraction had fallen to just over 2 per cent. To those figures might be added about another 4 per cent in 1850 and 3 per cent at the turn of the century to allow for the application of farm labour to building construction. See M. Primack, 'Land Clearing under Nineteenth Century Techniques', *Journal of Economic History*, XXII (December 1962), and the same author's 'Farm Construction as a Use of Farm Labor in the United States, 1850–1900', *Journal of Economic History*, XXV (March 1965).

60 'In the Middle West there was insufficient local capital in a form readily con-vertible into cash. The capital of the community was represented largely by farm improvements . . . In recognition of this condition, there was resort to barter, or exchange of the shares of railroad companies for land, labor, and materials' (Frederick A. Cleveland and Fred W. Powell, *Railroad Finance* (New York, 1912), reprinted in A. D. Chandler, Jr (ed.), *The Railroads: The Nation's First Big Business* (New York, 1965), 52).

61 In terms of the model discussed in note 41, the terms $R_1, R_2, \ldots, R_n$ would be replaced by terms of the form $(R_1 + LR_1), \ldots, (R_n + LR_n)$ where LR_n is the increase in the rental value of the land that is attributable to its location near the railroad or canal.

62 Cleveland and Powell, *Railroad Finance*, reprinted in Chandler (ed.), *The Rail-roads*, 48–58. This trend was supported by the willingness of the railroads to accept farm mortgages and/or materials as part or full payment for the shares.

63 See Lance E. Davis and D. North, *Institutional Change and American Economic Growth* (Cambridge, 1971), for the period 1857–60. Macauley's study shows that rates on railroad bonds averaged 9·3 per cent, while New England municipal bonds averaged 5·0 per cent; in the earlier period this difference must have been even more pronounced. Macauley, *Some Theoretical Problems suggested by the Movement of Interest Rates, Bond Yields and Stock Prices.*

64 In terms of the model the R_n terms were replaced by $(R_n + LS_n)$, and the result

was an increase in present value. In the case of the Illinois Central, for example, between 1854 and 1870 the railroad sold 2·2 million acres (of its 2·6-million-acre grant) for $24·8 million. Paul W. Gates, *The Illinois Central Railroad and Its Colonization Work* (Cambridge, Mass., 1934).

65 Fogel concludes that the public's assessment of the probability of failure of the Union Pacific scheme was 72 per cent. Robert W. Fogel, *The Union Pacific Railroad: A Case of Premature Enterprise* (Baltimore, Md, 1960).

66 The economic principles involved in complete price discrimination had been worked out by Charles Ellet when he attempted to design a rate structure for the James River and Great Kanawha Canal, but even that talented engineer and economist never discovered a practical way of implementing his structure. Charles Ellet, *An Essay on the Laws of Trade in Reference to the Works of Internal Improvement in the United States* (Richmond, Virginia, 1839).

67 See the discussion in Davis and North, *Institutional Change and American Economic Growth*.

68 Although there is still no general history of the growth of mortgage banks in the United States, A. Bogue has written a first-rate account of the rise of one such organization (the J. B. Watkins Land Mortgage Company of Lawrence, Kansas), and D. M. Frederiksen provides a good contemporary account of the general mortgage banking scene (Bogue, *Money at Interest*; Frederiksen, 'Mortgage Banking in the United States'). The Watkins Company had branches in New York City and in London, as well as sales agents in Buffalo, Albion, Batavia, Rochester, Syracuse, Rome, and Johnstown, New York; Wilmington, Delaware; Boston, Massachusetts; Warner, New Hampshire; and Ferrisburg, Vermont.

69 The first American saving bank was established in 1815; over the next decade, banks were opened in most cities of the Northwest. See Emerson W. Keyes, *A History of Savings Banks in the United States*, 2 vols. (New York, 1878), and F. P. Bennett, Jr, *The Story of Mutual Savings Banks* (Boston, 1924). For studies of individual bank behaviour see Charles E. Knowles, *History of the Bank for Savings in the City of New York, 1819–1829* (New York, 1929); P. L. Payne and Lance E. Davis, *The Savings Bank of Baltimore, 1818–1866: A Historical and Analytical Study* (Baltimore, Md, 1956); and J. M. Wilcox, *A History of the Philadelphia Savings Fund Society, 1816–1916* (Philadelphia, 1916).

70 See Lance E. Davis and P. L. Payne, 'From Benevolence to Business, the Story of Two Savings Banks', *Business History Review*, XXXII, 4 (Winter 1958), and Davis, 'Sources of Industrial Finance'.

71 US Comptroller of the Currency, *Annual Report* for 1916, section IV, vol. 1 (Washington, 1917). The increase in the number of depositors is equally impressive: in 1820 there were fewer than nine thousand; by 1910 the number was almost nine million.

72 Although the period of growth was later, the geographical spread of deposit banking was much wider, reaching as it did into every state and territory. By 1910 they had actually passed the mutuals, possessing at that time deposits of $3·7 thousand million. Almost all of that growth, however, came during the last two decades of the period.

73 Evans, *Business Incorporations*.

74 In 1905, for example, Frank Vanderlip, a New York banker, is quoted as saying, 'The whole great Mississippi Valley gives promise that in some day distant perhaps it will be another New England for investments. There is developing a bond market there which is of constant astonishment to eastern dealers' (quoted in G. Edwards, *The Evolution of Finance Capitalism* (London and New York, 1938)). Some feeling for change in the geographical distribution of investors can be obtained from

an examination of the regional distribution of interest payments on the federal debt. In 1870, per capita interest payments amounted to $4·25 in the New England states, $3·01 in the Middle Atlantic states, $0·76 in the East North Central region, $0·45 in the West North Central area, and $0·49 in the South. In 1900, the figures were $1·18, $1·31, $0·57, $0·45, and $0·24 respectively (Legler, 'Regional Distribution of Federal Receipts and Expenditures', 95). On the participation of middle America in the securities market, see William Z. Ripley, *Main Street and Wall Street* (Boston, 1927), and Margaret Myers, 'The Investment Market after 1919', in H. F. Williamson (ed.), *The Growth of the American Economy* (New York, 1944).

75 Robert Sobel, *The Big Board: A History of the New York Stock Market* (New York, 1965); Margaret Myers, *The New York Money Market*, 1 (New York, 1931); Navin and Sears, 'The Rise of the Market for Industrial Securities'; and Edwards, *The Evolution of Finance Capitalism*.

76 For a history of the growth of the investment banking industry, see Vincent P. Carosso, *Investment Banking in America: A History* (Cambridge, Mass., 1970).

77 Henrietta Larson, *Jay Cooke: Private Banker* (Cambridge, Mass., 1936).

78 Lewis Corey, *The House of Morgan* (New York, 1930); Frederick Lewis Allen, *The Great Pierpont Morgan* (New York, 1949); and J. R. T. Hughes, *The Vital Few* (Boston, 1966).

79 Albert O. Greef, *The Commercial Paper House in the United States* (Cambridge, Mass., 1938). Lance E. Davis, 'The Investment Market, 1870–1914: The Evolution of a National Market', *Journal of Economic History*, xxv, 3 (September 1965).

80 For a complete study of the Massachusetts Hospital Life Insurance Company see Gerald White, *A History of the Massachusetts Hospital Life Insurance Company*, (Cambridge, Mass., 1955) and Lance E. Davis, 'United States Financial Intermediaries in the Early Nineteenth Century' (unpublished Ph.D. dissertation, The Johns Hopkins University, 1956).

81 For the early period, see Davis, 'United States Financial Intermediaries', and Lester Zartman, *The Investment of Life Insurance Companies* (New York, 1906). For developments after the Civil War, see Douglass North, 'Capital Accumulation in Life Insurance between the Civil War and the Investigation of 1905', in W. Miller (ed.), *Men in Business* (Cambridge, Mass., 1952). There are also a number of studies of individual companies: particularly recommended are H. F. Williamson and O. Smalley, *Northwestern Mutual Life: A Century of Trusteeship* (Evanston, Illinois, 1957), and R. Buley, *The Equitable Life Assurance Society of the United States, 1859–1964* (New York, 1967).

82 There were, of course, two exceptions to this rule. The First and Second Banks of the United States had been chartered by special act of the United States Congress.

83 Hammond, *Banks and Politics in America*.

84 Paul B. Trescott, *Financing American Enterprise* (New York, 1963), Dewey, *Financial History of the United States*; Milton Friedman and Anna Schwartz, *A Monetary History of the United States, 1867–1960* (Princeton, 1963).

85 John A. James, 'The Evolution of the National Money Market, 1888–1911', *Journal of Economic History*, xxxvi, 1 (March 1976).

CHAPTER II

The United States: Evolution of Enterprise

1 The author gratefully acknowledges the assistance of the Alfred P. Sloan Foundation and the Division of Research at the Harvard Graduate School of Business Administration, which made this study possible.

2 *Metallurgical Review*, December 1877, 332-3.

3 Temin, *Iron and Steel in Nineteenth-Century America* (Cambridge, Mass., 1964), 165.

4 James H. Bridge, *The Inside History of the Carnegie Steel Company* (New York, 1903), 85.

5 *Transactions of the American Society of Mechanical Engineers*, VII (1886), 429-30.

6 From a talk entitled 'The Gospel of Industrial Steadiness', delivered in Boston on 25 May 1899, and published in James H. Bridge (ed.), *The Trust: Its Book* (New York, 1902), 87-8.

CHAPTER III

Capital Formation in Japan

1 We wish to express our gratitude to Nobukiyō Takamatsu for generous help in the preparation of this chapter.

Since the original draft of this chapter was completed, we have published a book in which many of the issues discussed in this chapter are treated in much greater detail: see Kazushi Ohkawa and Henry Rosovsky, *Japanese Economic Growth: Trend Acceleration in the Twentieth Century* (Stanford, Calif., 1973).

2 The Meiji era actually began in 1868 and ended in 1912, but from an economic point of view dating based on the reign of an emperor is meaningless.

3 This was undoubtedly the case in much of Africa and in some parts of Asia.

4 See Henry Rosovsky, 'Japan's Transition to Modern Economic Growth, 1868–1885', in H. Rosovsky (ed.), *Industrialization in Two Systems* (New York, 1966).

5 See Henry Rosovsky, 'Rumbles in the Rice Fields', *Journal of Asian Studies*, XXVII, 2 (1968). This review article deals mainly with the work of Professor James Nakamura.

6 Beginning in 1965, a research group at Hitotsubashi University began publishing a thirteen-volume series of historical statistics: K. Ohkawa, M. Shinohara, and M. Umemura (eds.), *Chōki keizai tōkei* [*Estimates of Long-Term Economic Statistics of Japan since 1868*] (these are the so-called '*LTES*' volumes). Agriculture is dealt with in vol. IX, M. Umemura *et al.*, *Nōringyō* [*Agriculture and Forestry*] (Tokyo, 1966): see especially p. 276. Other available volumes are: I: *Kokumin shotoku* [*National Income*] (1974); II: *Jinkō to rōdōryoku* [*Population and Labour Force*] (1973); III: *Shihon stokku* [*Capital Stock*] (1965); IV: *Shihon keisei* [*Capital Formation*] (1971); VI: *Kojin shōhi shishitsu* [*Personal Consumption Expenditures*] (1967); VII: *Zaisei shishitsu* [*Public Expenditures*] (1966); VIII: *Bukka* [*Prices*] (1965); X: *Kōkōgyō* [*Mining and Manufacturing*] (1972); XII: *Tetsudō to denryoku* [*Railways and Electrical Utilities*] (1965). (Other volumes are planned for Savings and Currency, Textiles, and Regional Economic Statistics.)

Virtually all of the quantitative information used in this chapter is based on those volumes. For the convenience of readers unacquainted with the Japanese language, most of our citations will refer to Ohkawa and Rosovsky, *Japanese Economic Growth*, where the Japanese sources are analysed and described in considerable detail.

7 It is very difficult to be more precise, because reliable aggregate product figures are not available for the nineteenth century.

8 To be more precise, gross domestic fixed private capital formation, excluding residential dwellings.

9 Both total product and capital stock measures entail greater statistical problems. In the former case, there are difficulties in estimating the output of tertiary production and the output of the handicraft sector. In the latter case, problems of valuation and depreciation create many obstacles.

10 Having identified the industries whose growth was most responsible for twentieth-century investment spurts, it would now be logical to discuss the experiences of individual industries. Unfortunately the data for this type of analysis are unavailable. The only exception applies to the period 1955–61. For this period, the Economic Planning Agency has provided figures which indicate an average annual real rate of growth of capital formation in manufacturing of 34·4 per cent. The individual rates are as follows: metal products, 50·4 per cent; transport machinery, 44·4 per cent; other machinery, 49·4 per cent; petroleum and coal products, 38·3 per cent; chemical products, 23·7 per cent; ceramics, 25·7 per cent; food and tobacco, 20·1 per cent; textiles, 13·7 per cent; other industries (timber, pulp and paper, printing, hides, rubber), 20·1 per cent.

11 These ideas were initially developed in Kazushi Ohkawa and Henry Rosovsky, 'A Century of Japanese Economic Growth', in W. W. Lockwood (ed.), *The State and Economic Enterprise in Japan* (Princeton, 1965), and the same authors' 'Postwar Japanese Economic Growth in Historical Perspective: A Second Look', in L. Klein and K. Ohkawa (eds.), *Economic Growth: The Japanese Experience since the Meiji Era* (New Haven, Conn., 1968).

12 The GDP figures which form the basis of these growth rates are still subject to future revision, especially in the case of tertiary production.

13 See Ohkawa and Rosovsky, *Japanese Economic Growth*, basic statistical Table 18, pp. 328–9.

14 *Ibid.*, Table 3.1, p. 47.

15 See K. Boulding and N. Sun, 'The Effects of Military Expenditures upon the Economic Growth of Japan' (mimeographed: Tokyo, 1967).

16 That these requirements were comparatively small is demonstrated by the fact that the absolute size of the gainfully employed labour force in agriculture remained stable until the Second World War. After the war it started to decrease, but even at present around 15 per cent of Japan's labour force is still gainfully employed in the primary sector.

17 Clearly, market conditions which would affect the capacity level of operations could lead to similar results.

18 However, we have noticed that a lag of varying duration may be present. Three points can be made in connection with this apparent discrepancy. First, our observations are based on five- or seven-year moving averages, and therefore a specific turning point must be thought of as a rather broad band of years. Secondly, investment spurts are here considered in the aggregate, but they begin in specific industries, and the mechanism which we describe applies especially to the leading industries. Thirdly, external factors – changes in demand, foreign markets, etc. – could precede, and set the conditions for, an investment spurt.

19 It has already been shown that the post-war decline of the aggregate capital–output ratio (K/Y) was steeper than at any previous time. Sectoral capital–output ratios are available mostly for the postwar period. They indicate the most marked declines in manufacturing, at rates about nine times as rapid as the average for the entire economy. (In agriculture, the capital–output ratio actually increased.) Within manufacturing, the most impressive declines occurred in the machinery, petroleum, and chemical sectors.

20 See Y. Shionoya, 'Patterns of Industrial Development', in Klein and Ohkawa (eds.), *Economic Growth*.

21 Our own research indicates that the aggregate residual grew over four times more rapidly following the Second World War, in comparison with the 1930s. Residuals grew most rapidly in manufacturing and facilitating industries. See Ohkawa and Rosovsky, *Japanese Economic Growth*, chaps. 3 and 4. For a quite similar perspec-

tive, see Edward F. Denison and William K. Chung, *How Japan's Economy Grew So Fast* (Washington, 1976).

22 The inclusion of foreign trade reinforces the arguments. Possibilities of exporting obviously raise the level of aggregate demand and improve the chances of obtaining economies of scale. On the supply side, the case for the direct or simple explanation is especially applicable as seen in the relative secular decline of export prices. After all, Japanese exports, since 1900, consisted almost entirely of modern manufactures – i.e. those products that benefited most from imported technology.

CHAPTER IV

Factory Labour and the Industrial Revolution in Japan

The following abbreviations are used in the notes:

ELTES Kazushi Ohkawa, Miyohei Shinohara, and Mataji Umemura (eds.), *Chōki keizai tōkei suikei to bunseki*, or *Estimates of Long-Term Economic Statistics of Japan since 1868*, 13 vols. (Tokyo, 1966– : see above, p. 504 note 6).

NRKN Rōmu Kanri Shiryō Hensankai [Society for the Compilation of Historical Materials on Work-Force Management], *Nihon rōmu kanri nenshi* [*The Chronicle of Work-Force Management*], 2 vols. (Tokyo, 1962).

NRUS Rōdō Undō Shiryō Iinkai [Committee on Historical Materials on the Labour Movement], *Nihon rōdō undō shiryō* [*Historical Materials on the Labour Movement in Japan*], 11 vols. (Tokyo, 1959– : 6 vols. published by 1968).

Shokkō jijō Japan, Ministry of Agriculture and Commerce, *Shokkō jijō* [*The Conditions of Factory Labour*], ed. T. Tsuchiya, 3 vols. (Tokyo, 1947: first published 1903).

1 The author wishes to acknowledge financial support from the East Asian Studies Center of Stanford University, which has made this study possible.

2 *ELTES*, I, 'National Income', 16.

3 Computed from *ELTES*, III, 'Capital Stock', Table 1, pp. 148–50. Since *ELTES*, II, 'Population and the Labor Force', was not available at the time of writing, the labour-force growth rate in the text was computed from data in Kazushi Ohkawa *et al.*, *The Growth Rate of the Japanese Economy since 1878* (Tokyo, 1958), chap. 5, part II.

4 The formula for this calculation is as follows:

$$G(Y) = aG(K) + (1 - a)G(N) + G(R)$$

which states that the growth rate of income (Y) is the sum of the weighted growth rates of capital (K) and of labour (N), the weights being relative shares of capital (a) and of labour ($1 - a$). When $G(Y)$ is not equal to this sum, a residual growth rate ($G(R)$) has to be recognized to balance the equation. For a thorough inquiry into the size of the residual in Japan, see Kazushi Ohkawa and Henry Rosovsky, *Japanese Economic Growth* (Stanford, Calif., 1973).

5 Henry Rosovsky, 'Japan's Transition to Economic Growth, 1868–1885', in H. Rosovsky (ed.), *Industrialization in Two Systems* (New York, 1966), 93.

6 Computed with the help of tables in *NRUS*, x, 154–65.

7 T. C. Smith, *The Agrarian Origins of Modern Japan* (Stanford, Calif., 1959), 112.

8 *Ibid.*, 113–14.

9 Toshio Furushima, 'Bakumatsuki no nōgyō hiyō rōdōsha' ['Paid Labour in the

Late Edo Period'], in Takamasa Ichikawa *et al.*, *Hōken shakai kaitaiki no koyō rōdō* [*Paid Labour during the Period of Disintegration of Feudal Society*] (Tokyo, 1961), 184.

10 *Ibid.*, 180–1.

11 Nobuo Watanabe, 'Shōgyōteki nōgyō ni okeru koyō rōdō' ['Paid Labour in Commercial Agriculture'], in Ichikawa *et al.*, *Paid Labour*, 54–7.

12 *Ibid.*, 81.

13 *Ibid.*, 80–103.

14 *NRUS*, I, 25–36.

15 *Ibid.*, 26–7.

16 Hideo Hayashi, 'Bisai ni okeru meiji kōhanki no koyō rōdō' ['Paid Labour in Western Aichi during the Late Meiji Era'], in Ichikawa *et al.*, *Paid Labour*, 235–7.

17 Takamasa Ichikawa, 'Nōson kōgyō ni okeru koyō rōdō' ['Paid Labour in Rural Industries'], in Ichikawa *et al.*, *Paid Labour*, 129–46.

18 *Ibid.*, 151.

19 T. C. Smith, *Political Change and Industrial Development in Japan: Government Enterprise, 1868–1880* (Stanford, Calif., 1955), chap. 6. See also *NRUS*, I, 136–47.

20 Mikio Sumiya, *Nihon chinrōdōshi ron* [*A Tract on the History of Wage Labour in Japan*] (Tokyo, 1955), 156.

21 Computed from the agrarian survey for the prefecture of Gunma, *NRUS*, I, 158–60.

22 Sumiya, *Tract on the History of Wage Labour*, 152–74; and Mitsuhaya Kajinishi *et al.*, *Seishi rōdōsha no rekishi* [*A History of Workers in the Raw Silk Industry*] (Tokyo, 1955), chap. 1.

23 Kajinishi *et al.*, *op. cit.*, 36–44. See also *NRUS*, I, 155–8.

24 Smith, *Political Change and Industrial Development*, chap. 1.

25 The rest of this section draws upon Hiroshi Hazama, *Nihon rōmu kanrishi kenkyū* [*Studies in the History of Work-Force Management*] (Tokyo, 1964), chap. 4; *NRKN*, I; *NRUS*, I, 97–118. For analyses and discussions of labour conditions in the government-owned heavy industries, see Sumiya, *Tract on the History of Wage Labour*, 208–39, and Masao Endo, 'Meiji shoki ni okeru rōdōsha no jōtai' ['The Conditions of Workers during the Early Meiji Era'], in M. Sumiya *et al.*, *Meiji zenki no rōdō mondai* [*Labour Problems in the Early Meiji Era*] (Tokyo, 1960), 43–95.

26 This information is from a report by François L. Verny (1837–1908), who built the Yokosuka Shipyard and supervised it until 1876. See Kunitaro Takahashi, *Oyatoi gaikokujin-gunji* [*Foreign Employees – Armed Services*] (Tokyo, 1968), 119.

27 Taichi Kinukawa, *Honpō menshi bōseki shi* [*The History of Japanese Cotton Textiles*], 7 vols. (Tokyo, 1937), II, chap. 12. See also Johannes Hirschmeier, 'Shibusawa Eiichi: Industrial Pioneer', in W. W. Lockwood (ed.), *The State and Economic Enterprise in Japan* (Princeton, 1965), chap. 5.

28 Keizo Fujibayashi, 'Meiji nijūnendai ni okeru waga bōsekigyō rōdōsha no idō genshō ni tsuite' ['The Mobility of Workers in Japanese Cotton Textiles in the Mid-Meiji Era'], in Sumiya *et al.*, *Labour Problems in the Early Meiji Era*, 137–76.

29 Kinukawa, *History of Japanese Cotton Textiles*, III, 179.

30 Kazuo Okochi, *Labor in Modern Japan* (Tokyo, 1958), 15. See also Wakizō Hosoi, *Jokō aishi* [*A Tragic History of Female Factory Workers*] (Tokyo, 1925), chaps. 7 and 8.

31 Gennosuke Yokoyama, *Nihon no kasō shakai* [*The Lower-Class Society of Japan*] (Tokyo, 1898), 200–1; Sumiya, *Tract on the History of Wage Labour*, 196–202; Hosoi, *A Tragic History*, chap. 4.

32 *NRUS*, I, 255–90.

33 *Ibid.*, 125–6.

34 For the state of this peculiar phenomenon before and around 1900, see Kashiro Saito, *La Protection ouvrière au Japon* (Paris, 1900); Ernest Foxwell, 'The Protection of Labour in Japan', *Economic Journal*, XI (1901), 106–124; and *Shokkō jijō*, vol. I. For its subsequent development, *NRUS*, I, 290–7; and Hosoi, *A Tragic History*, chap. 3.

35 Computed from data reported by the cotton textile employers' association (mentioned above): *NRUS*, I, 259–60. See also *Shokkō jijō*, I, 66–8.

36 *Shokkō jijō*, I, 5–18.

37 *Ibid.*, 69.

38 Japan, Prime Minister's Office, *Nihon teikoku tōkei zensho* [*Statistical Collection for the Empire of Japan*] (Tokyo, 1928), 23.

39 Computed from data in the official explanation of the need for the Factory Law: *NRUS*, III, 209–19.

40 This and other episodes in this paragraph are from *Shokkō jijō*, III, 166–92. For other incidents, see Hosoi, *A Tragic History*, chap. 11.

41 Prime Minister's Office, *Statistical Collection for the Empire of Japan*, 23–4.

42 Japan, Ministry of Commerce and Industry, *Kojō tōkei hyō* [*Factory Statistics*], I (Tokyo, 1909).

43 *Shokkō jijō*, I, 177–88 and 240–68. See also Kajinishi *et al.*, *History of Workers in the Raw Silk Industry*, chap. 2.

44 *Shokkō jijō*, I, 187.

45 *Ibid.*, 70.

46 *Ibid.*, 244–68.

47 Yokoyama, *The Lower-Class Society of Japan*, part II; and *NRUS*, II, 241–87.

48 Inferred from Endo, 'Conditions of Workers', 56–7, for the 1880s; *Shokkō jijō*, II, 5–7, for around 1900; and Ministry of Commerce and Industry, *Factory Statistics*, 1914.

49 *Shokkō jijō*, II, 36–8.

50 Mikio Sumiya, *Nihon rōdō undōshi* [*A History of the Labour Movement in Japan*] (Tokyo, 1966), 51.

51 *NRKN*, I, 109.

52 *NRUS*, II, 241–2. See also Yoshio Morita, *Wagakuni no shihonka dantai* [*Industrialists' Associations in Japan*] (Tokyo, 1926), 25–35.

53 Sumiya, *History of the Labour Movement*, 18. Benji Yamazaki, *Nihon shōhi kumiai undōshi* [*A History of Consumers' Co-operatives in Japan*] (Tokyo, 1932), 18.

54 For personalities involved in this movement, see Hyman Kublin, *Meiji rōdō undōshi no hitokoma* [*An Aspect of the History of the Meiji Labour Movement*] (Tokyo, 1959); and the same author's *Asian Revolutionary: The Life of Sen Katayama* (Princeton, 1964).

55 *Shokkō jijō*, II, 14.

56 This certainly offers an extreme contrast to Japanese workers' propensity to save after the Second World War. But see, for example, *Shokkō jijō*, II, 19–20.

57 Yamazaki, *History of Consumers' Co-operatives*, 46–53.

58 Sen Katayama, 'Labor Problem Old and New', *Far East*, October 1897 (reprinted in *NRUS*, II, 255–63); and *The Labor Movement in Japan* (Chicago, 1918), chaps. 1 and 2.

59 *Shokkō jijō*, III, 169–70.

60 See Yokoyama's observations reported in *Shinkōron* [*New Review*], September 1910 (reprinted in *NRUS*, III, 11–16).

61 R. P. Dore, *British Factory – Japanese Factory* (Berkeley, Calif., 1973), part III.

62 Herbert Passin, *Society and Education in Japan* (New York, 1965), chap. 4.

63 Japan, Ministry of Education, *Jitsugyō kyōiku gojūnenshi* [*Fifty Years of Vocational Education*] (Tokyo, 1934); Mamoru Sato *et al.*, *Totei kyōiku no kenkyū* [*Studies in Apprenticeship*] (Tokyo, 1962), part i.

64 R. P. Dore, *Education in Tokugawa Japan* (London, 1965), 321.

65 Kazushi Ohkawa, 'Nihon keizai no seisan bunpai 1905–1963' ['Production and Distribution in the Japanese Economy, 1905–1963'], *Keizai kenkyū* [*Economic Review*], XIX, 2 (April 1968), 136.

66 For further details, see Koji Taira, 'Education and Literacy in Meiji Japan: An Interpretation', *Explorations in Economic History*, VIII, 4 (July 1971), 371–94.

67 Inazo Nitobe, *Japan* (New York, 1931), 239–44. The 'curious fact' which Nitobe mentions in this connection is extremely illuminating: 'the blind man can be better educated than his more fortunate brethren who are endowed with good sight; for the former, by acquiring the forty-seven letters of the [*kana*] syllabary, through the Braille system, can read history, geography or anything written in that system; whereas he who has eyesight cannot read the daily papers unless he has mastered at least 2000 characters' (p. 242). For literacy tests administered to military conscripts, see Taketoshi Yamamoto, 'Meiji kōki no riterashi chōsa' ['Literacy Survey in the Late Meiji Era'], *Hitotsubashi ronsō* [*Hitotsubashi Review*], LXI, 3 (March 1969), 345–55.

68 Takano's article in *American Federationist*, I, 8 (October 1894) (reprinted in *NRUS*, I, 396–400).

69 *NRUS*, I, 403–5.

70 Data in this paragraph, unless otherwise noted, are from various volumes of *Shokkō jijō*.

71 According to a survey of the Osaka Education Society: *NRUS*, X, 170–1.

72 Ohkawa, 'Production and Distribution', 136.

73 Japan, Ministry of Home Affairs, *Saimin chōsa tōkeihyō tekiyō* [*Statistical Abstracts on the Survey of the Poor*] (Tokyo, 1912). See also *NRUS*, III, 85–101.

74 For data and sources, see Koji Taira, *Economic Development and the Labor Market in Japan* (New York, 1970), chap. 5. In addition, see Hazama, *Studies in the History of Work-Force Management*, chap. 3; *NRKN*, II, part i; and *NRUS*, III, 111–76.

75 For a brief biographical review of these modernizers of management, see Koji Taira, 'Factory Legislation and Management Modernization during Japan's Industrialization, 1886–1916', *Business History Review*, XLIV, 1 (Spring 1970), 84–109.

76 When these classics were reprinted after the Second World War, they received notes of introduction or recommendation from prominent scholars as follows: Yokoyama from Yasoji Kazahaya, *Shokkō jijō* from Takao Tsuchiya, and Hosoi from Kazuo Okochi.

77 S. B. Levine, 'Labor Market and Collective Bargaining in Japan', in W. W. Lockwood (ed.), *The State and Economic Enterprise in Japan* (Princeton, 1965), chap. 14. See also Ryu Nibuya, 'Nenkō seido no kaiko to tenbō' ['Reflections upon Nenkō seido'], *Nihon rōdō kyōkai zasshi* [*Monthly Journal of the Japan Institute of Labour*], VI, 12 (December 1964). The latest, most comprehensive study of the history of industrial relations and work-force management in Japan's heavy industry is Tsutomu Hyodo, *Nihon ni okeru rōshi-kankei no tenkai* [*The Development of Industrial Relations in Japan*] (Tokyo, 1971).

78 A report of the Mitsubishi Holding Company (1914), *NRUS*, III, 17–29 and 119–24; *NRKN*, II, 16–19 and 166–9.

79 Yokoyama (1910), *NRUS*, III, 12.

80 For example, the Tokyō-fu shokkō gakkō (Tokyo Prefectural Vocational School) was jointly utilized by the Ishikawajima Shipyard, the Shibaura Engineering Works, and others (Hazama, *Studies in the History of Work-Force Management*, 458).

81 Konosuke Odaka, 'A History of Money Wages in the Northern Kyūshū Industrial Area, 1898–1939', *Hitotsubashi Journal of Economics*, VIII, 2 (February 1968).

82 See a report on accidents and health hazards at the Tokyo Artillery Factory, in *NRUS*, I, 348–53.

83 Iwao F. Ayusawa, *A History of Labor in Modern Japan* (Honolulu, 1966), chaps. 3 and 4; Japan, Ministry of International Trade and Industry, *Shōkō seisakushi* [*A History of Commercial and Industrial Policies*], 25 vols. (Tokyo, 1962), VIII; *NRUS*, III, 178–256; Yasoji Kazahaya, *Nihon shakai Seisakushi* [*A History of Social Policy in Japan*], 2 vols. (Tokyo, 1951), I, chaps. 3, 4, and 5; R. P. Dore, 'The Modernizer as a Special Case: Japanese Factory Legislation, 1882–1911', *Comparative Studies in Society and History*, XI, 4 (October 1969), 443–50.

84 For further details, see Koji Taira, 'Labor Markets, Unions, and Employers in Interwar Japan', in Adolf Sturmthal and James G. Scoville (eds.), *The International Labor Movement in Transition* (Urbana, Illinois, 1973), 149–77.

85 Computed from data in *NRUS*, X, 426–7.

86 Japan, Prime Minister's Office, *Rōdō tōkei jitchi chōsa hōkoku* [*Report on the Survey of Labour Statistics*] (Tokyo, 1936).

CHAPTER V

Entrepreneurship, Ownership, an Management in Japan

1 Faced with subjects which could easily be expanded to several times the length of this chapter, I choose to emphasize those aspects which are not sufficiently dealt with in English and which are of interest to persons not specializing in Japanese economic history. Some sections of the chapter, as described in the text, are brief and only highlight uniquely Japanese or selected important aspects. Interested readers are referred to the Bibliography.

Throughout this chapter, Japanese names appear with surnames last, following Western usage.

2 Takao Tsuchiya, who wrote nearly a dozen volumes on related topics, put forth his view repeatedly with little or no variation. One of his books, from which the above quotation was taken, expressed his theme (which he has been expanding since the 1930s) as follows:

In the case of Japan, the feudalistic samurai or their sons shouldered the leadership role of the Meiji entrepreneurs. Unlike any other nation, the development of capitalism was guided by bureaucrats who were samurai and by business leaders who were also of samurai origin . . . Thus, the Meiji entrepreneurs were strongly motivated by the semi-feudal spirit of *shikon shōsai*. This, of course, was inevitable.

Takao Tsuchiya, *Gendai nihon keizaishi kōwa* [*Lectures on the Economic History of Modern Japan*] (Tokyo, 1958), 53.

3 George B. Sansom wrote: 'It was these men [samurai], and not the bourgeois, who laid the foundation of a capitalist structure and at the same time developed a political system that bore little resemblance to those which came into force in the advanced industrial countries of Western Europe under the influence of a powerful money class.' Sansom, *The Western World and Japan* (New York, 1951), 110–11.

4 George B. Sansom, *Japan: A Short Cultural History* (New York, 1943), 509.

5 One of the earliest and most influential works in this body of literature is Yasuzō

Horie, *Nihon shihonshugi no seiritsu* [*The Formation of Japanese Capitalism*] (Tokyo, 1938). Horie's English articles – 'An Outline of the Rise of Capitalism in Japan', *Kyoto University Economic Review*, XI (1936), and 'The Government and Industry in the Early Years of Meiji Era', *Kyoto University Economic Review*, XIV (1939) – have often been quoted by Western writers.

6 Eiichi Shibusawa, *Rongo to soroban* [*The Analects and the Abacus*] (Tokyo, 1928), 304. Takao Tsuchiya's views on Shibusawa, representative of writers of his generation, are found in his *Nippon shihonsugi no keieishiteki kenkyū* [*A Business History Study of Japanese Capitalism*] (Tokyo, 1954), 189. Johannes Hirschmeier, *The Origins of Entrepreneurship in Meiji Japan* (Cambridge, Mass., 1964), 167-75, and his 'Shibusawa Eiichi: Industrial Pioneer', in W. W. Lockwood (ed.), *The State and Economic Enterprise in Japan* (Princeton, 1965), 209-47, are useful, as Hirschmeier made full use of pre-war Japanese sources.

7 This is the major thesis of Tsuchiya's *Business History Study of Japanese Capitalism*.

8 Gustav Ranis, 'The Community-Centered Entrepreneur in Japanese Development', *Explorations in Entrepreneurial History*, XIII (1955), 81.

9 Michael Y. Yoshino, *Japan's Managerial System* (Cambridge, Mass., 1968), 50.

10 Hirschmeier, *Origins of Entrepreneurship*, 68.

11 *Ibid.*, 209.

12 *Ibid.*, 58. Hirschmeier, who made an extensive use of Japanese literature, again summarizes the pre-war Japanese view on this point.

13 For example, this figure has been quoted by Toshihiko Katō, *Hompō ginkōshi-ron* [*A History of Banking in Japan*] (Tokyo, 1957), 33, and in Takao Tsuchiya, *Chihō ginkō shōshi* [*A Brief History of Local Banks*] (Tokyo, 1961), 27. The original source is the Ministry of Finance, *Ginkō-kyoku dai niji hōkoku* [*The Second Report of the Banking Bureau*] (Tokyo, 1880), 129.

14 Thomas C. Smith, *Political Change and Industrial Development in Japan: Government Enterprise, 1868-1880* (Stanford, Calif., 1955), 63. However, Smith, unlike several other authors, is careful to exclude silk-reeling from this statement.

15 Martin Bronfenbrenner, 'Some Lessons of Japan's Economic Development, 1853-1938', *Pacific Affairs*, XXXIV, 1 (Spring 1961), 14.

16 Harold G. Moulton, *Japan: An Economic and Financial Appraisal* (Washington, 1931), 337.

17 For a detailed account of Yasuda's life, see Kozo Yamamura, 'A Re-examination of Entrepreneurship in Meiji Japan (1868-1912)', *Economic History Review*, 2nd ser., XXI, 1 (April 1968), 144-58.

18 '*Zaibatsu*' literally means a financial clique. Many economists have defined it, and the following three characteristics are usually attributed to pre-war zaibatsu: (1) a semi-feudal character, in that centralized control rests in a zaibatsu family, which extends its power through strategically arranged marriages and other personal knight–vassal types of relationships; (2) well-knit, tightly controlled relationships among the affiliated firms by means of holding companies, interlocking directorships, and mutual stock-holdings; and (3) extremely great financial power in the form of commercial credit, which is used as the central leverage to extend control in all industries. As will be shown, not all these characteristics become evident until after the First World War. For further discussion on the nature of zaibatsu, see: Kozo Yamamura, 'Zaibatsu, Prewar and Zaibatsu, Postwar', *Journal of Asian Studies*, XXIII, 4 (August 1964), 539-54.

19 For a fuller account of Iwasaki's life, see Kozo Yamamura, 'The Founding of Mitsubishi: A Case Study in Japanese Business History', *Business History Review*, XLI, 2 (Summer 1967), 141-60.

20 Kazuo Suehiro, *Kondō Rempei den oyobi ikō* [*The Life and Writings of Rempei*

Kondō] (Tokyo, 1926); and Kumakichi Uzaki, *Toyokawa Ryōhei* [*The Life of Ryōhei Toyokawa*] (Tokyo, 1922).

21 Hidemitsu Shiroyanagi, *Sumitomo monogatari* [*The Story of Sumitomo*] (Tokyo, 1931), 183-7.

22 Tsuchiya, *Business History Study of Japanese Capitalism*, 174.

23 Takao Tsuchiya, *Zaibatsu o kizuita hitobito* [*The Zaibatsu-Builders*] (Tokyo, 1955), 210.

24 Biographical accounts of these men are found in Kōkichi Mitani [*Motoki Shōzō and Tomiji Hirano*] (Tokyo, 1913); Tōyō Textile Company, *Tōyō Bōseki 70-nenshi* [*Seventy Years of the Tōyō Textile Company*] (Tokyo, 1953); Tsuchiya, *The Zaibatsu-Builders*, 77-8.

25 Tsuchiya, *The Zaibatsu-Builders*, 78.

26 Mitani, *Detailed Biographies*, 229.

27 In contrast to the view on the samurai class that is popularly held, especially among Japanese writers, Lockwood went as far as to say that

It is incorrect to contrast the Japanese samurai and the Chinese scholar official class as a whole, and to find here a key to the divergency of the two countries after 1868. Many samurai were as inert and obscurantist as the typical Chinese mandarin in the face of the western challenge. As a class they were more idle, more ignorant, more arrogant. Most of them sank into obscurity once their caste privileges were cancelled.

W. W. Lockwood, 'Japan's Response to the West: The Contrast with China', *World Politics*, IX, 1 (October 1956), 45-6.

28 James C. Abegglen and Hiroshi Mannari, 'Leaders of Modern Japan: Social Origins and Mobility', *Economic Development and Cultural Change*, IX (October 1960), 109-34.

29 Horie, *Formation of Japanese Capitalism*, 83.

30 Tsunehiko Yui, 'On *The Origins of Entrepreneurship in Meiji Japan* by J. Hirschmeier', *Japan Business History Review*, 1 (1966), 105-6.

31 Hirschmeier, *Origins of Entrepreneurship*, 47. His exact words are: 'The last decade of the Tokugawa period had done much to blur class distinctions with respect to education, patterns of thinking, and economic activity.'

32 The points made in this and the following paragraphs are based on Kozo Yamamura, 'The Role of the Samurai in the Development of Modern Banking in Japan', *Journal of Economic History*, XXVII, 2 (June 1967), 198-220, and several recent Japanese studies cited in that article.

33 Hugh T. Patrick, 'Japan, 1868-1914', in Rondo Cameron (ed.), *Banking in the Early Stages of Industrialization: A Study in Comparative Economic History* (New York, 1967), 249.

34 Toshio Furushima, *Sangyō-shi* [*A History of Industry*] (Tokyo, 1966), 237. He also writes: 'These delegates [sent from Matsushiro in Nagano prefecture] were denied permission to see the plant, and the same applied also to those from Okaya [also in Nagano prefecture] who came to see the plant.'

35 *Ibid.*, 236.

36 Shumpei Okada (ed.), *Meiji-shoki no zaisei kinyū seisaku* [*Fiscal and Monetary Policies of the Early Meiji Period*] (Tokyo, 1964), 250-1.

37 *Ibid.*, 253.

38 For a table including more detailed information and data, see *Ibid.*, 252.

39 Furushima, *History of Industry*, 235.

40 Now a part of Fukushima prefecture.

41 *Ibid.*, 236.

42 John E. Orchard, for example, wrote (in his *Japan's Economic Position* (New York, 1930), 93) that

Dissatisfied at this rate of progress, the government in 1879 began to encourage the spinning industry more actively and more directly. Orders for spinning machinery were placed abroad and model government mills of 2,000 spindles each were established in Aichi and Tochigi Prefectures. In the next five or six years, similar mills were established in the prefecture of Hiroshima, Nara, Hyōgo, Okayama, Mie, Yamanashi, Shizuoka, Miyagi, Osaka, and Nagasaki. These mills were later handed over to private enterprises and those located more favorably have increased in size and have become the nuclei of large companies of the present day.

43 The major sources on Itō's case are: Taiichi Kinukawa (ed.), *Itō Denhichi Ō* [*The Venerable Denhichi Itō*] (Tokyo, 1936), and Tōyō Textile Company, *Seventy Years*.

44 Kinukawa, *The Venerable Denhichi Itō*, 16.

45 Tōyō Textile Company, *Seventy Years*, 49.

46 Kinukawa, *The Venerable Denhichi Itō*, 126. The six letters written by Itō to the government asking for postponement of payment spell out his difficulties in painful detail: *ibid.*, 91–134.

47 *Ibid.*, 76–7.

48 Tōyō Textile Company, *Seventy Years*, 145–6.

49 The major sources used for this section are: Gorō Suzuki, *Suzuki Tōsaburō den: Kindai nihon sangyō no senku* [*A Biography of Tōsaburō Suzuki, A Pioneer of Modern Japanese Industry*] (Tokyo, 1956); Gorō Suzuki, *Reimei nihon no ichi kaitakusha: Chichi Suzuki Tōsaburō no isshō* [*A Pioneer of Japan's Dawn: The Life of My Father, Tōsaburō Suzuki*] (Tokyo, 1939); Dainihon Seitō KK, *Nittō saikin 25-nenshi* [*A History of the Japan Sugar Refining Company during the Past Twenty-Five Years*] (Tokyo, 1924); Dainihon Seitō KK, *Nittō 65-nenshi* [*Sixty-five Years of the Japan Sugar Refining Company*] (Tokyo, 1906). The first two are useful, though written by Suzuki's son, as he conscientiously attempted to maintain an objective tone. There are also many brief writings on Suzuki in relation to his inventions and his political career.

50 Hirschmeier notes that 'he decided to produce refined sugar because of his concern that all refined sugar was imported' (*Origins of Entrepreneurship*, 267). This is an uncritical acceptance of Gorō Suzuki's view (expressed in his *A Pioneer of Japan's Dawn*, 80). Although Suzuki expressed such a view in 1899, in a pamphlet which he wrote commemorating an increase in the capital of his company, I am inclined to believe this either was written for public consumption or else reflected what he himself had come to believe by this time. In 1885, when he began to plan for refining, his goal, I believe, was simply to obtain cheaper domestically produced raw material for his ice-sugar, and he was confident that he could successfully challenge his foreign competition as he had done with the Chinese sugar (Tōsaburō Suzuki, 'Nihon tōgyo ron' ['A Treatise on the Sugar Industry in Japan'], published in the daily *Tōyō Keizai Shimpō* [*Oriental Economic News*] on 15 June 1899, and reproduced *in toto* in Gorō Suzuki, *A Pioneer of Japan's Dawn*, 194–204).

51 David S. Landes, 'Japan and Europe: Contrasts in Industrialization', in W. W. Lockwood (ed.), *The State and Economic Enterprise in Japan*, 101–2.

52 Rosovsky would consider the 'institutional reform and financial policies' of the government 'during the years of transition (1868–1885)' to be of more long-run significance than the fact that the government 'operated factories, subsidized certain industries, imported technicians', etc. (Henry Rosovsky, 'Japan's Transition to Economic Growth, 1868–1885' in H. Rosovsky (ed.), *Industrialization in Two Systems* (New York, 1966), 133. See also Sydney Crawcour, 'The Tokugawa Period and

Japan's Preparation for Modern Economic Growth', paper given at the 1967 meeting of the American Historical Association in Montreal; and Hugh T. Patrick, 'Lessons for Underdeveloped Countries from the Japanese Experience of Economic Growth', *Indian Economic Journal*, x (October 1961).

53 Ronald P. Dore, 'Mobility, Equality, and Individuation in Modern Japan', in R. P. Dore (ed.), *Aspects of Social Change in Modern Japan* (Princeton, 1967); and Marius B. Jansen, 'Tokugawa and Modern Japan', in J. W. Hall (ed.), *Studies in the Institutional History of Early Modern Japan* (Princeton, 1968).

54 Dore, 'Mobility, Equality, and Individuation', 114.

55 Takao Tsuchiya, *Nihon no seishō* [*Japan's Political Merchants*] (Tokyo, 1956).

56 Tsuchiya, *The Zaibatsu-Builders*; and Hidemitsu Shiroyanagi, *Nakamigawa Hikojiro den* [*A Biography of Hikojiro Nakamigawa*] (Tokyo, 1950).

57 Dore, 'Mobility, Equality, and Individuation', 118.

58 Abegglen and Mannari, 'Leaders of Modern Japan', 120.

59 Hirschmeier, *Origins of Entrepreneurship*, 246–86.

60 Patrick, 'Japan, 1868–1914', 283.

61 E. H. Carr, *What is History?* (New York, 1967), 26.

62 Meiji Zaiseishi Hensankai [Editorial Committee of the Meiji Financial History], *Meiji zaiseishi* [*Meiji Financial History*], 15 vols. (Tokyo, 1904–5), XII, 328.

63 Katō, *History of Banking in Japan*, 18.

64 Article 1 of the Kawase Kaisha Act read in part: 'The *kawase kaisha* were established for the purpose of . . . enriching the nation and . . . the government shall exercise its authority when loans are not repaid upon the promised date.' The government directed *kawase kaisha* to lend money for 'international trade, tea-growing, and purchasing cocoons', all of which were risky long-term loans. (*Ibid.*, 22.)

65 Oji Paper Company, *Oji seishi shashi* [*The History of the Iji Paper Company*], 5 vols. (Tokyo, 1957), vol. I.

66 See Muneo Nitta, *Tokyo dentō kabushiki kaisha kaigyō 50-nenshi* [*The First Fifty Years of the Tokyo Electric Light Company*] (Tokyo, 1936), and the company's *Tokyo dentō kabushiki kaishashi* [*A History of the Tokyo Electric Light Company*] (Tokyo, 1956).

67 The very interesting case of Hirano is not discussed in this chapter because of space limitations. Those interested can examine Mitani, *Detailed Biographies*; Arai Gensui, *Tokyo Ishikawajima Zōsenjo 50-nenshi* [*A Fifty-Year History of the Tokyo Ishikawajimi Shipyard*] (Tokyo, 1930); and the Ishikawajimi Heavy Industry Company, *Ishikawajima jūkogyō kabushiki kaisha 108-nenshi* [*A 108-Year History of Ishikawajima Heavy Industries, Ltd*] (Tokyo, 1961).

68 See Yamamura, 'The Role of the Samurai'.

69 Patrick, 'Japan, 1868–1914', 279.

70 Here and elsewhere in this essay the discussions on Mitsui are based on the following sources, in addition to those works of Tsuchiya already cited (*Japan's Political Merchants*, *Business History Study*, and *The Zaibatsu-Builders*): Ryotarō Iwai, *Mitsui, Mitsubishi monogatari* [*The Stories of Mitsui and Mitsubishi*] (Tokyo, 1934); Mitsubishi Economic Research Institute, *Mitsui, Mitsubishi, Sumitomo* (Tokyo, 1955); Hidekichi Wada, *Mitsui kontserun dokuhon* [*The Story of the Mitsui 'Konzern'*] (Tokyo, 1937); Mitsuhaya Kajinishi, *Seishō* [*The Political Merchants*] (Tokyo, 1963); Mitsui Bank, *Mitsui ginkō 50-nenshi* [*A Fifty-Year History of the Mitsui Bank*] (Tokyo, 1926); Mitsui Bank, *Mitsui ginkō 80-nenshi* [*An Eighty-Year History of the Mitsui Bank*] (Tokyo, 1957).

71 For a fuller treatment and useful sources, see Yamamura, 'The Founding of Mitsubishi Zaibatsu'.

72 Tōyō Kaizai Shimpō-sha [Tōyō Economic Publishing Co.], *Meiji–Taisho kokusei sōran* [*A Survey of the National Economy in the Meiji–Taisho Periods*] (Tokyo,

1924), 12–13 and 36. The total amount of paid-in capital for each year is taken from Tōkeikyoku [Bureau of Statistics], *Teikoku tokei nenkan* [*Annual Report of Imperial Statistics*] for the respective years.

73 Japan Industrial Bank, *Nippon kōgyō ginkō 50-nenshi shi* [*A Fifty-Year History of the Japan Industrial Bank*] (Tokyo, 1957), 38.

74 Mitsui Bank, *An Eighty-Year History*, 405.

75 Mitsubishi Bank, *Mitsubishi ginkō shi* [*The History of the Mitsubishi Bank*] (Tokyo, 1954), 90.

76 Tōyō Textile Company, *Seventy Years*, 135–52.

77 Fumio Yamada, 'Capital for Japan's Cotton Textile Industry', *Keizaigaku Ronshū* [*Economic Essays*, University of Tokyo], VI, 2 (1962), 147.

78 Toshimitsu Imuda, 'Meijiki ni okeru kabushiki kaisha no hatten to kabunushi-sō no keisei' ['The Development of Incorporated Firms and the Formation of the Shareholder Class in the Meiji Period'], in Osaka Municipal University, Economic Research Institute, *Meijiki ho keizai hatten to keizai shutai* [*Economic Development and Its Leading Agents in the Meiji Period*] (Osaka, 1968). The same author, who made an extensive use of industrial and individual data, provisionally advanced the thesis that the financing patterns should be divided into the following five categories: (1) partnership; (2) mostly by relatives; (3) mostly by non-management shareholders; (4) by management and shareholders from two distinct groups, where the number of shareholders is not large; (5) the same as (4) but where the number of shareholders is large. One of his more important (though still tentative) conclusions is that 'although there was a difference in degree, the basic pattern of financing approximated the process of development of incorporated firms seen in advanced Western nations' (*Ibid.*, 141).

79 Data were obtained from the respective company histories, which the writer was able to obtain since 1962, and from the Yūshōdō Microfilms publication of 'The Annual Financial Reports of One Thousand Firms, 1868–1945' (Tokyo, 1962). As most Japanese writers agree, there were about eighty-five firms which were directly controlled by the four zaibatsu holding companies at the end of the 1920s; the sample of thirty-seven covers about 44 per cent of these firms. The zaibatsu affiliates which were controlled only to a limited degree by zaibatsu subsidiaries or by the zaibatsu holding companies are not included among the eighty-five firms classified as direct subsidiary firms.

80 Data are from the Yūshōdō Microfilms; see also Yasuichi Kimura (ed.), *Shibaura seisakusho 65-nenshi* [*A Sixty-five-Year History of the Shibaura Machine-Tool Industries*] Tokyo, 1940).

81 Data are from the Yūshōdō Microfilms, and from Dainihon Seruroido KK, *Dainihon seruroido kaishashi* [*A History of the Greater Japan Celluloid Company*] (Tokyo, 1952).

82 The Mitsui Gōmei (a legal entity organized by the Mitsui family) owned the Mitsui Bank before 1919. However, when a part of the bank shares were sold publicly in 1919, the Gōmei was observed by the bank.

83 Mitsui Bank, *An Eighty-Year History*, 210–11.

84 Yūshōdō Microfilms; and Oji Paper Company, *History*, vol. I.

85 Yūshōdō Microfilms; and Mitsubishi Shipbuilding Company, *Mitsubishi zōsen* [*History of the Mitsubishi Shipbuilding Company*] (Tokyo, 1958).

86 Yūshōdō Microfilms; and Saburō Fumoto, *Mitsubishi Iizuka tankōshi* [*The History of Mitsubishi Iziuka Coal Mines*] (Tokyo, 1961).

87 Yūshōdō Microfilms, and Nisshin Seifun KK, *Nisshin seifun kabushi kaishashi* [*The History of the Nisshin Flour-Milling Company*] (Tokyo, 1965).

88 The firms are Nihon Cement (Asano), Koga Mining (Koga), Mitsui Bussan,

Taiheiyō Coal-Mining (Mitsui), Hokkai Soda (Mitsui), Mitsubishi Papers, Nisshin Steamships (Mitsubishi), Meiji Sugar-Refining (Mitsubishi), Sumitomo Besshi Lead-Mining, Sumitomo Steel Pipes, the Sumitomo Steel Mill, Fujikura Electric Wires (Sumitomo), and Sumitomo Electric Wires.

89 Calculated from data contained in Mitsui Bank, *An Eighty-Year History*, 421–2.

90 Calculated from the Sumitomo Bank data in the Yūshōdō Microfilms.

91 K. Takahashi and J. Aoyama, *Nihon zaibatsu-ron* [*A Study of the Japanese Zaibatsu*] (Tokyo, 1938), 162.

92 Calculated from data contained in Japan Industrial Bank, *A Fifty-Year History*, 222–3, and the data sections of Nomura Securities Company of Japan, *Kōshasai nenkan* [*An Annual Report of Government and Company Bonds*] (Tokyo, 1930). The zaibatsu firms are identified by referring to Kamekichi Takahashi, *Nihon zaibatsu no kaibō* [*An Anatomy of Japanese Zaibatsu*] (Tokyo, 1930), 21–2, 55–60, and 140–1, and Ryukichi Minobe, *Karuteru, Torasuto, Kontserun* [*Cartels, Trusts, and Concerns*], 2 vols. (Tokyo, 1931), vol. II. Throughout this chapter, the expressions 'zaibatsu-controlled', 'zaibatsu firms', and 'zaibatsu groups' are used only for those cases which are clearly identifiable – i.e. those in which connections with zaibatsu families and banks can be readily shown by share-holding, interlocking directorships, or loans made. For the pre-1940 years, such identification is quite straightforward because of the evident dependence of zaibatsu subsidiaries and affiliates on the zaibatsu banks and other zaibatsu firms.

93 Takahashi, *An Anatomy of Japanese Zaibatsu*, 44–7.

94 From data contained in the history of each bank and the Yūshōdō Microfilms.

95 The necessary data and information were obtained from the histories of the banks mentioned. Here the procedure (well accepted by Japanese scholars) of separating long- and short-term loans is adopted to obtain the necessary ratios. The long-term loans are *kashitsukekin* (literally, 'money lent'), which are the sums of the loans made against various negotiable instruments (*tegata kashitsuke* and *shōken kashitsuke*). The total of loans includes – in addition to long-term loans – bills discounted (*waribiki tegata*), call loans, and overdrafts (*tōza kashikoshi*: literally, 'lent for the moment'). There are various difficulties concerning renewed short-term loans and some of the loans made for less than a year, which are put under the heading *tegata kashitsuke*, but adjustments made for these difficulties should not change the ratios observed here by more than a few percentage points.

96 The eight zaibatsu are Mitsui, Mitsubishi, Sumitomo, Yasuda, Daiichi (i.e. the Big Five, involving twenty-nine banks, four credit firms, four life-assurance companies, and nineteen other types of insurance companies), and the Kawasaki, Yamaguchi, and Kōnoike groups (involving twenty-one banks, three credit firms, seven life-assurance companies, and six other types of insurance firms). The last three zaibatsu are much smaller in size. Takahashi, *An Anatomy of Japanese Zaibatsu*, 39.

97 For detailed descriptions, see Mitsuhaya Kajinishi et al., *Nihon shihonshugi no botsuraku* [*The Fall of Japanese Capitalism*], vol. I (Tokyo, 1960), 185–90.

98 *Ibid.*, 157–61.

99 Kajinishi Mitsuhaya, *Zoku nihon shihonshugi hattatsu-shi* [*A Revised History of the Development of Japanese Capitalism*] (Tokyo, 1957), 49–50.

100 A detailed description of this merger is found in Yasuda Bank, *Yasuda ginkō 60-nenshi* [*A Sixty-Year History of the Yasuda Bank*] (Tokyo, 1940), 225–48.

101 Holding Company Liquidation Commission, *Nippon zaibatsu to sono kaitai* [*The Japanese Zaibatsu and Their Dissolution*], 2 vols. (Tokyo, 1962), vol. II (*Data*), 469.

102 *Ibid.*, 63.

103 *Ibid.*, 468–72.

104 *Ibid.*, 450–5.

105 This section on the post-war period is based on Kozo Yamamura, *Economic Policy in Postwar Japan: Growth Versus Economic Democracy* (Berkeley, California, 1967).

106 Yasuzō Horie, 'The Problem of *ie* in Japanese Business History', *Japan Business History Review*, II, 1 (July 1967), is a useful re-examination of the concept of *ie*. On many points made in this section, as well as on *ie*, Solomon B. Levine, 'Labor and Collective Bargaining' in W. W. Lockwood (ed.), *The State and Economic Enterprise in Japan*, 633–7, is excellent.

107 A leading student of Japanese history observed:

The oldest and in many ways the most deeply rooted of these historically ingrained systems of political organization grew out of the earliest period of Japanese history for which we can reconstruct the political community. We have called this the 'familial' system rather than use the more common term 'clan' which gives rise to too many ambiguous connotations... The familial ingredient in Japan's political heritage, while being transformed under changing conditions of culture and political ideology, nonetheless formed a constant and important element linking the social hierarchy to the power structure at all levels. The tendency of the Japanese to fictionalize superior–inferior relations by conceiving of them in familial terms is the best example of this.

John W. Hall, *Government and Local Power in Japan, 500 to 1700: A Study Based on Bizen Province* (Princeton, 1966), 6–7.

108 See Yamamura, 'The Founding of Mitsubishi Zaibatsu'.

109 Hiroshi Hazama, *Nihon rōmu kanrishi kenkyū [A Study of Japanese Labour Management]* (Tokyo, 1964), 15. In the area of labour management and the managerial system as a whole, this is the most useful and valuable book to appear since the end of the Second World War.

110 A thorough analysis of the *ringi* system is available in Akira Yamashiro (ed.), *Ringi-teki keiei to ringi seido [Ringi Management and Ringi System]* (Tokyo, 1966).

111 Ronald P. Dore, 'The Legacy of Tokugawa Education', in Marius B. Jansen (ed.), *Changing Japanese Attitudes Toward Modernization* (Princeton, 1965), 104.

CHAPTER VI

Capital Formation during the Period of Early Industrialization in Russia, 1890–1913

1 The author acknowledges his intellectual debts to Professor Simon Kuznets and to the late Albert Vainshtein. Dr Don Landau and Mrs Amy Knight have given generously of their ideas and time to process much of the amassed data. The study was supported by grants from the National Science Foundation and the University of Chicago College.

2 One could mention also the abolition of collective fiscal responsibility of the peasants in the communes in 1887, a measure which was reversed in 1893 and re-enacted later but was not followed up by allowing the peasants to leave the communes and set themselves up as independent farmers.

3 See S. G. Strumilin, *Statistiko-ekonomicheskie ocherki* (Moscow, 1958), 680. Strumilin estimated the domestic trade turnover for 1890 at 4,033 million roubles, and that for 1913 at 11,754 million roubles.

4 Grains, flax and hemp, oil-seeds, eggs, butter, and livestock are included in this

group. The export of those commodities constituted 70 per cent of total Russian exports in 1890, and 63·7 per cent of total exports in 1913.

5 The Population Census of 1897 already indicated that 46·5 per cent of the urban population of the Empire were born outside of the cities in which they resided. The fact that 31 per cent of the urban population were born outside of the district (*guberniia*) in which the city was located adds an illuminating characteristic of the migration process. See Central Statistical Committee, *Obshchyi svod po imperii rezultatov razrabotki dannykh pervoi vseobshchei perepisi naseleniia* (St Petersburg, 1905), I, pp. 84–113.

6 While the urban population of European Russia increased during the period 1890–1913 by 68·9 per cent, from 11,013,000 to 18,604,000, a sample of 103 localities (forty cities and sixty-three towns and factory settlements) indicates that for large-scale industry the growth rate of employment in the cities exceeded the growth rate of employment in the small towns and factory settlements by a wide margin (162 per cent as against 104 per cent for the years 1890–1914).

For the urban population data, see V. Zaitsev, 'Vlianie kolebanii urozhaev na estestvennoe dvizhenie naselenia', in V. G. Groman (ed.), *Vlianie neurozhaev na narodnoe khoziaistvo Rossii*, II (Moscow, 1927), 53. For the sample of factory employment in 103 localities, see V. I. Klimov, '103 vazhnieishykh tsentra fabrichno-zavodskoi promyshlennosti evropeiskoi Rossii v 1900–1914' in Istoricheskaia Geografia, *Voprosy Geografii*, L (Moscow, 1960), 209–10.

7 Goldsmith compared the average annual rates of growth of manufacturing and mining obtained by various methods from the basic data collected by N. D. Kondratiev (base = 1900):

	1888–1900	1900–13	1888–1913
Kondratiev Geometric Average	8·1	4·2	5·6
Kondratiev Arithmetic Average	7·2	4·4	5·3
Value-added weights			
Imputed weights	7·1	4·1	5·1
Unadjusted weights	6·7	4·0	4·9

See R. Goldsmith, 'The Economic Growth of Tsarist Russia, 1860–1913', *Economic Development and Cultural Change*, IX (1961), 465.

8 It is probably unfair to blame past generations for lacking the knowledge which was acquired by subsequent generations at a relatively high cost.

9 The gold reserves of the State Bank increased, from January 1890 to January 1898, from 475 million roubles to 1,185 million roubles, a rise of 150 per cent.

10 Although during most of this period most of the railway equipment was produced domestically, the government was forced to pay in foreign exchange the interests and guaranteed dividends to foreign bond-holders. As a guarantor of the railway loans for private companies, the government was under obligation to pay even when the companies suffered deficits. The total of railway bonds increased by 100 per cent during this period, from 1,200 million to 2,400 million.

11 This particular measure of government indebtedness was chosen because it possesses greater uniformity than the varying definitions of the national debt. Basically it includes government long-term borrowing, bonds and shares of the railway companies, and the bonds of the government-sponsored land banks.

12 Table 50 (Statistical Appendix, below) reflects the changes over time of government-guaranteed securities including state bonds, railway bonds, and bonds of the Nobility and Peasant Banks, the two major institutions of government-guaranteed land mortgages.

13 It is interesting to note that the largest branch of Russian industry, the textile industry, was relying largely on internal financing by its stockholders and owners

rather than upon borrowing in the market. Mining, metallurgy, and many other branches of manufacturing industries relied heavily upon sales of securities and bank borrowing.

In terms of both the number of securities quoted on the exchange and the volume of capital represented by such enterprises, one could rank the exchanges as follows: (1) St Petersburg, representing by the end of our period double the size of the next in rank; (2) Paris, with a preponderance of mining and metallurgy; (3) Brussels, with a heavy concentration on public utilities and local transportation; (4) London, representing oil and mining; and (5) Berlin, with a broad spectrum of the manufacturing industries.

14 The distribution between foreign-owned and domestically owned industrial assets is difficult to establish. Any Western scholar who bases his claims or opinions upon secondary Russian sources is a victim of a gross distortion of the actual distribution. The resolution of this problem must be left to further research based upon a re-examination of primary sources.

15 For example, such grandiose railway construction projects as the Trans-Siberian railway and a number of other railways in Asia were constructed at the expense of the government treasury. This does not preclude the possibility of a transfer from government foreign loans to railway construction, but it is significant that at least in the formal sense it came from the state budget.

16 During ten out of the twenty-four years of the period 1890–1913, the yearly net change in value of the railways (measured in current prices) exceeded the change in value of industrial capital.

17 This should be helpful when all of the material on capital formation in Russia is available and is analysed to permit comparison with the studies of Simon Kuznets and his associates of the NBER for the USA, of Richard Stone and Charles Feinstein for England, of Henry Rosovsky for Japan, or of Walther Hoffmann for Germany.

18 A comparison between the composition of the capital stock for 1913 in our study and the composition of the total capital stock estimates (exclusive of land) presented for 1913 by Albert Vainshtein yields the following results: (1) the share of construction is identical, and (2) there is a discrepancy between the relative shares of equipment and inventories. Our study underestimates equipment, which is understandable because of the omission of public utilities, railways, and government-owned installations. For the comparison we used Albert L. Vainshtein, *Narodnoe bogatstvo i narodnokhoziaistvennoe nakoplenie predrevolutsionnoi Rossii* (Moscow, 1960).

19 In many instances the insurance data have a broader coverage and are more detailed than the aggregate figures provided in the publications of government statistics. The insurance data, apart from their peculiar pitfalls, have a number of advantages. They reflect much more closely the actual utilization of the capital stock, whether the value of buildings and equipment or the levels of inventories. They tend also to mirror the market value of assets more closely than other estimates. The most extensive use of insurance data was made for the estimates of capital employed in industry and of urban residential structures.

20 During the period 1890–1906 the Russian peasantry paid a total of 1,437·3 million roubles in redemption payments, before these were discontinued under the pressure of the 1905–6 revolutionary situation, at a time when a radical change in agricultural policies took place.

21 Vainshtein estimated the distribution of some of the expenditures of the peasant population of the fifty districts of European Russia in 1912. The figures are instructive and support our contention about the effects of taxation. By re-grouping Vainshtein's data we obtain the following results: (1) direct taxes 221·7 million roubles; (2) excise taxes, the levy on alcohol, and the cost of tariff, 456·6 million; (3) payment of land

rents and purchases of land, 375·9 million – a total of 1,054·3 million roubles out of an estimated cash income of 2,750 million roubles. See Albert L. Vainshtein, *Oblozhenie i platezhi krestianstva v dovoyennoe i revolutsionnoe vremia* (Moscow, 1924), 148.

22 The data on the leasing of land by peasants are fragmentary and imprecise; the available estimates have a very broad range – 19·5 million *dessiatiny* to 48·8 million *dessiatiny* (1 *dessiatin* = 1·0925 hectares). While during the 1890s the amount of land leased by the peasants was most probably above 30 million *dessiatiny*, it declined after 1900 and remained within the range of 25 to 28 million *dessiatiny* until the First World War.

23 The data for the years 1911–13 are not precise and are of unknown coverage; therefore, the 1913 figure is an estimate for 1912 based upon Ministry of Finance, *Ezhegodnik Ministerstva Finansov za 1916 god* (Petrograd, 1917), 409.

In addition to sales by the nobility, there were also land sales to the peasants of government land, which accounts for a few million *dessiatiny*. Therefore, although the peasants were not the sole buyers of nobility land, their total land acquisition approximates the volume of net sales by the nobility.

24 In addition, changes in inventories of seed and feed would have to be included in the calculation of capital formation according to the definition of capital used in this chapter.

25 Apart from the incompleteness of official data on usable land, there was a strong, almost unanimous presumption among leading experts of agricultural statistics that the official data reporting the planted areas were underestimated by at least 5 per cent. Because no clear pattern of the bias could be found, the official data on the planted area are accepted here. A detailed analysis of capital in land would have to include the changes in the reported planted area, since the yearly additions to capital in absolute terms would be greater than the official figures would suggest.

26 Wheat and barley accounted for 10·0 million *dessiatiny* out of the reported 13·7 million increase in planted area for the fifty districts of European Russia, and for 20·4 million out of the reported 29·2 million for the seventy-two districts of Russia.

27 The estimate was derived on the assumption that the land improvements constitute 35 per cent of the current price of land.

28 The only exception to this rule was the existence of a special legal category of *majorat*, including a few hundred large landed estates which could not be subdivided and for which the status of indivisible inheritance was granted and preserved.

29 A notable shortcoming of the capital estimates is the assumption that when a new farm unit is created it is equipped with an average set of dwellings and buildings, while anyone even vaguely familiar with the agricultural scene knows that this process takes years to complete. Therefore, for purposes of analysis, three-year moving averages would be more realistic estimates of the changes in capital stock of farm structures than the reported year-to-year changes.

30 In part the results obtained are due to assumptions underlying the methods of calculation employed.

31 See Table 45 (Statistical Appendix, below) for growth of capital in farm structures.

32 While railways and water transportation were reducing the demand for overland transportation provided by animal power, the increased volume of goods entering the commercial channels tended to maintain the previous level of overland transportation services.

33 The data are available only for 15 July of each year, i.e. for the lowest level of stocks instead of the yearly average level. Secondly, data are available for the four major grains only and leave out all other commodities. Thirdly, the data cover only

sixty-four districts of Russia, and the series cannot be extended back beyond the year 1897.

34 In this connection it might be of interest to note that according to the 1897 population census 39·3 per cent of the labour force in construction was located in the cities. Even if we were to assume higher productivity on the part of construction labour in the cities, perhaps we should also have to assume that urban construction absorbed some of the labour of rural construction workers.

35 Farm and non-farm construction in Russia was not identical with rural and urban distribution, since a relatively large proportion of industry was located in rural areas.

36 Corresponding data for the Russian Empire, at least between 1897 and 1914, indicate even a somewhat higher rate of urban population growth for the Empire as a whole than for the fifty provinces of European Russia.

37 An important omission in our knowledge pertains to the 'velocity' of the mortgage funds in urban housing. We do not know what was the average length of an urban mortgage loan. Without data on the turnover of the loanable funds, it is difficult to establish the flow of actual investment capital provided by the mortgage loans.

38 Since the fire insurance excluded the foundations of buildings, here as in the case of urban housing and some categories of rural housing, the value of the foundation had to be estimated. For the same reason, the figures represented in Tables 48 and 49 (below) reflect inadequately the capital in enterprises which were engaged in mining operations, since the value of the mine was not included in the fire insurance.

39 According to one set of data, out of a total capital of newly established joint-stock companies during the period 1901–13 of 1,525·9 million roubles, 807·3 million could be accounted for by private firms which changed their status to corporations. Other data put the share of existing capital in newly formed corporations at an even higher percentage of the total. See I. F. Gindin, *Russkie kommercheskie banki* (Moscow, 1948), 450.

40 In the totals, non-industrial corporations such as banks and trading companies are also included.

41 This will become possible only when the archives of the Russian and foreign banks are opened to interested researchers.

42 Vainshtein, *Narodnoe bogatstvo*.

43 Military facilities included such items as factories and naval yards, structures, armaments, etc., which represent types of capital similar to the civilian sector.

44 When a production function for industry was constructed using the estimates for industrial capital, output, and labour input measured by the number of workers, each of the other series derived independently exhibited a strong collinearity with the data on total capital in industry.

45 For our purposes, an obvious shortcoming of the Varzar index (which was never published in its entirety) is that it is limited to the territory of the Soviet Union of the period before 1939. Curiously enough, Varzar did not exclude exports from his index, on the assumption that they were exchanged for foreign goods which entered into final consumption.

46 The higher growth rate could be explained in part by the differences in territorial coverage, since the areas of imperial Russia left out by the Varzar index (the Polish and Baltic Provinces) had a lower growth rate of output during this period than the territory accounted for by the Varzar index; but the required adjustment would account for a relatively small portion of the growth.

47 The subject of education and training is discussed further in chapter VIII below.

48 The approximation of male literacy for the agricultural labour force is based

upon the literacy rate of recruits for military service in the army, which increased from 32 per cent in 1890 to 68 per cent in 1913. For the female labour force, apart from the census data of 1897, there are data on school enrolment of females in the rural areas.

49 The data for 1897 are based upon the population census; the 1913 data are estimated from the 1918 census of the factory labour force.

CHAPTER VII

Labour and Industrialization in Russia

1 M. K. Rozhkova (ed.), *Ocherki ekonomicheskoy istorii Rossi pervoy poloviny XIX veka* (Moscow, 1959), 178, 182, and 196.

2 R. W. Goldsmith, 'The Economic Growth of Tsarist Russia, 1860–1913', *Economic Development and Cultural Change*, IX, 2 (1961), 441–75.

3 Russia, Ministerstvo Finansov, *Vestnik Finansov, Torgovli i Promyshlennosti* (hereafter cited as '*VF*'), 1912, no. 23, p. 493.

4 *Ibid.*, and on the basis of V. E. Varzar (ed.), *Statistika obrabatyvayushchey promyshlennosti za 1908 god*, 2 parts (St Petersburg, 1912), part 1; and Goldsmith, *op. cit.*

5 *VF*, *loc. cit.*, p. 492. According to United Nations, International Labour Office, *Employment and Economic Growth* (Geneva, 1964), section USSR, industry's share of employment in Russia in 1913 was 9 per cent, as against 15 per cent in Japan, 33 per cent in the USA in 1910, and 51 per cent in Great Britain in 1911 (even Egypt's share was higher, at 11 per cent).

6 C. Tilly and R. Tilly, 'Agenda for European Economic History in the 1970s', *Journal of Economic History*, XXXI, 1 (March 1971), 188ff, use the term 'proto-industry' for pre-factory industry, which they consider an educational experience which exposed men to some features of industrial life before the concentration of wage labour in factories. In this chapter the term applies to both pre-factory and pre-mechanized factory industry.

7 M. Zlotnikov, 'Ot manufaktury k fabrike', *Voprosy Istorii*, nos. 11–12 (1946), 31–48; J. T. Fuhrmann, *The Origins of Capitalism in Russia* (Chicago, 1972), 243.

8 E. I. Zaozerskaya, *U istokov krupnogo proizvodstva v russkoy promyshlennosti XVI–XVII vekov* (Moscow, 1970), 64 and 176; M. Ya. Volkov, 'Khozyaystvo kuptsa Srednego Povolzhya I. A. Miklyayeva v kontse XVII – pervoy chetverti XVIII v.', in S. D. Skazkin (ed.), *Problemy genezisa kapitalizma* (Moscow, 1970), 230.

9 Zaozerskaya, *op. cit.*, 150–1 and 170; Volkov, *op. cit.*, 227; N. I. Pavlenko, *Razvitiye metallurgicheskoy promyshlennosti Rossii v pervoy polovine XVIII veka* (Moscow, 1953), 354.

10 Fuhrmann, *op. cit.*, 75; Zaozerskaya, *op. cit.*, 178.

11 Pavlenko, *Razvitiye*, 190–3; Fuhrmann, *op. cit.*, 23 and 45ff.

12 Pavlenko, *Razvitiye*, 213ff.

13 N. I. Pavlenko, 'O nekotorykh storonakh pervonachalnogo nakopleniya v Rossii', *Istoricheskiye Zapisky*, LIV (1955), 213.

14 P. N. Milyukov, *Gossudarstvennoye khozyaystvo Rossii v pervoy chetverti XVIII stoletiya i reforma Petra Velikago* (St Petersburg, 1905), 476–7; A. A. Kizevetter, *Posadskaya obshchina v Rossi XVIII st.* (Moscow, 1903), 81; A. V. Pogozhev, 'Votchinnyye fabriki i ikh fabrichnyye', *Vestnik Yevropy*, VIII (1889), 15ff.

15 A. L. Shapiro, 'K istorii krest'yanskikh promyslov i krest'yanskoy manufaktury v Rossii v XVIII v.', *Istoricheskiye Zapisky*, XXXI (1950), 147; Pavlenko, *Razvitiye*,

351–3; V. G. Geyman, *Manufakturnaya promyshlennost' Peterburga petrovskogo vremeni*, (Moscow and Leningrad, 1947), 246 and 284.

16 Pavlenko, *Razvitiye*, 231; Rozhkova (ed.), *Ocherki*, 226; M. Tugan-Baranovsky, *Russkaya fabrika v proshlom i nastoyashchem*, 6th issue, reprinted from 3rd edn (Moscow and Leningrad, 1934), 105ff.

17 B. B. Kafengauz, *Istoriya khozyaystva Demidovykh* (Moscow, 1950), 204.

18 Pavlenko, 'O nekotorykh', 388.

19 Pavlenko, *Razvitiye*, 190–204.

20 Pavlenko, 'O nekotorykh', 204.

21 I. S. Kurutsin, 'Formirovaniye rabochey sily na tekstil'nykh manufakturakh v XVIII v.', *Istoricheskiye Zapisky*, v (1939), 145; K. A. Pazhitnov, *Ocherki istorii tekstil'noy promyshlennosti dorevolyutsyonnoy Rossii: Khlopchatobumazhnaya, l'nopenkovaya i sholkovaya promyshlennost'* (Moscow, 1958: cited hereafter as 'Ocherki tekstil'noy (1958)'), 208.

22 Pavlenko, *Razvitiye*, 195ff; R. Portal, *L'Oural au XVIIIe siècle* (Paris, 1950), 83ff.

23 Pavlenko, *Razvitiye*, 203ff.

24 *Ibid.*, 190ff; Kurutsin, *op. cit.*, 144–5.

25 Pavlenko, *Razvitiye*, 205.

26 Kurutsin, *op. cit.*, 146ff.

27 *Ibid.*, 143; P. G. Lyubomirov, *Ocherki po istorii russkoy promyshlennosti XVII, XVIII i nachala XIX veka* (Moscow, 1947), 78–9.

28 K. Lodyzhensky, *Istoriya russkago tamozhennago tarifa* (St Petersburg, 1886), 69; A. Kahan, 'Continuity in Economic Activity and Policy during the Post-Petrine Period in Russia', *Journal of Economic History*, xxv, 1 (March 1965).

29 Rozhkova (ed.), *Ocherki*, 174ff.

30 V. V. Semevsky, *Krest'yane v tsarstvovaniye imperatritsy Yekateriny II*, vol. 1 (St Petersburg, 1903), 584–5; M. L. de Tegoborski, *Commentaries on the Productive Forces of Russia*, 2 vols. (London, 1855), vol. 1, p. 85; V. Kabuzan, *Narodonaseleniye Rossii v XVIII – pervoy polovine XIX v.* (Moscow, 1963), 123; P. G. Lyubomirov (ed.), *A. N. Radishchev: materialy i izsledovaniya* (Moscow and Leningrad, 1936), 196.

31 A. V. Pogozhev, *Uchot chislennosti i sostava rabochikh v Rossii: materialy po statistike truda* (St Petersburg, 1906), 76 and 100; K. A. Pazhitnov, *Ocherki po istorii tekstil'noy promyshlennosti dorevolyutsyonnoy Rossii: sherstyanaya promyshlennost'* (Moscow, 1955: cited hereafter as 'Ocherki tekstil'noy (1955)'), 83–6; Tugan-Baranovsky, *op. cit.*, 87–91.

32 E. I. Zisel'son, 'K voprosu o formirovanii promyshlennykh kadrov na predpriyatiyakh Peterburga v 1801–1861', in V. Ya. Ovsyankin (ed.), *Istoriya rabochego klassa Leningrada* (Leningrad, 1962), 15; Pazhitnov, *Ocherki tekstil'noy* (1955), 92 and 112.

33 R. E. Zelnik, *Labor and Society in Tsarist Russia: The Factory Workers of St Petersburg 1855–1870* (Stanford, Calif., 1971), 36; Ovsyankin, *op. cit.*, 15ff; Lodyzhensky, *op. cit.*, 193–6.

34 Tugan-Baranovsky, *op. cit.*, 108–10; Rozhkova (ed.), *Ocherki*, 193–6.

35 Pazhitnov, *Ocherki tekstil'noy* (1955), 90; Rozhkova (ed.), *Ocherki*, 215; K. A. Pazhitnov, 'K voprosu o roli krepostnogo truda v doreformennoy promyshlennosti', *Istoricheskiye Zapisky*, vii (1946).

36 Zlotnikov, *op. cit.*, 31–48.

37 Pogozhev, *Uchot*, Table 22, p. 75; Tugan-Baranovsky, *op. cit.*, 45; G. von Schultze-Gaevernitz, *Ocherki obshchestvennago khozyaystva i ekonomicheskoy politiki Rossii* (St Petersburg, 1901: translated from the German original of 1899), 44; Pogozhev, 'Votchinnye'; E. M. Dement'yev, *Fabrika, chto ona dayot naseleniyu i chto ona u nego beryot* (Moscow, 1897), 46.

38 K. N. Serbina, 'Posluzhnyye spiski rabochikh Urala kak istorichesky istochnik', *Problemy Istochnikovedeniya*, VII (1959), 105–11.

39 Tugan-Baranovsky, *op. cit.*, 168; Pazhitnov, *Ocherki tekstil'noy* (1958), 205–6.

40 W. L. Blackwell, *The Beginnings of Russian Industrialization 1800–1860* (Princeton, 1968), 42.

41 S. Gvozdev, *Zapisky fabrichnago inspektora* (Moscow, 1911), 215; T. v. Laue, 'Russian Peasants in the Factory, 1892–1904', *Journal of Economic History*, XXI (1961), 67.

42 Karl Marx, *Capital*, I (Moscow, 1965), 168–9.

43 'Statute on the Relations between Factory-Owners and Hired Workers', in *Polnoye sobraniye zakonov Rossiykoy Imperii*, 2nd ser., vol. x, no. 8157, para. 10; N. S. Kinyapina, *Politika russkogo samoderzhaviya v oblasti promyshlennosti* (Moscow, 1960), 400.

44 P. Lokhtin, *Bezzemel'ny proletariat v Rossii* (Moscow, 1905), 30.

45 A. E. Lositsky, *Raspadeniye obshchiny* (St Petersburg, 1912), 8ff.

46 V. E. Postnikov, *Yuzhno-russkoye krest'yanskoye khozyaystvo*, 2nd edn (Moscow, 1907), especially chap. 2, pp. 34ff; S. Y. Keysler, 'Sel'skaya obshchina i eya sovremennoye polozheniye', *Vestnik Yevropy*, VII (1884).

47 A. Vesnin, 'Ob otmene krugovoy poruki', *Narodnoye Khozyaystvo*, VIII (1901), 14–15; Postnikov, *op. cit.*, chap. 2; A. M. Pankratova, 'Proletarizatsiya krest'yanstva i ego rol' v formirovanii promyshlennogo proletariata Rossii', *Istoricheskiye Zapiski*, LIV (1955), 202; L. M. Ivanov, 'Preyemstvennost' fabrichno-zavodskogo truda i formirovaniye proletariata v Rossii', in Ivanov (ed.), *Rabochy klass i rabocheye dvizheniye v Rossii 1861–1917* (Moscow, 1966), 88.

48 Calculated on the basis of N. P. Oganovsky (ed.), *Sel'skoye khozyaystvo Rossii v XX veke* (Moscow, 1923), 60ff; S. G. Strumilin, *Izbrannyye proizvedeniya* (5 vols. (Moscow, 1963–5), III, 306.

49 N. F. Rudnev, 'Promysly krest'yan v Yevropeyskoy Rossii', *Sbornik Saratovskago Zemstva*, no. 6 (Saratov, 1894), 190–1; A. N. Chelintsev, *Sel'sko-khozyaystvennaya geografiya Rossii* (Prague, 1924), 64–5.

50 S. Sagorsky, *Die Arbeiterfrage in der Südrussischen Landwirtschaft* (Munich, 1908), 142ff; *VF*, 1900, no. 35, p. 428; *VF*, 1904, no. 32, pp. 221ff; *VF*, 1910, no. 19, p. 283; *VF*, 1910, no. 36, p. 419.

51 Based on A. G. Rashin, *Naseleniye Rossii za sto let (1811–1913) gg.* (Moscow, 1956); *VF*, 1904, no. 26; *VF*, 1915, no. 7.

52 Rashin, *op. cit.*; V. K. Yatsunsky, 'Izmeneniya v razmeshchenii naseleniya Yevropeyskoy Rossii v 1724–1916 gg.', in *Istoriya SSSR*, no. 1 (1957), 192–224.

53 On the basis of Russia, Narodny Kommissariyat Finansov SSSR (ed.), *Narodnoye i gosudarstvennoye khozyaystvo* (Moscow, 1923), 17; Chelintsev, *op. cit.*, 73–5.

54 Chelintsev, *loc. cit.*; Yatsunsky, 'Izmeneniya', 217; P. G. Ryndzyunsky, 'Krest'yansky otkhod i chislennost' sel'skogo naseleniya v 80ykh godakh XIX v.', in Skazkin (ed.), *Problemy genezisa kapitalizma*, 413–35.

55 Rashin, *Naseleniye*, 98.

56 Pogozhev, *Uchot*, 8.

57 Goldsmith, *op. cit.*

58 *Ibid.*, M. Falkus, 'Russia's National Income: A Revaluation', *Economica*, n.s., XXXV, 137 (February 1968), 527–3; UN, International Labour Office, *op. cit.*, USSR.

59 Chelintsev, *op. cit.*, 64ff; T. Shanin, *The Awkward Class: Political Sociology of Peasantry in a Developing Society: Russia 1910–1925* (Oxford, 1972), 93; B. Markus, 'Abolition of Unemployment in USSR', *International Labour Review*, XXXIII (1935), 356; see also J. S. Wellisz, 'Dual Economies, Disguised Unemployment and the Unlimited Supply of Labour', *Economica*, n.s., XXXV, 137 (February 1968), 22–5; G.

Arrighi, 'Labour Supplies in Historical Perspective: A Study of the Proletarianization of the African Peasantry in Rhodesia', *Journal of Development Studies*, VI, 3 (April 1970), 203ff; W. A. Lewis, 'Economic Development with Unlimited Supply of Labour', *Manchester School* (May 1954), reprinted in A. N. Agarwala and S. P. Singh, *The Economics of Underdevelopment* (Oxford, 1958).

60 A. G. Rashin, *Formirovaniye rabochego klassa Rossii* (Moscow, 1958), Table 51, p. 172.

61 *Ibid.*, Tables 50–1, pp. 171–2; N. A. Troynitsky (ed.), *Chislennost' i sostav rabochikh v Rossii na osnovanii dannykh pervoy vseobshchey perepisi naseleniya rossiyskoy imperii 1897 g.* (St Petersburg, 1906); Pogozhev, *Uchot*, 15; on the basis of Russia, Ministerstvo Finansov, Departament okladnykh sborov [Department of Non-Repartitional Taxes] (ed.), *Materialy Vysochayshe uchrezhdyonnoy 16 noyabrya 1901 komissii po izsledovaniyu voprosa o dvizhenii s 1861 po 1900 g. blagosostoyaniya sel'skago naseleniya srednezemledel'cheskikh guberniy sravnitel'no s drugimi mestnostyami Yevropeyskoy Rossii*, 3 vols. (St Petersburg, 1903), vol. III.

62 Rudnev, *op. cit.*

63 On the basis of Z. M. Svavitsky and N. A. Svavitsky, *Zemskiye podvornyye perepisy, 1880–1913, pouyezdnyye itogi* (Moscow, 1926), 308 and 374.

64 Vladimirskoye Gubernskoye Zemstvo, Statistichesky Komitet, *Materialy dlya otsenki zemel' Vladimirskoy gubernii: Vladimirsky uyezd*, 3rd edn (Vladimir, 1912), p. 1; see also Sankt-Peterburgskoye Gubernskoye Zemstvo, Statistiko-ekonomicheskoye otdeleniye, *Materialy dlya otsenki zemel' S.-Peterburgskoy gubernii: Gdovsky uyezd* (St Petersburg, 1914), pp. 1 and 35–6.

65 Rashin, *Formirovaniye*, 327.

66 *Ibid.*, 329 and 333; and on the basis of Dept of Non-Repartitional Taxes *Materialy . . . 16 noyabrya 1901* (see note 61 above).

67 On the basis of *ibid.*, vol. III.

68 Table 53 is based on Rashin, *Formirovaniye*, Table 51, p. 172, and L. S. Gaponenko, 'Rabochy klass Rossii nakanune velikogo oktyabrya', *Istoricheskiye Zapisky*, LXXIII (1969), pp. 43–4.

69 B.V., 'K kharakteristike agrarnykh otnosheniy v yugo zapadnom kraye', *Narodnoye Khozyaystvo*, I (1903), 67–79; Y. I. Shatilov, 'Odno iz batrachnykh khozyaystv sredney Rossii', *Trudy imperatorskago Obshchestva Sel'skago Khozyaystva*, XVIII (Moscow, 1886); V. Y. Meyer, *Prilepskaya ekonomiya brat'yev baronov K. i A. Yegorovichey Meyendorf* (Moscow, 1896); *Entsiklopedichesky slovar*, Brokhauz i Efron, LI, 10–15; *VF*, 1910, no. 19, pp. 283ff, and no. 36, p. 419.

70 On the basis of Troynitsky (ed.), *op. cit.*; Chelintsev, *op. cit.*, 62; Pogozhev, *Uchot*, 30; A. A. Panov (ed.), *Dvizheniye rabochikh na zarabotki v 1910 g.: stroitelnyye i dorozhnyye raboty* (St Petersburg, 1911), 5.

71 P. Vikhlyayev, 'Ustoychivost' vnezemledel'cheskikh otkhozhe-promyslovykh zarabotkov sel'skago naseleniya v Rossii', *Narodnoye Khozyaystvo* (1900), III (1900), 78–80; Rashin, *Formirovaniye*, 117ff; Pogozhev, *Uchot*, 26; *VF*, 1910, no. 13, pp. 578–9, and no. 16, pp. 126–7.

72 *VF*, *ibid.*; Chelintsev, *op. cit.*, pp. 62ff; A. V. Prilezhayev, *Chto takoye kustarnoye proizvodstvo?* (St Petersburg, 1882), 69–72.

73 V. Levitsky, 'Znacheniye kustarnykh promyslov v narodnom khozyaystve', *Narodnoye Khozyaystvo*, VI (1902), 34–48; 'Kustarnaya promyshlennost', in *Entsiklopedichesky Slovar*, *op. cit.*, XXXIII, 121–7; Russia, Ministerstvo Finansov, Departament torgovli i manufaktur, *Trudy komissii po izsledovaniyu kustarnoy promyshlennosti v Rossii*, part 3 (St Petersburg, 1879–82); V. I. Kovalevsky (ed.), *Rossiya v kontse XIX v.*, 512ff; *VF*, 1902, no. 7, pp. 269–76; *VF*, 1911, no. 13, pp. 588ff.

74 *Entsiklopedichesky Slovar*, *loc. cit.*; *VF*, 1914, no. 42, p. 76, and no. 39, p. 137;

VF, 1912, no. 24, pp. 575–6; P. G. Ryndzyunsky, *Krest'yanskaya promyshlennost' v poreformennoy Rossii (60–80-ye gody XIX v.)* (Moscow, 1966), 230ff; Kovalevsky, *op. cit.*, 516ff.

75 Ryndzyunsky, *Krest'yanskaya*, 217ff; Tugan-Baranovsky, *op. cit.*, 396ff.

76 *Trudy komissii* (see note 73 above), 39ff; *Entsiklopedichesky Slovar*, *op. cit.*, XXXIII, 123.

77 H. Myint, 'Dualism and the Internal Integration of Underdeveloped Economies', *Banca nazionale del lavoro Quarterly Review*, no. 93 (June 1970), 128–56.

78 K. A. Pazhitnov, *Problema remeslennykh tsekhov v zakonodatel'stve russkogo absolutizma* (Moscow, 1952), 99, 103, and 110–12; Rozhhkova (ed.), *Ocherki*, 64–5.

79 Russia, Tsentral'ny statistichesky komitet, *Yezhegodnik Rossii za 1910 g.* (St Petersburg, 1911), 63; *VF*, 1916, no. 29, pp. 99–100; *VF*, 1911, no. 14, p. 7; *Pogozhev, Uchot*, 20 and 35.

80 Pogozhev, *ibid.*

81 Rashin, *Formirovaniye*, 143.

82 V. Alymov, 'K voprosu o polozhenii truda v remeslennom proizvodstve', *Narodnoye Khozyaystvo*, VI (1904), 1–27.

83 S. N. Prokopovich (ed.), *Opyt ischisleniya narodnago dokhoda 50 guberniy Yevropeyskoy Rossii v 1900–1913 g.* (Moscow, 1918).

84 Pogozhev, *Uchot*, 1–22.

85 *Ibid.*, 16.

86 V. E. Varzar (ed.), *Statistika*, part 1, p. 35.

87 *Ibid.*, 36.

88 Pogozhev, *Uchot*, 76–81.

89 A. F. Yakovlev, *Ekonomicheskiye krizisy v Rossii* (Moscow, 1955), 85; S. P. Sigov, *Ocherki po istorii gornozavodskoy promyshlennosti Urala* (Sverdlovsk, 1936), 208; K. A. Pazhitnov, *Ocherki tekstil'noy* (1955), 125ff; Kovalevsky, *op. cit.*, 289.

90 Rashin, *Formirovaniye*, 8–9; Tugan-Baranovsky, *op. cit.*, 239–45; Pazhitnov, *Ocherki tekstil'noy* (1958), 75ff.

91 Pogozhev, *Uchot*.

92 *Ibid.*; V. E. Varzar (ed.), *Statisticheskiye svedeniya o fabrikakh i zavodakh, ne oblozhennykh aktsizom za 1900 god* (St Petersburg, 1903: issued by Otdel promyshlennosti Ministerstva Finansov), pp. x–xi.

93 *Ibid.*

94 V. I. Lenin, *Razvitiye kapitalizma v Rossii*, in *Sochineniya*, III (Moscow, 1946), Appendix II.

95 Varzar (ed.), *Statisticheskiye svedeniya*, pp. x–xi; Russia, Ministerstvo Finansov, *Svod dannykh o fabrichno-zavodskoy promyshlennosti Rossii za 1897 god* (St Petersburg, 1900), *Vvedeniye*.

96 Calculated on the basis of P. A. Khromov, *Ekonomicheskoye razvitiye Rossii v XIX–XX vekakh* (Moscow and Leningrad, 1950), 27 and 31–2.

97 Based on *Svod Otchotov Fabrichnykh Inspektorov* for relevant years.

98 Rashin, *Formirovaniye*, 61.

99 *Ibid.*, 62–3.

100 *Ibid.*, and Varzar, *Statistika*.

101 In his view of Rashin's book in *Journal of Economic History*, XXI, 2 (June 1961), 209–10, G. V. Rimlinger reaches similar conclusions. In the USA, employment in manufacture grew from 1·3 million to 6·6 million during the period 1859–1914. During the period 1909–14, factory inspectors reported the mushrooming of small mechanical weaving sheds, and in general a relative increase in smaller units.

102 Based on Russia, Ministerstvo Finansov, Departament torgovli i manufaktur, *Itogi torgovli i promyshlennosti Rossii 1825–1855 gg.* (St Petersburg, 1896), 47–50.

103 On the basis of *ibid*.
104 A. V. Pogozhev, 'Sanitarnoye izsledovaniye fabrichnykh zavedeniy Bogorod-skago uyezda', *Sbornik statisticheskikh svedeniy po Moskosvskoy gubernii: otdel sanitarnoy statistiki*, III (Moscow, 1885), 6; V. P. Bezobrazov, *Narodnoye khozyaystvo Rossii: Moskovskaya tsentral'naya promyshlennaya oblast'*, 3 parts (St Petersburg, 1882), part 1, pp. 279 and 288-90.
105 V. N. Vasil'yev, 'Formirovaniye promyshlennogo proletariata Ivanovskoy oblasti', *Voprosy Istorii*, no. 6 (1952), 110; Rashin, *Formirovaniye*, 16-17; Pazhitnov, *Ocherki tekstil'noy* (1955), pp. 125ff, and Table 32, p. 140.
106 Ya. P. Garelin, *Gorod Ivanovo-Voznesensk, ili byvsheye selo Ivanovo i Voznesensky posad*, 2 vols. (Shuya, 1884-5), II, 59-60 and 100-1. On the basis of Varzar, *Statistika*, 24; Khromov, *op. cit.*, 105-6; Pazhitnov, *Ocherki tekstil'noy* (1955), 219ff; Pazhitnov, *Ocherki tekstil'noy* (1958), 276.
107 *VF*, 1914, no. 24, pp. 575ff.
108 R. S. Livshits, *Razmeshcheniye promyshlennosti v dorevolyutsyonnoy Rossii* (Moscow, 1955), 104-6 and 180ff; *Krenholmskaya manufaktura 1857-1907: Istorichesky ocherk* (St Petersburg, 1907), 16ff.
109 Based on Dept of Non-Repartitional Taxes, *Materialy . . . 16 noyabrya* (see note 61 above), vol. III; Khromov, *op. cit.*, 204ff; Pogozhev, *Uchot*.
110 On the basis of I. Glivits, *Zheleznaya promyshlennost' Rossii* (St Petersburg, 1911), *Prilozheniye*, pp. 7-8 and 12-13.
111 For 1897, from Ministerstvo Finansov, *Svod dannykh*, pp. xxi-xxxi; for 1908, from Varzar (ed.), *Statistika*.
112 I. Gindin, 'O nektorykh osobennostyakh ekonomicheskoy i sotsyal'noy struktury rossiyskogo kapitalizma v nachale XX v.', *Istoriya SSSR*, III (1966), 48-9; L. E. Shepelev, 'Aktsyonernoye uchreditel'stvo v Rossii', in M. P. Vyatkin (ed.), *Iz istorii imperializma v Rossii* (Moscow and Leningrad, 1959), 152-3.
113 Paul Gregory, in 'Economic Growth and Structural Change in Tsarist Russia: A Case of Modern Economic Growth', *Soviet Studies*, XXIII (1972), 431, similarly concludes that the sectoral distribution of GNP in Russia differed from that of advanced countries.
114 On the basis of J. H. Bater, 'The Industrial Geography of St Petersburg: 1850-1914' (unpublished Ph.D. thesis, University of London, 1969), 73.
115 On the basis of S. Bernshteyn-Kogan, *Chislennost, sostav i polozheniye metal-lurgicheskikh rabochikh*, Trudy studentov ekonomicheskogo otdeleniya SPb. Politekh-nicheskogo Instituta Imperatora Petra Velikago, no. 4 (St Petersburg, 1910), 28-9; Livshits, *op. cit.*, 206; V. K. Yatsunsky, 'Znacheniye ekonomicheskikh svyazey s Rossiyey dlya khozyaystvennogo razvitiya gorodov Pribaltiki v epoku kapitalizma', *Istoricheskiye Zapisky*, XLV (1954), 115 and 119.
116 Varzar (ed.), *Statistika*.
117 A. Raffalovich (ed.), *Russia: Its Commerce and Trade* (London, 1918), 115; Gindin, *op. cit.*
118 Rashin, *Formirovaniye*, 192-3.
119 On the basis of Livshits, *op. cit.*, Table 40, p. 205, footnote in *ibid.*, and pp. 263ff.
120 *Ibid.*, p. 264 and Table 36.
121 Pogozhev, *Uchot*, 83-4; Russia, Ministerstvo Torgovli i Promyshlennosti, Otdel promyshlennosti, *Dannyye o prodolzhitel'nosti i raspredelenii rabochego vremeni v promyshlennykh predpriyatiyakh, podchinyonnykh nadzoru fabrichnoy i gornoy inspektsii v 1913 g.* (Petrograd, 1914), 2.
122 *Svod Otchotov Fabrichnykh Inspektorov* for the relevant years.
123 *Ibid.*, 1913.

124 On the basis of Ministerstvo Torgovli, *Dannyye* ... (see note 121).

125 *Svod Otchotov Fabrichnykh Inspektorov*, 1907, vii–viii; *ibid.*, 1913, pp. xliii–xliv; *ibid.*, 1906, p. vii.

126 *Ibid.*, 1906, p. 7; S. Koehler, *Die russische Industriearbeiterschaft von 1905–1917*, Osteuropa-Institut in Breslau (Leipzig and Berlin, 1921), 25ff.

127 Troynitsky (ed.), *op. cit.*, pp. vi–vii; B. P. Kadomtsev, *Professyonal'ny i sotsyal'ny sostav naseleniya yevropeyskoy Rossii po dannym perepisi 1897 g.* (St Petersburg, 1909), 59–60; Bernshteyn-Kogan, *op. cit.*, 32; *VF*, no. 26 (1904), Table 3; N. F. Kudryavtsev, *Prishlyye sel'sko-khozyaystvennyye rabochiye na Nikolayevskoy yarmarke v m. Kakhovke v Tavricheskoy gubernii i sanitarny nadzor za nimi* (Kherson, 1896), 11; A. Yaroshko, *Rabochy vopros na yuge: Yego proshedsheye, nastoyashcheye i budushcheye* (Moscow, 1894), 121.

128 Bernshteyn-Kogan, *op. cit.*, 83–5; Russia, Ministerstvo Vnutrennikh Del, Tsentral'ny statistichesky komitet, *Sankt-Peterburg no perepisi 15 dekabrya 1890 g.*, *Naseleniye* (St Petersburg, 1891), part 1; Ministerstvo Vnutrennikh Del ..., *Sankt-Peterburg po perepisi naseleniya 15 dekabrya 1900 goda*, *Naseleniye* (St Petersburg, 1903), part 1; Ministerstvo Vnutrennikh Del ..., *Petrograd po perepisi naseleniya 15 dekabrya 1910 g.* (Petrograd, 1914); A. A. Chuprov (ed.), *Rechi i stat'i*, 4 parts (St Petersburg, 1909), part 1, pp. 193ff.

129 Sagorsky, *op. cit.*, 74–6.

130 P. A. Vikhlyayev (ed.), *Zemledel'cheskoye khozyaystvo i promysly krest'yanskago naseleniya: promysly*, part 2 (Moscow, 1908), 644; P. Nevolin, *Kustarnaya promyshlennost' vo Vladimirskoy gubernii* (Vladimir, 1912), 120.

131 Zelnik, *op. cit.*, 36–7.

132 On the basis of *ibid.*, 125ff.

133 Raffalovich, *op. cit.*, 147ff; O. Goebel, *Entwicklungsgang der russischen Industriearbeiter bis zur ersten Revolution (1905)*, Osteuropa-Institut in Breslau (Leipzig and Berlin, 1920), 14ff.

134 E. Andreyev, *Rabota maloletnikh v Rossii i v Zapadnoy Yevrope* (St Petersburg, 1884), 160; V. Yu Gessen, *Trud detey i podrostkov v fabrichnozavodskoy Rossii ot XVII veka do oktyabrskoy revolyutsii* (Moscow, 1927), vol. 1, pp. 50ff.

135 P. A. Peskov, *Fabrichny byt Vladimirskoy gubernii: otchot za 1882–1883* (St Petersburg, 1883), 30; Ya. T. Mikhaylovsky, *O deyatel'nosti fabrichnoy inspektsii: otchot glavnago fabrichnago inspektora* (St Petersburg, 1886), 76–7; V. V. Svyatlovsky, *Kharkovsky fabrichny okrug: otchot za 1885 god* (St Petersburg, 1886), 15.

136 Pogozhev, *Uchot*, 83–4.

137 On the basis of *Svod Otchotov Fabrichnykh Inspektorov* for the relevant years: see above.

138 On the basis of Ministerstvo Torgovli, *Dannyye* ... (see note 121), pp. xxxviiff.

139 Peskov, *op. cit.*, 18; Gvozdev, *op. cit.*, 48 and 50.

140 I. I. Yanzhul, *Fabrichny byt Moskovskoy gubernii: otchot za 1882–3* (St Petersburg, 1884), 5ff; Yanzhul, 'Detsky i zhensky fabrichny trud v Anglii i Rossii', *Otechestvennyye Zapisky*, nos. 2–4 (1880); F. F. Erisman (ed.), 'Sanitarnoye izsledovaniye fabrichnykh zavedeniy Moskovskago uyezda', in *Sbornik statisticheskikh svedeniy po Moskovskoy gubernii: otdel sanitarnoy statistiki*, IV (Moscow, 1885), part 1, pp. 288–9.

141 Erisman (ed.), *op. cit.*, 292; Gvozdev, *op. cit.*, 34; based on I. M. Koz'minykh-Lanin, *Gramotnost' i zarabotki fabrichno-zavodskikh rabochikh Moskovskoy gubernii* (Moscow, 1912: cited hereafter as '*Gramotnost'* (1912)').

142 On the basis of Russia, Ministerstvo Vnutrennikh Del, *Obshchy svod po imperii rezul'tatov razrabotki dannykh pervoy vseobshchey perepisi naseleniya, proizvedennoy 28 yanvarya 1897*, vol. 1 (St Petersburg, 1905), 97–100; Yu. Yanson, 'Naseleniye Peterburga, ego ekonomichesky i sotsyal'ny sostav po perepisi 1869 g.', *Vestnik Yevropy*,

no. 10 (1875), 617; Ministerstvo Vnutrennikh Del, Tsentral'ny statistichesky komitet, *Sankt-Peterburg po perepisi 10 dekabrya 1869 goda* (St Petersburg, 1872–5), vol. I, p. 110; *idem, Sankt-Peterburg po perepisi* . . . *1890*, 36; *idem, Sankt-Peterburg po perepisi* . . . *1900*, 32–3; *idem, Petrograd po perepisi* . . . *1910*, 3; A. S. Nifontov, 'Formirovaniye klassov burzhuaznogo obshchestva v russkom gorode', *Istoricheskiye Zapisky*, LIV (1950), 239ff.

143 Moscow, Gorodskaya Uprava, Statisticheskoye otdeleniye, *Perepis Moskvy 1882 g.: Naseleniye i zanyatiya* (Moscow, 1885), 38–42; Moscow, Gorodskaya Uprava . . ., *Perepis Moskvy 1902 goda, Naseleniye* (Moscow, 1904), 3 and 10; Russia, Tsentral'noye Statisticheskoye Upravleniye SSSR, *Statistichesky Yezhegodnik goroda Moskvy i Moskovskoy gubernii* (Moscow, 1927), Table 14.

144 On the basis of Ministerstvo Vnutrennikh Del . . ., *Petrograd po perepisi* . . . *1910*, Tables 14a and 15; Moscow, Gorodskaya Uprava . . ., *Perepis Moskvy 1902*, 11 and 63; Rashin, *Naseleniye*, 113, 139–40, 145, and 147; Nifontov, *op. cit.*, 240ff.

145 On the basis of L. M. Ivanov, 'O soslovno-klassovoy strukture gorodov kapitalisticheskoy Rossii', in L. M. Ivanov (ed.), *Problemy sotsyal'no-ekonomicheskoy istorii Rossii* (Moscow, 1971), 327; Baku, Gorodskaya Uprava, Statisticheskoye otdeleniye, *Baku po perepisi 22 oktyabrya 1903 g.*, vol. I (Baku, 1905), 38–48; *idem, Perepis Baku 1913 goda*, III (Baku, 1916), 7.

146 Chuprov, *op. cit.*, 193.

147 *VF*, 1904, no. 26, Tables 4–5, pp. 546–7

148 On the basis of Moscow, Gorodskaya Uprava . . ., *Perepis Moskvy 1902*, 2–7.

149 P. M. Shestakov, *Rabochiye na manufakture tovarishchestva 'Emil Tsindel' v Moskve: statisticheskoye izsledovaniye* (Moscow, 1900), 21–2; A. P., 'Rabochiye Sormovskikh zavodov', *Narodnoye khozyaystvo*, IV (1902), 92–3; Rashin, *Formirovaniye*, 286.

150 Bernshteyn-Kogan, *op. cit.*, 161, Appendix 1; A. Svavitsky and V. Sher, *Ocherk polozheniya rabochikh pechatnago dela v Moskve* (St Petersburg, 1909), 14–15.

151 Shestakov, *op. cit.*, 22; Svavitsky and Sher, *op. cit.*, 15–16.

152 S. M. Bogoslovsky, *Zabolevayemost' fabrichnykh rabochikh Bogorodsko-Glukhovskoy i Istominskoy manufaktur Bogorodskago uyezda za 1896–1900 gg.* (St Petersburg, 1901), 29; see also *VF*, 1910, no. 40, pp. 24ff.

153 S. Koehler, *op. cit.*, 37ff.

154 According to Chuprov, *op. cit.*, 193, in Paris and Berlin in 1880 the ratios were 1,020 and 1,060 women respectively per thousand men; Zelnik, *op. cit.*, 234.

155 Chuprov, *op. cit.*

156 Bernshteyn-Kogan, *op. cit.*, 53ff.

157 Soyuz Rabochikh po Metallu, *Materialy ob ekonomicheskom polozhenii i professyonal'noy organizatsii peterburgskikh rabochikh po metallu* (St Petersburg, 1909: based on inquiries of 1 September 1907 and 1 January 1908), 85ff; Russia, Statisticheskoye Byuro Sovyeta S'yezda Neftepromyshlennikov, *Zarabotnaya plata sluzhaschikh i rabochikh bakinskago promyshlennago rayona* (Baku, 1912), 11–13.

158 Yanzhul, *Fabrichny byt*, 119ff; Schultze-Gaevernitz, *op. cit.*, 120ff; V. I. Miropol'sky, *Voronezhsky fabrichny okrug-otchot za 1885 g.* (St Petersburg, 1886), 55ff; A. V. Shidlovsky, *Kazansky fabrichny okrug: otchot za 1885* (St Petersburg, 1886); Svyatlovsky, *op. cit.*, 120ff; Peskov, *op. cit.*, 31ff; Koehler, *op. cit.*, 30ff.

159 M. Lauwick, *L'Industrie dans la Russie Méridionale: sa situation – son avenir* (Brussels and Paris, 1907), 146.

160 Koehler, *op. cit.*, 32–3.

161 M. K. Rozhkova, 'Rabochiye Tryokhgornoy manufaktury vo vtoroy polovine XIX v.', in *Istoriya proletariata SSSR*, no. 1 (Moscow, 1930), 223 and 229; and M. K.

Rozhkova, 'Sostav rabochikh Tryokhgornoy manufaktury nakanune imperyalis-ticheskoy voyny', in *ibid.*, no. 5 (Moscow, 1931), 103.

162 L. M. Ivanov, 'Preyemstvennost' fabrichno-zavodskogo truda i formirovaniye proletariata v Rossii', in L. M. Ivanov (ed.), *Robochy klass i rabocheye dvizheniye v Rossii 1861–1917* (Moscow, 1966), 80.

163 *Ibid.*

164 Shestakov, *op. cit.*, 19, 25–7, and 37–9.

165 Svavitsky and Sher, *op. cit.*, 8–9 and 45.

166 *Ibid.*

167 Shestakov, *op. cit.*, 39; Pogozhev, *Uchot*, 101 and Chart 18.

168 A. M. Pankratova, 'Rabochy klass i rabocheye dvizheniye nakanune revolyut-sii 1905 g.', in M. N. Pokrovsky (ed.), *1905: Istoriya revolyutsyonnogo dvizheniya v otdel'nykh ocherkakh* (Moscow and Leningrad, 1925), 421; Laue, *loc. cit.*, 74.

169 Professor H. Kries, in *OEDC Publication no. 13557* (Paris, 1961), p. 26, com-ments that workers who have close ties with agriculture, as in Norway or Ireland, remain poorly adjusted to industrial life; employers report a tendency to absenteeism, greater fatigue, and less general integration in the firm; 'where the factory invites him to integrate into a consumer–wage economy, the paternal farm . . . keeps him to a subsistence economy'.

170 A. I. Tyumenev, *Ot revolyutsii k revolyutsii* (Leningrad, 1925), 204–5.

171 Ivanov, 'Preyemstvennost'', Table 6, p. 121; see also Russia, Uchonaya komissiya po izsledovaniyu istorii truda v Rossii, *Trud v SSSR: Spravochnik 1926–1930* (Moscow, 1930), 28–9.

172 Rashin, *Formirovaniye*, Table 143, p. 575.

173 Koehler, *op. cit.*, 38–44.

174 *Ibid.*; M. K. Palat, 'Tsarist Labour Policy', *Soviet Studies*, no. 2 (1973); V. Ya. Laverichev, *Tsarism i rabochy vopros v Rossii 1861–1917* (Moscow, 1972), 100–15 and 241ff.

175 G. Arrighi (*op. cit.*, 223) writes with reference to African peasants that 'stabil-ised labour commanded a premium determined by the difference between the cost of means of subsistence of single men during their working life in wage employment and the cost of means of subsistence of the worker's family over his life cycle'.

176 Pazhitnov, *Ocherki tekstil'noy* (1958), 129; *VF*, 1915, no. 15.

177 Goebel, *op. cit.*, 8.

178 Novitsky, *op. cit.*, 24–5; Laverichev, *op. cit.*, 82.

179 Novitsky, *op. cit.*, 19ff.

180 E. Kolodub, *Trud i zhizn' gornorabochikh na grushevskikh antratsitnykh rudnikakh*, 2nd edn (Moscow, 1907), 111–13.

181 *Ibid.*, 126.

182 *Ibid.*, 109–11.

183 Novitsky, *op. cit.*, 24.

184 Kolodub, *op. cit.*, 42ff; B. F. Brandt, *Torgovo-promyshlennyy krizis*, 2 vols. (St Petersburg, 1902), vol. I, pp. 184ff; Laverichev, *op. cit.*, 84–6.

185 Dement'yev, *Fabrika*, 38.

186 Peskov, *op. cit.*, 67; Novitsky, *op. cit.*, 44–9.

187 Peskov, *op. cit.*, 102–11; Novitsky, *op. cit.*, 25ff.

188 Peskov, *op. cit.*, 67; Novitsky, *op. cit.*, 37; Yanzhul, *Fabrichny byt*, 78–9, 90–3, 102, and 108.

189 Pogozhev, *Uchot*, p. 113 and Table 47.

190 S. G. Strumilin, *Izbrannyye proizvedeniya*, III, 367; *Svod Otchotov Fabrichnykh Inspektorov* for 1913.

191 Goebel, *op. cit.*, 13–14.

192 Schultze-Gaevernitz, *op. cit.*, 116–18.

193 Goebel, *op. cit.*, 14; Shestakov, *op. cit.*, 25; A. P. , 'Rabochiye', 90; Statisticheskoye Byuro, *Zarabotnaya plata*.

194 *Svod Otchotov Fabrichnykh Inspektorov* for 1909, 1910, 1911, etc.

195 Novitsky, *op. cit.*, 36–7; Peskov, *op. cit.*, 67–8; Yanzhul, *Fabrichny byt*, 79–80.

196 *Novitsky, op. cit.*, 36–7; *Svod Otchotov Fabrichnykh Inspektorov* for 1910.

197 Peskov, *op. cit.*, 68–71.

198 *Ibid.*, 71–2; Schultze-Gaevernitz, *op. cit.*, 131–2.

199 C. Kerr, J. T. Dunlop, F. H. Harrison, and C. A. Myers, *Industrialism and Industrial Man: The Problems of Labour and Management in Economic Growth* (Harmondsworth, 1973), 227ff; S. Pollard, 'Factory Discipline in the Industrial Revolution'. *Economic History Review*, 2nd ser., XVI, 2 (December 1963), 254–72.

200 I. Kh. Ozerov, *Politika po rabochemu voprosu za posledniye gody* (Moscow, 1906), especially chap. 4, pp. 112ff; Laverichev, *op. cit.*, especially chap. 3, pp. 117ff; V. P. Bezobrazov, 'Dnevnik, 1887 g.', *Russkaya Starina*, CLIV (1913), 273; V. P. Bezobrazov, *Nablyudeniya i soobrazheniya otnositel'no novykh fabrichnykh uzakoneniy i fabrichnoy inspektsii* (St Petersburg, 1888), 4–6 and 8–10; Tugan-Baranovsky, *op. cit.*, 318–19. For an intelligent treatment of the government's role, see G. von Rimlinger, 'Autocracy and the Factory Order in Early Russian Industrialization', *Journal of Economic History*, XX (1960), 67–92, especially 91–2.

201 Archives of International Harvester Company of Chicago (cited hereafter as 'IHA'), no. 1238, Report of B. A. Kennedy, 17 April 1909; W. Reay to C. S. Funk, 30 October 1909. I am obliged for copies of these documents to E. C. Pickering (see her 'The International Harvester Company in Russia: A Case Study of a Foreign Corporation in Russia from the 1860's to the 1930's', unpublished Ph.D. thesis, Princeton University, 1974). All further references to IHA material are by courtesy of Dr Pickering. Schultze-Gaevernitz, *op. cit.*, 137–8.

202 See, e.g., E. F. Denison, *Why Growth Rates Differ* (Washington, 1957); I. Adelman and C. F. Morris, *Society, Politics and Economic Development* (Baltimore, Md, 1957). On the other hand, there are those who argue that 'Capital, however financed, *is* the key development constraint, without which education merely produces educated unemployed.' (*Journal of Development Studies*, VI, 3 (1970), Review of D. Horowitz, *Hemispheres North and South and Economic Disparities Among Nations* (1967).)

203 Schultze-Gaevernitz, *op. cit.*, 137–8.

204 L. L. Gavrishev, 'O vliyanii obshchego obrazovaniya rabochikh na produktivnost' ikh truda', in *Trudy s'yezda deyateley po teknicheskomu i professyonal'nomu obrazovaniyu v Rossii 1895–1896 gg.*, section 4 (St Petersburg, 1898), 133–42; Gavrishev, 'Teknicheskoye obrazovaniye', in *Trudy vserossiyskago torgovo-promyshlennago s'yezda 1896 g. v Nizhnem-Novgorode*, VI (St Petersburg, 1897), 293–4; I. M. Koz'minykh-Lanin, *Gramotnost' rabochikh fabrichno-zavodskoy promyshlennosti Moskovskoy gubernii* (Moscow, 1911: cited hereafter as '*Gramotnost*' (1911)'), 13–14; Statisticheskoye Byuro, *Zarabotnaya plata*, 10.

205 S. G. Strumilin, 'Khozyaystvennoye znacheniye narodnogo obrazovaniya', *Planovoye Khozyaystvo*, 1924, nos. 9–10.

206 Tugan-Baranovsky, *op. cit.*, 397–8.

207 *Ibid.*; Moskovskoye Gubernskoye Zemstvo, Statistichesky otdel, *Moskovskaya guberniya po mestnomu obsledovaniyu 1898–1900 gg.*, vol. V: 'Promysly' (Moscow, 1901), 656–7.

208 N. S. Timashev, 'Overcoming Illiteracy: Public Education in Russia, 1880–1940', *Russian Review*, no. 2 (1942), 82–3; L. Stone, 'Literacy and education in England, 1640–1900', *Past and Present*, no. 42 (1969), 101.

209 On the basis of Ministerstvo Vnutrennikh Del, *Obshchy Svod*, vol. I, pp. 36–9.

210 *Ibid.*; also A. G. Rashin, 'Gramotnost' i narodnoye obrazovaniye v Rossii v XIX i nachale XX v.', *Istoricheskiye Zapisky*, XXXVII (1951), 49; Rashin, *Naseleniye*, 309–10.

211 Ministerstvo Vnutrennikh Del, *Obshchy Svod*, vol. I, pp. 44–7.

212 On the basis of Rashin, *Formirovaniye*, 586–7.

213 *Ibid.*, 588; E. M. Dement'yev, 'Sanitarnoye izsledovaniye fabrik i zavodov Kolomenskago uyezda', in *Sbornik statisticheskikh svedeniy po Moskovskoy gubernii: otdel sanitarnoy statistiki*, III (Moscow, 1885), 76–7 and 123–4.

214 On the basis of N. Hans, *History of Russian Educational Policy* (London, 1931), 242.

215 Rashin, 'Gramotnost'', 45; I. M. Bodganov, *Gramotnost' i obrazovaniye v dorevolyutsyonnoy Rossii i v SSSR, Istoriko-statisticheskiye ocherki* (Moscow, 1964), 55–6.

216 G. Guroff and S. F. Starr, 'A Note on Urban Literacy in Russia, 1890–1914', *Jahrbücher für Geschichte Osteuropas*, n.s., XIX, 4 (December 1971), 525.

217 Koz'minykh-Lanin, *Gramotnost'* (1911), 1–3.

218 On the basis of Russia, Tsentral'noye Statisticheskoye Upravleniye SSSR, *Fabrichno-zavodskaya promyshlennost' v period 1913–1918 gg.* (Moscow, 1922), 45ff.

219 M. Kaser, 'Education in Tsarist and Soviet Development', in C. Abramsky (ed.), *Essays in Honour of E. H. Carr* (London, 1974), 245.

220 N. V. Chekhov, *Narodnoye obrazovaniye v Rossii s 60ykh godov XIX v.* (Moscow, 1912), 145 and 155.

221 Koz'minykh-Lanin, *Gramotnost'* (1911), 13–14.

222 A. P., 'Rabochiye', 91ff; Shestakov, *op. cit.*, 14ff and 60.

223 Shestakov, *loc. cit.*

224 Dement'yev, *op. cit.*, III, 76–7 and 123–4; Carlo M. Cipolla, *Literature and Development in the West* (Baltimore, Md, 1969), 25–6; Peskov, *op. cit.*, 32. Peskov notes the role of retired soldiers in imparting literacy.

225 Guroff, *op. cit.*, 223.

226 Strumilin, 'Dinamika oplaty promyshlennogo truda v Rossii za 1900–1914 gg', *Planovoye Khozyaystvo*, 1926, no. 9.

227 Chekhov, *op. cit.*, 145.

228 N. Annensky, 'Voprosy truda na torgovo-promyshlennom s'yezde', *Russkoye Bogatstvo*, X (1896), 190; see, e.g. Novitsky, *op. cit.*, 88ff; Peskov, *op. cit.*, 27–37.

229 Blackwell, *op. cit.*, 326–7.

230 *VF*, 1903, no. 2, p. 48; *VF*, 1915, no. 12, pp. 549–51.

231 *Ibid.*

232 *Ibid.*; Russia, Ministerstvo Torgovli i Promyshlennosti, Uchebny otdel, *Materialy po tekhnicheskomu i remeslennomu obrazovaniyu* (Petrograd, 1917), 21–2; IHA, no. 1238, Report of B. A. Kennedy, 17 April 1909.

233 O. Crisp, 'The Financial Aspect of the Franco-Russian Alliance, 1894–1914', unpublished Ph.D. thesis, University of London, 1954, pp. 211ff; Lauwick, *op. cit.*, 136–40; B. F. Brandt, *Inostrannyye kapitaly: ikh vliyaniye na ekonomicheskoye razvitiye strany*, 3 vols. (St Petersburg, 1898–1901), II, 268–72; J. F. Fraser, *Russia of To-day* (New York, 1916), 183; J. P. McKay, *Pioneers for Profit: Foreign Entrepreneurship and Russian Industrialization, 1885–1913* (Chicago and London, 1970), 257ff.

234 Crisp, *op. cit.*, 212–13; Statisticheskoye Byuro, *Zarabotnaya plata*, 8–9. See also K. A. Pazhitnov, 'Razvitiye kamennougol'noy i metallurgicheskoy promyshlennosti na yuge Rossii', *Narodnoye Khozyaystvo*, 1905, no. 3, pp. 34–5.

235 IHA, no. 208, Report of Robert Walker, 23 April 1903; IHA, no. 1238 (see note 232 above); Pickering, 'International Harvester Company in Russia', 65–6.

236 IHA, no. 1238, Report of 22 July 1909; Kennedy to Funk, 17 August 1909.

237 *Ibid.*; Pickering, *op. cit.*, 139.

238 O. Crisp, Review of McKay, *op. cit.*, in *Soviet Studies* (Glasgow), July 1972; Pazhitnov, 'Razvitiye', shows how intending entrepreneurs started by soliciting government custom for a few years in advance and only then proceeded with the flotation of capital for the construction of a plant. Thus, the Nicopol–Maryupol Company, having secured an order for oil pipes for the Trans-Caucasian Railway, imported a whole plant from the USA and installed it in Maryupol.

239 A. S. Islavin, 'Obzor kamennougol'noy i zhelezodelatel'noy promyshlennosti Donetskago kryazha', *Gorny Zhurnal*, 1875, nos. 1–3, pp. 82ff; A. Lisyansky, 'Osnovaniye yuzovskogo zavoda', *Istoriya SSSR*, no. 5 (1964), 150–9; I. M. Lukomskaya, 'Formirovaniye promyshlennogo proletariata Donbassa', in V. V. Al'tman (ed.), *Iz istorii rabochego klassa i revolyutsyonnogo dvizheniya* (Moscow, 1958), 290–307; Pazhitnov, 'Razvitiye', 66; Brandt, *Inostrannyye kapitaly*, II, 261–2.

240 V. K. Yatsunsky, 'Rol' Peterburga v promyshlennom razvitii Rossii', *Voprosy Istorii*, no. 9 (1954), 95–105; Schultze-Gaevernitz, *op. cit.*, 202; Goebel, *op. cit.*, 21.

241 Lauwick, *op. cit.*, 179; Crisp, *op. cit.*, 212; McKay, *op. cit.*, 190ff; Pazhitnov, 'Razvitiye', 35.

242 Pazhitnov, *Ocherki tekstil'noy* (1958), 129; *VF*, 1913, no. 40, p. 10.

243 Goldsmith, *op. cit.*

244 Ministerstvo Finansov, *Svod dannykh*; *VF*, 1900, no. 5, pp. 210ff; Varzar (ed.), *Statistika*, 4; V. E. Varzar and L. B. Kafengauz, 'Dinamika fabrichno-zavodskoy promyshlennosti Rossii', in S. G. Strumilin (ed.), *Ocherki ekonomicheskoy istorii Rossii* (Moscow, 1960), Appendix 2.

245 On the basis of Varzar and Kafengauz, 'Dinamika'.

246 Recalculated from the index of wholesale prices of M. E. Podtyagin, quoted in Strumilin (ed.), *Ocherki*, 115.

247 On the basis of N. K. Prokopovich (ed.), *op. cit.*

248 On the basis of Varzar (ed.), *Statistika*, 21.

249 P. A. Khromov, *Ocherki ekonomiki perioda monopolisticheskogo kapitalizma* (Moscow, 1960), 38ff; *Narodnoye Khozyaystvo v 1913 g.* (St Petersburg, 1914), 337–8; K. A. Pazhitnov, *Ocherki po istorii bakinskoy neftepererabatyvayushchey promyshlennosti* (Moscow and Leningrad, 1940), 139 and 162.

250 Khromov, *Ocherki ekonomiki*, 45.

251 A. N. Shcherban, *Istoriya tekhnicheskogo razvitiya ugol'noy promyshlennosti Donbassa*, 2 vols. (Kiev, 1969), vol. I, pp. 72–3, 99, 103, 106, and 110; Pazhitnov, 'Razvitiye', 45ff and 56ff.

252 Russia, Sovet S'yezdov Predstaviteley Promyshlennosti i Torgovli, *Statistichesky Yezhegodnik na 1914 god* (Petrograd, 1914), 181; Khromov, *Ocherki ekonomiki*, 46.

253 Pazhitnov, 'Razvitiye', 50ff; *VF*, 1904, no. 16; *VF*, 1910, no. 39; *VF*, 1911, no. 12.

254 Khromov, *Ocherki ekonomiki*, 49; *VF*, 1913, no. 40.

255 On the basis of Khromov, *op. cit.*, 58; *VF*, 1914, no. 14, p. 49.

256 Schultze-Gaevernitz, *op. cit.*, 96.

257 *Ibid.*, 97; Russia, Ministerstvo Finansov, Departament torgovli i manufaktur, *The Industries of Russia*, ed. J. M. Crawford (St Petersburg, 1893: published for the World's Columbian Exposition, Chicago), p. 12.

258 Schultze-Gaevernitz, *op. cit.*, 97ff.

259 *Ibid.*; *The Industries of Russia* (see note 258), 21.

260 Schultze-Gaevernitz, *op. cit.*, 100; Russia, Ministerstvo Torgovli i Promyshlennosti, Otdel promyshlennosti, *Statsitika bumagopryadil'nago i tkatskago proizvodstva za 1900–1910 gg.* (St Petersburg, 1911), p. x; *VF*, 1915, no. 8.

261 IHA, no. 1238, 'Russian manufacturing' (Reay to Funk), 30 October 1909.

262 Varzar (ed.), *Statistika*, p. 7; Lauwick, *op. cit.*, 148; on the basis of Statistiche-skoye Byuro, *Zarabotnaya plata*, 136ff.

263 Lauwick, *op. cit.*, 148; Schultze-Gaevernitz, *op. cit.*, 99; Statisticheskoye Byuro, *op. cit.*, 136ff.

264 Varzar (ed.), *Statistika*, 6–7.

265 On the basis of *Svod Otchotov Fabrichnykh Inspektorov* for 1914; Strumilin, 'Dinamika'.

266 Baron von Haxthausen, *The Russian Empire, Its People, Institutions and Resources*, 2 vols. (London, 1856), vol. I, p. 147; Schultze-Gaevernitz, *op. cit.*, 119ff.

267 Pickering, *op. cit.*, 96.

268 Based on *Svod Otchotov Fabrichnykh Inspektorov* for the relevant years; Strum-ilin, 'Dinamika'.

269 Strumilin, *op. cit.*, 165.

270 *Ibid.*

271 *VF*, 1915, no. 7.

272 Based on A. Rykachev, 'Tseny na khlyeb i na trud v S.-Peterburge za 58 let', in *VF*, 1911, no. 3, utilizing the 'Vedomosti spravochnykh tsen v S.-Peterburge'.

273 Tugan-Baranovsky, *op. cit.*, 332.

274 A. I. Chuprov and A. S. Posnikov (eds.), *Vliyaniye urozhayev i khlyebnykh tsen na nekotoryye storony russkago narodnago khozyaystva*, 2 vols. (St Petersburg, 1897).

275 V. N. Grigor'yev in *ibid.*, II, 134; Schultze-Gaevernitz, *op. cit.*, 137.

276 Rykachev, *op. cit.*, graph on p. 205; L. V. Khodsky, *Po povodu knigi 'Vliyaniye urozhaev i khlebnykh tsen na nekotoryye storony russkago narodnago khozyaystva'* (St Petersburg, 1897), 25ff.

277 *Ibid.*, p. 206 and Table A, p. 201.

278 *Ibid.*

279 Tugan-Baranovsky, *op. cit.*, graph following p. 244.

280 Rykachev, *op. cit.*, 202.

281 *Ibid.*, 178. In the Lyubertsy works, which International Harvester acquired from another American company in 1909, the average daily earnings (not including the manager, heads of departments, and office staff) were 120 kopecks, which the International Harvester representative in Russia considered low in view of the 'class of work', this being a machine-construction works: Pickering, *op. cit.*, 85. Strumilin, *Izbrannyye proizvedeniya*, III, 277.

282 On the basis of *ibid.*, 279.

283 S. N. Prokopovich, 'Krest'yanstvo i poreformennaya fabrika', in A. K. Dzivelegov *et al.* (eds.), *Velikaya reforma: obshchestvo i krest'yansky vopros i proshlom i nastoyeshchem*, VI (Moscow, 1911), 171; see also Bernshteyn-Kogan, *op. cit.*, 53ff; Koehler, *op. cit.*, 23.

284 Tugan-Baranovsky, *op. cit.*, 350.

285 *Ibid.*, 295–6.

286 On the basis of *VF*, 1910, no. 5, p. 216; *Svod Otchotov Fabrichnykh Inspektorov* for 1912.

287 T. C. Smith, 'Pre-modern Economic Growth: Japan and the West', *Past and Present*, no. 60 (August 1973), 127–81.

288 R. Mabro, 'Employment and Wages in Dual Agriculture', *Oxford Economic Papers*, n.s., XXIII, 3 (November 1971), 402; S. Zak, *Promyshlenny kapitalizm v Rossii* (Moscow, 1908), 66–71.

289 S. Swianiewicz, *Forced Labour and Economic Development* (Oxford, 1965), 62.

290 *Ibid.*

291 IHA, no. 1225, Kennedy to Funk, 24 February–6 March 1910; Pickering, *op. cit.*, 80.

292 Myint, *op. cit.*

293 Varzar (ed.), *Statistika*, 22.

294 Falkus, *op. cit.*

CHAPTER VIII

Russian Entrepreneurship

1 The four modest areas where market relationships obtain are listed by G. Grossman, 'Gold and the Sword: Money in the Soviet Command Economy', in H. Rosovsky (ed.), *Industrialization in Two Systems* (New York, 1966), 207.

2 R. Campbell, 'On the Theory of Economic Administration', in *ibid.*, 203.

3 J. P. Hardt and T. Frankel, 'The Industrial Managers', in H. G. Skilling and F. Griffiths (eds.), *Interest Groups in Soviet Politics* (Princeton, 1971), 171 and 191.

4 B. Csikós-Nagy, *Socialist Economic Policy* (London, 1973), 75.

5 Herman Aubin, 'The Lands East of the Elbe and German Colonization Eastwards', in *Cambridge Economic History*, I (Cambridge, 1941), 454; in the twelfth century 'a regular body of entrepreneurs developed who organized colonization to profit by it'.

6 Robert S. Lopez, 'The Trade of Medieval Europe: The South', in *Cambridge Economic History*, II (Cambridge, 1952), 260.

7 See especially Alfred Marshall, *Principles of Economics*, ed. C. W. Guillebaud, 9th (variorum) edn, 2 vols. (London, 1961), I, Appendix A, 745-7.

8 See especially 'Conversion of Commodity Capital and Money Capital into Commercial Capital and Money-lending Capital', in Marx, *Capital*, ed. F. Engels, transl. from 3rd German edn by S. Moore and E. Aveling, 3 vols. (Moscow, 1961-2), III, part IV, chap. 16.

9 J. Hicks, *A Theory of Economic History* (Oxford, 1969), 141.

10 Given a trade network in active existence and the fungibility of assets (*ibid.*, 142-4).

11 *Ibid.*, 21.

12 *Ibid.*, 10-11.

13 J. H. Bater, *St Petersburg – Industrialization and Change* (London, 1976), 67.

14 Hicks, *Theory of Economic History*, 155.

15 O. Crisp, *Studies in the Russian Economy before 1914* (London, 1976), 10.

16 Roger Portal, 'The Industrialization of Russia', in *Cambridge Economic History*, VI (Cambridge, 1965), 826.

17 L. Volin, *A Century of Russian Agriculture* (Cambridge, Mass., 1970), 21; Volin shows why the 19 million 'Crown peasants' (or 'state peasants') were as near serfdom as the 22 million in bondage to the gentry or the Imperial family.

18 Alexander Gerschenkron, 'Agrarian Policies and Industrialization', in *Cambridge Economic History*, VI, 721.

19 Portal, 'Industrialization of Russia', 754-5.

20 A. Gerschenkron, *Continuity in History and Other Essays* (Cambridge, Mass., 1968), 130, quotes in this connection the Russian proverb 'If you do not cheat, you will not sell'.

21 A study of the Soviet period suggests that it is only in the second half of the twentieth century that 'the capacity to promote technological innovation' has been

accorded real prominence (J. S. Berliner, *The Innovation Decision in Soviet Industry* (Cambridge, Mass., 1976), p. xi).

22 P. I. Lyashchenko, *Istoriya narodnogo khozyaistva SSSR*, 1st edn (Moscow, 1939) and 3rd edn, 2 vols. (Moscow, 1952), chaps. 3–4. References hereafter to the Russian text are to the 2nd edition (1947–8) or the 3rd (which was completed in 1956 by a posthumous third volume on the Soviet period), cited below as 'Lyashchenko, *Istoriya*, 2nd edn' or '. . . *Istoriya*, 3rd edn'. The translation by L. M. Herman (*History of the National Economy of Russia to the 1917 Revolution* (New York, 1949), from the Russian 1st edition) is cited hereafter as 'Lyashchenko, *History*, 1st edn'.

23 I. S. Golubnichy, A. Pogrebinsky, and I. N. Shemyakin (eds.), *Ekonomicheskaya istoriya SSSR*, 1st edn (Moscow, 1963) and 2nd edn (Moscow, 1967), chap. 2. (The two editions are cited hereafter as 'Golubnichy *et al.*, *Ekonomicheskaya istoriya*, 1st edn' and '. . . *istoriya*, 2nd edn'.)

24 P. A. Khromov, *Ekonomicheskoe razvitie Rossii* (Moscow, 1967), 42. This work is cited hereafter as 'Khromov, *Ekonomischeskoe razvitie* (1967)', as distinct from his *Ekonomicheskoe razvitie Rossii v XIX–XX vekakh* (Moscow, 1950), cited as 'Khromov, *Ekonomicheskoe razvitie* (1950)'.

25 Lenin's pioneering and scholarly study is *Razvitie kapitalizma v Rossii* (St Petersburg, 1899), but he reflected on the genesis of feudalism also in his polemic *What Are These 'Friends of the People' and How Do They Fight the Social Democrats?*

26 See 'Introduction' in Khromov, *Ekonomicheskoe razvitie* (1967), and Lyashchenko, *History*, 1st edn, chap. 5 (the discussion is omitted from the 2nd edn).

27 Lyashchenko, *Istoriya*, 2nd edn, 125 (not in the 1st edn).

28 Golubnichy *et al.*, *Ekonomicheskaya istoriya*, 1st edn, 64; 2nd edn, 72 and 76.

29 *Ekonomicheskoe razvitie* (1967), 278.

30 M. Tugan-Baranovsky, *Russkaya fabrika v proshlom i nastoyashchem*, I: *Istoricheskoe razvitie russkoy fabriki v XIX veke*, 3rd edn (Moscow, 1926), 17. A translation by A. Levin and C. Levin, supervised by G. Grossman (*The Russian Factory in the 19th Century* (Homewood, Ill., 1970)), appeared after material had been collected for this chapter, and references are therefore to the Russian text unless otherwise stated.

31 V. N. Yakovtsevsky, *Kupechesky kapital v feodal'no-krepostnicheskoi Rossii* (Moscow, 1953), 19.

32 Khromov, *Ekonomicheskoe razvitie* (1967), 117–18; Khromov's view seems exaggerated in the light of the assessment by H. Pirenne, *Histoire économique de l'Occident médiéval* (Bruges, 1951), 192–6, of the eighth-century urban economy in the West.

33 B. A. Rybakov, *Remeslo drevnei Rusi* (Moscow, 1948), 517–18.

34 The text of the treaty, with commentary, is in I. Sorlin, 'Les Traités de Byzance avec la Russie au Xe siècle', *Cahiers du Monde Russe et Soviétique*, II, 4 (1961), 446–75.

35 On the general Byzantine silk prohibition see Steven Runciman in *Cambridge Economic History*, II, 94.

36 Golubnichy *et al.*, *Ekonomicheskaya istoriya*, 35 (the text cited is the same in both editions).

37 The Hanseatic Peterhof described by Michael Postan in *Cambridge Economic History*, II, 225–6.

38 '*Delo*' in Russian is the equivalent of the French '*affaires*' and does not only connote private business. At the height of the movement for economic devolution in the 1960s, the Soviet weekly *Ekonomicheskaya gazeta* ran a regular feature entitled '*Delovoi klub*', promoting 'businesslike' dealings among state enterprises.

39 M. Kaser, *Soviet Economics* (London and New York, 1970), 47.

40 *Ibid.*, 47–9. On *tovarishchi* and consumption as the criterion for medieval

Russian land ownership, see R. E. F. Smith, 'Russia', in *Cambridge Economic History*, I, 2nd edn (Cambridge, 1966), 538–9 and 546–7.

41 J. Hobson, *The Evolution of Modern Capitalism* (London, 1949), 2 and 22–3, drawing particularly on the concept of *homo oeconomicus* in Hume (*Essays*, II, 57).

42 J. A. Schumpeter, *The Theory of Economic Development* (Cambridge, Mass., 1934), 84 and 89.

43 Even today something of this difference between Western and Russian entrepreneurship is epitomized in the floor-plans of Moscow's two leading department stores – now state-run but built privately within a few years of each other at the turn of this century. TsUM, founded as Muir and Mirrlees, is as typical as its original British ownership implies of the integrated Victorian emporium which was 'one of the forms of penetration of finance capital into retail trade': see *Bol'shaya sovetskaya entsiklopediya*, 2nd edn (Moscow, 1949–58), XLIV, 236 (hereafter cited as '*BSE2*'; the 1st edn (Moscow, 1926–49) and the 3rd edn (Moscow, 1970– , in progress) are cited as '*BSE1*' and '*BSE3*' respectively). GUM, on the other hand, is a congeries of over a thousand individual shops ranged in three two-storeyed arcades – the 'Upper Trading Rows' before the Revolution, reopened as a store in 1953. For a brief description of the *gostiny dvor*, see *BSE2*, XII, 281. On the associations, see below, pp. 426–8, and the major study of early merchant groups, J. Kaufmann-Rochard, *Origines d'une bourgeoisie russe, XVIe et XVIIe siècles* (Paris, 1969), 43–9.

44 The lay population was divided into 'men of service' (*sluzhilye lyudi*) and 'men of the land' (*zemskie lyudi*).

45 For a brief history of the Strogonovs, see *Entsiklopedichesky slovar'* (St Petersburg and Moscow, 1890–1907), LXII, 803–5 (hereafter cited as 'Brokgauz', from the name of its principal publisher); and on their rights as *imenitye lyudi*, see *ibid.*, XXIV, 947. The entry in *BSE1*, LIII, 45, adds that they began as salters in the early sixteenth century, but the entry in *BSE2* is less comprehensive.

46 In the Muscovite state only the two highest classes, boyars and *okol'nichie*, had the right *pisat'sya s vichem* ('to have their names written with a -*vich*'), though by the end of the seventeenth century the patronymic was already a polite form for those of higher standing: B. O. Unbegaun, *Russian Surnames* (Oxford, 1972), 12. This usage is of course now general among Russians and virtually all Soviet citizens.

47 Brokgauz, XVIII, 523.

48 Pointing to the significance of etymology, G. Wheeler, *Racial Problems in Soviet Muslim Asia* (London, 1960), observes that the Russians 'profited greatly from the *pax Mongolica* and from Mongolian government institutions' (p. 1). The present writer (*Soviet Economics*, 94) finds a heritage from Tatar taxation in the Soviet 'nonparametric' command economy.

49 Redistribution (*peredel*) principally of land but also of current supplies. The annual dividend of firewood has endowed Russian with a single word, '*perezhech*'', for 'to burn more than the household's quota of fuel'.

50 The collective '*sotnya*' (now restricted to the meaning of a unit of one hundred roubles) was originally a military company of one hundred men under a *sotnik* (centurion); the title of the individual commercial group '*sto*' is the standard term for one hundred. '*Sotnya*' was also employed as a territorial unit (cf. the English 'hundred') and for a category of Crown peasant in Galicia and Volhynia in the fourteenth to nineteenth centuries: see V. D. Grekov, *Krest'yanie na Rusi s drevneishikh vremen do XVII veka*, 2nd edn (Moscow, 1952–4), I, pp. 360–1.

51 *Sukonnoe rylo* (from '*sukno*', 'cloth') was not restricted to drapers, though that was its origin. Bibliographies on the various hundreds are annexed to the relevant entries in the *Encyclopedia*: *Gost*, *BSE2*, XII, 282, and *BSE3*, VII, 150; *Sotni*, *BSE2*, XL, 133; *Surozhane*, *BSE2*, XLI, 312 (and L, 134).

52 Because of its Crimean members from Surozh (now Sudak) and Kafa (Feodosiya); see Golubnichy *et al.*, *Ekonomicheskaya istoriya*, 2nd edn, 49–50.

53 Literally, 'traders' plough', but the plough in this context is a measure for tax division: Kaufmann-Rochard, *Origines*, 76–8.

54 On measures to regain migrant *posadskie*, see *ibid.*, 71; they reached self-defeating proportions in an *ukaz* of 1658 which imposed capital punishment on such fugitives: A. Leroy-Beaulieu, *L'Empire des tsars et les russes*, 3 vols. (Paris, 1881–9), I, p. 294.

55 Although compulsory migration might be imposed in the interests of the ruler: that from Novgorod after its annexation to towns within the Muscovite state (*ibid.*, 71–2) was the largest but may have been dictated by the political need to diminish the status of the 'trade side' of the city (*torgovaya storona*) in relation to the 'cathedral side' (*sofiyskaya storona*); on their rivalry, see J. Fennell, *The Emergence of Moscow, 1304–1369* (London, 1968), 249.

56 Although the standard dictionary translation of '*tsekh*' in its historical usage is 'guild' or 'corporation', the essential pettiness of the grouping may be seen through its derivative '*tsekhovshchina*', 'narrow professionalism'.

57 The Moscow *Serebryany ryad* (Silversmiths' Row) was a monopolist in the city and even, partially, in the Kremlin, and it had its hallmark for quality control (Kaufmann-Rochard, *Origines*, 78). There were some 100 specialized *ryady* in Moscow by the late seventeenth century, and a dozen in most other towns (Golubnichy *et al.*, *Ekonomicheskaya istoriya* (1967), 75).

58 The *posad* itself was originally outside the city wall and corresponds precisely to the medieval *forisburgus* or *faubourg* (see Pirenne, *Histoire économique*, 194).

59 'Free' or 'privileged' (*svobodny*, 'free'); see A. Eck, *Le Moyen Age russe* (Paris, 1933), 568.

60 The armourers of Tula, for example, from whom came the Demidovs, the ironmasters of the Urals; see Kaufmann-Rochard, *Origines*, 79, and below.

61 See M. Dobb, *Studies in the Development of Capitalism* (London, 1946), 96–7.

62 See the sources cited in *BSE2*, XLVI, 586; '*tsekh*' was used after 1722 for the unit of the abortive guild movement introduced by Paul I (1799), and in the capitalist and Soviet period for the lowest level of intra-factory administration (translatable as 'shop'). Khromov, *Ekonomicheskoe razvitie* (1967), 131, emphasizes the spontaneous establishment of *tsekhi* in Russia before the Mongol invasion, but he finds the guild form more common in the peripheral areas (Poland, Transcaucasus, Central Asia, and Western Russia).

63 V. I. Sergeevich, *Russkaya yuridicheskaya drevnost'*, 1 (St Petersburg, 1890).

64 Tugan-Baranovsky, *Russkaya fabrika*, 11.

65 W. Treue, *Wirtschaftsgeschichte der Neuzeit, 1700–1760* (Stuttgart, 1962), 262, comments that the lack of development after the adoption of Magdeburg City Rights by some Russian cities disproved the old German saying that 'the city air makes one free'.

66 *BSE2*, XXXIX, 232, citing V. E. Syroechkovsky, *Gosti-surozhane* (Moscow and Leningrad, 1935).

67 In their 1st edition, Golubnichy *et al.* ventured on an exact estimate – thirty merchants to the average group of *gosti* and 158 to a *gostinaya sotnya* (*Ekonomicheskaya istoriya*, 1st edn, 74–5); in their 2nd edition, the former is suggested as fifteen to thirty merchants, with the *gostinaya* and *sukonnaya sotni* having 100 to 150 (2nd edn, 76). The numbers in a *skladnichestvo* 'did not exceed four' (*BSE2*, XXXIX, 232).

68 H. Storch, *Historisch-statistisches Gemälde des russischen Reiches am Ende des achtzehnten Jahrhunderts*, 8 vols. (Riga, 1797–1803), III, 178. The 'merchants' to which he refers are the *skupshchiki*, defined (by Kaufmann-Rochard, *Origines*, 278) primarily

as such price-setters but also 'as suppliers of raw materials, and thus as entrepreneurs of the putting-out system'. The term also covers any wholesaler but is to be distinguished from *zakazchik*, a client for a bespoke order. The translation and full bibliographical source for Storch and for Korsak and Kostomarov (below) are from the Levin edition of Tugan-Baranovsky, *Russkaya fabrika*; like so many of his contemporaries, as much in Russia as in England (cf. Yurovsky or Pigou), Tugan-Baranovsky seldom gave full references.

69 His authorities are A. K. Korsak, *O formakh promyshlennosti voobshche i o znachenii domashnego proizvodstva v zapadnoi Evrope i Rossii* (Moscow, 1861), and N. I. Kostomarov, *Ocherki torgovli Moskovskogo gosudarstva v XVI i XVII stoletiyakh* (St Petersburg, 1862).

70 *BSE2*, xxix, 594; for a bibliography see *ibid.*, xlix, 643, which, however, ignores the work of P. A. Ostroukhov, doubtless because he emigrated to Prague; also Kaufmann-Rochard, *Origines*, 48–9.

71 *Ibid.*, 254.

72 Some of its trade concessions, derived from Ivan the Terrible in 1554, had been withdrawn in 1570, and the opposition of Russian merchants had prevented their full restitution. Among political events conducing to the expulsion of 1649 were the Company's own involvement in the Polono-Swedish conspiracy of 1612 and the regicide of 1649 in England (see below, p. 448).

73 Yakovtsevsky, *Kupechesky kapital*, 19, believes that the gradual displacement of *corvée* by quit-rent did not affect the gentry's attitude, but Khromov follows Lenin more closely (*Sochenenie*, 4th edn (Moscow, 1941–67, English transl. 1960–70), I, 496) in stating that the landlords' profit increased with the transfer to quit-rent. The latter, particularly when paid by a household (as *tyaglo*) rather than by the commune, increased the volume of artefacts against farm produce, as also did the growth of seasonal non-farm activity (*otkhozhye*); these, as O. Shimkin shows ('The Entrepreneur in Tsarist and Soviet Russia', *Explorations in Entrepreneurial History*, II (1949), 24–34), prepared the way for the serf–entrepreneur.

74 Yakovtsevsky, *Kupechesky kapital*, 20.

75 J. Kulischer, 'Die kapitalistischen Unternehmer in Russland (insbesondere die Bauern als Unternehmer) in den Anfangsstadien des Kapitalismus', *Archiv für Sozialwissenschaft und Sozialpolitik*, lxv (1931), 309–55, thus considers that the founder of the Romanov dynasty has a prior claim over Peter in respect of foreign industrialists.

76 Shimkin, 'The Entrepreneur', seems to be alone in believing that serf *arteli* fostered the experience necessary for entrepreneurship.

77 In rejecting the 'historical inevitability' of its abolition, A. Gerschenkron (*Cambridge Economic History*, VI, 707) points out that although free labour is more productive than that of serfs, its excess must be very large before a serf-owner finds it more profitable to hire workers than to keep manpower gratis. In the present context this can be applied to a preference to consume from such gratis suppliers (the serf *kustar'*) rather than to buy from outside. Such a trend was enforced by making a virtue of self-sufficiency, on which Kaufmann-Rochard, *Origines*, 25, cites the sixteenth-century *Domostroi* (French transl., M. E. Duchène (Paris, 1910), 93 and 98), and by the Russian's predilection for copying for himself what little he could have bought from outside (Leroy-Beaulieu, *L'Empire*, I, pp. 291–2).

78 A. Shonfield, 'Thinking about the Past' (a review of Hicks, *Theory of Economic History*), *Encounter*, October 1972, 37.

79 *Ibid.*, 38.

80 Hicks, *Theory of Economic History*, 112. See also a comparison of these ratios in England after the Black Death, in Russia at the time of the imposition of serfdom, and

in the ante-bellum South of the USA: E. Domar, 'The Causes of Slavery or Serfdom: A Hypothesis', *Journal of Economic History*, xxx (1970), 18–32.

81 L. Makkai, 'Die Hauptzüge der wirtschaftlich–sozialen Entwicklung Ungarns im 15.–17. Jahrhundert', *Studia Historica*, no. 53 (Budapest, 1953), especially 38–46.

82 Khromov, *Ekonomicheskoe razvitie*, 120; and Grekov, *Krest'yanie na Rusi*, ii, 127.

83 Lyashchenko, *History*, 1st edn, 186, and *Istoriya*, 3rd edn, 232 and 244.

84 A. I. Nikitinsky, *Istoriya ekonomicheskogo byta Velikogo Novgoroda* (Moscow, 1893), 84.

85 N. D. Rychkov, 'On Corporations in Russia and Western Europe', *Russky Vestnik*, xvii (1862); N. Stepanov, *Sravnitel'no-istorichesky ocherk organizatsii remeslennoi promyshlennosti v Rossii i zapadnoevropeiskikh gosudarstvakh* (Kiev, 1864); I. I. Dityatin, *Ustroistvo i upravlenie gorodov Rossii*, i (St Petersburg, 1875); and Korsak, *O farmakh*, iii.

86 Lyashchenko, *History*, 1st edn, 208, *Istoriya*, 3rd edn, i, p. 263; and K. A. Pazhitnov, *Problema remeslennykh tsekhov v zakonodatel'stve russkogo absolutizma* (Moscow, 1952), 169.

87 V. Leshkov, *Russky narod i gosudarstvo* (Moscow, 1958).

88 Khromov, *Ekonomicheskoe razvitie* (1967), 129–30, marshals his own conclusions and those of M. Dovnar-Zapol'sky, and T. Efimenko before the Revolution and M. Tikhomirov, K. Serbina, S. Yushkov, and B. Rybakov subsequently.

89 *Ibid.*, 131.

90 Lyashchenko, *History*, 1st edn, 99.

91 B. A. Rybakov, *Remeslo drevney Rusi*, 330.

92 Leroy-Beaulieu, *L'Empire*, i, p. 215.

93 Crisp, *Studies in the Russian Economy*, 9.

94 Leroy-Beaulieu, *L'Empire*, i, pp. 294–5.

95 *Ibid.*, 254.

96 Lyashchenko, *History*, 1st edn, 283.

97 B. B. Kafengauz, 'Some Problems of the Genesis of Capitalism in Russia', in V. V. Mavrodin (ed.), *Voprosy genezisa kapitalizma v Rossii* (Leningrad, 1960), 7–11.

98 S. G. Strumilin, *Ocherki ekonomicheskoi istorii Rossii* (Moscow, 1960), 260–313.

99 Yakovtsevsky, *Kupechesky kapital*, 182. Reference has already been made to Marx's general treatment of 'merchant's' capital; he went on (in chap. 20) to conclude that Russian merchant's capitalism had left the Asiatic mode of production untouched, but Engels remarked (in annotating the posthumous edition) that 'Russia has been making frantic exertions to develop its own capitalist production' (*Capital*, iii, 329).

100 Yakovtsevsky, *Kupechesky kapital*, a view following Lenin, *Sochenenie*, 4th edn, i, p. 461 (*The Economic Content of Narodism*), and iii, 151 (*The Development of Capitalism in Russia*).

101 The assistance of Dr Milan Hauner is gratefully acknowledged for research underlying sections III and IV.

102 W. Sombart, *Der moderne Kapitalismus*, 3 vols. (Munich, 1919), i–ii, chap. 55.

103 Whose relevance to Russian development he perceived (*ibid.*, 864).

104 M. Weber, *Wirtschaft und Gesellschaft*, 2 vols. (Tübingen, 1956), i, p. 292; *The Protestant Ethic and the Spirit of Capitalism*, transl. T. Parsons (New York, 1957), 39 and 189–90.

105 A. Gerschenkron, *Europe in the Russian Mirror* (Cambridge, 1970), 9–61; and see below, pp. 452–3.

106 Peter's model differed from Stalin's in that the latter used specific regulation (whereby each order in a command economy must be addressed to a particular recipient) in combination with an incentive, such as the bonus paid to the manager of a Soviet enterprise when a specified plan target is achieved.

107 A life of indolence made possible by unearned income, as portrayed in Goncharov's novel *Oblomov*.

108 Awareness of the inequity was a chief cause of the Pugachev rising of 1773–4; for three views, see N. Dubrovin, *Pugachev i ego soobshchniki*, 3 vols. (St Petersburg, 1884); A. Gaissinovitch, *La Révolte de Pougatchev* (Paris, 1938); and *Pugachevshchina*, 3 vols. (Moscow and Leningrad, 1926–31).

109 The reiteration of the inefficiencies arising from automatic promotion is sufficiently frequent in Solzhenitsyn's *August 1914* as to suggest that the novelist is drawing a parallel with Soviet bureaucracy.

110 The terms are the concepts of T. Burns and G. M. Stalker, *The Management of Innovation* (London, 1961), whose thought the paragraph here largely follows.

111 *From Max Weber: Essays in Sociology*, eds. H. M. Garth and C. Wright Mills (New York, 1958), 231.

112 *Ibid.*, 238.

113 B. Pares, *A History of Russia*, 5th edn (London, 1962: first published 1926), 226.

114 Treue, *Wirtschaftsgeschichte*, 265.

115 W. M. Pinter, 'The Social Characteristics of the Early Nineteenth-Century Russian Bureaucracy', *Slavic Review*, XXIX, 3 (September 1970), 443. See also D. M. Rowney, 'Study of the Russian Ministry of Internal Affairs in the Light of Organization Theory', in R. Kanet (ed.), *Behavioral Revolution and Communist Studies* (New York, 1970), and D. I. Shindzikashvili, *Ministerstvo Vnutrennikh Del tsarskoi Rossii v period imperializma – Struktura, funktsii, reaktsionaia sushchnost' i sviaz' s drugimi ministerstvami* (Omsk, 1974).

116 M. Raeff, 'Imperial Russia: Peter I to Nicholas I', in R. Auty and D. Obolensky (eds.), *Companion to Russian Studies*, I: *An Introduction to Russian History* (Cambridge, 1976), 153.

117 At Peter's death in 1725 there were 336 industrial establishments in Russia, of which 43 per cent were owned by the state (E. I. Zaorskaya, *Manufaktura pre Petre I* (Moscow, 1947), 9–10); and 223 were set up during his reign (Tugan-Baranovsky, *Russkaya fabrika*, 15).

118 *Istoriya SSSR s drevneyshikh vremen do nashikh dnei*, 12 vols., in progress (Moscow, 1966– ; hereafter cited as '*Istoriya SSSR*'), III, 196–9.

119 Grossman ('Gold and the Sword', 231–6) and the present writer (*Soviet Economics*, chaps. 4–6) mention the importance of demonetization in 'classic' Soviet planning; but E. Ames, 'Theories of Economic Planning', in W. Gumpel and D. Keese (eds.), *Probleme des Industrialismus in Ost und West* (Olten, 1973), 15–44, analyses it as run by financial articulation.

120 Pares, *History of Russia*, 229 and 240.

121 Significantly, some Soviet historians use in relation to the Institute the same word for 'verification' ('*kontrol*') which is today applied to the Ministry of State Control of the USSR (*Istoriya SSSR*, III, 230; but Khromov, *Ekonomicheskoe razvitie* (1967), 261, avoids the word).

122 *Istoriya SSSR*, III, 231–4.

123 *Ibid.*, 234.

124 *Ibid.*, 233.

125 See *BSE2*, XXX, 9; W. L. Blackwell, *The Beginnings of Russian Industrialization, 1800–1860*, I (Princeton, 1968), 150–4. The latter's description of the Department of State Economy, as 'primarily an information gathering and advisory body . . . [with] no executive power' ('p. 151), could be applied to Gosplan before 1930.

126 A State Planning Section was set up within Vesenkha in December 1917 and was transferred (as Gosplan) to the Council of Labour and Defence (STO) in February 1921; Vesenkha was liquidated in January 1932 and the STO in April 1937.

127 With an employment of 3,440, it was the largest unit in the capital's munitions and naval works, which occupied over 7,800 (Strumilin, *Ocherki*, 354–7).

128 Examples from *Istoriya SSSR*, III, 204.

129 See Treue, *Wirtschaftsgeschichte*, 260.

130 S. Ya. Borovoy, 'The State debt as source of primitive accumulation in Russia', in Mavrodin (ed.), *Voprosy genezisa kapitalizma*, 217–28.

131 See especially F. Polyansky, *Pervonachal'noe nakoplenie kapitala v Rossii* (Moscow, 1958), and A. Gerschenkron, *Economic Backwardness in Historical Perspective* (Cambridge, Mass., 1962), 99–106.

132 There were to be ten such 'revisions', the last in 1859 before the first census proper of 1897. They constitute an entrepreneurial function of the state in enumerating a saleable asset, namely serfs.

133 See Lyashchenko, *History*, 1st edn, 269; Golubnichy *et al.*, *Ekonomicheskaya istoriya*, 2nd edn, 120.

134 Khromov, *Ekonomicheskoe razvitie* (1967), 260–1.

135 O. Crisp. 'Russia, 1860–1914', in R. Cameron (ed.), *Banking in the Early Stages of Industrialization* (Oxford, 1967), 169, 186, and 189.

136 There was also a trivial volume of deposits after 1770 in the case of the Nobility Bank; see G. Garvy, 'Banking under the Tsars and under the Soviets', *Journal of Economic History*, XXII (1972), 875, and his extensive references to studies on Tsarist banking, 873–4. Small savings had been accepted from the nobility since 1722 and later from others by the *Prikazy obshestvennogo prizreniya* (Public Trustee Offices): *ibid.*, 875.

137 *Ibid.*, 876.

138 *Ibid.*

139 *Ibid.*, 874. Garvy's reference to the Soviet measure is to the credit reform of 1930, which forbade all mercantile credit outside the State Bank system; the term 'monobank' is his coinage – in his *Money, Banking and Credit in Eastern Europe* (New York, 1966) – and refers to the network of specialized state banks under the aegis of the Ministry of Finance.

140 Lyashchenko, *History*, 1st edn, 292; Tugan-Baranovsky, *Russkaya fabrika*, 16.

141 On the booms under Peter and Catherine and the intervening stagnation, see Blackwell, *Beginnings of Industrialization*, 19–22; Strumilin, *Ocherki*, 331–44 and 335–6; and R. Portal, *L'Oural au XVIIIe siècle* (Paris, 1950), 306–15.

142 Blackwell, *Beginnings of Industrialization*, 21.

143 Thus, in 1719 the Turchaninov textile mill (see below, p. 441) was given the right to employ 'the women and girls held in Moscow and the provinces undergoing punishment for their deeds' (Tugan-Baranovsky, *Russkaya fabrika*, Levin transl., 16–17).

144 Decree cited *ibid.*, 83.

145 Lyashchenko, *History*, 1st edn, 294; *Istoriya*, 2nd edn, 392.

146 *Istoriya SSSR*, III, 207.

147 Tugan-Baranovsky (*Russkaya fabrika*, 83) criticizes L. N. Nisselovich, *Istoriya zavodsko-fabrichnogo zakonodatel'stva Rossiskoi Imperii* (St Petersburg, 1883), II, 52.

148 Under Soviet planning this principle applied throughout manufacturing only to output of side-line consumer goods (the *shirpotrebfond*), although there is a further parallel in the retention of above-plan profits; moreover, the principle is the legal foundation of collective-farm procurement in the USSR.

149 It is not irrelevant that the compulsory procurement quota for Soviet collective farms was until 1976 also linked with an assured labour force because the farmer entered membership by birth into a farm household, had (as noted above, pp. 417 and 467) no internal passport which would allow him to settle in a town (a three-day

visit was the maximum stay in an urban area), needed the permission of a general assembly of households in order to resign membership, and had to perform a minimum of work (usually 150 days) on collective land or stock.

150 M. A. Gorlovsky and A. N. Pyatnitsky, *Iz istorii rabochego dvizhenia na Urale* (Sverdlovsk, 1954), 39 and 55 (cited in Blackwell, *Beginnings of Industrialization*, 158).

151 The proportions are of course reversed. S. Swianiewicz (*Forced Labour and Economic Development* (London, 1965), 39) suggests 8 per cent as the share of forced labour in Soviet employment in 1939; but this feature belongs more to the chapter in this volume devoted to labour.

152 Kulischer, 'Die kapitalistischen Unternehmer', 320; see also Blackwell, *op. cit.*, 155–63.

153 A. M. Pankratova, in *Rabochee dvizhenie v Rossii v XIX veke* (Moscow, 1955), I, part 1, p. 106 (cited in Blackwell, *op. cit.*, 159).

154 M. E. Falkus, *The Industrialisation of Russia, 1700–1914* (London, 1972), 21–2, dates the change from the second decade of the eighteenth century, noting the promotion of domestic consumer-goods production and the strongly protective tariff of 1724.

155 Pares, *History of Russia*, 263–4.

156 Tugan-Baranovsky, *Russkaya fabrika*, 17–20.

157 *Ibid.*, Lyashchenko's analysis (*History*. 1st edn, 292–3) follows his.

158 The new owners were accorded the authority to hire skilled native and foreign staff 'paying them fair wages for their labour'; on the controversy over the respective shares of free and serf labour see Gerschenkron, *Europe in the Russian Mirror*, 78.

159 See further, Tugan-Baranovsky, *Russkaya fabrika*, 19–20 and 23; Lyashchenko, *History*, 1st edn, 293.

160 Kulischer, 'Die kapitalistischen Unternehmer', 309–11.

161 Falkus, *Industrialisation of Russia*, 24.

162 Tugan-Baranovsky, *Russkaya fabrika*, 31; Kulischer, 'Die kapitalistischen Unternehmer', *passim*; Blackwell, *op. cit.*, 25–7 and 198–209; Lyashchenko, *History*, 1st edn, 215–16; N. I. Pavlenko, 'On the Question of the Evolution of the Gentry in the Seventeenth and Eighteenth Centuries', in Mavrodin (ed.), *Voprosy genezisa kapitalizma*, 54–75; and A. Kahan, 'The Costs of "Westernization" in Russia: The Gentry and the Economy in the Eighteenth Century', *Slavic Review*, XXV (1966), 55.

163 Tugan-Baranovsky, *Russkaya fabrika*, Levin transl., 25.

164 The major studies are M. Confino, *Domaines et seigneurs en Russie vers la fin du XVIIIe siècle* (Paris, 1963), and Jerome Blum, *Lord and Peasant in Russia from the Ninth to the Nineteenth Century* (Princeton, 1961).

165 Blackwell, *Beginnings of Industrialization*, 203–4, citing A. N. Nasonov, 'From the History of Manorial Serfs in the Nineteenth Century in Russia', *Izvestiya Akademii Nauk SSSR*, 1926, ser. VI, p. 504.

166 Blackwell, *op. cit.*, 202.

167 Tugan-Baranovsky, *Russkaya fabrika*, 78.

168 Among many discussions, see P. Struve, *Krepostnoye khozyaistvo* (St Petersburg, 1913), 74–112; I. V. Stepanov, 'Workers of the Volga Region in the Seventeenth Century', and I. G. Shul'ga, 'The Development of Trade in Left-Bank Ukraine in the Second Half of the Eighteenth Century', both in Mavrodin (ed.), *Voprosy genezisa kapitalizma*, 90–109 and 157–69 respectively; H. Rosovsky, 'The Serf Entrepreneur in Russia', *Explorations in Entrepreneurial History*, VI, 4 (1953–4), 210ff; G. P. G. Sinzheimer, 'Les Industries kustar': Un Châpitre de la révolution industrielle en Russie', *Cahiers du Monde Russe et Soviétique*, VIII, 2 (1967); and, briefly, Lyashchenko, *History*, 1st edn, 296.

169 Grachev had paid Sheremetev 130,000 roubles for his freedom in 1795, three

years earlier. On this and later innovations see Rosovsky, 'The Serf Entrepreneur', 219ff; Tugan-Baranovsky, *Russkaya fabrika*, 80–7.

170 Lyashchenko, *Istoriya*, 2nd edn, II, 19; Rosovsky, 'The Serf Entrepreneur'; Blackwell, *Beginnings of Industrialization*, 205–12.

171 Tugan-Baranovsky, *Russkaya fabrika*, 81; Rosovsky, 'The Serf Entrepreneur'; Blackwell, *op. cit.*, 205–12; Lyashchenko, *Istoriya*, 2nd edn, II, 442; V. T. Bill, *The Forgotten Class: The Russian Bourgeoisie to 1900* (New York, 1959), 15–35.

172 Yakovtsevsky, *Kupechesky kapital*, 19.

173 It is for this reason significant that the English were allowed to continue trade at Archangel but nowhere else. It was the country's sole seaport, with a turnover (1653) of 1·06 m. roubles, or approximately 18 m. gold roubles of 1900 purchasing power (*Istoriya SSSR*, III, 26).

174 Lyashchenko, *Istoriya*, 2nd edn, 397. *BSE3*, VI, 521, points out that *gil'diya* was first officially used by the *Kommerts-kollegia* in 1719. See also P. G. Ryndzyunsky, *Gorodskoe grazhdanstvo doreformennoi Rossii* (Moscow, 1958).

175 Blackwell (*Beginnings of Industrialization*, 104) cites the Urban Regulation of 1785 as defining the *meshchanstvo* as 'middling sort of people'.

176 *Ibid.*, 102.

177 Data for 1765 and 1849–50 respectively (Yakovtsevsky, *Kupechesky kapital*, 172).

178 A. Kopanev, *Naselenie Peterburga v pervoi polivine XIX veka* (Moscow and Leningrad, 1957), 110–13.

179 Blackwell, *Beginnings of Industrialization*, 196; '*kuplya*', for example, can only mean 'buying'.

180 *Istoriya SSSR*, IV, 52–4.

181 Blackwell, *op. cit.*, 104; see also *Istoriya SSSR*, IV, 54.

182 Falkus, *Industrialisation of Russia*, 36. Without regard for his narrow vision on economic dynamism, Pares (*History of Russia*, 369) commends 'honest' Kankrin for 'a wide administrative experience and . . . as a watchdog of the resources of the state'.

183 Cited in *BSE2*, XX, 10.

184 E. V. Spiridonova, *Ekonomicheskaya politika i ekonomicheskie vzglady Petra I* (Moscow, 1952), 63.

185 *Nakaz Ekaterina Vtoroy* (St Petersburg, 1893), 186; Pares (*History of Russia*, 283) attributes 250 of the articles in her *Instruction* to Montesquieu's *The Spirit of Law* and 100 to Beccaria's *Crimes and Punishments*.

186 Reprinted in *Yuridicheskie proizvedeniya progressivnykh russkikh mysliteley: vtoraya polovina XVIII veka*, ed. S. A. Pokrovsky (Moscow, 1959), 140.

187 The lineage of this and other propositions of Desnitsky and his fellow student Ivan Tret'yakov is traced by A. H. Brown, 'Adam Smith's First Russian Followers', in T. Wilson (ed.), *Adam Smith: Critical Essays* (Oxford, 1974). On Smith's link (relevant to the Russian case) between monopoly by privilege and price-fixing (as opposed to Ricardo's monopolistic supply-fixing) see M. Bowley, *Studies in the History of Economic Theory before 1870* (London, 1973), 158–61.

188 A. Kahan, 'Continuity in Economic Activity and Policy during the Post-Petrine Period in Russia', *Journal of Economic History*, XXV, 1 (March 1965), 82.

189 A. Kahan, 'A Proposed Mercantilist Code in the Russian Iron Industry, 1734–36', *Explorations in Entrepreneurial History*, 2nd ser., II, 2 (Winter 1965), 85.

190 N. I. Pavlenko, *Razvitie metallurgicheskoi promyshlennosti Rossii v pervoi polovine XVIII veka* (Moscow, 1953), 483, cited by Kahan, *op. cit.*

191 The proposed role of the 'charge master', employed by the plant but nominated by the state, has something in common with that of the chief accountant (*glav-*

bukhalter) of the Soviet enterprise, the only staff member under the director to be appointed by the supervising Ministry, for the very reason that his function is to supervise accounts in the interests of the state.

192 Blackwell, *Beginnings of Industrialization*, 236.

193 Little is known about the economic role of the indigenous Jews, ancient or medieval immigrants chiefly to the Caucasus and Central Asia (which were annexed to the Empire in the nineteenth century).

194 'First Guild' transactions by Jews outside the Pale were permitted only from 1859.

195 Gerschenkron, *Europe in the Russian Mirror*, 11.

196 Blackwell, *op. cit.*, 212, drawing on his article 'The Old Believers and the Rise of Private Industrial Enterprise in Early Nineteenth-Century Moscow', *Slavic Review*, XXIV (1965), 407–24. See also Bill, *The Forgotten Class*, 81–108, and *BSE1*, LII, 718–23.

197 Innovations in Russia due to Old Believers include the Jacquard loom (Rogozhin), oil-drilling in Baku (Kokorev), and the cotton machinery of the Morozovs (mentioned above, p. 446).

198 Fedor Guchkov founded a woollen mill in the Preobrazhensky Old Believer community and made it one of the largest in Russia. His descendants typify the process of assimilation: one of his great-grandsons was Mayor of Moscow and another was chairman of the Octobrist Party, President of the Third Duma, and Minister of War in the Provisional Government of 1917.

199 Gerschenkron, *Europe in the Russian Mirror*, 36.

200 See S. W. Baron, *The Russian Jew under Tsars and Soviets* (New York, 1964); Blackwell's discussion (*Beginnings of Industrialization*, 230–40) notes that Sombart, in *The Jews and Modern Capitalism* (transl. M. Epstein (New York, 1913) from *Die Juden und das Wirtschaftsleben* (Leipzig, 1911)), made no reference to those in Russia, apart from one brief mention (p. 333).

201 Sombart, *The Jews*, 176.

202 See the 'Introduction' by R. P. Bartlett to A. A. Klaus, *Nashi Kolonii: opyt i materialy po istorii i statistike inostrannoy kolonizatsi v Rossii* (St Petersburg, 1869; reprinted Cambridge, Mass., 1972); and 'Foreign Settlement in Russia under Catherine II', *New Zealand Slavonic Journal*, new ser., I, 1 (1974), 1–22. An authorized translation of Klaus (by J. Toews), with additional text, was published as *Unsere Kolonien: Studien und Materialen zur Geschichte und Statistik der ausländischen Kolonisation in Russland* (Odessa, 1887); the first study on this topic was F. Matthäi, *Die deutsche Ansiedlungen in Russland: Ihre Geschichte und ihre volkswirtschaftlicher Bedeutung für die Vergangenheit und Zukunft* (Leipzig, 1866).

203 Yakovtsevsky, *Kupechesky kapital*, 19–20.

204 S. Blanc, 'The Economic Policy of Peter the Great', in W. L. Blackwell (ed.), *Russian Economic Development from Peter the Great to Stalin* (New York, 1974), 33 (transl. from *Cahiers du Monde Russe et Soviétique*, III (1962), 122–39).

205 E.g. Golubnichy *et al.*, *Ekonomicheskaya istoriya*, in their 2nd edition omit the lengthy defence of the national nature of technology which figured in their 1st edition, pp. 100–1 (chap. 7 in the 1st edn and chap. 6 in the 2nd edn). On technology in pre-Reform Russia see A. Vucinich, *Science in Russian Culture: A History to 1860* (Stanford, Calif., 1963), V. V. Danilevsky, *Russkaya tekhnika* (2nd edn, Leningrad, 1948) and V. S. Verginsky, *Tvortsy novoi tekhniki v krepostnoy Rossii* (Moscow, 1957).

206 Blackwell, *Beginnings of Industrialization*, 29.

207 L. E. Shepelev, *Aktsionernye kompanii v Rossii* (Leningrad, 1973), 55.

208 The list had taken three years to draw up, so confused were the Ministry's records (*ibid.*, 59).

209 *Ibid.*, 63.

210 Lyashchenko, *History*, 1st edn, 334.

211 Bater, *St Petersburg*, 48.

212 Blackwell's excellent survey of these and other foreign entrepreneurs includes (*Beginnings of Industrialization*, 250) the name of Louis Gaver, which seems likely to be Geyer (see S. Kieniewicz and W. Kula (eds.), *Historia Polski* (Warsaw, 1956), II, part 2, p. 571 (chap. 83, by J. Jedlicki), although he calls him French. K. C. Thalheim, 'Die wirtschaftliche Entwicklung Russlands', in G. Katkov *et al.* (eds.), *Russlands Aufbruch ins 20. Jahrhundert* (Olten, 1970), 89–103, surveys the innovatory and capital inflows of the first half of the nineteenth century (calling Geyer a Saxon).

213 G. von Schulze-Gaevernitz, *Volkswirtschaftliche Studien aus Russland* (Leipzig, 1899), quoted in Blackwell, *Beginnings of Industrialization*, 241.

214 Strumilin, *Ocherki*, 434–6; Tugan-Baranovsky, *Russkaya fabrika*, 55–6; and Blackwell, *op. cit.*, 241–61, who draws particularly on B. Ishchanian, *Die ausländischen Elemente in der russischen Volkswirtschaft* (Berlin, 1913); and E. Amburger, *Die Anwerbung ausländischer Fachkräfte für die Wirtschaft Russlands vom 15. bis in das 19. Jahrhundert* (Wiesbaden, 1968).

215 Kieniewicz and Kula (eds.), *Historia Polski*, II, part 2, pp. 51–3 (chap. 45, by G. Missalowa); A. Jezierski, *Handel zagraniczny królestwa polskiego 1815–1914* (Warsaw, 1967), 34, 37.

216 Near enough to, but not under the control of, the Warsaw municipality; conservative elements in Cracow were opposed to industrialization (the installation of the Nowa Huta steelworks after the Second World War was a deliberate attempt to proletarianize the city).

217 Kieniewicz and Kula (eds.), *Historia Polski*, II, part 2, pp. 270–1 (chap. 61, by W. Długoborski).

218 *Ibid.*, 52.

219 An extensive bibliography on the textile industry of the period 1829–34 is given by G. Missalowa, 'Les Crises dans l'industrie textile au royaume de Pologne à l'époque de la révolution industrielle', *Studia Historiae Oeconomicae*, no. 8 (Poznan, 1973), 286–7.

220 *Ibid.*, 297–9. 'Trading capitalism' is 'merchant's capitalism' (as on p. 419 above).

221 A. V. Chayanov, *The Theory of Peasant Economy*, transl. and ed. D. Thorner, B. Kerblay, and R. E. F. Smith (Homewood, Ill., 1966), 258.

222 *Ibid.*, 257.

223 D. A. Milyutin, memorandum, 'The Danger of Continuing Military Activities in 1856' (see *Istoriya SSSR*, IV, 561–2).

224 See G. V. Rimlinger, 'The Expansion of the Labour Market in Capitalist Russia, 1861–1917', *Journal of Economic History*, XXI (1961); in his 'Autocracy and the Factory Order in Early Russian Industrialization', *Journal of Economic History*, XX (1960), especially 67–8, he draws attention to the legacy of serfdom which led workers in the period after Emancipation to appeal to governmental authority against their employers rather than going directly to the latter.

225 Golubnichy *et al.*, *Ekonomicheskaya istoriya*, 1st edn, 196; Khromov, *Ekonomicheskoe razvitie* (1967), 321.

226 *Razvitie kapitalizma v Rossii* (*Works*, 5th edn, III, 128).

227 Many of the intellectuals who deplored the economic power of the state would have preferred its replacement by a disaggregated system of peasant and handicraft enterprise; this Slavophile or populist view was of course opposed by the 'Westernizers', who desired decentralization within a capitalist market.

228 The famine – the last of the Tsarist period – had further significance in public debate on the reform of the economic system: Tolstoy's advocacy (as a populist) of

relief work was denounced by Plekhanov, heading the Marxist school of 'worse means better' – that is, peasant impoverishment promotes revolution.

229 T. K. von Laue, *Sergei Witte and the Industrialization of Russia* (New York, 1963), 192.

230 Portal, in *Cambridge Economic History*, VI, 812–19. The railways were themselves a school of entrepreneurship and even of economic government (both Vishnegradsky and Witte worked their way to the Ministry of Finance through the railways).

231 Thus M. V. Ptukha (*Ocherki po istorii statistiki v SSSR*, 2 vols. (Moscow, 1955 and 1959), II, 5) stresses the importance of the creation (1845) of an independent collector of data, the Russian Geographical Society, and in general the statistical research in universities; E. A. Mashikhin and V. M. Simchera ('The History of Statistical Yearbooks in Russia, USSR and USA', in T. V. Ryabushkin *et al.* (eds.), *Ocherki po istorii statistiki SSSR* (Moscow, 1972), 120) consider the *Statistichesky vremmenik Rossiskoi imperii* (1866) as the first proper yearbook.

232 Lyashchenko, *Istoriya*, Russian 1st edn (see note 22 above), II, 159–60; Blackwell, *Beginnings of Industrialization*, 270–311; *Istoriya SSSR*, V, 310–22.

233 *Cambridge Economic History*, VI, 803 and 813.

234 As implied in the title of a recent paper which both analyses the reforms and describes the relatively scanty previous writing on the topic: W. G. Wagner, 'Tsarist Legal Policies at the End of the Nineteenth Century: A Study in Inconsistencies', *Slavonic and East European Review*, LIV (July 1976), 371–92.

235 *Ibid.*, 393.

236 *BSE2*, IV, 194.

237 *Istoriya SSSR*, V, 144.

238 Von Laue, *Sergei Witte*, 96. There were 4·8 m. accounts by 1900 (861 m. roubles), compared with 1·1 m. in 1892 (239 m. roubles): *ibid.*, 174.

239 Shepelev, *Aktsionernye kompanii*, 99–107.

240 The Petersburg Bourse Committee had been established in 1816, and that of Moscow in 1837 (*BSE2*, III, 381).

241 G. A. Hosking, *The Russian Constitutional Experiment: Government and Duma, 1907–1914* (Cambridge, 1973), 18; and H. D. Mehlinger and J. M. Thompson, *Count Witte and the Tsarist Government in the 1905 Revolution* (Bloomington, Indiana, 1972), 314–16.

242 Collective responsibility for payment of taxes was, however, abolished entirely.

243 On the passport laws of 1894 and 1906, see *Cambridge Economic History*, VI, 754 and 787–8.

244 Cited by von Laue, *Sergei Witte*, 223. It figures in his draft programme of 1906 after the revolution of 1905 (cf. Hosking, *The Russian Constitutional Experiment*, 18).

245 Gerschenkron's translation of '*zemsky nachal'nik*' as 'land captain' (in *Cambridge Economic History*, VI) is also frequently found.

246 Von Laue, *Sergei Witte*, 174.

247 Witte's critique of the potentially conflicting instructions on the peasant was echoed sixty years later in another context when Khrushchev defended the abolition of machine-tractor stations (1958) because they and their directors and the local authorities (*raiispolkom*) were two 'bosses' – *khozyain* – over the collective farm.

248 Gerschenkron, in *Cambridge Economic History*, VI, 783.

249 *Ibid.*

250 Farmers were permitted free movement in 1946 (see p. 418 above).

251 For details, see Volin, *A Century of Russian Agriculture*, 242 and 382.

252 Lyashchenko, *Istoriya*, 2nd edn, 675.

253 *Cambridge Economic History*, VI, 851 and 849 respectively.

254 Gerschenkron, 'The Modernization of Entrepreneurship', in *Continuity in History and Other Essays*, 128–39. He has argued (in 'Criticism from Afar: A Reply', *Soviet Studies*, XXV (1973), 182–4) against Olegina's critique of the investment bank as 'substitute' (I. N. Olegina, 'Capitalist and Socialist Industrialization in the Treatment of A. Gerschenkron', *Istoriya SSSR*, no. 2 (1971), especially 188–9).

255 On the 'native' genesis and localism of the Moscow entrepreneur against the attachment to foreign approaches and investment through Russia favoured in St Petersburg, see J. D. White, 'Moscow, Petersburg and the Russian Industrialists', *Soviet Studies*, XXIV (1973), 414–15.

256 See Crisp, 'Russia, 1860–1914', chap. 7; Lyashchenko, *History*, 1st edn, 475–8; P. N. Stopyansky, *Zhizn' i byt Peterburgskoy fabriki 1704–1914* (Leningrad, 1925); I. Kh. Ozerov, *Ekonomicheskaya Rossiya i ee finansovaya politika na iskhode XIX i v nachale XX veka* (St Petersburg, 1905); and Khromov, *Ekonomicheskoe razvitie* (1950), chap. 2. *BSE2*, XXVIII, 373 states that three named Moscow banks received Ministry of Finance support, but this may well be referring to the rescue operations after the recession.

257 The calculation is by Crisp ('Russia, 1860–1914', 226), from data in P. V. Ol', *Inostrannye kapitaly v Rossii* (Petrograd, 1922), 146–255.

258 Gerschenkron, 'The Modernization of Entrepreneurship'.

259 Lyashchenko, *History*, 1st edn, 160 (and see Table 73 below).

260 J. P. McKay, *Pioneers for Profit: Foreign Entrepreneurship and Russian Industrialization, 1885–1913* (Chicago, 1970), 384.

261 *The Times* (London), 14 May 1969, 14.

262 McKay, *Pioneers*, 385.

263 *Materialy po istorii SSSR*, VI: *Dokumenty po istorii monopolisticheskogo kapitalizma v Rossii* (Moscow, 1959), 173–95 (transl. von Laue, *Journal of Modern History*, XXVI (1954), 60–75).

264 Cited by McKay, *op. cit.*, 19.

265 See *ibid.*, 30–1.

266 A. Kahan, 'Government Policies and the Industrialization of Russia', *Journal of Economic History*, XXVII (1967), 466. Khromov, *Ekonomicheskoe razvitie* (1950), 498–503, shows the small share of public outlay on railway-building.

267 *Pioneers*, 8.

268 The Post Office made systematic losses.

269 *Pioneers*, 380–3.

270 Cf. the variety of other uses to which the Russian generation of proprietors put their profits (pp. 463 and 470, above).

271 Pares, *History of Russia*, 466.

272 In addition to the extensive involvement of German and other West European firms in Silesian mining and metals there was French, German, Italian, and Austrian capital in Galician oil, French and Belgian in textiles and German, Swiss and Belgian in electricity and tramways (I. Ihnatowicz, in B. Zientara, A. Maczak, I. Ihnatowicz, and Z. Landau, *Dzieje gospodarcze Polski do 1939 g.* (Warsaw, 1965), 450).

273 Z. Landau and J. Tomaszewski, *Bank Handlowy w Warszawie S.A.: Historia i rozwój, 1870–1970* (Warsaw, 1970), 33.

274 *Ibid.*, 37.

275 Hosking, *The Russian Constitutional Experiment*, 160–244.

276 There are many recent Polish studies of this period: W. Rusiński, *Rozwój gospodarczy ziem polskich* (Warsaw, 1963), 238–346; B. Bajer, *Przemysł włókienniczy na ziemiach polskich od początku XIX wieku do 1939 roku* (Łódź, 1958); *Ekonomika górnictwa i hutnictwa w królestwie polskim 1840–1910*, ed. W. Kula, 2 vols. (Warsaw, 1959 and 1961); L. Łukasiewicz, *Przewrót techniczny w przemyśle królestwa polskiego 1857–1886*

(Warsaw, 1963); I. Ihnatowicz, *Przemysł Łódski w latach 1860–1900* (Wrocław, 1965), 76–87; I. Pietrzak-Pawłowski, *Królestwo polskie w początkach imperializmu 1900–1905* (Warsaw, 1955), 186–212; and I. Kostrowicka, Z. Landau and J. Tomaszewski, *Historia gospodarcza Polski XIX i XX wieku* (Warsaw, 1966), part 3.

277 See, among many works, Baron, *The Russian Jew*; S. M. Dubnow, *History of the Jews in Russia and Poland*, 2 vols. (Philadelphia, 1916 and 1920); Yu. Gessen, *Istoriya yevreiskogo naroda v Rossii*, 2 vols. (Leningrad, 1925 and 1927); and L. Greenberg, *The Jews in Russia*, 2 vols. (New Haven, Conn., 1944 and 1951).

278 B. A. Romanov, *Rossia v Mandzhurii* (Moscow, 1955), 273, cited by von Laue (*Sergei Witte*, 245).

279 See von Laue, *op. cit.*, 181–7.

280 S. Galai, *The Liberation Movement in Russia, 1900–1905* (Cambridge, 1973), 182–4, who also cites the numerous other analyses of *Zubatovshchina*.

281 V. S. Ziv, *Inostrannye kapitaly v russkikh aksioniernykh predpriyatiyakh*, 1: *Germanskie kapitaly* (Petrograd, 1915), 1–9.

282 *Inostrannye kapitaly v Rossii* and *Inostrannye kapitaly v narodnom khozyaistve*.

283 Ziv, *Inostrannye kapitaly*, 36–57. There have recently been Soviet and East German re-examinations of the weight of German economic influence: B. V. Ananich *Rossiya i mezhdunarodny kapital 1897–1914: ocherki istorii finansovykh otnoshenii* (Leningrad, 1970); J. Mai, *Das deutsche Kapital in Russland, 1850–1894* (East Berlin, 1970). Other East German studies which touch on the question are by J. Nötzold, 'Agrarian Questions and Industrialization in Russia on the Eve of the First World War', *Saeculum*, XVII (1966), 170–92; and Nötzold, *Wirtschaftspolitische Alternativen der Entwicklung Russlands in der Äre Witte und Stolypin* (East Berlin, 1966).

284 M. Miller, *The Economic Development of Russia, 1905–1914* (London, 1926; 2nd edn, 1967), 121; she cites Keynes's article in the *Manchester Guardian Commercial Supplement: Reconstruction of Europe*, no. 4 (27 July 1922), which is not reproduced in the extracts from that *Supplement*, no. 5, in *The Collected Writings of J. M. Keynes*, IX (London, 1972), 59–75; but the figure is given as £766 m. for Russian indebtedness to other Allies in *The Economic Consequences of the Peace* (*ibid.*, 22).

285 Some eight thousand Danes emigrated to Russia in the second half of the nineteenth century, but only 1,478 declared themselves to be Danes at the 1897 census. S. Å. Christensen, L. P. Poulsen-Hansen, B. Renne, and M. Tangaard, *Den dansk emigration til Russland 1875–1914* (Copenhagen, 1970).

286 J. N. Westwood, 'John Hughes and Russian Metallurgy', *Economic History Review*, 2nd ser., XVII, 3 (1965), 569.

287 Introduced in four provinces in 1894 and in the remainder by 1914. On these cartels, see Miller, *op. cit.*, 237–40.

288 R. Hare, *Portraits of Russian Personalities between Reform and Revolution* (London, 1959), 306.

289 See von Laue, *Sergei Witte*, 93–4 and 182.

290 *Ibid.*, 677.

291 A. Nove, 'Internal Economies', *Economic Journal*, LXX, 280 (December 1960), 852.

292 Lenin, *Works*, 4th edn, English transl. (Moscow, 1961), VI, 21 and 54 respectively.

293 See Z. Pustula, *Początki kapitału monopolistycznego w przemyśle hutniczo-metalowym królestwa polskiego 1882–1900* (Warsaw, 1968); and, more generally, Kula (ed.), *Ekonomike górnictwa*.

294 The cartelization of industry and the transition from 'industrial' to 'finance' capitalism has occupied the attention of many Russian economic historians, notably E. L. Granovsky, *Monopolistichesky kapitalizm v Rossii* (Leningrad, 1929); A. Finn-

Enatoevsky, *Sovremennoe khozyaistvo Rossii* (St Petersburg, 1911); Ya. I. Livshin, *Monopolii v ekonomike Rossii* (Moscow, 1961); G. Tsyperovich, *Sindikaty i tresty v Rossii*, 1st edn (Petrograd, 1918); N. Vanag, *Finansovy kapital v Rossii* (Moscow, 1925); N. Vanag and S. Tomsinsky, *Ekonomicheskoe razvitie Rossii*, I: *Epokha promyshlennogo kapitalizma*, and II: *Epokha finansogo kapitalizma* (Moscow and Leningrad, 1928 and 1930); and S. S. Zak, *Promyshlenny kapitalizm v Rossii* (Moscow, 1908). There is a history of Prodamet, A. L. Tsukernik, *Sindikat 'Prodamet': istoriko-ekonomichesky ocherk 1902–1914 g.* (Moscow, 1959), and numerous factory histories which throw light on their relations with the central sales agency. Lyashchenko, *History*, 1st edn, 677–85, has a summary survey.

295 V. Ya. Lavrichev, 'The All-Russian Union of Trade and Industry', *Istoricheskie zapiski*, LXX (1961), 38, cited in White, 'Moscow, Petersburg and the Russian Industrialists', 416.

296 As claimed by White, *ibid.*, but countered by R. A. Roosa, 'United Russian Industry', *Soviet Studies*, XXIV (1973), 423–4.

297 *Ibid.*, 422–3.

298 Gerschenkron, 'The Modernization of Entrepreneurship', in *Continuity in History*, 128–39.

299 Cited by S. O. Zagorsky, *State Control of Industry in Russia during the War* (New Haven, Conn., 1928), 84.

300 *Ibid.*, 182.

301 Roosa, 'United Russian Industry', 425.

302 Zagorsky, *State Control*, 90.

303 *Ibid.*, 93.

304 *Ibid.*, 98; and White, 'Moscow, Petersburg and the Russian Industrialists', 439.

305 See A. L. Siderov, *Ekonomicheskoe polozhenie Rossii v gody pervoi mirovoi voiny* (Moscow, 1973); and research by L. Siegelbaum, as yet unpublished (except as a review of Siderov's book in *Soviet Studies*, XXVII, 2 (1975), 309–11).

306 For details, see Zagorsky, *State Control*, 125, 152, 156, and 209, and Appendixes.

307 *Ibid.*, 183–9.

308 E. H. Carr, *The Bolshevik Revolution, 1917–1923*, II: *The Economic Order* (London, 1952), 81.

309 Individual expropriations continued until the very eve of the July nationalization, the last being the Guzhon Metallurgical Works in Moscow (renamed 'Hammer and Sickle' in 1922).

310 A. V. Venediktov, *Organizatsiya gosudarstvennoi promyshlennosti v SSSR*, 2 vols. (Leningrad, 1957 and 1961), I, pp. 25 and 40.

311 Tsyperovich, *Sindikaty i tresty*, 3rd edn (Petrograd, 1920), 187.

312 *Ibid.*, 6–7. The first edition of 1918 (subtitled *Popularny ocherk*, 'A Popular Outline') had been strictly historical and did not reproduce the resolution cited above.

313 Tsukernik, *Sindikat 'Prodamet'*, 9.

314 Carr, *The Economic Order*, 81 and 84.

315 *Ibid.*

316 *Ibid.*, 394.

317 Proceedings of the Second All-Russian Congress of Soviets, cited *ibid.*, 395.

318 I. A. Gladkov, *Ocherki stroitel'stva sovietskogo planovogo khozyaistva v 1917–1918 gg.* (Moscow, 1950), 94.

319 Carr, *The Economic Order*, 77.

320 'Urgent Tasks of Soviet Power' (*Pravda*, 28 April 1918), in *Sochinenie*, 5th (Russian) edn, XXXVI, 185.

321 I. A. Gladkov (ed.), *Natsionalizatsiya promyshlennosti v SSSR, sbornik dokumentov i materialov 1917–1920 gg.* (Moscow, 1954), 15. Gladkov uses exactly the same

words in his *Ocherki sovietskoi ekonomiki 1917–1920 gg.* (Moscow, 1956), 67, except that the last phrase is 'the Leninist platform for the socialist transformation of Russia'.

322 I. A. Gladkov, *Voprosy planirovaniya sovietskogo khozyaistva v 1918–1920 gg.* (Moscow, 1951), 8.

323 Venediktov, *Organizatsiya*, I, pp. 182–6; M. Dobb, *Soviet Economic Development since 1917*, 4th edn (London, 1957), 88–96. V. V. Kabanov, 'State Capitalism in 1918–19', in M. P. Kim (ed.), *Novaya ekonomicheskaya politika* (Moscow, 1974), 89–90, notes that Soviet economic historians used to identify state capitalism with NEP, but argues that a transitional form emerged in 1918. *Istoriya sotsialisticheskoi ekonomiki SSSR*, 6 vols. (Moscow, 1976– ; in progress), I, p. 44, considers that the nationalization 'was combined with the Lenin plan for a broad use of state capitalism'.

324 Dobb, *Soviet Economic Development*, 94; Carr, *The Economic Order*, chap. 16.

325 *Works*, 4th edn, xxvii (Moscow, 1965), 325–54 (the original appeared in *Pravda*, 9–11 May 1918).

326 Quoted in Dobb, *Soviet Economic Development*, 93.

327 See especially Cz. Bobrowski, *Formation du système soviétique de planification* (Paris, 1956), 18–20.

328 A. Nove, *An Economic History of the USSR* (London, 1969), 52; F. Samokhvalov, *Sovety narodnogo khozyaistva v 1917–32 gg.* (Moscow, 1964), 27.

329 Lenin, *Works*, 4th edn, xxvii, 335–6.

330 *Ibid.*, 318; and M. Dobb, 'The Discussions of the 1920s about Building Socialism', *Annali dell'Instituto G. Feltrinelli*, 1967 (Milan, 1967), 136–7.

331 *Istoriya SSSR*, vii, 305. Among numerous shorter accounts of the 'coming of nationalization', see A. Baykov, *The Development of the Soviet Economic System* (Cambridge, 1946), chap. 1; Portal, in *Cambridge Economic History*, vi, 868; Golubnychy *et al.*, *Ekonomicheskaya istoriya*, 2nd edn, chap. 15; V. T. Chuntunov, *Ekonomicheskaya istoriya SSSR* (Moscow, 1969), chap. 4; and the entry 'Nationalization' in *BSE2*, xxix, 283–5.

332 Nearly two-thirds of the enterprises then taken over were producers of capital or intermediate goods (Venediktov, *Organizatsiya*, I, 229).

333 The qualification ('*tsenz*') for statistical report as 'large' was thirty employed, or sixteen if motive power was used; this group was known as '*tsensovaya promyshlennost*', often loosely translated as 'census industry'. W. Nutter, *The Growth of Industrial Production in the Soviet Union* (Princeton, 1962), 187–91, notes that in 1928–9 private workshops (i.e. those with fewer than three employees if power were used) then accounted for 75 per cent of employment in small-scale industry as defined for statistical returns.

334 A. Kaufman, *Small-Scale Industry in the Soviet Union* (New York, 1962), 19.

335 The distinction between the two groups and a description of each is in Sinzheimer, 'Les Industries kustar'', 205–22.

336 See D. J. Male, *Russian Peasant Organisation before Collectivisation* (Cambridge, 1971), chaps. 2 and 3.

337 For detailed rules see Baykov, *Development of the Soviet Economic System*, 105–6; and on finance, see A. Z. Arnold, *Banks, Credit and Money in Soviet Russia* (New York, 1937), 99–110.

338 *Ibid.*, 107.

339 Akademiya nauk SSSR, Institut ekonomiki, *Sovietskoe narodnoe khozyaistvo v 1921–1925 gg.* (Moscow, 1960), 514. The series, of which five volumes have appeared, is under the general editorship of Gladkov.

340 Documentation in Soviet sources is especially deficient: the main calendar of economic events, *Ekonomicheskaya zhizn' SSSR: khronika sobytii i faktov 1917–1965*, I: *1917–50*, 2nd edn (Moscow, 1967), 115, mentions only the first decree, but neither

this nor any later measure figures in *Direktivy KPSS i sovetskogo pravitel'stva po khozyaistvennym voprosam*, I: *1917–1928* (Moscow, 1957) or *Istoriya industrializatsii SSSR 1926–1941 gg.: dokumenty i materialy*, I: *1926–1928* (Moscow, 1969). The list of contemporary acronyms for economic bodies in the latter (pp. 520–2) omits Glavkontsesskom.

341 A. C. Sutton, *Western Technology and Soviet Economic Development, 1917–1930* (Stanford, Calif., 1968); the present writer commented on Sutton's methods of quantification in a review in *Journal of Development Studies*, VII (1971), 159–61.

342 Sutton, *op. cit.*, 8–9.

343 As president of the Occidental Petroleum Corporation of Los Angeles, Hammer undertook in May 1973 to arrange contracts for the production of ammonia and urea from Siberian natural gas.

344 Sutton, *op. cit.*, 8–9

345 Baykov, *Development of the Soviet Economic System*, 126–7.

346 E. H. Carr and R. W. Davies, *Foundations of a Planned Economy, 1926–1929*, I (London, 1969), 778.

347 *Ibid.*, 950. The peak for foreign capital was 1926 when the foreign share of equity in mixed companies was 5·9 m. roubles as against a Soviet participation of 8·0 m. (*ibid.*, 717).

348 The practice may be compared to the 'lump' (self-employed subcontractors in the building industry of the UK during the sixties, which the Finance Act of 1971 was intended to eliminate).

349 *Ibid.*, 392.

350 *Ibid.*, 395.

351 *Works*, 4th edn, XXVII, 154.

352 Among many explanations of Lenin's concept of 'democratic centralism' in this context, see Gladkov, 'The Planned Development of the Soviet Economy', in L. M. Gatovsky *et al.* (eds.), *Sovietskaya sotsialisticheskaya ekonomika 1917–1957* (Moscow, 1957), 44–5.

353 Venediktov, *Organizatsiya*, I, p. 500.

354 Glavtop for fuel, Glavzemkhoz for state farms, and Glavkustprom for handicrafts (*ibid.*, 501–3).

355 Which had just been converted into an autonomous *tsentr* and thus became the forerunner of today's Gossnab.

356 Lyashchenko, *Istoriya*, 2nd edn, III, 153.

357 Venediktov, *Organizatsiya*, II, 28 and 83–9.

358 *Ibid.*, 55–6.

359 The Kramatorsk Engineering and Metallurgical Works, set under Donugol' in 1922, was declared 'autonomous' in December 1924 and was freed wholly of any subordination to Donugol' in October 1925, being put directly under Glavmetal (*ibid.*, II, 73).

360 Carr and Davies, *Foundations of a Planned Economy*, I, 384.

361 It might be observed that the editor of a recent symposium, S. Holland (*The State as Entrepreneur* (London, 1972), 34–9), stresses the market environment in seeing the modern public sector as reinforcing competition in a substantial and parallel private sector.

362 See, for example, the statements of Zinoviev and Trotsky cited in Carr, *The Economic Order*, 262–3 and 381–3.

363 The arguments are cogently presented by P. C. Roberts, *Alienation and the Soviet Economy* (Albuquerque, New Mexico, 1971).

364 Autonomous finance was not to be extended to the *glavk* level until the latter were converted to *ob"edinenie* in 1973.

365 Among many studies of the introduction of *khozrashet* see Akademiya nauk SSSR, Institut ekonomiki, *Postroenie fundamenta sotsialisticheskoi ekonomiki v SSSR 1926–1932 gg.* (Moscow, 1960), chap. 7; S. Mawrizki, *L'Industrie lourde en Union Soviétique: Système de direction et de planification* (Geneva and Paris, 1961), chaps. 1–4; and E. Verre, *L'Entreprise industrielle en Union Soviétique* (Paris, 1965), chap. 1.

366 See M. Kaser, 'Soviet Planning and the Price Mechanism', *Economic Journal*, LX (1950), 81–91.

367 N. K. von Meck, cited in N. Jasny, *Soviet Economists of the Twenties* (Cambridge, 1972), 32.

368 *Istoriya SSSR*, VIII, 414; that chapter is the official historians' record of 'The Exclusion of Private Capital from Industry and Trade' (pp. 414–24).

369 See Resolution of the Sixth Congress of Soviets, 12 March 1931, cited by Jasny, *op. cit.*, 38.

370 Gerschenkron, 'Industrial Enterprise in Soviet Russia', in S. Mason (ed.), *The Corporation in Modern Society* (Cambridge, Mass., 1960), reprinted in *Economic Backwardness in Historical Perspective*, 288–9.

371 M. McAuley, in a review of H. H. Höhmann, M. C. Kaser, and K. C. Thalheim (eds.), *The New Economic Systems of Eastern Europe* (London and Berkeley, Calif., 1975), in *Economic Journal*, LXXXVI, 343 (September 1976), 653–4.

Bibliographies

EDITORS' NOTE

In accordance with the established practice of the Cambridge series of histories, the bibliographies printed below are selective and incomplete. Their purpose is not to list all the publications bearing directly or indirectly on the subject, but to enable the readers to study some of the topics in greater detail. As a rule, books and articles superseded by later publications have not been included, and references to general treatises indirectly relevant to the subject-matter of individual chapters have been reduced to the minimum. As most of the chapters are not new pieces of research, but summaries and interpretations of knowledge already available in secondary literature, references to original sources have either been left out altogether or have been confined to the principal and most essential classes of evidence.

Within the limits set by those general principles, the individual contributors were given the freedom of composing and arranging bibliographies as they thought best. The 'layout' of the bibliographical lists, therefore, varies from chapter to chapter.

CHAPTER I

Capital Formation in the United States during the Nineteenth Century

ABRAMOVITZ, M., and P. DAVID. 'Economic Growth in America: Historical Realities and Neoclassical Parables', *De Economist*, CXXI, 3 (1973).

ALLEN, FREDERICK LEWIS. *The Great Pierpont Morgan*. New York, 1949.

ANDREANO, RALPH (ed.). *The Economic Impact of the American Civil War*. rev. edn. Cambridge, Mass., 1967.

BENNETT, F. P., JR. *The Story of Mutual Savings Banks*. Boston, 1924.

BIGELOW, E. B. *The Tariff Question Considered in Regard to the Policy of England and the Interests of the United States*. Boston, 1862.

BOGUE, A. *Money at Interest*. Ithaca, N.Y., 1955.

BRADY, DOROTHY S. 'Price Deflators for Final Product Estimates', in Brady (ed.), *Output, Employment, and Productivity*.

BRADY, DOROTHY S. (ed.). *Output, Employment, and Productivity in the United States after 1800*. Studies in Income and Wealth, 30. New York, 1966.

BRENNER, Y. S. *Theories of Economic Development and Growth*. London, 1966.

BROWN, MURRAY (ed.). *The Theory and Empirical Analysis of Production*. Studies in Income and Wealth, 31. New York, 1967.

BUCK, S. J. *The Granger Movement*. Cambridge, Mass., 1913.

BULEY, R. *The Equitable Life Assurance Society of the United States, 1859–1964*. New York, 1967.

BURMEISTER, E., and S. J. TURNOVSKY. 'Capital Deepening Response in an Economy with Heterogeneous Capital Goods', *American Economic Review*, LXII, 5 (December 1972).

CAROSSO, VINCENT P. *Investment Banking in America: A History*. Cambridge, Mass., 1970.

CHANDLER, A. D., JR (ed.). *The Railroads: The Nation's First Big Business*. New York, 1965.

CLEVELAND, F. A., and F. W. POWELL. *Railroad Finance*. New York, 1912 (reprinted in Chandler (ed.), *The Railroads*).

CONFERENCE ON RESEARCH IN INCOME AND WEALTH. *Output, Input, and Productivity Measurement*. Studies in Income and Wealth, 25. Princeton, 1961.

COREY, LEWIS. *The House of Morgan*. New York, 1930.

CREAMER, D., SERGEI P. DOBROVOLSKY, and ISRAEL BORENSTEIN. *Capital in Manufacturing and Mining*. Princeton, 1960.

DAVID, PAUL A. 'The Growth of Real Product in the United States before 1840: New Evidence and Controlled Conjectures', *Journal of Economic History*, XXVII, 2 (June 1967).

DAVIS, LANCE E. 'United States Financial Intermediaries in the Early Nineteenth Century'. Unpublished Ph.D. dissertation, The Johns Hopkins University, 1956.

—— 'Sources of Industrial Finance: The American Textile Industry – A Case Study', *Explorations in Entrepreneurial History*, IX, 4 (April 1957).

—— 'Stock Ownership in the Early New England Textile Industry', *Business History Review*, XXXII, 2 (Summer 1958).

—— 'The Investment Market, 1870–1914: The Evolution of a National Market', *Journal of Economic History*, XXV, 3 (September 1965).

DAVIS, LANCE E., and R. E. GALLMAN. 'The Share of Savings and Investment in Gross National Product during the 19th Century, United States of America', in F. C. Lane (ed.), *Fourth International Conference of Economic History* (Bloomington, Indiana, 1968). Paris, 1973.

DAVIS, LANCE E., and D. NORTH. *Institutional Change and American Economic Growth*. Cambridge, 1971.

DAVIS, LANCE E., and P. L. PAYNE. 'From Benevolence to Business: The Story of Two Savings Banks', *Business History Review*, XXXII, 4 (Winter 1958).

DAVIS, LANCE E., RICHARD A. EASTERLIN, WILLIAM N. PARKER, et al. *American Economic Growth: An Economist's History of the United States*. New York, 1972.

DE CANIO, STEPHEN J., and JOEL MOKYR. 'Inflation and the Wage Lag during the American Civil War.' Yale University Department of Economics Discussion Paper no. 32, October 1975 (mimeographed).

DENISON, E. F. *The Sources of Economic Growth in the United States.* New York, 1962.

DEWEY, DAVIS R. *Financial History of the United States.* New York, 1915.

DURAND, E. D. *The Finances of New York City.* New York, 1898.

EASTERLIN, R. A. 'Interregional Differences in Per Capita Income, Population and Total Income, 1840–1950', in Parker (ed.), *Trends in the American Economy.*

EDWARDS, G. *The Evolution of Finance Capitalism.* London and New York, 1938.

ELLET, C. *An Essay on the Laws of Trade in Reference to the Works of Internal Improvement in the United States.* Richmond, Virginia, 1839.

ENGERMAN, STANLEY. 'The Economic Impact of the Civil War', *Explorations in Entrepreneurial History*, 2nd ser., III, 3 (Spring/Summer 1966), reprinted in Andreano (ed.), *Economic Impact of the American Civil War.*

EVANS, G. HEBERTON. *Business Incorporations in the United States, 1800–1943.* New York, 1948.

FISHLOW, ALBERT. *American Railroads and the Transformation of the Ante-bellum Economy.* Cambridge, Mass., 1965.

—— 'Levels of Nineteenth-Century American Investment in Education', *Journal of Economic History*, XXVI, 4 (December 1966).

FOGEL, ROBERT W. *The Union Pacific Railroad: A Case of Premature Enterprise.* Baltimore, Md, 1960.

FREDERIKSON, D. M. 'Mortgage Banking in America', *Journal of Political Economy*, II (1894).

FRIEDMAN, MILTON, and ANNA SCHWARTZ. *A Monetary History of the United States, 1867–1960.* Princeton, 1963.

FUCHS, V. R. (ed.). *Production and Productivity in the Service Industries.* Studies in Income and Wealth, 34. New York, 1969.

GALLMAN, ROBERT E. 'Commodity Output, 1839–1899', in Parker (ed.), *Trends in the American Economy.*

—— 'Gross National Product in the United States, 1834–1909', in Brady (ed.), *Output, Employment, and Productivity.*

—— 'Trends in the Size Distribution of Wealth in the Nineteenth Century: Some Speculations', in Soltow (ed.), *Six Papers.*

—— 'The Statistical Approach: Fundamental Concepts as Applied to History', in Taylor and Ellsworth (eds.), *Approaches to American Economic History.*

—— 'Changes in Total U.S. Agricultural Factor Productivity in the Nineteenth Century', *Agricultural History*, XLVI, 1 (January 1972).

—— 'The Agricultural Sector and the Pace of Economic Growth: U.S. Experience in the Nineteenth Century', in Klingaman and Vedder (eds.), *Essays in Nineteenth Century Economic History.*

GALLMAN, ROBERT E., and EDWARD S. HOWLE. 'Fixed Reproducible Capital in the United States, 1840–1900'. Unpublished paper presented to Seminar on the Application of Economic Theory and Quantitative Methods to Problems of Economic History, Purdue University, February 1965 (mimeographed).

GALLMAN, ROBERT E., and THOMAS J. WEISS. 'The Service Industries in the 19th Century', in Fuchs (ed.), *Production and Productivity.*

GATES, P. W. *The Illinois Central Railroad and Its Colonization Work.* Cambridge, Mass., 1934.

GOLDSMITH, RAYMOND W. 'The Growth of Reproducible Wealth of the United States of America from 1805 to 1950', in Kuznets (ed.), *Income and Wealth of the United States.*

—— *A Study of Savings in the United States.* 3 vols. Princeton, 1955.

GOODRICH, C. *Government Promotion of American Canals and Railroads, 1800–1890.* New York, 1960.

GREEF, ALBERT O. *The Commercial Paper House in the United States.* Cambridge, Mass., 1938.

GREEN, G. *Finance and Economic Development in the Old South: Louisiana Banking, 1804–1865*. Palo Alto, Calif., 1972.

GRILICHES, ZVI. 'Research Cost and Social Returns: Hybrid Corn and Related Innovations', *Journal of Political Economy*, LXVI, 5 (October 1958).

HAMMOND, BRAY. *Banks and Politics in America from the Revolution to the Civil War*. Princeton, 1957.

HIBBARD, B. H. *A History of the Public Land Policies*. Madison, Wisconsin, 1965.

HICKS, J. D. *The Populist Revolt*. Minneapolis, Minn., 1931.

HOLMES, G. K., and J. S. LORD. 'Report on Real Estate Mortgages in the United States'. US Census Office, issued as Final Census Report, vol. XII, the 11th Census. Washington, [1890].

HOLT, C. F. 'The Role of State Government in the Nineteenth Century American Economy, 1820–1902: A Quantitative Study'. Unpublished Ph.D. dissertation, Purdue University, 1970.

HUGHES, J. R. T. *The Vital Few*. Boston, 1966.

JAMES, JOHN A. 'The Evolution of the National Money Market, 1888–1911', *Journal of Economic History*, XXXVI, 1 (March 1976).

JOHNSON, A. M., and B. E. SUPPLE. *Boston Capitalists and Western Railroads*. Cambridge, Mass., 1967.

JUSTER, F. T., and R. LIPSEY. 'A Note on Consumer Asset Formation in the United States', *Economic Journal*, LXXVII, 308 (1967).

KEYES, EMERSON W. *A History of Savings Banks in the United States*. 2 vols. New York, 1878.

KLINGAMAN, D. C., and R. K. VEDDER (eds.). *Essays in Nineteenth Century Economic History*. Athens, Ohio, 1975.

KNOWLES, CHARLES E. *History of the Bank for Savings in the City of New York, 1819–1829*. New York, 1929.

KUZNETS, SIMON. 'Economic Growth and Income Inequality', *American Economic Review*, XLV, 1 (March 1955).

—— *Capital in the American Economy: Its Formation and Financing*. Princeton, 1961.

—— 'Quantitative Aspects of the Economic Growth of Nations, Part X', *Economic Development and Cultural Change*, XV, 2 (January 1967).

KUZNETS, SIMON (ed.). *Income and Wealth of the United States: Trends and Structure*. Income and Wealth, series II. Cambridge, 1952.

LADIN, J. 'Mortgage Credit in Tippecanoe County, Indiana, 1865–1880', *Agricultural History*, XLI (1967).

LARSON, HENRIETTA. *Jay Cooke: Private Banker*. Cambridge, Mass., 1936.

LEBERGOTT, S. 'Wage Trends, 1800–1900', in Parker (ed.), *Trends in the American Economy*.

LEGLER, J. B. 'Regional Distribution of Federal Receipts and Expenditures in the Nineteenth Century: A Quantitative Study'. Unpublished Ph.D. dissertation, Purdue University, 1967.

LEWIS, W. A. *The Theory of Economic Growth*. London, 1955.

MACAULEY, FREDERICK R. *Some Theoretical Problems suggested by the Movement of Interest Rates, Bond Yields, and Stock Prices in the United States since 1856*. New York, 1938.

McGOULDRICK, PAUL F. *New England Textiles in the Nineteenth Century: Profits and Investment*. Harvard Economic Studies, 131. Cambridge, Mass., 1968.

MARTIN, J. G. *Seventy-Three Years' History of the Boston Stock Market*. Boston, 1871.

MEYER, B. H., C. MACGILL, et al. *History of Transportation in the United States before 1860*. Carnegie Institution of Washington publication no. 215C. Reprinted Forge Village, Mass., 1948.

MILLER, W. (ed.). *Men in Business*. Cambridge, Mass., 1952.

MYERS, MARGARET. *The New York Money Market*, I. New York, 1931.

—— 'The Investment Market after 1919', in H. F. Williamson (ed.), *The Growth of the American Economy*.

NAVIN, T., and M. SEARS. 'The Rise of the Market for Industrial Securities, 1887–1902', *Business History Review*, XXX (1955).

NORTH, DOUGLASS. 'Capital Accumulation in Life Insurance between the Civil War and the Investigation of 1905', in Miller (ed.), *Men in Business*.

PARKER, WILLIAM N. (ed.). *Trends in the American Economy in the Nineteenth Century*. Studies in Income and Wealth, 24. Princeton, 1960.

PAYNE, P. L., and LANCE E. DAVIS. *The Savings Bank of Baltimore, 1818–1866: A Historical and Analytical Study*. Baltimore, Md, 1956.

POOR, HENRY V. *History of the Railroads and Canals of the United States of America*, I. New York, 1860.

POPPLE, C. S. *The Development of Two Bank Groups in the Central Northwest*. Cambridge, Mass., 1944.

PRIMACK, MARTIN. 'Land Clearing under Nineteenth Century Techniques', *Journal of Economic History*, XXII (December 1962).

—— 'Farm Construction as a Use of Farm Labor in the United States, 1850–1900', *Journal of Economic History*, XXV (March 1965).

RIPLEY, WILLIAM Z. *Main Street and Wall Street*. Boston, 1927.

ROSENBERG, N. 'Technological Change in the Machine Tool Industry, 1840–1910', *Journal of Economic History*, XXIII, 4 (December 1963).

ROSTOW, W. W. *The Stages of Economic Growth*. 2nd edn. Cambridge, 1971.

SEVERSON, R. F., Jr. 'The Source of Mortgage Credit for Champaign County, 1865–1880', *Agricultural History*, XXXVI (July 1962).

SOBEL, R. *The Big Board: A History of the New York Stock Market*. New York, 1965.

SOLMON, L. C. 'Capital Formation and Expenditures on Education, 1880 and 1890'. Unpublished Ph.D. dissertation, University of Chicago, 1969.

SOLOW, ROBERT M. 'A Contribution to the Theory of Economic Growth', *Quarterly Journal of Economics*, LXX (1956).

SOLTOW, LEE. 'Evidence on Income Inequalities in the United States, 1866–1965', *Journal of Economic History*, XXIX, 2 (June 1969).

—— 'Economic Inequalities in the United States in the Period from 1790 to 1860', *Journal of Economic History*, XXXI, 4 (December 1971).

SOLTOW, LEE (ed.). *Six Papers on the Size Distribution of Wealth and Income*. Studies in Income and Wealth, 33. New York, 1969.

TAYLOR, GEORGE ROGERS, and LUCIUS F. ELLSWORTH (eds.). *Approaches to American Economic History*. Charlottesville, Virginia, 1971.

TEMIN, PETER. 'General Equilibrium Models in Economic History', *Journal of Economic History*, XXXI, 1 (March 1971).

TRESCOTT, P. B. *Financing American Enterprise*. New York, 1963.

TRUE, A. C. *A History of Agricultural Experimentation and Research in the United States, 1607–1925, including a History of the United States Department of Agriculture*. USDA Miscellaneous Publication no. 251. Washington, 1937.

ULMER, M. J. *Capital in Transportation, Communications, and Public Utilities: Its Formation and Financing*. Princeton, 1960.

UNITED STATES. Bureau of the Census. *Historical Statistics of the United States: Colonial Times to 1957*. Washington, 1960.

—— Comptroller of the Currency. *Annual Report, 1916*. Washington, 1917.

—— Department of Commerce. *Standard Industrial Classification Manual*. Washington, 1945.

USELDING, PAUL. 'Conjectural Estimates of Gross Human Capital Inflows to the American Economy, 1790–1860', *Explorations in Economic History*, IX, 1 (Fall 1971).

—— 'Factor Substitution and Labor Productivity Growth in American Manufacturing, 1839–1899', *Journal of Economic History*, XXXII, 3 (September 1972).

WHITE, GERALD. *A History of the Massachusetts Hospital Life Insurance Company*. Cambridge, Mass., 1955.

WILCOX, J. M. *A History of the Philadelphia Savings Fund Society, 1816–1916*. Philadelphia, 1916.

WILLIAMSON, H. F. (ed.). *The Growth of the American Economy*. New York, 1944.

WILLIAMSON, H. F., and O. SMALLEY. *Northwestern Mutual Life: A Century of Trusteeship.* Evanston, Illinois, 1957.

WILLIAMSON, JEFFREY. 'Watersheds and Turning Points: Conjectures on the Long-Term Impact of Civil War Financing', *Journal of Economic History*, XXXIV, 3 (September 1974).

ZARTMAN, L. *The Investment of Life Insurance Companies.* New York, 1906.

CHAPTER II

The United States: Evolution of Enterprise

As a rule, books on individual businessmen and firms are not listed in this bibliography, because all are cited in the more general studies listed below.

THE SPECIALIZATION OF TRADITIONAL ENTERPRISE – 1790S TO 1840S

General Studies

BRUCHEY, STUART. *The Roots of American Economic Growth.* London, 1965.

CLARK, VICTOR S. *History of Manufactures in the United States*, I: *1607–1860.* New Haven, Conn., 1929.

NORTH, DOUGLASS C. *The Economic Growth of the United States, 1790–1860.* Englewood Cliffs, N.J., 1961.

TAYLOR, GEORGE ROGERS. *The Transportation Revolution, 1815–1860.*

Specific Studies

ALBION, ROBERT G. *The Rise of New York Port.* New York, 1939.

ATHERTON, LEWIS E. 'The Pioneer Merchant in Mid-America', *University of Missouri Studies*, XIV, 2 (April 1939).

—— *The Southern Country Store, 1800–1860.* Baton Rouge, Louisiana, 1949.

BAILYN, BERNARD. *The New England Merchant in the Seventeenth Century.* Cambridge, Mass., 1955.

BRUCHEY, STUART. *Robert Oliver, Merchant of Baltimore, 1793–1819.* Baltimore, Md, 1956.

CLARK, JOHN G. *The Grain Trade in the Old Northwest.* Urbana, Illinois, 1966.

COLE, ARTHUR H. *The American Wool Manufacture.* 2 vols. Cambridge, Mass., 1926.

—— 'The Tempo of Mercantile Life in Colonial America', *Business History Review*, XXXIII (1959), 277–99.

GILCHRIST, DAVID T. (ed.). *The Growth of the Seaport Cities, 1790–1825.* Charlottesville, Virginia, 1967.

HARRINGTON, VIRGINIA. *The New York Merchant on the Eve of the Revolution.* New York, 1935.

HUNTER, LOUIS C. *Steamboats on the Western Waters.* Cambridge, Mass., 1949.

JONES, FRED M. *Middlemen in the Domestic Trade of the United States.* Urbana, Illinois, 1937.

REDLICH, FRITZ. *The Molding of American Banking, Men and Ideas.* 2 vols. New York, 1947–51.

SCARBOROUGH, WILLIAM K. *The Overseer: Plantation Management in the Old South.* Baton Rouge, Louisiana, 1966.

SCHREIBER, HARRY M. *The Ohio Canal Era: A Case Study of Government and the Economy, 1820–1861.* Athens, Ohio, 1969.

SHAW, RONALD E. *Erie Waters West: A History of the Erie Canal, 1782–1854.* Lexington, Kentucky, 1966.

WARE, CAROLINE F. *The Early New England Cotton Manufacture.* Boston and New York, 1931.
WOODMAN, HAROLD G. *King Cotton and His Retainers.* Lexington, Kentucky, 1968.

Sources

APPLETON, NATHAN, and SAMUEL BATCHELDER. *The Early Development of the American Cotton Textile Industry,* ed. George Rogers Taylor. New York, 1969 (first published 1858).
MONTGOMERY, JAMES. *A Practical Detail of the Cotton Manufacture of the United States of America.* New York and Glasgow, 1840.
UNITED STATES. 22nd Congress, First Session. *Documents Relative to Manufactures in the United States,* House Document no. 308 (The McLane Report on Manufactures). 2 vols. Washington, 1833.

THE RISE OF MODERN ENTERPRISE: 1840S TO THE FIRST WORLD WAR

General Studies

BRADY, DOROTHY S. (ed.). *Output, Employment and Productivity in the United States after 1800.* Studies in Income and Wealth, 30. Princeton, 1966. (See especially Albert Fishlow, 'Productivity and Technological Change in the Railroad Sector'.)
CLARK, VICTOR S. *History of Manufactures in the United States,* II: *1860–1893.* New Haven, Conn., 1929.
—— *History of Manufactures in the United States,* III: *1893–1928.* New Haven, Conn., 1929.
HABAKKUK, H. J. *American and British Technology in the Nineteenth Century.* Cambridge, 1962.
KIRKLAND, EDWARD C. *Industry Comes of Age.* New York, 1961.
PARKER, WILLIAM N. (ed.). *Trends in the American Economy in the Nineteenth Century.* Studies in Income and Wealth, 24. Princeton, 1960.
SCHURR, SAM H., *et al. Energy in the American Economy, 1850–1975.* Baltimore, Md, 1960.

Specific Studies

Transportation and Communication

CAMPBELL, EDWARD G. *The Reorganization of the American Railroad System, 1893–1900.* New York, 1938.
CHANDLER, ALFRED D., JR. *Henry Varnum Poor: Business Editor, Analyst and Reformer.* Cambridge, Mass., 1956.
—— 'The Railroads: Pioneers in Modern Corporate Management', *Business History Review,* XXXIX, 1 (Spring 1965), 16–40.
—— 'Anthracite Coal and the Beginnings of the Industrial Revolution in the United States', *Business History Review,* XLVI (1972), 141–81.
CHANDLER, ALFRED D., JR, with STEPHEN SALSBURY. 'The Railroads: Innovators in Modern Management', in Bruce Mazlish (ed.), *The Railroad and the Space Program.* Cambridge, Mass., 1965.
COCHRAN, THOMAS C. *Railroad Leaders, 1845–1890.* Cambridge, Mass., 1953.
KIRKLAND, EDWARD C. *Men, Cities and Transportation.* Cambridge, Mass., 1948.
RIPLEY, WILLIAM Z. *Railroads: Rates and Regulation.* New York, 1913.
—— *Railroads: Finance and Organization.* New York, 1915.
STOVER, JOHN F. *The Railroads of the South, 1865–1900.* Chapel Hill, N.C., 1955.
TAYLOR, GEORGE ROGERS, and IRENE D. NEU. *The American Railroad Network.* Cambridge, Mass., 1956.
THOMPSON, ROBERT L. *Wiring a Continent: The History of the Telegraph Industry in the United States, 1832–1866.* Princeton, 1947.

Mass Marketing, Mass Production, and the Integrated Industrial Enterprise

AITKEN, HUGH G. *Taylorism at Watertown Arsenal: Scientific Management in Action, 1908–1915.* Cambridge, Mass., 1960.
BARGER, HAROLD. *Distribution's Place in the American Economy.* Princeton, 1955.
BRIEF, RICHARD P. 'The Origins and Evolution of Nineteenth-Century Asset Accounting', *Business History Review*, XL, 1 (Spring 1966), 1–23.
CALHOUN, DANIEL C. *The American Civil Engineer: Origins and Conflict.* Cambridge, Mass., 1960.
CALVERT, MONTE A. *The Mechanical Engineer in America, 1830–1910.* Baltimore, Md, 1967.
CHANDLER, ALFRED D., JR. 'The Beginnings of "Big Business" in American Industry', *Business History Review*, XXXIII, 1 (Spring 1959), 1–31.
CHANDLER, ALFRED D., JR, and STEPHEN SALSBURY. *Pierre S. du Pont and the Making of the Modern Corporation.* New York, 1971.
CLARK, THOMAS D. *Pills, Petticoats and Plows.* Indianapolis, Indiana, 1944.
EICHNER, ALFRED. *The Emergence of Oligopoly: Sugar as a Case Study.* Baltimore, Md, 1969.
LITTERER, JOSEPH A. 'Systematic Management: Design for Organizational Recoupling in American Manufacturing Firms', *Business History Review*, XXXVII (1963), 369–91.
LIVERMORE, SHAW. 'The Success of Industrial Mergers', *Quarterly Journal of Economics*, L (1935), 68–96.
NELSON, RALPH L. *Merger Movements in American Industry, 1895–1956.* Princeton, 1959.
PORTER, GLENN, and HAROLD C. LIVESAY. *Merchants and Manufacturers: Studies in the Changing Structure of Nineteenth-Century Marketing.* Baltimore, Md, 1971.
RIPLEY, WILLIAM Z. *Trusts, Pools and Corporations.* Boston, 1905.
ROE, JOHN W. *American and English Tool Builders.* New Haven, Conn., 1916.
ROSENBERG, NATHAN. 'Technological Change in the Machine Tool Industry, 1840–1910', *Journal of Economic History*, XXIII (1963), 414–43.
TEMIN, PETER. *Iron and Steel in Nineteenth-Century America: An Economic Inquiry.* Cambridge, Mass., 1964.
THORELLI, HANS. *The Federal Anti-trust Policy.* Baltimore, Md, 1955.
WILKINS, MIRA. *The Emergence of Multinational Enterprise.* Cambridge, Mass., 1970.
WILLIAMSON, HAROLD F. *Winchester: The Gun that Won the West.* Washington, 1952.
WILLIAMSON, HAROLD F., et al. *The American Petroleum Industry*, I: *The Age of Illumination, 1859–1899.* Evanston, Illinois, 1959.
—— *The American Petroleum Industry*, II: *The Age of Energy, 1899–1959.* Evanston, Illinois, 1963.

Original Sources

BRIDGE, JAMES H. *The Inside History of the Carnegie Steel Company.* New York, 1903.
CHANDLER, ALFRED D., JR (ed.). *The Railroads: The Nation's First Big Business.* New York, 1965. (Includes reprinted pieces by Daniel C. McCallum, Albert Fink, Charles Francis Adams, and others.)
FITCH, CHARLES H. 'Report on Manufacture of Interchangeable Mechanisms', in United States, Department of Interior, Census Office, *Report on the Manufactures of the United States at the Tenth Census* (1 June 1880). Washington, 1883.
HADLEY, ARTHUR T. *Railroad Transportation.* New York, 1885.
METCALFE, HENRY. 'The Shop Order System of Accounts', *Transactions of the American Society of Mechanical Engineers*, VII (1886), 440–88.
POOR, HENRY V. *History of the Railroads and Canals of the United States.* New York, 1860.
ROSENBERG, NATHAN (ed.). *The American System of Manufactures: The Report of the Committee on Machinery of the United States 1855 and the Special Reports of George Wallis and Joseph Whitworth 1854.* Edinburgh, 1969.
TAYLOR, FREDERICK W. 'A Piece Rate System, Being a Step Towards a Partial Solution of the Labor Problem', *Transactions of the American Society o Mechanical Engineers*, XVI (1895), 856–87.

TAYLOR, FREDERICK W. *Shop Management*. New York, 1911.
—— *The Principles of Scientific Management*. New York and London, 1911.
TOWNE, HENRY R. 'The Engineer as Economist', *Transactions of the American Society of Mechanical Engineers*, VII (1886), 428–32.
—— 'Gain-Sharing', *Transactions of the American Society of Mechanical Engineers*, X (1889), 600–26.

MODERN BUSINESS ENTERPRISE SINCE THE FIRST WORLD WAR

General Studies

BERLE, ADOLF A., JR, and GARDINER C. MEANS. *The Modern Corporation and Private Property*. Chicago, 1932.
GALBRAITH, JOHN KENNETH. *The New Industrial State*. Boston, 1969.
KAPLAN, A. D. H. *Big Enterprise in a Competitive System*. Washington, 1954.
NUTTER, G. WARREN, and HENRY A. EINHORN. *Enterprise Monopoly in the United States, 1899–1958*. New York, 1959.

Specific Studies

AVERITT, ROBERT T. *The Dual Economy*. New York, 1968.
BRADY, ROBERT A. *Organization, Automation and Society*. Berkeley, Calif., 1961.
CHANDLER, ALFRED D., JR. 'Development, Diversification and Decentralization', in Ralph E. Freeman (ed.), *Postwar Economic Trends in the United States*. New York, 1960.
—— *Strategy and Structure: Chapters in the History of the Industrial Enterprise*. Cambridge, Mass., 1962.
—— 'The Structure of American Industry in the Twentieth Century: An Historical Overview', *Business History Review*, XLIII (1969), 355–98.
GORT, MICHAEL. *Diversification and Integration in American Industry*. Princeton, 1962.
MASON, EDWARD S. (ed.). *The Corporation in Modern Society*. New York, 1959.
NEWCOMER, MABEL. *The Big Business Executive*. New York, 1955.
SERVAN-SCHREIBER, JEAN-JACQUES. *The American Challenge*. New York, 1968.
TERLECKYJ, NESTER E., assisted by Harriet J. Helper. *Research and Development: Its Growing Composition*. New York, 1963.

Sources

CHANDLER, ALFRED D., JR (ed.). *Giant Enterprise: Ford, General Motors, and the Automobile Industry*. New York, 1967. (Provides numerous sources and documents.)
THORP, WILLARD. *The Integration of Industrial Operations*. Washington, 1924.
UNITED STATES. 89TH CONGRESS, FIRST SESSION. *Economic Concentration: Hearings before the Sub-Committee on Antitrust and Monopoly of the Committee on the Judiciary, United States Senate*, parts 1–3. Washington, 1963–5.
—— 91ST CONGRESS, FIRST SESSION. *Economic Report on Corporate Mergers, part 8A: Hearings before the Sub-Committee on Antitrust and Monopoly of the Committee on the Judiciary, United States Senate*. Washington, 1969.

As relatively few scholarly analyses have been made on the evolution of enterprise since the First World War, major sources of information are from business journals, particularly *Fortune* and *Business Week*. Recent historical developments are compiled in two case studies used at the Harvard Business School, one on the multinational since the Second World War and the other on the conglomerate. Both were prepared by Alfred D. Chandler, Jr, and are available through the Intercollegiate Case Clearing House, Soldiers Field, Boston, Mass.

CHAPTER III

Capital Formation in Japan

BOULDING, K., and N. SUN. 'The Effects of Military Expenditures upon the Economic Growth of Japan'. Unpublished paper, Tokyo, 1967 (mimeographed).

DENISON, EDWARD F., and WILLIAM K. CHUNG. *How Japan's Economy Grew So Fast.* Washington, 1976.

KLEIN, L., and K. OHKAWA (eds.). *Economic Growth: The Japanese Experience since the Meija Era.* New Haven, Conn., 1968.

OHKAWA, K., and H. ROSOVSKY. 'A Century of Japanese Economic Growth', in W. W. Lockwood (ed.), *The State and Economic Enterprise in Japan.* Princeton, 1965.

—— 'Postwar Japanese Economic Growth in Historical Perspective: A Second Look', in Klein and Ohkawa (eds.), *Economic Growth.*

—— *Japanese Economic Growth: Trend Acceleration in the Twentieth Century.* Stanford, Calif., 1973.

OHKAWA, K., M. SHINOHARA, and M. UMEMURA (eds.). *Chōki keizai tōkei Estimates of Long-Term Economic Statistics of Japan since 1868.* 13 vols., in progress. Tokyo, 1965– . (See p. 504 note 6 above for details.)

ROSOVSKY, HENRY. 'Japan's Transition to Modern Economic Growth, 1868–1885', in H. Rosovsky (ed.), *Industrialization in Two Systems.* New York, 1966.

—— 'Rumbles in the Rice Fields', *Journal of Asian Studies*, XXVII, 2 (1968).

SHIONOYA, Y. 'Patterns of Industrial Development', in Klein and Ohkawa (eds.), *Economic Growth.*

CHAPTER IV

Factory Labour and the Industrial Revolution in Japan

SOURCES IN JAPANESE

COMMITTEE ON HISTORICAL MATERIALS ON THE LABOUR MOVEMENT (Rōdō Undō Shiryō Iinkai). *Nihon rōdō undō shiryō* [*Historical Materials on the Labour Movement in Japan*]. 11 vols. Tokyo, 1959– (not yet completed). (Cited as '*NRUS*'.)

ENDO, M. 'Meiji shoki ni okeru rōdōsha no jōtai' ['The Conditions of Workers during the Early Meiji Era'], in Sumiya *et al.*, *Labour Problems in the Early Meiji Era*, 43–95.

FUJIBAYASHI, KEIZO. 'Meiji nijūnendai ni okeru waga bōsekigyō rōdōsha no idō genshō ni tsuite' ['The Mobility of Workers in Japanese Cotton Textiles in the Mid-Meiji Era'], in Sumiya *et al.*, *Labour Problems in the Early Meiji Era.*

FURUSHIMA, TOSHIO. 'Bakumatsuki no nōgyō hiyō rōdōsha' ['Paid Agricultural Labour in the Late Edo Period'], in Ichikawa *et al.*, *Paid Labour during the Period of Disintegration of Feudal Society.*

HAYASHI, H. 'Bisai ni okeru meiji kōhanki no koyō rōdō' ['Paid Labour in Western Aichi during the Late Meiji Era'], in Ichikawa *et al.*, *Paid Labour during the Period of Disintegration of Feudal Society.*

HAZAMA, H. *Nihon rōmu kanrishi kenkyū* [*Studies in the History of Work-Force Management*]. Tokyo, 1964.

HOSOI, WAKIZŌ. *Jokō aishi* [*A Tragic History of Female Factory Workers*]. Tokyo, 1925.

HYODO, TSUTOMU. *Nihon ni okeru rōshi-kankei no tenkai* [*The Development of Industrial Relations in Japan*]. Tokyo, 1971.

ICHIKAWA, T. 'Nōson kōgyō ni okeru koyō rōdō' ['Paid Labour in Rural Industries'], in Ichikawa *et al.*, *Paid Labour during the Period of Disintegration of Feudal Society.*

ICHIKAWA, T., *et al.* *Hōken shakai kaitaiki no koyō rōdō* [*Paid Labour during the Period of Disintegration of Feudal Society*]. Tokyo, 1961.

JAPAN. MINISTRY OF AGRICULTURE AND COMMERCE. *Shokkō jijō* [*The Conditions of Factory Labour*], ed. T. Tsuchiya. 3rd edn. 3 vols. Tokyo, 1947 (first published 1903). (Cited as '*Shokkō jijō*'.)

—— MINISTRY OF COMMERCE AND INDUSTRY. *Kōjō tōkei hyō* [*Factory Statistics*]. Quinquennial 1909–19; annual thereafter.

—— MINISTRY OF EDUCATION. *Jitsugyō kyōiku gojūnenshi* [*Fifty Years of Vocational Education*]. Tokyo, 1934.

—— MINISTRY OF HOME AFFAIRS. *Saimin chōsa tōkeihyō tekiyō* [*Statistical Abstracts on the Survey of the Poor*]. Tokyo, 1912.

—— MINISTRY OF INTERNATIONAL TRADE AND INDUSTRY. *Shōkō seisakushi* [*A History of Commercial and Industrial Policies*]. 25 vols. Tokyo, 1962.

—— PRIME MINISTER'S OFFICE. *Nihon teikoku tōkei zensho* [*Statistical Collection for the Empire of Japan*]. Tokyo, 1928.

—— —— *Rōdō tōkei jitchi chōsa hōkoku* [*Report on the Survey of Labour Statistics*]. Tokyo, 1936.

KAJINISHI, M., *et al*. *Seishi rōdōsha no rekishi* [*A History of Workers in the Raw Silk Industry*]. Tokyo, 1955.

KAZAHAYA, YASOJI. *Nihon shakai seisakushi* [*A History of Social Policy in Japan*]. 2 vols. Tokyo, 1951.

KINUKAWA, T. *Honpō menshi bōseki shi* [*The History of Japanese Cotton Textiles*]. 7 vols. Tokyo, 1937.

KUBLIN, H. *Meiji rōdō undōshi no hitokoma* [*An Aspect of the History of the Meiji Labour Movement*]. Tokyo, 1959.

MORITA, Y. *Wagakuni no shihonka dantai* [*Industrialists' Associations in Japan*]. Tokyo, 1926.

NIBUYA, RYU. '*Nenkō seido no kaiko to tenbō*' ['*Reflections upon Nenkō seido*'], *Nihon rōdō kyōkai zasshi* [*Monthly Journal of the Japan Institute of Labour*], VI, 12 (December 1964).

NRKN: see Society for the Compilation of Historical Materials on Work-Force Management.

NRUS: see Committee on Historical Materials on the Labour Movement.

OHKAWA, K. '*Nihon keizai no seisan bunpai 1905–1963*' ['Production and Distribution in the Japanese Economy, 1905–1963'], *Keizai kenkyū* [*Economic Review*], XIX, 2 (April 1968).

SATO, M., *et al*. *Totei kyōiku no kenkyū* [*Studies in Apprenticeship*]. Tokyo, 1962.

Shokkō jijō: see Japan, Ministry of Agriculture and Commerce.

SOCIETY FOR THE COMPILATION OF HISTORICAL MATERIALS ON WORK-FORCE MANAGEMENT (Rōmu Kanri Shiryō Hensankai). *Nihon rōmu kanri nenshi* [*The Chronicle of Work-Force Management*]. 2 vols. Tokyo, 1962.

SUMIYA, M. *Nihon chinrōdōshi ron* [*A Tract on the History of Wage Labour in Japan*]. Tokyo, 1955.

SUMIYA, M., *et al*. *Meiji zenki no rōdō mondai* [*Labour Problems in the Early Meiji Era*]. Tokyo, 1960.

TAKAHASHI, I. *Oyatoi gaikokujin-gunji* [*Foreign Employees – Armed Services*]. Tokyo, 1968.

WATANABE, N. '*Shōgyōteki nōgyō ni okeru koyō rōdō*' ['Paid Labour in Commercial Agriculture'], in Ichikawa *et al*., *Paid Labour during the Period of Disintegration of Feudal Society*.

YAMAMOTO, T. '*Meiji kōki no riterashi chōsa*' ['Literacy Survey in the Late Meiji Era'], *Hitotsubashi ronsō* [*Hitotsubashi Review*], LXI, 3 (March 1969).

YAMAZAKI, B. *Nihon shōhi kumiai* [*A History of Consumers' Co-operatives in Japan*]. Tokyo, 1932.

YOKOYAMA, GENNOSUKE. *Nihon no kasō shakai*. [*The Lower-Class Society of Japan*]. Tokyo, 1898.

Sources in English, etc.

Ayusawa, I. F. *A History of Labor in Modern Japan*. Honolulu, 1966.

Dore, R. P. *Education in Tokugawa Japan*. Berkeley, Calif., 1965.

—— *British Factory – Japanese Factory*. Berkeley, Calif., 1973.

Foxwell, E. 'The Protection of Labour in Japan', *Economic Journal*, xi (1901), 106–24.

Hirschmeier, Johannes. 'Shibusawa Eiichi: Industrial Pioneer', in Lockwood (ed.), *The State and Economic Enterprise in Japan*.

Katayama, Sen. 'Labor Problem Old and New', *Far East*, October 1897 (reprinted in *NRUS*, ii, 255–63).

—— *The Labor Movement in Japan*. Chicago, 1918.

Kublin, H. *The Life of Sen Katayama*. Princeton, 1924.

Levine, S. B. 'Labor Market and Collective Bargaining in Japan', in Lockwood (ed.), *The State and Economic Enterprise in Japan*.

Lockwood, W. W. *The Economic Development of Japan: Growth and Structural Change, 1868–1938*. Princeton, 1954.

Lockwood, W. W. (ed.). *The State and Economic Enterprise in Japan*. Princeton, 1965.

Nitobe, I. *Japan*. New York, 1931.

Odaka, K. 'A History of Money Wages in the Northern Kyushu Industrial Area, 1898–1939', *Hitotsubashi Journal of Economics*, viii, 2 (February 1968).

Ohkawa, K., et al. *The Growth Rate of the Japanese Economy since 1878*. Tokyo, 1958.

Ohkawa, K., and H. Rosovsky. *Japanese Economic Growth*. Stanford, Calif., 1973.

Ohkawa, K., M. Shinohara, and M. Umemura (eds.). *Estimates of Long-Term Economic Statistics of Japan since 1868*. 13 vols. Tokyo, 1966–   (in progress). (Cited in the notes as '*ELTES*'.)

Okochi, Kazuo. *Labor in Modern Japan*. Tokyo, 1958.

Passin, H. *Society and Education in Japan*. New York, 1965.

Rosovsky, H. 'Japan's Transition to Economic Growth, 1868–1885', in H. Rosovsky (ed.), *Industrialization in Two Systems*. New York, 1966.

Saito, K. *La Protection ouvrière au Japon*. Paris, 1900.

Smith, T. C. *Political Change and Industrial Development in Japan: Government Enterprise, 1868–1880*. Stanford, Calif., 1955.

—— *The Agrarian Origins of Modern Japan*. Stanford, Calif., 1959.

Sturmthal, A., and J. Scoville (eds.). *The International Labor Movement in Transition*. Urbana, Illinois, 1973.

Taira, K. *Economic Development and the Labor Market in Japan*. New York, 1970.

—— 'Factory Legislation and Management Modernization during Japan's Industrialization, 1886–1916', *Business History Review*, xliv, 1 (Spring 1970), 84–109.

—— 'Education and Literacy in Meiji Japan: An Interpretation, *Explorations in Economic History*, viii, 4 (1971), 371–94.

—— 'Labor Markets, Unions and Employers in Interwar Japan', in Sturmthal and Scoville (eds.), *The International Labor Movement in Transition*.

CHAPTER V

Entrepreneurship, Ownership, and Management in Japan

Sources in English

Abeggle, James C. *The Japanese Factory: Aspects of Its Social Organization*. New York, 1958.

Abeggle, James C., and Hiroshi Mannari. 'Leaders of Modern Japan: Social Origins and Mobility', *Economic Development and Cultural Change*, ix (1960).

ALLEN, GEORGE C. *A Short Economic History of Modern Japan, 1867–1937.* 2nd edn. London, 1962.
—— 'The Industrialization of the Far East: I. Japan and Manchuria', in *Cambridge Economic History of Europe*, VI, part 2. Cambridge, 1965.
BELLAH, ROBERT. *Tokugawa Religion: The Values of Industrial Japan.* New York, 1957.
BENNETT, JOHN W., and IWAO ISHINO. *Paternalism in the Japanese Economy.* Minneapolis, Minn., 1963.
BISSON, T. A. *Zaibatsu Dissolution in Japan.* Berkeley, Calif., 1954.
BROADBRIDGE, SEYMOUR A. *Industrial Dualism in Japan.* Chicago, 1966.
BRONFENBRENNER, MARTIN. 'Some Lessons of Japan's Economic Development, 1853–1938', *Pacific Affairs*, XXXIV, 1 (Spring 1961).
BROWN, DELMER M. *Nationalism in Japan: An Introductory Historical Analysis.* Berkeley, Calif., 1955.
CAIN, LOUIS P., and PAUL J. USELDING (eds.). *Business Enterprise and Economic Change.* Kent, Ohio, 1973.
CAMERON, RONDO (ed.). *Banking in the Early Stages of Industrialization: A Study in Comparative Economic History.* New York, 1967.
COWAN, CHARLES D. (ed.). *The Economic Development of China and Japan.* London, 1962.
CRAWCOUR, SYDNEY. 'Documentary Sources of Tokugawa Economic and Social History', *Journal of Asian Studies*, XX (1961).
—— 'The Development of a Credit System in Seventeenth Century Japan', *Journal of Economic History*, XXI (1961).
—— 'Changes in Japanese Commerce in the Tokugawa Period', *Journal of Asian Studies*, XXII (1963).
—— 'The Tokugawa Period and Japan's Preparation for Modern Economic Growth'. Paper given at the 1967 meeting of the American Historical Association, Montreal.
DORE, RONALD P. *Education in Tokugawa Japan.* Berkeley, Calif., 1965.
—— 'The Legacy of Tokugawa Education', in Jansen (ed.), *Changing Japanese Attitudes.*
—— 'Mobility, Equality, and Individuation in Modern Japan', in Dore (ed.), *Aspects of Social Change in Modern Japan.*
DORE, RONALD P. (ed.). *Aspects of Social Change in Modern Japan.* Princeton, 1967.
EMI, KOICHI. *Government Fiscal Activity and Economic Growth in Japan, 1868–1960.* Tokyo, 1963.
HALL, JOHN W. *Government and Local Power in Japan, 500 to 1700: A Study Based on Bizen Province.* Princeton, 1966.
HALL, JOHN W. (ed.). *Studies in the Institutional History of Early Modern Japan.* Princeton, 1968.
HALL, JOHN W., and R. K. BEARDSLEY. *Twelve Doors to Japan.* New York, 1965.
HAROOTUNIAN, HARRY D. 'The Economic Rehabilitation of the Samurai in the Early Meiji Period', *Journal of Asian Studies*, XIX (1960).
HAROOTUNIAN, HARRY D., and BERNARD S. SILBERMAN (eds.). *Japan in Crisis.* Princeton, 1973.
HIRSCHMEIER, JOHANNES. *The Origins of Entrepreneurship in Meiji Japan.* Cambridge, Mass., 1964.
—— 'Shibusawa Eiichi: Industrial Pioneer', in Lockwood (ed.), *The State and Economic Enterprise.*
HIRSCHMEIER, JOHANNES, and TSUNEHIKO YUI. *The Development of Japanese Business, 1600–1793.* Cambridge, Mass., 1975.
HONJŌ, EIJIRŌ. *The Social and Economic History of Japan.* Kyoto, 1935.
HORIE, YASUZŌ. 'An Outline of the Rise of Capitalism in Japan', *Kyoto University Economic Review*, XI (1936).
—— 'The Government and Industry in the Early Years of Meiji Era', *Kyoto University Economic Review*, XIV (1939).
JANSEN, MARIUS B. (ed.). *Changing Japanese Attitudes Toward Modernization.* Princeton, 1965.
KOMIYA, R. (ed.). *Postwar Economic Growth in Japan.* Berkeley, Calif., 1967.

LANDES, DAVID S. 'Japan and Europe: Contrasts in Industrialization', in Lockwood (ed.), *The State and Economic Enterprise*.

LEVINE, SOLOMON B. *Industrial Relations in Postwar Japan*. Urbana, Illinois, 1958.

—— 'Labor and Collective Bargaining', in Lockwood (ed.), *The State and Economic Enterprise*.

LOCKWOOD, WILLIAM W. *The Economic Development of Japan: Growth and Structural Change, 1868–1938*. Princeton, 1954.

—— 'Japan's Response to the West: The Contrast with China', *World Politics*, IX, 1 (October 1956).

LOCKWOOD, WILLIAM W. (ed.). *The State and Economic Enterprise in Japan*. Princeton, 1965.

McMASTER, J. 'The Takashima Mine: British Capital and Japanese Industrialization', *Business History Review*, XXXVII, 3 (1963).

MARSHALL, BYRON K. *Capitalism and Nationalism in Prewar Japan*. Stanford, Calif., 1968.

MIYAMOTO, M., Y. SAKUDO, and Y. YASUBA. 'Economic Development in Pre-industrial Japan, 1859–1894', *Journal of Economic History*, XXV (1965).

MOULTON, HAROLD G. *Japan: An Economic and Financial Appraisal*. Washington, 1931.

NODA, K. 'Postwar Japanese Executives', in Komiya (ed.), *Postwar Economic Growth*.

NORMAN, HERBERT. *Japan's Emergence as a Modern State*. New York, 1948.

ŌKŌCHI, KAZUO. *Labor in Modern Japan*. Tokyo, 1958.

ORCHARD, JOHN E. *Japan's Economic Position*. New York, 1930.

PATRICK, HUGH T. 'Lessons for Underdeveloped Countries from the Japanese Experience of Economic Growth', *Indian Economic Journal*, X (1961).

—— 'Japan, 1868–1914', in Cameron (ed.), *Banking in the Early Stages of Industrialization*.

RANIS, GUSTAV. 'The Community-Centered Entrepreneur in Japanese Development', *Explorations in Entrepreneurial History*, XIII (1955).

ROSOVSKY, HENRY. *Capital Formation in Japan, 1868–1940*. New York, 1961.

—— 'Japan's Transition to Economic Growth, 1868–1885', in H. Rosovsky (ed.), *Industrialization in Two Systems*. New York, 1966.

SANSOM, GEORGE B. *Japan, A Short Cultural History*. New York, 1943.

—— *The Western World and Japan*. New York, 1951.

SHELDON, CHARLES D. *The Rise of the Merchant Class in Tokugawa Japan*. New York, 1958.

SILBERMAN, BERNARD S. 'The Bureaucracy and Economic Development in Japan', *Asian Survey*, V (1965).

SMITH, THOMAS C. *Political Change and Industrial Development in Japan: Government Enterprise, 1868–1880*. Stanford, Calif., 1955.

—— 'Landlords and Rural Capitalists in the Modernization of Japan', *Journal of Economic History*, XVI, 2 (June 1956).

—— *The Agrarian Origins of Modern Japan*. Stanford, Calif., 1959.

—— 'Landlords' Sons in Business Elite', *Economic Development and Cultural Change*, IX, 1, part 2 (October 1960).

SUMIYA, MIKIO. *Social Impact of Industrialization in Japan*. Tokyo, 1963.

TAIRA, K. 'The Labor Market in Japanese Development', *British Journal of Industrial Relations*, II (1964).

VOGEL, EZRA F. *Japan's New Middle Class: The Salary Man and His Family in a Tokyo Suburb*. Berkeley, Calif., 1963.

WILLIAMSON, H. F. (ed.). *Managerial Strategies: A Multi-National Comparison*. Wilmington, Delaware, 1974.

YAMAMURA, KOZO. 'Zaibatsu, Prewar and Zaibatsu, Postwar', *Journal of Asian Studies*, XXIII (1964).

—— *Economic Policy in Postwar Japan: Growth Versus Economic Democracy*. Berkeley, Calif., 1967.

—— 'The Role of the Samurai in the Development of Modern Banking in Japan', *Journal of Economic History*, XXVII, 2 (June 1967).

YAMAMURA, KOZO. 'The Founding of Mitsubishi: A Case Study in Japanese Business History', *Business History Review*, XLI (1967).
—— 'A Re-examination of Entrepreneurship in Meiji Japan (1868–1912)', *Economic History Review*, 2nd ser., XXI, 1 (April 1968).
—— 'The Japanese Economy, 1911–1930: Concentration, Conflicts, and Crisis', in Harootunian and Silberman (eds.), *Japan in Crisis*.
—— 'Economic Responsiveness in Japanese Industrialization', in Cain and Uselding (eds.), *Business Enterprise and Economic Change*.
—— *A Study of Samurai Income and Entrepreneurship*. Cambridge, Mass., 1974.
—— 'Compromise with Culture: Transformation of Japanese Managerial System', in Williamson (ed.), *Managerial Strategies*.
YOSHINO, MICHAEL Y. *Japan's Managerial System*. Cambridge, Mass., 1968.
YUI, TSUNEHIKO. 'On *The Origins of Entrepreneurship in Meiji Japan* by J. Hirschmeier' (review article), *Japan Business History Review*, 1 (1966).

Sources in Japanese

AIHARA, SHIGERU (ed.). *Nippon no dokusen shihon* [*Monopolistic Capital of Japan*]. Tokyo, 1959.
AKASHI, TERUO. *Meiji ginkōshi* [*A History of Banking in Meiji Japan*]. Tokyo, 1935.
AKASHI, TERUO, and NORIHISA SUZUKI. *Nihon-kinyushi, Meiji-hen* [*A History of Japanese Banking, Meiji Volume*]. Tokyo, 1957.
ARISAWA, HIROMI (ed.) *Gendai nihon sangyō kōza* [*A Compendium on Contemporary Japanese Industry*]. 8 vols. Tokyo, 1959–60. Vol. 1: *Sōron: Kindai sangyō no hatten* [*Summary: The Development of Modern Industry*].
ASAKURA, KOICHI. *Meijizenki nippon kinyū kōzō-shi* [*A History of the Financial Structure in Meiji Japan*]. Tokyo, 1961.
FUKUZAWA, YUKICHI. *Fukuzawa Yukichi zenshū* [*The Collected Works of Yukichi Fukuzawa*]. Tokyo, 1926.
FUMOTO, SABURŌ. *Mitsubishi Iizuka tankōshi* [*The History of Mitsubishi Iizuka Coal Mines*]. Tokyo, 1961.
FURUSHIMA, TOSHIO. *Sangyō-shi* [*A History of Industry*]. Tokyo, 1966.
GENSUI, ARAI. *Tokyo Ishikawajima Zōsenjo 50-nenshi* [*A Fifty-Year History of the Tokyo Ishikawajimi Shipyard*]. Tokyo, 1930.
GIGA, SŌICHIRŌ. *Gendai nippon no dokusen kigyō* [*Monopolistic Enterprises of Modern Japan*]. Tokyo, 1962.
GREATER JAPAN CELLULOID COMPANY (Dainihon Seruroido KK). *Dainihon seruroido kaishashi* [*A History of the Greater Japan Celluloid Company*]. Tokyo, 1952.
HATTORI, SHISŌ (ed.), *Kindai nihon jimbutsu keizaishi* [*A Biographical Economic History of Modern Japan*]. 2 vols. Tokyo, 1955.
HATTORI, SHISŌ, and YOSHINAGA IRIMAJIRI (eds.), *Kindai nihon jimbutsu keizaishi* [*A Biographical Economic History of Modern Japan*]. 2 vols. Tokyo, 1965.
HAZAMA, HIROSHI. *Nihon rōmu kanrishi kenkyū* [*A Study of Japanese Labour Management*]. Tokyo, 1964.
HIGUCHI, HIROSHI. *Zaibatsu no fukkatsu* [*The Revival of Zaibatsu*]. Tokyo, 1953.
HOLDING COMPANY LIQUIDATION COMMISSION. *Nippon zaibatsu to sono kaitai* [*The Japanese Zaibatsu and Their Dissolution*]. 2 vols. Tokyo, 1962.
HORIE, YASUZŌ. *Nihon shihonshugi no seiritsu* [*The Formation of Japanese Capitalism*]. Tokyo, 1938.
—— 'Nihon keiei-shi ni okeru ie no mondai' ['The Problem of *ie* in Japanese Business History'], *Japan Business History Review*, II, 1 (July 1967).
IMUDA, TOSHIMITSU. 'Meijiki ni okeru kabushiki kaisha no hatten to kabunushi-sō keisei' ['The Development of Incorporated Firms and the Formation of the Shareholder Class in the Meiji Period'], in Osaka Municipal University, Economic Research Institute, *Meijiki no keizai hatten to keizai shutai* [*Economic Development and Its Leading Agents in the Meiji Period*]. Osaka, 1968.

IWAI, RYOTARŌ. *Mitsui, Mitsubishi monogatari* [*The Stories of Mitsui and Mitsubishi*]. Tokyo, 1934.
—— *Mitsubishi konzern dokuhon* [*The Story of the Mitsubishi Konzern*]. Tokyo, 1938.
JAPAN. BUREAU OF STATISTICS (Tōkeikyoku). *Teikoku tokei nenkan* [*Annual Report of Imperial Statistics*].
—— MINISTRY OF FINANCE. *Ginkō-kyoku dai niji hōkoku* [*Second Report of the Banking Bureau*]. Tokyo, 1880.
—— MINISTRY OF RAILWAYS. *Nihon tetsudōshi* [*A History of Japanese Railways*]. Tokyo, 1935.
JAPAN ECONOMIC HISTORY ASSOCIATION. *Kindai nihon jimbutsu keizaishi* [*A Biographical Economic History of Japan*]. Tokyo, 1955.
JAPAN INDUSTRIAL BANK. *Nippon kōgyō ginkō 50-nenshi* [*A Fifty-Year History of the Japan Industrial Bank*]. Tokyo, 1957.
JAPAN SUGAR-REFINING COMPANY (Dainihon Seitō KK). *Nittō 65-nenshi* [*Sixty-five Years of the Japan Sugar-Refining Company*]. Tokyo, 1906.
—— *Nittō saikin 25-nenshi* [*A History of the Japan Sugar-Refining Company during the Past Twenty-five Years*]. Tokyo, 1924.
KAJINISHI, MITSUHAYA. *Nihon ni okeru sangyō shihon* [*The Formation of Industrial Capital in Japan*], Tokyo, 1949.
—— *Sangyōshi no hitobito* [*Men in the History of Industry*]. Tokyo, 1954.
—— *Nihon sihoshugi hattatsushi* [*A History of the Development of Japanese Capitalism*], Tokyo, 1957.
—— *Zoku nihon shihonshugi hattatsu-shi* [*A Revised History of the Development of Japanese Capitalism*]. Tokyo, 1957.
—— *Seishō* [*The Political Merchants*]. Tokyo, 1963.
KAJINISHI, MITSUHAYA, et al. *Nihon shihonshugi no botsuraku.* [*The Fall of Japanese Capitalism*]. Vol. I. Tokyo, 1960.
KANNO, WATARŌ. *Nihon kaisha kigyō hasseishi no kenkyū* [*Studies in the Development of Incorporated Firms in Japan*]. Tokyo, 1931.
KATŌ, TOSHIHIKO. *Hompō ginkōshi-ron* [*A History of Banking in Japan*]. Tokyo, 1957.
KATŌ, TOSHIHIKO, and T. OUCHI (eds.). *Kokuritsuginkō no kenkyū* [*A Study of National Banks*]. Tokyo, 1963.
KIMURA, YASUICHI (ed.). *Shibaura seisakusho 65-nenshi* [*A Sixty-five-Year History of the Shibaura Machine-Tool Industries*]. Tokyo, 1940.
KINUKAWA, TAIICHI. *Hompō menshi bōsekishi* [*A History of Japanese Cotton-Spinning*]. 7 vols. Osaka, 1937.
KINUKAWA, TAIICHI (ed.). *Itō Denhichi Ō* [*The Venerable Denhichi Itō*]. Tokyo, 1936.
MANNARI, HIROSHI. *The Business Elite: Nihon ni okeru keieisha no jōken* [*The Business Elite: The Background of Business Leaders in Japan*]. Tokyo, 1965.
MATSUNARI, Y., T. MIWA, and Y. CHŌ. *Nippon ni okeru ginkō no hattatsu* [*The Development of Banks in Japan*]. Tokyo, 1959.
MEIJI FINANCIAL HISTORY EDITORIAL COMMITTEE (Meiji Zaiseishi Hensankai). *Meiji zaiseishi* [*Meiji Financial History*], 15 vols. Tokyo, 1904–5.
MINOBE, RYUKICHI. *Karuteru, Torasuto, Kontserun* [*Cartels, Trusts, and Concerns*]. 2 vols. Tokyo, 1931.
MITANI, KŌKICHI, *Motoki Shōzō to Hirano Tomiji shōden* [*Detailed Biographies of Shōzō Motoki and Tomiji Hirano*]. Tokyo, 1923.
MITSUBISHI BANK. *Mitsubishi ginkō shi* [*The History of the Mitsubishi Bank*]. Tokyo, 1954.
MITSUBISHI ECONOMIC RESEARCH INSTITUTE. *Mitsui, Mitsubishi, Sumitomo.* Tokyo, 1955.
MITSUBISHI, SHIPBUILDING COMPANY. *Mitsubishi zōsen* [*History of the Mitsubishi Shipbuilding Company*]. Tokyo, 1958.
MITSUI BANK. *Mitsui ginkō 50-nenshi* [*A Fifty-Year History of the Mitsui Bank*]. Tokyo, 1926.
—— *Mitsui ginkō 80-nenshi.* [*An Eighty-Year History of the Mitsui Bank*]. Tokyo, 1957.
MIYAMOTO, MATAJI. *Osaka chōnin* [*The Merchants of Osaka*]. Tokyo, 1957.
NISHINO, KIYŌ. *Sumitomo kontserun tokuhon* [*The Story of the Sumitomo Concern*]. Tokyo, 1937.

NISHINOIE, AIICHI, *Asano, Shibusawa, Okawa, Furukawa, kontserun tokuhon* [*The Story of the Asano, Shibusawa, Okawa, and Furukawa Concerns*]. Tokyo, 1937.
NISSHIN FLOUR-MILLING COMPANY (Nisshin Seifun KK). *Nisshin seifun kabushi kaishashi* [*The History of the Nisshin Flour-Milling Company*]. Tokyo, 1965.
NITTA, MUNEO. *Tokyo dentō kabushiki kaisha 50-nenshi* [*The First Fifty Years of the Tokyo Electric Light Company*]. Tokyo, 1936.
NODA, KAZUO. *Ninon no jūyaku* [*Business Executives in Japan*]. Tokyo, 1960.
NOMURA SECURITIES COMPANY OF JAPAN. *Kōshasai nenkan* [*An Annual Report of Government and Company Bonds*]. Tokyo, 1930.
ODA, SHIGEO. *Ningen Yasuda Zenjirō* [*The Man Zenjirō Yasuda*]. Tokyo, 1953.
OJI PAPER COMPANY. *Oji seishi shashi* [*The History of the Oji Paper Company*]. 5 vols. Tokyo, 1957.
OKADA, SHUMPEI (ed.). *Meiji-shoki no zaisei kinyū seisaku* [*Fiscal and Monetary Policies of the Early Meiji Period*]. Tokyo, 1964.
SAKADA, YOSHIO. *Shikon shōsai* [*The Samurai Spirit and Business Talent*]. Tokyo, 1964.
SHIBUSAWA, EIICHI. *Rongo to soroban* [*The Analects and the Abacus*]. Tokyo, 1928.
SHIROYANAGI, HIDEMITSU. *Nihon fugō hasseigaku* [*A Study of the Emergence of the Japanese Rich*]. Tokyo, 1920.
—— *Sumitomo monogatari* [*The Story of Sumitomo*]. Tokyo, 1931.
—— *Zaikai taiheiki* [*A History of the Tranquil World of Finance*]. Tokyo, 1947.
—— *Nakamigawa Hikojiro den* [*A Biography of Hikojiro Nakamigawa*]. Tokyo, 1950.
SUEHIRO, KAZUO. *Kondō Rempei den oyobi ikō* [*The Life and Writings of Rempei Kondō*]. Tokyo, 1926.
SUZUKI, BUNJI. *Rōdō ubdō nijūnen* [*Twenty Years in the Labour Movement*]. Tokyo, 1931.
SUZUKI, GORŌ. *Reimei nihon no ichi kaitakusha: Chichi Suzuki Tōsaburō no isshō* [*A Pioneer of Japan's Dawn: The Life of My Father Tōsaburō Suzuki*]. Tokyo, 1939.
—— *Suzuki Tōsaburō den: Kindai nihon sangyō no senku* [*A Biography of Tōsaburō Suzuki, A Pioneer of Modern Japanese Industry*]. Tokyo, 1956.
SUZUKI, TŌSABURŌ. 'Nihon tōgyo ron' ['A Treatise on the Sugar Industry in Japan'], *Tōyō Keizai Shimpō* [*Oriental Economic News*], 15 June 1899 (reprinted on Gōrō Suzuki, *A Pioneer of Japan's Dawn*).
—— *Nippon dokusen shihon no kaibō* [*The Anatomy of Japanese Monopolistic Capital*]. Tokyo, 1935.
TAKAHASHI, KAMEKICHI. *Nihon zaibatsu no kaibō* [*An Anatomy of Japanese Zaibatsu*]. Tokyo, 1930.
—— *Meiji–Taishō sangyō hattatsushi* [*A History of Industrial Development in the Meiji–Taisho Periods*]. Tokyo, 1932.
—— *Waga kuni kigyō no shiteki hatten* [*The Historical Development of Japan's Enterprises*]. Tokyo, 1956.
TAKAHASHI, KAMEKICHI, and J. AOYAMA. *Nihon zaibatsu-ron.* [*A Study of the Japanese Zaibatsu*]. Tokyo, 1938.
TANAKA, SŌGORŌ. *Iwasaki Yatarō den* [*A Biography of Yatarō Iwasaki*]. Tokyo, 1955.
TŌHATA, S., and T. TAKAHASHI (eds.). *Meijizenki no ginkō seido* [*The Banking System in Early Meiji Japan*]. Tokyo, 1965.
TOKYO ELECTRIC LIGHT COMPANY. *Tokyo dentō kabushiki kaishashi* [*A History of the Tokyo Electric Light Company*]. Tokyo, 1956.
TŌYŌ ECONOMIC PUBLISHING COMPANY (Tōyō Kaizai Shimpō-sha). *Meiji–Taisho kokusei sōran* [*A Survey of the National Economy in the Meiji–Taisho Periods*]. Tokyo, 1924.
TŌYŌ TEXTILE COMPANY. *Tōyō Bōseki 70-nenshi* [*Seventy Years of the Tōyō Textile Company*]. Tokyo, 1953.
TSUCHIYA, TAKAO. *Nippon Shihonshugi no keieishiteki kenkyū* [*A Business History Study of Japanese Capitalism*]. Tokyo, 1954.
—— *Zaibatsu o kizuita hitobito* [*The Zaibatsu-Builders*]. Tokyo, 1955.
—— *Nihon no seishō* [*Japan's Political Merchants*]. Tokyo, 1956.
—— *Nihon ni okeru keieisha seishin no hattatsu* [*The Development of Managerial Mentalities in Japan*]. Tokyo, 1957.

—— *Gendai nihon keizaishi kōwa* [*Lectures on the Economic History of Modern Japan*]. Tokyo, 1958.
—— *Nihon no keieisha seishin* [*Managerial Spirit in Japan*]. Tokyo, 1959.
—— *Chihō ginkō shōshi* [*A Brief History of Local Banks*]. Tokyo, 1961.
UZAKI, KUMAKICHI. *Toyokawa Ryōhei* [*The Life of Ryōhei Toyokawa*]. Tokyo, 1922.
WADA, HIDEKICHI. *Mitsui kontserun dokuhon* [*The Story of the Mitsui 'Konzern'*]. Tokyo, 1937.
YAMADA, FUMIO. 'Capital for Japan's Cotton Textile Industry', *Keizaigaku Ronshū* [*Economic Essays*, University of Tokyo], VI, 2 (1962).
YAMAJI, AIZAN. *Gendai kinkenshi* [*A History of Modern Economic Power*]. Tokyo, 1908.
YAMASHIRO, AKIRA (ed.), *Ringi-teki keiei seido* [*Ringi Management and Ringi System*]. Tokyo, 1966.
YANO, FUMIO. *Yasuda Zenjirō den* [*The Biography of Yasuda Zenjiro*]. Tokyo, 1925.
YASUDA BANK. *Yasuda ginkō 60-nenshi* [*A Sixty-Year History of the Yasuda Bank*]. Tokyo, 1940.

CHAPTER VI

Capital Formation during the Period of Early Industrialization in Russia, 1890–1913

GINDIN, I. F. *Russkie kommercheskie banki*. Moscow, 1948.
GOLDSMITH, R. 'The Economic Growth of Tsarist Russia, 1860–1913', *Economic Development and Cultural Change*, IX (1961).
KLIMOV, V. I. '103 vazhnieishykh tsentra fabrichno-zavodskoi promyshlennosti evropeiskoi Rossii v 1900–1914' in Istoricheskaia Geografia, *Voprosy Geografii*, L (Moscow, 1960).
MASLOV, P. P. *Kriticheskii analiz burzhuaznykh statisticheskich publikatsii*. Moscow, 1955.
RUSSIA. CENTRAL STATISTICAL COMMITTEE. *Obshchyi svod po imperii rezultatov razrabotki dannykh pervoi vseobshchei perepisi naseleniia*. St Petersburg, 1905.
—— MINISTRY OF FINANCE. *Ezhegodnik Ministerstva Finansov za 1916 god*. Petrograd, 1917.
STRUMILIN, S. G. *Statistiko-ekonomicheskie ocherki*. Moscow, 1958.
VAINSHTEIN, A. L. *Oblozhenie i platezhi krestianstva v dovoyennoe i revolutsionnoe vremia*. Moscow, 1924.
—— *Narodnoe bogatstvo i narodnokhoziastvennoe nakoplenie predrevolutsionnoi Rossii*. Moscow, 1960.
ZAITSEV, V. 'Vlianie kolebanii urozhaev na estestvennoe dvizhenie naselenia', in V. G. Groman (ed.), *Vlianie neurozhaev na narodnoe knoziaistvo Rossii*, II. Moscow, 1927.

CHAPTER VII

Labour and Industrialization in Russia

ADELMAN, I., and C. F. MORRIS. *Society, Politics and Economic Development*. Baltimore, Md, 1957.
ALYMOV, V. 'K voprosu o polozhenii truda v remeslennom proizvodstve', *Narodnoye Khozyaystvo*, VI (1904) 1–27.
ANDREYEV, E. *Rabota maloletnikh v Rossii i v Zapadnoy Yevrope*. St Petersburg, 1884.
ANNENSKY, N. 'Voprosy truda na torgovo-promyshlennom s'yezde', *Russkoye Bogatstvo*, X (1896).

ARRIGHI, G. 'Labour Supplies in Historical Perspective: A Study of the Proletarianization of the African Peasantry in Rhodesia', *Journal of Development Studies*, VI, 3 (April 1970).

BAKU. GORODSKAYA UPRAVA. STATISTICHESKOYE OTDELENIYE. *Baku po perepisi 22 oktyabrya 1903 g.*, I. Baku, 1905.

—— —— *Perepis Baku 1913 goda.* Baku, 1916.

BATER, J. H. 'The Industrial Geography of St Petersburg: 1850–1914'. Unpublished Ph.D. thesis, University of London, 1969.

BERNSHTEYN-KOGAN, S. *Chislennost', sostav i polozheniye metallurgicheskikh rabochikh.* Trudy studentov ekonomicheskago otdeleniya SPb. Politekhnicheskago Instituta Imperatora Petra Velikago, no. 4. St Petersburg, 1910.

BEZOBRAZOV, V. P. *Narodnoye khozyaystvo Rossii: Moskovskaya tsentral'naya promyshlennaya oblast'.* 3 parts. St Petersburg, 1882.

—— *Nablyudeniya i soobrazheniya otnositel'no novykh fabrichnykh uzakoneniy i fabrichnoy inspektsii.* St Petersburg, 1888.

—— 'Dnevnik, 1887 g.', *Russkaya Starina*, CLIV (1913).

BLACKWELL, W. L. *The Beginnings of Russian Industrialization, 1800–1860.* Princeton, 1968.

BOGDANOV, I. M. *Gramotnost' i obrazovaniye v dorevolyutsyonnoy Rossii i v SSSR, Istoriko-statisticheskiye ocherki.* Moscow, 1964.

BOGOSLOVSKY, S. M. *Zabolevayemost' fabrichnykh rabochikh Bogorodsko-Glukhovskoy i Istominskoy manufaktur Bogorodskago uyezda za 1896–1900 gg.* St Petersburg, 1901.

BRANDT, B. F. *Inostrannyye kapitaly: ikh vliyaniye na ekonomicheskoye razvitiye strany.* 3 vols. St Petersburg, 1898–1901.

—— *Torgovo-promyshlenny krizis.* St Petersburg, 1902.

CHEKHOV, N. V. *Narodnoye obrazovaniye v Rossii s 60ykh godov XIX v.* Moscow, 1912.

CHELINTSEV, A. N. *Sel'sko-khozyaystvennaya geografiya Rossii.* Prague, 1924.

CHUPROV, A. A. (ed.). *Rechi i stat'i.* 4 parts. St Petersburg, 1909.

CHUPROV, A. I., and A. S. POSNIKOV (eds.). *Vliyaniye urozhayev i khlyebnykh tsen na nekotovyye storony russkago narodnago khozyaystva.* 2 vols. St Petersburg, 1897.

CIPOLLA, CARLO M. *Literacy and Development in the West.* Baltimore, Md, 1969.

CRISP, O. 'The Financial Aspect of the Franco-Russian Alliance, 1894–1914'. Unpublished Ph.D. thesis, University of London, 1954.

DEMENT'YEV, E. M. *Fabrika, chto ona dayot naseleniyu i chto ona u nego beryot.* Moscow, 1897.

DEMENT'YEV, E. M. (ed.). 'Sanitarnoye izsledovaniye fabrik i zavodov Kolomenskago uyezda', in *Sbornik statisticheskikh svedeniy po Moskovskoy gubernii: otdel sanitarnoy statistiki*, III (issued by Moskovskaya Gubernskaya Zemskaya Uprava). Moscow, 1885.

DENISON, E. F. *Why Growth Rates Differ.* Washington, 1957.

ERISMAN, F. F. (ed.). 'Sanitarnoye izsledovaniye fabrichnykh zavedeniy Moskovskago uyezda', in *Sbornik statisticheskikh svedeniy po Moskovskoy gubernii: otdel sanitarnoy statistiki*, IV (issued by Moskovskaya Gubernskaya Zemskaya Uprava). Moscow, 1885.

FALKUS, M. 'Russia's National Income: A Revaluation', *Economica*, n.s., XXXV, 137 (February 1968), 52–73.

FRASER, J. *Russia of To-day.* New York, 1916.

FUHRMANN, J. T. *The Origins of Capitalism in Russia.* Chicago, 1972.

GAPONENKO, L. S. 'Rabochy klass Rossii nakanune velikogo oktyabrya', *Istoricheskiye Zapisky*, LXXIII (1969), 3–22.

GARELIN, YA. P. *Gorod Ivanovo-Voznesensk, ili, byvsheye selo Ivanovo i Voznesensky posad.* 2 vols. Shuya, 1884–5.

GAVRISHEV, L. L. 'Tekhnicheskoye obrazovaniye', in *Trudy vserossiyskago torgovo-promyshlennago s'yezda 1896 g. v Nizhnem-Novgorode*, VI. St Petersburg, 1897.

—— 'O vliyanii obshchego obrazoveniya rabochikh na produktivnost' ikh truda', in *Trudy s'yezda deyateley po tekhnicheskomu i professyonal'nomu obrazovaniyu v Rossii 1895–1896 gg.*, section 4. St Petersburg, 1898.

GESSEN, V. YU. *Trud detey i prodrostkov v fabrichnozavodskoy promyshlennosti Rossii ot XVII veka do oktyabrskoy revolyutsii.* Moscow, 1927.

GEYMAN, V. G. *Manufakturnaya promyshlennost' Peterburga petrovskogo vremeni.* Moscow and Leningrad, 1947.
GINDIN, I. 'O nekotorykh osobennostyakh ekonomicheskoy i sotsyal'noy struktury rossiyskogo kapitalizma v nachale XX v.', *Istoriya SSR*, III (1966).
GLIVITS, I. *Zheleznaya promyshlennost' Rossii.* St Petersburg, 1911.
GOEBEL, O. *Entwicklungsgang der russischen Industriearbeiter bis zur ersten Revolution (1905)* (Osteuropa-Institut in Breslau). Leipzig and Berlin, 1920.
GOLDSMITH, R. W. 'The Economic Growth of Tsarist Russia, 1860–1913', *Economic Development and Cultural Change*, IX, 2 (1961), 441–75.
GREGORY, PAUL. 'Economic Growth and Structural Change in Tsarist Russia: A Case of Modern Economic Growth', *Soviet Studies*, XXIII (January 1972), 418–34.
GUROFF, G., and S. F. STARR. 'A Note on Urban Literacy in Russia 1890–1914', *Jahrbücher für Geschichte Osteuropas*, n.s., XIX, 4 (December 1971).
GVOZDEV, S. *Zapiski fabrichnago inspektora.* Moscow, 1911.
HANS, N. *History of Russian Educational Policy.* London, 1931.
HAXTHAUSEN, BARON VON. *The Russian Empire, Its People, Institutions and Resources.* 2 vols. London, 1856.
ISLAVIN, A. S. 'Obzor kamennougol'noy i zhelezodelatel'noy promyshlennosti Donetskago kryazha', *Gorny Zhurnal*, 1875, nos. 1–3.
IVANOV, L. M. 'Preyemstvennost' fabrichno-zavodskogo truda i formirovaniye proletariata v Rossii', in L. M. Ivanov (ed.), *Robochy klass i rabocheye dvizheniye v Rossii 1861–1917.* Moscow, 1966.
——'O soslovno-klassovoy strukture gorodov kapitalisticheskoy Rossii', in L. M. Ivanov (ed.), *Problemy sotsyal'no-ekonomicheskoy istorii Rossii.* Moscow, 1971.
KABUZAN, V. *Narodonaseleniye Rossii v XVIII – pervoy polovine XIX v.* Moscow, 1963.
KADOMTSEV, B. P. *Professyonal'ny i sotsyal'ny sostav naseleniya yevropeyskoy Rossii po dannym perepisi 1897 g.* St Petersburg, 1909.
KAFENGAUZ, B. B. *Istoriya khozyaystva Demidovykh.* Moscow, 1950.
KAHAN, A. 'Continuity in Economic Activity and Policy during the Post-Petrine Period in Russia', *Journal of Economic History*, XXV, 1 (March 1965).
KASER, M. 'Education in Tsarist and Soviet Development', in C. Abramsky (ed.), *Essays in Honour of E. H. Carr.* London, 1974.
KERR, C., J. T. DUNLOP, F. H. HARBISON, and C. A. MYERS. *Industrialism and Industrial Man: The Problems of Labour and Management in Economic Growth.* Harmondsworth, 1973.
KEYSLER, S. Y. 'Sel'skaya obshchina i eya sovremennoye polozheniye', *Vestnik Yevropy*, VII (1884).
KHODSKY, L. V. *Po povodu knigi 'Vliyaniye urozhayev i khlebnykh tsen na nekotoryye storony russkago narodnago khozyaystva'.* St Petersburg, 1897.
KHROMOV, P. A. *Ekonomicheskoye razvitiye Rossii v XIX–XX vekakh.* Moscow and Leningrad, 1950.
——*Ocherki ekonomiki perioda monopolisticheskogo kapitalizma.* Moscow, 1960.
KINYAPINA, N. S. *Politika russkogo samoderzhaviya v oblasti promyshlennosti.* Moscow, 1968.
KIZEVETTER, A. A. *Posadskaya obshchina v Rossii XVIII st.* Moscow, 1903.
KOEHLER, S. *Die russische Industriearbeiterschaft von 1905–1917* (Osteuropa-Institut in Breslau). Leipzig and Berlin, 1921.
KOLODUB, E. *Trud i zhizn' gornorabochikh na grushevskikh antratsitnykh rudnikakh.* 2nd edn. Moscow, 1907.
KOVALEVSKY, V. I. (ed.). *Rossiya v kontse XIX veka.* St Petersburg, 1900 (reprinted by Mouton, 1969).
KOZ'MINYKH-LANIN, I. M. *Gramotnost' rabochikh fabrichno-zavodskoy promyshlennosti Moskovskoy gubernii.* Moscow, 1911. (Cited as 'Gramotnost' (1911)'.)
——*Gramotnost' i zarabotki fabrichno-zavodskikh rabochikh Moskovskoy gubernii.* Moscow, 1912. (Cited as 'Gramotnost' (1912)'.)
Krenholmskaya manufaktura 1857–1907: istorichesky ocherk. St Petersburg, 1907.
KUDRYAVTSEV, N. F. *Prishlyye sel'sko-khozyaystvennyye rabochiye na Nikolayevskoy*

yarmarke v m. Kakhovke v Tavricheskoy gubernii i sanitarny nadzor za nimi. Kherson, 1896.

KURITSIN, I. S. 'Formiroveniye rabochey sily na tekstil'nykh manufacturakh v XVIII v.', *Istoricheskiye Zapisky*, V (1939).

LAUE, T. VON. 'Russian Peasants in the Factory, 1892–1904', *Journal of Economic History*, XXI (1961), 61–80.

LAUWICK, M. *L'Industrie dans la Russie Méridionale: sa situation – son avenir.* Brussels and Paris, 1907.

LAVERICHEV, V. YA. *Tsarism i rabochy vopros v Rossii (1861–1917).* Moscow, 1972.

LENIN, V. I. *Razvitiye kapitalizma v Rossii*, in *Sochineniya*, III. Moscow, 1946.

LEVITSKY, V. 'Znacheniye kustarnykh promyslov v narodnom khozyaystve', *Narodnoye Khozyaystvo*, VI (1902), 34–48.

LEWIS, W. A. 'Economic Development with Unlimited Supply of Labour', *Manchester School*, May 1954; reprinted in A. N. Agarwala and S. P. Singh (eds.), *The Economics of Underdevelopment* (Oxford, 1958).

LISYANSKY, A. 'Osnovaniye yuzovskogo zavoda', *Istoriya SSSR*, no. 5 (1964), 150–9.

LIVSHITS, R. S. *Razmeshcheniye promyshlennosti v dorevolyutsyonnoy Rossii.* Moscow, 1955.

LODYZHENSKY, K. *Istoriya russkago tamozhennago tarifa.* St Petersburg, 1886.

LOKHTIN, P. *Bezzemel'ny proletariat v Rossii.* Moscow, 1905.

LOSITSKY, A. E. *Raspadeniye obshchiny.* St Petersburg, 1912.

LUKOMSKAYA, I. M., 'Formirovaniye promyshlennogo proletaryata Donbassa', in V. V. Al'tman (ed.), *Iz istorii rabochego klassa i revolyutsyonnogo dvizheniya.* Moscow, 1958.

LYUBOMIROV, P. G. *Ocherki po istorii russkoy promyshlennosti: XVII, XVIII i nachalo XIX veka.* Moscow, 1947.

LYUBOMIROV, P. G. (ed.). *A. N. Radishchev: materialy i izsledovaniya.* Moscow and Leningrad, 1936.

MABRO, R. 'Employment and Wages in Dual Agriculture', *Oxford Economic Papers*, n.s., XXIII, 3 (November 1971).

McKAY, J. P. *Pioneers for Profit: Foreign Entrepreneurship and Russian Industrialization, 1885–1913.* Chicago and London, 1970.

MARKUS, B. 'Abolition of Unemployment in USSR', *International Labour Review*, XXXIII (1935).

MARX, KARL. *Capital*, vol. I. Moscow, 1965.

MEYER, V. Y. *Prilepskaya ekonomiya brat'yev baronov K. i A. Yegorovichey Meyendorf.* Moscow, 1896.

MIKHAYLOVSKY, YA. T. *O deyatel'nosti abrichnoy inspektsii: otchot glavnago fabrichnago inspektora.* St Petersburg, 1886.

MILYUKOV, P. N. *Gossudarstvennoye khozyaystvo Rossii v pervoy chetverti XVIII stoletiya i reforma Petra Velikago.* St Petersburg, 1905.

MIROPOL'SKY, V. I. *Voronezhsky fabrichny okrug: otchot za 1885 g.* St Petersburg, 1886.

MOSCOW. GORODSKAYA UPRAVA. STATISTICHESKOYE OTDELENIYE. *Perepis Moskvy 1882 g.: Naseleniye i zanyatiya.* Moscow, 1885.

—— —— —— *Perepis Moskvy 1902 goda: Naseleniye.* Moscow, 1904.

—— GUBERNSKOYE ZEMSTVO. STATICHESKY OTDEL. *Moskovskaya guberniya po mestnomu obsledovaniyu 1898–1900 gg.*, V: 'Promysly'. Moscow, 1901.

MYINT, H. 'Dualism and the Internal Integration of Underdeveloped Economies', *Banca nazionale del lavoro Quarterly Review*, no. 93 (June 1970), 128–56.

NEVOLIN, P. *Kustarnaya promyshlennost' vo Vladimirskoy gubernii.* Vladimir, 1912.

NIFONTOV, A. S. 'Formirovaniye klassov burzhuaznogo obshchestva v russkom gorode', *Istoricheskiye Zapisky*, LIV (1955), 239 ff.

NOVITSKY, I. O. *Kievsky fabrichny okrug: otchot za 1885.* St Petersburg, 1886.

OGANOVSKY, N. P. (ed.). *Sel'skoye knozyaystvo Rossii v XX veke.* Moscow, 1923.

OZEROV, I. KH. *Politika po rabochemu voprosu za posledniye gody.* Moscow, 1906.

P., A. 'Rabochiye Sormovskikh zavodov', *Narodnoye Khozyaystvo*, IV (1902), 84–101, and V (1903), 81–94.

PALAT, M. K. 'Tsarist Labour Policy', *Soviet Studies*, no. 2 (1973).

PANKRATOVA, A. M. 'Rabochy klass i rabocheye dvizheniye nakanune revolyutsii 1905 g.', in M. N. Pokrovsky (ed.), *1905: Istoriya revolyutsyonnogo dvizheniya v otdel'nykh ocherkakh*. Moscow and Leningrad, 1925.

—— 'Proletarizatsiya krest'yanstva i ego rol' v formirovanii promyshlennogo proletariata Rossii', *Istoricheskiye Zapisky*, LIV (1955).

PANOV, A. A. (ed.). *Dvizheniye rabochikh na zarabotki v 1910 g.: stroitelnyye i dorozhnyye raboty*. St Petersburg, 1911.

PAVLENKO, N. I. *Razvitiye metallurgicheskoy promyshlennosti Rossii v pervoy polovine XVIII veka*. Moscow, 1953.

—— 'O nekotorykh storonakh pervonachalnogo nakopleniya v Rossii', *Istoricheskiye Zapisky*, LIV (1955).

PAZHITNOV, K. A. 'Razvitiye kamennougol'noy i metallurgicheskoy promyshlennosti na yuge Rossii', *Narodnoye Khozyaystvo*, III (1905).

—— *Ocherki po istorii bakinskoy neftepererabatyvayushchey promyshlennosti*. Moscow and Leningrad, 1940.

—— 'K voprosu o roli krepostnogo truda v doreformennoy promyshlennosti', *Istoricheskiye Zapisky*, VII (1946).

—— *Problema remeslennykh tsekhov v zakonodatel'stve russkogo absolutizma*. Moscow, 1952.

—— *Ocherki po istorii tekstil'noy promyshlennosti dorevolyutsyonnoy Rossii: sherstyanaya promyshlennost'*. Moscow, 1955. (Cited as '*Ocherki tekstil'noy* (1955)'.)

—— *Ocherki istorii tekstil'noy promyshlennosti dorevolyutsyonnoy Rossii: khlopchatobumazhnaya, l'nopenkovaya i sholkovaya promyshlennost'*. Moscow, 1958. (Cited as '*Ocherki tekstil'noy* (1958)'.)

PESKOV, P. A. *Fabrichny byt Vladimirskoy gubernii: otchot za 1882–1883*. St Petersburg, 1884.

PICKERING, E. C. 'The International Harvester Company in Russia: A Case Study of a Foreign Corporation in Russia from the 1860's to the 1930's'. Unpublished Ph.D. thesis, Princeton University, 1974.

POGOZHEV, A. V. 'Votchinnyye fabriky i ikh fabrichnnyye', *Vestnik Yevropy*, VIII (1889).

—— *Uchot chislennosti i sostava rabochikh v Rossii: materialy po statistike truda*. St Petersburg, 1906.

POGOZHEV, A. V. (ed.). 'Sanitarnoye izsledovaniye fabrichnykh zavedeniy Bogorodskago uyezda', in *Sbornik statisticheskikh svedeniy po Moskovskoy gubernii: otdel sanitarnoy statistiki*, III (issued by Moskovskaya Gubernskaya Zemskaya Uprava). Moscow, 1885.

POKROVSKY, M. N. (ed.). *1905: Istoriya revolyutsyonnogo dvizheniya v otdel'nykh ocherkakh*. Moscow and Leningrad, 1925.

POLLARD, S. 'Factory Discipline in the Industrial Revolution', *Economic History Review*, 2nd ser., XVI, 2 (December 1963).

PORTAL, R. *L'Oural au XVIIIe siècle*. Paris, 1950.

POSTNIKOV, V. E. *Yuzhno-russkoye krest'yanskoye khozyaystvo*. 2nd edn. Moscow, 1907.

PRILEZHAYEV, A. V. *Chto takoye kustarnoye proizvodstvo?* St Petersburg, 1882.

PROKOPOVICH, S. N. 'Krest'yanstvo i poreformennaya fabrika', in A. K. Dzhivelegov et al. (eds.), *Velikaya reforma: Russkoye obshchestvo i krest'yansky vopros v proshlom i nastoyashchem*, VI. Moscow, 1911.

PROKOPOVICH, S. N. (ed.). *Opyt ischisleniya narodnago dokhoda 50 guberniy Yevropeyskoy Rossii v 1900–1913 gg*. Moscow, 1918.

RAFFALOVICH, A. (ed.). *Russia: Its Commerce and Trade*. London, 1918.

RASHIN, A. G. 'Gramotnost' i narodnoye obrazovaniye v Rossii v XIX i nachale XXV.', *Istoricheskiye Zapisky*, XXXVII (1951).

—— *Naseleniye Rossii za sto let (1811–1913) gg*. Moscow, 1956.

—— *Formirovaniye rabochego klassa Rossii*. Moscow, 1958.

RIMLINGER, G. VON. 'Autocracy and the Factory Order in Early Russian Industrialization', *Journal of Economic History*, XX (March 1960), 67–92.

ROZHKOVA, M. K. 'Rabochiye Tryokhgornoy manufaktury vo vtoroy polovine XIX v.', *Istoriya proletariata SSSR*, no. 1. Moscow, 1930.

—— 'Sostav rabochikh Tryokhgornoy manufaktury na kanune imperyalisticheskoy voyny', *Istoriya proletariata SSSR*, no. 5. Moscow, 1931.

ROZHKOVA, M. K. (ed.). *Ocherki ekonomicheskoy istorii Rossii pervoy poloviny XIX veka.* Moscow, 1959.

RUDNEV, N. F. 'Promysly krest'yan v Yevropeyskoy Rossii', *Sbornik Saratovskago Zemstva*, no. 6 (Saratov, 1894).

RUSSIA. MINISTERSTVO FINANSOV. *Vestnik Finansov, Torgovli i Promyshlennosti.* Various dates. (Cited as '*VF*'.)

—— —— *Svod dannykh o fabrichno-zavodskoy promyshlennosti Rossii za 1897 god.* St Petersburg, 1900.

—— —— *Narodnoye khozyaystvo v 1913 g.* Petrograd, 1914.

—— —— DEPARTAMENT OKLADNYKH SBOROV [Department of Non-Repartitional Taxes]. *Materialy Vysochayshe uchrezhdyonnoy 16 noyabrya 1901 komissii po izsledovaniyu voprosa o dvizhenii s 1861 po 1900 g. blagosostoyaniya sel'skago naseleniya srednezemledel'-cheskikh guberniy sravnitel'no s drugimi mestnostyami Yevropeyskoy Rossii.* 3 vols. St Petersburg, 1903.

—— —— DEPARTAMENT TORGOVLI I MANUFAKTUR. *Trudy komissii po izsledovaniyu kustarnoy promyshlennosti v Rossii*, part 3. St Petersburg, 1879–82.

—— —— —— *The Industries of Russia*, ed. J. M. Crawford. Published for the World's Columbian Exposition, Chicago. St Petersburg, 1893.

—— —— —— *Itogi torgovli i promyshlennosti Rossii 1825–1855 gg.* St Petersburg, 1896.

—— MINISTERSTVO TORGOVLI I PROMYSHLENNOSTI. OTDEL PROMYSHLENNOSTI. *Svod Otchotov Fabrichnykh Inspektorov . . .* St Petersburg, various dates.

—— —— —— *Statistika bumagopryadil'nago i tkatskago proizvodstva za 1900–1910 gg.* St Petersburg, 1911.

—— —— —— *Dannyye o prodolzhitel'nosti i raspredelenii rabochego vremeni v promy-shlennykh predpriyatiyakh, podchinyonnykh nadzoru fabrichnoy i gornoy inspektsii v 1913 g.* Petrograd, 1914.

—— —— UCHEBNY OTDEL. *Materialy po tekhnicheskomu i remeslennomu obrazovaniyu.* Petrograd, 1917.

—— MINISTERSTVO VNUTRENNIKH DEL. *Obshchy svod po imperii rezul'tatov razrabotki dannykh pervoy vseobshchey perepisi naseleniya, proizvedennoy 28 yanvarya 1897*, I. St Petersburg, 1905.

—— —— TSENTRAL'NY STATISTICHESKY KOMITET. *Sankt-Peterburg po perepisi 10 dekabrya 1869 goda.* St Petersburg, 1872–5.

—— —— —— *Sankt-Peterburg po perepisi 15 dekabrya 1890 g., Naseleniye.* St Petersburg, 1891.

—— —— —— *Sankt-Peterburg po perepisi naseleniya 15 dekabrya 1900 goda, Naseleniye.* St Petersburg, 1903.

—— —— —— *Petrograd po perepisi naseleniya 15 dekabrya 1910 g.* Petrograd, 1914.

—— —— —— *Yezhegodnik Rossii za 1910 g.* St Petersburg, 1911.

—— NARODNY KOMMISSARIYAT FINANSOV SSSR. *Narodnoye i gosudarstvennoye khozyay-stvo.* Moscow, 1923.

—— SOVET S'YEZDOV PREDSTAVITELEY PROMYSHLENNOSTI I TORGOVLI. *Statistichesky Yezhegodnik na 1914 god.* Petrograd, 1914.

—— STATISTICHESKOYE BYURO SOVYETA S'YEZDA NEFTEPROMYSHLENNIKOV. *Zarabotnaya plata sluzhashchikh i rabochikh bakinskago promyshlennago rayona.* Baku, 1912.

—— TSENTRAL'NOYE STATISTICHESKOYE UPRAVLENIYE SSSR. *Fabrichno-zavodskaya promyshlennost' v period 1913–1918 gg.* Moscow, 1922.

—— —— *Statistichesky Yezhegodnik goroda Moskvy i Moskovskoy gubernii.* Moscow, 1927.

—— UCHONAYA KOMISSIYA PO IZSLEDOVANIYU ISTORII TRUDA V ROSSII. *Trud v SSSR: Spravochnik 1926–1930.* Moscow,

RYKACHEV, A. 'Tseny na khlyeb i na trud v. S.-Peterburge za 58 let', in *VF*, 1911, no. 3.

RYNDZYUNSKY, P. G. *Krest'yanskaya promyshlennost' v poreformennoy Rossii (60–80-ge gody XIX v.).* Moscow, 1966.

—— 'Krest'yansky otkhod i chislennost' sel'skogo naseleniya v 80ykh godakh XIX v.', in S. D. Skazkin (ed.), *Problemy genezisa kapitalizma* (Moscow, 1970), 413–35.

SAGORSKY, S. *Die Arbeiterfrage in der Südrussischen Landwirtschaft.* Munich, 1908.

ST PETERSBURG. Gubernskoye Zemstvo. Statistiko-ekonomicheskoye otdeleniye.

Materialy dlya otsenki zemel' S.-Peterburgskoy gubernii: Gdovsky uyezd. St Petersburg, 1914.

SCHULTZE-GAEVERNITZ, G. VON. *Ocherki obshchestvennago khozyaystva i ekonomicheskoy politiki Rossii* (translated from the German original of 1899). St Petersburg, 1901.

SEMEVSKY, V. V. *Krest'yane v tsarstvovaniye imperatritsy Yekateriny II,* I. St Petersburg, 1903.

SERBINA, K. N. 'Posluzhnyye spiski rabochikh Urala kak istorichesky istochnik', *Problemy Istochnikovedeniya,* VII (1959).

SHANIN, T. *The Awkward Class: Political Sociology of Peasantry in a Developing Society: Russia 1910–1925.* Oxford, 1972.

SHAPIRO, A. L. 'K istorii krest'yanskikh promyslov i krest'yanskoy manufactury v Rossii v XVIII v.', *Istoricheskiye Zapisky,* XXXI (1950).

SHATILOV, Y. I. 'Odno iz batrachnykh khozyaystv sredney Rossii', *Trudy Imperatorskago Obshchestva Sel'skago Khozyaystva,* XVIII (Moscow, 1886).

SHCHERBAN, A. N. *Istoriya tekhnicheskogo razvitiya ugol'noy promyshlennosti Donbassa.* 2 vols. Kiev, 1969.

SHEPELEV, L. E. 'Aktsyonernoye uchreditel'stvo v Rossii', in M. P. Vyatkin (ed.), *Iz istorii imperializma v Rossii.* Moscow and Leningrad, 1959.

SHESTAKOV, P. M. *Rabochiye na manufakture tovarishchestva 'Emil Tsindel' v Moskve: statisticheskoye izsledovaniye.* Moscow, 1900.

SHIDLOVSKY, A. V. *Kazansky fabrichny okrug otchot za 1885.* St Petersburg, 1886.

SIGOV, S. P. *Ocherki po istorii gornozavodskoy promyshlennosti Urala.* Sverdlovsk, 1936.

SKAZKIN, S. D. (ed.). *Problemy genezisa kapitalizma.* Moscow, 1970.

SMITH, T. C. 'Pre-modern Economic Growth: Japan and the West', *Past and Present,* no. 60 (August 1973).

SOYUZ RABOCHIKH PO METALLU. *Materialy ob ekonomicheskom polozhenii i professyonal'noy organizatsii peterburgskikh rabochikh po metallu.* St Petersburg, 1909.

STONE, L. 'Literacy and Education in England, 1640–1900', *Past and Present,* no. 42 (February 1969).

STRUMILIN, S. G. 'Khozyaystvennoye znacheniye narodnogo obrazovaniya', *Planovoye Khozyaystvo,* 1924, nos. 9–10.

—— 'Dinamika oplaty promyshlennogo truda v Rossii za 1900–1914 gg.', *Planovoye Khozyaystvo,* 1926, no. 9.

—— *Izbrannyye proizvedeniya.* 5 vols. Moscow, 1963–5.

STRUMILIN, S. G. (ed.). *Ocherki ekonomicheskoy istorii Rossii.* Moscow, 1960.

SVAVITSKY, A., and V. SHER. *Ocherk polozheniya rabochikh pechatnago dela v Moskve.* St Petersburg, 1909.

SVAVITSKY, Z. M., and N. A. SVAVITSKY. *Zemskiye podvornyye perepisy, 1880–1913, pouyezdnyye itogi.* Moscow, 1926.

SVYATLOVSKY, V. V. *Kharkovsky fabrichny okrug: otchot za 1885 god.* St Petersburg, 1886.

SWIANIEWICZ, S. *Forced Labour and Economic Development.* Oxford, 1965.

TEGOBORSKI, M. L. DE. *Commentaries on the Productive Forces of Russia.* 2 vols. London, 1855.

TILLY, C., and R. TILLY. 'Agenda for European Economic History in the 1970s', *Journal of Economic History,* XXXI (March 1971).

TIMASHEV, N. S. 'Overcoming Illiteracy: Public Education in Russia, 1880–1940', *Russian Review,* no. 2 (1942).

TROYNITSKY, N. A. (ed.). *Chislennost' i sostav rabochikh v Rossii na osnovanii dannykh pervoy vseobshchey perepisi naseleniya rossiyskoy imperii 1897 g.* St Petersburg, 1906.

TUGAN-BARANOVSKY, M. *Russkaya fabrika v proshlom i nastoyashchem.* 3rd edn. Moscow and Leningrad, 1934.

TYUMENEV, A. I. *Ot revolyutsii k revolyutsii.* Leningrad, 1925.

UNITED NATIONS. International Labour Office. *Employment and Economic Growth.* Geneva, 1964.

V., B. 'K kharakteristike agrarnykh otnosheniy v yugo zapadnom kraye', *Narodnoye Khozyaystvo,* I (1903), 67–79.

VARZAR, V. E. (ed.). *Statisticheskiye svedeniya o fabrikakh i zavodakh, ne oblozhennykh aktsizom za 1900 god*, issued by Otdel promyshlennosti Ministerstva Finansov. St Petersburg, 1903.
—— *Statistika obrabatyvayushchey promyshlennosti za 1908 god*. 2 parts. St Petersburg, 1912.
VARZAR, V. E., and L. B. KAFENGAUZ. 'Dinamika fabrichno-zavodskoy promyshlennosti Rossii', in S. G. Strumilin (ed.), *Ocherki ekonomicheskoy istorii Rossii* (Moscow, 1960), Appendix 2.
VASIL'YEV, V. N. 'Formirovaniye promyshlennogo proletariata Ivanovskoy oblasti', *Voprosy Istorii*, no. 6 (1932), 99–117.
VESNIN, A. 'Ob otmene krugovoy poruki', *Narodnoye Khozyaystvo*, VIII (1901).
VF: see Russia, Ministerstvo Finansov.
VIKHLYAYEV, P. 'Ustoychivost' vnezemledel'cheskikh otkhozhe-promyslovykh zarabotkov sel'skago naseleniya v Rossii', *Narodnoye Khozyaystvo*, III (1900).
VIKHLYAYEV, P. A. (ed.). *Zemledel'cheskoye khozyaystvo i promysly krest'yanskago naseleniya: promysly*. Moscow, 1908.
VLADIMIR. Gubernskoye Zemstvo. Statistichesky komitet. *Materialy dlyn otsenki zemel' Vladimirskoy gubernii: Vladimirsky uyezd*. Vladimir, 1912.
VOLKOV, M. YA. 'Khozyaystvo kuptsa Srednego Povolzhya I. A. Miklyayeva v kontse XVII – pervoy chetverti XVIII v.', in S. D. Skazkin (ed.), *Problemy genezisa kapitalizma* (Moscow, 1970).
WELLISZ, J. S. 'Dual Economies, Disguised Unemployment and the Unlimited Supply of Labour', *Economica*, n.s., XXXV, 137 (February 1968), 22–51.
YAKOVLEV, A. F. *Ekonomicheskiye krizisy v Rossii*. Moscow, 1955.
YANSON, YU. 'Naseleniye Peterburga, ego ekonomichesky i sotsyal'ny sostav po perepisi 1869 g.', *Vestnik Yevropy*, no. 10 (1875), 607–39.
YANZHUL, I. I. 'Detsky i zhensky fabrichny trud v Anglii i Rossii', *Otechestvennyye Zapisky*, nos. 2–4 (1880).
—— *Fabrichny byt Moskovskoy gubernii: otchot za 1882–3*. St Petersburg, 1884.
YAROSHKO, A. *Rabochy vopros na yuge: yego proshedsheye, nastoyashcheye i budushcheye*. Moscow, 1894.
YATSUNSKY, V. K. 'Rol' Peterburga v promyshlennom razvitii Rossii', *Voprosy Istorii*, no. 9 (1954).
—— 'Znacheniye ekonomicheskikh svyazey s Rossiyey dlya khozyaystvennogo razvitiya gorodov Pribaltiki v epokhu kapitalizma', *Istoricheskiye Zapisky*, XLV (1954).
—— 'Izmeneniya v razmeshchenii naseleniya Yevropeyskoy Rossii v 1724–1916 gg.', *Istoriya SSSR*, no. 1 (1957), 192–224.
ZAK, S. *Promyshlenny kapitalizm v Rossii*. Moscow, 1908.
ZAOZERSKAYA, E. I. *U istokov krupnogo proizvodstva v russkoy promyshlennosti XVI–XVII vekov*. Moscow, 1970.
ZELNIK, R. E. *Labor and Society in Tsarist Russia: The Factory Workers of St Petersburg 1855–1870*. Stanford, Calif., 1971.
ZISEL'SON, E. I. 'K voprosu o formirovanii promyshlennykh kadrov na predpriyatiyakh Peterburga v 1801–1861', in V. Ya Ovsyankin (ed.), *Istoriya rabochego klassa Leningrada*. Leningrad, 1962.
ZLOTNIKOV, M. 'Ot manufaktury k fabrike', *Voprosy Istorii*, nos. 11–12 (1946), 31–48.

CHAPTER VIII

Russian Entrepreneurship

ADLER-KARLSSON, G. *Western Economic Warfare, 1947–1967*. Stockholm, 1968.
AKADEMIYA NAUK SSSR. Institut ekonomiki. *Postroenie fundamenta sotsialisticheskoi ekonomiki v SSSR 1926–1932 gg*. Moscow, 1960.
—— *Sovietskoe narodnoe khozyaistvo v 1921–1925 gg*. Moscow, 1960.

AMBURGER, E. *Die Anwerbung ausländischer Fachkräfte für die Wirtschaft Russlands vom 15. bis in das 19. Jahrhundert.* Wiesbaden, 1968.
AMES, E. 'Theories of Economic Planning', in Gumpel and Keese (eds.), *Probleme des Industrialismus.*
ANANICH, B. V. *Rossiya i mezhdunarodny kapital 1897–1914: ocherki istorii finansovykh otnoshenii.* Leningrad, 1970.
ARNOLD, A. Z. *Banks, Credit and Money in Soviet Russia.* New York, 1937.
AUBIN, H. 'The Lands East of the Elbe and German Colonization Eastwards', in *Cambridge Economic History*, I. Cambridge, 1941.
AUTY, R., and D. OBOLENSKY (eds.). *Companion to Russian Studies*, I: *An Introduction to Russian History.* Cambridge, 1976.
BAJER, B. *Przemysł włókiennicny na ziemach polskich od początku XIX wieku do 1939 roku.* Łódź, 1958.
BARON, S. W. *The Russian Jew under Tsars and Soviets.* New York, 1964.
BARTLETT, R. P. 'Foreign Settlement in Russia under Catherine II', *New Zealand Slavonic Journal*, new ser., I (1974).
BATER, J. H. *St Petersburg – Industrialization and Change.* London, 1976.
BAYKOV, A. *The Development of the Soviet Economic System.* Cambridge, 1946.
BERLINER, J. S. *The Innovation Decision in Soviet Industry.* Cambridge, Mass., 1976.
BILL, V. T. *The Forgotten Class: The Russian Bourgeoisie to 1900.* New York, 1959.
BLACKWELL, W. L. 'The Old Believers and the Rise of Private Industrial Enterprise in Early Nineteenth-Century Moscow', *Slavic Review*, XXIV (1965).
—— *The Beginnings of Russian Industrialization, 1800–1860.* Princeton, 1968.
BLACKWELL, W. L. (ed.). *Russian Economic Development from Peter the Great to Stalin.* New York, 1974.
BLANC, S. 'The Economic Policy of Peter the Great', in Blackwell (ed.), *Russian Economic Development.*
BLUM, J. *Lord and Peasant in Russia from the Ninth to the Nineteenth Century.* Princeton, 1961.
BOBROWSKI, Cz. *Formation du système soviétique de planification.* Paris, 1956.
Bol'shaya sovetskaya entsiklopediya, 1st edn: Moscow, 1926–49; 2nd edn: Moscow, 1949–58; 3rd edn (in progress): Moscow, 1970–.
BOROVOY, S. YA. 'The State Debt as a Source of Primitive Accumulation in Russia', in Mavrodin (ed.), *Voprosy genezisa kapitalizma.*
BOWLEY, M. *Studies in the History of Economic Theory before 1870.* London, 1973.
BROKGAUZ: see *Entsiklopedichesky slovar'.*
BROWN, A. H. 'Adam Smith's First Russian Followers', in T. Wilson (ed.), *Adam Smith: Critical Essays.* Oxford, 1974.
BURNS, T., and G. M. STALKER. *The Management of Innovation.* London, 1961.
CAMPBELL, R. 'On the Theory of Economic Administration', in Rosovsky (ed.), *Industrialization in Two Systems.*
CARR, E. H. *The Bolshevik Revolution, 1917–1923.* 3 vols. II: *The Economic Order.* London, 1952.
CARR, E. H., and R. W. DAVIES. *Foundations of a Planned Economy, 1926–1929*, II. London, 1969.
CHAYANOV, A. V. *The Theory of Peasant Economy*, transl. and ed. D. Thorner, B. Kerblay, and R. E. F. Smith. Homewood, Ill., 1966.
CHRISTENSEN, S. Å., et al. *Den dansk emigration til Russland, 1875–1914.* Copenhagen, 1970.
CHUNTUNOV, V. T. *Ekonomicheskaya istoriya SSSR.* Moscow, 1969.
CONFINO, M. *Domaines et seigneurs en Russie vers la fin du XVIIIe siècle*, Paris, 1963.
CRISP, O. 'Russia, 1860–1914', in R. Cameron (ed.), *Banking in the Early Stages of Industrialization.* Oxford, 1967.
—— *Studies in the Russian Economy before 1914.* London, 1976.
CSIKÓS-NAGY, B. *Socialist Economic Policy.* London, 1973.
DANILEVSKY, V. V. *Russkaya tekhnika.* 2nd edn. Leningrad, 1948.
Direktivy KPSS i sovetskogo pravitel'stva po khozyaistvennym voprosam, I: *1917–1928.* Moscow, 1957.

DITYATIN, I. I. *Ustroistvo i upravlenie gorodov Rossii.* 2 vols. St Petersburg, 1875, and Yaroslavl', 1877.
DOBB, M. *Studies in the Development of Capitalism.* London, 1946.
—— *Soviet Economic Development since 1917.* 4th edn. London, 1957.
—— 'The Discussions of the 1920s about Building Socialism', *Annali dell'Instituto G. Feltrinelli.* Milan, 1967.
DOMAR, E. 'The Causes of Slavery or Serfdom: A Hypothesis', *Journal of Economic History,* XXX (1970).
Domostroi, transl. M. E. Duchène. Paris, 1910.
DUBNOW, S. M. *History of the Jews in Russia and Poland.* 2 vols. Philadelphia, 1916 and 1920.
DUBROVIN, N. *Pugachev i ego soobshchniki.* 3 vols. St Petersburg, 1884.
ECK, A. *Le Moyen Age russe.* Paris, 1933.
Ekonomicheskaya zhizn' SSSR: khronika sobytii i faktov 1917–1965, I: *1917–50.* 2nd edn. Moscow, 1967.
Entsiklopedichesky slovar'. St Petersburg and Moscow, 1890–1907.
EVENTOV, L. YA. *Inostrannye kapitaly v russkom promyshlennosti.* Moscow, 1931.
FALKUS, M. E. *The Industrialisation of Russia, 1700–1914.* London, 1972.
FENNELL, J. *The Emergence of Moscow, 1304–1369.* London, 1968.
FINN-ENATOEVSKY, A. *Sovremennoe khozyaistvo Rossii.* St Petersburg, 1911.
GAISSINOVITCH, A. *La Révolte de Pougatchev.* Paris, 1938.
GALAI, S. *The Liberation Movement in Russia, 1900–1905.* Cambridge, 1973.
GARVY, G. *Money, Banking and Credit in Eastern Europe.* New York, 1966.
—— 'Banking under the Tsars and under the Soviets', *Journal of Economic History,* XXII (1972).
GATOVSKY, L. M., *et al.* (eds.). *Sovietskaya sotsialisticheskaya ekonomika 1917–1957.* Moscow, 1957.
GERSCHENKRON, A. *Economic Backwardness in Historical Perspective.* Cambridge, Mass., 1962.
—— 'Agrarian Policies and Industrialization', in *Cambridge Economic History,* VI. Cambridge, 1965.
—— *Continuity in History and Other Essays.* Cambridge, Mass., 1968.
—— *Europe in the Russian Mirror.* Cambridge, 1970.
—— 'Criticism from Afar: A Reply', *Soviet Studies,* XXV (1973).
GESSEN, YU. *Istoria yevreiskogo naroda v Rossii.* 2 vols. Leningrad, 1925 and 1927.
GLADKOV, I. A. *Ocherki stroitel'stva sovetskogo planovogo khozyaistva v 1917–1918 gg.* Moscow, 1950.
—— *Voprosy planirovaniya sovetskogo khozyaistva v 1918–1920 gg.* Moscow, 1951.
—— *Ocherki sovetskoi ekonomiki 1917–1920 gg.* Moscow, 1956.
—— 'The Planned Development of the Soviet Economy', in Gatovsky *et al.* (eds.), *Sovietskaya sotsialisticheskaya ekonomika.*
GLADKOV, I. A. (ed.). *Natsionalizatsiya promyshlennosti v SSSR, sbornik dokumentov i materialov 1917–1920 gg.* Moscow, 1954.
GOLUBNICHY, I. S., A. POGREBINSKY, and I. N. SHEMYAKIN (eds.). *Ekonomicheskaya istoriya SSSR.* 1st edn: Moscow, 1963; 2nd edn: Moscow, 1967.
GORLOVSKY, M. A., and A. N. PYATNITSKY. *Iz istorii rabochego dvizhenia na Urale.* Sverdlovsk, 1954.
GRANOVSKY, E. L. *Monopolistichesky kapitalizm v Rossii.* Leningrad, 1929.
GREENBERG, L. *The Jews in Russia.* 2 vols. New Haven, Conn., 1944 and 1951.
GREKOV, V. D. *Krest'yanie na Rusi s drevneishikh vremen do XVII veka.* 2 vols. Moscow, 1952 and 1954.
GROSSMAN, G. 'Gold and the Sword: Money in the Soviet Command Economy', in Rosovsky (ed.), *Industrialization in Two Systems.*
GUMPEL, W., and D. KEESE (eds.). *Probleme des Industrialismus in Ost und West.* Olten, 1973.
HARDT, J. P., and T. FRANKEL. 'The Industrial Managers', in Skilling and Griffiths (eds.), *Interest Groups in Soviet Politics.*
HARE, R. *Portraits of Russian Personalities between Reform and Revolution.* London, 1959.

Hicks, J. *A Theory of Economic History*. Oxford, 1969.
Hobson, J. *The Evolution of Modern Capitalism*. London, 1949.
Höhmann, H. H., M. C. Kaser, and K. C. Thalheim (eds.). *The New Economic Systems of Eastern Europe*. London and Berkeley, Calif., 1975.
Holland, S. (ed.). *The State as Entrepreneur*. London, 1972.
Hosking, G. A. *The Russian Constitutional Experiment: Government and Duma, 1907–1914*. Cambridge, 1973.
Ihnatowicz, I. *Przemysł Łódksi w latach 1860–1900*. Wrocław, 1965.
Ishchanian, B. *Die ausländischen Elemente in der russischen Volkswirtschaft*. Berlin, 1913.
Istoriya industrializatsii SSSR 1926–1941 gg.: dokumenty i materialy, I: *1926–1928*. Moscow, 1969.
Istoriya sotsialisticheskoi ekonomiki SSSR. 6 vols. Moscow, 1976–   : in progress.
Istoriya SSSR s drevneyshikh vremen do nashikh dnei. 12 vols. Moscow, 1966–   : in progress.
Jasny, N. *Soviet Economists of the Twenties*. Cambridge, 1972.
Jezierski, A. *Handel zagraniczny królestwa polskiego 1815–1914*. Warsaw, 1967.
Kabanov, V. V. 'State Capitalism in 1918–19', in Kim (ed.), *Novaya ekonomicheskaya politika*.
Kafengauz, B. B. 'Some Problems of the Genesis of Capitalism in Russia', in Mavrodin (ed.), *Voprosy genezisa kapitalizma*.
Kahan, A. 'Continuity in Economic Activity and Policy during the Post-Petrine Period in Russia', *Journal of Economic History*, xxv, 1 (March 1965).
—— 'A Proposed Mercantilist Code in the Russian Iron Industry, 1734–36', *Explorations in Entrepreneurial History*, 2nd ser., ii, 2 (Winter 1965).
—— 'The Costs of "Westernization" in Russia: The Gentry and the Economy in the Eighteenth Century', *Slavic Review*, xxv (1966).
—— 'Government Policies and the Industrialization of Russia', *Journal of Economic History*, xxvii (1967).
Kaser, M. 'Soviet Planning and the Price Mechanism', *Economic Journal*, lx (1950).
—— *Soviet Economics*. London and New York, 1970.
Katkov, G., et al. (eds.). *Russlands Aufbruch ins 20. Jahrhundert*. Olten, 1970.
Kaufman, A. *Small-scale Industry in the Soviet Union*. New York, 1962.
Kaufmann-Rochard, J. *Origines d'une bourgeoisie russe, XVIe et XVIIe siècles*. Paris, 1969.
Kennan, G. *Russia and the West under Lenin and Stalin*. Boston, 1960.
Khromov, P. A. *Ekonomicheskoe razvitie Rossii v XIX–XX vekakh*. Moscow, 1950.
—— *Ekonomicheskoe razvitie Rossii*. Moscow, 1967.
Kieniewicz, S., and W. Kula (eds.). *Historia Polski*. Warsaw, 1956.
Kim, M. P. (ed.). *Novaya ekonomicheskaya politika*. Moscow, 1974.
Klaus, A. *Nashi Kolonii: opyt i materialy po istorii i statistike inostrannoy kolonizatsi v Rossii*. St Petersburg, 1869; reprinted Cambridge, Mass., 1972. (Transl. J. Toews, as *Unsere Kolonien: Studien und Materialen zur Geschichte und Statistik der ausländischen Kolonisation in Russland*. Odessa, 1887.)
Kopanev, A. *Naselenie Peterburga v pervoi polovine XIX veka*. Moscow and Leningrad, 1957.
Korsak, A. K. *O formakh promyshlennosti voobshche i o znachenii domashnego proizvodstva v zapadnoi Evrope i Rossii*. Moscow, 1861.
Kostomarov, N. I. *Ocherki torgovli Moskovskogo gosudarstva v XVI i XVII stoletiyakh*. St Petersburg, 1862.
Kostrowicka, I., Z. Landau, and J. Tomaszewski. *Historia gospodarcza Polski XIX i XX wieku*. Warsaw, 1966.
Kula, W. (ed.). *Ekonomika górnictwa i hutnictwa w królestwie polskim 1840–1910*. 2 vols. Warsaw, 1959 and 1961.
Kulischer, J. 'Die kapitalistischen Unternehmer in Russland (insbesondere die Bauern als Unternehmer) in den Anfangsstadien des Kapitalismus' *Archiv für Sozialwissenschaft und Sozialpolitik*, lxv (1931).
Landau, Z., and J. Tomaszewski. *Bank Handlowy w Warszawie S.A.: Historia i rozwój, 1870–1970*. Warsaw, 1970.

LAUE, T. K. VON. *Sergei Witte and the Industrialization of Russia.* New York, 1963.

LAVRICHEV, V. YA. 'The All-Russian Union of Trade and Industry', *Istoricheskie zapiski,* LXX (1961).

LENIN. V. I. *Razvitie kapitalizma v Rossii.* St Petersburg, 1899.

—— *Sochenenie.* 4th edn, 45 vols.: Moscow, 1941–67; 5th edn, 55 vols.: Moscow, 1958–65.

—— *Works.* English transl. of 4th Russian edn. Moscow, 1960–70.

LEROY-BEAULIEU, A. *L'Empire des tsars et les russes.* 3 vols. Paris, 1881–9.

LESHKOV, V. *Russky narod i gosudarstvo.* Moscow, 1858.

LIVSHIN, YA. I. *Monopolii v ekonomike Rossii.* Moscow, 1961.

LOPEZ, R. S. 'The Trade of Medieval Europe: The South', *Cambridge Economic History,* II. Cambridge, 1952.

ŁUKASIEWICZ, L. *Przewiót techniczny w przemysle królestwa polskiego 1857–1886.* Warsaw, 1963.

LYASHCHENKO, P. I. *Istoriya narodnogo khozyaistva SSSR.* 2 vols. 1st edn: Moscow, 1939; 2nd edn: Moscow, 1947–8; 3rd edn: Moscow, 1952. (Transl. L. M. Herman, as *History of the National Economy of Russia to the 1917 Revolution.* New York, 1949. The Russian text is cited in the notes as 'Lyashchenko, *Istoriya,* 2nd edn' or '. . . *Istoriya,* 3rd edn'; the English translation (after the Russian text of 1939) is cited as 'Lyashchenko, *History,* 1st edn'.)

MCKAY, J. P. *Pioneers for Profit: Foreign Entrepreneurship and Russian Industrialization, 1885–1913.* Chicago, 1970.

MAI, J. *Das deutsche Kapital in Russland, 1850–1894.* East Berlin, 1970.

MAKKAI, L. 'Die Hauptzüge der wirtschaftlich-sozialen Entwicklung Ungarns im 15–17. Jahrhundert', *Studia Historica,* no. 53 (Budapest, 1953).

MALE, D. J. *Russian Peasant Organisation before Collectivisation.* Cambridge, 1971.

MARSHALL, A. *Principles of Economics,* ed. C. W. Guillebaud. 9th (variorum) edn. 2 vols. London, 1961.

MARX, K. *Capital,* ed. F. Engels, transl. S. Moore and E. Aveling. 3 vols. Moscow, 1961–2.

MASHIKHIN, E. A., and V. M. SIMCHERA. 'The History of Statistical Yearbooks in Russia, the USSR, and the USA', in Ryabushkin *et al.* (eds.), *Ocherki po istorii statistiki SSSR.*

Materialy po istorii SSSR, VI: *Dokumenty po istorii monopolisticheskogo kapitalizma v Rossii.* Moscow, 1959. (Transl. T. K. von Laue, *Journal of Modern History,* XXVI (1954).)

MAVRODIN, V. V. (ed.). *Voprosy genezisa kapitalizma v Rossii.* Leningrad, 1960.

MAWRIZKI, S. *L'Industrie lourde en Union Soviétique: Système de direction et de planification.* Geneva and Paris, 1961.

MEHLINGER, H. D., and J. M. THOMPSON. *Count Witte and the Tsarist Government in the 1905 Revolution.* Bloomington, Indiana, 1972.

MILLER, M. *The Economic Development of Russia, 1905–1914.* London, 1926; 2nd edn, 1967.

MISSALOWA, G. 'Les Crises dans l'industrie textile au royaume de Pologne à l'époque de la révolution industrielle', *Studia Historiae Oeconomicae,* no. 8 (Poznan, 1973).

Nakaz Ekaterina Vtoroy. St Petersburg, 1893.

NASONOV, A. N. 'From the History of Manorial Serfs in the Nineteenth Century in Russia', *Izvestiya Akademii Nauk SSSR,* 1926, ser. VI.

NIKITINSKY, A. I. *Istoriya ekonomicheskogo byta Velikogo Novgoroda.* Moscow, 1893.

NISSELOVICH, L. N. *Istoriya zavodsko-fabrichnogo zakonodatel'stva Rossiskoi Imperii.* St Petersburg, 1883.

NÖTZOLD, J. *Wirtschaftspolitische Alternativen der Entwicklung Russlands in der Äre Witte und Stolypin.* East Berlin, 1966.

—— 'Agrarian Questions and Industrialization in Russia on the Eve of the First World War, *Saeculum,* XVII (1966).

NOVE, A. 'Internal Economies', *Economic Journal,* LXX (1960).

—— *An Economic History of the USSR.* London, 1969.

NUTTER, W. *The Growth of Industrial Production in the Soviet Union.* Princeton, 1962.

OL', P. V. *Inostrannye kapitaly v Rossii.* Petrograd, 1922.

—— *Inostrannye kapitaly v narodnom khozyaistve dovoennoi Rossii*. Leningrad, 1925.

OLEGINA, I. N. 'Capitalist and Socialist Industrialization in the Treatment of A. Gerschenkron', *Istoriya SSSR*, no. 2 (1971).

OZEROV, I. KH. *Ekonomicheskaya Rossiya i ee finansovaya politika na iskhode XIX i v nachale XX veka*. St Petersburg, 1905.

PARES, B. *A History of Russia*. 5th edn. London, 1962 (first published 1926).

PAVLENKO, N. I. *Razvitie metallurgicheskoi promyshlennosti Rossii v pervoi polovine XVIII veka*. Moscow, 1953.

—— 'On the Question of the Evolution of the Gentry in the Seventeenth and Eighteenth Centuries', in Mavrodin (ed.), *Voprosy genezisa kapitalizma*.

PAZHITNOV, K. A. *Problema remeslennykh tsekhov v zakonodatel'stve russkogo absolutizma*. Moscow, 1952.

PIETRZAK-PAWŁOWSKI, I. *Królestwo polskie w początkach imperializmu 1900–1905*. Warsaw, 1955.

PINTER, W. M. 'The Social Characteristics of the Early Nineteenth-Century Russian Bureaucracy', *Slavic Review*, XXIX, 3 (September 1970).

PIRENNE, H. *Histoire économique de l'Occident médiéval*. Bruges, 1951.

POKROVSKY, S. A. (ed.). *Yuridicheskie proizvedeniya progressivnykh russkikh mysliteley: vtoraya polovina XVIII veka*. Moscow, 1959.

POLYANSKY, F. *Pervonachal'noe nakoplenie kapitala v Rossii*. Moscow, 1958.

PORTAL, R. *L'Oural au XVIIIe siècle*. Paris, 1950.

—— 'The Industrialization of Russia', in *Cambridge Economic History*, VI. Cambridge, 1965.

POSTAN, M. M. 'The Trade of Medieval Europe: The North', in *Cambridge Economic History*, II. Cambridge, 1952.

PTUKHA, M. V. *Ocherki po istorii statistiki v SSSR*. 2 vols. Moscow, 1955 and 1959.

Pugachevshchina. 3 vols. Moscow and Leningrad, 1926–31.

PUSTULA, Z. *Początki kapitału monopolistycznego w przemyśle hutniczometalowym królestwa polskiego 1882–1900*. Warsaw, 1968.

Rabochee dvizhenie v Rossii v XIX veke. Moscow, 1955.

RAEFF, M. 'Imperial Russia: Peter I to Nicholas I', in Auty and Obolensky (eds.), *Companion to Russian Studies*, I.

RIMLINGER, G. V. 'Autocracy and the Factory Order in Early Russian Industrialization', *Journal of Economic History*, XX (1960).

—— 'The Expansion of the Labor Market in Capitalist Russia, 1861–1917', *Journal of Economic History*, XXI (1961).

ROBERTS, P. C. *Alienation and the Soviet Economy*. Albuquerque, New Mexico, 1971.

ROMANOV, B. A. *Rossiya v Mandzhurii*. Moscow, 1955.

ROOSA, R. A. 'United Russian Industry', *Soviet Studies*, XXIV (1973).

ROSOVSKY, H. 'The Serf Entrepreneur in Russia', *Explorations in Entrepreneurial History*, VI (1953–4).

ROSOVSKY, H. (ed.). *Industrialization in Two Systems*. New York, 1966.

ROWNEY, D. M. 'Study of the Russian Ministry of Internal Affairs in the Light of Organization Theory', in R. Kanet (ed.), *Behavioral Revolution and Communist Studies*. New York, 1970.

RUNCIMAN, S. 'Byzantine Trade and Industry', in *Cambridge Economic History*, II. Cambridge, 1952.

RUSIŃSKI, W. *Rozwój gospodarczy ziem polskich*. Warsaw, 1963.

RYABUSHKIN, T. V., *et al.* (eds.). *Ocherki po istorii statistiki SSSR*. Moscow, 1972.

RYBAKOV, B. A. *Remeslo drevnei Rusi*. Moscow, 1948.

RYCHKOV, N. D. 'On Corporations in Russia and Western Europe', *Russky Vestnik*, XVII (1862).

RYNDZYUNSKY, P. G. *Gorodskoe grazhdanstvo doreformnennoi Rossii*. Moscow, 1958.

SAMOKHVALOV, F. *Sovety narodnogo khozyaistva v 1917–32 gg*. Moscow, 1964.

SCHULZE-GÄVERNITZ, G. VON. *Volkswirtschaftliche Studien aus Russland*. Leipzig, 1899.

SCHUMPETER, J. A. *The Theory of Economic Development*. Cambridge, Mass., 1934.

SERGEEVICH, V. I. *Russkaya yuridicheskaya drevnost'*. 3 vols. St Petersburg, 1890–1903.

SHEPELEV, L. E. *Aktsionernye kompanii v Rossii*. Leningrad, 1973.

SHIMKIN, O. 'The Entrepreneur in Tsarist and Soviet Russia', *Explorations in Entrepreneurial History*, II (1949).

SHINDZIKASHVILI, D. I. *Ministerstvo Vnutrennikh Del tsarskoi Rossii v period imperializma – Struktura, funktsii, reaktsionaia sushchnost' i sviaz' s drugimi ministerstvami*. Omsk, 1974.

SHONFIELD, A. 'Thinking about the Past', *Encounter*, October 1972.

SHUL'GA, I. G. 'The Development of Trade in Left-Bank Ukraine in the Second Half of the Eighteenth Century', in Mavrodin (ed.), *Voprosy genezisa kapitalizma*.

SIDEROV, A. L. *Ekonomicheskoe polozhenie Rossii v gody pervoi mirovoi voiny*. Moscow, 1973.

SINZHEIMER, G. P. G. 'Les Industries kustar': Un Châpitre de la révolution industrielle en Russie', *Cahiers du Monde Russe et Soviétique*, VIII (1967).

SKILLING, H. G., and F. GRIFFITHS (eds.). *Interest Groups in Soviet Politics*. Princeton, 1971.

SMITH, R. E. F. 'Russia', in *Cambridge Economic History*, I. 2nd edn. Cambridge, 1966.

SOMBART, W. *The Jews and Modern Capitalism*, transl. M. Epstein, from *Die Juden und das Wirtschaftsleben* (Leipzig, 1911). New York, 1913.

—— *Der moderne Kapitalismus*. 3 vols. Munich, 1919.

SORLIN, I. 'Les Traités de Byzance avec la Russie au Xe siècle', *Cahiers du Monde Russe et Soviétique*, II (1961).

SPIRIDONOVA, E. V. *Ekonomicheskaya politika i ekonomicheskie vzglady Petra I*. Moscow, 1952.

STEPANOV, I. V. 'Workers of the Volga Region in the Seventeenth Century', in Mavrodin (ed.), *Voprosy genezisa kapitalizma*.

STEPANOV, N. *Sravnitel'no-istorichesky ocherk organizatsii remeslennoi promyshlennosti v Rossii i zapadnoevropeiskikh gosudarstvakh*. Kiev, 1864.

STOPYANSKY, P. N. *Zhizn' i byt Peterburgskoy fabriki 1704–1914*. Leningrad, 1925.

STORCH, H. *Historisch-statistisches Gemälde des russischen Reiches am Ende des achtzehnten Jahrhunderts*. 8 vols. Riga, 1797–1803.

STRUMILIN, S. G. *Ocherki ekonomicheskoi istorii Rossii*. Moscow, 1960.

STRUVE, P. *Krepostnoye khozyaistvo*. St Petersburg, 1913.

SUTTON, A. C. *Western Technology and Soviet Economic Development, 1917–1930*. Stanford, Calif., 1968.

SWIANIEWICZ, S. *Forced Labour and Economic Development*. London, 1965.

SYROECHKOVSKY, V. E. *Gosti-surozhane*. Moscow and Leningrad, 1935.

THALHEIM, K. C. 'Die wirtschaftliche Entwicklung Russlands', in Katkov *et al.* (eds.), *Russlands Aufbruch ins 20. Jahrhundert*.

TREUE, W. *Wirtschaftsgeschichte der Neuzeit, 1700–1760*. Stuttgart, 1962.

TSUKERNIK, A. L. *Sindikat 'Prodamet': istoriko-ekonomichesky ocherk 1902–1914 g.* Moscow, 1959.

TSYPEROVICH, G. *Sindikaty i tresty v Rossii*. Petrograd, 1918; 3rd edn, 1920.

TUGAN-BARANOVSKY, M. *Russkaya fabrika v proshlom i nastoyashchem*, I: *Istoricheskoe razvitie russkoy fabriki v XIX veke*. 3rd edn. Moscow, 1926. (Transl. A. Levin and C. Levin, supervised by G. Grossman, as *The Russian Factory in the 19th Century*. Homewood, Ill., 1970.)

UNBEGAUN, B. O. *Russian Surnames*. Oxford, 1972.

VANAG, N. *Finansovy kapital v Rossii*. Moscow, 1925.

VANAG, N., and S. TOMSINSKY. *Ekonomicheskoe razvitie Rossii*, I: *Epokha promyshlennogo kapitalizma*, and II: *Epokha finansogo kapitalizma*. Moscow and Leningrad, 1928 and 1930.

VENEDIKTOV, A. V. *Organizatsiya gosudarstvennoi promyshlennosti v SSSR*. 2 vols. Leningrad, 1957 and 1961.

VERGINSKY, V. S. *Tvortsy novoi tekhniki v krepostnoy Rossii*. Moscow, 1957.

VERRE, E. *L'Entreprise industrielle en Union soviétique*. Paris, 1965.

VOLIN. L. *A Century of Russian Agriculture*. Cambridge, Mass., 1970.

VUCINICH, A. *Science in Russian Culture: A History to 1860*. Stanford, Calif., 1963.

WAGNER, W. G. 'Tsarist Legal Policies at the End of the Nineteenth Century: A Study in Inconsistencies', *Slavonic and East European Review*, LIV, 3 (July 1976).

WEBER, M. *Wirtschaft und Gesellschaft.* 2 vols. Tübingen, 1956.
—— *The Protestant Ethic and the Spirit of Capitalism,* transl. T. Parsons. New York, 1957.
—— *From Max Weber: Essays in Sociology,* ed. H. M. Garth and C. W. Mills. New York, 1958.
WESTWOOD, J. N. 'John Hughes and Russian Metallurgy', *Economic History Review,* 2nd ser., XVII, 3 (1965).
WHEELER, G. *Racial Problems in Soviet Muslim Asia.* London, 1960.
WHITE, J. D. 'Moscow, Petersburg and the Russian Industrialists', *Soviet Studies,* XXIV (1973).
YAKOVTSEVSKY, V. N. *Kupechesky kapital v feodal'no-krepostnicheskoi Rossii.* Moscow, 1953.
ZAGORSKY, S. O. *State Control of Industry in Russia during the War.* New Haven, Conn., 1928.
ZAK, S. S. *Promyshlenny kapitalizm v Rossii.* Moscow, 1908.
ZAORSKAYA, E. I. *Manufaktura pri Petre I.* Moscow, 1947.
ZIENTARA, B., A. MACZAK, I. IHNATOWICZ, and Z. LANDAU. *Dzieje gospodarcze Polski do 1939 g.* Warsaw, 1965.
ZIV, V. S. *Inostrannye kapitaly v russikh aksioniernykh predpriyatiyakh,* I: *Germanskie kapitaly.* Petrograd, 1915.

INDEX

A&P (Great Atlantic & Pacific Tea Co.), 98

Abegglen, James C., 237

absenteeism, 530n169; in Tsarist Russia, 380, 382, 383, 384; methods of control (Japan), 201–2

accident insurance, 373

accounting

Russia, 484; Soviet Russia, 492, 544n191

United States: in early times, 83–5; in modern times, 125; accounting firms, 123; cost-accounting, 91, 92–3; double-entry, 83; in organization of enterprise, 113–16, 117; for railway companies, 90–1, 102–3; shop accounting, 104

administration

'administrative economy' of Soviet Russia, 416, 492; cost of, in Russian industry, 404; discriminatory, in Tsarist and Soviet Russia, 416

administrative network in USA, 132, 133; techniques for, 100, 119, 125, 129

Administration of the Mines (Russia), 342, 348

advertising, 98, 108, 114, 463

aeroplanes, 122; air transport, 124, 126; aircraft carriers, 127

African peasants, 530n175

agriculture

Japan, 134; agricultural technology, 137; capital formation, 153–4; commercial agriculture, 170; growth rates, 145, 146; improvements: irrigation, 149, seed selection, 145, 146; labour force, 168, 170–1, 505n16, surplus for industry, 256; labour inputs, 146; loans from banks, 239; output, 146, 147; peasant agriculture, 137–8, 145–6; regional differences, 146; in Tokugawa era, 137–8, 145–6; trade associations, 191; traditional character of, 159

Russia: agrarian reforms, 467, 475; agricultural banks, 465; agricultural holdings, 286; capital accumulation, 266, formation, 276–83, stock, 275, 290, 300, 301; capitalism and, 459; commercialization, 265, 268, 269–70, 271, 274, 280, 282; crisis in, 266–7, 270; dual (estate and peasant) agriculture, 325–6; education and, 394; exports, 270, 293; foreign settlers in, 454; growth, 265, 270, a giant sector, 309, intensification, 278; improvements, 277–8, 294, irrigation, 278; incomes, 374; labour force, 312, 329, 350, 521n48, hired, 327, 332, 333, 334, surplus for industry, 413, 415, women, 358–9; labour inputs, 413; labour mobility, 265; machinery and equipment, 280, 300, 301, 334, 355, 359, 482; Ministry of Agriculture, 436–7; monoculture, 334; peasant agriculture, 267, 325, 327, 334, 375–6, 413, three-field system, 266, 267; People's Commissariat of Agriculture, 437; population, 267; private agriculture in Soviet Russia, 486; produce market, 329; seasonal nature of, 374; sharecropping, 267; share of national income, 328–9, 415; Special Council for Agriculture (First World War), 480; wages, 411

United States: agricultural colleges, 42–4; agricultural crops, 97–8, processing for, 101; capital–output ratios, 18–19, 21; commercial agriculture, 75; demand for products, 131; depression of 1890s, 51; equipment and machinery, 29, 103; improvements, 29, 55; loans for, 51; movement away from, 49, 50, 65–6; states' expenditure on, 45, 46

see also crops; farms and farming; grain

Aichi, 172, 183, 513n42

Akema, F., Dutch entrepreneur, 311

Alabama, 42, 76, 499n49

alcohol, 76, 86, 101, 342; tax on, 519n21 beer, 86, 101, 108; vodka, 384; whisky, 75, 101, 110; wines, 76

Alexander I, Tsar of Russia: prefigures First Five-Year Plan, 436–7; refuses Kankrin's emancipation proposal, 450; reopens University of Tartu, 455; revokes right to buy populated villages for factories, 320; settles German colonists in South Russia, 341; toleration for Skoptsy and Jews, 454

Alexander II, Tsar of Russia: educational reforms, 389; rules for foreign entrepreneurs, 455–6

Alexei Mikhailovich, Tsar of Russia, 448

Alexei Romanov, Tsar of Russia, 429

Allied Command, policy of 'economic democratization' in Japan, 250–1, 263

Alsace, French prisoners from, 398

aluminium, 122

organization (*cont.*)
 tion, 176; 'second-best' only available, 139; techniques imported, 164
 Russia: American concept of, in Russia, 397; East–West bifurcation in, 430; in *gosti* enterprise, 425; Hicksian analysis applied to Russia, 419–20; impetus from Peter the Great, 432–59; not native to Russians, 424; planned, in communist programme, 478, 484; peasant 'spontaneous' co-operatives, 429; pre-Petrine, 428–32; in Western guilds, 427
 United States: organizational design, 71–2, 86, 100; for consolidated properties, 112; internal, 88; in metal-working industries, 101, 103–4; for railroads, 92; organizational revolution, 133, in mass distribution, 98–9
Orthodox Church, 452, 454; churches, 426; ecclesiastical serfs, 443; elementary schools, 294, 307; heretics, 452; saints, 427; secularization of estates, 443
Osaka
 employers, 182–3; agricultural employment, 171; employment contracts, 170
 engineering works, 198
 textile workers, 180, 181, 183, 185, 187, 198, 513n42
 urban vigour, 141
 wage payments, 201
Osaka Cotton Textile Co., 180, 220, 230; finance for, 243; *see also* Tōyō Textile Co.
output
 Japan: growth, 157, 162, 256; trend acceleration, 163
 Russia: and the consumption basket, 293; of factories, 345; industrial, 341; invoiced to state officials, 435; poor quality of, 317; of serf labour, 444; value of, as criterion of a factory, 342; per worker, 399–404, in agriculture, 329
 United States: elasticity of, in relation to capital, 7–8, 10, 11; heterogeneous outputs, 496n7; increase in, after 1790, 78–9; inputs and outputs, 71, 72, 131, 133
 see also production; productivity
out-workers, 352
overheads, 352, 414, 415
overseers, *see* foremen
ownership
 Japan: and control, 238–54, changing

patterns, 262–4; concentration, 250; economic democratization, policy of Allied Command, 250–1, reversed on restoration of sovereignty, 251; 'revolution' in shareholding, 251–2
 Russia: of land, 425; ownership status, 287; of productive factors, 421; of serfs, 426, 445; of works, 313
  in Soviet revolution, 484–5, 487; private ownership abolished, 417, 492
 United States, 68, 70, 109, and control, 83, 112, 130; owners and managers, 36, 37, 72
oyakata (filler of parental role), 189, 190, 192, 193–4; modernized into supervisor of work force, 205; in Nagasaki shipyard, 205–7

Pacific Ocean, reached by railroad (1869), 87, by telegraph (1861), 88; war in, 166, 213
packaged goods, 107, 110
Pale of Settlement, 453, 476; Jewish banks, 454
Pankratev family, entrepreneurs, 431
Pankratova, A. M., 371
paper and pulp industry
 Japan: capital formation, 505; merchant enterprise in, 234; paper mills, 220; zaibatsu enterprise, 515n88
 Russia: juvenile labour, 361; possessional factories, 321; share of total employment and production, 354; wages, 412
 United States: capital–output ratio, 20; diversification, 126–7; mergers, 110; technological innovation, 103
Pares, Bernard, 441, 544nn182, 185
Paris, 220, 470, 529; stock exchange, 518n13
parish priests, *see* religion
Parker, William N., 2
partnerships, 62, 131, 445, 472
passports (Russia): family, 362; workers', 332, 334, 338, 370, 381–2, 388, 542n149, 547n243
 identity cards, 466
Patrick, Hugh T., 226, 239
Paul I, Tsar of Russia; Corporation Code, 448–9; guilds, 538n62; restrictions on foreign enterprise, 455
Paulsen, Zacharias, silk and velvet factory, 429
Pavlenko, N. I., 315
Pawtucket (R.I.), textile mill, 80